FEMINIST JUDGMENTS

What would United States Supreme Court opinions look like if key decisions on gender issues were written with a feminist perspective? *Feminist Judgments* brings together a group of scholars and lawyers to rewrite, using feminist reasoning, the most significant U.S. Supreme Court cases on gender from the 1800s to the present day. The twenty-five opinions in this volume demonstrate that judges with feminist viewpoints could have changed the course of the law. The rewritten decisions reveal that previously accepted judicial outcomes were not necessary or inevitable and demonstrate that feminist reasoning increases the judicial capacity for justice. *Feminist Judgments* opens a path for a long overdue discussion of the real impact of judicial diversity on the law as well as the influence of perspective on judging.

Kathryn M. Stanchi is a Professor of Law and Affiliated Professor of Women's Studies at Temple University Beasley School of Law.

Linda L. Berger is Family Foundation Professor of Law and the Associate Dean for Faculty Development and Research at the University of Nevada, Las Vegas, William S. Boyd School of Law.

Bridget J. Crawford is a Professor of Law at Pace University School of Law.

Feminist Judgments

REWRITTEN OPINIONS OF THE UNITED STATES SUPREME COURT

KATHRYN M. STANCHI
Temple University Beasley School of Law

LINDA L. BERGER
University of Nevada, Las Vegas,
William S. Boyd School of Law

BRIDGET J. CRAWFORD
Pace University School of Law

CAMBRIDGE
UNIVERSITY PRESS

CAMBRIDGE
UNIVERSITY PRESS

One Liberty Plaza, 20th Floor, New York, NY 10006, USA

Cambridge University Press is part of the University of Cambridge.

It furthers the University's mission by disseminating knowledge in the pursuit of education, learning, and research at the highest international levels of excellence.

www.cambridge.org
Information on this title: www.cambridge.org/9781107565609

© Cambridge University Press 2016

First published 2016

Printed in the United States of America by Sheridan Books, Inc.

A catalogue record for this publication is available from the British Library.

Library of Congress Cataloguing in Publication Data
Names: Crawford, Bridget J., author. | Berger, Linda L., author. |
Stanchi, Kathryn M., author.
Title: Feminist judgments : rewritten opinions of the United States
Supreme Court / Bridget J. Crawford, Pace University School of Law,
Linda L. Berger, University of Nevada, Las Vegas, William S. Boyd School of Law,
Kathryn M. Stanchi, Temple University Beasley School of Law.
Description: New York NY : Cambridge University Press, 2016. |
Includes bibliographical references and index.
Identifiers: LCCN 2016008441 | ISBN 9781107126626 (hardback)
Subjects: LCSH: Women – Legal status, laws, etc. – United States – Cases. |
Feminist jurisprudence – United States – Cases. | Equality before the law –
United States – Cases. | Discrimination – Law and legislation –
United States – Cases. | Feminism – United States – History – 20th century.
Classification: LCC KF478.C74 2016 | DDC 349.73082–dc23
LC record available at http://lccn.loc.gov/2016008441

ISBN 978-1-107-12662-6 Hardback
ISBN 978-1-107-56560-9 Paperback

For Eddie, Kaitlyn, Paolo and Gianluca – KMS
For Tom and Michael – LLB
For my daughter – BJC

Contents

Notes on contributors

Jamie R. Abrams is a Law Professor at the University of Louisville Brandeis School of Law where she teaches Family Law, Women & Law, and Torts. She received her LL.M. from Columbia University and her J.D. from American University. Her scholarship focuses on military integration, gendered citizenship, and birthing autonomy. She has published in various top law journals, including recent articles on the "Illusion of Autonomy in Women's Medical Decision-Making" in the *Florida State Law Review* and on "Debunking the Myth of Universal Male Integration" in the *University of Michigan Journal of Law Reform*. Thanks to Corey Shiffman and Jeremy Woodruff for research and editing.

Erez Aloni is an Assistant Professor at Whittier Law School, where he teaches courses in contracts and domestic relations. Prior to joining Whittier, he was a fellow at the Center for Reproductive Rights and Columbia Law School. He received his LL.M. and S.J.D. from the University of Pennsylvania Law School. His articles have appeared in the *UCLA Law Review*, the *Tulane Law Review*, and the *Harvard Journal of Law and Gender*, among others. He would like to thank Carlos Ball for helpful remarks on the commentary and for consistent, thoughtful, feminist-spirited mentoring.

Carlos A. Ball is Distinguished Professor and Judge Frederick Lacey Scholar at the Rutgers University Law School. His books include *The First Amendment and LGBT Equality* (forthcoming); *Same-Sex Marriage and Children: A Tale of History, Social Science, and Law* (2014); *The Right to be Parents: LGBT Families and the Transformation of Parenthood* (2012); and *From the Closet to the Courtroom: Five LGBT Lawsuits That Have Changed Our Nation* (2010). He is also the editor of *After Marriage Equality: The Future of LGBT Rights* (New York University Press 2016).

Ann Bartow is Director of the Franklin Pierce Center for Intellectual Property and Professor of Law at the University of New Hampshire School of Law. She is a graduate of Cornell University and the University of Pennsylvania Law School. She also holds an LL.M. in Legal Education from Temple University's Beasley School of Law. She primarily writes and teaches in the Copyright Law, Patent Law and Trademark Law areas, often integrating feminist legal theory into these subjects. She dedicates the chapter she contributed to this book to Alida Starr Gebser, who showed amazing courage in the face of great injustice.

Linda L. Berger is the Family Foundation Professor of Law and the Associate Dean for Faculty Development and Research at UNLV Boyd School of Law. She teaches courses in legal communication and rhetoric. She received her B.S. from the University of Colorado and her J.D. from Case Western Reserve University School of Law. Berger is the President of the Legal Writing Institute and a founder of the peer-reviewed journal *Legal Communication & Rhetoric*. Her scholarship on rhetorical theory, study, and practice can be found in the *Journal of Legal Education*, the *Journal of Law and Policy*, the *Michigan State Law Review*, and the *Southern California Interdisciplinary Law Journal*, among others.

Patricia A. Broussard is a Professor of Law at Florida A & M University College of Law in Orlando, Florida. She teaches courses in Constitutional Law, Advanced Appellate Advocacy, and Advanced Topics of Women and the Law. She received her B.S. from Northwestern University and her J.D. from Howard University School of Law. Professor Broussard serves on the Board of the Society of American Law Teachers and is a Fulbright Scholar with a specialty in the study of female genital mutilation.

Dale Margolin Cecka is a Clinical Professor of Law and Director of the Family Law Clinic at the University of Richmond School of Law. She received her B.A. from Stanford University and her J.D. from Columbia University School of Law. Her scholarly articles have appeared in *Catholic University Law Review* and *West Virginia Law Review*, among others. She is a former Skadden Fellow and serves on the Board of Directors of the Virginia State Bar Section on Education of Lawyers.

Martha Chamallas holds the Robert J. Lynn Chair in Law at Ohio State's Moritz College of Law where she teaches Gender and the Law, Torts, and Employment Discrimination. She is the author of *The Measure of Injury: Race, Gender and Tort Law* (2010) (with Jennifer B. Wriggins) and *Introduction to Feminist Legal Theory* (3d. ed. 2013). She is the author of more than forty articles and book chapters appearing in law journals such as the *Michigan Law Review*, *The University of Chicago Law Review*, the *University of Pennsylvania Law Review* and the *Southern California Law Review*. Many thanks to Allison Haugen for her terrific research assistance.

David S. Cohen is a Professor of Law at the Drexel University Thomas R. Kline School of Law where he teaches courses in Constitutional Law and Sex, Gender, and the Law. He is the co-author of *Living in the Crosshairs: The Untold Stories of Anti-Abortion Terrorism* (2015) and several articles about masculinity and sex segregation. Professor Cohen graduated from Columbia Law School and Dartmouth College. He thanks Suraji Wagage for her truly excellent research assistance.

Bridget J. Crawford is a Professor of Law at Pace University School of Law. She teaches courses in Feminist Legal Theory, Taxation, and Wills, Trusts & Estates. She received her B.A. from Yale University, her J.D. from the University of Pennsylvania Law School and her Ph.D. from Griffith University in Australia. Crawford is an elected member of the American Law Institute and the American College of Trust and Estate Counsel. She is the co-editor (with Anthony C. Infanti) of *Critical Tax Theory: An Introduction* and the subject of a profile in *What the Best Law Professors Do* (2013).

Karen Syma Czapanskiy, Professor of Law at the University of Maryland Francis King Carey School of Law, teaches courses on family law, property and families raising disabled children. She has written about family law, gender bias, family violence, welfare reform, special education, and public input in South Africa's legislative process. She served as chair of the Association of American Law Schools Section on Women in Legal Education and on the board of the Society of American Law Teachers. Active in electoral politics, she has served on the Montgomery County Democratic Central Committee and worked on behalf of candidates in local, state, and national elections.

Cynthia Hawkins DeBose is a Professor at Stetson University College of Law where she teaches courses in Family Law, Adoption Law, Child Welfare Law, Domestic Violence Law & Policy, and Family Law Mediation. She earned her B.A. degree from Wellesley College and her J.D. degree from Harvard Law School. Professor Hawkins DeBose is the author of *Mastering Adoption Law and Policy* (2015). She is a Florida Supreme Court Certified Family & Civil Law Mediator. She is a Former Chair of the Association of American Law Schools Women in Legal Education Section. She is licensed to practice law in Pennsylvania and Washington, D.C.

Andrea Doneff, at the time she wrote this Commentary, was an Associate Professor at Atlanta's John Marshall Law School (AJMLS). At AJLMS she was Director of the Legal Skills and Professionalism Program, and taught Dispute Resolution, Mediation, Legal Writing, Transactional Drafting, and Civil Procedure. She wrote primarily on dispute resolution, including arbitration and negotiation. Since writing this Commentary, Andrea has left AJMLS and joined the Kinnard Mediation Center at the United States Court of Appeals for the Eleventh Circuit as a Circuit Mediator. This Commentary reflects solely her own views and does not in any way reflect the views of the Court.

Ilene Durst is an Associate Professor of Law and the Director of Persuasive Legal Writing at Thomas Jefferson School of Law where she teaches courses in legal methods and communication, immigration and refugee law, and law and literature. She received her B.A. from the State University of New York at Albany, her J.D. from New York Law School, and her M.F.A. from University of California, Irvine.

Lucinda M. Finley is the Frank Raichle Professor of Law at the State University of New York at Buffalo Law School. Her teaching and research interests are in the areas of feminist theory, reproductive rights, gender and tort law, and employment discrimination. She has published widely on these topics in leading law reviews and in book collections. She is also an experienced federal appellate advocate who has successfully argued cases in the U.S. Supreme Court and in several federal circuit courts of appeal. From 2005 through 2014 she served in a top leadership position in the central administration of her University, as Vice Provost for Faculty Affairs.

Iselin M. Gambert is Associate Director and Associate Professor of Legal Writing at The George Washington University Law School. She teaches courses in legal communication and rhetoric and directs the legal Writing Center. Iselin received her B.A. from Pomona College and her J.D. from GW Law. She thanks Karen Thornton for inspiring her to pursue this project, Ryan Fletcher for his support and encouragement, Renee Reasoner for revision assistance, and Justice Ginsburg for making her private papers available. Iselin dedicates her commentary to her mother, Gry Gambert – the first feminist she ever met, and the most extraordinary person she has ever known.

Cynthia Godsoe is an Assistant Professor of Law at the Brooklyn Law School. She teaches courses in family law, criminal law, professional responsibility, and public interest lawyering. Her scholarship centers on the regulation of intimate behavior, gender and sexuality through family and criminal law, and her work has appeared in the *Tulane Law Review, Yale Law Journal Forum,* and *Cardozo Law Review*. Professor Godsoe graduated from Harvard Law School in 1998, and received her Bachelor of Arts from Harvard College in 1993. She thanks Kaitlyn Devenyns for excellent research assistance and Liz Schneider and Bennett Capers for thoughtful comments.

Phyllis Goldfarb is the Jacob Burns Foundation Professor of Clinical Law and Associate Dean for Clinical Affairs at George Washington University Law School. Formerly she was a Professor of Law at Boston College Law School, teaching Criminal Justice Clinic, Gender and Legal Theory, and other courses. She serves as an Editor-in-Chief of the *Clinical Law Review* and has published articles on various topics, including her representation of women who killed batterers (*George Washington Law Review*) and feminism's ethical relationship to clinical education (*Minnesota Law Review*). She holds a B.A. (Brandeis), an Ed.M. (Harvard), a J.D. (Yale), and an LL.M. (Georgetown).

Deborah Gordon is an Associate Professor of Law at the Drexel University Thomas R. Kline School of Law. She teaches courses in Legal Methods and Wills, Trusts and Estates. She received her B.A. from Williams College and her J.D. from New York University Law School, where she served as editor-in-chief of the Law Review. She is the current secretary of the Association of American Law Schools Section on Trusts & Estates.

Leslie C. Griffin is the William S. Boyd Professor of Law at UNLV Boyd School of Law. She teaches constitutional law, law and religion, and bioethics. She received her J.D. from Stanford Law School and her Ph.D. in Religious Studies from Yale University.

Cassandra Jones Havard is a Professor of Law at the University of Baltimore School of Law. She teaches courses in banking, corporate and commercial law. She earned a B.A. with highest honors from Bennett College and a J.D. from the University of Pennsylvania where she was editor-in-chief of the *Black Law Journal*. After law school, Jones Havard clerked on the Third Circuit Court of Appeals for the Honorable A. Leon Higginbotham, Jr. At Baltimore, she serves on the Faculty Senate and is the Director of the Charles Hamilton Houston Scholars Program, a pipeline program for underrepresented minority and economically disadvantaged undergraduates interested in a legal career.

Berta Esperanza Hernández-Truyol is the Levin, Mabie & Levin Professor of Law at the University of Florida Levin College of Law and an affiliate professor at the Center for Women's and Gender Studies and the Center for Latin American Studies. She teaches international law, international human rights, and specialized, interdisciplinary, graduate seminars on human rights. Her scholarly work explores issues of gender, race, culture, sexuality, and language and their interconnections. Her publications include: *Just Trade; Moral Imperialism*; and close to 100 articles and chapters. She is a member of the American Law Institute and the American Society of International Law; she serves on the Board of Southern Legal Counsel.

Kimberly Holst teaches legal writing and skills courses at the Sandra Day O'Connor College of Law at Arizona State University. Her scholarship focuses on the intersection of educational pedagogy and traditional law school pedagogy and the development of law school pedagogy in the global context. She has also written in the areas of intellectual property law and criminal procedure. Professor Holst serves on the Board of Directors for the Legal Writing Institute and as a Co-Managing Editor for *Legal Writing: The Journal of the Legal Writing Institute*, and is a past Chair of the Association of American Law Schools Section on Legal Writing, Reasoning, and Research.

Margaret E. Johnson is an Associate Professor and Co-Director for the Center on Applied Feminism at the University of Baltimore School of Law. Her scholarship focuses on social justice and systemic reform issues relating to domestic violence and the legal system as well as feminist legal theory and gender justice. Her scholarly articles have appeared in the *UC Davis Law Review*, the *BYU Law Review*, the *Cardozo Law Review*, and the *Villanova Law Review*, among others. She thanks Addie Crawford for her able research assistance and Kathy Stanchi and Ann McGinley for their comments.

Margo Kaplan is an Associate Professor at Rutgers Law School, where she teaches courses on criminal law, health law and policy, and sex crimes. Her research explores legal limitations on intimate decisions, particularly the use of criminal law in areas of sex and health. Professor Kaplan's publications have examined topics such as sex-positive law, HIV-exposure criminalization, sexual assault, and pedophilia. She holds a joint appointment with the Department of Public Policy and Administration.

Inga N. Laurent is an Associate Professor and Director of the Externship Program at Gonzaga University School of Law. She is engaged with initiatives to help diversify the legal profession and to reform the criminal justice system. Prior to joining academia, she worked as a staff attorney with Southeastern Ohio Legal Services (SEOLS) under a grant from the federal Violence Against Women Act. While at SEOLS, she provided holistic civil legal services to victims of domestic violence and worked to systematically address domestic violence issues.

Pamela Laufer-Ukeles is Professor of Law at the University of Dayton School of Law. From 2014 to 2016 she has also been affiliated with Bar-Ilan University and Shaarei Mishpat College of Law in Israel. Her scholarship and teaching are in the fields of family law, reproductive rights, bioethics, gender and the law, and torts. She has published numerous law review articles and book chapters including articles in the *Indiana Law Journal, Connecticut Law Review, Harvard Journal of Gender and the Law,* and the *American Journal of Law and Medicine.* Her current work explores the nature of relational rights and commercial intimacy. She is a graduate of Harvard Law School and Columbia College.

Aníbal Rosario Lebrón is a Puerto Rican attorney, linguist, and photographer currently serving as an Assistant Professor of Lawyering Skills at Howard University School of Law. He works also as a Consultant to the Solicitor General of the Commonwealth of Puerto Rico. He holds a B.S. in Biology, a J.D., and a Post-Graduate Certificate in Linguistics from the University of Puerto Rico as well as a LL.M. in Legal Theory from New York University. He would like to thank his research assistant, Aaron P. Riggs, for his insightful comments and dedication to this project.

Maya Manian is a Professor of Law at the University of San Francisco School of Law. She teaches courses on Constitutional Law, Family Law, and Gender and the Law. Professor Manian received her B.A. from the University of Michigan and her J.D. from Harvard Law School. Her research focuses on access to reproductive health care. Her scholarly articles have appeared in the *Washington and Lee Law Review,* the *Ohio State Law Journal,* and the *Duke Journal of Gender Law & Policy,* among others. She thanks Amy Wright for excellent services as research librarian.

Kris McDaniel-Miccio, Professor of Law at the Sturm College of Law, University of Denver, is also a research faculty member at the Centre for Gender and Women Studies, Trinity College Dublin and the Equality Institute, University College Dublin, Ireland. While a Fulbright, Marie Curie and Trinity College Scholar, she conducted research on freedom-to-marry movements in the U.S., Northern Ireland, and Ireland. In Ireland, she lectured and debated issues specific to the Irish Marriage Equality Referendum. In the U.S., Professor McDaniel-Miccio and her wife were the lead plaintiffs in a successful lawsuit challenging Colorado's mini DOMA. Her scholarship has been published in law review and peer-reviewed scholarly journals in the U.S. and Ireland. And finally, she is an ordained rabbi!

Ann C. McGinley, the William S. Boyd Professor of Law at the UNLV Boyd School of Law, is an internationally recognized scholar in gender, employment discrimination, and disability law and a leader in Multidimensional Masculinities Theory. She is a co-editor of *Masculinities and the Law: A Multidimensional Approach* (2012) (with Frank Rudy Cooper) and a co-author of *Disability Law: Cases, Materials, Problems* (5th ed.) (with Laura Rothstein). Her most recent book, *Through a Different Lens: Perspectives on Masculinity and Employment Discrimination Law* is forthcoming in 2016.

Teri McMurtry-Chubb is an Associate Professor of Law at Mercer University School of Law. She researches, teaches, and writes in the areas of discourse analysis and rhetoric, critical race theory/feminism, hegemony studies, and legal history. Professor McMurtry-Chubb is the co-founder of the Center for Law, Diversity & Justice at Fairhaven College of Interdisciplinary Studies in Bellingham, Washington, and the author of *Legal Writing in the Disciplines: A Guide to Legal Writing Mastery* (2012). She thanks God, her colleagues who read and supported this work, and her husband Mark A. Chubb for jumping the broom over nineteen years ago.

Maria Isabel Medina is the Ferris Family Distinguished Professor of Law at Loyola University New Orleans College of Law. She teaches and writes about gender, constitutional law, and immigration law, and is a past co-chair of the Constitutional Law Section and past chair of the Immigration Law Section of the Association of American Law Schools. She is an elected member of the American Law Institute. She thanks Chelsea Rice for research assistance, commentator Patricia Broussard, editor Linda Berger, and the participants of the Tulane Law School's Faculty Summer Workshop series, in particular Shu-Yi Oei, Catherine Hancock, John Lovett, and John Blevins.

Kimberly M. Mutcherson is Vice Dean and Professor of Law at Rutgers School of Law, where she teaches courses in family law, bioethics, health law and policy. She received her B.A. from the University of Pennsylvania and her J.D. from Columbia Law School. Her work appears in numerous scholarly journals and she speaks nationally and internationally as an expert on assisted reproduction. She thanks David Cohen, Bridget Crawford, Jody Lyneé Madeira, Rachel Rebouché, and Priscilla Smith for their helpful edits and comments.

Maria L. Ontiveros is Professor of Law and co-director of the labor and employment law program at University of San Francisco School of Law. She holds an A.B. from University of California, Berkeley; a J.D. from Harvard Law School; an M.I.L.R. from Cornell; and a J.S.D. from Stanford Law

School. Her research focuses on organizing immigrant workers, workplace harassment of women of color, and modern-day applications of the Thirteenth Amendment. Catherine Tran, USF 2014, and Lee Ryan, reference librarian, both provided excellent research help.

Angela Onwuachi-Willig is the Kierscht Professor of Law at the University of Iowa and a graduate of Grinnell College, University of Michigan Law School, and Yale Graduate School of Arts and Sciences. She authored *According to Our Hearts:* Rhinelander v. Rhinelander *and the Law of the Multiracial Family* (2013). Her articles have appeared in journals such as the *Yale Law Journal* and *California Law Review*. She is an elected American Law Institute member, a recipient of the Association of American Law Schools Minority Groups Section's Clyde Ferguson Award and Derrick Bell Award, and a former Iowa Supreme Court finalist. She thanks Kristen Tiscione and Kathryn Stanchi.

Sandra S. Park is a Senior Staff Attorney in the ACLU Women's Rights Project. She engages in litigation and policy advocacy at the national and local levels to advance the human rights and civil liberties of women and girls. Sandra's current focus includes challenging discrimination faced by survivors of gender-based violence in housing, law enforcement, schools, and the military. She also represented twenty medical organizations, geneticists, and patients to win a unanimous 2013 ruling from the U.S. Supreme Court invalidating human gene patents. She graduated *magna cum* laude from Harvard College and New York University School of Law.

Nancy D. Polikoff is Professor of Law at American University Washington College of Law where she teaches Family Law and a seminar on Children of LGBT Parents. For forty years, she has been writing about, teaching about, and working on litigation and legislation about LGBT families. Her book, *Beyond (Straight and Gay) Marriage: Valuing All Families under the Law*, was published in 2008. Professor Polikoff is a member of the National Family Law Advisory Council of the National Center for Lesbian Rights. In 2011, she received the National LGBT Bar Association's Dan Bradley award, the organization's highest honor.

Lisa R. Pruitt is a Professor of Law at the University of California, Davis, Martin Luther King, Jr. School of Law, where she teaches torts, feminist legal theory, and law and rural livelihoods, among other courses. Much of Professor Pruitt's scholarship theorizes the legal relevance of rural socio-spatiality, with specific attention to the junctures at which rural women encounter law and legal institutions. She has written extensively about abortion access for rural women, including *Toward a Feminist Theory of the Rural* (2007) and *Urbanormativity, Spatial Privilege, and Judicial Blind Spots in Abortion Law* (2015).

Dara E. Purvis is an Assistant Professor of Law at the Pennsylvania State University School of Law. She teaches courses in family law, sexuality and the law, and contracts. She received her J.D. from Yale, her M.Phil. from the University of Cambridge, and her B.A. from the University of Southern California.

Rachel Rebouché is an Associate Professor at Temple University Beasley School of Law. She teaches Family Law, Health Law, and Comparative Family Law. Her current research focuses on reproductive health, collaborative divorce, genetic testing, and governance feminism. She received a J.D. from Harvard Law School, LL.M. from Queen's University, Belfast, and B.A. from Trinity University. She was an associate director of adolescent health programs at the National Partnership for Women & Families and a Women's Law and Public Policy Fellow at the National Women's Law Center. Professor Rebouché clerked for Justice Kate O'Regan on the Constitutional Court of South Africa.

Deborah L. Rhode is the Ernest W. McFarland Professor of Law and Director of the Center on the Legal Profession at Stanford University. She is the former Chair of the American Bar Association Commission on Women in the Legal Profession, and former Director of Stanford's Institute for Research on Women and Gender. Her recent books on gender include *What Women Want* (2014), *The Beauty Bias* (2010) and *Gender and Law* (with Katharine Bartlett and Joanna Grossman, 2013).

Ruthann Robson is Professor of Law and University Distinguished Professor at the City University of New York (CUNY) School of Law, where she has taught since 1990 primarily in the areas of constitutional law and sexuality and law. Her books include *Dressing Constitutionally: Hierarchy, Sexuality, and Democracy* (2013); *Sappho Goes to Law School* (1998); *Gay Men, Lesbians, and the Law* (1996); and *Lesbian (Out)Law: Survival Under the Rule of Law* (1992). She is the editor of the casebook *First Amendment Cases, Controversies, and Contexts* and the three volume set, *International Library of Essays in Sexuality and Law* (2011). She is one of the twenty-six professors selected for inclusion in *What the Best Law Teachers Do* (Harvard University Press 2013).

Laura Rosenbury is the Dean and Levin, Mabie & Levin Professor of Law at University of Florida Levin College of Law. Her scholarship focuses on law's participation in the construction of gender. She has explored law's relationship to friendship, intimacy, sex, marriage, and childrearing, analyzing the ways such personal relationships shape legal and cultural understandings of male and female roles. Dean Rosenbury is also the co-author of the fourth edition of the *Feminist Jurisprudence* casebook, along with Cynthia Bowman, Deborah Tuerkheimer, and Kimberly Yuracko. She welcomes all feminist inquiries at rosenbury@yahoo.com.

Macarena Sáez is a Fellow in International Legal Studies and the Director of the Center for Human Rights and Humanitarian Law at American University Washington College of Law. She teaches Family Law, Comparative Family Law and Human Rights Strategic Litigation. She has written extensively in the areas of gender, sexuality and the law. She is the co-editor of the first casebook on gender and the law in Latin America. Professor Sáez was one of the main attorneys in the first case on sexual orientation before the Inter-American System of Human Rights.

Shaakirrah R. Sanders teaches Constitutional Law, Criminal Procedure, and the First Amendment at the University of Idaho College of Law. She has appeared in *The New York Times*, Associated Press, Al Jazeera America, Northwest and Boise State Public Radio, and Boise's KTVB News 7, KITV News 9, and KBOI News 2. She earned a B.S. from Trinity College (Hartford, Connecticut) and a J.D. from Loyola University New Orleans College of Law. She served as a judicial law clerk in the United States District Court for the Eastern District of Louisiana and the United States Court of Appeals for the Eighth Circuit.

Michelle S. Simon is a Professor at Pace Law School, where she served as Dean from 2007 to 2014. She currently teaches civil procedure, torts, conflicts and education law. She received her B.A. from SUNY Albany and her J.D. from Syracuse Law School. She thanks Anastazia Sienty for helpful research and editorial assistance.

Brenda V. Smith is a Professor of Law and Director of the Project on Addressing Prison Rape at American University, Washington College of Law. She received her B.A. from Spelman College and J.D. from Georgetown University Law Center. Her scholarly articles have appeared in *University of California, Los Angeles Law Review, North Carolina Law Review, Yale Journal of Law and Feminism, Columbia Journal of Gender and Law* and the *American University Journal of Gender, Social Policy and Law*. She served as Commissioner on the National Prison Rape Elimination Commission from 2003 to 2009. She thanks Emma Burgess Roy for invaluable research assistance.

Kathryn M. Stanchi is a Professor of Law and Affiliated Professor of Women's Studies at Temple University Beasley School of Law. She teaches writing courses, including courses in feminism and advocacy, her main scholarly areas of concentration. Her articles have appeared in the *Washington Law Review*, the *Harvard Civil Rights-Civil Liberties Law Review* and the *Berkeley Women's Law Journal*, among others. She attended Bryn Mawr College and the University of Pennsylvania, both of which influenced her feminist consciousness in different ways. She received her J.D., *magna cum laude*, from Boston University School of Law.

Tracy A. Thomas is Associate Dean for Institutional Excellence and Seiberling Chair of Constitutional Law at The University of Akron School of Law. She teaches courses on family law, dispute resolution, and remedies, and also directs the Constitutional Law Center. She is past chair of the Association of American Law Schools Section on Remedies. Professor Thomas is co-editor of the *Gender and the Law Prof Blog* and editor of the annual *Women and the Law*.

Kristen Konrad Tiscione is a Professor of Legal Research and Writing at Georgetown University Law Center. She has taught in the J.D. and LL.M. programs for twenty years. She received her B.A. from Wellesley College and her J.D. from Georgetown. She is a member of the Board of Directors of the Legal Writing Institute and the Secretary of the Association of Legal Writing Directors. She is also serving a second term as a member of the Editorial Board of *Legal Writing: The Journal of the Legal Writing Institute*. Her scholarly interests include classical rhetoric, feminist legal theory, and employment discrimination.

Christine M. Venter is the Director of the Legal Writing Program at Notre Dame Law School, where she also teaches Gender Issues and is a research faculty member in the Gender Studies program. She obtained her undergraduate and law degrees from the University of Cape Town in South Africa and a Masters and Doctorate in International Human Rights from Notre Dame Law School. She is the author of *International Women's Rights: Equality and Justice* (2012).

Valorie K. Vojdik is a Professor of Law at the University of Tennessee College of Law. She teaches Sex, Gender and Justice; Civil Procedure; Civil Rights; and related courses. Her research and scholarship focuses on feminist legal theory, masculinities theory, gender and war, and international women's rights. She received her J.D. from New York University School of Law and her

A.B. *magna cum laude* from Brown University. She has litigated cases involving gender discrimination and was lead counsel to Shannon Faulkner in the federal lawsuit that successfully challenged the male-only admission policy of The Citadel in South Carolina.

Mary Ziegler is the Stearns, Weaver, Miller Professor at Florida State University College of Law, where she teaches courses in reproduction, gender, and sexuality, family law, employment law, and torts. She received her B.A. and J.D. from Harvard University. In addition to more than twenty articles, she is the author of *After Roe: The Lost History of the Abortion Debate* (2015). She would like to thank Linda Berger and Leslie Griffin for their editorial assistance.

Advisory panel

Kathryn Abrams
Herma Hill Kay Distinguished Professor of Law
University of California, Berkeley, School of Law

Katharine T. Bartlett
A. Kenneth Pye Professor of Law
Duke University School of Law

Devon W. Carbado
The Honorable Harry Pregerson Professor of Law
University of California, Los Angeles, School of Law

Mary Anne Case
Arnold I. Shure Professor of Law
The University of Chicago Law School

Erwin Chemerinsky
Dean of the School of Law
Distinguished Professor of Law
Raymond Pryke Professor of First Amendment Law
University of California, Irvine, School of Law

April L. Cherry
Professor of Law
Cleveland-Marshall College of Law

Kimberlé W. Crenshaw
Distinguished Professor of Law
University of California, Los Angeles, School of Law
Professor of Law, Columbia Law School

Martha Albertson Fineman
Robert W. Woodruff Professor of Law
Emory University School of Law

Margaret E. Johnson
Associate Professor of Law
University of Baltimore School of Law

Sonia Katyal
Professor of Law
University of California, Berkeley, School of Law

Nancy Leong
Associate Professor
University of Denver Sturm College of Law

Catharine A. MacKinnon
Elizabeth A. Long Professor of Law, University of Michigan Law School
James Ames Barr Visiting Professor, Harvard Law School

Rachel Moran
William H. Neukom Fellows Research Chair
American Bar Foundation

Melissa Murray
Professor of Law
University of California, Berkeley, School of Law

Angela Onwuachi-Willig
Charles M. and Marion J. Kierscht Professor of Law
The University of Iowa College of Law

Nancy D. Polikoff
Professor of Law
American University Washington College of Law

Dorothy E. Roberts
George A. Weiss University Professor of Law and Sociology and the Raymond
Pace and Sadie Tanner Mossell Alexander Professor of Civil Rights
University of Pennsylvania Law School

Daniel B. Rodriguez
Dean and Harold Washington Professor
Northwestern University School of Law

Susan Deller Ross
Professor of Law
Georgetown University Law Center

Vicki Schultz
Ford Foundation Professor of Law and Social Sciences
Yale Law School

Dean Spade
Associate Professor of Law
Seattle University School of Law

Robin L. West
Frederick J. Haas Professor of Law and Philosophy
Georgetown University Law Center

Verna L. Williams
Judge Joseph P. Kinneary Professor of Law
University of Cincinnati College of Law

Preface

What would United States Supreme Court opinions look like if key decisions on gender issues were written with a feminist perspective? To begin to answer this question, we brought together a group of scholars and lawyers to rewrite, using feminist reasoning, the most significant U.S. Supreme Court cases on gender from the 1800s to the present day. While feminist legal theory has developed and even thrived within universities, and feminist activists and lawyers are responsible for major changes in the law, feminist reasoning has had a less clear impact on judicial decision making. Doctrines of *stare decisis* and judicial language of neutrality can operate to obscure structural bias in the law, making it difficult to see what feminism could bring to judicial reasoning.

The twenty-five opinions in this volume demonstrate that judges with feminist viewpoints could have changed the course of the law. The rewritten decisions show that previously accepted judicial outcomes were not necessary or inevitable and demonstrate that feminist reasoning increases the judicial capacity for justice, not only for women but for many other oppressed groups. The remarkable differences evident in the rewritten opinions also open a path for a long overdue discussion of the real impact that judicial diversity has on law and of the influence that perspective has in judging.

Kathryn M. Stanchi
Linda L. Berger
Bridget J. Crawford

Acknowledgments

The U.S. Feminist Judgments Project has received support from many different people and institutions. Our project would not have been possible without the vision of the women who created the Women's Court of Canada and the U.K. Feminist Judgments Project. Special thanks go to Erika Rackley and Rosemary Hunter of the U.K. Feminist Judgments Project for guiding us and answering our many questions.

We wish to thank Jamie R. Abrams, David S. Cohen, and Kristen Konrad Tiscione who were an integral part of the early process of thinking about the book's content and organization. We are indebted to the members of our Advisory Panel who provided excellent counsel on which cases to include in this book.

We received technical and administrative support from Maria Campos, Caitlin Harrington, Judy Jaeger, Shyam Nair, and Rebecca Schatschneider.

We could not have accomplished what we did without superb research help from our professional librarians and our student research assistants: Michael Ahlert, Elliot Anderson, Sheila Arjomandi, Matthew Beckstead, Dana Bonfiglio, Rhiannon DiClemente, Elizabeth Dolce, Stephanie Grey, Rosemarie Hebner, Noa Kaumeheiwa, Ryan Koleda, Dina Kopansky, Katie LaDow, Andrea Orwoll, Aakash Patel, Chad Schatzle, Amy Skiles, and Breeana Somers.

We are grateful to John Berger for his guidance and assistance throughout the publication process.

Finally, each of us would like to thank those people who supported and inspired us throughout the hard work of this project. Kathy would like to thank her husband, Frank Fritz, whose strength and support of this project was unflagging; she also would like to thank her family, who supported her in all their different ways, but especially her parents, for sacrificing much to educate her even though they grew up in a time and culture that believed it a waste of time and money to educate girls. Linda Berger thanks Terry Pollman, Ann McGinley, Leslie Griffin, Andi Orwoll, Maria Campos, Dan Hamilton, and Boyd School of Law. Bridget Crawford thanks Horace Anderson, Lolita Buckner Inniss, Catharine MacKinnon, Dan Renkin, and Michelle Simon.

About the cover art

On the cover, *Little Girl from Harlem* © Soraida Martinez

Soraida Martinez is a New York-born artist of Puerto Rican heritage who, since 1992, has been known for creating the art of "Verdadism," a contemporary form of the style of hardedge painting where every painting is accompanied by a written social commentary. Soraida's paintings depict her life experiences for the purpose of promoting peace, tolerance, and understanding. Soraida's Verdadism art can be seen at soraida.com.

Commentary on Little Girl from Harlem

As a little girl living in Harlem, I always knew that Harlem was some kind of exile. What I didn't know was why I had to be there. There were happy times as well as sad times … but, to escape, I would always daydream. I would daydream of a backyard, of growing up and going to art school, and of moving away. As an adult, I was always embarrassed to say that I was born in Harlem and that I had lived there until I turned fourteen … because people were quick to judge me. Most people assume that I grew up middle-class and came from a middle-class neighborhood. Little do they know that there are lots of people from Harlem that are just like me.

– Soraida Martinez 1995

Table of cases

PART I

Introduction and overview

1

Introduction to the U.S. feminist judgments project

Kathryn M. Stanchi, Linda L. Berger, and Bridget J. Crawford

How would U.S. Supreme Court opinions change if the justices used feminist methods and perspectives when deciding cases? That is the central question that we sought to answer by bringing together a group of scholars and lawyers to carry out this project. To answer it, they would use feminist theories to rewrite the most significant gender justice cases decided by the U.S. Supreme Court from the passage of the final Civil Rights Amendment in 1870 to the summer of 2015.

As an initial matter, we provided no guidance to our contributors on what we meant by "feminism." We wanted our authors to be free to bring their own vision of feminism to the project. Yet it would be disingenuous to suggest that we ourselves do not have a particular perspective on what "feminism," "feminist reasoning," or "feminist methods" are. Indeed, without such a perspective, we would not have undertaken the project.

We recognize "feminism" as a movement and perspective historically grounded in politics, and one that motivates social, legal, and other battles for women's equality. We also understand it as a movement and mode of inquiry that has grown to endorse justice for all people, particularly those historically oppressed or marginalized by or through law.[1] We believe that "feminism" is not the province of women only, and we acknowledge and celebrate the multiple, fluid identities contained in the category "woman."[2] Within this broad view, we acknowledge that feminists can disagree (and still be feminist) and that there are no unitary feminist methods or reasoning processes. So when we refer to feminist methods or feminist reasoning processes, we mean

---

[1] So-called "third-wave" feminists particularly see feminism as a broader social justice issue. *See, e.g.,* Bridget J. Crawford, *Toward a Third-Wave Feminist Legal Theory: Young Women, Pornography and the Praxis of Pleasure,* 14 Mich. J. Gender & L. 99, 102 (2007); Kristen Kalsem and Verna L. Williams, *Social Justice Feminism,* 18 UCLA Women's L.J. 131, 169–72 (2010).

[2] *See* Katharine T. Bartlett, *Feminist Legal Methods,* 103 Harv. L. Rev. 829, 830 (1990).

"methods" and "reasoning processes" *plural*, all the while acknowledging that there is a rich and diverse body of scholarship that has flourished under the over-arching label "feminist legal theory." Indeed, those are the methods and reasoning processes examined and employed by many of the authors represented in the book.

Nevertheless, in shaping the project from its early stages through the finished pages, we as editors have been motivated by a broad and expansive view of what "feminism" is. This capacious understanding undoubtedly shaped the project in many ways, including our choice of cases, our selection of authors, and our edits, even if we did not define feminism for our contributors. We leave it to readers to explore the varieties of feminism that are reflected in these pages.

Feminist legal theory and scholarship have developed and even thrived within universities over the last thirty to forty years. Feminist activists and lawyers are responsible for major changes in the law of employment discrimination, sexual harassment, marital rape, reproductive rights, family relationships, and equitable distribution, to name just a few areas. Feminism has had a less discernable impact on judging, however, and it is relatively rare to see explicitly feminist reasoning in judicial decisions. More common are judicial reliance on the doctrine of *stare decisis* and judicial use of the language of apparent neutrality. Both of these moves tend to obscure embedded and structural biases in the law, making it difficult to recognize that feminism offers a critical expansion of the field for judicial decision making.

The twenty-five opinions in this volume demonstrate that judges who are open to feminist viewpoints could have arrived at different decisions or applied different reasoning to reach the same (or different) results in major decisions of the U.S. Supreme Court. As the authors reworked their opinions related to gender, they applied feminist theory or methods. The resulting feminist judgments demonstrate that neither the initial outcome nor the subsequent development of the law was necessary or inevitable. Feminist reasoning expands the judicial capacity for equal justice and can help make more attainable political, economic, and social equality for women and other disadvantaged groups.

GOALS OF THE PROJECT

Although the project has a number of goals, one priority is to uncover that what passes for neutral law making and objective legal reasoning is often bound up in traditional assumptions and power hierarchies. That is, all legal actors – judges, juries, litigants, lawyers – engage in their decision making within a situated perspective that is informed by gender, race, class, religion, disability, nationality, language, and sexual orientation. For judges, that (often unacknowledged) situated perspective can be crucial to the reasoning and the outcome of cases. The situated perspective of the decision maker may drive American jurisprudence as much as – if not more than – *stare decisis* does. A judge's worldview may inform the choices that the judge makes about the doctrinal basis for an opinion. For example, a judge may need to choose whether a lawsuit should be decided as a substantive due process case about privacy rights or as an equal protection case about gender equality. Recognizing that all decision making involves a situated perspective reveals that decision makers are affected by assumptions and expectations of norms relating to gender, race, class, sexuality, and other characteristics. Despite the alleged neutrality of the rules and processes of decision making within the U.S. judicial system, values and beliefs shaped by experience may exert a significant, if difficult-to-see, influence on the judges' interpretation and application of the law.

The U.S. Feminist Judgments Project turns attention to the U.S. Supreme Court. Contributors to this volume challenge the formalistic concepts that U.S. Supreme Court opinions are, or should be, written from a neutral vantage point and that they are, or should be, based on deductive logic or "pure" rationality. When the project's authors brought their own feminist consciousness or philosophy to some of the most important (and supposedly "neutral") decisions and assertions about gender-related issues, the judicial decisions took on a very different character. Feminist consciousness broadens and widens the lens through which we view law and helps the decision maker overcome the natural tendency to see things the same way or do things "the way they've always been done." Through this project, we hope to show that systemic inequalities are not intrinsic to law, but rather may be rooted in the subjective (and often unconscious) beliefs and assumptions of the decision makers. These inequalities may derive from processes and influences that tend to reinforce traditional or familiar approaches, decisions, or values. In other words, if we can broaden the perspectives of the decision makers, change in the law is possible.

In addition to exposing the contextual nature of judicial decision making, another goal of the project was to learn what "feminist" judging and decision making would look like, both from a substantive and rhetorical standpoint. What would the world look like if women and men with self-identified feminist consciousness were judges? With regard to substance, we wondered which of the many feminist theories would have practical application in judging and decision making and which laws contained the greatest potential for feminist application. Would we see some feminist theories or methods more frequently used than others? Which ones?

In terms of language, we wondered whether some feminist judges might use language or rhetorical strategies that differed from the original opinions in describing the facts or issue of a case, or the applicable law or reasoning.[3] To some scholars, the very label "feminist judgments" will suggest a particular feminist language, but the idea that feminists might speak in a "different" language or voice is a controversial one.[4] As our sister-editors in the U.K. observed, law is "a powerful and productive social discourse that *creates* and reinforces gender norms ... [L]aw does not simply operate on pre-existing gendered realities, but contributes to the construction of those realities."[5] We wanted our book to open a small vista on what law might look like if feminists were able to contribute, in a meaningful way, to that powerful, constitutive discourse.

INTELLECTUAL ORIGINS OF THE PROJECT

The U.S. Feminist Judgments Project is inspired by a similar project in the United Kingdom. In 2013, Kathy Stanchi attended the Applied Legal Storytelling Conference in London where she heard Professor Erika Rackley speak about the U.K. Feminist Judgments project, a volume of rewritten decisions from the House of Lords and Court of Appeal. The U.K. Project, itself inspired by the Women's Court of Canada,[6] united fifty-one feminist professors, practitioners, and research fellows to supply the "missing" feminist voice in British jurisprudence by rewriting, using feminist reasoning, key cases on parenting, property and markets, criminal law, public law, and equality. The

---

3   Some legal scholars have criticized certain traditional aspects of the judicial voice as intertwined with the class, race, and gender bias in the law. *See, e.g.,* Lucinda M. Finley, *Breaking Women's Silence in Law: The Dilemma of the Gendered Nature of Legal Reasoning,* 64 *Notre Dame L. Rev.* 886, 888 (1989); Kathryn M. Stanchi, *Feminist Legal Writing,* 39 *S.D. L. Rev.* 387, 402–03 (2002).

4   *Compare* Carrie Menkel-Meadow, *Portia in a Different Voice: Speculations on a Women's Lawyering Process,* 1 *Berkeley Women's L.J.* 39 (1985); Suzanna Sherry, *Civic Virtue and the Feminine Voice in Constitutional Adjudication,* 72 *Va. L. Rev.* 543, 592–613 (1986) *with* Catharine A. MacKinnon, Feminism Unmodified: Discourses on Life and Law 45 (1987) ("take your foot off our necks, then we will hear in what tongue women speak").

5   Feminist Judgments: From Theory to Practice 6–7 (Rosemary Hunter, Clare McGlynn and Erika Rackley eds., 2010) (referencing Carol Smart, Feminism and the Power of Law (1989)).

6   The Women's Court of Canada brought together a group of academics and practitioners who rewrote several cases involving section 15 (the equality clause) of the Canadian Charter of Rights and Freedoms. Their opinions are now online. *Decisions of the Women's Court of Canada,* TheCourt.ca (Sept. 9, 2015, 12:52 PM), www.thecourt.ca/decisions-of-the-womens-court-of-canada/.

U.K. Project has spawned similar projects covering Irish, Australian, and New Zealand law, as well as a project devoted to the field of international law.[7]

Having long wondered why feminist legal theory, despite its rich and vibrant academic history in the U.S., had not made greater inroads into American jurisprudence, we realized that the body of U.S. common law was overdue for feminist rewriting. Kathy Stanchi, Linda Berger, and Bridget Crawford agreed to serve as the project's editors, and a group of informal advisors organized by Kathy Stanchi met at the 2014 Annual Meeting of the Association of American Law Schools to discuss how many and which cases to choose for rewriting. Searching for a unifying theme that would tie the cases together, Bridget Crawford suggested limiting the selection to U.S. Supreme Court cases because of the Court's influence on the legal knowledge and awareness of the American public. Although restricting the project to U.S. Supreme Court cases limited the doctrinal coverage and excluded important state and lower court cases, the benefit of a unifying focus outweighed the detriments.

The editors realized early on that this could be the first of many U.S. feminist judgment projects. Like the U.K. project, the U.S. project might inspire feminist treatment of the decisions of other courts or other subject matters. For example, future projects might focus on decisions of state courts, appellate courts, and administrative agencies. Alternatively, future projects might be organized by following traditional subject-matter lines (e.g., torts, criminal law, property, civil procedure), or by developing areas of interest (e.g., entertainment law, farming law), or by applying additional critical theories (e.g., critical race theory, Lat Crit, critical tax theory). We welcome and invite such future work.

METHODOLOGY

Even after deciding to limit the project to decisions of the U.S. Supreme Court, we still had to narrow the scope. Beginning with the active duty of Chief Justice John Jay in 1789, the U.S. Supreme Court has decided more than 1,700 cases. In keeping with the impetus for the project, we decided to limit our pool of potential cases to those related to gender, although we all agreed that many other cases could benefit from a feminist rewriting. Our initial list contained nearly sixty cases.

[7] *See* Feminist Judgments Project, www.kent.ac.uk/law/fjp/ (last visited Sept. 9, 2015); Northern/Irish Feminist Judgments Project, www.feministjudging.ie/ (last visited Sept. 9, 2015); Australian Feminist Judgments Project, www.law.uq.edu.au/the-australian-feminist-judgments-project (last visited Sept. 9, 2015).

To minimize the influence of personal preferences and to benefit from the views of a range of diverse and knowledgeable experts, we assembled an Advisory Panel to help us select the cases most appropriate for rewriting. The panel included twenty-three scholars with expertise in feminist theory, constitutional law, or both. Its members were diverse in race, gender, sexuality, and academic background. We were honored to have the advisory participation of Kathryn Abrams, Katharine Bartlett, Devon Carbado, Mary Anne Case, Erwin Chemerinsky, April Cherry, Kimberlé Crenshaw, Martha Albertson Fineman, Margaret Johnson, Sonia Katyal, Nancy Leong, Catharine MacKinnon, Rachel Moran, Melissa Murray, Angela Onwuachi-Willig, Nancy Polikoff, Dorothy Roberts, Daniel Rodriguez, Susan Deller Ross, Vicki Schultz, Dean Spade, Robin West, and Verna Williams. We asked them to evaluate all sixty cases for possible feminist rewriting. Their feedback was surprisingly consistent, and we narrowed our initial list of sixty to thirty potential cases.

Having decided to follow the U.K. model of publishing a rewritten opinion accompanied by an expert commentary that would frame and provide context for the revision, we next issued a public call inviting potential authors to apply to rewrite one of the thirty cases or to comment on a rewritten opinion. Providing commentary for each rewritten opinion was important because the original opinions would not be included in the volume. The commentary describes the original decision, places it within its historical context, and assesses its continuing effects. Equally important, the commentary analyzes the rewritten feminist judgment, emphasizing how it differs both in process and effect from the original opinion. By following this format of matching rewritten opinion and commentary throughout the writing and editing process, we were able not only to include additional voices but also to gain the benefits of productive collaboration among opinion writers, commentators, and editors.

In response to the call for authors, we received more than one hundred applications, mostly from law professors, but also from practitioners, clerks, and others. Our applicants represented a range of subject-matter specialties, expertise, and experience. They were well-known feminist legal theorists of established reputation and standing as well as more junior scholars, both tenured and untenured. Some were firmly grounded in theory while others were more familiar with the substance and methods of law practice, including practicing attorneys, clinicians, and legal writing professors.

As editors, we were committed to diversity on many levels. In terms of cases, our almost-final list of twenty-four cases was chosen to represent a range of gender-related issues. In terms of authors, we sought contributors who were diverse in perspective, expertise, and status as well as race, sexuality, and gender.

In addition to the forty-eight authors selected to write the twenty-four opinions and their matching commentaries, we invited Professor Berta Esperanza Hernández-Truyol to write a chapter that would provide an overview of feminist legal theory and an account of feminist judging. The project was well underway in June 2015 when the U.S. Supreme Court decided *Obergefell v. Hodges*,[8] a landmark case on the constitutionality of same-sex marriage. We immediately added that case, along with the authors of *Obergefell*'s rewritten opinion and commentary, to the book. The final volume thus includes twenty-five cases and represents the contributions of fifty-one authors and the three editors.

GUIDELINES FOR THE OPINIONS AND COMMENTARY

The purpose of the U.S. Feminist Judgments Project is to show, in a practical and realistic way, that U.S. Supreme Court decisions could have been decided differently had the justices approached their decisions from a more complex and contextualized vantage. To illustrate this point, we asked the opinion writers to engage in a re-envisioning of the decision-making process, drawing on their own knowledge of feminist methods and theories, but bound by the facts and law that existed at the time. Opinion authors were limited as well to 8,000 words (far less than many U.S. Supreme Court opinions) but were free to choose to write a majority opinion, a dissent, or a concurrence, depending on their goals. A major practical difference between this project and real judging is that our authors were not constrained by the necessity of persuading other justices. It would have been unrealistic to require, across the board, that the authors speculate (in some uniform way) about what might have been accomplished through the formal (but not uniform) give-and-take that traditionally happens between justices at conference and in the more informal discussions among peers in the halls and chambers.

Authors were limited in the sources they could use in writing their opinions. They could draw only on facts and law in existence at the time of the original opinion. Many of our authors chafed at this constraint. But we felt strongly that such a source constraint, one of the hallmarks of the U.K. project, was essential to the legitimacy and goals of the U.S. project. To make the point that law may be driven by perspective as much as *stare decisis*, it was critical that the feminist justices be bound, just as the original justices were, to the law and precedent in effect at the time.

---

[8] *Obergefell v. Hodges*, 135 S. Ct. 2584 (2015).

In terms of materials other than the facts and law in existence at the time of the opinion, we recognized that our opinion writers likely would be unable to avoid using feminist arguments and critiques that emerged after the original opinion. This was especially true with respect to cases decided before the 1970s, when the modern women's liberation movement gained traction in the United States. Opinion writers could draw upon theories and philosophies that became familiar and widely used after the original decision, but they were required to cite only to contemporaneous sources. This struck us as a fair compromise. After all, we believe that it is an inherent and unavoidable aspect of judging that the decision makers bring to the law their own cultural and social assumptions (often uncited). So like any judges, our authors could espouse cultural or social views and bring their perspectives to their interpretation and application of the law.

As it turned out, these restrictions on sources of authority were less inhibiting than expected. Many of our authors reported that, to their surprise, the feminist analyses, social theories, and arguments that they wished to rely on were in circulation at the time of the original decision, and sometimes even well represented in the amicus briefs before the Court. This was true even of our oldest decision in *Bradwell v. Illinois*,[9] a U.S. Supreme Court case denying a woman admission to the bar. Professor Phyllis Goldfarb, the author of the revised opinion in *Bradwell*, reports that advocates of women's rights in the late 1800s had introduced into the mainstream public discourse feminist egalitarian ideals about women's participation in professional and public life, and they made strong arguments within the existing legal framework to advance these ideals. Reports like this from our authors confirm that our initial hypothesis had been correct: it is not that feminist arguments did not exist at the time of particular decisions, but rather that feminist consciousness has often been ignored or erased in U.S. Supreme Court jurisprudence.

We asked the opinion rewriters to employ a judicial voice and to observe the conventions of appellate opinion writing. Accepting the limitations of the genre, we wanted the opinions to sound like opinions – not like legal scholarship or advocacy, which is what most of our authors are accustomed to writing. This was important to the project's realism. Some of our authors found this requirement to be both liberating and constraining.[10] While the judicial voice is powerful, commanding and declarative, it is also a public voice in which

---

[9] *Bradwell v. Illinois*, 83 U.S. 130 (1873).
[10] As noted in the U.K. Feminist Judgments Introduction, "writing a judgment imposes certain expectations and constraints on the writer that inevitably affect – even infect – her theoretical purposes." Feminist Judgments, *supra* note 5, at 5.

the judge speaks not just for herself but also for her office. This public, official characteristic has traditionally required a certain dignity and forbearance in tone as well as a writing style that conveys candor, fairness, and dispassion. And while we wanted our authors to have the freedom to write as feminists, however they defined the term, we also asked them to honor legal conventions such as procedural rules and traditions. For example, while the authors could expand on the factual narrative contained within the original opinion, they had to limit themselves to the legal record before the Court, unless it was appropriate to use judicial notice for an easily verifiable fact.[11]

The authors of the commentaries had a formidable task, one perhaps even more difficult than that of the authors of rewritten opinions. Besides providing a summary of and context for the original opinion, the commentary also had to shed light on the feminist and theoretical underpinnings of the rewritten feminist judgment. Thus, when the feminist justice implicitly relied on non-precedential authority, such as theories or studies that were published after the date of the opinion, we encouraged the commentary author to discuss and cite those works to give credit to the feminist thinkers who made the reasoning possible. The commentators had to accomplish all this in 2,000 words.[12]

Within these guidelines, the contributors were free to pursue their particular feminist visions. Mindful of the many diverse feminist views, as noted above we did not define what "feminism" is or what the preferred feminist view of a particular case should be. While our edits occasionally suggested that authors consider the implications of certain works or theories, we did not interfere with their freedom to see the case, and its importance, in their own ways. Again within the constraints of the judicial opinion writing style already noted, we allowed authors to use the argument frameworks, wording choices, and writing style that they determined were most consistent with their feminist approach to the case.

In some cases, we as editors disagreed strongly with a contributor's approach. And, in several cases, the opinion writer and the commentator disagreed with each other. We expressed views in multiple rounds of edits, but each

---

[11] This also was potentially constraining, as feminist legal theorists have argued that the law often dismisses as irrelevant facts, circumstances, and contexts relevant to an outsider perspective. *See* Kim Lane Scheppele, *Just the Facts, Ma'am: Sexualized Violence, Evidentiary Habits, and the Revision of Truth*, 37 N.Y.L. Sch. L. Rev. 123 (1992). We recognized this problem, of course, but, on balance, decided that any project could not address every problem of outsider invisibility.

[12] The Australian Feminist Judgments Project offered an interesting alternative: opinion and commentary together could be 7,000 words, and the author and commentator could split that up however they saw fit.

contribution reflects its author's view and choices. The reader will see occasional evidence of disagreements between opinion writers and commentators, or might detect a failed compromise between the editors, on the one hand, and a particular contributor, on the other, with respect to a piece's substance, tone or style. Rather than suppress these disagreements, though, we celebrate them as part of, and a worthy extension of, the rich and diverse debate that marks a dynamic field like feminist legal theory.

TOPICS AND ORGANIZATION OF CASES

The twenty-five cases cover a wide range of doctrinal areas, but a majority concern constitutional law doctrines, such as equal protection and due process, or interpretation of federal statutory law such as Title VII and Title IX. Nearly half raise equal protection issues, and six address Title VII claims. The cases touch on numerous legal issues related to justice and equality, including reproductive rights, privacy, violence against women, sexuality, and economic and racial justice. Included are core cases related to gender and feminism that are familiar and expected (like *Roe*,[13] *Meritor*,[14] *Geduldig*[15]), but also some less well-known cases that were nevertheless worthy of feminist attention, in part to demonstrate that issues of subordination can arise indirectly as well as directly. Thus, we also included cases on immigration (*Nguyen*[16]), the Commerce Clause (*Morrison*[17]), and pensions (*Manhart*[18]), to name just three.

The cases appear in the volume in chronological order from the earliest (1873, *Bradwell*) to the most recent (2015, *Obergefell*). This will allow readers to consider the evolution of feminism and feminist thought, both in the types of legal issues that the Court addressed and the manner in which the issues are approached. We considered alternatives for organizing the cases, such as by doctrinal categories (e.g. "Equal Protection" and "Substantive Due Process") or by traditional areas of feminist inquiry (e.g. "Reproductive Freedom" or "The Regulation of Sexuality"). We determined that these divisions were artificial for most of the innovative rewrites in the volume.[19] Most of the feminist

---

[13] *Roe v. Wade*, 410 U.S. 113 (1973).
[14] *Meritor Sav. Bank v. Vinson*, 477 U.S. 57 (1986).
[15] *Geduldig v. Aiello*, 417 U.S. 484 (1974).
[16] *Nguyen v. INS*, 533 U.S. 53 (2001).
[17] *United States v. Morrison*, 529 U.S. 598 (2000).
[18] *City of L.A. Dep't of Water & Power v. Manhart*, 435 U.S. 702 (1978).
[19] The cases in the U.K. feminist judgments book are separated into traditional doctrinal categories such as "Parenting," "Property and Markets," and "Criminal Law and Evidence."

judgments exceed the boundaries of both traditional legal categories and more feminist ones. We embraced the chronological organization as the most neutral and free from editorial influence.

As we expected given the diversity of feminist thought, the feminist judgments vary widely in their approaches. In the sections that follow, we have attempted to identify common feminist themes and methods used in the rewritten judgments. Although we have categorized the theories and methods used by the authors of the opinions, this categorization is loose at best. All of the opinions cut across boundaries or fall into multiple categories.

In categorizing the common themes that emerged, we found that we covered some of the same theoretical ground as Professor Berta Hernández-Truyol does in Chapter 2. To the extent our description or analysis of the theories differs from that of Professor Hernández-Truyol, we note again the wide variety of perspectives and interpretations that can arise within the feminist legal community. We acknowledge that our views, experience, and situated perspectives as editors influenced our creation of theoretical and methodological categories as well as our decisions about which opinions to place in which category.

The volume contains fifteen re-imagined majority opinions, four concurring opinions, five dissenting opinions, and one partial concurrence/dissent.

The majority opinions are almost equally divided between those that changed the ruling (eight), and those that changed the reasoning but not the ruling (seven). One author of a majority opinion, Professor Deborah Rhode in *Johnson v. Transportation Agency*, attempted to write an opinion that could have garnered a majority of votes based on the composition of the Court at the time. Most majority authors, however, wrote as if their opinions were persuasive enough to have garnered enough votes of their colleagues without regard to the practical or political realities of the time. Authors pursuing the first approach made somewhat limited feminist changes to the original opinion or incorporated changes that reflected substantial compromises while authors in the second group tended to write more expansive opinions with the potential for transformative results.

Similarly, many of the feminist authors cite to feminist scholarship more liberally than mainstream American jurisprudence does, taking the implicit view that feminist scholarship is a legitimate and appropriate source of authority. Citation to feminist scholarship as an authoritative source can be seen in Professor Aníbal Rosario Lebrón's dissenting opinion in *United States v. Morrison* and Professor Angela Onwuachi-Willig's majority opinion in *Meritor v. Vinson,* among others.

In terms of substance, the feminist authors in many of the opinions decided the case on the same legal grounds as the original, such as substantive due process or hostile work environment under Title VII. Others, however, changed the legal basis for the opinion or added additional rationales. Interestingly, these rationales often raised equality and liberty points in cases where the U.S. Supreme Court seemingly did not. For example, Professor Laura Rosenbury's *Griswold v. Connecticut* rejects the famous "penumbra" privacy analysis of the original, finding that the contraception ban at issue implicated equal protection and personal liberty. Similarly, Professor Kim Mutcherson's concurring opinion in *Roe v. Wade* rejects Justice Blackmun's controversial "trimester approach." She acknowledges that abortion raises privacy concerns, emphasizing that government efforts to control the reproductive decisions of women and not men violates equal protection. Similar changes in the legal underpinning of the decision occur in Professor Ruthann Robson's *Lawrence v. Texas,* Professor Carlos Ball's *Obergefell v. Hodges,* Professor Phyllis Goldfarb's *Bradwell v. Illinois,* and Professor Leslie Griffin's *Harris v. McRae.*

Judging from the substance of their opinions, the dissenting authors found a true freedom in being able to write separately. In her dissent in *Dothard v. Rawlinson,* for example, Professor Maria Ontiveros would have made *Dothard* the first U.S. Supreme Court opinion to recognize and endorse a Title VII claim for hostile work environment sexual harassment. Similarly, Professor Ann Bartow takes an unusual approach in her dissent in *Gebser v. Lago Vista Independent School District,* focusing almost wholly on the problems with the majority's treatment of the story of the case and only partly on the troublesome legal standard. In writing a dissenting opinion in *Michael M. v. Superior Court,* Professor Cynthia Godsoe found that a gender-specific statutory rape law violated the Equal Protection Clause. These dissenting opinions add a feminist voice where previously there was none.[20]

---

[20] Three of the cases in which the authors dissented, *Michael M. v. Superior Court, Gebser v. Lago Vista Independent School District,* and *United States v. Morrison,* were decided on a 5–4 vote. While it is impossible to know, such close votes invite speculation about whether the addition of a feminist justice (in *Michael M.,* decided by all men, or in *Gebser* and *Morrison,* in which Justice Ruth Bader Ginsburg dissented) might have changed the results in these important cases.

FEMINIST METHODS

A. *Feminist practical reasoning*

Feminist practical reasoning recognizes that what counts as a problem and effective resolutions of that problem will depend on "the intricacies of each specific factual context."[21] It brings together the voices and stories of individual women's lived experiences with the broader historical, cultural, economic, and social context described in historical and social science research. Feminist practical reasoning rejects the notion that there is a monolithic source for reason, values and justifications, a notion that is often a hallmark of traditional legal reasoning (consider the ubiquitous "reasonable person" in tort law). Rather, feminist practical reasoning seeks to identify sources of legal reasoning and values by drawing on the perspectives of "outsiders," or those excluded from or less powerful in the dominant culture. It also is more open to conceding the bias inherent in any form of human reasoning or decision making, including its own.[22] Professor Lucinda Finley's opinion in *Geduldig v. Aiello* is an example of feminist practical reasoning as are the feminist rewrite of Professor Pamela Laufer-Ukeles in *Muller v. Oregon* and the feminist rewrite of *Town of Castle Rock v. Gonzales* by Professor Maria Isabel Medina.

B. *Narrative feminist method*

Related to feminist practical reasoning is the use of narrative to illuminate the effects of the law on individual plaintiffs. While feminist practical reasoning may address both the individual story of the case and the broader context in which the law is applied, narrative feminist method focuses on presenting the facts of the particular case as a story. The story of the case is critical to the legal outcome; how the decision maker sees the story, what that person sees as relevant and irrelevant, and what inferences the decision maker draws from the facts often drive the ultimate decision.[23] Because of the centrality of story to law, feminists and other critical legal scholars have embraced narrative as a distinctive method of subverting and disrupting the

---

[21]   Bartlett, *supra* note 2, at 851.

[22]   *Id.* at 857–58.

[23]   *See, e.g.*, Brian J. Foley and Ruth Anne Robbins, *Fiction 101: A Primer for Lawyers on How to Use Fiction Writing Techniques to Write Persuasive Fact Sections*, 32 Rutgers L.J. 459 (2001); Brian J. Foley, *Applied Legal Storytelling, Politics, and Factual Realism*, 14 Leg. Writing 17 (2008).

dominant legal discourse. Feminist narrative method seeks to reveal and oppose the bias and power dynamics inherent in the law's purported neutrality by including and asserting the relevance of facts that are important to those outside the mainstream account in law. Feminist narrative also shines a light on facts or topics that the law often shies away from or euphemizes, such as sexuality, the law's racism, or the details of rape or other violence against women. By euphemizing or obscuring ugly truths about society, legal arguments and legal decisions allow them to proliferate because they remain invisible.[24] Narrative method also humanizes the law by focusing on the actual people involved in the cases and the harms done to them rather than on abstract rules and ideals.

Many of the authors expanded on, added to, or structurally altered the factual recitations of the original opinions. While our guidelines, in accordance with legal convention, restricted the authors to the record before the U.S. Supreme Court, many authors delved into that record to uncover facts that had been overlooked, dismissed as legally irrelevant, or otherwise deleted from the narrative on which the decision was ultimately based. Expanded or re-envisioned narratives are used in several feminist judgments, including those by Professor Deborah Rhode in *Johnson v. Transportation Agency*, Professor Ann McGinley in *Oncale v. Sundowner Offshore Services, Inc.*, Professor Ann Bartow in *Gebser v. Lago Vista Independent School District*, Professor Teri McMurtry-Chubb in *Loving v. Virginia*, and Professor Lucinda Finley in *Geduldig v. Aiello*.

C. *Breaking rhetorical conventions*

Some feminist authors used conventional and traditional judicial tone and language, but others pushed the boundaries of the genre. The editors flagged the oppositional language and discussed it among ourselves and with the authors and commentators. On balance, however, the editors honored the author's wishes if the author felt that the language was essential to her feminist vision. Several of our authors argued that it was sometimes important to depart from conventional language and rhetoric because the bias inherent in the substance of the opinions is likely to be reflected, or further obscured, by the conventions of judicial writing that counsel in favor of neutral word choices

---

[24] *See* Kathryn Abrams, *Hearing the Call of Stories*, 79 Cal. L. Rev. 971, 971–73 (1991). *See also* Margaret E. Montoya, *Mascaras, Trenzas, y Greñas: Un/Masking the Self While Un/braiding Latina Stories and Legal Discourse*, 17 Harv. Women's L.J. 185 (1994).

and a judicious, impersonal tone. In other words, they could not conform to those conventions and fully realize their feminist vision.[25]

Thus, in some of the narratives of the feminist judgments, readers will see an unusual level of frankness as well as a conscious use of bold and explicit language or a humbler approach to the Court's power. So, for example, in Professor Ruthann Robson's rewrite of *Lawrence v. Texas*, readers will see the U.S. Supreme Court explicitly apologize for the damage caused by a mistaken prior ruling in *Bowers v. Hardwick*,[26] an unprecedented rhetorical approach in U.S. Supreme Court jurisprudential history. In *United States v. Virginia*, Professor Valorie Vojdik states that the Virginia Women's Institute for Leadership, the remedy offered by VMI to cure its male-only policy, is not a remedy, but "misogyny," marking the first time that the U.S. Supreme Court would have used the word "misogyny" in this way. Finally Professor Laura Rosenbury's opinion in *Griswold v. Connecticut* uses explicit sexual language, including a reference to orgasm and the joy of sexual relationships, to convey a refreshing endorsement and approval of sexuality as a core liberty and relational interest.

D. Widening the lens[27]

Although some authors took an unconventional approach to judicial opinion writing, many wrote opinions that are indistinguishable in style, tone, and structure from prototypical judicial decisions. In this category, we place opinions in which the authors shifted their focus by looking at what assumptions were being made and whose interests were at stake in the original opinions.[28] While staying within the boundaries of existing legal doctrine and using recognizably paradigmatic modes of legal reasoning, they relied on alternative legal rules; they framed issues more narrowly or more broadly; and they presented different rationales. In this category, we would put Professor Phyllis Goldfarb's *Bradwell v. Illinois*, Professor Tracy Thomas's *City of Los Angeles Department of Water & Power v. Manhart*, and Professor Martha Chamallas's *Price Waterhouse v. Hopkins*, among others.

---

[25] *See, e.g.*, Finley, *supra* note 3, at 888; Stanchi, *supra* note 3, at 404.

[26] *Bowers v. Hardwick*, 478 U.S. 186 (1986).

[27] Similar results may be seen when the authors engage in the feminist method that Katharine Bartlett describes as asking the woman question: "identifying or challenging those elements of existing legal doctrine that leave out or disadvantage women and members of other excluded groups." Bartlett, *supra* note 2, at 831.

[28] *See generally id.* at 848.

FEMINIST THEORIES

A. *Formal equality*

Given the history of sex discrimination, many of the opinions confront laws that explicitly differentiate on the basis of sex (e.g., *Frontiero*,[29] *Manhart*[30]) and consequently, the feminist judgments rest on notions of formal equality. Formal equality is among the earliest of feminist legal philosophies. It grew out of a time when sex differences were seen as inherent and unchangeable, and as a result, discrimination based on sex was acceptable and overt. Formal equality seeks to fix explicit sex discrimination by asserting that similarly situated people should be treated the same regardless of sex or gender and that invidious use of a sex classification is presumptively unlawful.[31]

Several feminist judgments rely on formal equality principles, including Professor Cynthia Godsoe in *Michael M. v. Superior Court* and Professor Karen Czapanskiy in *Stanley v. Illinois*. Two of the majority opinions dealing with equality, Professor Dara Purvis's *Frontiero v. Richardson* and Professor Lisa Pruitt's *Planned Parenthood v. Casey*, explicitly mandate strict scrutiny for gender classifications, a change that would no doubt have effected a major transformation in law and culture. In *Frontiero*, four of the nine justices in the original decision voted for strict scrutiny, so only one additional vote was needed to change the course of legal history. That close vote certainly invites speculation about "what could have been" had the justices come from a more diverse cross-section of society.

B. *Anti-subordination/dominance feminism*

Although formal equality succeeded in eradicating most of the explicitly discriminatory laws, many feminist advocates realized that formal equality's "sex neutral" approach was little help in dealing with more subtle or ingrained structural oppressions. As Catharine MacKinnon notes, gender neutrality in law will always favor men because "society advantages them before they get into court, and law is prohibited from taking that preference into account

---

[29] *Frontiero v. Richardson*, 411 U.S. 677 (1973).
[30] *City of L.A. Dep't of Water & Power v. Manhart*, 435 U.S. 702 (1978).
[31] *See* Katie Eyer, Brown, *Not Loving*, 125 *Yale L. J. F.* 1, 1–2 (2015) ("In the statutory domain, [formal equality] generally takes the form of an explicit statutory proscription on discrimination on the basis of a particular characteristic, and, in the contemporary constitutional domain, generally takes the form of 'protected class' status triggering heightened scrutiny.")

because that would mean taking gender into account ... So the fact that women will live their lives, as individuals, as members of the group women, with women's chances in a sex discriminatory society, may not count, or else it is sex discrimination."[32] The limitations of formal equality were first apparent in the context of pregnancy, but, as many of the cases in this volume show, the doctrine is entrenched in law, often to women's detriment. As a result, many of the feminist judgments in this volume embrace anti-subordination doctrine and related theories such as substantive equality and structural feminism. In several of the judgments, the influence of Catharine MacKinnon's work is also apparent.

Anti-subordination feminism is a theory based on the recognition of social oppression of certain groups. The theory posits that even facially neutral policies are invidious and illegal if they perpetuate existing oppressions and hierarchies based on categories like race and sex.[33] This theory seeks to eradicate the more subtle forms of discrimination and injustice without sacrificing helpful laws that differentiate based on group affiliation, such as affirmative action. Like anti-subordination theory, the related structural feminism locates the primary sources of oppression in social structures such as patriarchy and capitalism.[34] Professor MacKinnon's work adds a layer to these theories, positing that not only are there manifest power imbalances between men and women rooted in the basic building blocks of law and society, but also that these power imbalances are eroticized and sexualized to women's detriment, particularly in laws related to rape, spousal abuse and pornography.[35]

These theories, often in conjunction with others, appear throughout several of the feminist judgments, including Professor Valorie Vojdik's concurring opinion in *United States v. Virginia* and Professor Angela Onwuachi-Willig's majority opinion in *Meritor v. Vinson*, among others.

---

[32] Catharine A. MacKinnon, *On Difference and Dominance, in* Feminism Unmodified 35 (1987) ("whenever a difference is used to keep us second class and we refuse to smile about it, equality law has a paradigm trauma and it's crisis time for the doctrine").

[33] Ruth Colker, *Anti-Subordination Above All: Sex, Race, and Equal Protection*, 61 N.Y.U. L. Rev. 1003, 1007–10 (1986).

[34] *See generally* MacKinnon, *supra* note 32; Nancy Levit, *Feminism for Men: Legal Ideology and the Construction of Maleness*, 43 UCLA L. Rev. 1037, 1098–99 (1996).

[35] *See generally* MacKinnon, *supra* note 32. Some refer to Professor MacKinnon's work under the heading "dominance feminism," but she herself does not like that term, saying "it's as much about subordination as dominance." Emily Bazelon, *The Return of the Sex Wars*, N.Y. Times Magazine at 56, September 10, 2015, www.nytimes.com/2015/09/13/magazine/the-return-of-the-sex-wars.html?_r=o. On power imbalances and related issues, see also Kathryn Abrams, *Songs of Innocence and Experience: Dominance Feminism in the University*, 103 Yale L.J. 1533, 1549 (1994).

C. Anti-stereotyping

Anti-stereotyping doctrine critiques the law's adherence to sex roles and its normative judgments about what a woman (and a man) should be. Related to anti-essentialism, anti-stereotyping seeks to disrupt the law's reinforcement of traditional roles for men and women. Some commentators credit Ruth Bader Ginsburg with bringing anti-stereotyping doctrine to U.S. jurisprudence in the 1970s. They argue that fighting gender roles was at the core of Ginsburg's litigation strategy.[36] Perhaps due to Ginsburg's efforts, anti-stereotyping has found its way into U.S. Supreme Court jurisprudence to a certain extent, most notably in *Price Waterhouse v. Hopkins*[37] as well as Ginsburg's opinion in *United States v. Virginia*.[38] This provided a rich foundation for our authors to build upon for their revised versions as they rejected common, fixed impressions of men and women widely held in American society and law. Anti-stereotyping theory is evident in Professor David Cohen's majority opinion in *Rostker v. Goldberg*, and Professor Maria Ontiveros's concurrence/dissent in *Dothard v. Rawlinson*, among others.

In the anti-stereotyping realm, several of the feminist judgments employ and cite social science data, readily available at the time of the opinion, that undermine widely held beliefs about women and men. The use of contemporaneous social science data is a critical tool to demonstrate that law and legal reasoning are often intertwined with and based on unsupported and stereotypical normative assumptions about sex roles, masculinity and femininity. A key foundation for Professor Martha Chamallas's concurring opinion in *Price Waterhouse v. Hopkins*, for example, is that courts should carefully examine and credit expert testimony by social scientists over the mechanical application of traditional ideas about sex and sex roles.

Masculinities theory, a relative newcomer to feminist legal theory, also plays a strong role in some of the rewritten opinions. Masculinities theory is an anti-stereotyping theory, but where some of the early anti-stereotyping theory focused exclusively on women's idealized roles, masculinities theory posits that damaging stereotypical assumptions about manhood also infect our culture, and, consequently, our laws. The theory focuses on deconstructing the norm of masculinity as damaging not just to women, but also to men who fail to conform to that norm. Still recognizing that as a group, men have

---

[36] Cary Franklin, *The Anti-Stereotyping Principle in Constitutional Sex Discrimination Law*, 85 N.Y.U. L. Rev. 83, 88–96 (2010).

[37] *Price Waterhouse v. Hopkins*, 490 U.S. 228 (1989).

[38] *United States v. Virginia*, 518 U.S. 515 (1996).

more power than women, masculinities also encapsulates the idea that men competing to prove an idealized notion of manhood often use women and non-conforming men as "props" to enhance their own status power within the masculinist hierarchy and to denigrate women and the feminine.[39] The masculinities branch of anti-stereotyping theory is evident in Professor Ann McGinley's revised majority opinion in *Oncale v. Sundowner*, for example.

D. Multi-dimensional theories: anti-essentialism and intersectionality

Another common theme in some of the judgments was anti-essentialism – challenging the notion, prevalent in law and in much of early feminist theory, that there is a fixed and identifiable "essence" that characterizes a certain set of human beings, such as women.[40] Relatedly, some of the feminist judgments explore themes of intersectionality, a legal approach that recognizes that gender is only one potential axis of discrimination and that discrimination against women is often combined with and compounded by oppression based on race, sexuality, class, and ethnicity. Beyond the recognition of multiple forms of oppression, intersectionality provides a theoretical framework through which the law can recognize and remedy those multiple oppressions instead of forcing a case into one distilled category of discrimination.[41] These theories are evident in the opinions of Professor Lisa Pruitt in her rewritten majority opinion in *Planned Parenthood v. Casey*, Professor Teri McMurtry-Chubb in her majority opinion in *Loving v. Virginia*, and Professor Ilene Durst in her majority opinion in *Nguyen v. INS*, among others.

E. Autonomy and agency

Several authors also relied on agency and autonomy rationales, noting that in addition to arguments based on deprivations of liberty under the Due Process Clause, the Constitution provides support for the argument that the government must act affirmatively to provide opportunities for full citizenship.

---

[39] Masculinities and the Law: A Multidimensional Approach 1–5 (Frank Rudy Cooper and Ann C. McGinley eds., 2012).

[40] *See* Angela Harris, *Race and Essentialism in Feminist Legal Theory*, 42 Stan. L. Rev. 581 (1990).

[41] Kimberlé Crenshaw, *Demarginalizing the Intersection of Race and Sex: A Black Feminist Critique of Antidiscrimination Doctrine, Feminist Theory and Antiracist Politics*, 1989 U. Chi. Legal F. 139; Devon W. Carbado and Mitu Gulati, *The Fifth Black Woman*, 11 J. Contemp. Legal Issues 701, 702 (2001) ("particular social groups (e.g., black people) are constituted by multiple status identities (e.g., black lesbians, black heterosexual women, and black heterosexual men)" and the different status identity holders within any given social group face discrimination that is different in both quantity and quality from discrimination faced by others).

Related to agency and autonomy, a true joy in sexual awareness and liberation can be seen in several of the feminist judgments. This sex-positive feminism is often attributed to third-wave feminists, who celebrate the joy of sexuality and sexual agency and tend to reject the tropes of passive victimhood that some associate with the second wave.[42] Though, to be fair, the emphasis on the centrality of sexual experience is related to, and may have developed from, ideas of relational, or hedonic, feminists, who criticize feminism for ignoring women's happiness and emphasize the importance of human relationships to women's approach to life and law.[43] Sexual autonomy rationales appear in Professor Carlos Ball's majority opinion in *Obergefell v. Hodges* and Professor Kim Mutcherson's majority opinion in *Roe v. Wade,* among others. They are especially vivid in Professor Laura Rosenbury's rewrite of *Griswold v. Connecticut.*

CONCLUSION

The richness and diversity of the rewritten opinions, as well as the incisive analysis of the commentaries, exceeded our expectations and goals. The opinions and commentaries reveal the breadth and depth of feminism and demonstrate the viability and practicality of using feminist legal theories and feminist methods to decide legal questions. Illustrating applied feminism, the opinions and commentaries reflect their authors' informed and distinctive choices about the grounds of legal reasoning, the forms of legal arguments, and the effects of language use. The volume reveals clearly the situated perspective inherent in judging, but also shows that widening the range of potential perspectives can make a significant difference. In other words, the law can be a dynamic and vibrant source of change, especially if its interpretation and formation includes judges of different experiences, backgrounds, and worldviews. We hope that the book will be an instructive, educational, and even inspirational resource for academics, students, lawyers, and judges alike.

The volume is both an academic text and a practical illustration of applied feminism. We hope it will arouse interest beyond the legal academic market. The book embraces an educational function regardless of audience. Students might learn about the law and feminism. The legal community and the wider public might learn about the way law works, what cases mean, and how the identity and philosophy of judges matter. For every reader, the book is an

---

[42] Crawford, *supra* note 1, at 117–22.
[43] *See, e.g.,* Robin L. West, *The Difference in Women's Hedonic Lives: A Phenomenological Critique of Feminist Legal Theory,* 3 Wisc. Women's L.J. 81 (1987).

opportunity to contemplate the arc of justice, and the important role that feminism can play in achieving it for women and all people who challenge traditional gender roles.

A final note on the order of the editors' names. Because Kathy Stanchi brought the three of us together as editors, we decided that her name should be listed first. A coin toss determined the order of the other two editors' names.

From the time the three of us began to work together on the project, this has been a collaborative endeavor to which we contributed equally. In keeping with our feminist philosophy, we aimed to achieve unanimity on all editorial decisions. Thus, while we know that citation conventions traditionally use only the first editor's name, this convention does not reflect accurately the equal contributions of the editors to the project. Accordingly, we ask that those citing our work use all three editors' names in the citation. Feminism should make a difference not only in judging, but also in scholarship and the conventions of attribution.

We hope that you are as pleased and excited as we are at the results of this collaborative project. Enjoy!

2

Talking back[1]: From feminist history and theory to feminist legal methods and judgments

Berta Esperanza Hernández-Truyol

INTRODUCTION

Not all women or people of color, in all or some circumstances or indeed in any particular case or circumstance but enough people of color in enough cases, will make a difference in the process of judging ... I would hope that a wise Latina woman with the richness of her experience would more often than not reach a better conclusion than a white male who hasn't lived that life.[2]

Perspective, context, and experience are relevant to judging. That is the essence of the Feminist Judgments Project and of these observations by Justice Sonia Sotomayor, the third of only four women and the only woman of color ever appointed to the U.S. Supreme Court. And while feminist judging will likely have its most obvious impact on exposing and eradicating women's subordination, as is evident from Justice Sotomayor's statement, women are multidimensional. Thus, the core goal of the Feminist Judgments Project is to dismantle hierarchies, no matter whether they are based on gender, sex, sexuality, race, ethnicity, class, religion, nationality, language, culture, or ability.

This chapter provides background on and context for three important elements of the Feminist Judgments Project: history, theory, and method. It traces the historical and cultural contexts within which the feminist movements emerged and evolved, and it presents the development of feminist theoretical frameworks and feminist methods. To explore women's judging, the chapter chronicles the appointment of women to the federal judiciary and reviews studies about the impact of women's presence on the bench. Finally, considering the purpose of the project, as prelude to the reconstructed judgments,

---

[1] Bell hooks, *Talking Back, in* Making Face, Making Soul/Haciendo Caras 207 (Gloria Anzaldúa ed., 1990).
[2] Sonia Sotomayor, *A Latina Judge's Voice*, 13 *Berkeley La Raza L.J.* 87, 91–92 (2002).

the chapter explores the questions of what it takes to judge, what makes a judgment feminist, and what difference feminist judging might make in the process or outcome of cases.

Multiple feminist perspectives, based on divergent philosophies, have led to a resistance to adopting any one definition of feminism. Feminism may be defined in multiple ways: as the "ideology of women's liberation,"[3] as "an analysis of women's subordination for the purpose of figuring out how to change it,"[4] and as "a *critical* social practice directed toward better understanding and improving the position of women in diverse social locations."[5]

Despite varied meanings and diverse participants, feminisms throughout time have sought to better the conditions of women's lives, to advocate for the rights of women, to pursue women's equality, and to liberate women and all sexes from cultural, legal, social, economic, and political subordination. A feminist philosophy views women as entitled to having their voices heard, their goals met, their desires fulfilled, their participation accepted, their contributions acknowledged, and their presence respected. The identities and interests of the women who have led the movements, and the concept of what and who is a woman, have shifted and evolved. "Woman" is a social construct that does not have a singular or homogeneous essence and necessarily remains fluid.[6] "Woman" is a multidimensional concept that recognizes no essential woman, but rather that women are different and diverse along the axes of gender, sex, sexuality, race, ethnicity, class, religion, nationality, language, culture, and ability.

HISTORICAL BACKGROUND – THE DEVELOPMENT OF FEMINIST LEGAL THEORY AND METHODS

Tracing the historical development of feminisms and feminist legal thought provides context for a project highlighting the difference that feminist judging can make. With a topic as complex as feminist history and feminist legal theory, any overview will be inherently limited. By highlighting developments in feminist thinking, however inchoately or cursorily, this section demonstrates how diverse and multi-faceted feminism is and how much potential it has as a transformative tool.

---

[3] Maggie Humm, The Dictionary of Feminist Theory 74 (1st ed. 1990).
[4] Linda Gordon, *The Struggle for Reproductive Freedom: Three Stages of Feminism, in* Capitalist Patriarchy and the Case for Socialist Feminism 107 (Zillah R. Eisenstein ed., 1979).
[5] Susan Archer Mann, Doing Feminist Theory: From Modernity to Postmodernity, at xvi (2012).
[6] *See, e.g.,* Judith Butler, *Performative Acts and Gender Constitution: An Essay in Phenomenology and Feminist Theory*, 40 *Theatre J.* 519 (1988).

A. *The emergence of feminist movements*

1. The arc of history

Feminism must be understood as a fluid, multidimensional methodology and practice. It crosses boundaries of gender, sex, sexuality, race, ethnicity, class, religion, nationality, language, culture, and ability. The goal of feminism is to create a world in which women – a category constructed differently across cultures and contexts – enjoy full personhood.

The first identified use of *feminism* occurred in 1837 in France by Charles Fourier, a philosopher who believed that women's liberty was a marker of social progress.[7] The first use of the term in the United States was in 1906, and after 1910 it was more widely utilized.[8] Because of the term's roots in the European enlightenment era and the Western, bourgeois character of nineteenth- and twentieth-century feminism, some groups within the women's movements have rejected the use of the term *feminist* and opted for alternative labels.[9] For example, some Black feminists in the U.S. have adopted the label "womanist" to signal that they have a simultaneous focus on race and gendered aspects of women's oppression. Similarly, some Latinas have opted for the label "Xicanista" to reflect their work within a post-colonial historical tradition. The diversities in the labels used to describe work for women's equality hint at the difficulties in describing a single, uniform feminist legal theoretical inquiry or methodological approach.

In its early days, feminist theory focused on the "woman question": to what extent does gender bias underlie the development of apparently neutral structures and norms in society and what impact have those developments had on women? Feminist legal theory focuses on how gender bias has affected the development of the law and legal structures as well as the different experiences that men and women have with the law. Feminist inquiry unveils the law as being complicit in women's subordination. Gender bias is not an accident in the law, but rather a central force in its development.[10]

Although the woman question is a critical tool for examining gender bias, its very name and focus invite questions about the category *woman*. As reflected in the alternative self-labeling of racially and ethnically diverse feminists, to ask the *woman* question involves a degree of intellectual essentialism. Some women of color, lesbians, women of differing and questioning sexualities, and

---

[7] Mann, *supra* note 5, at 2.
[8] *Id.*
[9] *Id.* at 7, 8.
[10] Martha Chamallas, Introduction to Feminist Legal Theory 2 (1st ed. 1999).

women who experience gender along a continuum have felt excluded from the scope and mode of this inquiry. They point out that "women" have not had a monolithic experience with the law or in society.

Methodologically, feminist analysis can overcome these divides by recognizing and valuing all women's different experiences in family, society, the workplace, and politics. Out of the diversity of women's experiences comes richness and strength. In the legal system, feminist legal theories and methods can recognize that philosophical and nuanced experiential differences among legal actors (plaintiffs, defendants, counsel, judges, and other representatives such as legislators) are relevant to process and outcomes.[11]

Like their counterparts in the social sciences, feminist legal theorists seek to effect change. Their focus is on reforming law and legal structures by unearthing the locations that effect or preserve women's subordinated status, asking why and whether they are persistent across time and cultures, and seeking to change these manifestations of inequality.[12] The range of relevant concerns includes not only discrimination, but also limitations imposed on women's participation in economic, political, social, intellectual, cultural, and family life as well as issues of reproductive rights, sex-based violence, and exploitation.[13] Working to reveal hidden bias and to ask how laws affect men and women differently, feminist legal scholars currently work in just about every area of law – from torts to trusts and estates, from corporations to tax, from family law to criminal law, from contracts to international law.

2. Feminist movements: the waves

For intellectual convenience, some scholars refer to the first, second, third, and even fourth "waves" of feminism in the United States.[14] The wave metaphor serves as a sort of shortcut for understanding broad trends in history, but the imagery is admittedly imperfect. To give just one example, the "waves" cannot be differentiated by clearly delineated starting and ending points or by their agendas; they incorporate fluid timelines and concepts. Indeed, feminist goals cut across the "waves," and many feminists criticize the metaphor as divisive and unhelpful.[15] To be sure, the label fails to account for "pre-wave"

---

[11] *See* Christina L. Boyd, Lee Epstein and Andrew D. Martin, *Untangling the Causal Effects of Sex on Judging*, 54 Am. J. Pol. Sci. 389 (2010).

[12] *See, e.g.*, Clare Dalton, *Where We Stand: Observations on the Situation of Feminist Legal Thought*, 3 Berkeley Women's L.J. 1, 2 (1989).

[13] Chamallas, *supra* note 10, at chs. 7–9.

[14] *See, e.g.*, Patricia Cain, *Feminist Jurisprudence: Grounding the Theories*, in Feminist Legal Theory: Foundations 359, 359–62 (D. Kelly Weisberg ed., 1993).

[15] *See* Jane Wong, *The Anti-Essentialism v. Essentialism Debate in Feminist Legal Theory: The Debate and Beyond*, 5 Wm. & Mary J. Women & L. 273, 275 (1999); Edna Kaeh Garrison,

contributions of indigenous societies that existed before colonialism and conquest or early Western writings.

Acknowledging these limitations, the wave designation allows for a shorthand way to discuss the progression – although it has not been linear – of the movement for women's equality in the U.S. The so-called first wave emerged in the nineteenth and early twentieth centuries[16] at a time when women had very few legal rights – no right to vote, to education, to work, or even to their earnings and other property if they were married. First-wave feminism can be understood as an outgrowth of liberal political philosophy which focused on equality, the rationality of man, and the "rights of man" including autonomous individualism, private property rights, and citizens' rights to participate in government.[17] Advocates focused on gaining formal legal rights for women, especially the franchise. First-wave feminism culminated with the passage of the Nineteenth Amendment in 1920.[18] Subsequent critics of first-wave feminism have pointed to its preoccupation with issues of concern primarily to middle- and upper-class white women and the racial tensions that certain woman suffragists sought to exploit to their advantage in their effort to gain formal legal rights for white women.

U.S. feminism's second wave grew out of many women's experiences with the anti-war and civil rights movements of the 1960s. Women questioned their persistent marginalization and subordination in culture, society, politics, economics, and law. Through individual consciousness-raising, women became empowered to address male norms and dominance in personal and public life. During this time, feminists began to harness the power of the law to achieve greater equality for women. Significant legal successes in the 1960s and 1970s included the passage of the Equal Pay Act of 1963; Title VII

Are We On a Wavelength Yet? On Feminist Oceanography, Radios and Third Wave Feminism, in Different Wavelengths: Studies of the Contemporary Women's Movement 237 (Jo Reger ed., 2005).

[16] Hester Eisenstein, Contemporary Feminist Thought, at xiv (1983); Judith Lorber, Gender Inequality, Feminist Theories and Politics 1–3 (5th ed. 2012); Berta E. Hernández-Truyol, *Human Rights Through a Gendered Lens: Emergence, Evolution, Revolution, in* Women's International Human Rights: A Reference Guide 3 (Kelly Askin and Dorean Koenig eds., 1999).

[17] Eisenstein, *supra* note 16, at xiv; Lorber, *supra* note 16, at 1; *see also* Hernández-Truyol, *supra* note 16 (noting international human rights foundation in liberalism, and the meaning of liberal ideology); Berta E. Hernández-Truyol and Sharon Rush, *Foreword: Culture, Nationhood, and the Human Rights Ideal*, 33 U. Mich. J.L. Reform 233 (2000) (critique of liberalism from, among other perspectives, a feminist lens).

[18] Lorber, *supra* note 16, at 2; *see* U.S. Const. amend. XIX. Most women in Europe obtained the right to vote after World War I, but French women did not obtain this right until after World War II.

of the Civil Rights Act of 1964 (non-discrimination in employment); a 1967 executive order extending affirmative action rights to women; Title IX (1972) (non-discrimination in education); the Women's Educational Equity Act of 1975; and the Pregnancy Discrimination Act of 1978. Women lawyers and their allies brought impact litigation in the areas of reproductive rights and access to higher education, to name just two areas. Second-wave feminists were behind the unsuccessful push for an Equal Rights Amendment. Feminism suffered a major setback with its 1982 defeat.

Some scholars trace the origins of third-wave feminism to the response to the nomination of Clarence Thomas to the U.S. Supreme Court in 1991.[19] The hearings came during a period of political, social, and economic conservatism. Feminism had been declared "dead."[20] But women all over America were galvanized by the perceived bias of official Washington in responding to the allegations that Judge (now Justice) Thomas had harassed Professor Anita Hill when she worked with him as a junior attorney. At the same time, non-academic culture was providing new venues for cultural expressions by women. Out of much of that writing emerged what some have called the "third wave" of feminism, marked by a rejection of traditional binary thinking about sex, sexuality, gender, and race.

Some themes emerge from third-wave feminist work, taken together: all identity categories are socially constructed; media reproduce particular versions of culture; technology shapes how the self and politics are performed. Third-wave feminists deconstruct dualisms, reject identity categories as restrictive and essentialist, opt for polyvocality, support multidimensionality, embrace hybridity, and insist on the importance of individual identity.[21] Because of its general rejection of categories and the individual lens it employs, some refer to third-wave feminism as the "anything goes" feminism, and others criticize its individualistic focus for neglecting the history of various feminisms in encouraging community and common purpose. Third-wave feminism's focus on individual perspectives and individual resistance exists simultaneously with a fierce commitment to coalition building among social justice movements and activism. Third-wave feminist commitments have not necessarily translated into the legal arena yet (or at all) in a way that is recognizable.[22]

---

[19] Mann, *supra* note 5, at 278.

[20] *Id.* at ch. 7 *passim.*

[21] *Id.* at 5, 274.

[22] *See* Bridget J. Crawford, *Toward a Third-Wave Feminist Legal Theory: Young Women, Pornography and the Praxis of Pleasure*, 14 *Mich. J. of Gender & L.* 99 (2007) (positing various reasons why third-wave feminism has not permeated the law).

Coexisting with the growth of feminism, and existing across the so-called waves, significant tensions along identity lines have resulted in rich critiques of any conception of unitary feminism. Excluded from and invisible in white, heteronormative feminist discourses that failed to incorporate or support matters of concern such as racism, homophobia, and issues of class, women of color, lesbians, and young women, to name just three groups, have advocated for alternative frameworks and positions. In *Sister/Outsider*, Audre Lorde underscored the myriad ways white feminists ignored issues of race and class when they should instead have developed alternative theoretical frameworks.[23] Intersectionality scholars, who rejected single-axis theoretical frameworks as rendering invisible the multidimensionality of the concerns and experiences of women of color, insisted that these divisive topics be included in the ongoing conversations.[24]

B. *Major branches of feminism*

The various theoretical strands within feminism reflect some of the rich historical context. The borders within feminism are not static, however, and the rewritten opinions in this volume represent different (and sometimes multiple) theoretical strands.[25] Labeling different strands within feminist theory inevitably simplifies their richness and invites critique of how aptly any one scholar fits (or not) under a particular label. What this overview might describe as one "brand" or "strand" of feminism will not be fully consistent with a different scholarly account. But regardless of what label is assigned to a particular feminist theory, what all feminist theory (and indeed all the opinions in this book) share is a commitment to identifying and achieving the conditions necessary to enable women to experience full personhood, in all its complexity.

1. Liberal feminism

Liberal feminism dates to 1779 when Mary Wollstonecraft published *A Vindication of Rights of Women*,[26] based upon classical liberal philosophy of

---

[23] Audre Lorde, Sister/Outsider 115–16, 119 (1st ed. 1984).
[24] Kimberlé Crenshaw, *Demarginalizing the Intersection of Race and Sex: A Black Feminist Critique of Antidiscrimination Doctrine, Feminist Theory and Antiracist Politics*, 1989 U. Chi. Legal F. 139.
[25] *See, e.g.*, Eisenstein, *supra* note 16, at xx.
[26] Jane C. Ollenburger and Helen A. Moore, A Sociology of Women: The Intersection of Patriarchy, Capitalism, and Colonization 17–18 (2d ed. 1998).

equal rights, individualism, liberty, and justice.[27] In the law, liberal feminist theory focuses on individual autonomy, and this strand of feminism had particular prominence in early impact litigation in the 1970s.[28] Liberal feminism posits that, like men, women are entitled to core freedoms, including equality in the public sphere,[29] and that equal access to the professions and politics is necessary to achieve that equality.[30] Liberal feminists work within the existing structures, and many early liberal feminists believed that incremental change in the law was the best way to secure and advance women's rights.

The "similarly situated" focus of liberal feminist legal theory[31] was challenged because its central claim was that women are just like men. If so, then the women who will be most likely to advance are the ones whose life experiences most resemble men's. And notwithstanding the successes of some equal protection litigation, the liberal feminist "sameness" paradigm can obscure the gendered nature of the existing social, economic, legal, and political rules and structures.[32] For that reason, some feminists turned their focus to women's differences from men, in particular their biological differences and the ability to become pregnant. They also drew attention to the distinction between biological sex and *gender*, the latter being socially performed and learned roles of femaleness or maleness.[33] In some analyses, the resulting emphasis on gender better exposed the subordinated position of women that results from stereotyping, job stratification, and the glass ceiling.

2. Radical feminism

Pointing to the ubiquity of women's subjugation, radical feminism "holds that gender oppression is the oldest and most profound form of exploitation, predating and underlying all other forms including those of race and class"[34] and sexual orientation.[35] Radical feminism posits that, beyond discrimination,

[27] Sonya Andermahr, Terry Lovell, C. Wolkowitz, A Glossary of Feminist Theory 149 (1st ed. 1997); *see also* Ollenburger and Moore, *supra* note 26, at 17.

[28] Mary Becker, *Patriarchy and Inequality: Towards a Substantive Feminism*, 1999 U. Chi. Legal F. 21, 32.

[29] Hilary Charlesworth and Christine Chinkin, The Boundaries of International Law: A Feminist Analysis 39 (2000).

[30] Lorber, *supra* note 16, at 23; *see also* Ollenburger and Moore, *supra* note 26, at 17.

[31] Cain, *supra* note 14, at 238; Mary Becker, *Strength in Diversity: Feminist Theoretical Approaches to Child Custody and Same-Sex Relationships*, 23 Stetson L. Rev. 701, 704 (1994).

[32] Chamallas, *supra* note 10, at 25–26; Charlesworth and Chinkin, *supra* note 29, at 38 n.56. *See also* Eisenstein, *supra* note 16, at xx.

[33] *See* Mann, *supra* note 5, at 69.

[34] Eisenstein, *supra* note 16, at xix–xx; Andermahr *et al.*, *supra* note 27, at 222–23.

[35] Ollenburger and Moore, *supra* note 26, at 21; Mann, *supra* note 5, at 88.

patriarchal oppression includes violence against women such as rape and other forms of physical abuse.[36] Consequently, radical feminism insists that the only way to end women's subjugation is to undo patriarchy. This may require close examination of sexuality's role in women's subordinate status or even abolishing the binary distinctions based on gender.[37] Critics of radical feminism observe that the focus on sexuality ignores race, class, and sexual orientation at its peril, perpetuating myriad existing inequalities.[38]

Radical feminism emphasizes structural inequalities and observes the need to deconstruct and reconstruct existing structures and values in society, politics, and economics.[39] A principal objective is to debunk the gendered social order as socially constructed and not naturally or biologically preordained.[40] This approach reveals how gendered subordination exists in law, medicine, religion, and other social institutions.[41] Radical feminism exposes the existing social and political structures as imbued with gender bias.

3. Marxist and socialist feminism

Although Marxist and socialist feminisms have not garnered much support since the 1990s and the rise of globalization, the theories are worthy of brief mention because they draw attention to significant concerns about class and separate economic spheres. Marxist feminism, while committed to women's emancipation, roots women's subordination in economic forces. These include changes in the organization of work and family structures and the development of the concept of private property, which created the home as a separate female sphere. Socialist feminism, on the other hand, holds that for women to attain equality, both capitalism and patriarchy must be eradicated.[42]

4. Lesbian feminism

Lesbian feminism locates the source of women's inequality in the oppressive structures of and linkages between heterosexuality and male domination.[43] The movement emerged in the late 1960s and early 1970s because lesbians, a

---

[36] Lorber, *supra* note 16, at 124; Ollenburger and Moore, *supra* note 26, at 21; Andermahr *et al.*, *supra* note 27, at 222–23.
[37] *See, e.g.*, Catharine A. MacKinnon, Sex Equality 32–33 (2d ed. 2001).
[38] Cain, *supra* note 14, at 239 n.162.
[39] Chamallas, *supra* note 10, at 26.
[40] Andermahr *et al.*, *supra* note 27, at 222–23.
[41] Lorber, *supra* note 16, at 124.
[42] *Id.* at 33. *See also* Eisenstein, *supra* note 16, at xx.
[43] Lorber, *supra* note 16, at 151.

diverse group that cannot be constructed homogenously along identity lines, were outsiders to and marginalized by strains of heteronormativity within the mainstream women's movement and the male centrism of the predominantly white and male gay liberation movement.[44] Lesbians had always been a strong force in the women's movement, but some leaders were less than welcoming. Betty Friedan, for example, called lesbianism a "lavender menace." At one point NOW refused to engage issues of concern to lesbians.[45] Lesbian legal theory, while not extensive, centers lesbians' perspectives and seeks to render lesbians visible.[46] This is a noteworthy move with continued importance because, notwithstanding the U.S. Supreme Court's recognition of marriage equality, LGBT people have unequal recourse if they are dismissed from jobs, denied housing, and subjected to violence and other deleterious treatment, such as being denied visitation rights to partners and children. The lesbian feminism paradigm forces the evaluation and deconstruction of norms and their application not only as male or patriarchal but also as heteropatriarchal. Such a move benefits all women because it takes sexuality out of the private realm into the public realm and unveils persisting inequities in education, work, society, and politics.

5. Cultural feminism

Cultural feminists celebrate women's differences from men and embrace the existence of a separate "women's culture"[47] with distinctive characteristics and attributes related to women's everyday experiences that are otherwise devalued by patriarchal attitudes.[48] These traits include "intimacy, persuasion, warmth, caring and sharing"[49] as well as mothering, spirituality, and moral reasoning.[50] Cultural feminists have made significant use of Carol Gilligan's research on the ways that women and men perceive and navigate the world. Focusing on the moral development and decision-making processes of men and women, Gilligan observed that while men appear to reach decisions in a linear manner, with individual autonomy as a foremost consideration, women appear to form their decisions in the context of the social institutions that are affected,

---

[44] Andermahr *et al.*, *supra* note 27, at 147–48.
[45] *See* Mann, *supra* note 5, at 92.
[46] *See, e.g.*, Ruthann Robson, Lesbian (Out)law: Survival Under the Rule of Law (1992); Cain, *supra* note 14.
[47] Eisenstein, *supra* note 16, at xx.
[48] Andermahr *et al.*, *supra* note 27, at 47–48.
[49] Lorber, *supra* note 16, at 75.
[50] Andermahr *et al.*, *supra* note 27, at 47.

including school and family.[51] Cultural feminism, like the other strands, has been critiqued as essentialist, falsely universalizing all women into a single model and privileging particular elements of women's complex identities.[52]

In law, cultural feminism specifically incorporates a so-called woman's lens in problem solving, identity construction, perspective,[53] and relationships.[54] Cultural legal feminism challenges the law's structural privileging of the patriarchal, hierarchical, advocative, and adversarial. It suggests instead a contextual approach to resolving disputes in the guise of "rationality, objectivity and abstractness."[55] To further the goal of women's equality, cultural feminism seeks to eliminate gendered binaries and superior valuation of male (and correlative devaluation of female) methodologies and attributes.[56] In a Feminist Judgments Project, cultural feminism supports the giving of voice to women's different positions, encourages valuing women's perspectives, and provides the tools to deconstruct male norms and structures. At the same time, cultural feminism acknowledges that the claim to a unitary "woman" is on theoretically shaky ground.

6. Women-of-color feminism

Women-of-color feminism or multiracial feminism (more commonly known in legal scholarship as intersectional feminism) focuses on the multidimensional nature of discrimination against women of color. Multiple "others" exist within intertwined hierarchies that operate not only on the basis of sex and gender inequalities, but also on the grounds of race, color, sexuality, ethnicity, culture, disability, and class. An individual who experiences multiple "otherness" faces exacerbated effects of marginalization and subordination.

The intersectional feminism framework rejects the atomizing,[57] essentializing,[58] or universalizing of the experiences of women. These moves give primacy to gender bias over prejudice based on race, class, or sexuality. The

---

[51] See generally Carol Gilligan, In a Different Voice: Psychological Theory and Women's Development (reissue ed. 1993).

[52] See Andermahr et al., supra note 27, at 82.

[53] Chamallas, supra note 10, at 27. Interestingly, in legal theory, as contrasted to the social sciences, cultural feminists ignore the lesbian experience. See Cain, supra note 14, at 361.

[54] Cain, supra note 14, at 241.

[55] Charlesworth and Chinkin, supra note 29, at 40–41.

[56] Id.

[57] Berta E. Hernández-Truyol, Borders (En)Gendered: Normativities, Latinas, and a LatCrit Paradigm, 72 N.Y.U. L. Rev. 882, 885, 924 (1997).

[58] Katharine T. Bartlett and Angela P. Harris, Gender and Law: Theory, Doctrine, Commentary 1007–1009 (2d ed. 1998); see also Chamallas, supra note 10, at 87.

intersectional argument is that the existing system is based upon an "additive model of oppression" that is grounded in "Eurocentric, masculinist thought" and as a result does not reflect the reality that "race, class, and gender [are] interlocking systems of oppression" that constitute a "matrix of domination."[59] Other traits – including age, ability, ethnicity, sexual orientation, culture, and religion – also constitute part of the matrix. Economic, political, legal, and social structures support the existing systems of oppression.

In law, intersectional feminist analysis challenges law's single-axis analytical approach. Like radical feminism, it recognizes differences between men and women, but admittedly most intersectional feminism has not been concerned with exploring the male–female binary. It acknowledges and centers differences between and among women on the bases of race, class, ethnicity, culture, and sexuality, while simultaneously making some universal claims about the experiences of "Black women," for example. Differences between and among women are significant, sometimes conflicting, and often lead to different priorities and strategies. For example, depending on one's lived experience or the historic experience of one's racial group, some women might articulate abortion as a priority in a reproductive rights agenda while other women might advocate a focus on the "freedom to give birth, to keep their children and not have to have contraception forced upon them."[60] Because the constitutional paradigm is a single-axis framework, advancing an intersectional approach in impact litigation is especially challenging.

7. Postmodern feminism[61]

Postmodern feminism contests all group categories as misleadingly essentialist and rejects the existence of any category's objective reality beyond the individual's perspective. This framework recognizes group identities as social constructs,[62] and postmodernists conclude that what appears to be the truth depends upon a person's experience.[63] The postmodernism model critiques as male the claim that there can be only one answer to a question or only one truth that can explain all questions.[64] The postmodern challenge to

---

[59] Patricia Hill Collins, Black Feminist Thought: Knowledge, Consciousness, and the Politics of Empowerment 225 (1990); *see also* Lorber, *supra* note 16, at 75.

[60] Mann, *supra* note 5, at 189; *see also id.* at 167.

[61] *See* Andermahr *et al.*, *supra* note 27, at 207; *see also* Mann, *supra* note 5, at ch. 6 *passim*.

[62] Mann, *supra* note 5, at 21.

[63] Cain, *supra* note 14, at 242.

[64] Patricia Smith, *Feminist Jurisprudence and the Nature of Law, in* Feminist Jurisprudence 6 (Patricia Smith ed., 1993).

feminism is to ask the complex woman question in a non-universalized and non-essentialized manner while still confronting categories of subordination. Significantly, for the postmodern feminist inquiry – unlike the liberal, radical, lesbian, or even intersectional feminist inquiry – issues of sameness or difference are irrelevant as "illusions caused by the flawed structural frameworks that generate them."[65] Postmodernists believe that "[e]quality will come when there are so many recognized sexes, sexualities, and genders that one cannot be played against the other."[66]

In the legal context, postmodern feminism has had a limited application, as the law's decision-making processes revolve around questions of sameness or difference. But postmodern feminism rejects the concept that "categorical, abstract theories derived through reason and assumptions about the essence of human nature can serve as the foundation of knowledge."[67] It recognizes that the legal system excludes many perspectives, including multiple women's perspectives, and urges that we search for the myriad women's realities not reflected in the law.[68] Moreover, postmodernists point out, the existing hierarchy embeds and recreates gender inequality in all social structures.

Postmodernists unveil the impact of mass culture and cultural texts in producing, reproducing, and entrenching beliefs and images about gender, gender roles, and expectations;[69] they challenge the normativity of heterosexuality; and they seek representation and acceptance of alternative sexual expressions in the social sphere.[70] To postmodern feminists, no system can address all structural gender deficiencies, and a complex analytical framework is necessary to attain equality. Without rejecting the concept of binding legal precedent, postmodern feminism recognizes that every new set of facts is different from the precedential facts and may warrant a different evaluation.

C. Feminist legal methods

As Justice Sotomayor's "wise Latina" observation suggests, feminist methodology is a process – an approach to research, writing, analyzing, and theorizing that feminists employ. It has a particular goal of knowing and incorporating the realities of women's lives; asks certain types of questions; raises particular

[65] *Id.*
[66] Lorber, *supra* note 16, at 285.
[67] Smith, *supra* note 64, at 6; *see also* Katharine T. Bartlett, *Gender Law*, 1 *Duke J. Gender L. & Pol'y* 1 (1994).
[68] Charlesworth and Chinkin, *supra* note 29, at 45.
[69] Lorber, *supra* note 16, at 284–85.
[70] *Id.*

topics and concerns; and embraces insight and knowledge obtained by viewing the world through a feminist lens.

Justice Ginsburg's partial dissent in *Safford Unified School District v. Redding*[71] provides a glimpse as to how deploying a feminist lens could change the applicability of precedent. Justice Ginsburg would have denied official immunity to the assistant principal who ordered a strip search of a thirteen-year-old girl suspected of possessing forbidden drugs (ibuprofen). During oral argument, Justice Ginsburg expressed concern that her colleagues, all male, were insensitive to the lasting effect of the strip search. She observed during a later interview that her colleagues had not "quite understood," having never been a thirteen-year-old girl, that a strip search could be traumatic.[72] In Justice Ginsburg's view, the facts of the case: the nature of the violation, the thin grounds for suspicion, and the girl's "age and sex" rendered the decision to order a strip search irreconcilable with the supposedly controlling precedent.

The techniques to deploy the feminist method include storytelling, conversation, group discussion, participant observation, and seeking out and listening to life stories. The purpose of the feminist method is to uncover women's experiences and to claim them as valid, even (or especially) when those experiences may differ based on race, class, sexuality, or other identity markers. Women engage in these explorations to improve the position of women in social, economic, political, legal, and cultural spheres.

Feminist legal methodology incorporates feminist perspectives into the typical legal methods that lawyers, judges, and academics employ to write, analyze, apply, and interpret law. Embracing the substantive concerns expressed by one or more of the branches of feminism, a feminist judgment also may employ a feminist reasoning process.

Katharine Bartlett has identified three feminist legal methods: asking the woman question, feminist practical reasoning, and consciousness-raising.[73] To ask the woman question in law is to identify the gendered biases of rules and practices that pose as neutral and to uncover how they can disadvantage women. Feminist practical reasoning builds on the Aristotelian concept of practical reasoning – a holistic model that seeks to reach the best possible solution in the context of complex situations by focusing on the context of the practices and values relevant to a specific problem. Feminist

---

[71] 557 U.S. 364, 375 (2009).
[72] Joan Biskupic, *Ginsburg: Court Needs Another Woman*, USA Today (Oct. 5, 2009), http://usatoday30.usatoday.com/news/washington/judicial/2009-05-05-ruthginsburg_N.htm.
[73] Katharine T. Bartlett, *Feminist Legal Methods*, 103 *Harv. L. Rev.* 829 (1990).

practical reasoning specifically and mindfully incorporates the context of women's concerns and values into legal reasoning. This incorporation of women's concerns and values exposes hidden biases and injustices. Finally, consciousness-raising is an interactive and collaborative method by which women articulate their experiences and find meaning in them. It provides a structure both for asking the woman question and for engaging in feminist practical reasoning.

Martha Chamallas identifies six "moves" or theoretical tools used by feminists to engage in critical analysis of the law.[74] First is the significance of recognizing women's experience so as to expose the locations where law has effected the subordination or exclusion of women.[75] Second is being aware of intersectionality and multiple dimensions in order to guard against the assumption that all women have shared essential common experiences. In this way, feminists are able to take into account the multiple dimensions that create complex personal identities.[76] Third is asking the woman question to unearth "male bias in rules, standards, and concepts that appear neutral or objective on their face."[77] This inquiry unveils the maleness of law by scrutinizing how the law, even the laws that pose as neutral, can be detrimental to women. In other words, asking the woman question establishes that the status quo is not a neutral position.

The fourth move is the recognition of a "double bind" or "catch 22" where "women constantly face dilemmas in which they are forced to predict which less-than-ideal course of action will prove to be the least hazardous."[78] This move derives from the dilemma of difference arising from the structural male bias embedded into most institutions' rules and regulations.[79] The fifth move – "reproducing patterns of male domination" – is the recognition "that change is not inherently progressive and that even substantial shifts in rhetoric and rules may not bring about major improvements in women's lives."[80] Finally, the sixth move, "unpacking women's choice," replaces the myth that women lack the intellect or the moral force to be public actors with the idea that women have full agency to make choices "without denying or minimizing the distinctive constraints placed on women in a male-dominated society."[81]

---

[74] Martha Chamallas, Introduction to Feminist Legal Theory 4–15 (3d ed. 2013).
[75] *Id.* at 4–6.
[76] *Id.* at 6–7.
[77] *Id.* at 8.
[78] *Id.* at 10.
[79] Chamallas, *supra* note 74, at 11.
[80] *Id.* at 11–13.
[81] *Id.* at 13–15.

While feminist legal methods are of great value in unearthing intrinsic and structural biases in law and the legal system, their application should be consciously non-essentialist. As many strands of feminism have insisted, the category "woman" is a social construction that crosses the borders of gender, sex, sexuality, race, ethnicity, class, religion, nationality, language, culture, and ability. Critiques of the feminist methods literature reveal that a feminist method that embraces the "universal woman" trope generally privileges some experiences over others, thus rendering invisible key components of women's identities. A more robust feminist theory embraces the diversity that otherwise is lost in a focus on the cisgender over queer, male over female, heterosexual over LGBT,[82] White over people of all colors,[83] Anglos over people of all ethnicities, English-speaking over multilingualism, U.S. citizens over non-citizens, middle- or upper-class over working class or poor, able-bodied over disabled. In sum, feminist legal methods traditionally aim to unearth and eliminate the unconscious bias that imbues law with a male perspective. The most insightful and useful feminist methods also embrace the rich and complex multiplicity of women's experiences to incorporate a multidimensional analysis.

BRIEF HISTORY OF WOMEN IN THE JUDICIARY

The Feminist Judgments Project focuses on whether and how feminist judging matters. It acknowledges that experiences shape people's understandings. The project recognizes that personal perspectives and other critical identity characteristics are relevant to judging because in the law there is ample room for interpretation. Jurists fill in the gaps by drawing upon, among other things, their personal knowledge and life experiences. Such understanding explains Justice Ginsburg's empathy for the thirteen-year-old girl subjected to an intrusive strip search; she, unlike her colleagues, understood that the situation appears differently within the context of knowing that "[i]t's a very sensitive age for a girl."[84]

Similarly, in *Wheaton College v. Burwell*,[85] the U.S. Supreme Court split along gender lines. The all-male majority ruled that a Christian college in Illinois could refrain from following the Affordable Care Act's contraception mandate. The female justices joined in a sharp dissent on the basis that

[82] Cain, *supra* note 14, at 360–62.
[83] *See* Angela P. Harris, *Race and Essentialism in Feminist Legal Theory*, 42 Stan. L. Rev. 581 (1990).
[84] Adam Liptak, *Supreme Court Says Child's Rights Violated by Strip Search*, N.Y. Times (June 26, 2009), www.nytimes.com/2009/06/26/us/politics/26scotus.html.
[85] 134 S. Ct. 2806 (2014).

the promise of health insurance coverage for women was rendered illusory by the majority's stance. Just three days before *Wheaton College*, the five male Catholic justices had written the majority opinion in *Burwell v. Hobby Lobby*,[86] ruling that closely held corporations were not obligated to provide certain forms of contraception to which the corporation had religious objections. Here, too, the three female justices, this time joined by Justice Breyer, vehemently dissented, noting that when religious entities voluntarily enter into commercial activity, the religious beliefs of their owners should not exempt them from statutory obligations.

Of course, being a female judge does not automatically translate to being a feminist judge. Similarly, a male judge is not automatically anti-feminist: after all, August Bebel raised the woman question – a question about women's equality and women's role in society – in his 1910 book, *Women and Socialism*.[87] Still, to the extent that judging comes out of experience, it is worth discussing the numbers of women in the U.S. judiciary.

A. *Women on the bench*

It was not until 1928, almost fifty years after *Bradwell v Illinois*,[88] almost forty years after the federal court system was established, and after the first wave of feminism had receded from public prominence, that President Calvin Coolidge appointed Genevieve Rose Cline to the U.S. Customs Court (now known as the U.S. Court of International Trade), making her the first woman named to the federal bench.[89] In 1934, Franklin Roosevelt appointed Florence Allen, the only woman in her University of Chicago Law School class, to serve on the Sixth Circuit, making her the first woman to serve on an Article III appellate court.[90] Five years later, President Dwight D. Eisenhower nominated Mary Honor Doulon, a Cornell Law School graduate and the first female partner at a Wall Street law firm, to the U.S. Customs Court to fill the vacancy left by Genevieve Rose Cline.[91] In 1950,

---

[86] 134 S. Ct. 2751 (2014).

[87] August Bebel, *Introduction in* Woman and Socialism (Meta L. Stern (Hebe) trans., Socialist Literature Co. 1910) (1879), www.marxists.org/archive/bebel/1879/woman-socialism/index .htm?utm_source=lasindias.info.

[88] *Bradwell v. Illinois*, 83 U.S. 130 (1873) (upholding the decision by Illinois that a woman should not be licensed to practice law).

[89] Women's History Month, United States Courts, www.uscourts.gov/aboutfederal-courts/ educational-resources/annual-observances/womens-history-month (last visited July 14, 2015).

[90] *Id. See also* Sally J. Kenney, Gender and Justice: Why Women in the Judiciary Really Matter 70 (2013).

[91] United States Courts, *supra* note 89.

President Harry Truman appointed Burnita Shelton Matthews, a George Washington University evening school graduate, to be the first woman to serve as a District Court judge in D.C.[92] In 1961, President John F. Kennedy appointed Sarah Tilgham Hughes, like Burnita Shelton Matthews a night school graduate of George Washington University, to the District Court for the Northern District of Texas.[93] Thereafter, President Nixon appointed Cornelia Groefsema Kennedy, President Ford appointed Mary Anne Richey, and President Johnson appointed three women: June Lazenby Green, Shirley Ann Mount Hufstedler, and in 1966, Constance Baker Motley, who became the first Black woman ever appointed to the federal bench.[94]

When Jimmy Carter ran for President, his campaign promises included increasing representation of women in the federal government.[95] When he took office in 1977, there were only eight women on the federal bench,[96] with only one out of ninety-seven on federal courts of appeal, making women less than 1 percent of the total federal judiciary, despite being 9.2 percent of all lawyers, and 15 percent of recent law school graduates. In 1978, the Omnibus Judgeship Act created 150 new positions, providing Carter the opportunity to diversify the judiciary with appointments of women and minority group members.[97] During his tenure, Carter appointed forty women judges, of whom seven were African American and one was Latina.[98] These appointments included eleven women, one of whom was African American, to federal appeals courts.[99]

President Ronald Reagan kept his campaign promise to appoint a woman to the U.S. Supreme Court by appointing Sandra Day O'Connor in 1981, the year he took office.[100] Of his 358 appointments to federal courts, however, only twenty-nine[101] were women, of whom one was Latina, and one

[92] History of the Federal Judiciary: Milestones of Judicial Service, Federal Judicial Center, www.fjc.gov/history/home.nsf/page/judges_milestones.html (last visited May 13, 2015).
[93] United States Courts, *supra* note 89.
[94] History of the Federal Judiciary: Biographical Directory of Federal Judges, Federal Judicial Center, www.fjc.gov/history/home.nsf/page/judges_milestones.html (last visited May 13, 2015).
[95] Kenney, *supra* note 90, at 71–73.
[96] Nancy Scherer, *Diversifying the Federal Bench: Is Universal Legitimacy for the U.S. Justice System Possible?*, 105 Nw. U. L. Rev. 587, 588 (2011). *But see* Kenney, *supra* note 90, at 71 (providing that there were only five women, making it less than 1%).
[97] Kenney, *supra* note 90, at 82.
[98] Jennifer Segal Diascro and Rorie Spill Solberg, *George W. Bush's Legacy on the Federal Bench: Policy in the Face of Diversity*, 92 Judicature 289, 292 tbl. 1 (2009).
[99] *Id.* at 295 tbl. 4. *But see* Erwin Chemerinsky, The Case Against the Supreme Court 301 (2014) (noting only nine appointments to courts of appeals).
[100] Kenney, *supra* note 90, at 83.
[101] *Id.*

Black.[102] By the end of Reagan's term, the percentage of women in the federal judiciary had risen from 6.5 percent to 8.7 percent.[103]

President George H.W. Bush appointed a total of thirty-six women (19.5 percent) to the federal bench, most during the 1992 election year.[104] Of the thirty-six, three were Latinas and two were African American.[105] Most of his female appointments consisted of promotions for women originally appointed by Reagan.[106]

Even though since 1992 the number of women in law school has risen dramatically, approaching 50 percent of students, only approximately 25 percent of sitting federal Article III judges are women.[107] Thus, despite the changing demographics in law schools and the legal profession, women remain underrepresented in the judiciary. While during his tenure President Bill Clinton made 104 female appointments, which included fifteen African Americans, five Latinas and one Asian American,[108] his successor President George W. Bush made only fifty female appointments, which included eight African American women.[109]

As of March 2015, President Barack Obama had appointed 129 female judges, including two women to the U.S. Supreme Court, more than any President to date.[110] His other appointees include seven women to federal courts of appeals and seventeen to U.S. District Courts where women had never served before. Even with Obama's appointments, only 35 percent (sixty of the 171) of active judges sitting on federal courts of appeals are women, only 33 percent of active judges in District Courts are women, and seven District Courts have yet to see a single female judge.[111]

President Obama has appointed more than twice as many women of color to the federal bench as any previous president. Eighty women of color

---

[102] Segal Diascro and Solberg, *supra* note 98, at 292 tbl. 1. *But see* Eric Lichtblau, *Reagan Record on Naming Women Judges Hit*, L.A. Times (February 3, 1988), http://articles.latimes.com/1988-02-03/news/mn-27231_1_women-lawyers (providing that Reagan appointed 367 judges of whom thirty-one were women).

[103] Lichtblau, *supra* note 102. The number of black judges fell from 8% to 6.3% in the same time. *Id. See also* Segal Diascro and Solberg, *supra* note 98.

[104] Lichtblau, *supra* note 102.

[105] Segal Diascro and Solberg, *supra* note 98, at 292 tbl. 1.

[106] Lichtblau, *supra* note 102.

[107] *Women in the Federal Judiciary: Still a Long Way to Go*, National Women's Law Center (August 4, 2015), www.nwlc.org/resource/women-federal-judiciary-still-long-way-go-1.

[108] Segal Diascro and Solberg, *supra* note 98, at 292 tbl. 1.

[109] *Id.; see also* Scherer, *supra* note 96.

[110] National Women's Law Center, *supra* note 107.

[111] *Id.* at 1 n.2.

currently serve as federal judges, including forty-two African-Americans, twenty-five Latinas, ten Asian-Americans, one Native-American, one Latina/ Asian-American woman, and one Latina/African-American.[112] Yet, there are only eleven women of color sitting on federal Courts of Appeals, of whom five sit on the Ninth Circuit, two on the D.C. Circuit, and one each on the First, Fourth, Sixth, and Seventh Circuits,[113] leaving seven federal Courts of Appeals without a single female judge of color.[114] Three women, Ruth Bader Ginsburg, Sonia Sotomayor, and Elena Kagan – the latter two being Obama appointments – currently serve on the U.S. Supreme Court. There are no records of appointments by sexuality or class.

B. Do women make a difference?

Since the time that President Jimmy Carter took office in 1977 and set out to diversify the federal judiciary by appointing more women, there has been a proliferation of studies analyzing the impact of sex on judging.[115] Overall, these studies fail to show any definitive pattern with respect to gendered differences in judging. For example, one 1983 study evaluating the voting of Carter's Courts of Appeals appointees over a two-year period found that there was little difference between men and women on decisions affecting the rights of accused and prisoners, but some differences in outcomes for lawsuits for race and sex discrimination.[116]

In a recent compilation, researchers reported on more than thirty studies of the impact of women on the bench in both state and federal courts.[117] Supporting Justice Ginsburg's claim that "at the end of the day, a wise old man and a wise old woman reach the same judgment,"[118] these studies found no difference between men and women judges in decisions on search and seizure or obscenity, civil rights and prisoners' rights, alimony, sentencing guidelines, affirmative action, sexual harassment, age discrimination, criminal and civil rights, sentencing, criminal law, and the Voting Rights Act.[119]

[112] *Id.* at 1.
[113] *Id.*
[114] *Id.*
[115] *See* Christina L. Boyd, Lee Epstein and Andrew D. Martin., *Web Appendix to Untangling the Causal Effects of Sex on Judging*, http://epstein.wustl.edu/research/genderjudgingapp.pdf (hereinafter "Appendix").
[116] Kenney, *supra* note 90.
[117] *See* Appendix, *supra* note 115.
[118] *See* Biskupic, *supra* note 72.
[119] Appendix, *supra* note 115, at 2–5.

Some differences were found based on the combination of sex and the
judges' political party affiliation. A 1999 study of Courts of Appeals decisions
found that Republican female judges were more likely to support labor unions
than Republican men, although no such difference emerged between female
and male Democratic judges. A 2000 study of state court decisions on obscenity and the death penalty found that Democratic women judges were more
liberal than Democratic men judges, but that there was no difference between
Republican men and Republican women judges. A 2002 study of Internal
Revenue Service disputes concluded that Democratic women were more
likely than other judges to favor the taxpayer.[120]

Studies on discrimination cases show that women's presence matters to those
cases. The 1993 study that showed no differences between male and female
judging on matters of search and seizure and obscenity did find that female
judges were more likely to support the plaintiff in employment discrimination
cases, an outcome confirmed in a 1999 study of Courts of Appeals decisions
on sex and race discrimination cases. Other studies corroborate at least some
differences in discrimination lawsuits. For example, women judges are more
willing to strike laws adverse to gays, women judges are more inclined to rule
for the claimant in statutory sex discrimination cases, and women judges have
higher settlement rates in personal injury cases and civil rights termination
cases than their male counterparts.[121]

The studies are inconclusive on the existence of a "panel effect," that is,
whether the presence of a woman or women on a panel makes a difference in
the outcome of discrimination cases. The 1999 study mentioned earlier found
no panel effects. However, a 2004 study of Courts of Appeals employment
discrimination cases and the 2005 study on statutory sex discrimination cases
found that men judges sitting on a panel with women judges were more likely
to find for the plaintiff. Similarly, a 2006 study on sex discrimination cases
heard in the state courts found that the more women who were on the court,
the more likely there would be a ruling for the plaintiff.[122]

The few studies on criminal cases show haphazard results. A 1999 study of
criminal sentencing in state trial courts found that women judges are more
likely to incarcerate defendants and give longer sentences. A 2000 study of various criminal law cases in state trial courts found that men are more likely to
find for defendants. In criminal procedure and civil rights, a study of Courts of
Appeals decisions between 1977 and 1996 found that women judges are more

[120] Id. at 5.
[121] Id. at 2, 5.
[122] Id. at 2–5.

conservative than their male counterparts in criminal matters but more liberal in civil rights. This study also found a panel effect: male judges on panels with women vote more similarly to the women. And, a 2005 study on police brutality concluded that female judges were more likely to find for the defendant.[123]

As for family law, the 1995 study of state trial court divorce cases heard between 1978 and 1984 found no difference in alimony awarded, but did find that women judges awarded more child support. Twenty years later, a 2005 study of divorce cases decided between 1998 and 1999 by states' highest courts found that women judges more often ruled for mothers over fathers. It also found that having a woman on the court increased the chances of male judges ruling in favor of the mother.[124]

One study published in 2010 analyzed sex-based effects in thirteen areas of law.[125] The researchers' review of matched data revealed "no significant effects" of having a female judge in ADA, capital punishment, sexual harassment, or abortion cases. However, data showed significant differences in sex discrimination suits.[126] Moreover, data analysis on panel effects of women judges showed no significant differences in areas such as sexual harassment and affirmative action although "strong and systematic panel effects emerge" in sex discrimination claims.[127]

FEMINIST JUDGMENTS

Feminist perspectives apply beyond opinion writing and decision making. Judging is a multi-faceted responsibility. Judges manage the courtroom and preside over the proceedings. They consider both law and fact in making decisions, they interpret and apply the law, and they assess evidence in light of the law.

The Code of Conduct for United States judges provides a framework describing how judges are expected to analyze the facts and law.[128] This code includes five canons – "rules of reason" – that operate alongside treaties, custom, the Constitution, statutes, common law, rules of courts, and precedent. A feminist inquiry would ask first whether and how the canons are structurally

[123] *Id.*
[124] *Id.*
[125] Boyd *et al.*, *supra* note 115, at 389.
[126] *Id.* at 401.
[127] *Id.* at 402–06 (noting that "the likelihood of a male judge ruling in favor of the plaintiff increases by 12% to 14% when a female sits on the panel").
[128] Guide to Judiciary Policy Vol. 2: Ethics & Judicial Conduct, Pt. A: Codes of Conduct, Ch. 2: Code of Conduct for U.S. Judges, www.uscourts.gov/uscourts/RulesAndPolicies/conduct/vol02a-ch02.pdf.

biased based on sex or gender. For example, the notion of a "rule of reason" is itself based on male norms and traditions. Until Mary Wollstonecraft, reason had been viewed exclusively as a male trait, juxtaposed to the female trait of emotion. Using a reconstructed, non-gendered model, the canons, in particular canons 1 through 3,[129] may still provide a framework for exploring the parameters of feminist judging.

Canon 1 provides that "[a] Judge should uphold the integrity and independence of the judiciary." This norm is aimed at ensuring that judges act "without fear or favoritism in a manner free from self-interest or bias." Feminist judging specifically seeks to achieve justice in a non-gender-biased way by listening to narratives, contextualizing disputes, and utilizing knowledge acquired through life experiences. It aims at unearthing biases in legal, social, economic, and other structures that get in the way of equality in law and fact.

Canon 2 urges that judges "avoid impropriety and the appearance of impropriety in all activities." Canon 2A elaborates by providing that judges must respect and comply with the law; 2B explains that "[a] judge should not allow family, social, political or financial, or other relationships to influence judicial conduct or judgment"; and 2C forbids membership in organizations that "discriminate[] on the basis of race, sex, religion or national origin" because such membership may give the impression that the obligation to be impartial is impaired. While 2C's requirement of nondiscrimination is fully aligned with the feminist judging model, 2A and B require more attention.

Regarding 2A, while judges must respect the law, feminist judging requires an initial analysis to uncover hidden biases or foundations that can have the effect of reinforcing or perpetuating the subordination of women. Similarly, 2B is not problematic if it means that specific personal relationships of the judge should not influence the judge in a particular case. However, feminist judging, in particular cultural feminism, urges that a judge should consider relationships more generally when they are relevant to a case.

Canon 3 requires that judges act "fairly, impartially and diligently." This canon suggests an answer is needed first to whether judging from a feminist perspective is intrinsically biased or partial. Rather than being partial, feminist approaches simply unearth gender hierarchies and the role of gender in laws and legal systems that result in disadvantages to women. Like any other judicial philosophy such as originalism, a feminist judicial philosophy must work within the framework of legal rules and the facts of a particular case. Being aware of and recognizing the role of gender may lead to fairer and

[129] Canon 4 addresses permissible extrajudicial activity and Canon 5 directs judges to refrain from engaging in political activity.

more impartial results because the judge identifies, analyzes, and understands whether biases exist that would prejudice women. Such decision making may well correct an injustice otherwise masked by concealed gendered prejudices or partialities, as shown by the example of Justice Ginsburg's recognition in *Safford* of how a thirteen-year-old girl might react to the strip search.

Moreover, no judge is a clean slate. All judges have life experiences that shape their perceptions and reasoning. These include family, education, and work experience as well as interactions with society that are framed by their identities with respect to gender, sex, sexuality, race, ethnicity, class, religion, nationality, language, culture, and ability. In the past, perhaps because the face of the judiciary was homogeneous, there was less awareness of these human realities and diversities among judges. Male norms created a sense that they captured a neutral and impartial way of seeing. For example, in *Bradwell v. Illinois*, male bias and gender subordination ideology were deployed in the context of establishing the separate spheres as "natural" and dictated by the "divine" order, undermining the law's claim of neutrality and impartiality.[130]

Despite this long history of judges being influenced by their life experiences and ideologies, the media have focused on the three female justices' 2014 dissents in several Affordable Care Act cases, writing articles about the "female justices issu[ing] [a] searing dissent over new contraceptive case."[131] These stories suggest that the justices' sex determined their reasoning and that their sex matters because the issue is contraception. In neither case did the media focus on the sex of the male majority or the combination of their male sex and Catholic religion as the possible reason for the majority outcome, suggesting that their decision in contrast was neutral and unbiased. In cases in which there was a religious objection to the law and the majority justices aligned with their own religion's teachings, the media gave

[130] *Bradwell v. Illinois*, 83 U.S. 130, 141 (1873).
[131] *See* Irin Carmon, *Female Justices Issue Searing Dissent Over New Contraceptive Case*, MSNBC (July 3, 2014), www.msnbc.com/msnbc/sotomayor-blistering-dissent-contraception-case; Brett Logiurato, *Female Justices Issue Scathing Dissent in the First Post-Hobby Lobby Birth Control Exemption*, Bus. Insider (July 3, 2014), www.businessinsider.com/sotomayor-ginsburg-kagan-dissent-wheaton-college-decision-supreme-court-2014-7; Mark Sherman, *3 Female Justices Dissent in First Post-Hobby Lobby Contraceptive Case* TPM News (July 3, 2014), talkingpointsmemo.com/news/3-female-justices-dissent-in-first-post-hobby-lobby-contraception-case; Bill Mears and Tom Cohen, *Supreme Court Women Lash Out at Birth Control Decision* CNN (July 5, 2014), www.cnn.com/2014/07/04/politics/supreme-court-women/; Nia-Malika Henderson, *How Justice Ginsburg's Hobby Lobby Dissent Helps Shape the Debate About Reproductive vs. Religious Rights*, Washington Post (July 1, 2014), www.washingtonpost.com/blogs/she-the-people/wp/2014/07/01/how-justice-ginsburgs-hobby-lobby-dissent-helps-shape-the-debate-about-reproductive-and-religious-rights/.

the impression by their silence that the majority's decisions were influenced only by neutral principles.

By choosing sports analogies to describe the role of judges, the American Bar Association (ABA) presents an example of the use of a gendered perspective under the guise of neutral storytelling: "Judges are like umpires in baseball or referees in football or basketball." The description continues by referencing baseball and noting that judges, "[l]ike the ump ... call 'em as they see 'em ... ."[132] While the ABA notes that the "calling" has to be based upon facts and law, without consideration of the popularity or unpopularity of a particular position or whether the judge agrees with the law, the choice of language, perhaps inadvertently, recognizes that judges are not clean slates. "Calling them as they see them" implies that there can be different views of the same play.

In rendering their decisions, judges draw on knowledge about the world that is pertinent to the case but extrinsic to its facts. Jurists often take "judicial notice" of such common knowledge in deciding cases – a common knowledge that masquerades as fact but may be anything but. In this regard, feminist judges, like all judges, can deploy their feminist knowledge and thought process in filling the gaps and engaging in discretionary acts to analyze the meaning or proper application of the law. Significantly, the feminist's common knowledge may differ from the knowledge of her or his colleagues, and such additional "common knowledge" may serve to assist the pursuit of justice.

Given that judging evaluates substance as well as procedure, what would feminist judging methods look like? One feminist inquiry is the "woman question." This question, posed by Wollstonecraft more than two centuries ago, is still relevant and valid. In the legal context, asking the woman question involves examining whether rules, norms, and practices that are posing as neutral are in fact gendered and thereby complicit in the subordination of women. Beyond the woman question, other characteristics distinguish a feminist-method approach to judging: flexibility, equality, multidimensionality, interdisciplinary, contextuality, and anti-subordination. Derived from and supported by the various feminist theoretical frameworks, these methods further the judicial goal of fair and impartial justice.

Flexibility refers to the approach to be taken in judging facts and law. The facts must be analyzed so that one voice is not privileged over another. The rules need to be read so that they can be applied justly. This requires that a

---

[132] ABA, Div. for Pub. Educ., How Courts Work – Courts and Legal Procedure: The Role of Judges, www.americanbar.org/groups/public_education/resources/law_related_education_network/how_courts_work/judge_role.html.

judge unearth biases in the rules themselves and confront the notion of the normativity of maleness in law.

Equality includes the promotion of not only formal equality but also the goal of substantive equality. It is not fair or impartial to compare unlikes to likes. Realities of life such as pregnancy can only be labeled as unique or a disability from the normative stance of one who cannot perform that task. Equality in life and law can only be attained by pursuing both formal and substantive equality.

Multidimensionality entails embracing the different conditions of different women in myriad contexts in which women may encounter the law. It rejects the single-axis method that does not account for the complex realities of people's lives. It rejects the male–female binary model and its inscribed hierarchy of power, upends essentialism within feminism, and topples the traditional legal approach. Multidimensionality recognizes that power is multidirectional. It seeks to ground jurisprudence and its outcomes by looking to and centering the marginalized, the invisible, and the voiceless in order to ensure that they, too, receive justice. Thus, when evaluating the existence of sex-based bias, feminist judging understands that what defines a woman is much more than her sex or gender. Both women (and men) also have identities relating to class, education, race, ethnicity, religion, sexuality, and more. These identities not only inform their interactions with and in society but also likely have preordained their location in society. Some or all of these identity characteristics might be relevant to the analysis of the current legal matter. Here, the human rights model of the indivisibility and interdependence of rights may be used to support the move away from the traditional uni-dimensional legal analysis.

Feminist judging should be interdisciplinary. Women (and men) live in a world that is not bound solely by law. Social, political, economic, and cultural realities concretely inform the circumstances that surround the event that is being judged. Because these other locations are gendered male or at least may reflect male bias, the judge must analyze how these realities have interacted with the law. Thus, different works from the social sciences, political science, medicine, economics, history, philosophy, art, and popular culture may provide a more complete frame for the legal landscape.

While interdisciplinarity provides both legal and extra-legal information, feminist judging uses contextualization to understand the information within the particular case. For example, feminist judging would explore whether the story would be told differently from a different perspective, one that is not privileged. Consideration of timing and relationships changes the way actions are viewed and understood. Contextual material allows the judge to analyze the situation from different locations. Especially important to feminist judging is to welcome the introduction of narratives traditionally excluded, thus giving voice to the voiceless.

Feminist judging adopts an anti-subordination philosophy. This expands on equality, interdisciplinarity and contextualization by examining the relative power of the actors in their relationships with each other as well as to society. The anti-subordination stance reveals structural inequalities that lead to unjust outcomes because they pose as neutral. An anti-subordination approach often requires historically specific analysis, and it expands the range of feminist issues because a panoply of economic subordinations plague women disproportionately.

In sum, feminist judging is a conscious methodology that liberates what Foucault labels "subjugated knowledges" and raises the non-essential woman's experience.[133] Feminist judging can liberate and enrich the law by unearthing otherwise hidden factors and considering a fuller narrative.

While reflecting a commitment to pursuing women's equality and deploying certain methods, feminist judging is not outcome determinative. Feminist arguments can and have supported different outcomes on topics as varied as reproductive rights, pornography, and surrogacy. In reproductive technologies and surrogacy matters, for example, sex, race and class hierarchies often come into play. For instance, in India there is a booming industry in which well-to-do Western, white couples, gay and straight alike, use poor Indian women as surrogates. During pregnancy the Indian women often live in dorms and have their bodies controlled by the clinic to carry their white babies to term. Feminists on one side condemn such practice. They reject the commodification of women, the "rental" of the womb, and deplore the normalization of what some call a modern form of slavery of poor women of color. The other side argues that the surrogate woman is exercising agency in making a choice that makes economic sense for her and her family, provides her with health care and food, and pays her more than she could earn in another probably more risky job. Both sides cite feminist arguments. Both divergent stances are fully supportable by existing feminist theories and analysis.

CONCLUSION

Feminist theories and methods promote fairness. Feminist judging is fair and impartial because it examines the law itself, as well as the institutional, social, and historical contexts of any dispute, to find structural biases that would lead to an unjust result. Feminist judgments make a difference because judges with

---

[133] Mann, *supra* note 5, at 220.

feminist perspectives are able to turn a different lens on the world and the law, one that reflects the point of view of an outsider, a foreigner, an expert with a different life experience. Feminist judgments result from methods that are flexible; promote equality; are multidimensional, contextual and interdisciplinary; and promote anti-subordination.

The male perspective pervades the normative fabric of law and legal structures. It naturalizes and normalizes male-gendered views, values, and hierarchies. Through this lens, women are the "other," outsiders existing in the shadows of the law. Women of color, lesbians, and poor women often comprise multiple others, more distanced outsiders, invisible in the long shadows. Feminist theory and methods provide the tools for feminist judging to deploy a critical, counter-hegemonic narrative that exposes and eradicates the male bias in ostensibly neutral ways of seeing. Feminist judging liberates all women, and all sexes, from the intertwined subordinations of gender, sex, sexuality, race, ethnicity, class, religion, nationality, language, culture, and ability. Feminist judging embraces all people as fully human and deserving of real equality

PART II

The feminist judgments

3

Commentary on *Bradwell v. Illinois*

Kimberly Holst

BACKGROUND

When the U.S. Supreme Court upheld the denial of a law license to Myra Bradwell,[1] two historical currents were diverted. First, the decision was a setback for the nineteenth-century wave of feminism focusing on formal equality. As evidenced by the nascent woman suffrage movement,[2] these feminists were working to eliminate sex-based barriers to women's exercise of civil and political rights.[3] Second, the decision undermined the development of an expansive interpretation of the Reconstruction Amendments adopted after the Civil War. The Court apparently feared that the restructuring contemplated by these Amendments would dangerously shift the balance of power from the states to the federal government. Between 1870 and 1873, the Court retreated from endorsing the exercise of federal power and increasingly invalidated Acts of Congress while refusing to restrict discriminatory state actions.[4]

Myra Bradwell was the founder and editor-in-chief of the *Chicago Legal News*[5] and a feminist. Under her leadership, Chicago's weekly legal newspaper published all new statutes and judicial decisions.[6] Bradwell's columns

---

[1]   *Bradwell v. Illinois*, 83 U.S. 130, 139 (1873).

[2]   Jane M. Friedman, America's First Woman Lawyer 22 (1993). Later known as the women's suffrage movement, the movement began with the formation in 1869 of the National Woman Suffrage Association (NWSA) led by Elizabeth Cady Stanton and Susan B. Anthony, and the American Woman Suffrage Association (AWSA), led by Lucy Stone, Henry Blackwell, and Julia Ward Howe.

[3]   *See, e.g.*, Martha E. Chamallas, Introduction to Feminist Legal Theory 9–15 (3d ed. 2012).

[4]   Charles Warren, *The Slaughterhouse cases and the death of Chase: 1873, in* The Supreme Court in United States History 255–57 (1926).

[5]   Friedman, *supra* note 2, at 77. Bradwell secured a special charter from the Illinois legislature that freed her from the legal handicaps that typically encumbered married women and allowed her to run the business.

[6]   *Id.* at 79–80.

advocated women's rights and other social and legal advancements.[7] When she decided to become an attorney, Bradwell apprenticed under her husband, James Bradwell.[8] There were no female attorneys in the United States in 1860 and very few in 1869,[9] the year that Bradwell took and passed the Illinois bar exam and applied for admission to the Illinois bar.

At first, the Illinois Supreme Court denied Bradwell's admission because she suffered from a "disability imposed by [her] married condition."[10] The reasoning relied upon the law of coverture – that is, a married woman's legal existence was incorporated through her husband, impairing her right to enter into legal agreements and her ability to practice law.[11] After Bradwell challenged the denial, the Illinois Supreme Court rejected her application again in January 1870, asserting that it could not act contrary to the intention of the Legislature.[12] The Illinois court apparently feared that admission of a woman might lead to women, married or single, holding public office. Their decision thus expanded Bradwell's "disability" for law practice from her status as a married woman to her status as a woman.[13]

In her legal memorandum to the Illinois Supreme Court, Bradwell inserted two federal constitutional issues that would enable her later to petition the U.S. Supreme Court. These were novel legal arguments because the courts had not yet decided any cases under the newly adopted Fourteenth Amendment. Bradwell argued that denying her application to the state bar violated her right to "full and equal benefit of the law," a claim that was never addressed by the courts below.[14] Her second claim, based on the right "to carry on a trade," as protected by the Privileges and Immunities Clause, became the focus of the U.S. Supreme Court opinion.[15]

Required to retain a member of the U.S. Supreme Court bar to handle her argument, Bradwell hired Matthew Hale Carpenter, a well-known constitutional lawyer. Carpenter argued that, absent any limiting language, the Privileges and Immunities Clause protected the fundamental civil rights of all people. His short brief distinguished Bradwell's bid for admission to the

---

[7] *Id.* at 78.

[8] *Id.* at 18.

[9] Nancy T. Gilliam, *A Professional Pioneer: Myra Bradwell's Fight to Practice Law,* 5 L. & Hist. Rev. 105, 107 (1987).

[10] Friedman, *supra* note 2, at 19.

[11] *Id.*

[12] Gilliam, *supra* note 9, at 111 (quoting *In re Bradwell,* 55 Ill. 535, 538 (1869)).

[13] *Id.* at 112.

[14] *Id.* at 114.

[15] *Id.* at 115. Bradwell made an interstate citizenship claim based on her previous citizenship in Vermont. This claim was not analyzed.

bar from arguments related to women's suffrage,[16] apparently fearing that a perceived link would harm Bradwell's chances.[17] Arguing for an expansive interpretation of the Fourteenth Amendment in Bradwell's case, Carpenter simultaneously argued for a narrow interpretation in the *Slaughter-House Cases*, where he had been hired to present the contrary argument.[18]

Bradwell and the *Slaughter-House Cases* took approximately three years to decide,[19] and the lengthy *Slaughter-House* decision was announced with great fanfare in 1873, delaying the *Bradwell* decision until the next day. Not kept informed of the status or outcome of her case, Bradwell would find out that she had lost when she received a copy of the opinion in a telegram.[20]

THE ORIGINAL OPINION

Myra Bradwell's lawsuit would never be considered separately, on its own merits. Instead, it would always be tied to the *Slaughter-House Cases*,[21] a group of consolidated lawsuits filed by independent butchers who argued that a Louisiana statute granting a monopoly to a single corporate slaughterhouse violated the Fourteenth Amendment by impeding the butchers' conduct of their trade. Together, *Bradwell* and the *Slaughter-House Cases* would require the Court to interpret the developing Fourteenth Amendment.[22] Ultimately, the Court chose to frame its decision in *Bradwell* in the shadow of its *Slaughter-House* opinion.

In the *Slaughter-House Cases*, the Court adopted a narrow view of the Fourteenth Amendment's Privileges and Immunities Clause, disregarding its historical meaning as a guarantee of fundamental civil rights in general, and of the right to pursue a livelihood in particular. The majority further asserted that despite its broader language, the Fourteenth Amendment's Equal Protection Clause prohibited unequal treatment only when the inequality was based on race.[23] Consistent with this limited interpretation, the brief majority opinion in *Bradwell*, drafted by Justice Miller, concluded that "admission to

---

[16] Robert M. Spector, *Woman Against the Law: Myra Bradwell's Struggle for Admission to the Illinois Bar*, 68 J. Ill. State Hist. Soc'y 235 (1975).

[17] *See* Gilliam, *supra* note 9, at 120.

[18] *Id.* at 118.

[19] *See id.* at 105, 122–24; Richard L. Aynes, *Kate Chase, the "Sphere of Women's Work," and Her Influence upon Her Father's Dissent in* Bradwell v. Illinois, 117 *Ohio Hist.* 31, 35 (2010).

[20] Gilliam, *supra* note 9, at 127.

[21] *Slaughter-House Cases*, 83 U.S. (16 Wall.) 36 (1873).

[22] Gilliam, *supra* note 9, at 117.

[23] *Id.* at 125; *Slaughter-House Cases*, 83 U.S. at 73–77.

practice in the courts of a State" is not a privilege or immunity belonging to citizens of the United States.[24]

Bradwell is perhaps best known for the concurrence written by Justice Bradley, joined by Justices Field and Swayne, each of whom had dissented in the *Slaughter-House Cases*. Addressing the role of women in society, the concurrence relies on the "wide difference in the respective spheres and destinies of man and woman."[25] Determining that "harmony … to the family institution is repugnant to the idea of a woman adopting a distinct and independent career from that of her husband,"[26] the concurrence calls on the "law of the Creator" and tradition in stating that the "paramount destiny and mission of woman are to fulfill the noble and benign offices of wife and mother."[27]

THE FEMINIST JUDGMENT

The *Bradwell* decision failed to recognize the broader, historically sound interpretation of the Fourteenth Amendment and to differentiate Myra Bradwell's arguments from those of the butchers in the *Slaughter-House Cases*. In the feminist dissent, Professor Phyllis Goldfarb, writing as Justice Goldfarb, remedies these errors and corrects the Court's substitution of ideological assumptions for legal reasoning.

First, the feminist dissent adopts the interpretation of the Fourteenth Amendment intended by its drafters. Goldfarb relies on both the language of the text and the historical context surrounding the adoption of the Reconstruction Amendments. She clarifies that the original intention of the Fourteenth Amendment was to protect equality for all and to limit group subordination. Throughout the opinion, Goldfarb acknowledges that race and gender subordination operate differently, but she finds that the underlying principles of formal equality are not limited to racial equality.

Next, the feminist opinion distinguishes *Bradwell* from the *Slaughter-House Cases*. Goldfarb emphasizes the flaw inherent in framing both cases as simply "restrict[ing] the right of a person to pursue his chosen occupation."[28] While Louisiana's slaughterhouse monopoly affected how independent butchers conducted their business, the butchers were not entirely precluded from pursuing their livelihoods because of their identities. Bradwell, however, was completely excluded from the practice of law solely because of her sex.

---

[24] *Bradwell*, 83 U.S. at 139.
[25] *Id.* at 141 (Bradley, J., concurring).
[26] *Id.*
[27] *Id.*
[28] Gilliam, *supra* note 9, at 105.

Third, the feminist opinion exposes the ideological basis of the concurring justices' reliance on the concept of separate spheres for men and women's lives. Goldfarb illustrates that this image was inaccurate, not only because the boundaries had routinely been crossed but also because the description of separate spheres did not cover the lives of many women at the time. By exposing the fallacy that separate spheres imagery applies to all women, the feminist dissent demonstrates that the majority's reasoning is based not on universal neutral principles, but on particular ideological beliefs.

The feminist dissent further reveals the role of gender ideology by highlighting the inconsistencies between the concurrence in *Bradwell* and the dissents by the same justices in the *Slaughter-House Cases*. For example, the dissent by Justice Bradley in the *Slaughter-House Cases* finds that "the right to follow such profession or employment as each one may choose" is a fundamental privilege of American citizenship, yet he denies that right to Myra Bradwell.[29] The feminist dissent suggests that the concurring justices' views of gender differences were so passionately held that they overrode their views of the fundamental rights protected by the Fourteenth Amendment. Goldfarb illustrates that gender-differentiated power operates through paternalistic claims that women need men's protection and structural claims that the laws are "natural," thus legitimizing gender hierarchy by attempting to erase men's role in creating it.

Finally, Goldfarb more centrally brings into focus the individuals who are asking for recognition of their rights; she identifies Bradwell by name, shows concern for the consequences of the decision on individual people's lives, and demonstrates an awareness of what the law may have looked like from the perspective of Bradwell and other women.

CONCLUSION

While awaiting the outcome, Bradwell helped pass an Illinois statute that allowed all persons, regardless of sex, the freedom to select their occupation, profession, or employment.[30] As a result, a woman was admitted to the Illinois bar in 1873. Bradwell did not try again to obtain her license, but in 1890, the Illinois Supreme Court acted on its own motion and admitted Bradwell to the

---

[29] This feminist point echoes comments by Bradwell published in the *Chicago Legal News* in response to the opinion in 1873. Gilliam, *supra* note 9, at 127–28.

[30] Friedman, *supra* note 2, at 134; The Revised Statutes of the State of Illinois 169 (Harvey B. Hurd comp. and ed., Springfield, Illinois Journal Co. 1874).

Illinois state bar. Bradwell was admitted to practice before the U.S. Supreme Court in 1892, just before she died of cancer.[31]

Had the *Bradwell* Court adopted a more expansive view of the Fourteenth Amendment, the currents moving women's equality forward might have gained force a century earlier.[32] Adopted by the Court, Goldfarb's dissent would have created a constitutional foundation for women to advance in political and social spheres. A finding for Bradwell based on the feminist dissent's broad reading of the Fourteenth Amendment might have secured civil rights and liberties decades earlier not only for women but also for other subordinated groups.

As it was, it would take another fifty years for the ratification of the Nineteenth Amendment granting women the right to vote. It would take another century for the Court to find a constitutional prohibition against sex-based discrimination.

Bradwell v. Illinois, 83 U.S. 130 (1873)

Justice Phyllis Goldfarb, dissenting.

This term marks the Court's first occasion to give meaning to America's new national structure, as enshrined in three constitutional amendments adopted in 1868 in the aftermath of our terrible and protracted Civil War. Designed to alter the political dynamics of our union, these Amendments establish fundamental freedoms protected by federal power.

The Fourteenth Amendment, a bright new star in this constitutional firmament, speaks expansively. It is a deep honor and a profound responsibility to announce initial interpretations of its high-minded words. The importance of exercising our constitutional responsibility to interpret the Fourteenth Amendment scrupulously cannot be overstated, as our first words on its application will reverberate for generations to come on what it means to be a citizen of America.

Today the Court decides what American citizenship means for the Petitioner, a prominent legal publisher in the state of Illinois, a woman who has passed the state bar examination, and who possesses both the desire to obtain a license to practice law and every ability and qualification that the state demands of her to do so. Yet the Illinois Supreme Court has upheld the denial of her license on but one ground: she is not a man. Under the newly

---

[31] Spector, *supra* note 16, at 240–41.
[32] Gilliam, *supra* note 9, at 105. *See Adkins v. Children's Hospital*, 261 U.S. 525 (1923) and *Reed v. Reed*, 404 U.S. 71 (1971).

adopted Fourteenth Amendment, may a state lawfully prevent a qualified person from entering a chosen vocation exclusively because of her sex? That is the question we decide today.

To my dismay, eight justices of this Court decide the question in the affirmative. I view the flaws in the stated reasoning of the majority and concurring opinions to reveal a failure to apprehend in a meaningful way the new constitutional imperatives our nation has forged from the social, political, and legal upheavals it has so recently endured. Grounding my reasoning, as I must, in the democratic and egalitarian principles of the constitutional structure of our postwar union, and having endeavored to comport my legal judgments with the letter and spirit of our reconstructed constitutional design, I respectfully dissent.

I

Procedural history

Myra Bradwell, editor and publisher of the *Chicago Legal News*, passed the Illinois bar examination with "high honors" in August 1869. After submitting a certificate attesting to her good moral character, and all other materials required to become a member of the bar, Bradwell asked the Illinois Supreme Court to issue her a license to practice law. In support of her application, she filed briefs arguing that: (1) the governing statute makes admission to law practice open to all persons and the legislature's own rules of construction demonstrate that its use of male pronouns should be understood as referring either to men or women; (2) recent cases and statutes support her admission to the bar because they modify the common law to allow women – including married women – to transact business, control their earnings, and pursue employment; and (3) the Fourteenth Amendment of the United States Constitution protects her right as a citizen to choose her vocation. In January 1870, the Illinois Supreme Court denied Bradwell's application for a license to practice law, holding that although she was well-qualified and the statute governing admission to the bar does not require the exclusion of women, the court should not exercise its discretion to admit to law practice any class of persons whom the legislature did not intend to be admitted. Thereafter, Bradwell sought review of the Illinois Supreme Court decision in the U.S. Supreme Court.

When Bradwell petitioned this Court for relief in January of 1870, nearly three years ago, the Court was also considering petitions from a group of independent Louisiana butchers. The latter petitions asserted that a partial slaughterhouse monopoly granted to a single corporation by the Louisiana legislature

impaired the independent butchers' right to practice their livelihood, a right
for which they claimed protection from the three primary constitutional safeguards found in Section One of the Fourteenth Amendment. Despite marked
differences between their circumstances and those of Petitioner Bradwell, this
Court has focused on the overlap in constitutional claims and determined to
decide these cases simultaneously. The Court's choice to link the two matters
ties the fate of Bradwell's law license and the equality of women before the
law to the Court's reception of the arguments of the Louisiana butchers in the
Slaughter-House Cases, 83 U.S. (16 Wall.) 36 (1873).

II

The text of Amendment XIV, Section One, of the
United States Constitution

Bradwell asks us to overturn the Illinois Supreme Court's decision upholding
the denial of her license to practice law. Her argument is based on the not-
yet-five-year-old text of Section One of the Fourteenth Amendment. Section
One reads as follows:

> All persons born or naturalized in the United States, and subject to the juris-
> diction thereof, are citizens of the United States and of the state wherein
> they reside. No State shall make or enforce any law which shall abridge the
> privileges and immunities of citizens of the United States; nor shall any State
> deprive any person of life, liberty, or property, without due process of law; nor
> deny to any person within its jurisdiction the equal protection of the laws.
>
> U.S. Const. amend. XIV, § 1.

Section One is broad and unqualified. Its language requires equality before
the law, allowing no class-based distinctions such as those of race or sex.
According to Section One, all former slaves born in the United States are citizens. So too is Petitioner Bradwell, who according to the record was born in
the state of Vermont. Having moved to Chicago, she has transferred her state
citizenship to Illinois. Her state of residence matters only insofar as it establishes, for constitutional purposes, that she is a citizen of the United States.[33]

---

[33] In the Illinois Supreme Court, Bradwell suggested that the state's decision to withhold her
law license discriminated against her under the second section of Article IV that provides "the
citizens of each state shall be entitled to all the privileges and immunities of the citizens in the
several States." U.S. Const. art. IV, § 2, cl. 1. I do not refer to that argument here, as I agree with
the majority – and apparently with Petitioner and her counsel who relied on other arguments
to this Court – that Art. IV, § 2 is not applicable to the claims and circumstances of this case.

What is the meaning of United States citizenship? The second sentence of Section One bears at least part of the answer: citizens have privileges – freedom to do things – and immunities – freedom from state restrictions in exercising their privileges. In short, the Privileges and Immunities Clause tells us that citizens like Bradwell have rights that all states – while showing regard for equal protection and due process of law – must protect. In sum, through the operation of the Fourteenth Amendment, the Constitution now restricts state governments, not just the federal government, from impeding civil rights and individual liberties.

The concept of "privileges and immunities" first appeared on our shores in colonial charters, then in the Articles of Confederation, and subsequently in Article IV, Section Two of the Constitution, which reads, "the citizens of each State shall be entitled to all the privileges and immunities of the citizens in the several States." U.S. Const. art. IV, § 2, cl. 1. We have read that clause to mean that states cannot discriminate in their laws against persons from other states. But the language of the Fourteenth Amendment is different, indicating that by virtue of their *federal* citizenship, all Americans have rights, and that both state and federal governments must respect these rights of citizenship. As Justice Field affirms in his *Slaughter-House* dissent: "The amendment ... assumes that there are such privileges and immunities which belong of right to citizens as such, and ordains that they shall not be abridged by State legislation." *Slaughter-House Cases*, 83 U.S. at 96 (Field, J., dissenting).

The privileges and immunities of citizenship encompass the fundamental civil rights found in common law. In his well-known opinion in *Corfield v. Coryell*, Justice Washington asserts that protected privileges and immunities are those "which are, in their nature, fundamental; which belong of right, to the citizens of all free governments." 6 F. Cas. 546, 551–52 (C.C.E.D. Pa. 1823) (No. 3230). These include "protection by the government; the enjoyment of life and liberty, with the right to acquire and possess property ... and to pursue and obtain happiness and safety; subject nevertheless to such restraints as the government may justly prescribe for the general good of the whole." *Id.* at 552.

Congress knew Justice Washington's words well, echoing them in the Civil Rights Act of 1866, which guaranteed racial equality with respect to the common law rights "to make and enforce contracts, to sue, be parties, and give evidence, to inherit, purchase, lease, sell, hold, and convey real and personal property, and to full and equal benefit of all laws and proceedings for the security of person and property, as is enjoyed by white citizens." Civil Rights Act of 1866, ch. 31, § 1, 14 Stat. 27 (1866). Through this language, the Civil Rights Act of 1866 evinces an awareness that a central injustice of slavery was its denial of the fundamental right of all people, regardless of race, to own their own labor, to contract for gainful employment, and to reap the fruits of their labors. Justice Field confirms this view in his dissenting opinion in *Slaughter-House*, writing: "The abolition of slavery and involuntary servitude was intended [to accord] the right to pursue the ordinary avocations of life without other restraint than such as affects all others ... ." *Slaughter-House Cases*, 83 U.S. at 90 (Field, J., dissenting).

Stripped of the formally superior status that slavery gave them, many in the former Confederate states responded by enacting discriminatory laws, Black Codes, that sought to recreate racial hierarchy and enforce racial inequality by denying fundamental civil rights to large populations of freed slaves. The Civil Rights Act of 1866, passed over President Johnson's veto, was designed to outlaw these discriminatory practices. Because the risk remained that the Act might be repealed by a future congressional majority or struck down by a U.S. Supreme Court that thought it beyond congressional authority, Congress determined to constitutionalize the achievements of the Act through the passage of the Fourteenth Amendment. But the language of the Fourteenth Amendment is broader than the underlying statutory language, protecting the privileges and immunities of all classes of citizens, who are understood to be equal classes before the law. Hence the Fourteenth Amendment, propelled in part by an inclusive concern for the human right to labor on one's own behalf, now raises a challenge to other hierarchical social relationships that implicate these and related concerns.

Congress intended the Fourteenth Amendment to be wider in scope than the Civil Rights Act. Indeed, like the statute that inspired it, the first draft of the Fourteenth Amendment submitted to Congress in 1866 limited its prohibitions solely to discrimination on the basis of race. While race discrimination was – and remains – a critical concern of the moment, Congress rejected the race-specific draft in favor of a more general one. Providing a constitutional basis for racial equality as well as the equality of other classes of persons, the Fourteenth Amendment protects members of subordinated groups from law's disfavor. The provision, extending across the ages a principle of equality writ large, authorizes federal power to invalidate discriminatory laws and practices, including those enacted by states, that treat classes of people as less than full citizens. Because the Amendment does not recognize degrees or tiers of citizenship, and all citizens have fundamental rights, post-Civil War America can no longer have second-class citizens under law.

Whether Bradwell will be granted an attorney's license depends on this Court's determination of whether she is a citizen in possession of rights that the Fourteenth Amendment directs all states to honor and honor equally. As I have described above, in my view, the remarkable breadth of the hard-won language of Section One of the Fourteenth Amendment, its inclusive grant of citizenship, its focus on citizens' individual rights, its concern with equality, its grounding in ownership of one's labor, and its reallocation of power and responsibility between the states and the federal government require this Court to overturn the Illinois court's refusal to issue the license to practice law that Bradwell so richly deserves. Unfortunately, the majority's miserly reading of the Fourteenth Amendment in the *Slaughter-House Cases* now poses an obstacle to this outcome.

III

The Slaughter-House Cases

Having read the *Slaughter-House* opinions in draft, I find myself in sharp disagreement with the five justices whose majority opinion offers a cramped reading of the Fourteenth Amendment. Now the Court has compounded the error – dispensing with Bradwell's petition in short order and with nary a mention of the rights of women – by relying on the faulty reasoning of the majority in *Slaughter-House*. In its cursory opinion in *Bradwell*, the majority merely references its *Slaughter-House* decision, offering no further explication of its reasoning, or its application to Bradwell's claims.

As a consequence of the Court's decision to chain *Bradwell* to *Slaughter-House*, I must justify my *Bradwell* dissent by explaining first how the Court erred in *Slaughter-House*. If the majority in the *Slaughter-House Cases* had fully appreciated the intended message of Section One of the Fourteenth Amendment, and had decided in accord with its purpose, *Slaughter-House* would support rather than undermine Bradwell's quest for a law license. Subsequently, I will demonstrate that even under the Fourteenth Amendment as narrowed by the *Slaughter-House Cases*, Bradwell's constitutional claims are stronger than the Louisiana butchers' claims, and therefore she still should prevail.

Given the current state of interpretive development of this new constitutional provision, I believe – contrary to the *Slaughter-House* majority – that Bradwell's strongest case sounds in the Privileges and Immunities Clause. The Equal Protection Clause offers great promise as well. And the overall import of Section One, including not just these Clauses but the Due Process Clause too, will be realized only when the law protects the equality of all people, regardless of race, sex, and other class or caste distinctions.

IV

The privileges and immunities clause

In construing the Fourteenth Amendment to uphold the slaughtering business monopoly created in 1869 by the Louisiana legislature, the five justices
comprising the bare *Slaughter-House* majority assert that the privileges and
immunities of United States citizens are few. They comprise only those rights
that affect a citizen's relationship with the federal government, such as the
right to access the federal courts or to petition the federal government for
redress of grievances. Despite the clarity of Congress's contrary intention, the
majority cannot fathom that the Privileges or Immunities Clause was intended
"as a protection to the citizen of a state against the legislative power of his own
State." *Id.* at 74 (majority opinion).

This restrictive reading of the Clause flies in the face of our own recent
history, as I have recited it above. The privileges and immunities guaranteed
to the citizens of a state have long been understood to be their fundamental
civil rights at common law. Bradwell's right to pursue a livelihood for which
she is well qualified would certainly fall within those common law privileges
and immunities that the Fourteenth Amendment empowered federal courts to
protect from the sort of state interference that Illinois has presented.

Moreover, the Supremacy Clause of Article Six, Section Two, already prohibits states from abridging their citizens' federal rights.[34] U.S. Const. art. VI,
§ 2, cl. 2. If the Fourteenth Amendment now protects only those privileges and
immunities that were already protected from state violations, then, as Justice
Field wrote in his *Slaughter-House* dissent, "it was a vain and idle enactment
which accomplished nothing, and most unnecessarily excited Congress and
the people on its passage." *Slaughter-House Cases*, 83 U.S. at 96 (Field, J.,
dissenting).

Because Congress surely would not have bothered to craft, with great fanfare, a meaningless and redundant Amendment, I can only conclude that
Justice Miller, and the four justices who join his *Slaughter-House* opinion,
are mistaken in asserting that the Fourteenth Amendment's Privileges and
Immunities Clause means nothing new. Nonetheless, their erroneous reading, smothering the Clause just as it was taking its first breath, now disrupts

---

[34] "This Constitution, and the Laws of the United States which shall be made in Pursuance
thereof; and all Treaties made, or which shall be made, under the Authority of the United
States, shall be the supreme Law of the Land; and the Judges in every State shall be bound
thereby, any Thing in the Constitution or Laws of any State to the Contrary notwithstanding."

Bradwell's claim for its protection of her right to pursue the occupation she has chosen.

Beyond oppression by a centralized power, such as the British monarch that America had overthrown, the circumstances that led to the Civil War taught us about decentralized oppression by states as well. Because recent experience has shown that federal power can serve as a check on state tyranny, the Fourteenth Amendment deliberately recalibrates the relationship between the federal government and the states. Apparently, Justice Miller objects to the new federal–state balance, maintaining that a finding on behalf of the plaintiffs' constitutional rights in *Slaughter-House* "would constitute this court a perpetual censor upon all legislation of the States, upon the civil rights of their own citizens, with authority to nullify such as it did not approve as consistent with those rights." *Id.* at 78 (majority opinion). He expresses discomfort with "so great a departure from the structure and spirit of our institutions; when the effect is to fetter and degrade the State governments by subjecting them to the control of Congress … when in fact it radically changes the whole theory of the relations of the State and Federal governments to each other and of both these governments to the people." *Id.*

I concede that these are bold new federal powers. But the results Justice Miller complains of, that lead him to be "convinced that no such results were intended," *id.*, are precisely those that Congress sought to achieve. They are the Fourteenth Amendment's *raison d'etre*. Unlike Justice Miller, I trust that Congress meant what it said when it undertook to grant federal constitutional protection of individual rights from trespass by the states. In the aftermath of the Civil War, the turbulent circumstances in our nation warrant this important constitutional innovation.

We cannot shrink from the responsibilities that Congress has bestowed upon us. States retain complete discretion to exercise their police power and regulatory authority as they choose, so long as they do not infringe upon Fourteenth Amendment freedoms, such as the privileges and immunities of citizenship, "which of right belong to the citizens of all free governments." *Id.* at 97 (Field, J., dissenting). Where states infringe these rights, as I believe Louisiana has done in the *Slaughter-House Cases* and Illinois has done in the *Bradwell* case, federal courts are required to identify these violations and to secure the rights of American citizenship.

Under *Corfield*, the Civil Rights Act of 1866, and now the Fourteenth Amendment, one of the primary rights of citizenship is the right to pursue a vocation. Yet in *Slaughter-House*, the five-justice majority finds the Louisiana legislature's grant of a partial slaughterhouse monopoly to a single corporation to be a legitimate exercise of its police powers in regulating the health and safety of its citizens with respect to a potentially noxious industry. Because I believe the butchers' right to pursue their vocation is impeded by their restriction, upon payment of fees, to using the corporate slaughterhouse, I disagree. Section One of the Fourteenth Amendment, centered on equality, does not countenance such special-interest legislation that favors the few at the expense of the fundamental liberties of many.

V

Distinctions between Bradwell *and the* Slaughter-House Cases

Nonetheless, having decided the *Slaughter-House Cases* as they did, the majority asserts that, in the name of consistency, they are now required to uphold the denial of Bradwell's right to practice law. I cannot assent to this proposition. Although the *Slaughter-House* decision makes it more difficult for Bradwell to prevail, I believe that she has presented us a stronger Fourteenth Amendment claim than have the Louisiana butchers. Focusing on pertinent distinctions between the claims in *Slaughter-House* and in *Bradwell* would enable the five justices in the *Slaughter-House* majority to rule in Bradwell's favor.

While the right of independent butchers to practice their trade was burdened by the Louisiana legislation creating a slaughterhouse monopoly, and the conditions under which the butchers might continue to work were altered, the plaintiffs were not entirely prohibited by law from engaging in their occupation. Additionally, even after Justice Washington recognized fundamental common law rights to practice an occupation, *Corfield* permitted favored treatment of oyster harvesters from New Jersey when pursuing their trade in New Jersey waters, much like the *Slaughter-House* majority now upholds the favored treatment of some in the Louisiana slaughtering industry. In this respect, each of these cases stands in contrast to *Bradwell*, in which the plaintiff faces a complete ban on engaging in her chosen profession. Even if the privileges and immunities of United States citizenship as guaranteed by the Fourteenth Amendment are more limited than I believe they are, if they are deemed to protect to any degree the common law right to devote one's labor to a calling, and to receive the benefits of that labor, then Bradwell's privileges and immunities of citizenship have been abridged to a greater extent than the abridgment challenged by the *Slaughter-House* plaintiffs.

There are other significant distinctions between the *Bradwell* case and the *Slaughter-House Cases* as well. The *Slaughter-House* majority was reluctant to assume the authority to overturn an act of a state legislature. Yet here the act at issue is a decision of a state court to withhold the grant of a professional license to a female applicant, despite legislative silence on its legitimacy. Overturning a state court decision should not raise structural concerns of the same magnitude as nullifying the laws passed by a legislative body. Choosing to use a more modest form of institutional authority to uphold a stronger claim of constitutional right can serve to justify a finding for Bradwell, regardless of the holding of *Slaughter-House*.

Finally, *Bradwell* presents a more paradigmatic case for Fourteenth Amendment protection. The immediate impetus for Section One of the Fourteenth Amendment was the denial of civil rights, on the basis of race, to the large population of freed slaves. But the language of the Amendment is not limited to race-based denials of civil rights. This suggests that Congress understood denials of civil rights to former slaves of African descent as one virulent species of a broader problem: discrimination against identifiable classes of people based on physical or personal characteristics. In this regard, discrimination on the basis of sex is similar in relevant respects to discrimination on the basis of race. Unlike the Louisiana butchers who were not in this sense an identifiable class subject to discrimination, Bradwell experienced the evisceration of a fundamental privilege and immunity of her American citizenship – occupational freedom – because she was a woman, a situation analogous in certain ways to that of slaves who had been deprived of control over their labor because of race. Because Congress understood the Fourteenth Amendment as an instrument for preventing the creation of subordinate classes – especially subordinate labor classes – and Bradwell's absolute exclusion from her chosen profession highlighted and reinforced her subordinate status, withholding her license to practice law falls squarely within the proscriptions of the Fourteenth Amendment.

VI

Other Fourteenth Amendment arguments

To the extent that I derive a decision in Bradwell's case from a particular constitutional directive, I have elaborated what I deem to be powerful arguments for finding support for her claims in the Privileges and Immunities Clause of Section One of the Fourteenth Amendment. While Bradwell's counsel relied primarily on that Clause in his argument before this Court, I have already noted the important equality principles that underlie not just the Privileges and Immunities Clause, but other clauses of the Fourteenth Amendment, and Section One as a whole. I now turn to those other Fourteenth Amendment arguments.

Once again, the *Slaughter-House* majority has made my task challenging, as it has drained meaning not only from the Privileges and Immunities Clause but also from other aspects of the Fourteenth Amendment. I repeat my conviction that they are wrong to do so, for they are defying the equality principles that animate the postwar constitutional enterprise. Even so, despite the impediments they raise, their reductive efforts still leave room for Bradwell to prevail in her mission to obtain a license to practice law.

A

The Equal Protection Clause

In her brief to the Illinois Supreme Court on December 31, 1869, Bradwell claims that the Fourteenth Amendment generally accords her "full and equal benefit of all laws" and a right to "follow the profession of an attorney-at-law upon the same terms, conditions, and restrictions as are applied to and imposed upon every other citizen of the State of Illinois." Tr. of Record at 9, *Bradwell v. Illinois*, 83 U.S. (16 Wall.) 130 (1873) (No. 487). Having fulfilled all state requirements for admission of attorneys, she maintains that "it is contrary to the true intent and meaning" of the Fourteenth Amendment to refuse her a license to practice law. *Id.*

The Equal Protection Clause of the Fourteenth Amendment holds special resonance for her claim. For what Bradwell seeks is to be equally protected by the laws of Illinois that prescribe the requirements for obtaining a law license, all of which she has fulfilled. The Fourteenth Amendment's general requirement that states must provide to all persons equal protection of the laws would forbid the state of Illinois from withholding a law's protection from freed slaves of African descent, women, or other identifiable classes. Equal treatment under law, regardless of race, sex, or other distinctive characteristics, is the new constitutional command. All are to be equal before the law. No class can be subordinate to another in the eyes of the law.

State regulations for granting law licenses are designed to protect the public by ensuring that only qualified applicants are admitted to the bar. It is appropriate for the law to discriminate in the issuance of law licenses against those who have not exhibited the qualifications for admission. But Bradwell has proven herself as qualified as any male applicants to become an attorney. She stands before the law in an equal position with other qualified candidates, male or female. Denying her admission to the bar is a form of discriminatory treatment that does not advance the purpose of the relevant regulations for granting law licenses. Therefore, it is an unreasonable and unjust denial of the equal protection of the laws to which all persons are entitled under the dictates of the Fourteenth Amendment.

Despite the logical relevance of the Equal Protection Clause to the situation before us, the *Slaughter-House* majority holds that the Clause is directed only at discrimination on the basis of race. Since Congress specifically rejected proposed language that so limited the Clause, this is an unwarranted conclusion. The universal application of the Equal Protection Clause to all persons suggests to me that our nation's experience with the brutalities of race-based chattel slavery revealed to us the importance of principles of human equality in a democratic republic and the evil of group subordination under law. Group subordination, the hierarchy of some classes of people over others, is the offense that Congress sought to eradicate through provisions of the Fourteenth Amendment like the Equal Protection Clause. That Clause would forbid the denial of law's benefits to women solely because they are women.

Thus, a finding under the Equal Protection Clause that Bradwell should have been granted a law license is not precluded by the *Slaughter-House Cases*. After the majority opinion states that the Equal Protection Clause was designed to combat discriminatory treatment on the basis of race, Justice Miller observes that the Clause is "so clearly a provision for that race and that emergency, that a strong case would be necessary for its application to any other." *Slaughter-House Cases*, 83 U.S. at 81. I submit that *Bradwell* is such a strong case. Our democracy will not prosper if qualified participants are denied opportunities solely on the basis of sex. Nor will it be a democracy, which depends for its sustenance on the consent of the governed, male and female alike. The principle of equal justice to which our nation has newly committed itself requires granting Myra Bradwell the law license she has earned.

B

The Due Process Clause

The Due Process Clause of the Fourteenth Amendment may offer additional support to this conclusion. Bradwell produced her qualifications to become an attorney under a law of general applicability, yet on the basis of sex, the Illinois state courts denied the law's application to her. This is not the fair application of the law that the Due Process Clause affords to all persons. Instead it can be appropriately understood as a Fourteenth Amendment deprivation of liberty and property without due process of law. As Justice Bradley avers in his *Slaughter-House* dissent: "[A] law which prohibits a large class of citizens from adopting a lawful employment ... does deprive them of liberty as well as property, without due process of law." *Slaughter-House Cases*, 83 U.S. at 122 (Bradley, J., dissenting).

C

The Amendment as a whole

Rather than elaborate further on the application of the Due Process Clause in the circumstances before us, I prefer to note again that the three key clauses of Section One – guaranteeing the privileges and immunities of citizenship, equal protection of the laws, and due process of law – follow one upon the other, their meaning and purpose intertwined. As a whole, Section One of the Fourteenth Amendment establishes an inherent pattern, a unifying theme, a larger purpose: equality of all before the law. In Justice Bradley's words, "Equality before the law is undoubtedly one of the privileges and immunities of every citizen." *Id.* at 118.

This short sentence captures the intersecting aims of Section One and underscores the constitutional deprivation that Petitioner Bradwell suffered. As a woman equal to the men granted law licenses in Illinois, Bradwell is protected by the connected and interdependent values of our new constitutional structure. Denying her the right to choose a livelihood for which she is well suited is forbidden by Section One of the Fourteenth Amendment, both in the fullness of its related meanings and in its component parts.

VII

Inconsistent opinions

The *Slaughter-House Cases* sparked passionate dissents. In his dissent, Justice Field writes: "That only is a free government, in the American sense of the term, under which the inalienable right of every citizen to pursue his happiness is unrestrained except by just and impartial laws." *Slaughter-House Cases*, 83 U.S. at 111 (Field, J., dissenting). Justice Swayne observes, "These amendments are all consequences of the late civil war ... They are a bulwark of defence, and can never be made an engine of oppression. The language employed is unqualified in its scope. There is no exception in its terms, and there can be properly none in their application ... This court has no authority to interpolate a limitation that is neither expressed nor implied." *Id.* at

128–29 (Swayne, J., dissenting). Justice Bradley declares that the Fourteenth Amendment prohibits states from restricting citizenship "to any classes or persons," that a citizen of the United States has "an equality of rights with every other citizen; and the whole power of the nation is pledged to sustain him in that right," and that "the right to choose one's calling is an essential part of that liberty which it is the object of government to protect." *Id.* at 112–13, 116 (Bradley, J., dissenting).

Citizenship confers privileges, he tells us, "and among these, none is more essential and fundamental than the right to follow such profession or employment as each one may choose, subject only to uniform regulations equally applicable to all." *Id.* at 119.

Yet eight justices of this Court – including Justices Field, Swayne, and Bradley – would deny to Myra Bradwell the Fourteenth Amendment's guarantee of the inalienable right of every citizen to choose a calling. For Bradwell, this decision makes the Fourteenth Amendment, adopted to combat oppression, another engine of oppression. To deny her rights that others possess is to limit Fourteenth Amendment safeguards in a way that exceeds our authority. Viewing this Court's opinions in *Bradwell* from the perspective of women in general and Petitioner in particular, I fear that the law appears to be an unjust and partial instrument, despite the Fourteenth Amendment's assurance to the contrary.

On what grounds do the justices who share my understanding of the Fourteenth Amendment's expansive meaning and purpose base their decision to deny relief to this worthy Petitioner? Justice Bradley indicates that deciding which occupations shall be filled exclusively by men "fairly belongs to the police power of the State." *Bradwell v. Illinois*, 83 U.S. at 142 (Bradley, J., concurring). When addressing arguments in the *Slaughter-House Cases* about whether it is within the proper police power of the state to grant a corporation an exclusive charter to operate a slaughterhouse, and require other butchers to pay fees to use it, Justice Bradley finds that the police power cannot justify such state action as it is "onerous, unreasonable, arbitrary, and unjust" and violates the fundamental freedom of citizens to pursue a chosen profession. *Slaughter-House Cases*, 83 U.S. at 119 (Bradley, J., dissenting). Yet when Bradwell complains in parallel that complete exclusion from her chosen profession is onerous, unreasonable, arbitrary, unjust, and therefore violative of her privileges and immunities of citizenship, Justice Bradley, joined by Justices Field and Swayne, reports that the state's decision to use its police power to reserve the legal profession for men is founded on "nature, reason, and experience." *Bradwell*, 83 U.S. at 142 (Bradley, J., concurring).

VIII

The ideology of separate spheres

The view that women should remain at home and men should have a
near-exclusive monopoly on the activities of civic life is one of long vintage.
Under the doctrine of coverture, British common law and custom rendered
married women subjects of their husband's rule. As Justice Bradley notes, a
woman's civic identity was subsumed into her husband's. *Bradwell*, 83 U.S. at
141 (Bradley, J., concurring). She had no economic rights and, without her
husband's consent, could not make contracts or hold property in her own
name. Through the operation of these legal norms, women were excluded
from the public sphere.

At the same time, our law has admitted of many exceptions to the strict
rules of coverture, and the boundaries of the separate spheres have been much
traversed. Slave women, pioneer women, women who settled the frontiers
of this vast nation, women who managed lands and businesses while men
were fighting the Civil War, all have demonstrated their skills as laborers.
Single women, widowed women, women separated from their husbands have,
by necessity, become wage-earners and business people, showing their apti-
tude for self-support. In various circumstances before the courts, judges have
recognized these realities and granted women, single and married, an independent civic status, modifying common law proscriptions to enable women
to sue and be sued, to contract, to earn wages, to inherit, to own property.
Married Women's Property Acts – passed in many states, including Illinois –
have endorsed these changes. Indeed, in operating her publishing business,
Bradwell has been empowered by the Illinois legislature to make all manner
of contracts, to retain her own earnings, and to hold her own property. The
legislature has recognized the quality of her work, and by extension her talent
in the sphere of civic and professional life, by authorizing all Illinois courts to
admit into evidence the contents of her weekly legal publication.

In light of these liberalizations, it is not entirely fair to say, as Justice Bradley
does, that experience points only in the direction of women's separate domestic sphere. *Id.* There are too many counter-examples, including that of this
Petitioner, to support his general assertion that "the natural and proper timidity
and delicacy which belongs to the female sex evidently unfits it for many of the
occupations of civil life." *Bradwell*, 83 U.S. at 141 (Bradley, J., concurring). In
fact, the language of the concurring justices, dissenters all in *Slaughter-House*,
shows less concern for principled doctrinal consistency than for the imag-
ined specter of gender equality. Their expressed belief in a hierarchical social

order in which men and women should forever and always operate in separate spheres appears to cloud their Fourteenth Amendment vision, so elegantly expressed in other contexts. When their separate spheres ideology allies itself, as here, with those who misread the Fourteenth Amendment to allow states to infringe the fundamental rights of citizens, women become less than the full citizens that the Constitution entitles them to be.

In his concurring opinion in *Bradwell*, Justice Bradley declares that "the sterner sex," *id.* at 142, should be "woman's protector and defender," *id.* at 141. He wishes to shelter women from the harsh demands of public life, such as those entailed in the practice of law. This kind of paternalism represents a peculiar form of protection, for it imprisons women in men's purported high esteem for them. Man becomes a defender only of woman's dependency, and she is relegated to the status of his inferior. Barred from public pursuits, with no authority, no economic power, and no enforceable rights, she is at the mercy of his beneficence (which is not forthcoming in all instances). Such a system is a description not of family harmony but of gender hegemony.

The concurring justices in *Bradwell* appeal to powers even more authoritative than the United States Constitution to support the separate spheres philosophy by which they would adjudicate Bradwell's case. They appeal to "the general constitution of things" as dictated by "nature," *id.* at 142, which "has always recognized a wide difference in the respective spheres and destinies of man and woman," *id.* at 141. They invoke "the divine ordinance," which "indicates the domestic sphere as that which properly belongs to the domain and functions of womanhood." *Id.* These irrebuttable forces are "repugnant to the idea of a woman adopting a distinct and independent career from that of her husband." *Id.* They comprise "the law of the Creator." *Id.*

Men, not God, are the creators of these laws. Men who make laws in the legislature, men who enforce laws, and men who adjudicate them on this and all other courts are also the principal beneficiaries. They guarantee freedom to themselves, and compel women to support men in the exercise of freedoms that women are denied. While I certainly understand why men may be reluctant to relinquish these arrangements that establish for themselves a position of social dominance – just as many broke from and fought the Union before relinquishing their slaves – I see no basis for assuming that the Creator, with a capital "C," shares that reluctance.

The hierarchies of gender reside less in nature and more in the hearts of men. Lawmakers and judges produce what they call the natural order by enforcing separate spheres, and erasing from their minds any awareness of their role in creating it. Women's "natural" fitness for the home is undoubtedly shaped by laws that have long confined them there. And if separate spheres are the natural order of things, why are laws required to enforce them? Why have women organized to draft a Declaration of Sentiments to advance their rights? *See Declaration of Sentiments* (1848).[35] Why does Myra Bradwell, with her husband's blessing, operate a thriving business in legal publishing and seek a license to practice law? The natural order will take its course only when oppressive laws are removed and all people can exercise equally their fundamental liberties, including the liberty to choose their callings.

In our country today, only men hold political and economic power, and men's power is affected by advances in women's liberty. This reality makes it all the more noteworthy that, after the war, Congress adopted constitutional provisions that guarantee civil rights in universal terms independent of gender. Evidently, the liberal ideal of universal equality has a stronger pull, and a stronger claim to fairness, than does the separate spheres ideology of gender. Unfortunately, the Court's opinion in *Bradwell* perpetuates the conflation of gender ideology and law, despite constitutional moorings that would enable us to disentangle them.

IX

Conclusion

Just as it will take an extended span of years to shake off the ideologies of white supremacy that for centuries supported American slavery – understood as a form of domestic relations – so too will it take an extended span of years to break the yoke of gender ideology that underlies the domestic relations of men and women and blocks both our nation's promise and its progress. But the Fourteenth Amendment beckons us toward greater freedom. Egalitarian democracy – of the sort that our best selves and our best rhetoric espouse – lies over the horizon, if only we can summon the strength to hold true to the humane course that our new Constitution charts.

For now, however, this Court places the imprimatur of law on woman's confinement to the private sphere, no matter her desires or talents. To advance in this way inequality under law is to invert the meaning and purpose of the new constitutional design that it is our duty to respect. I trust that the clarity of the Fourteenth Amendment's purpose, and its vision of equality for all before the

---

[35] Modeled after the Declaration of Independence, this document – drafted principally by Elizabeth Cady Stanton in Seneca Falls, New York at the first convention organized to address the civil and political rights of women – listed the restrictions on women's liberty that establish men's "absolute tyranny" over women and asserted the need to advance women's rights to equality with men.

law, will ultimately prevail. Given the importance and urgency of the issue to our democratic future, I hope the day is not too far distant when all our laws and institutions recognize the fundamental rights and equality of women, and all other classes who are treated as subordinate citizens. Until then, I respectfully dissent.

4

Commentary on *Muller v. Oregon*

Andrea Doneff

INTRODUCTION

Allowing the State of Oregon to enact workplace legislation protecting only women, the U.S. Supreme Court in *Muller v. Oregon*[1] accepted women's greater need for protection as a fact established by social science research. *Muller* is important to the history and theory of feminism for two reasons. First, it is known for the *Brandeis brief* filed on behalf of the State of Oregon by then-attorney and later U.S. Supreme Court Justice Louis Brandeis. A Brandeis brief emphasizes social science research to bolster the factual argument made in support of the legal analysis. While it is common today to make policy arguments based on non-legal research or to provide expert analysis of surrounding facts, it was not nearly so common before *Muller*.[2]

Second was *Muller's* acceptance of the state's argument that it could use its police powers to create protectionist laws for women based on the facts of women's weaker nature and man's historical domination and role as protector of women.[3] The feminist dissent by Professor Pamela Laufer-Ukeles, writing as Justice Laufer-Ukeles, points out that protecting workers based on sweeping generalizations cannot be justified at the expense of equality for women.

---

[1] *Muller v. Oregon*, 208 U.S. 412 (1908).

[2] Some debate whether the Brandeis brief was actually a new concept and whether it made any difference in the Court's opinion. *See, e.g.*, David E. Bernstein, *Brandeis Brief Myths*, 15 *Green Bag 2d* 9, 12 (2011); Henry Wolf Biklé, *Judicial Determination of Questions of Fact Affecting the Constitutional Validity of Legislative Action*, 38 *Harv. L. Rev.* 6 (1924).

[3] 208 U.S. at 422.

THE ORIGINAL OPINION

In *Muller*, a laundry owner was fined for violating an Oregon law limiting the number of hours women could work in factories or laundries to ten hours per day. Oregon justified the use of its police power on the basis that working long hours in laundries was bad for women's health, safety, and morals.[4] Oregon's brief spent just a few of its more than 100 pages discussing the law; the rest of the brief presented research and quotes from a wide variety of experts on the impact of long hours of factory work on women, especially its effects on their ability to bear and raise children and care for their families.

The brief cited and quoted numerous reports and statements from around the world. For example, one report entitled the *Specific Evil Effects on Childbirth and Female Functions* found that "[t]he evil effect of overwork before as well as after marriage upon childbirth is marked and disastrous."[5] The brief asserted that shorter hours were the only possible protection against such harms because "[a] decrease in the intensity of exertion is not feasible."[6]

It was essential that Oregon offer such evidence rather than purely legal arguments because in 1905, the U.S. Supreme Court had found unconstitutional a similar New York law limiting hours for all employees in bakeries.[7] In *Lochner v. New York*, the Court held that the state could not justify its interference with the freedom to create contracts guaranteed by the Fourteenth Amendment because it could not show that the state's police power was necessary to protect "the safety, the morals, [or] the welfare, of the public."[8]

To distinguish its legislation from that in *Lochner*, Oregon had to show that the state's exercise of its police power was "fair, reasonable, and appropriate."[9] The U.S. Supreme Court could easily have followed *Lochner*, holding that the statute restricting women's work hours interfered with the right to contract. The *Muller* Court acknowledged that Oregon had created an equal right to contract for men and women,[10] but nonetheless upheld the statute, justifying the state's use of its police power in this instance on the need to protect women. The Court explained that the right to equality between the sexes was

[4] Br. for the State of Oregon at 12, *Muller v. Oregon*, 208 U.S. 412 (1908) (No. 107).

[5] *Id.* at 36.

[6] *Id.* at 56.

[7] *Lochner v. New York*, 198 U.S. 45 (1905). The Court had previously upheld maximum hours for miners and for people working on public projects, and laws regulating how workers were paid. *Lochner* may have been an anomaly. Bernstein, *supra* note 2, at 9–10.

[8] 198 U.S. at 57.

[9] *Muller*, 208 U.S. at 422–23.

[10] *Id.*

"not of itself decisive. The reason runs deeper, and rests in the inherent difference between the two sexes, and in the different functions in life which they
perform."[11] Concluding that "woman's physical structure and the performance
of maternal functions place her at a disadvantage in the struggle for subsistence," the Court found that the statutory limitations were imposed not only
for the woman's benefit, "but also largely for the benefit of all."[12]

Addressing the social science research only in a footnote, the Court
appeared to take judicial notice of it as fact. The Court summed up its reasoning by quoting one expert: "The reasons for the reduction of the working
day to ten hours – (a) the physical organization of women, (b) her maternal
functions, (c) the rearing and education of the children, (d) the maintenance
of the home – are all so important and so far reaching that the need for such
reduction need hardly be discussed."[13]

The *Muller* decision was a product of the Progressive Era, which occurred
between 1870 and 1920.[14] During this era, the country moved from a mostly
agrarian society to an industrial one, with people moving into cities to work
in factories instead of working for themselves or in small businesses. Newly
educated middle- and upper-class women searched for meaningful work in
a society that restricted opportunities for women by limiting the kind of work
they could do and expecting them to leave work when they got married.[15]
Women engaged in social activism to address issues such as the sources of
poverty, disease, and poor living and working conditions.[16]

Legislation like Oregon's resulted from "an entering wedge" strategy.[17] This
strategy had the goal of using progress achieved in protecting women in the workforce to change the laws regarding men (and thus protecting all workers) sometime in the future.[18] The *Muller* decision "helped pave the way for later cases that
upheld maximum hour and minimum wage legislation for all workers. Protective
labor legislation for all workers thus got its foot in the door through women."[19]

---

[11] *Id.* at 423.
[12] *Id.* at 421–22.
[13] *Id.* at 419 n. 1.
[14] Arianne Renan Barzilay, *Women at Work: Towards an Inclusive Narrative of the Rise of the
      Regulatory State*, 31 Harv. J. L. & Gender 169, 175 (2008).
[15] *Id.* at 176.
[16] *Id.*
[17] *Id.* at 186. In her dissent, Laufer-Ukeles notes that during the ten years before *Muller*, organ-
      ized labor had been engaged in repeated efforts to limit employer power over workers. *See*
      Price V. Fishback and Shawn Everett Kantor, *The Adoption of Workers' Compensation in the
      United States 1900–1930*, 41 J. L. & Econ. 305, 310 (1998); Steven P. Garvey, *Freeing Prisoners'
      Labor*, 50 Stan. L. Rev. 339, 358, 366 (1998).
[18] Barzilay, *supra* note 14, at 181.
[19] Marcia McCormick, *Consensus, Dissensus, and Enforcement: Legal Protection of Working
      Women From the Time of the Triangle Shirtwaist Factory Fire to Today*, 14 N.Y.U. J. Legis. &

Not surprisingly, legislative action setting maximum hours was only a first step.[20] *Muller* did not, for example, help improve deplorable working conditions for women working in factories.[21] The fire at the Triangle Shirtwaist Factory in 1911 and the subsequent investigation into the conditions that created the tragedy may have been much more instrumental than *Muller* in encouraging legislatures to pass laws focused on safety and sanitation in workplaces.[22] The passage of federal worker protections in the New Deal era (1930s to 1940s) also advanced the cause.[23] In one sense, however, *Muller* was essential to all these reforms: after *Muller*, courts were not likely to overturn worker protections enacted into legislation, at least for women.[24]

THE FEMINIST JUDGMENT

Although feminists in 1908 may have favored the Oregon legislation, the dissent by Laufer-Ukeles reflects modern feminist thought in striking down protectionist legislation based on stereotypically essential feminine characteristics. Rather than stereotypes, the feminist dissent relies on facts showing that women in the early 1900s were far less dependent upon and subordinate to men than they ever had been in their history.[25] They had recently won the right to own property and to enter into contracts. Most women had attained a high school education and some women had even become engaged in the "learned professions," such as law.[26] Laufer-Ukeles observes that "[w]omen's intellectual capabilities are not less than their brothers.'" Such a statement is a bold attack on the Court's approval of the protectionist legislation rejected so quickly in *Lochner* and adopted so readily in *Muller*.

Pub. Pol'y 645, 654 (2011). *See Bunting v. Oregon*, 243 U.S. 426 (1917) (upholding an Oregon law restricting work hours to ten hours per day for all industrial workers).

[20] McCormick, *supra* note 19, at 654.

[21] *Id.* at 658.

[22] *Id.* (noting that it took some time for the laws to be enforced effectively).

[23] *Id.*

[24] *Id.*

[25] The feminist judgment relies on contemporaneously reported facts as well as later-compiled reports of the facts that existed at the time of the opinion. *See* Charles P. Neill, Report on the Condition of Women and Child Wage-Earners in the United States, S. Rep. No. 645, at 62, 64–65 (2d Sess. 1912); Marital Status of Women in the Civilian Labor Force: 1900–2002, U.S. Census Bureau, Mini-Historical Statistics, Statistical Abstract of the United States 52–53 tbl. HS-30 (2003) (in 1900, approximately 20 percent of women were in the workforce, approximately 6–8 percent of those were married); Florence Kelley, Some Ethical Gains Through Legislation (1905).

[26] These data in the feminist judgment come from later-compiled reports. *See, e.g.*, James P. Smith and Michael P. Ward, *Time-Series Growth in the Female Labor Force*, 3 J. Labor Econ. S59, S78 (1985) (describing that by the early 1900s a high school education was typical for girls).

The approach taken by Laufer-Ukeles follows the modern feminist approach of skepticism toward broad gender-based protectionist legislation and replaces the broad brush with legislation pinpointed to address specific workplace problems. As Justice Ruth Bader Ginsburg noted in an address 100 years after *Muller*,[27] "Having grown up in years when women, by law or custom, were protected from a range of occupations, including lawyering, and from serving on juries, I am instinctively suspicious of women-only protective legislation. Family-friendly legislation, I believe, is the sounder strategy."[28]

In the dissent, Laufer-Ukeles acknowledges that the party most advantaged by striking down the Oregon legislation is the employer. Still, she concludes, leaving the law intact hurts all women "by demeaning them in the eyes of the law and impeding the momentum of the law and history towards recognizing women's intellectual equality and significant ability to contribute to the work force." Equal treatment for all, she argues, takes priority over protections for some, especially where those protections harm women's ability to be treated equally, as required by the Constitution.

If the feminist dissent had become the majority opinion in 1908, it might have advanced equal rights for women. But without the *Muller* precedent upholding Oregon's legislation, other courts may not have been able to chip away at U.S. Supreme Court precedent (the *Lochner* rule) and other legislatures may not have been able to limit work hours or improve working conditions for everyone over time. The dissent could easily be read along with *Lochner* to assert that legislatures should forgo protection for all employees except in very limited areas.

On the other hand, in suggesting that specific protections based on identifiable needs might be permissible, the dissent might well have set the stage earlier for the Family and Medical Leave Act,[29] the Pregnancy Discrimination Act,[30] and perhaps the Americans with Disabilities Act.[31] Legislatures might have focused on protecting workers whose specific conditions made them vulnerable, such as pregnant women or people with disabilities. Moreover, the feminist dissent might have set the stage for the Civil Rights Act of 1964,[32] which prohibits discrimination on the basis of race, sex, religion, national origin, or color. The dissent also presages 42

---

[27] Ruth Bader Ginsburg, Muller v. Oregon: *One Hundred Years Later*, 45 *Willamette L. Rev.* 359 (2009).

[28] *Id.* at 379.

[29] 29 U.S.C. § 2601.

[30] 42 U.S.C. § 2000e(k).

[31] 42 U.S.C. § 12101.

[32] 42 U.S.C. § 2000e.

U.S.C. § 1981, which guarantees all individuals the right to contract on the same basis as white citizens.

Equal protection challenges like this one do not preclude the legislature from addressing the problems that all employees face; they simply require that the legislation address specific needs rather than generalizing. Laufer-Ukeles encourages the legislature to find the right level of protection matched with the constitutionally required level of equality and autonomy.

Muller v. Oregon, 208 U.S. 412 (1908)

Justice Pamela Laufer-Ukeles, dissenting.

BACKGROUND

I respectfully dissent from the decision of the Court. I find the reasoning of the majority faulty on a number of grounds. I will restate the logical basis for the majority opinion and specify my objections to the reasoning. I will attempt to provide an alternative understanding of the important precedent at stake here. Because I believe this alternative reasoning better describes the nature of this case, I dissent in the result and believe the conviction of the defendant should be overturned. In sum, because the Oregon legislation is overbroad and differentiates between men and women in a manner that cannot be justified by the state's police power, violating the Due Process Clause as well as the Equal Protection Clause of the Fourteenth Amendment and embedding unjustified discrimination against women in legal precedent, the reasoning of the majority must be rejected.

The legislature of the State of Oregon passed an act providing that "no female [shall] be employed in any mechanical establishment or factory or laundry in this State more than ten hours during the twenty-four hours of any one day." Or. Rev. Stat. §§ 653.255–653.275, 653.990 (1903). Moreover, the law states that "any employer who shall require any female to work in any of the places mentioned" for more than the prohibited amount of time "shall be guilty of a misdemeanor, and upon conviction therefore shall be" punished. *Id.*

The defendant was convicted for a violation of this act by requiring a female to work more than the time allowed by the law in a laundry. The Supreme Court of the State of Oregon confirmed this conviction. *State v. Muller*, 48 Or. 252 (1906). The state court decision settled the constitutionality of the act under the State Constitution of Oregon. The defendant appeals this conviction, arguing that the Oregon law violates the U.S. Constitution because it

(1) violates the Due Process Clause of the Fourteenth Amendment; (2) is class legislation that does not apply equally to all persons similarly situated under the Equal Protection Clause of the Fourteenth Amendment; and (3) is not a valid exercise of police power.

In the past decade, organized labor has repeatedly attempted to restrain capitalist employers by limiting employer power over working people through legislation. These laws were intended to protect working people from work conditions that were considered too burdensome by labor organizations. Laws that limited working hours are among these new initiatives. We invalidated the bulk of these laws, at least as applied to men, in *Lochner v. New York*, 198 U.S. 45 (1905), based on liberty interests possessed by individuals to set their own working hours through freedom of contract, property rights, and individual freedoms established by the Due Process Clause of the U.S. Constitution. In this challenge to the Oregon law, the majority has decided not to revisit the holding of *Lochner* and thus this Court must abide by the precedent set therein. I do not disagree with the relevance and applicability of the *Lochner* precedent.

THE QUESTIONS PRESENTED

This Court is faced with the question of whether the Oregon legislation has a substantial relation to the object of the statute or whether it should be deemed unreasonable, amounting to an arbitrary interference with the right to contract. More specifically, is it less arbitrary to limit women's working conditions as provided in the Oregon statute than to limit men's working conditions in a manner that would clearly be prohibited by *Lochner* as arbitrary and unconstitutional? Or, alternately, is the Oregon statute a valid exercise of the state's police powers? This question can further be divided into two parts based on the police powers at issue in this case: (1) Are women's health concerns so fundamentally different from a man's health concerns as to justify abridging women's rights of contract and their liberty and property rights to engage in paid labor in a manner impermissible when applied to men? and (2) Is women's autonomy fundamentally different from a man's autonomy such that her liberty is more readily curtailed in order to protect her in bargaining for wage labor? While these two inquiries are considered in an intertwined manner in the majority opinion, it is helpful to consider each state justification for the law separately. Although they are of course interrelated as they both pertain to the question of when and on what basis women can be legitimately differentiated from men, women's health and autonomy present different conceptual bases upon which to justify the Oregon law despite the holding in *Lochner*.

There is both a due process and equal protection element to this claim under the Fourteenth Amendment to the U.S. Constitution; although the inquiries overlap, both elements need to be kept in mind. The holding in *Lochner* makes clear that constraining rights to contract to labor may violate the Due Process Clause by infringing on basic liberties. 198 U.S. at 45–47. In addition, while women may be treated differently than men due to their differences, the Equal Protection Clause demands that any two classes of people be treated similarly to the extent that they are similar. *See Barbier v. Connolly*, 113 U.S. 27, 31 (1885) ("equal protection and security should be given to all under like circumstances in their employment of their personal and civil rights"); *see also Bell's Gap R. Co. v. Commonwealth of Pennsylvania*, 134 U.S. 232, 238 (1890) (attesting to the constitutional requirement that persons must be equally burdened to the extent they are in similar situations and under similar conditions). Under this law, women are treated and therefore categorized differently than men. Thus, this law establishes a classification that is used to treat the established classes differently. Classification for purposes of state legislation must be reasonable, and must rest upon some ground of difference having a fair and substantial relation to the object of the legislation, so that all persons similarly circumstanced shall be treated alike. Broadly stating that men and women are different is insufficient; specific differences relevant to the object of the classification must be explored.

Responding to this inquiry necessitates first understanding the scope of the holding in *Lochner* and then determining whether such reasoning applies to women as well or whether women can be differentiated from men for valid reasons.

Lochner v. New York

In *Lochner*, we found that state prosecution of a bakery for employing a worker for more than sixty hours per week under a New York statute, 1897 N.Y. Laws art. 8, ch. 415, § 110, as a misdemeanor, second offense, violated the U.S. Constitution. 198 U.S. at 45–47. In determining the constitutionality of the state law, the Court balanced on the one hand the right of contract, interpreted as "the right to purchase or to sell labor" as is protected in the Due Process Clause of the Fourteenth Amendment, against the police powers of the state to limit such liberties based on the "safety, health, morals, and general welfare of the public." *Id.* at 53. In *Lochner*, the police power was characterized as a broad and far-reaching power but not without limitations. *Id.*

The first interest used to justify the state's police power in *Lochner* is the state's interest in its citizens' health. This interest has been held to be a valid

state interest justifying legislation that limits personal freedom. *See, e.g.,
Holden v. Hardy*, 169 U.S. 366 (1898). In *Holden v. Hardy*, the right to contract for labor was held to be rationally limited in the context of the number
of hours workmen can be required to work underground in mines due to the
effect underground work in mines has on a citizen's health. Thus, the Court
recognized that if particularly significant repercussions on a laborer's physical health from certain working conditions could be proven, the state police
power in limiting those conditions would be justified and would therefore be
considered non-arbitrary. *Jacobson v. Massachusetts*, 197 U.S. 11 (1904).

However, this health justification was rejected as arbitrary in *Lochner*. As
this Court explained, laws that regulate the working conditions of miners have
been considered acceptable constitutional limitations on a person's ability to
sell his labor. *Lochner*, 198 U.S. at 54 (citing *Holden v. Hardy*, 169 U.S. 366).
However, we distinguished cases involving mining regulations due to the particular exposure to dangers inherent in working in refining ores and smelt-
ing. *Id.* Thus, we left open the possibility of limiting an employee's freedom
to sell his labor when particular health dangers are involved. However, the
health considerations must be particularly severe and precisely articulated.
Moreover, even under such severe conditions, the statute at issue in *Holden*
provided an exception for emergency conditions. *Id.* at 54–55. We interpreted
this exception for emergency circumstances to be significant in meeting the
constitutional standard for when labor rights can be constitutionally limited.
Id. We thus interpreted the police powers of the state to protect the health
of workers narrowly, under closely tailored circumstances, leaving maximum
liberty to individuals to engage in wage labor at their own discretion. *Id.* The
freedoms protected here are both those of the laborer and the employer. *Id.*
at 56. The employer has the freedom to hire and set conditions as will be
accepted by the employee without government interference.

Moreover, separate from the state's power to police individuals' power to
contract based on health concerns, legislation that limits working hours has
been justified as involving the state's police power to protect individuals from
making certain bargains that the state deems are not in their best interests.
This protective legislation can be justified by the more vulnerable positions
of most workers as compared to employers and their inability to garner equal
bargaining power. *Id.* at 57.

However, in *Lochner*, this Court declared such reasoning to be an arbitrary violation of the liberties and autonomies protected by the Due Process
Clause. *Id.* at 56–59. In *Lochner*, we stressed the power and breadth of the
Due Process Clause based on the belief that each individual has the right to
engage in the labor market without the government imposing arbitrary limits

that infringe a person's property and liberty rights in his wage labor. *Id.* This Court held that the Constitution demands that each person be permitted to determine what is best for that person rather than have the state interfere to make such decisions for the person. *Id.* at 58–59. The Court declared that it is fundamental to the freedoms of substantive due process that individuals retain the liberty to make such bargains as they believe are in their own best interests. *Id.* at 56–58; *see also Leep v. Railway Co.*, 58 Ark. 407 (1894) ("When the subject of contract is purely and exclusively private, unaffected by any public interest or duty to person, to society, or government, and the parties are capable of contracting, there is no condition existing upon which the legislature can interfere for the purpose of prohibiting the contract or controlling the terms thereof."). The *Lochner* holding is a decision grounded in preserving autonomy and treating individuals as equals in intelligence and capacity when it comes to their ability to enter into contracts. 198 U.S. at 57. Thus, in *Lochner*, we rejected the argument that the state has valid interests in preventing employees from making exploitative bargains in selling their labor due to uneven bargaining power. *Id.*

The *Lochner* Court declared that as applied to men, both health concerns and the interest in protecting employees from the threat of bad bargains are insufficient to justify restrictive legislation due to the liberty protections of the Due Process Clause. *Id.* at 58.

APPLICATION OF THE HOLDING OF *LOCHNER* TO THE OREGON LAW

Since we are dealing with nearly identical legislation that is applied solely to women, the justifications for the police power to protect workers' health and protect workers from making bad bargains due to gaps in bargaining power are the same justifications that are applicable here. Therefore, it is left to determine whether these state interests, rejected when justifying protection for men, can be used to justify protection for women.

The first question is whether women's health concerns are particularly implicated in laundries and factories so as to justify working hour restrictions similar to the case of miners in *Holden v. Hardy*, 169 U.S. 366, and unlike bakers' working hours in *Lochner*. And, the second question is whether there is something about the capacity of women that justifies further intrusion into their decision-making power than is permitted for men.

Determining whether the justifications rejected for men can be applied to women first requires determining whether women's due process rights are equal to those of men, and second whether such justifications are substantively different when applied to men as compared to when applied to women. As the majority states, it is the law of Oregon that women, whether married or single, have equal contractual and individual rights as men. *First Nat'l Bank of So. Oregon v. Leonard*, 36 Or. 390, 396 (1900). These contractual rights give them the same rights as men under the Due Process Clause. *Id.* I agree with the majority, therefore, that men and women share the same due process rights. Thus, it is left to be determined whether legislation based on the same interests held to be insufficient for justifying interference with the due process rights of men – health and protection from gaps in bargaining power – does not also infringe those same rights for women. Or whether, due to women's differences, such legislation can be justified as pertaining to women.

PRECEDENTIAL IMPACT

Before considering the nature of women's difference from men, I will clarify the considerable precedential impact that this decision is bound to have. If this decision were to strike down such legislation, it has the potential to invalidate present and future legislation designed to limit women's working hours and improve women's working conditions. On the other hand, upholding the legislation, as the majority decision does, provides significant support for legislation intended to protect women's working conditions. The legislation introduced by Oregon that is being scrutinized today is similar to quite a few other cases of protective legislation specifically designed for women in other states. *See, e.g., State v. Buchanan*, 29 Wash. 602 (1902) (limiting work hours for women); *see also* Br. for the State of Or. App. 11–17 (listing all legislation that would be either overturned or called into question by declaring the statute in this case unconstitutional). *But see Ritchie v. People*, 155 Ill. 98 (1895) (law limiting women's work hours held to violate the Due Process Clause of the U.S. Constitution). However, some of the statutes that have been upheld in other states are less restrictive than the Oregon law under review. *See, e.g., Commonwealth v. Hamilton Mfg. Co.*, 120 Mass. 383 (1876) (upholding constitutionality of law that prohibited a particular employer from requiring a woman to work more than ten hours a day or sixty hours a week but allowed her to work at multiple establishments if she so chose, thus imposing limitation on the employer and not the individual).

Indeed, the nature of women's status in the workplace, including her rights, protections and freedoms, will be greatly affected by this decision. Nonetheless, this Court is required to make its determinations based on constitutional arguments and precedent and not on the basis of its belief in the manner in which such legislation would or would not benefit women in the short term or the long term. This decision, as it is given in the shadow of *Lochner*, must deal squarely with the issue of the constitutionality of classifying women as different from men in the context of health concerns and the capacity to engage in labor contracts and not make policy judgments about whether social welfare reform that protects laborers would be beneficial to women. Instead, this Court must determine whether justifications for protections already held to be unconstitutionally impermissible when applied to men can nonetheless be used to protect women.

EXPLORING WOMEN'S DIFFERENCES

It is commonly understood that women are on average of more slight build than men and therefore, on average, may tire more easily when performing certain tasks or may be less well suited for more difficult lifting; perhaps, although this is certainly arguable, they may even be injured more readily. *See* Br. for the State of Or. App. 24–32; *see also People v. Williams*, 101 N. Y. Supp. 562 (Sup. Ct. App. Div. 1st Dep't 1906) ("We may all be prepared to agree that for physical reasons, a woman cannot, speaking generally, work as long or as hard as a man, and, if we had to consider a statute limiting the number of hours, per day or per week, during which a woman might work, the arguments now set forth to sustain the clause under consideration would be apposite and persuasive."). This distinction between men and women is supported by legal precedent offered by the State as well as numerous empirical studies. *See, inter alia*, Br. for the State of Or. App. 18–36.

Moreover, women are uniquely positioned to become pregnant and provide the important service of childbearing. Pregnancy can cause a woman to be tired and sore and make long hours particularly burdensome. As there are no special permissions in the law for women who are pregnant in the workforce, women may be forced to leave their jobs when pregnant if the condition affects their ability to function in the workplace. *Id.* at 33–42 (citing studies on the detrimental effect of prolonged work hours on pregnant women).

Furthermore, in addition to these physical differences between men and women, women are also as a matter of culture and tradition primarily responsible for the rearing of children. Therefore, after long days at work, women may also need to care for their children in the evenings, as well as keep house and execute other chores pertaining to the home and child care. Even if women work in factories or outside the house, it is still their primary responsibility to care for and raise their children. Again, this difference also may make such legislation beneficial to women in easing their burdens at work, and thus giving them more time to work in the home. Although the majority does not describe these differences in detail, it apparently relies on them to justify the differences in the outcome for protective legislation regarding women as opposed to men.

FAILURE TO ACCOUNT FOR DIFFERENTIATION
AMONG WOMEN: RELYING ON STEREOTYPES AND
"ESSENTIALIZING" WOMEN'S ROLE AS CHILD-BEARERS

Despite these potentially significant differences between men and women that may justify different protective measures by the state in order to protect women's health, it must be kept in mind that not *all* women are different in these ways. While generalities may be acknowledged, so must exceptions be recognized. There are women who are stronger physically than men; women who do not choose to or cannot become pregnant; and women who do not raise children in any event. There are women who never marry and women who can work many more hours than men without feeling tired or frail. Simply put, generalities do not account for the whole picture of women's presence in the work force. There are men of slight frame who would not be protected by social welfare legislation under *Lochner* and women of sturdy and athletic build who do not need protections but would receive them under the majority opinion in this case. There are women in the workforce who are beyond child-bearing years or are infertile, women who are unmarried, and women who are not caring for children. The numbers for whom these differences pertain are neither exceptional nor arcane, but significant and relevant, although exact numbers are hard to locate. *See, e.g.,* Florence Kelley, *Some Ethical Gains Through Legislation* (1905).

   Allowing states to enact legislation intended to protect women can perhaps be best justified by the physical differences involved in pregnancy. Pregnant women indeed suffer from an onset of hormonal changes and physical transformations that may make long physical labor difficult. However, assuming that these differences apply to the vast majority of women who are in the market who are not pregnant is illogical and problematically infringes these women's freedom. Furthermore, distinguishing between pregnant women and non-pregnant women can be done relatively easily through women's own testimony or, if necessary, through physical examination to support her own indications. Although such physical examination may be fallible at the beginning of a pregnancy, clear physical indication can allow easy differentiation. If a woman is pregnant, then protective legislation to protect frailty caused by pregnancy can be justified at her election. But, for readily identifiable non-pregnant women, such protective legislation cannot be justified.

Given the particularly narrow exception for curtailing due process liberties allowed by the police power to protect health as enunciated in *Lochner*, 198 U.S. at 54, and *Holden*, 169 U.S. at 386–87, 397–98, only labor restrictions for pregnant women could survive constitutional review. All women do not need protective regulation based on their pregnant status.

Indeed, of the women employed in the paid workforce in factories and offices at the turn of the century – roughly 20 percent of women participated in the labor force – about 6 to 8 percent were married. Most employed wage-earning women were single or widowed, and thus they either were not caring for children or if they were, they very much needed the wage labor they were selling in order to care for those children. Indeed, roughly half of single women and about one-third of widowed or divorced women participate in the labor force. Thus, the Oregon legislation is too broad, assuming gender makes a difference when the difference is narrower than gender. Given the strict constitutional standard we announced in *Lochner* and *Holden* for legislating protective regulation based on health concerns, such legislation regarding women must be more narrowly tailored to women's specific health concerns, providing a more limited exception to the fundamental liberties protected by the Due Process Clause.

Not all women can be reduced to caregivers who have duties after work that make them more in need of protection or carriers of fetuses who are in need of protection based on their health, even though both caring for children and bringing children into the world are exceedingly important jobs. Women who need to work and who are able to do so must also be considered. And for them, such protective health-based justifications for limiting their ability to contract may not apply. More particularized legislation that protects women's actual health needs and does not broadly protect all women whether they have specific health concerns or not may pass constitutional muster. However, as currently written, Oregon's legislation is too broad to be considered non-arbitrary.

BENEFITS BECOME BURDENS

The Oregon law could help all women who suffer at the hands of burdensome labor conditions. However, in light of the *Lochner* precedent that this Court has established outlawing identically justified legislation to protect men, such legislation can be justified only when it is based on real differences from men. On the one hand, the Oregon law would help women who do indeed live different lives based on these physical and cultural differences and such differences could justify different treatment of men and women. In particular, as stated, woman's responsibility for child-raising and the physical condition of pregnancy can make long working hours very burdensome upon her.

However, the effect of this law as it is broadly applied to all women would be to burden women who are not actually different in these ways from men with limitations on their freedom to contract that men do not have. These so-called social benefits could then become significant burdens upon them, making them unattractive to employers and unlikely to be hired when competing with men for similar jobs. Indeed, even though many women rely on such work to feed their families and themselves, employers could just as easily decide to hire no women at all. Benefits can make women's lives easier but they can also be burdens – here are two sides to a benefit that is not evenly distributed among all market workers. When protective legislation is fairly and justifiably distributed among employees, it can empower them. However, when an entire class of laborers is "protected" and thus made less attractive to employers who have to comply with those protections, such protective benefits can be burdensome. Moreover, even for women who do lead lives that are significantly different from men, this legislation would put a burden upon them and make them less attractive to employers. Here, the majority indicates that "woman's physical structure and the performance of maternal functions place her at a disadvantage in the struggle for subsistence." *Muller*, 208 U.S. at 421. This may be true. However, such legislation as Oregon proposes may only deepen her difficulty.

Legislation can protect women in a more nuanced manner without making them appear to be less attractive as workers. For instance, regulations can be tailored to cover only pregnant women or to provide benefits for all disabilities or infirmities that may make workers of either sex unable to meet certain standards and for which health-related protections can be justified. Moreover, such regulations can be drafted to actually protect pregnant women by preserving their place in the workforce if they require health-related absences and providing them with maternity leave after the child is born as opposed to merely restricting their employment hours. By specifically tailoring protective efforts, legislation can conform to the spirit of *Lochner*, 198 U.S. at 54–56, narrowly restricting working conditions only when context justifies such restrictions in the specific instance and allowing exceptions when these restrictions are not suitable. In this regard, the importance of emergency exceptions referred to in *Lochner* can be readily analogized to the non-pregnant, non-married female worker. *Id.* Moreover, universalizing working restrictions in a manner that applies both to men and women will protect women from being exceptionalized and discriminated against, both important considerations where women already face much discrimination and inequality in the workforce.

One might point out that only women are employed in certain factories and for certain jobs such as laundry work and thus the competition is unlikely to keep them out of the market. However, there is no reason that men cannot or will not do laundry and they will if the pay and job opportunities are good. Given the discrimination women face in the workforce and the importance of their equal protection of the law under the Fourteenth Amendment, the law should err on the side of maintaining equality and not assume that the free market will benefit women in the same manner it does men.

WOMEN'S INCAPACITY AND THE "MIRROR METHOD"

Aside from health concerns, some have argued that legislation is needed to protect women because of a woman's lesser capacity to negotiate working conditions on her own behalf. The court in *Lochner* stresses that it is arbitrary to protect male laborers from employment contracts in which they have freely engaged because "[t]here is no contention that bakers as a class are not equal in intelligence and capacity to men in other trades or manual occupations, or that they are not able to assert their rights and care for themselves without the protecting arm of the state, interfering with their independence of judgment and action." *Lochner*, 198 U.S. at 57. Perhaps the majority in this case believes that women are not equally able to take care of themselves, justifying differentiating legislation. As the majority explains, "she still looks to her brother and depends upon him" and further concludes that "the well-being of the race [justifies] legislation to protect her from the greed as well as the passion of man." *Muller*, 208 U.S. at 422.

The majority reflects on the historical perception that "history discloses the fact that woman has always been dependent upon man." *Id.* at 421. The majority compares women to minors in that "she has been looked upon in the courts as needing especial care that her rights may be preserved." *Id.* Although acknowledging that many limitations on her personal freedom have been removed, the Court concludes that her position is not one of equality. *Id.* at 422. And, the majority finds that this lack of equality will affect her ability to bargain and make contracts on her own behalf because "there is that in her disposition and habits of life which will operate against a full assertion of those rights." *Id.* This kind of reasoning depends upon a reflection of the way the law treated women in the past, and then reinforces this historical understanding by mirroring that reasoning going forward. Change can only happen if we stop mirroring the past and focus on how the law can create a better and less discriminatory future.

These characterizations of woman, which have in the past been used to
exclude her from various professions as well as property ownership, need to
be rejected and the process of doing so has already begun. *See, e.g., Bradwell
v. Illinois*, 55 Ill. 535, 539 (1869) (barring women from the legal profession);
Lelia Robinson, *Women Lawyers in the United States*, 2 Green Bag 10 (1890)
(describing the advent of women lawyers). Women are increasingly educated,
employed and proficient in professional fields. This changing reality must
increasingly be the basis for legal precedent as opposed to reliance on the
old reality of incapacity from which we have come so far already. *Ritchie*, 155
Ill. at 112–13 (recounting the changes in the law that provide for and recognize equality in due process rights for women). The states of the union have
roundly rejected women's incapacity during marriage based on the doctrine
of coverture and have affirmatively acknowledged all women's rights to hold
property and to engage in contracts. *See, e.g.*, Rev. St. Ill. C. 68 §§ 1, 6, 7
(1893). Women have the right to choose their profession and vocation. *Ritchie*,
155 Ill. at 112; *In re Leach*, 134 Ind. 665 (1893). Merely being a woman does not
make women less capable. Indeed, she shares the freedoms of autonomy and
liberty in a manner equivalent to men. *People v. Williams*, 189 N.Y. 131, 136–37
(1907) ("In the gradual course of legislation upon the rights of a woman, in
this state, she has come to possess all of the responsibilities of the man and she
is entitled to be placed upon an equality of rights with the man.").

The assumptions that women have lowered capacities to make decisions
on their own behalf and in their own best interests keep women subordinate
and fail to reflect the modern awareness and reality that women are increasingly educated and capable. We have come far in respecting the capacities
of women but we are always in danger of slipping backwards. These dangers
must always be kept in mind.

First, relying on history to determine a woman's liberty interests going forward recreates the past through future-oriented legislation. Although it may
be true that in the past, women have been viewed as dependent and unable
to assert their own rights, unless there is something essentially incapable
about women, such past tendencies will only serve to perpetuate incapacity if
allowed to further inform legislation and case law. And, if past practices have
made women more dependent and less capable of exerting their rights and
thereby not similarly situated to men, legislation should aim to help women
better exert their rights, not paternalistically remove them from them.

Second, there is no basis in fact or science to substantiate women's differences in asserting one's liberty and freedom of contract. Women have the
capacity to contract to sell their labor. That women bear and raise children
and may thereby become financially dependent on men does not make them

in any way incapable of contracting on their own behalf. Women's intellectual capabilities are not less than their brothers'.

Third, the analogy of women to children is invalid. Women are not wards of the state. Therefore, the reasoning of such courts as the Nebraska Supreme Court in *Wenham v. State*, which analogizes children with women and argues that legislation is for their own protection, cannot be validated on the basis of women's incapacity. 65 Neb. 394, 425–26 (1902).

However, women's real differences can compromise their freedom of choice due to the differences of pregnancy and child-rearing that women experience. Women who are pregnant and have responsibilities for child care cannot work the hours that men work and may need consideration for physical limitations. Therefore, in order to secure and promote her autonomy and capacity to make good bargains in the labor market, legislation can seek to benefit a woman by providing her with support and the environment she needs to make good choices. Such legislation, however, does not include restricting her capacity to bargain about her work hours in ways that are permitted to men. Instead labor protections seeking to promote women in the workplace can prohibit the terminating of women's work due to pregnancy, provide reduced hours for pregnant women, or mandate leaves for women during pregnancy or after childbirth. Additionally, legislation could provide emergency benefits to women in the labor force who have sick children. Such measures would support women and look to accept their differences while helping them navigate their pregnancy and child-rearing responsibilities.

These forms of legislation are acceptable in that they take into account both due process concerns and equal protection concerns. They seek to promote women's continued autonomy and due process guarantees and treat a woman differently from men only to the extent she is indeed different. Such carefully tailored legislation is essential to women's advancement in the workforce. This differentiating legislation should be narrow and focused, targeting only women who actually need it due to their pregnant conditions, thus ensuring the strong liberty interests that *Lochner* protects for both men and women. Moreover, such legislation could be sensitive to equal protection issues, ensuring that women's role in the workplace is not overly burdened by the protective legislation involved as compared to men.

Indeed, both men and women are vulnerable and need protection at various times in their lives. Women may become pregnant and undertake more child care during certain years, limiting their options for market work, but men and women both become ill, suffer from overwork and stress, suffer from loss and physical and emotional challenges over their lifetimes. Employees may not expect these future hardships or they may not have the ability to forgo employment due to financial pressures. Legal protection for all employees that seeks to recognize and protect against such vulnerabilities is constitutionally justified by the state for the purpose of protecting its citizens' health and well-being and is certainly not arbitrary. However, since the question that is raised in this case is whether women can be broadly protected in a manner in which men cannot, the legislation at issue here is not constitutional. Perhaps it is time to reconsider the broader holding of *Lochner* or at least the ramifications it has had on stifling legislation that protects employees. But such reconsideration has not been raised in this case, which focuses only upon the vulnerability of women and asks this Court to reinforce a broad scheme of differentiation between men and women.

It should be noted that many women's groups support this legislation for the protection it gives to women, and by extension protections that should be given to all persons in the labor market. The advisability of such legislation for all persons must be left for another day since the precedent of *Lochner* binds this Court. While the individual who would benefit immediately if my dissent became law is the male employer who can be said to be taking advantage of working women by employing them for an exorbitant number of hours, the majority opinion hurts all women in the long run by demeaning them in the eyes of the law and impeding the momentum of the law and history towards recognizing women's intellectual equality and significant ability to contribute to the work force. While I am sympathetic to the concerns of women's groups who seek to protect vulnerable women, and by extension chip away at *Lochner* and ultimately protect vulnerable men as well, this Court cannot make decisions based on policy when it is bound by precedent. In the shadow of *Lochner*, calling all women different from men so as to justify their protection based on their more feeble health and bargaining capacities, thereby calling into question the autonomy and capacity of women as a whole, should not be a rationale relied upon by this Court. We have moved beyond the days in which women were as a class considered feeble-minded and weak, and thus in need of a man's protection and guidance. U.S. Supreme Court precedent must lead the cause in rooting out such discrimination even if unpopular among men and women alike. This Court cannot uphold legislation that unjustifiably discriminates between men and women by using broad classifications that are stereotypes and thereby arbitrary, but must instead insist that legislatures differentiate carefully and justifiably. Even the short-term advancement of working conditions of women in factories cannot justify legally precedential and unjustified discrimination.

CONCLUSION

In sum, the Oregon statute is unconstitutionally broad and should be struck down as violating both the Due Process and Equal Protection Clauses.

First, the legislation fails to give sufficient respect to the ways in which men and women are similar and the ways that they are dissimilar. The law should be specifically tailored to take into account differences without essentializing all women as child bearers and caregivers and all men as market earners. Just as the Court in *Lochner* was careful to allow health justifications only in narrow circumstances to protect the broader issue of men's bargaining power, 198 U.S. 54–55, so too in this case, only when women are actually different and more vulnerable than men can their due process rights be limited due to health concerns. Such distinctions when not narrowly tailored threaten to entrench history and burden women, preventing them from providing important contributions to the market environment in our increasingly industrial world. Because the Oregon legislation at issue does not carefully account for the differences between men and women and results in a broad classification of men and women in different categories vis-à-vis their right to contract for their labor, the Oregon law violates women's equal protection guarantees by its arbitrary classifications.

Second, as women have the same liberty interests and capacities for autonomy, women's due process rights are violated by this statute because it is arbitrary to circumvent her liberty interests in contracting her labor in a manner that is not allowed for men.

I recognize the difficulties of the workplace for pregnant women and women responsible for child care. Legislation recognizing those difficulties would be constitutional if narrowly tailored to deal with women's particular physical and cultural differences and intended to promote women's autonomy and participation in the workforce. And I suggest that protective legislation needed to promote the wellbeing of all persons male and female can be justified when narrowly tailored to protect their health and to preserve their resilience in times of hardship. However, a state that truly wants to support women's ability to work must devise legislation that actually protects women when pregnant or weak and that treats her role as a caregiver in a manner that respects her autonomy and liberty as well as her claims to equality.

5

Commentary on *Griswold v. Connecticut*

Cynthia Hawkins DeBose

INTRODUCTION

Is there any reason why women should not receive clean, harmless, scientific knowledge on how to prevent conception? … The woman of the upper middle class has all available knowledge and implements to prevent conception. The woman of the lower middle class is struggling for this knowledge.

– Margaret Sanger[1]

Within the family law canon, *Griswold v. Connecticut*[2] is heralded as foreshadowing the modern right to privacy. In *Griswold*, the U.S. Supreme Court struck down the Connecticut law banning contraceptive use due to its unconstitutional intrusion upon marital privacy. By upholding a married couple's right to use contraception, the Court established that procreation is not the sole or defining purpose of marriage.

Griswold's legacy includes the notable privacy cases *Eisenstadt v. Baird*,[3] *Roe v. Wade*,[4] and *Carey v. Population Services International*.[5] Indeed, "*Griswold's* story demonstrates how conflict over the right to privacy – one of the most fiercely contested rights of the modern constitutional canon – has helped to entrench the right to privacy, to make it endure, and to imbue it with evolving meaning."[6]

---

[1] *The Prevention of Conception*, The Woman Rebel, Mar. 1914. Margaret Sanger was the founder of the Birth Control League (later re-named Planned Parenthood).
[2] *Griswold v. Connecticut*, 381 U.S. 479 (1965).
[3] 405 U.S. 438 (1972).
[4] 410 U.S. 113 (1973).
[5] 431 U.S. 678 (1977).
[6] Reva Siegel, *How Conflict Entrenched the Right to Privacy*, 124 Yale L.J. Forum 316, 316 (2015).

In contrast, in the feminist judgment, Professor Laura Rosenbury, writing as Justice Rosenbury, rejects the privacy frame, and somewhat jarringly catapults forward to a world of sexual liberty regardless of relationship status. Justice Rosenbury also explicitly ties contraception to women's ability to participate in civic and political life, emphasizing that control over one's reproductive future is crucial to equal citizenship regardless of gender, race, or class. The feminist *Griswold* therefore propels the opinion out of the marital bedroom into a world of sexual pluralism that challenges traditional divides between public and private.

CONNECTICUT'S CONTRACEPTION BAN – RELICS OF THE COMSTOCK ACT (1873)

As Rosenbury explains, the statutes in *Griswold* were vestiges of the 1873 Comstock Act, a federal law that prohibited the delivery or transportation of obscene or immoral material, which included any methods of, or information pertaining to, birth control. The Comstock Act was openly moralistic, and its true purpose was to link sex and procreation – any separation of the two was "obscene."[7] The law's namesake, Anthony Comstock, was a so-called morality crusader. By early 1874, it was publicized that Comstock had seized 130,000 pounds of books, 194,000 pictures and photographs, and 60,300 "articles made of rubber for immoral purposes, and used by both sexes."[8] The ACLU described Comstock's efforts as "religious-moral zealotry" and Comstock himself as "a zealot who believed that 'anything remotely touching on sex' was obscene."[9]

At least twenty-four state legislatures, including Connecticut, enacted laws mirroring the federal Comstock Act. By 1965, however, Connecticut was the only state with a comprehensive ban on contraception: sections 53–32 and 54–196 of the General Statutes of Connecticut (hereafter "the statutes"). Planned Parenthood referred to the statutes as "an archaic remnant of 'obscenity' legislation passed three-quarters of a century ago."[10]

---

[7] An Act for the Suppression of Trade in, and Circulation of, Obscene Literature and Articles of Immoral Use, ch. 258. 17 Stat. 598 (1873) (repealed 1909) (Comstock Act of 1873).

[8] Anthony Comstock, Traps for the Young xi (Robert Bremner ed., 1967).

[9] Motion for Leave to File Brief for ACLU and the Connecticut Civil Liberties Union as Amici Curiae and Amici Curiae Brief at 11, *Griswold v. Connecticut*, 381 U.S 479 (No. 496) (hereinafter "Br. for ACLU").

[10] Motion for Leave to File a Brief with Brief and Appendices as Amicus Curiae for Planned Parenthood Federation of America, Inc., at 25, *Griswold v. Connecticut*, 381 U.S 479 (No. 496) (hereinafter "Br. for Planned Parenthood"). *See generally*, Catherine Roraback, Griswold v. Connecticut: *A Brief Case History*, 16 *Ohio Northern Univ. L. Rev.* 395 (1989).

THE CONNECTICUT CASES – IF AT FIRST YOU DON'T SUCCEED

The Connecticut Comstock Law had a long and volatile history in the
Connecticut courts and was twice the subject of U.S. Supreme Court review
prior to *Griswold*.[11] It was against this backdrop that the U.S. Supreme Court
agreed to hear the *Griswold* case.

GRISWOLD – THE SUPREME COURT OPINION

In a 7–2 decision written by Justice William O. Douglas, the U.S. Supreme
Court found the statutes unconstitutional. The Court famously found
that "penumbras" of rights, emanating from the First, Fourth, Fifth, and
Ninth Amendments, protect the private use of contraception from governmental intrusion.[12] *Griswold's* holding was firmly grounded in the privacy
within marriage, a right the Court referred to as "sacred" and "older than
the Bill of Rights."[13] The Court determined that the statutes violated this
"sacred" right, condemning as "repulsive" the image of police searching
"the sacred precincts of marital bedrooms for telltale signs of the use of
contraceptives."[14]

The focus of *Griswold* was not women's equality. After all, in 1965, constitutional protections against sexual discrimination were as yet undeclared and
undiscovered by the U.S. Supreme Court. Although the ACLU's Amicus Brief
argued that the Equal Protection Clause protected married women who chose
"to work in industry, business, the arts, and the professions[,]" the majority
opinion in *Griswold* ignored this rationale.[15] Even Planned Parenthood did not
make a sex discrimination argument in its brief, instead focusing on the law's
discriminatory effect on and application to "the indigent and under-educated"
who utilized public clinics and, in the absence of publicly supported contraceptive planning, were left to seek illegal (and dangerous) abortions and
unhealthy sterilization.[16]

[11] *See generally State v. Nelson*, 11 A.2d 856 (1940); *Tileston v. Ullman*, 26 A.2d 582 (1942), *appeal
      dismissed*, 318 U.S. 44 (1943); *Trubek v. Ullman*, 165 A.2d 158 (1960), *appeal dismissed and cert.
      denied*, 367 U.S. 907 (1961); Melissa Murray, *Overlooking Equality on the Road to* Griswold,
      124 Yale L.J. Forum 324 (2015) (arguing that *Trubek* was a missed opportunity for the U.S.
      Supreme Court to address sex equality).
[12] *Griswold*, 381 U.S. at 483.
[13] *Id.* at 486.
[14] *Id.* at 485.
[15] Br. for ACLU, *supra* note 9, at 16.
[16] Br. for Planned Parenthood, *supra* note 10, at 20.

SEXUAL FREEDOM AND EQUALITY VIA *GRISWOLD*: THROUGH THE
ROSE-COLORED GLASSES OF A FEMINIST JUSTICE

Rosenbury's opinion squarely rejects marital privacy as a basis for her reasoning. She eschews the "penumbra" privacy analysis and firmly grounds
her opinion in gender equality and the right to sexual liberty. Relying on the
liberty protected by the Fifth and Fourteenth Amendments, particularly the
Due Process and Equal Protection Clauses, although quite far-reaching for
the 1960s, Rosenbury finds a constitutional liberty interest in the development
and formation of adult personal relationships and extends this liberty interest
to all sexual activity among consenting adults – regardless of marital status or
sexual orientation.

This liberty analysis combines aspects of liberal, relational, dominance, and
sex-positive feminisms, resulting in a thoroughly postmodern feminist judgment that – in 1965 – would have been practically inconceivable. Rosenbury's
emphasis on liberty as opposed to privacy foreshadows the decades-later decision in *Lawrence v. Texas*, which states that "[l]iberty presumes an autonomy
of self that includes freedom of thought, belief, expression, and certain intimate conduct."[17]

Lawrence heralds that "[i]t is a promise of the Constitution that there is
a realm of personal liberty which the government may not enter,"[18] but also
situates "intimate conduct" as "but one element in a personal bond that is
more enduring."[19] Rosenbury goes even farther than *Lawrence* by finding that
"intimate conduct" and the "realm of personal liberty" include all manner
of adult sexual expression and activity, whether in or out of a relationship,
thereby extending the liberal frame of *Lawrence*.

At the same time, Rosenbury emphasizes that personal relationships –
including but not limited to sexual ones – often make individual autonomy
possible. This aspect of her analysis mirrors the "rights as relationship" interpretation of the Constitution, which rejects an understanding of constitutional rights as protection from intrusion by others, instead viewing such rights
as "structuring the relations between individuals and the sources of collective
power so that autonomy is fostered rather than undermined."[20]

Throughout the opinion, Rosenbury appears sensitive to the sexual power
dynamics long analyzed by dominance feminists, particularly during an era

---

[17] *Lawrence v. Texas*, 539 U.S. 558, 562 (2003).
[18] *Id.* at 578 (quoting *Planned Parenthood of Se. Pa. v. Casey*, 505 U.S. 833, 847 (1992)).
[19] *Id.* at 567.
[20] Jennifer Nedelsky, *Reconceiving Rights as Relationship*, 1 Rev. of Const. Stud./Revue D'études
     Constitutionnelles 1, 8 (1993).

with meager rape laws.[21] Therefore, it is startling that Rosenbury simultaneously takes a sex-positive focus, positioning herself squarely within what is now called the "cultural cliteracy" approach. That approach "establishes and places in a larger context the law's silence about women's sexual pleasure, while also revealing the promise of ... 'environments in which a woman defines sex according to her own values, desires, and pleasures.' "[22] As illustrated by Rosenbury's opinion, however, cultural cliteracy and dominance feminism both reject family privacy as "a vehicle for enshrining the control of the strongest family members over the weak ... permitt[ing] exploitation, abuse, and even spousal rape."[23]

Cultural cliteracy, like Rosenbury's opinion, then diverges from dominance feminism in its quest to bring sexual pleasure out from the dark recesses of current law and policy. Although such an argument would have seemed outrageous to most jurists at the time of *Griswold*, it certainly would have found support from the counter-culture and free love movements of the 1960s, which were fomented by the on-going Vietnam War (1955–1975) and the re-emergence of the women's movement.[24]

In addition to her liberty analysis, Rosenbury also finds that the Connecticut statutes violate the Equal Protection Clause by relegating women, particularly poor women and women of color, to "second class economic and political lives." Rosenbury therefore embraces an intersectional analysis in this section of the opinion, noting that while the text of the statutes does not discriminate against women or the poor on its face, it has a significant disparate impact.

In recognizing this disparate impact, Rosenbury seeks to stave off the Court's subsequent holding in *Washington v. Davis*, which limited constitutional challenges to claims of intentional discrimination.[25]

Moreover, the impact of the statutes on women's citizenship is, in Rosenbury's view, "dire" because mothers inordinately bear caregiving responsibilities for children, which impedes their ability to participate as full citizens in civil society. In this aspect of her opinion, Rosenbury finds grounding in

---

[21] *See* Catharine A. MacKinnon, *Feminism, Marxism, Method, and the State: Toward Feminist Jurisprudence*, 8 *Signs* 515, 535 (1983).

[22] Susan Frelich Appleton, *Towards a "Culturally Cliterate" Family Law?*, 23 *Berkeley J. Gender L. & Just.* 267, 270 (2008).

[23] *Id.* at 289.

[24] *See* Jane Gerhard, Desiring Revolution: Second-Wave Feminism and the Rewriting of American Sexual Thought 1920 to 1982 (2001).

[25] *Washington v. Davis*, 426 U.S. 229 (1976).

the decisions of the Warren Court, which had begun to take notice of, and address, law's disparate impact on the poor.[26]

CONCLUSION

Liberty finds no refuge in a jurisprudence of doubt.[27]

Rosenbury's well-reasoned, relationally and culturally based, postmodern feminist re-dux of the *Griswold* opinion exemplifies this poetic phrase from *Casey*. Her feminist judgment, if adopted at the time, would have created a firm foundation for women's broader right to control their reproductive futures. This foundation would have included state financial assistance for those women who could not otherwise afford such services. With this support, women likely would have broken through traditional public/private divides at a much faster rate than that witnessed since 1965.

In addition, Rosenbury's opinion firmly establishes a jurisprudence of sexual pluralism, one that seeks to free men and women regardless of sexual orientation from moralistic, sex-negative laws. While shocking at times, her frank discussion of sexual expression illustrates the ways that even recent marriage equality victories remain tied to a relatively narrow understanding of personal life. If her opinion had been adopted in 1965, marriage equality in 2015 would be a quaint footnote in the nation's family law canon.

Unfortunately, due to its far-reaching tone, tenor, content, and reasoning, Rosenbury's opinion would not likely have been penned in 1965.

Griswold v. Connecticut, 381 U.S. 479 (1965)

Justice Laura Rosenbury delivered the opinion of the Court.

In this case we are asked to consider the state's role in policing sexual interactions between adults. Estelle Griswold, the Executive Director of the Planned Parenthood League of Connecticut, and C. Lee Buxton, a licensed physician and professor at Yale Medical School who served as the Medical Director of the League's New Haven office for the ten days it was permitted to operate, appeal their convictions under §§ 53–32 and 54–196 of the Conn. Gen. Stat. (1958 rev.). Appellants argue that the statutes unconstitutionally abridge the rights of women and men to manage the terms and consequences

---

[26] *See generally, Griffin v. Illinois,* 351 U.S. 12 (1956); *Gideon v. Wainwright,* 372 U.S. 335 (1963); and *Douglas v. California,* 372 U.S. 353 (1963). *See also* Cary Franklin, Griswold *and the Public Dimension of the Right to Privacy,* 124 *Yale L.J. Forum* 332 (2015).

[27] *Planned Parenthood of Se. Pa. v. Casey,* 505 U.S. 833, 844 (1992).

of consensual sexual activity. We agree that the statutes unconstitutionally limit sexual liberty and perpetuate inequality. We therefore reverse the
convictions below.

The statutes challenged in this case can be traced back to a dark period of
our nation's past. In 1873, Congress enacted what is commonly known as the
Comstock Law. That law, among other things, made it a crime to possess "any
drug or medicine, or any article whatever, for the prevention of contraception
or for causing unlawful abortion" in territories within the exclusive jurisdiction of the United States or to use the U.S. mail to distribute or advertise
such contraceptives. 17 Stat. 598–99 (1873). Twenty-four states subsequently
enacted their own laws extending the reach of the Comstock Law. The statutes
considered today were part of Connecticut's efforts to do so.

First appearing in 1879, as part of "An Act to Amend an Act Concerning
Offenses against Decency, Morality and Humanity," the challenged statutes
have remained largely unchanged in the intervening decades. Section 53–32
of the Conn. Gen. Stat. provides:

> Any person who uses any drug, medicinal article or instrument for the pur-
> pose of preventing conception shall be fined not less than fifty dollars or
> imprisoned not less than sixty days nor more than one year or be both fined
> and imprisoned.

Section 54–196 of the Conn. Gen. Stat. provides:

> Any person who assists, abets, counsels, causes, hires or commands another
> to commit any offense may be prosecuted and punished as if he were the
> principal offender.

Together, these statutes have long banned contraceptive use and distribution
in any context within the state. Connecticut has sporadically enforced this
comprehensive ban despite decades-old decisions severely limiting the reach
of the original federal law. *See, e.g., United States v. One Package*, 86 F.2d 737
(2d Cir. 1936).

The ongoing utility of these statutes is disputed, but the motivations beyond
their passage are not. By criminalizing contraceptive distribution and use,
the Comstock Law and its state extensions attempted to limit the context and
content of sexual relations between adults. Without legal access to contraception, men and women seeking to engage in vaginal-penile sexual intercourse
could abstain from that activity or face the risk of either prosecution or pregnancy. The statutes therefore attempted to inextricably tie sex with procreation, greatly limiting sexual agency and possibility. The Connecticut statutes

at issue in this case, and others like them, continue to perpetuate this narrow construction of sex even as sexual mores have gradually changed.

These attempts to link sex with procreation were motivated by more than a desire to limit sexual freedom. The Comstock Law and its state extensions also enforced a separate spheres ideology, whereby women's place was in the home while men participated in the market and political life. *See* Br. for ACLU *et al.* as Amicus Curiae at 15–16. Because public life was built around male needs and norms, with no accommodation for pregnancy, women had little ability to engage fully in the market and organizations outside of the family unless they could control the consequences of their sexual relations with men. Contraceptive bans like Connecticut's ensured that law-abiding women could cross over into public life only if they both abstained from engaging in sexual activity with men *and* were able to successfully fend off any unwanted sexual advances from male colleagues. In addition to imposing the physical consequences of pregnancy on women, then, contraceptive bans preserved a gendered division of labor throughout society, disproportionately limiting women's participation in the public sphere.

Advocates of the Comstock Law and its state extensions targeted the behavior of some women more than others, however. Advocates expressed particular concern that native-born white women were not procreating at the same rate as immigrant women and women of color. Contraceptive bans therefore became a crucial part of strategies to stave off so-called "race suicide." *See, e.g., Take Chicagoans in Federal War on Race Suicide*, Chi. Trib., Nov. 21, 1912, at 1. The desire to maintain the gender order thus dovetailed with desires to maintain the racial and class order. When relatively wealthy white women could not be trusted to fulfill their domestic duties, and preserve the race, the criminal law stepped in.

It is against this backdrop that the State of Connecticut arrested Appellants on November 10, 1961. Ms. Griswold and Dr. Buxton had opened their New Haven center ten days earlier, offering medical exams to women and prescribing various forms of contraception based on each woman's needs. Most of their patients were relatively poor women, which at the height of anxiety about race suicide may have boded against prosecution. By the time of the instant case, however, the State of Connecticut primarily targeted public health clinics when enforcing the law. *See* Br. for Planned Parenthood Fed. of Am. as Amicus Curiae at 21. These clinics were readily visible to authorities in ways that the private doctors who prescribed contraception for wealthier women were not. Despite its origins, then, the brunt of Connecticut's contraceptive ban came to be borne by poor women and the doctors and clinic operators who served them.

Connecticut prosecuted Ms. Griswold and Dr. Buxton under §§ 54–196, and they waived their right to a jury trial. During the subsequent bench trial, three women from New Haven testified that they had visited the Appellants' center, had received contraception and instruction about how to use it from either or both of the Appellants, and had subsequently used that contraception during vaginal-penile intercourse with their husbands. The state did not prosecute these women or their husbands, choosing to prosecute the Appellants only. The lower court found Appellants guilty as accessories to contraceptive use and fined them $100 each.

Upon direct appeal, the Supreme Court of Errors of Connecticut relied on the testimony described above to hold that "there is no doubt that, within the meaning of Section 54–196, the [Appellants] did aid, abet and counsel married women in the commission of an offense under Section 53-32." 151 Conn. 544, 546 (1964). The Supreme Court of Errors also rejected the Appellants' constitutional arguments, emphasizing that "courts may not interfere with the exercise by a state of the police power to conserve the public safety and welfare, including health and morals, if the law has a real and substantial relation to the accomplishment of those objects." *Id.* at 546–47. The appellate court deferred to the legislature's views of the laws required to preserve public safety and welfare and, finding those views to be neither arbitrary nor unreasonable, concluded that section 54–196 did not invade Appellants' constitutional rights. *Id.* at 547.

We granted certiorari to consider whether Connecticut's contraceptive ban violates the Fourteenth Amendment. In doing so, we reject the rational basis framework employed by the Supreme Court of Errors. Appellants do not ask us to review the wisdom, need, and propriety of statutes that touch economic problems, business affairs, or social conditions. Instead, Appellants ask us to review statutes that criminalize one aspect of personal relationships between adults. Because these relationships are vital to realizing the liberty and equality protected by the Constitution, we subject the statutes to more rigorous review.

Although neither the Constitution nor the Bill of Rights mentions personal relationships, this Court has long recognized the importance of such relationships in securing the liberty guaranteed by the Fifth and Fourteenth Amendments. Those amendments protect certain personal liberties from being abridged by the federal government or the states. *See, e.g., Bolling v. Sharpe,* 347 U.S. 497 (1953); *Cantwell v. Connecticut,* 310 U.S. 296 (1940). As Justice Harlan has previously emphasized, "'liberty' is not a series of isolated points," but rather "is a rational continuum which, broadly speaking, includes a freedom from all substantial arbitrary impositions and purposeless restraints." *Poe v. Ullman*, 367 U.S. 497, 543 (1961) (Harlan, J., dissenting). Because liberty is thus protected by the Fifth and Fourteenth Amendments, "certain interests require particularly careful scrutiny of the state needs asserted to justify their abridgment." *Id.* The interest to form the personal relationships of one's choice certainly lies among the liberty interests requiring that careful scrutiny.

Indeed, this Court has already protected the liberty to form and maintain certain relationships. In *Meyer v. Neb.*, 262 U.S. 390 (1923), and *Pierce v. Soc'y of Sisters*, 268 U.S. 510 (1925), we recognized the liberty interests of teachers and schools in forming relationships with parents and their children, holding that states may not criminalize the teaching of foreign languages, *Meyer*, 262 U.S. at 400–03, or require parents to send their children to public schools, *Pierce*, 268 U.S. at 534–35. In doing so, we also recognized and affirmed the liberty at the heart of the parent–child relationship itself. Parents may direct the upbringing of their children, free from undue state interference, only if parents have the liberty to engage the teachers and schools of their choice.

The states thus must respect a zone of liberty for parents and children to develop their relationships as they see fit. *See, e.g., Prince v. Mass.*, 321 U.S. 158, 166 (1944). Although many have interpreted *Meyer* and *Pierce* as affirming only parents' authority, parental rights encompass much more than individual choices about how to live life free from governmental control. The decision to have children initially implicates autonomy interests, but once a child is born, autonomy no longer suffices to explain parents' right to custody and control. Parents' rights instead come into being through the relationships they have with their children. Our holdings therefore affirm that the content of parent–child relationships must be left to parents and children themselves, with states intervening solely to ensure that children receive the care and education they need to become full participants in our democracy.

We see no reason to limit the zone of liberty to form personal relationships to the parent–child relationship. Although children must necessarily rely on their relationships with parents and other adults for financial and physical support, the need for personal relationships is not extinguished upon reaching the age of majority. Indeed, limiting protection of personal relationships to parent–child relationships would imply that the parent–child relationship is a one-way relation, with parents providing care and support and receiving nothing in return. Yet it is beyond dispute that parents often find their lives greatly enriched by the companionship and love provided by their children as well as by the sense of accomplishment they experience as they help their children develop into citizens themselves.

Just as adults form important relationships with children, they also form important relationships with other adults. These personal relationships cannot be divorced from the individual liberty protected by the Fifth and Fourteenth Amendments. Instead, these relationships make individual autonomy possible. Individuals rely on each other for care, support, and inspiration as they go about determining and achieving their own goals. It is often only through interactions with others that adults develop an understanding of their individual paths. Moreover, many adults choose life paths that center around, or at least include, personal relationships with family members, friends, and other loved ones. The freedom to form such relationships, and to develop one's identity through them, undoubtedly falls within the zone of liberty protected by the Fourteenth Amendment. *Cf. NAACP v. Alabama ex rel. Patterson*, 357 U.S. 449, 460 (1958) ("It is beyond debate that freedom to engage in association for the advancement of beliefs and ideas is an inseparable aspect of the 'liberty' assured by the Due Process Clause of the Fourteenth Amendment.").

Sexual activity between consenting adults may play an important role in both this process of individual discovery and the development of meaningful personal relationships. Extensive research in the fields of medicine, sociology, and psychology has documented the value of sexual exploration and pleasure, including but not limited to orgasm. *See, e.g.*, Alfred C. Kinsey, *et al.*, *Sexual Behavior in the Human Male* (1948); Alfred C. Kinsey, *et al.*, *Sexual Behavior in the Human Female* (1953). Although some forms of sexual exploration and pleasure may be achieved on one's own, other forms may come into being only in the presence of another individual. Sexual activity between consenting adults therefore can be an important aspect of individual identity and self-expression. At times, such activity may also deepen other aspects of the participants' relationships, including emotional and other bonds.

When sexual activity involves a man and a woman, however, these possibilities are often circumscribed by the possibility of pregnancy. Although at any given time some women and men may seek to conceive a child, others seek to experience sexual pleasure and connection while delaying conception or forgoing it altogether. In other words, they may seek to develop short- or long-term sexual relationships with one another without creating the new relationship that pregnancy often entails.

Access to contraceptives therefore is a necessary prerequisite for many men and women who seek to engage in mutual sexual activity in order to develop their identity, to deepen their relationships, or to simply experience pleasure and release. By criminalizing all use and distribution of contraception, the State of Connecticut has foreclosed this important aspect of liberty or made it unduly risky, therefore limiting individuals' liberty to interact with others in the ways they desire. Although some individuals may choose to develop their identity and relationships through the abstinence urged by the state, others will choose to do so through sexual activity. The state may not use its coercive power to limit this choice.

We therefore hold that the statutes at issue in this case deprive individuals of the liberty guaranteed by the Fourteenth Amendment. The State of Connecticut may express an interest in population growth and in the health and safety of its citizens, but, by enforcing a comprehensive ban on contraception, the state seeks to achieve its goals by means having a maximum destructive impact upon some forms of sexual interaction. Such laws cannot stand in light of the familiar principle, so often applied by this Court, that a "governmental purpose to control or prevent activities constitutionally subject to state regulation may not be achieved by means which sweep unnecessarily broadly and thereby invade the area of protected freedoms." *NAACP v. Alabama ex rel. Flowers*, 377 U.S. 288, 307 (1964).

We also hold that the statutes at issue in this case deprive women of the equal protection of law guaranteed by the Fourteenth Amendment. Although the statutes do not distinguish between men and women on their face, they together with other state statutes differentially deprive women of the means to control their reproductive futures. This disparate impact violates the very essence of the equal protection clause.

Connecticut concedes that, in contrast to the statutes at issue, no state law prohibits the use of condoms. Although Connecticut has long justified this distinction as necessary for the prevention of disease, *see, e.g., Tileston v. Ullman*, 26 A.2d 582 (Conn. 1942), no aspect of state law prevents any individual from using condoms to prevent conception. Men thus have access to a form of contraception tailored to their anatomy whereas women are denied access to forms of contraception tailored to their anatomy, including diaphragms, intra-uterine devices, and what are now commonly called birth control pills.

Both men and women may purchase and use condoms in the state, of course, but this formal equality obscures an underlying substantive inequality. Condoms by definition must be used with the consent and acquiescence of the men wearing them. Given differences in anatomy, if men choose not to wear a condom, women have no means to wear the condom themselves. Because Connecticut criminalizes the distribution and use of other forms of contraception, women seeking to manage the reproductive consequences of vaginal-penile intercourse are therefore left to the mercy of their male partners. When a man refuses to wear a condom, women have little recourse. Even women who wish to abstain from unprotected sex may be unable to stop a man who wishes to engage in it. And Connecticut provides no effective mechanism to punish men who force women to engage in unprotected sex, as rape laws do not apply to spouses, *see, e.g.,* *State v. Volpe,* 113 Conn. 288 (1931), and are rarely enforced against other acquaintances, *see* Ralph Slovenko and Cyril Phillips, *Psychosexuality and the Criminal Law,* 15 Vand. L. Rev. 797 (1962). Men face no similar dilemma in their sexual relations with women.

Connecticut's ban on all forms of contraception other than condoms therefore relegates women to a second-class status in the state. By wearing condoms, men may engage in vaginal-penile intercourse with minimal risk of pregnancy. Women seeking to engage in vaginal-penile intercourse have no comparable legal means of minimizing the chances of pregnancy. Moreover, women have no means of protecting themselves against pregnancy when they are forced to have unprotected sex against their will. This in and of itself is impermissible under the Equal Protection Clause of the Fourteenth Amendment.

But the impact on women's citizenship is even more dire. In addition to being solely responsible for the gestation and birth of children as a matter of biology, women have long been expected to engage in the bulk of caregiving post-birth. *See, e.g.,* Thomas A. Mahoney, *Factors Determining the Labor-Force Participation of Married Women,* 14 Indus. & Lab. Rel. Rev. 563 (1961). Although the State of Connecticut does not mandate this connection between childbearing and caregiving, it also does nothing to disrupt it. The state offers neither childcare for preschool children nor incentives for fathers to care for children on the same terms as mothers. State law does require married fathers to support their children financially, but state law often imposes no financial obligations on men who are not married to the women they impregnate. *See* Conn. Gen. Stat. §§ 52–435 (1960 rev.). Indeed, under the state's so-called bastardy laws, children born outside of marriage may have no legal father at all. *Id.* Moreover, state law requires no father, married or not, to provide children with the daily, time-intensive care they need.

Men who choose to engage in vaginal-penile intercourse without a condom likely will not bear the brunt of caring for any resulting children. Unhindered by such caregiving responsibilities, men may continue to participate in government activities, civil society, and the market economy as they did before conception. Under Connecticut's existing law, women have no similar freedom of choice. If women engage in vaginal-penile intercourse without a condom, either on their own volition or because their male partners decline to wear a condom, they have no legal option for preventing pregnancy. In turn, any resulting pregnancy will lead to additional caregiving responsibilities. Such caregiving responsibilities may prevent women from fully participating as equal citizens in government, the market economy, and other aspects of life outside of the family.

The statutes at issue therefore perpetuate two tiers of citizenship in the State of Connecticut. Some women will be able to mitigate the harms of this gendered hierarchy by relying on the financial support of their husbands, friends, or family members. Such women may even have the financial resources to obtain contraceptive devices outside of the State of Connecticut or through private doctors in the state willing to evade the law. Other women, however, will be relegated to second-class economic and political lives. Poor women, women of color, and immigrant women are already disadvantaged in our market economy. By opening the New Haven office of the Planned Parenthood League of Connecticut, Appellants sought to provide such women with tools to manage their fertility so that they could better support themselves and their existing family members. By closing the office and prosecuting Appellants, the State of Connecticut perpetuated existing inequalities among women and between women and men in violation of the Equal Protection Clause of the Fourteenth Amendment.

It is true that women may avoid aspects of these inequalities by eschewing vaginal-penile intercourse, instead engaging in sex with other women or sex with men that does not involve vaginal-penile intercourse, such as oral or anal sex. Other women may forgo genital contact altogether. Nothing in this opinion should be read as foreclosing such options or elevating vaginal-penile intercourse over these other ways of life. Same-sex sexual activity brings pleasure and meaning to many individuals, as does oral sex or anal stimulation with members of the same or different sex. Other individuals may derive meaning through celibacy or by otherwise prioritizing personal relationships that do not hinge on sexual activity.

As we emphasized in the previous section, however, such choices are part of the liberty protected by the Fourteenth Amendment. If women are abstaining from vaginal-penile intercourse or engaging in other forms of sexual activity because they do not have access to contraception, their liberty has been greatly constrained. That violation of the Due Process Clause cannot cure the state's unequal protection of law. Moreover, many women may be forced to engage in vaginal-penile intercourse without a condom, making it impossible to avoid the inequalities imposed by law.

We therefore hold that the Connecticut statutes at issue in this case deprive women of the equal protection of law guaranteed by the Fourteenth Amendment. Connecticut's comprehensive ban on contraception limits women's reproductive choices in ways men's reproductive choices are not, with dire consequences for women's citizenship. The statutes therefore relegate women to a second-class status in the state, in violation of the Equal Protection Clause.

Although Connecticut asks us to uphold the statutes at issue in their entirety, the state argues in the alternative that any constitutional infirmity should extend to married couples only. The witnesses in the case below were in fact married women assisted by the Appellants, but we see no reason to confine our analysis to married couples. The statutes extend to the consequences of vaginal-penile intercourse between married and unmarried couples alike. Our analysis accordingly concerns the management of those consequences, not marriage.

Some believe that marriage is a coming together for better or for worse, hopefully enduring, and intimate to the degree of being sacred. Amici therefore urge us to respect the privacy of the marital relationship, including private decisions about sex and reproduction within marriage. *See, e.g.,* Br. for ACLU, *supra,* at 7; Br. for Planned Parenthood, *supra,* at 12. As set forth above, we agree that individuals must be free to make decisions about such matters without interference from the state. But we have never held that marriage is a prerequisite for the exercise of such liberty. Indeed, in *Meyer, Pierce,* and *Prince,* we protected the parent–child relationship without regard to marriage. In holding that states must respect a zone of liberty for parents and children, we at no point asked whether a child's parents were married to each other, married to others, or living outside of marriage. Given that the Fourteenth Amendment generally protects parent–child relationships post-birth, we see no need to limit the protection of reproductive decision making pre-birth.

Under our existing family law system, moreover, married couples may have less need for contraception than do individuals living outside of marriage. Marriage involves more than a negative right to be free from government intrusion. Marriage instead is an affirmative legal status entitling a couple to preferential government treatment. States originally extended this preferential treatment to husbands as a reward for their ongoing financial support of their wives and children. Today, states bestow benefits upon married couples more generally, but such benefits continue to reinforce the private welfare function of marriage. The benefits attaching to marriage incentivize individuals to privately address the dependencies that arise when adults care for children and for one another. In other words, states affirmatively recognize and reward marriage in order to minimize families' reliance on state and federal coffers. Marriage privatizes dependency.

Pursuant to this regime, married couples have more resources to respond to pregnancy and childbirth than do unmarried individuals. Whereas spouses privatize dependency through marriage, non-spouses must privatize dependency through careful reproductive planning. Access to contraception is a vital part of such planning. When that planning is thwarted by contraceptive bans like Connecticut's, unmarried mothers often struggle to care for their children because unmarried fathers are not required to provide for their so-called illegitimate children. If the state had to limit contraception to a particular group, then it would make sense to limit it to those women living outside of marriage as they do not benefit from other laws privatizing dependency.

But we see no need to limit our holding to married or unmarried individuals. Contraception is not a limited or scarce resource; indeed, contraception is made scarce only when states criminalize its use. When not criminalized, contraception can be an important tool for sustaining the health and welfare of families living in and out of marriage. Indeed, the General Assembly of the United Presbyterian Church and other denominations have approved contraceptive use because of the multiple ways it may contribute to the economic welfare of families. *See* George Dugan, *Church Backs Use of Birth Control*, N.Y. Times, May 28, 1959, at 20. In order to respect the liberty and equality of all individuals seeking to form personal relationships, we decline to confine our holding to married, or unmarried, individuals.

We therefore hold that the state statutes at issue in this case violate both the Due Process Clause and Equal Protection Clause of the Fourteenth Amendment. Contraception need not be rationed among groups of individuals, but it also may not be imposed on individuals. Instead, decisions about contraceptive use must lie with the individual and her loved ones. States may neither intrude upon this zone of liberty nor provide differential access on the basis of gender, class, or marital status. We accordingly *reverse* the holding below and order the State of Connecticut to permit Appellants to resume operation of the New Haven office of the Planned Parenthood League of Connecticut post-haste.

6

Commentary on *Loving v. Virginia*

Inga N. Laurent

INTRODUCTION

Loving v. Virginia,[1] perhaps the most aptly named case in the history of the U.S. Supreme Court, is often celebrated as a landmark decision that helped to shape our country by eradicating long-standing, discriminatory laws that barred interracial marriage. Based on Chief Justice Earl Warren's recognition that these laws violated the central meaning of the Equal Protection Clause, the U.S. Supreme Court ended a nearly 300-year history prohibiting interracial marriage in various states.[2] Although some scholars believe that the decision was too little, too late,[3] there is no disagreement that the *Loving* opinion marked a major shift in the legal recognition of interracial marriage. Professor Kevin Noble Maillard memorialized this important moment: "In the collective memory of the United States, mixed race did not exist until 1967. By giving legal recognition to interracial marriage, *Loving v. Virginia* established a new context for racial possibilities in the United States."[4] The feminist judgment in *Loving* weaves together a heroic tale of love juxtaposed against long-standing definitions of marriage that were shaped by White supremacy and patriarchy.

[1] *Loving v. Virginia*, 388 U.S. 1 (1967).
[2] Renee Romano, Loving v. Virginia *in Historical Context*, Brooklyn Historical Society, http://cbbg.brooklynhistory.org/learn/loving-v-virginia-historical-context (last visited August 17, 2015).
[3] *See generally* Richard Delgado, Naim v. Naim, 12 *Nev. L.J.* 525 (2012); Peter Wallenstein, Race, Sex, and the Freedom to Marry: *Loving v. Virginia* (2014).
[4] Kevin Noble Maillard, *The Multiracial Epiphany, or How to Erase an Interracial Past, in* Loving v. Virginia *in A Post Racial World: Rethinking Race, Sex and Marriage* 91 (Kevin Noble Maillard and Rose Cuison Villazor eds., 2012).

THE STORY OF MILDRED AND RICHARD LOVING

Loving's outcome, striking down Virginia's anti-miscegenation law, is well known, but the details of the personal story and the long, difficult struggle leading up to the U.S. Supreme Court's decision are often lost.[5] Mildred Delores Jeter, a Black woman, and Richard Loving, a White man, married on June 2, 1958. Mildred, who was called "Stringbean" or "Bean," and Richard had known each other for most of their lives, as their families lived and worked in close proximity. Although the couple lived in Virginia, they were married in Washington, D.C. About a month after they were married, Caroline County Sheriff R. Garnett Brooks entered the Lovings' home in the middle of the night and arrested the couple for violating Virginia's ban on interracial marriage.[6]

As a result of their arrests, convictions, and impending punishment of jail or banishment, the couple fled from the only home they had ever known to live in Washington, D.C. While there, Richard struggled to find work and Mildred missed being with her family and yearned for the country: "I just missed being at home ... I missed being with my family and friends ... I wanted my children to grow up in the country, where they could run and play, and where I wouldn't worry about them so much. I never liked much about the city."[7] After an arduous legal battle that lasted for almost eight years, the U.S. Supreme Court overturned the Lovings' convictions and declared that Virginia's anti-miscegenation law was unconstitutional.

THE HISTORICAL, SOCIAL, AND POLITICAL CONTEXT
OF THE ORIGINAL OPINION

By the time of the *Loving* decision, social and political trends seemed to favor striking down the Virginia law and others like it. There were a significant number of interracial couples. The area where the Lovings had grown up had been a "visibly mixed race community since the 19th century ... [and] by the

---

[5] Robert A. Pratt, *The Case of Mr. and Mrs. Loving: Reflections on the Fortieth Anniversary of Loving v. Virginia, in* Family Law Stories 7, 11 (Carol Sanger ed., 2007).

[6] In order to tell a fuller story of the lives of Mildred Jeter and Richard Loving, the feminist judgment relies on scholarly analysis of the original opinion, including the following: Susan Dudley Gold, *Loving v. Virginia*: Lifting the Ban on Interracial Marriage 7 (2007); Phyl Newbeck, Virginia Hasn't Always Been for Lovers: Interracial Marriage Bans and the Case of Richard and Mildred Loving 135 (2008); Robert A. Pratt, *Crossing the Color Line: A Historical Assessment and Personal Narrative of Loving v. Virginia*, 41 How. L.J. 229, 234–35 (1998) [Pratt, *Crossing the Color Line*].

[7] Pratt, *supra* note 5, at 15.

time Richard and Mildred had begun to date in the 1950s, they had lived their whole lives in a community that had made an art form of evading Jim Crow restrictions on relationships."[8]

Richard Delgado asserts that interracial relationships were almost "passé" by the time the *Loving* decision was issued in 1967.[9] Public criticism of anti-miscegenation laws was mounting, and only sixteen states still had laws that barred interracial marriage.[10] "Federal courts were striking down discriminatory laws and practices in a host of settings, ranging from segregated buses to golf courses, public beaches, bathhouses and swimming pools, while Congress was enacting legislation banning discrimination in housing, employment and voting."[11] The National Association for the Advancement of Colored People (NAACP) had scored an important victory in *McLaughlin*.[12] There, the U.S. Supreme Court overruled *Pace v. Alabama*, invalidating laws regulating sex between people of different races, but it failed to reach the specific question of laws banning interracial marriage. And "the very idea that some races were biologically superior to others lost respectability and legitimacy in the wake of the racial genocide in the Holocaust."[13]

The *Loving* lawsuit also came at a time when the tide was turning from peaceful, non-violent protests calling for civil rights to a more militant demand for those rights. "By then, Black Power had appeared on the scene ... Blacks in civil rights organizations were beginning to insist that whites cede leadership."[14] In the midst of these tensions, the Warren Court delivered its unanimous opinion, holding that "we have consistently denied the constitutionality of measures which restrict the rights of citizens on account of race. There can be no doubt that restricting the freedom to marry solely because of racial classifications violates the central meaning of the Equal Protection Clause."[15] Moreover, Chief Justice Warren found that the law violated the Due Process Clause because it deprived the Lovings of their liberty interests: the "freedom to marry has long been recognized as one of the vital personal rights essential to the orderly pursuit of happiness by free men."[16]

---

[8] Brent Staples, Loving v. Virginia *and the Secret History of Race*, N.Y. Times, May 14, 2008, at A22.

[9] Delgado, *supra* note 3, at 529.

[10] Romano, *supra* note 2.

[11] Delgado, *supra* note 3, at 525.

[12] *McLaughlin v. Florida*, 379 U.S. 184 (1964).

[13] Romano, *supra* note 2.

[14] Delgado, *supra* note 3, at 528.

[15] *Loving*, 388 U.S. at 11–12.

[16] *Id.* at 12.

After years of exile and struggle, Richard and Mildred Loving were able to return home and she declared, "I feel free now."[17]

THE FEMINIST JUDGMENT

The importance of Professor Teri McMurtry-Chubb's judgment for feminist thought is that it unmasks – and renders unavoidable – the link between America's history of White supremacy and patriarchy and America's legal structures for regulating marriage and families. Writing as Justice McMurtry-Chubb, she reaches the same conclusion as the original opinion: Virginia's anti-miscegenation law could show "no legitimate overriding [state] purpose independent of invidious racial discrimination" and should be struck down. But the feminist opinion differs radically from the original in its reliance on the legal history of marriage and family relationships among and between Blacks and Whites during the colonial, antebellum, and postbellum eras in the American South.[18] The judgment voices the destruction that White supremacy and patriarchy has wrought upon Black and White, males and females.

McMurtry-Chubb's feminist judgment closely examines Virginia's long history of enacting and enforcing laws that regulated interracial marriage and sexual relationships. While the original opinion mentions that the maintenance of White supremacy is the only possible rationale for the Virginia statute – and declares that it is an illegitimate one[19] – the feminist judgment uses history as a tool to reveal the underlying gender classifications and the ways that marriage was designed to confer racial benefits through the patriarchal ties of matrimony.

First, in her Equal Protection Clause analysis, McMurtry-Chubb shows that the anti-miscegenation statutes were part of a long and complex history

[17] Pratt, *supra* note 5, at 15.
[18] The feminist judgment relies on original sources as well as later accounts, including John Hope Franklin and Alfred A. Moss, Jr., From Slavery to Freedom: A History of African Americans 129 (7th ed. 1994); Evelyn Brooks Higginbotham, Righteous Discontent: The Women's Movement in The Black Baptist Church, 1880–1920 189–90 (1993); Patricia Morton, Disfigured Images: The Historical Assault on Afro-American Women 71–72 (1991); J. Douglas Smith, *The Campaign for Racial Purity and the Erosion of Paternalism in Virginia, 1922–1930: "Nominally White, Biologically Mixed, and Legally Negro,"* 68 J. of S. Hist. 65, 65–66, 69–70, 71–73 (2002).
[19] "The fact that Virginia prohibits only interracial marriages involving white persons demonstrates that the racial classifications must stand on their own justification, as measures designed to maintain White Supremacy … There can be no doubt that restricting the freedom to marry solely because of racial classifications violates the central meaning of the Equal Protection Clause." *Loving*, 388 U.S. at 11–12.

of intersecting racism and sexism. She emphasizes that though the statutes appeared neutral as to race and gender on their face, both the intent and the results were discriminatory on racial and gender bases. For example, the statutes were rooted in social and legal prohibitions on White women engaging in sexual relationships with and giving birth to children by Black men. Moreover, the statutes were based on the patriarchal notion that only fathers have the power to "legitimate" children. In other words, the historical goal of the statutes was the continuation of White supremacy through the regulation of Black and White women's bodies and procreative choices.

Because of the intersection of racism and sexism embedded in the history she recounts, McMurtry-Chubb finds the Virginia statute is suspect and subject to strict scrutiny review. As she notes: "It matters not that sections 20–58 and 20–59, on their face, criminalize Black and White males and females equally for interracial marriage; what matters is that these statutes are meant to deny access to the benefits of whiteness to all but legally White children who are White because they were fathered by White men and came through a White woman's womb." Because "the purpose of the Fourteenth Amendment was to destroy the maintenance of White supremacy in all of its forms," the Virginia statute violated the Equal Protection Clause.

Second, McMurtry-Chubb turns again to history to find that the Virginia statute denied the Lovings their fundamental right to marry under the Due Process Clause. Quoting an earlier U.S. Supreme Court decision that called marriage "one of the basic civil rights of man" and concluded that "[m]arriage and procreation are fundamental to the very existence and survival of the race,"[20] McMurtry-Chubb points out that Blacks were denied this basic right until Emancipation. Moreover, prior to the legalization of their marriages, procreation for Black men and women was supported because it aided the survival of the plantation system, not because it was essential to the survival of Black men and women.

Had it become the judgment at the time, McMurtry-Chubb's opinion would have made a difference in the future development of the law. The feminist judgment remedies the long-standing inability of equal protection doctrine to address intersecting issues of race and gender by subjecting to strict scrutiny any classification that results in the maintenance of White supremacy and patriarchy and the resulting subordination of women and men of color, White women, and LGBTQ persons of any race. Similarly, the feminist judgment avoids the problems associated with "color-blind" jurisprudence because it differentiates between those classifications whose purpose is to perpetuate

[20] *Skinner v. Oklahoma ex rel. Williamson*, 316 U.S. 535, 540 (1942).

advantages based on White patriarchal privilege and those whose purpose is to provide opportunities for equal access to rights previously enjoyed solely by White citizens as a result of their race and gender.

Ultimately, the real heroes of *Loving* were not the attorneys or the Warren Court, but the two people who fought to stay together and triumphed despite overwhelming obstacles. Their love story tragically ended when a drunk driver killed Mr. Loving in 1975, not even ten years after the decision.[21] Mildred Loving never remarried; she avoided almost all requests for interviews and lived the remainder of her days in the house that her husband built for her and their three children: Sidney, Donald, and Peggy. Without the Lovings' resolve, it may have been years or decades before the Court found that the time had come to eliminate the barriers of state-imposed racial classifications prohibiting the marriage of two people who desperately wanted to commit themselves to one another. Richard Loving's simple and poignant request provides the best summary of the battle and the ultimate conclusion of the case: "Tell the Court I love my wife, and it is just unfair that I can't live with her in Virginia."[22]

Loving v. Virginia, 388 U.S. 1 (1967)

Justice Teri McMurtry-Chubb delivered the opinion of the Court.

I

Facts and procedural posture

Mildred Delores Jeter, the unnamed African American spouse of the plaintiff in this action, grew up in Central Point, Caroline County, Virginia. Richard Perry Loving, the White man who had become Ms. Jeter's friend through childhood and adolescence and later became her husband, also grew up in Central Point, Caroline County, Virginia. This particular locale in Virginia is

---

[21] To recount the story of the Lovings, the feminist judgment draws upon the sources already mentioned, *supra* note 6, in addition to sources published after the deaths of those involved, including the obituaries of Mildred Loving, *available at* www.legacy.com/ns/mildred-loving-obituary/109079408 (last visited May 27, 2015); Sidney Clay Jeter, *available at* www.tributes.com/show/Sidney-Clay-Jeter-88464382 (last visited May 27, 2015); and Donald Lendberg Loving, *available at* www.findagrave.com/cgi-bin/fg.cgi?page=gr&GRid=26690546 (last visited May 27, 2015), as well as Phyl Newbeck, *Mr. and Mrs. Loving: The Caroline County Couple Who Reluctantly Changed History*, Style Wkly. (August 18, 2004), www.styleweekly.com/richmond/mr-and-mrs-loving/Content?oid=1360711.

[22] Pratt, *Crossing the Color Line*, *supra* note 6, at 239.

known for its White and African American residents' habitual practice of interracial coupling and creating children of both European and African descent.

Mildred Jeter and Richard Loving's friendship began when Mildred was
eleven and Richard was seventeen. The friendship became a courtship and
then a romance, consummated and subsequently memorialized by the birth
of the couple's son Sidney Clay Jeter on January 27, 1957. Just over a year later,
Mildred became pregnant with the couple's second child. At eighteen years of
age and approximately five months into her pregnancy, Mildred travelled with
Richard to Washington, D.C., and on June 2, 1958, the two married legally.
They travelled back to Caroline County, Virginia where their marriage was
illegal. For the next nine days, they stayed with Mildred's parents at their house
and lived as husband and wife. On June 12, 1958, their tenth day as newly-
weds, the two were roused from their marriage bed and arrested on charges of
violating Virginia's anti-miscegenation laws. Richard was released on bail, but
Mildred stayed in jail for another four days, until she was arraigned and her
case was set for hearing. Richard's hearing was set for July 17, 1958. Mildred's
hearing was set for October 13, 1958. She would give birth to her and Richard's
second child, a boy, Donald Lendberg Loving, five days before, on October
8, 1958.

In October of 1958, a grand jury for the Circuit Court of Caroline County
issued an indictment charging the Lovings with violating Virginia's ban on
interracial marriages. The indictment stated:

> [T]he said Richard Perry Loving, being a white person and the said Mildred
> Dolores [sic] Jeter being a colored person, did unlawfully and feloniously
> go out of the State of Virginia, for the purpose of being married, and with
> the intention of returning to the State of Virginia and were married out of
> the State of Virginia, to-wit, in the District of Columbia on June 2, 1958,
> and afterwards returned to and resided in the County of Caroline, State of
> Virginia, cohabitating as man and wife against the peace and dignity of the
> Commonwealth.

On January 6, 1959, the Lovings pleaded guilty to the charge and were sentenced to one year in jail; however, the trial judge suspended the sentence for
a period of twenty-five years on the condition that the Lovings leave the state
and not return to Virginia together for twenty-five years. The judge stated in
his opinion that:

> Almighty God created the races white, black, yellow, malay, and red, and he
> placed them on separate continents. And but for the interference with his
> arrangement, there would be no cause for such marriages. The fact that he
> separated the races shows that he did not intend for the races to mix.

After their convictions, the Lovings vacated the State of Virginia with their two sons and went to live with Mildred's family in the District of Columbia. Mildred gave birth to their third child and only girl, Peggy Loving, in 1960. Richard, trained as a bricklayer, commuted to Caroline County from Washington, D.C. to continue work as the family's sole breadwinner.

The Lovings' time in the District was spent in the shadow of the Civil Rights Movement. The nation watched as Reverend Dr. Martin Luther King, Jr. became the tangible, public embodiment for the movement and delivered his "I Have A Dream" speech at the March on Washington for Jobs and Freedom in Washington, D.C., on August 28, 1963. Dr. King's speech and the push for civil rights legislation did not go unnoticed by one of Mildred's cousins, who urged her to write to Attorney General Robert F. Kennedy, a public advocate for civil rights and the end of segregation, and tell him her and Richard's story. Kennedy informed Mildred that the bill that would become the Civil Rights Act of 1964 would not ameliorate her situation, but urged her to enlist the help of the American Civil Liberties Union (ACLU). Mildred Loving penned the following letter to the ACLU:

Dear Sir,

I am writing to you concerning a problem we have. Five years ago, my husband and I were married here in the District. We then returned to Virginia to live. My husband is White. I am part Negro and part Indian. At the time we did not know there was a law in Virginia against mixed marriages. Therefore we were jailed and tried in a little town of Bowling Green [Virginia]. We were to leave the state to make our home.

The problem is we are not allowed to visit our families. The judge said if we enter the state within the next thirty years, that we will have to spend one year in jail. We know that we can't live there, but we would like to go back once and awhile to visit our families and friends. We have three children and cannot afford an attorney.

We wrote to the Attorney General, he suggested that we get in touch with you. Please help us if you can. Hope to hear from you real soon.

Yours Truly,

Mr. and Mrs. Richard Loving

Mildred's letter helped the Lovings secure ACLU counsel. On November 6, 1963, the Lovings filed a motion in the state trial court to vacate the judgment and set aside the sentence on the ground that the statutes they violated were repugnant to the Fourteenth Amendment. Two years later, on January 22, 1965, the state trial judge denied the motion to vacate the sentences. Because the motion was not decided by October 28, 1964, the Lovings had leave to institute a class action in the United States District Court for the Eastern District of Virginia requesting a three-judge court to be convened to declare the Virginia anti-miscegenation statutes unconstitutional, and to enjoin state officials from enforcing their convictions. They subsequently perfected an appeal to the Supreme Court of Appeals of Virginia. On February 11, 1965, the three-judge District Court continued the case to allow the Lovings to present their constitutional claims to the highest state court.

The Supreme Court of Appeals upheld the constitutionality of the anti-miscegenation statutes and, after modifying the sentence, affirmed the convictions. The Lovings appealed this decision, and we noted probable jurisdiction on December 12, 1966. *Loving v. Virginia*, 385 U.S. 986 (1966).

The Lovings are charged with violating Virginia Annotated Code sections 20–58 and 20–59 (1950). The sections provide as follows:

> § 20–58. *Leaving State to evade law.* If any white person and colored person shall go out of the State for the purpose of being married, and with the intention of returning, and be married out of it, and afterwards return to and reside in it, cohabiting as man and wife, they shall be punished as provided in § 20–59, and the marriage shall be governed by the same law as if it had been solemnized in this State. The fact of their cohabitation here as man and wife shall be evidence of their marriage.

> § 20–59. *Punishment for marriage.* If any white person intermarry with a colored person, or any colored person intermarry with a white person, he shall be guilty of a felony and shall be punished by confinement in the penitentiary for not less than one nor more than five years.

The issue presented by the case before us is as follows: Do laws governing marriage violate the Due Process and Equal Protection Clauses of the Fourteenth Amendment to the United States Constitution when they are based on gender classifications that serve as a conduit for preferential racial benefits? We answer that question in the affirmative, as such classifications perpetuate invidious racial discrimination based on white patriarchal privilege. The Fourteenth Amendment Due Process Clause prohibits a state from encroaching upon a citizen's fundamental right to marry. *Skinner v. Oklahoma ex rel. Williamson*, 316 U.S. 535, 540 (1942). The guarantee of this protection is among the Constitution's strongest, and it applies when a state, like Virginia, seeks to limit a person's choice of spouse for the sole purpose of limiting access to white patriarchal privilege and its attendant economic, social, and political benefits.

Likewise, the Equal Protection Clause subjects classifications based on race to a "most rigid scrutiny." *Korematsu v. United States*, 323 U.S. 214, 216

(1944). There should be no less scrutiny applied when gender classifications funnel the benefits of whiteness through patriarchal structures such as marriage, all in the service of maintaining White supremacy. Because marriage in the State of Virginia since the seventeenth century has been based on such classifications, it is necessary to closely examine the legal history of marriage in both the American South and Virginia, particularly with regard to marriage among and between the races during the colonial, antebellum, and postbellum eras. A close examination of this history illuminates the gender classifications implicit in Virginia's anti-miscegenation statutes. It lays bare how marriage as contemplated by the Virginia legislature, as well as states with the same or similar statutes, was designed to confer racial benefits through the patriarchal ties of matrimony as expressed by racialized gender roles.

II

A brief legal history of slave marriages

Marriage in the context of slavery was a struggle over access to and control of Black bodies. Permission to marry or not controlled who had access to and control over Black male and female bodies and any children nurtured and birthed by Black female bodies. Just over a century ago, when the institution of slavery figured prominently in the laws governing and lives of Virginia's citizens, the plantation was the womb of White supremacy. The planter was the patriarch who seeded that womb and perpetuated White supremacy through his oversight and management of the property in land and people. Slaves were the property of their masters. Simply, "[s]ubmission [was] required of the slave, not only to the will of his Master, but to the will of all white persons." William Goodell, *The American Slave Code In Theory And Practice: Its Distinctive Features Shown By Its Statutes, Judicial Decisions and Illustrative Facts* 305 (1853).[23] Because submission implies perceived inferiority, slaves were viewed as morally inferior to White planters, plantation mistresses, and their children. This perceived inferiority was especially highlighted in the areas of sexuality and sexual relationships. Planters granted slave couples permission to engage in symbolic marriages

---

[23] *See also Dred Scott v. Sandford*, 60 U.S. (19 How.) 393, 407 (1857), *superseded by constitutional amendment*, U.S. Const. amend. XIV. There, this Court stated that: "[Blacks] had for more than a century before been regarded as beings of an inferior order, and altogether unfit to associate with the white race, either in social or political relations; and so far inferior, that they had no rights which the white man was bound to respect." 60 U.S. at 407.

to temper the stereotypical and well-publicized sexual lasciviousness of enslaved women and the sexual predatory nature of enslaved men.

To avoid the implications of the rights bundled in the marriage union and emanating from it, the State of Virginia has argued that marriage is not a civil right, but a moral imperative. Citing the Tenth Circuit Court of Appeals decision in *Stevens v. United States*, Virginia contends that "[marriage] is a domestic relation having to do with the morals and civilization of a people." Br. of Appellee at 33 (citing 46 F.2d 120, 123 (10th Cir. 1944)). However, the legal history of marriage in Virginia and throughout the South leads to the opposite conclusion. Legally, marriage has been consistently viewed as a contract. In fact, the contractual view of marriage was the stated legal basis upon which slaves were prohibited to marry. *Lemon v. Harris*, 80 S.E. 740, 741 (Va. 1914).

Although enslaved men and women were permitted to enter into symbolic marriages, called contubernal relationships, with the consent of their masters, they were prevented by law from entering into civil contracts and owning personal property. *Scott v. Raub*, 14 S.E. 178, 180 (Va. 1891);[24] *Hall v. United States*, 92 U.S. 27, 30 (1875). Thus, enslaved men and women were expressly denied the civil, contractual right to marry. Goodell, *supra*, at 93; *Hall*, 92 U.S. at 30 (citing *Hall v. Mullen*, 5 H. & J. 190 (Md. 1821)); *Gregg v. Thompson*, 2 S.C.L. (1 Mill) 331 (1818); *Jenkins v. Brown*, 25 Tenn. (6 Hum.) 299 (1845); *Jackson v. Lervey*, 5 Cow. 397 (N.Y. Sup. Ct. 1826); *Emerson v. Howland*, 1 Mas. (1 Will.) 45 (1805); *Bland v. Dowling*, 9 G. & J. 19 (Md. 1837). The law also barred slaves from renting, owning, or transferring real property. Goodell, *supra*, at 90–92. Additional legal prohibitions blocked slaves from inheriting property or receiving gifts, even if that gift was their own freedom. *Id. See Trotter v. Blocker*, 6 Port. 269, 290 (Ala. 1838); *Haywood v. Cravens*, 4 N.C. (Car. L. Rep.) 360 (1816).

These barriers to the ownership and transfer of legal property denied slaves control over themselves, children, and spouses. Goodell, *supra*, at 114. Such control is required to establish a family unit for the purposes of protecting and caring for spouses and children, and building and transferring wealth. Accordingly, as William Jay wrote in his *Inquiry Into the Character and Tendencies of American Colonization and American Anti-Slavery Societies*:

> A necessary consequence of slavery is the absence of the marriage relation … A slave may indeed be formally married, but so far as legal rights and

[24] In *Scott v. Raub*, the court explained that: "while a slave had no legal capacity to assent to a contract, with the consent of their masters they might marry, and had the moral capacity to enter into such a connection; yet while they remained in a state of slavery, it could produce no civil effect." 14 S.E. at 180.

obligations are concerned, it is an idle ceremony. Of course, these laws do not recognize the parental relation, as belonging to slaves. A slave has no more legal authority over his child than a cow has over her calf.

> Goodell, *supra*, at 113 (citing William Jay, *Inquiry* 132 (1835)).

Civil, contractual marriage was a legal impossibility in slavery, because slave owners required full control over the bodies of slaves to make a plantation profitable. Male and female slave labor was necessary for planting and harvesting crops, and for running the plantation household. Additionally, female slaves provided labor that male slaves could not; enslaved women provided reproductive labor that added bodies to the workforce or the auction block, both for the planter's profit. Regardless of the race of the male who impregnated her, the children of enslaved women were slaves, and their care, maintenance, and control the sole privilege of the slave master. As one Congressman from Virginia explained:

> [T]he [white slave] master forgoes the service of his female slave, has her nursed and tended during the period of her gestation, and raises the helpless infant offspring. The value of the property justifies the expense, and I do not hesitate to say that in its increase consists much of our wealth.
>
> Goodell, *supra*, at 83.

On February 1, 1865, the Thirteenth Amendment to the United States Constitution made slavery unconstitutional and divested plantation owners of their land and slave masters of their labor force, both physical and reproductive. U.S. Const. amend XIII, § 1. Emancipation brought with it a comprehensive system of legislation (e.g., the Civil Rights Acts of 1866 and 1870, and the Fourteenth (1868) and Fifteenth (1870) Amendments to the United States Constitution) designed to give the formerly enslaved access to the individual and collective rights of White citizens, the benefits of whiteness. The Civil Rights Act of 1866, which incorporated the language of the Thirteenth Amendment in its introduction, gave the newly emancipated the right to contract and to "inherit, purchase, lease, sell, hold, and convey real and personal property." Civil Rights Act of 1866, 14 Stat. 27 (1866). Subsequent to its passage, the Virginia Legislature amended its Constitution and enacted law to recognize contubernal relationships (slave marriages) and to legitimize the children from those marriages. Article 11 section 7 of the Virginia Constitution stated that:

> [T]he children of parents, one or both of whom were slaves at the period of cohabitation, and who were recognized by the father as his children, and whose mother was recognized by such father as his wife, and was

cohabited with as such, shall be capable of inheriting any estate whereof such father may have died seised or possessed as though they were born in lawful wedlock.

Scott v. Raub, 14 S.E. at 179.

By Act passed on February 27, 1866, Virginia legislators further provided:

[T]hat when colored persons, before the passage of this act, shall have undertaken and agreed to occupy the relation of husband and wife, and shall be cohabiting together as such at the time of its passage, whether the rites of marriage shall have been celebrated between them or not, they shall be deemed husband and wife, and be entitled to the rights and privileges and subject to the duties and obligations, of that relation, in like manner as if they had been duly married by law, and all their children shall be deemed legitimate, whether born before or after the passage of this act; and when the parties have ceased to cohabit before the passage of this act in consequence of the death of the woman, or from any other cause, all the children of the woman recognized by the man to be his shall be deemed legitimate.

Id. at 179–80.

As both the constitutional and statutory provisions demonstrate, marital relationships carried with them inherent rights and benefits that inured based on gender. Virginia's recognition of slave marriages as legal and binding and the legitimacy of children in those marriages was dependent upon whether the father and husband in the marriage chose to accept those roles. In slavery, slave husbands had no rights to the reproductive labor of their wives, control over their children, or the physical labor of either; they had no patriarchal rights. Slave women, Black women, who were reproductively sound were called "breeders," and the slave master had the sole right to her "brood," regardless of who actually fathered her children. Goodell, *supra*, at 82–83.

Abolitionist and pastor George B. Cheever was accurate in his remarks to slave "husbands":

Husbands, beware of imagining that you have any rights, any authority, in regards to the chattel you are permitted to live with; beware of ever so loving them as to be unwilling to sacrifice them at a moment's warning to the avarice, the need, or the passions of your owners. Ye are not permitted to love, but only in subjection to the price of the market, the necessities of your master, and the grand rule of your domestic institution, the slave and its increase.

George B. Cheever, *The Fire and Hammer of God's Word Against the Sin of Slavery*, Address at the Anniversary of the American Abolition Society (May 1858).

In the aftermath of the Civil War, most Southern planters were destitute and without a workforce to help them subsist or regain their former wealth. Given this context, Virginia's legalization of slaves' contubernal relationships transferred social and financial control over Black women and financial responsibility for their children off the plantation, from White male masters, and to Black fathers and husbands. In Emancipation, Black men and Black men alone had the sole legal ability to legitimate children born of Black women, regardless of whether the biological father was the White slave master. In Emancipation, Black men gained patriarchal rights. The stakes were too high for Virginia legislators to allow White men to legitimate the children of interracial unions; with such legitimation would come access to the rights and benefits of whiteness on a generational scale.

III

A brief legal history of interracial marriage in Virginia

Despite masquerading as a case about the right to marry, the efficacy of the Lovings' marriage is yet another conversation in the continuing dialogue about which male, White or Black, holds the right to legitimate the children born of Black and White women's wombs. White male planters and masters, both patriarchs of their personal plantation holdings and the plantation system itself, learned that the route to perpetuating the system of slavery traversed Black women's wombs. Pre-Emancipation barriers to slave marriages effectively gave White male plantation owners ownership and control of Black women's children, fathered by the slave master or slave, while effectively blocking them from the legitimacy and access to property rights and wealth that White fatherhood would bring.

In the evolution of Virginia's laws barring interracial marriage, a period stretching from 1662–1924, legislation focused on the power of White women's wombs as the sole vessel for legally White, legitimate children with access to the benefits of whiteness as transferred via families through generations. Only White men could legitimate children birthed from White women's wombs. Only children of these unions could own, rent, sell, transfer, and inherit property, including slaves, which were the vehicles to wealth and power in the antebellum South. Breaking with the European legal tradition that the status of the child follows the status of the father, Virginia legislators codified this access to wealth based on the "color" of the womb where the children resided through laws that made the status of children dependent on the status of the mother. These laws began in the colonial era, gained momentum in the antebellum era, and continue into the present day. In December of 1662, the Virginia legislature passed its first Act of this kind:

> Whereas some doubts have arisen whether children got by any Englishman upon a negro woman shall be slave or ffree [sic], Be it therefore enacted and declared by this present grand assembly, that all children borne [sic] in this country shalbe [sic] held bond or free only according to the condition of the mother, And that if any [White male or female] christian [sic] shall commit ffornication [sic] with a negro man or woman, hee [sic] or shee [sic] soe [sic] offending shall pay double the ffines [sic] imposed by the former act.
>
> 2 William Waller Hening, *The Statutes at Large, Being a Collection of All the Laws of Virginia, from the First Session of the Legislature, in the Year 1619: Published Pursuant to an Act of the General Assembly of Virginia, Passed on the Fifth Day of February One Thousand Eight Hundred and Eight* 170 (1810).

By the text of this Act, White men and women were punished monetarily for challenging the White patriarchal privilege of legitimating White children. Subsequent statutory provisions that punished illicit relationships between White female indentured servants and their White masters further underscored White male primacy in legitimating White children. In 1753, the Virginia legislature passed "Rules as to [White] women servants having bastard children." In this section, Section XII, of the Act:

> [I]f any woman servant shall be got with children by her master, neither said master, nor his executors, administrators, nor assigns, shall have any claim of service against her, for, or by reason of such child, but she shall, when her time due to her said master, by indenture, custom, or order of court, shall be expired, be sold by the church wardens for the time being, of the parish wherein such child shall be born, for one year, or pay one thousand pounds of tobacco; and the said one thousand pounds of tobacco, or whatever she shall be sold for, shall be employed by the vestry, to the use of said parish.
>
> *Id.* at 360–61.

With this language, the legislature punished White women for challenging the boundaries of White patriarchy, as it existed within a legal and duly solemnized marriage relationship to which she was not a part. The Act protected a White woman from further servitude by the master or his heirs or assigns, but fined her by further service or goods in kind (tobacco) for her sexual dalliances beyond the marital bed. The master and his children from this union were exempt from fine or punishment.

Concurrent legislation in the 1753 Act continued the punishment for challenging White patriarchal privilege, but unlike its 1662 counterpart focused punishment solely on White female transgressors for coupling with Black male slaves. Section XII of the 1753 Act further provided:

> And if any woman servant shall have a bastard child by a negroe [sic] or mulattoe [sic], over and above the year's service due to her master or owner, she shall immediately upon the expiration of her time, to her then present master or owner, pay down to the church-wardens of the parish wherein such child shall be born, for the use of said parish, fifteen pounds current money of Virginia, or be by them sold for five years to the use aforesaid; and in [this case], the church wardens shall bind the said child until it shall be thirty one years of age.
>
> *Id.*

The same legislation provided parallel punishment for non-indentured White women:

> And if any free christian [sic] white woman shall have such bastard child by a negroe [sic], or mulattoe [sic], for every such offence, she shall, within one month after her delivery of such bastard child, pay the church wardens for the time being, of the parish wherein such child shall be born, for the use of said parish, fifteen pounds current money of Virginia, or be by them sold for five years to the use aforesaid; and in [this case], the church wardens shall bind the said child until it shall be thirty one years of age.
>
> *Id.*

Again, these statutory provisions punished White women for sullying their wombs with Black children. Because the condition of these children followed their mothers, without this legislation, the mixed race children would otherwise have been able to access some of the benefits of whiteness that their mothers enjoyed. Such access would be a threat to White patriarchal privilege, which exalted White women's bodies as the sole route for legitimate, legal, White children. Accordingly, Section XII of the 1753 Act not only criminalized White women's sexual behavior, whether they were free or indentured, by binding the mothers over to service for five years, but also exempted their children from the legitimating force of White patriarchy by binding them over for thirty-one years. *Id.*

Section XIV of the Act extended the reach of White patriarchal control into marital relationships by placing a legal bar to interracial marriage. Both males

and females were punished by a prison term of six months (without bail eligibility) and a fine of ten pounds Virginia currency for attempting to marry Black
or Mulatto men and women. *Id.* at 361–62. These same anti-miscegenation
laws were re-enacted by the Virginia legislature and gained broader appeal
when framed in the context of the 1924 "Act to Preserve Racial Integrity"
(hereinafter the "1924 Racial Integrity Act"). 2 W.A. Plecker, *The New Virginia
Law to Preserve Racial Integrity*, Virginia Health Bulletin (1924).

IV

The 1924 Racial Integrity Act, scientific racism, and rational basis review

One hundred and ten years ago, this Court stated in *Dred Scott v. Sandford*
that "[Black people were not] included, and were not intended to be
included, under the word 'citizens' in the Constitution, and [could] therefore
claim none of the rights and privileges which the instrument provides for
and secures to the citizens of the United States." *Dred Scott v. Sandford*, 60
U.S. at 404–05.[25] Amidst the early twentieth century instability of immigration,
World War I, and American industrialization, the noted lawyer and eugeni-
cist Madison Grant, author of *The Passing of the Great Race*, reasoned that
because the founders viewed themselves as superior to them, African slaves
were beyond the social imagination of the Founding Fathers in formulating
the U.S. Constitution. Viewing their superiority to everyone else as a given,
the Founding Fathers were more concerned about proving their equality to
Englishmen. Madison Grant, *The Passing of the Great Race or The Racial
Basis of European History* xx–xxi (4th ed. 1921).

Grant's work was foundational for the American eugenics movement, a
movement that equated the physical characteristics of race (i.e., skin color,
skull size, body type, facial characteristics) to the social characteristics a person exhibited, whether real or stereotypical. Together, physical appearance
linked with perceived social characteristics became the basis and justification
for awarding social, political, and legal benefits or punishments to particular
groups of people. Grant, *supra*, at xx–xxi, 13–14. Key in Grant's theories was
that Western European men and their descendants were qualified by "birth,

---

[25] This Court stated that Black people at the time the Constitution was ratified were "considered
as a subordinate and inferior class of beings, who had been subjugated by the dominant race,
and, whether emancipated or not, yet remained subject to their authority, and had no rights or
privileges but such as those who held the power and the Government might choose to grant
them." 60 U.S. at 404–05.

education, and integrity" to lead and acquire wealth. *Id.* at 5–6. Slavery was the means by which superior men hurled the enslaved, willing or not, into civilization for their own good. *Id.* at 5–7. Western European men and their descendants were superior by virtue of lineage and intellect. Accordingly, it was imperative to keep them "pure" and distinct from the lower men and their inferior characteristics, lest "disharmonic combinations" result. *Id.* at 13–14. Ultimately, races required separation; race mixing would dilute the "most valuable classes" of men and end in societal ruin. *Id.* at 46–48. Particularly perilous were interracial marriages and the resulting children. Of these unions, Grant wrote:

> When it becomes thoroughly understood that the children of mixed mar-
> riages between contrasted races belong to the lower type, the importance
> of transmitting in unimpaired purity the blood inheritance of ages will be
> appreciated at its full value, and to bring halfbreeds [sic] into the world will
> be regarded as a social and racial crime of the first magnitude. The laws
> against miscegenation must be greatly extended if the higher races are to be
> maintained.
>
> *Id.* at 60.

The 1924 Racial Integrity Act was the culmination of Grant's work and lobbying efforts through his protégé Ernest Sevier Cox, co-founder (along with composer and segregationist John Powell) of the Anglo-Saxon Clubs of America and author of the anti-miscegenation tome *White America.* Cox translated Grant's work in Southern, racial terms:

> The difference between the white man, who has produced all civilizations,
> and the Negro, who has few cultural possessions save those which he has
> received from the white man, is not a color difference merely. Pigmentation
> affects the skin only, white civilized culture is the product of the mind's mas-
> tery over things material and spiritual. It so happens that white skin accom-
> panies the culturally capable, while black skin accompanies the culturally
> deficient.
>
> Ernest Sevier Cox, *White America* 54 (rev. ed. 1937).

By painting people of African descent as biologically deficient, Cox created a mural in which only people of European descent were worthy of legitimation and access to full citizenship rights, White citizenship rights.

It comes as no surprise that the primary platform of the Anglo-Saxon Clubs of America was to prevent miscegenation. Cox worked with Powell and Dr. Walter Ashby Plecker, the Virginia Department of Health's Registrar of Vital Statistics, to create legislation to keep the races separate and provide harsher penalties for interracial marriage. *Id.* at 73–74. In Amherst and Bedford Counties, two Virginia counties where White racial identity was challenged by a large presence of biracial persons, Plecker directed the registrars there to register persons with "even a trace of negro blood on either side" as legally Black. *Id.* at 74–75. His ability to do so, in contravention of Virginia law defining Blacks as those with 1/16 Black blood, demonstrates Plecker's heft and his authority to place Grant and Cox's "science" within his purview as one of Virginia's chief health officers. *Id.* at 71. Cox, Powell, and Plecker's work bore its first fruits when on March 8, 1924, Senate Bill 219 "To Preserve Racial Integrity" passed in the Virginia House of Representatives and was made law, the 1924 Racial Integrity Act.

Again, as in the antebellum period, regulating marriage and children was how "racial integrity" was maintained, and it was how access to the benefits of whiteness was controlled. Although the Racial Integrity Act drew on scientific theories to bolster White supremacist claims to wealth, and social and political benefits, it reified the antebellum legal framework that made the bodies of White men and women the only route to these items. The Act was touted as a means to protect the health and welfare of Virginia's citizens by preventing race mixture. Based on Grant and Cox's pseudo-scientific theories about inherent racial superiority and inferiority, the Racial Integrity Act was, in actuality, a means to deny Virginia's Black citizens access to essential rights of citizenship and full participation in a democracy, including education. The justifications preceding the full text of the Act are telling in this regard. Plecker articulated the reasons for the law just prior to its text as it appears on the books:

> It is estimated that there are in the State from 10,000 to 20,000 possibly more, near white people, who are known to possess an intermixture of colored blood, in some cases to a slight extent it is true, but still enough to prevent them from being white.
>
> In the past it has been possible for these people to declare themselves as white, or even to have the Court so declare them. *Then they have demanded the admittance of their children into the white schools*, and in not a few cases have intermarried with white people.
>
> ...
>
> In any large gathering or school of colored people, especially in the cities, many will be observed who are scarcely distinguishable as colored.
>
> These persons, however, are not white in reality, not by the new definition of this law, that a white person is one with no trace of the blood of any other race, except that a person with one-sixteenth of the American Indian, if there is no other race mixture, may be classed as white.

Their children are likely to revert to the distinctly negro type even when all apparent evidence of the mixture has disappeared.

The Virginia Bureau of Vital Statistics has been called upon within one month for evidence by two lawyers employed to assist people of this type *to force their children into the whole public schools*, and by another employed by the school trustees of the district to prevent this action.

In each case evidence was found to show that either the people themselves or their connections were reported to our office to be of mixed blood.

1924 Racial Integrity Act (emphasis added).

Calling on Grant and Cox's eugenics research, Plecker stated the "scientific" reasons to bar interracial marriage:

Unless radical measures are used to prevent it, Virginia and other parts of the Nation must surely in time go the way of all other countries in which people of two or more races have lived in close contact. With the exception of the Hebrew race, complete intermixture or amalgamation has been the inevitable result.

To succeed, the intermarriage of the white race with mixed stock must be made impossible. But that is not sufficient, public sentiment must be so aroused that intermixture out of wedlock will cease.

The public must be led to look with scorn and contempt upon the man who will degrade himself and do harm to society by such abhorrent deeds.

The Bureau of Vital Statistics, *Clerks who issue marriage licenses, and the school authorities are the barriers placed by law between the danger and the safety of the Commonwealth.*

Id. (emphasis added).

The Lovings were convicted under the law barring interracial marriage that was justified by Plecker's words and re-enacted under the same. Given the historical context for the law, as set forth *supra* and in the preceding sections, this Court cannot review sections 20–58 and 20–59 of Virginia's criminal code as laws passed in the exercise of Virginia's police power to protect the health, safety, and welfare of Virginians. Faulty scientific justifications for state laws concerning "health" call into question a rational basis review of such laws. Laws are not about "health" simply because a state insists, in the face of historical and material evidence to the contrary, that its citizens are in physical danger. *McLaughlin v. Florida,* 379 U.S. 184, 191 (1964). This is especially true when "health" is a proxy for diverting the financial, educational, and political resources to one race, here Whites, at the expense of another, Blacks.

V

Fourteenth Amendment Equal Protection Clause and
Virginia's anti-miscegenation laws

As the history of slave marriages and interracial marriage indicates, White male and Black female couplings provide access to the benefits of whiteness for Black women and their children. In contrast, Black male and White female couplings challenge White male ownership of White women's reproductive ability. For their choice of Black men as partners and fathers, White women and their biracial children are punished; these unions dilute the benefits of whiteness and widen access to whiteness to more than legally White persons. The laws criminalizing interracial unions limit access to the benefits of White supremacy through gender to perpetuate White patriarchal privilege.

It matters not that sections 20–58 and 20–59, on their face, criminalize Black and White males and females equally for interracial marriage; what matters is that these statutes are meant to deny access to the benefits of whiteness to all but legally White children who are White because they were fathered by White men and came through a White woman's womb. The implicit gender classifications in sections 20–58 and 20–59 by which the State seeks to confer racial benefits advance no less than the invidious discrimination that the Fourteenth Amendment was designed to prohibit. *Slaughter-House Cases*, 83 U.S. 36 (1873); *Strauder v. State of West Virginia*, 100 U.S. 303, 307–08 (1880); *Ex parte Virginia*, 100 U.S. 339, 344–45 (1880); *Shelley v. Kraemer*, 334 U.S. 1 (1948); *Burton v. Wilmington Parking Authority*, 365 U.S. 715 (1961); *McLaughlin*, 379 U.S. at 192. Thus, the State of Virginia's argument that the equal application of the law is harmonious with the Equal Protection Clause of the Fourteenth Amendment must fail.

Because rational basis review is not appropriate for sections 20–58 and 20–59, we must next determine the appropriate level of review by which to assess the constitutionality of these laws. Sections 20–58 and 20–59 are criminal laws that contain gender classifications through which racial benefits are distributed. Like our review of the criminal statutes at issue in *McLaughlin v. Florida*, which contained racial classifications, our review of Virginia anti-miscegenation statutes must thoroughly examine the goals of the Equal Protection Clause to secure for all persons the equal protection of the laws. 379 U.S. at 192. Our work is especially pressing because of the burden criminal laws place on individual rights and liberty. *Id.* In *Korematsu v. United States*, we determined that classifications based on race are suspect and subject to the "most rigid scrutiny." 323 U.S. at 216.

The anti-miscegenation statutes at issue grant preferential racial benefits based on gender classifications; thus, they perpetuate invidious racial discrimination based on White patriarchal privilege. When laws inequitably allocate preferential racial benefits based on gender, these classifications are suspect and must survive a strict scrutiny review. Accordingly, the Virginia legislature must provide some evidence that sections 20–58 and 20–59 were created to meet a purpose distinct from perpetuating invidious discrimination based on White patriarchal privilege. Otherwise it will not avoid a finding that these statutes are unconstitutional.

The legal history of Virginia's marriage laws illustrates that the state's regulation of marriage was for the sole purpose of restricting preferential racial benefits to White men and women by legitimating only those children from White wombs who were fathered by White men. If Virginia's anti-miscegenation statutes are allowed to stand, Mildred Loving's three children, nurtured and birthed from a Black womb and fathered by a White man, would be denied the legitimating force of White fatherhood and excluded from the benefits of Richard Loving's whiteness. Because the purpose of the Fourteenth Amendment was to destroy the maintenance of White supremacy in all of its forms, these statutes violate the essence of the Equal Protection Clause and are unconstitutional.

VI

Fourteenth Amendment Due Process Clause and the freedom to marry

Lastly, sections 20–58 and 20–59 impinge upon both Mildred and Richard Loving's freedom to marry the person of their choice. Of statutes that seek to regulate marriage, we stated in *Skinner v. Oklahoma ex rel. Williamson* that "[w]e are dealing here with legislation which involves one of the basic civil rights of man. Marriage and procreation are fundamental to the very existence and survival of the race." 316 U.S. at 540. The same is true in this case, but with several clarifications. First, Black people in the United States were denied this "basic civil right of man" until the Emancipation period. Second, procreation for Black men and women prior to the legalization of marriage between them was for the survival of the plantation system, not for the survival of Black people. We must take into consideration these distinctions when articulating exactly what freedom is at issue here.

For Mildred Loving, a Black woman, sections 20–58 and 20–59 impermissibly encroach upon her right to choose a spouse regardless of the type of benefits, racial or patriarchal, her choice might bring. By restricting Mrs. Loving to a Black spouse as the sole source of her and her children's legitimation, Virginia anti-miscegenation laws restrict her and her children to the benefits of Blackness, more specifically Black patriarchy. Likewise, these statutory provisions impermissibly encroach upon Richard Loving's right to choose a spouse regardless of the type of racial and patriarchal benefits his choice requires him to bestow. Virginia's anti-miscegenation laws restrict him to sharing the benefits of White patriarchy with only White women. To deny both Mildred and Richard Loving the freedom to choose a spouse based on the maintenance of White patriarchal privilege contravenes the promise of equity in the letter and spirit of the Fourteenth Amendment. Thus, we find Virginia's miscegenation statutes an unconstitutional violation of the Fourteenth Amendment Due Process Clause.

These convictions must be reversed.

It is so ordered.

7

Commentary on *Stanley v. Illinois*

Nancy D. Polikoff

INTRODUCTION

Joan Stanley died of cancer in 1968, leaving behind her unmarried partner of eighteen years, Peter Stanley, and their two young children, Kimberly, one and a half years old, and Peter Jr., two and a half years old.[1] In Illinois, a legal "parent" included both married and unmarried mothers but only married fathers. Therefore, the State of Illinois instituted a court proceeding to make the children wards of the state because they lacked parents.

The hearing that followed was brief. The evidence showed that Peter and Joan Stanley were not married, that Peter Stanley was the father of the children and had lived with and supported them, and that at some point after Joan Stanley's death, Peter Stanley had arranged for the toddlers to live with his friends, the Nesses. The state's attorney did not allege that Peter Stanley had neglected the children. The judge concluded that the children lacked parents as a matter of law, made them wards of the state, and appointed the Nesses as guardians.

Stanley appealed to the Illinois Supreme Court, where he again lost. He then obtained review in the U.S. Supreme Court, where he argued that declaring his children to be wards of the state without a showing of his parental unfitness violated his right to due process under the Fourteenth Amendment. He prevailed.[2] The Court determined that Stanley had a substantial interest in "the children he had sired and raised."[3] The Court had never before made such a statement about a nonmarital father. It ruled that as a matter of due process, all parents, including Peter Stanley, were constitutionally entitled to a

---

[1]   A seventeen-year-old daughter, Karen, had been found neglected in an earlier case and was in a foster home at the time of the hearing in this case. Her custody was not challenged.

[2]   *Stanley v. Illinois*, 405 U.S. 645 (1972).

[3]   *Id.* at 651.

hearing on fitness before the state could assume custody of their children. The Court rejected the state's argument that unmarried fathers were so seldom fit that it was administratively inefficient to provide them all hearings. It reasoned that "the Constitution recognizes higher values than speed and efficiency."[4]

LARGER CONTEXT

For hundreds of years, a set of laws had punished sex outside of marriage, imposed catastrophic consequences for bearing children outside of marriage, assumed and fostered "separate spheres" for men and women, and imposed gendered requirements within marriage. By the end of the 1970s, those laws had changed, with the U.S. Supreme Court playing a major role in the legal transformation. Several of the most important cases were decided in the two-year period that included *Stanley*.

In *Reed v. Reed*, the U.S. Supreme Court for the first time struck down a sex-based classification.[5] An Idaho statute presumed that men were more capable than women of administering a deceased's estate. The state supreme court had upheld the statute, noting that "nature itself" created the distinction between men and women and that the legislature could assume that men would be more qualified. The U.S. Supreme Court reversed under the Equal Protection Clause, heralding a decade during which it would invalidate numerous sex-based distinctions.

The Court also issued two opinions giving women greater control over childbearing and therefore over their sexuality. In *Eisenstadt v. Baird*, it declared unconstitutional a prohibition on the distribution of contraceptives to unmarried women.[6] In *Roe v. Wade*, it struck down criminal prohibitions on abortion.[7] It further invalidated the amendment to a federal statute extending food stamps only to households of related individuals, a requirement enacted explicitly to exclude "hippie communes," a subculture that openly embraced free love.[8] The Court reasoned that "a bare congressional desire to harm a politically unpopular group cannot constitute a legitimate governmental interest."[9] It also invalidated a Louisiana workers' compensation law that extended survivors' benefits primarily to "legitimate" children.[10]

---

[4] *Id.* at 656.
[5] *Reed v. Reed*, 404 U.S. 71 (1971).
[6] *Eisentstadt v. Baird*, 405 U.S. 438 (1972).
[7] *Roe v. Wade*, 410 U.S. 113 (1973).
[8] *U.S. Dept. of Agriculture v. Moreno*, 413 U.S. 528 (1973).
[9] *Id.* at 534. Two decades later the Court would invoke this exact language to strike down laws discriminating against lesbian women and gay men. *See Romer v. Evans*, 517 U.S. 620 (1996).
[10] *Weber v. Aetna Casualty and Surety Co.*, 406 U.S. 164 (1972).

These constitutional rulings evidenced a dramatic departure from centuries in which women's sexuality was tightly controlled and enforced through harsh measures affecting both them and their nonmarital children.

THE FEMINIST CONCURRENCE

The concurrence of Professor Karen Czapanskiy, writing as Justice Czapanskiy, reaches the same conclusion as the original *Stanley* majority that the Illinois statute is unconstitutional. It does not, however, agree that all parents are entitled to a hearing on their fitness; it extends a full hearing only to parents who can first show that they have assumed parental responsibilities through financial support or caretaking. Peter Stanley met this test. Czapanskiy's concurrence insists on gender equality by requiring both mothers and fathers to make this preliminary showing. To the extent that it narrows the group of fathers with constitutional rights to their nonmarital children, the feminist concurrence foreshadows subsequent case law.

Stanley was not a case about adoption, but both the state and the amicus Child Care Association of Illinois warned that extending rights to unmarried fathers would interfere with the state's interest in prompt and stable adoption placements. The U.S. Supreme Court ignored these concerns. Before *Stanley*, states required the consent of only the mother of a nonmarital child, except under very limited circumstances. *Stanley*'s revolutionary recognition of the relationship between an unmarried father and his biological child meant that those statutes might be unconstitutional.

The U.S. Supreme Court heard three cases after *Stanley* involving consent to adoption statutes. In all, the mother married a man who sought a stepparent adoption. The Court upheld the adoption without the biological father's consent in two of the cases, *Quilloin v. Walcott*[11] and *Lehr v. Robertson*,[12] finding in each that the father had failed to assume sufficient responsibility for the child to merit the constitutional right to block the adoption. In the third case, *Caban v. Mohammed*,[13] the father and mother had raised their children together, yet the statute required only the mother's consent to an adoption. The Court invalidated the statute as unconstitutional sex discrimination. The constitutional test now for determining whether a nonmarital biological father can block an adoption is whether he "grasps th[e] opportunity [to develop a

---

[11] *Quilloin v. Walcott*, 434 U.S. 246 (1978).
[12] *Lehr v. Robertson*, 463 U.S. 248 (1983).
[13] *Caban v. Mohammed*, 441 U.S. 380 (1979).

relationship with his offspring] and accepts some measure of responsibility for the child's future."[14]

On the other hand, state statutes are not written in the gender-neutral way the feminist concurrence demanded; they still require the consent of all mothers before an adoption can take place, even if a mother has abandoned a newborn. Without her consent an agency must go through a much more lengthy and onerous process, the very impediment to swift and stable adoptions that some feared would result from granting rights to nonmarital fathers. The U.S. Supreme Court upheld such a gender-based distinction in *Lehr*, reasoning that the statute, in spite of its gendered language, did not really classify on the basis of sex but rather on whether the parent had an established custodial relationship with the child.

Czapanskiy's feminist concurrence represents the strand of feminist thought that emphasizes formal equality. Requiring both mothers and fathers to show that they have acted as parents rebuffs overbroad generalizations about men, women, and caretaking. Formal equality also means that the mother and father stand on equal footing at the moment the child is born, the first moment at which either has the opportunity to care for the child.

But their different circumstances prior to birth pose a challenge for formal equality. The most troubling scenario looks something like this: An unmarried woman gets pregnant and does not want to raise a child. She has the option and the right to choose abortion, or she can place the child for adoption. She has to make that decision early in the pregnancy. She may believe the man has no interest in raising a child. He may have told her so directly; he may be married to another woman and planning to stay with her; he may have moved away and shown no interest in whether their sexual relationship resulted in a pregnancy. She may have no reason to believe he would thwart a plan to place the child for adoption.

But what if he changes his mind? His family may pressure him or he may simply reconsider. The pregnant woman's adoption plan included a full termination of her rights. If the man assumes custody, she remains the child's mother. She will not be able to put her pregnancy behind her with the finality of an abortion or adoption. She will have an obligation to support the child. If the father lives in the same town, she may be unable to avoid seeing the child.

A feminist approach to this scenario yields two different possibilities. Equality of treatment pursuant to the Czapanskiy concurrence gives the father, if he comes forward when the child is born, an equal right to raise the

[14] *Lehr*, 463 U.S. at 262.

child and therefore the ability to thwart the woman's plan to place the child for adoption. That she would have had an abortion had she known his intentions earlier may be cause for empathy, but it would not be a reason for deviation from the principle that the parents have equal rights.

On the other hand, a feminist might conclude that the different lived experience of the woman and the man points to a different result. The woman was obligated to decide early in the pregnancy whether to carry to term. The closest it may be possible to come to equality is to demand that the man express his intentions during that same period of time. He would have the obligation to determine if there were a pregnancy and to assert his interest in raising the child while an abortion is still possible. If he fails to do so, he would not have the right to block the woman's decision to place the child for adoption. This feminist approach views pregnancy as a difference between men and women that the law must incorporate.

Both the *Stanley* court and the feminist concurrence involve a child's biological parents. Today, states define legal parentage to include nonbiological parents in numerous situations. What constitutional protection might the feminist concurrence afford such relationships?

Most commonly, and without controversy, adoption creates legal parentage, as does a husband's consent to his wife's insemination with donor semen. The following individuals are also parents under some state laws: a wife, or nonmarital partner of either sex, who consents to a woman's insemination with donor semen; a man or woman who receives a child into his/her home and holds the child out as his/her own; a man or woman who develops a "de facto" parental relationship with a child with the full consent of the child's parent; a couple who are the intended parents of a child born to a surrogate. Some jurisdictions allow a child to have more than two legal parents. These definitions have been critical to the recognition of parent–child relationships in the families formed by same-sex couples.

The feminist concurrence makes the presence of an actual parent–child relationship necessary to the constitutional recognition of parenthood. It should also be read as signaling that the presence of such a relationship, when formed with the consent of the child's parent, is sufficient to create parentage entitled to constitutional protection. The feminist concurrence, like *Stanley* itself, also emphasizes that a marital relationship is not a prerequisite for conferring legal parentage. With the era of same-sex marriage now upon us, it is more important than ever to reaffirm that principle, lest the children of unmarried same-sex parents find themselves without the protection conferred upon all children with married parents.

Stanley v. Illinois, 405 U.S. 645 (1972)

Justice Karen Syma Czapanskiy, concurring.

This Court has held that Peter Stanley, an unmarried father, was denied equal protection under the law when his children were removed from his care without a hearing on his fitness, while married parents and unmarried women would be entitled to a hearing. I concur in the judgment. I write separately to comment on what process is due to parents when the state seeks to declare their children wards of the state.

Because of this Court's decision, Peter Stanley will have access to the same level of due process that the State of Illinois provides in cases involving married parents and unmarried mothers. The Court's decision focuses exclusively on the deprivation of rights suffered by the father. In my view, however, the focus should be on the relationship of the parent and the child. In other words, what process is due to a parent should turn on the answer to this question: what kind of process is needed to ensure that the essential relationship of the parent and child is not severed unnecessarily?

The Court's decision requires Illinois and many other states to modify their statutes to ensure that unmarried fathers are not denied their rights. States may focus their changes, as did this Court, solely on expanding rights for unmarried fathers. If the focus were on the relationship of the parent and the child instead, legislatures would be asking, "What kind of process should be provided to all parents?"

My concern is informed by the history of parental rights. Recognition of parental rights was once accorded only to married white fathers. Gradually, recognition was extended to married white mothers, to unmarried mothers, and to fathers who had formerly been enslaved. *See* Jacobus tenBroek, *The Thirteenth Amendment to the Constitution of the United States: Consummation to Abolition and Key to the Fourteenth Amendment*, 39 Cal. L. Rev. 171, 177–180 (1951).

As they extended recognition, earlier lawmakers, unlike this court, did not look exclusively at the desires of parents. Instead, a common argument was that children's needs would be better served by according their parents legal recognition. In other words, extending parental rights usually turned on the relationship of the parent and the child, not solely the needs of the parent or the child. For example, a New York court concluded in 1840 that, contrary to the common law of England, the exclusive right of the married father to custody of his children had to yield to a right of custody in the mother when the children were young and she was a fit person to care for them. *Ahrenfeldt v. Ahrenfeldt,*

1 Hoff. Ch. 497 (N.Y. Ch. 1840). In an earlier Massachusetts case in which the unmarried father of a child sued the mother for custody, the Supreme Judicial Court said, "In legal contemplation, a bastard is generally considered as the relative of no one. But, to provide for his support and education, the mother has a right to the custody and control of him, and is bound to maintain him, as his natural guardian." *Wright v. Wright*, 2 Mass. 109, 110 (1806).

The case of Peter Stanley allows consideration of a new question: now that all categories of parents with formal ties to children have been accorded some level of recognition, must all parents be treated alike, or is there some legitimate ground for treating them differently? Since, historically, changes in legal recognition of parents have turned on the relationship of the parent and child, I suggest that legislators responding to today's decision look to history for insight. Extending the same rights to all unmarried fathers could turn out, as the State argued in this case, to empower many men who had never before taken much of an interest in their children. The resulting possibilities for litigation, confusion and delay are real. What the state's argument misses, however, is that its existing statute empowered numerous parents who had taken little interest in their children. While the statute empowers every mother, not every mother provides care for her child and some desert children at birth. The statute also empowers every married father, even though some never live with their children or provide for them financially.

My suggestion, therefore, is that legislators consider a two-step process for all parents. Before the state can declare a child to be a ward of the state or declare a child free for adoption, a preliminary inquiry should be undertaken to determine whether any person or persons who enjoy formal parental rights have exercised responsibility for the child. Different parents do different things for children, and all manner of responsibility should count. Some parents, for example, provide physical care. Others provide financial care. Some parents represent the child in the community, such as in the child's relationship with school, medical care providers and daycare providers. Some parents do all of these. In my view, any parent who has exercised responsibility in any of these ways or in any other serious way should be accorded the kind of due process rights that Mr. Stanley will enjoy as the result of the Court's decision. On the other hand, no parent should be presumed to have exercised responsibility, regardless of whether that parent is the mother or the father, and regardless of whether the parents were married or unmarried.

The two-step process will relieve the state of litigating dependency in cases where the nominal parent has done so little that a finding of unfitness based on neglect is inevitable. The two-step process also allows children to be freed for adoption without input from a parent who has never stepped into the role. Further, it reinforces the Court's willingness today and in other recent cases to stop distinguishing between parents on the basis of their marital status. *See Glona v. Am. Guar. & Liab. Ins. Co,* 391 U.S. 73 (1968).

By treating all parents alike, regardless of gender and marital status, the two-step process discourages stereotyping. Not every unmarried man is an uncaring sperm provider; nor is every woman a responsible mother; nor is every married man an actively engaged father. As the Court said when overturning a mandatory preference for a father over a mother in the appointment of an executor for the estate of their child,

> To give a mandatory preference to members of either sex over members of the other, merely to accomplish the elimination of hearings on the merits, is to make the very kind of arbitrary legislative choice forbidden by the Equal Protection Clause of the Fourteenth Amendment; and whatever may be said as to the positive values of avoiding intra-family controversy, the choice in this context may not lawfully be mandated solely on the basis of sex.
>
> *Reed v. Reed,* 404 U.S. 71, 76–77 (1971).

The two-step process eliminates the opportunity for a full hearing where the parent has failed to demonstrate a minimum degree of parental responsibility in the past. While the preliminary hearing could reduce the judicial time spent on dependency decisions, the savings may come at the cost of denying a full hearing to some men and women without adequate justification. For example, despite a statute that is appropriately inclusive about parental conduct, decision makers might apply stereotypes about mothers and fathers to deny parents of both sexes a fair outcome. A woman who supports a child financially but does little hands-on nurturing could be found to have failed as a mother, even though she has not failed as a parent. A man who changes diapers but earns no income could be subject to the opposing stereotype that he has failed as a father, even though he has not failed as a parent. Women could face credibility problems, particularly about issues such as domestic violence, and be denied a full opportunity to litigate the adequacy of their parental conduct toward a child. Men and women who live in poverty could lose guardianship of their children because they lack adequate representation, rather than because the evidence is against them. Unfortunately, all of these problems could arise in the full hearing process, so I am not convinced that they are sufficient reason to require a full hearing in every case.

Plainly, Mr. Stanley has exercised responsibility for his children to a sufficient degree to satisfy the first step of a two-step process. (Indeed, assuming the state on remand alleges no reason to declare the children dependent other than the death of their mother, Mr. Stanley should not be subject to any further inquiry about his guardianship, since no other parent would be.) The young children who were the subjects of the dependency hearing were Peter Stanley, Jr., and Kimberly Stanley. Their parents, Joan and Peter Stanley, had been involved with each other for nearly two decades at the time of Joan Stanley's death. At the hearing, the evidence was conflicting about whether Joan and Peter Stanley had lived together continuously during all of that time, and the court was informed of a neglect case against Peter Stanley involving an older child, but there was no conflict in the evidence about Peter living in the household continuously from the time of Peter Jr.'s birth and continuing to live with and care for Kimberly and Peter, Jr. after Joan Stanley's death. Not long before the dependency hearing, Mr. Stanley placed the children with some old friends. There was no evidence that he stopped seeing or caring for the children after they began living in the home he selected for them. Further, the court approved of his appointed substitutes, as can be seen by its decision to name the couple to be the guardians of the children.

Based on the record before the trial court, Mr. Stanley has demonstrated a history of exercising responsibility for his children. He lived with them before and after the death of their mother and cared for them exclusively for some time after that. When he decided that keeping the children in his care was inadvisable, he found suitable people to help him by taking in his children. This is not a picture of a man whose only involvement with his children was being present at their conception or who demonstrated no interest in them after their birth. It is instead the picture of a man who acted responsibly enough as a parent and who should be deprived of their guardianship only after a full and fair hearing on the question of whether his children had been neglected.

8

Commentary on *Roe v. Wade*

Rachel Rebouché

There have been thousands of law review articles and countless books interpreting, contesting, or explaining *Roe v. Wade*,[1] decided in 1973.[2] In that
case, the U.S. Supreme Court held that criminal laws banning abortion were
an infringement of a constitutional right to privacy under the Due Process
Clause of the Fourteenth Amendment.[3] The Court held that women, in consultation with their physicians, may terminate a pregnancy for any reason
during the first trimester, or the first thirteen weeks of gestation.[4] In the second trimester, the Court ruled, a state may "regulate the abortion procedure
in ways that are reasonably related to maternal health."[5] And in the last trimester, the state interests in protecting "the potentiality of human life" and
"the life or health of the mother" justify the strictest regulation, and even
bans, of abortion.[6]

The concurrence of Professor Kimberly Mutcherson, writing as Justice
Mutcherson, sets a new course for abortion rights, drawing on important,
post-*Roe* jurisprudential and theoretical developments. Specifically, Justice
Mutcherson offers an equality argument for abortion. After explaining how
her concurrence comports with and departs from the original majority opinion, this Commentary considers how post-*Roe* abortion jurisprudence might
have differed if *Roe* had been based on equality considerations.

---

[1] *Roe v. Wade*, 410 U.S. 113 (1973).
[2] *See, e.g.*, What *Roe v. Wade* Should Have Said (Jack M. Balkin ed., 2005).
[3] 410 U.S. 113, 153, 164–66 (1973).
[4] *Id.* at 164.
[5] *Id.*
[6] *Id.*

BUILDING ON BLACKMUN

Mutcherson agrees with Justice Blackmun that the right to abortion is a privacy right, and, like Blackmun, she cites prior decisions of the Court protecting rights to bodily integrity and personal or familial privacy.[7] However, Mutcherson departs from Blackmun's opinion by rejecting the trimester framework and grounding a constitutional right to abortion in both due process and equal protection. The trimester framework, according to Mutcherson, is doomed to fail: technological advances will make abortion safer earlier in pregnancy, and viability as the boundary for state regulation accords misguided protection for fetuses. Because the fetus is not a person bearing constitutional rights, Mutcherson concludes that there are no state interests that justify restricting the decision of a woman to end her pregnancy at any point. Instead, she argues that a state may encourage women to bring their pregnancies to term by enacting policies that lessen the costs of motherhood but protect women's health and promote gender equality. The distinction between *encouragement* and *coercion* can be difficult to discern, and Mutcherson suggests that a strict scrutiny test should police the difference. The test she imagines would not permit states to enact waiting periods or biased informed consent laws, for example. The best way to protect fetal life, Mutcherson says, is for the state to "consider the needs of the pregnant woman."

In explaining abortion as a due process right, Mutcherson emphasizes the constitutional right to bodily integrity; pregnancy is a unique condition requiring a woman to sustain the life of another. Mutcherson clarifies the intersection of pregnancy and the Constitution's protection from physical restraint. Pregnancy is a physical and psychological sacrifice that many women willingly make, but the choice to surrender one's bodily resources for the benefit of another is one that the state cannot compel. Mutcherson analogizes abortion bans to laws that would force an individual to undergo medical treatment or to save the life of another person. In this vein, she advances a feminist approach to bioethics that would develop in the years after *Roe*.

INTRODUCING EQUAL PROTECTION

Treading new ground in sex equality, Mutcherson's concurrence holds that abortion bans penalize women, and only women, by forcing them to become mothers. The expectation that women become mothers carries professional and educational disadvantages because pregnancy exacts costs and imposes

---

[7]   *Id.* at 130–38, 152–53.

burdens that are not evenly distributed between the sexes. Foreshadowing
the influence of the reproductive justice movement, Mutcherson notes that
abortion restrictions have disproportionate consequences for women with low
incomes, women of color, or otherwise marginalized women. Specifically, the
state-by-state legalization of abortion, as was occurring when the Court decided
Roe, privileges women with means to travel and penalizes women who cannot
afford to take time off work, cross state borders, or secure transportation.

True to the era, Mutcherson's opinion focuses on the biological differences
between men and women. This binary has driven sex-equality jurisprudence,
and it has been definitional to constitutional protection under the Equal
Protection Clause. Mutcherson reasons, as academics have subsequent to
Roe, that the problem with abortion bans is that they depend on gender stereotypes about women's duties to serve as wives and mothers.[8] When women
cannot decide to terminate a pregnancy, law presumes motherhood is natural,
altruistic, and non-negotiable.[9] The Equal Protection Clause is the constitutional tool for challenging laws that perpetuate women's second-class citizenship because of their biological capacity to have children.

Mutcherson's equal protection holding would have been a significant
departure from the original opinion's reasoning and a striking step in equality
jurisprudence given what had and what had not happened by 1973. Congress
had passed the Equal Rights Amendment, but it was not yet clear that states
would fail to ratify it. As of 1973, the Court had yet to decide a series of cases
that subjected sex classifications to heightened scrutiny under the Equal
Protection Clause.[10] The year after *Roe*, the U.S. Supreme Court decided
Geduldig v. Aiello and held that discrimination based on pregnancy is not
sex-based discrimination.[11] The congressional response to *Geduldig* – the
Pregnancy Discrimination Act – did not become law until 1978. Among other
requirements, the Act mandates employers treat pregnant women the same as
applicants or employees who are similar in their ability to work.[12]

How an equality basis for abortion rights might have changed the legal
discourse has been the subject of debate since *Roe*.[13] And it is a debate that

---

[8] *See* Reva Siegel, *Siegel, J., concurring, in* What *Roe v. Wade* Should Have Said (Jack Balkin, ed., 2005).
[9] *See, e.g.,* Reva Siegel, *Reasoning From the Body: An Historical Perspective on Abortion Regulation and Questions of Equal Protection*, 44 Stan. L. Rev. 261 (1992).
[10] *See* Leslie Harris and June Carbone, Family Law 78–83 (2014) (summarizing constitutional limits on gender-based classifications).
[11] *Geduldig*, 417 U.S. 484 (1974).
[12] 42 U.S.C. § 2000(e) *et seq.* Congress had not enacted the Family and Medical Leave Act, providing for twelve weeks of unpaid maternity leave. 29 U.S.C. §§ 2601–2654 (1993).
[13] *See* Ruth Bader Ginsburg, *Some Thoughts on Autonomy and Equality in Relation to* Roe v. Wade, 63 N.C. L. Rev. 375 (1985).

has left an imprint on subsequent abortion jurisprudence. A plurality of the Court upheld and revised *Roe* in *Planned Parenthood of Southeastern Pennsylvania v. Casey* in 1992.[14] In *Casey*, the Court referred to the importance of abortion rights to women's equality in "economic and social life" in ways that *Roe* did not.[15] Mutcherson's test under the Equal Protection Clause, so early in the life of sex-discrimination cases, does not announce explicitly the level of constitutional scrutiny for gender-based classifications. Yet her concurrence could have paved the way for heightened scrutiny and offers rationales for strict scrutiny review. Mutcherson argues that there is no compelling state interest in restricting pregnant women's abortion decisions, and, perhaps more interestingly, she offers a substantive view of constitutional equality. The government not only must justify why it "treats like things in a disparate manner"; it must also consider the effects of laws that reinforce gender *in*equality.

Mutcherson's opinion also reflects (and attempts to harmonize) theoretical conflicts among feminists about the role of pregnancy. The core of Mutcherson's concurrence is that pregnancy plays a "dichotomous role" in women's lives: pregnancy "marks some women as special and worthy of praise and protection"; but pregnancy can be medically risky, is mentally taxing, and threatens employment and educational opportunities. Her reasoning illustrates a longstanding tension in feminist legal theory.[16] At the risk of oversimplification, liberal feminist theorists have emphasized that equality rights allow women to reject caregiving roles and to pursue advancement in public life on the same footing with men. Cultural feminist theorists contend that the problem is not that law treats women as mothers or caregivers, but that law and public institutions do not value (and instead make invisible) women's caregiving roles.[17] Mutcherson's concurrence captures both positions – the "blessing but burden" of pregnancy. She makes the observation that law fails pregnant women as mothers: there is no safety net for caregivers, no promise of assistance with child care, and no guarantee of continued education or pay.[18] But she also focuses on how pregnancy – for any woman – can be a significant obstacle to personal and professional development.

---

[14] *Planned Parenthood of Se. Pa. v. Casey*, 505 U.S. 833, 856 (1992).
[15] *Id.*
[16] June Carbone: From Partners to Parents: The Second Revolution in Family Law 21–26 (2001) (juxtaposing the scholarship of Susan Muller Okin and Martha Fineman).
[17] *Id.* at 21.
[18] *See also* Siegel, *Siegel, J., concurring, supra* note 8, at 81–82.

ABORTION RIGHTS REIMAGINED

Mutcherson's concurrence may not have stemmed the tide of anti-abortion activism and legislation or the backlash against women's changing societal roles. But it might have provided future courts stronger language for grounding abortion protections in the rights of women. Justice Blackmun, writing a concurrence in *Casey*, arrived where Mutcherson starts: the state cannot force women "to accept the 'natural' status and incidents of motherhood" without "triggering the protection of the Equal Protection Clause."[19]

Imagine if the Court in *Casey* focused less on rejecting regulation by trimester because Mutcherson's concurrence already had predicted that it would become outdated. We might still have *Casey's* undue burden test. But the Court in *Casey* might have acknowledged that such a test is a departure from the heightened scrutiny of state laws that restrict women's fundamental rights. Justice Mutcherson's opinion could have influenced the Court's developing equality jurisprudence and provided a basis for interpreting the right to end pregnancy as a right to opt out of prescribed gender roles that can support discrimination based on sex and sexuality.

Rights related to sexuality bear mention as Mutcherson's concurrence could have been cited in cases that extended equality rights for groups beyond pregnant women. As *Roe* briefly acknowledged,[20] abortion implicates the stereotypes and stigma attendant to women's sexual intercourse with men. To be sure, constitutional protection for intimate sexual conduct is not part of *Roe's* reasoning. Nor did the Court foresee, in 1973, constitutional protections for same-sex individuals' or couples' sexual expression. Even so, Mutcherson's concurrence could have informed the extension of equal protection (as well as due process) rights for gay, bisexual, transsexual, transgender, and queer persons. Cases like *Lawrence v. Texas*[21] and *United States v. Windsor*,[22] which relied on rational basis review and left unclear the scope of an equal protection right to sexuality, did not have the benefit of Mutcherson's concurrence.[23] The same is true of *Obergefell v. Hodges*, although in that opinion equality arguments appear to more clearly buttress the constitutional right to marriage for couples of the same sex.[24]

---

[19] *Planned Parenthood of Se. Pa. v. Casey*, 505 U.S. 833, 928 (1992).
[20] *Roe*, 410 U.S. at 148 (noting the argument that abortion bans "discourage illicit sexual conduct").
[21] *Lawrence v. Texas*, 539 U.S. 558 (2003).
[22] *United States v. Windsor*, 133 S. Ct. 2675 (2013).
[23] See Jill Lepore, *To Have and to Hold: Reproduction, Marriage, and the Constitution*, New Yorker, May 25, 2015, at 38–39.
[24] *Obergefell v. Hodges*,135 S. Ct. 2584 (2015).

Constitutional rights to equality are, of course, not enough. Announcing constitutional protection does not necessarily mean its beneficiaries will gain access to the social and economic benefits that rights promise. Even with the limitations of rights in mind, a reimagined *Roe* and these twenty-first century cases highlight the Court's role in affirming evolving concepts of gender or sex and in dismantling the state control of procreative or relational decision making. Justice Kennedy wrote in *Obergefell*, "the Court has recognized that new insights and societal understandings can reveal unjustified inequality within our most fundamental institutions that once passed unnoticed and unchallenged."[25] The reasoning that undermines laws that fix women's place as mothers can also help untether sexuality from procreation or from hetero-sexuality. Were Mutcherson's concurrence the law, her opinion could have set the United States on the path of realizing that future.

Roe v. Wade, 410 U.S. 113 (1973)

Justice Kimberly M. Mutcherson, concurring.

I

I concur in the Court's judgment and join Parts I–VIII of the Court's opinion, in which Justice Blackmun holds that the right to privacy found in the Fourteenth Amendment extends to a woman's decision to terminate a pregnancy. I write separately to disagree with the Court's rigid trimester framework for determining the extent to which the state can interfere with that right, to explicate further the nature of the fundamental right to terminate a pregnancy that we find today, and to hold that the right to an abortion is constitutionally protected under the Equal Protection Clause of the Fourteenth Amendment.

Before proceeding to the merits, I note that this case does not require this Court to decide whether any individual woman should have an abortion – that decision can be made only by a competent pregnant woman. Only she can weigh the rewards and risks of pregnancy. The decision to end a pregnancy, like so many medical decisions, is not amenable to judicial fiat. At this time, we are spared the task of deciding whether any particular physician must perform abortions or deciding how any faith tradition must counsel its adherents about the practice of abortion. Our decision today cannot and should not hold sway over how religious leaders interact with their adherents. Finally, we are not tasked with solving the ethical and moral conundrums attendant to the

---

[25] *Id.* at 20.

termination of fetal life via abortion. Even with the parameters of our decision thus cabined, I am mindful that no matter the decision that issues from this Court, some will consider abortion always to be an unqualified moral wrong and others will find the moral failure in refusing to allow women, and women alone, to determine their reproductive fate at all stages of pregnancy. Neither camp can claim today's decision as an unreserved victory.

In this matter, we must determine whether individual women or the state will decide the circumstances in which a woman must carry a pregnancy to term. Despite the passionate feelings that abortion engenders, the role of this Court is to interpret a living document whose most basic tenets are implicated by the ruling that we make today. Deciding what role the government can play in determining the uses to which a woman puts her body and on whose behalf implicates a range of rights protected by our Constitution including a right to bodily integrity, *Rochin v. California*, 342 U.S. 165 (1952), a right to privacy as articulated in cases like *Griswold v. Connecticut*, 381 U.S. 479 (1965), and *Eisenstadt v. Baird*, 405 U.S. 438 (1972), including the right to make intimate decisions about procreation and parenting without unjustified interference by the government, *Skinner v. Oklahoma ex rel. Williamson*, 316 U.S. 535 (1942), *Meyer v. Nebraska*, 262 U.S. 390 (1923), and a right to equal protection that extends to protection from unjustified gender-based discrimination, *e.g.*, U.S. Const. amend. XIX. With full respect for these rights that the Constitution grants to all, today we decide that the Texas statutory scheme regulating access to abortion is invalid.

II

Appellant Jane Roe began this action as an unmarried pregnant woman who wished to terminate her pregnancy, but who could not legally do so in the State of Texas because of that state's restrictive abortion laws. *Roe v. Wade*, 410 U.S. 113, 120 (1973). She sued on behalf of herself and all other women "who have sought, are seeking, or in the future will seek to obtain a legal, medically safe abortion, but whose lives are not critically threatened by the pregnancy." Br. for Appellants at 9. Like many other women who find themselves pregnant when pregnancy and parenting are not compatible with their present circumstances, Ms. Roe sought pregnancy termination because of the financial hardship attendant to pregnancy and parenting as a single parent and because of the significant social stigma attached to a pregnancy outside of marriage. *Id.* As a woman with a 10th grade education and no employment sufficiently remunerative to allow her to travel to a state with legalized abortion, Ms. Roe found herself in dire circumstances.

Ms. Roe initiated this litigation against the State of Texas alleging deprivation of fundamental liberties secured to her and other women under the Constitution and previously articulated by this Court. Specifically, she claimed that the criminal abortion restrictions in Texas violated her right to appropriate and safe medical advice related to the decision whether to carry a given pregnancy to term, *id.* at 10, the fundamental right of all women to choose the circumstances of pregnancy and childbearing, *id.* at n.5, the right of physicians to practice medicine within the bounds of applicable professional standards, and the right to personal privacy. *Id.*

The statutory scheme in Texas does not subject a woman to criminal penalties for seeking an abortion, but physicians who perform abortions without satisfying the restrictions contained in the statute are subject to a felony conviction and up to five years in prison for violations of the statute, 2A Tex. Penal Code art. 1191, at 429 (1961), as well as cancellation of a medical license. 12B Tex. Rev. Civ. Stat. Ann. art. 4505, at 541 (1961). Hospitals can lose their operating licenses for permitting illegal abortions to be performed within their facilities. 12B Texas Civ. Stat. Ann. art. 4437f § 9, at 216 (1966). Thus, while a woman does not risk a prison sentence for her decision to terminate her pregnancy, the statutory scheme makes it impossible or unlikely that she will be able to secure an abortion from a licensed medical provider if the pregnancy does not pose a sufficient risk to her life so as to meet the requirements of the Texas abortion laws. Thus, women like Ms. Roe are effectively barred from legally accessing pregnancy termination procedures in their home state.

Like the majority, I do not question that Jane Roe has standing to pursue this claim on her own behalf and on behalf of similarly situated women. *Roe,* 410 U.S. at 125. I also agree that a fair reading of the Constitution and our case law must lead to the conclusion that Ms. Roe, and all women, have a constitutional right to terminate their pregnancies. This is so both as a matter of due process under the Fourteenth Amendment and as a matter of equal protection under the same Amendment. Those statutes, like many in effect around the country, create significant barriers for women accessing abortions, including banning the procedure for large groups of women who would otherwise choose to terminate their pregnancies. These statutes are not just an inconvenient obstacle to care that women must surmount. Rather, they are an impenetrable and unnecessary barrier that forces women, against their will, to endure a life-changing, risky, and physically taxing experience. This is a state of affairs that should not stand.

I agree with the majority to the extent that it holds that the right to terminate a pregnancy is a fundamental right under the Fourteenth Amendment of the Constitution, which emanates from the right to privacy that this Court has previously found to be part and parcel of that Amendment. *Roe*, 410 U.S. at 152–153. I would also hold that denying women the right to refuse to carry a pregnancy to term is a violation of equal protection under the Fourteenth Amendment as it demands that women, and only women, accede to the use of their bodies in a way that demeans them and that subjects them to significant personal, professional, and social obstacles only as a consequence of their sex. Therefore, I hold that the Texas abortion law, which makes abortion a crime except in the case of an abortion to save the life of the pregnant woman, whether supported or not by compelling interests of the state, is too broadly impactful to survive the highest level of constitutional scrutiny and it must therefore fall in its entirety.

III

Whether termed a right to bodily integrity or a more broadly construed right to privacy, the right for which Appellant Roe argues is one that this Court has articulated as being foundational in our democracy across a range of issues and in a range of cases. In *Union Pacific Railway Co. v. Botsford*, we declared: "No right is held more sacred, or is more carefully guarded, by the common law, than the right of every individual to the possession and control of his own person, free from all restraint or interference of others, unless by clear and unquestionable authority of law." *Union Pac. R. Co. v. Botsford*, 141 U.S. 250, 251 (1891); *Terry v. Ohio*, 392 U.S. 1, 9 (1968). More recently, in *Eisenstadt v. Baird*, 405 U.S. 438 (1972), we asserted that: "If the right of privacy means anything, it is the right of the individual, married or single, to be free from unwarranted governmental intrusion into matters so fundamentally affecting a person as the decision whether to bear or beget a child." *Id.* at 453. In *Stanley v. Georgia*, 394 U.S. 557, 564 (1969), we wrote: "[A]lso fundamental is the right to be free, except in very limited circumstances, from unwanted governmental intrusions into one's privacy." Thus, the right to end a pregnancy falls well within the purview of other personal rights to which this Court and several others have accorded constitutional significance. *See, e.g., Poe v. Menghini*, 339 F. Supp. 986 (1972); *YWCA v. Kugler*, 342 F. Supp. 1048 (D.N.J. 1972); *Babbitz v. McCann*, 310 F. Supp. 293 (E.D. Wis. 1970), appeal dismissed, 400 U.S. 1 (1970); *People v. Belous*, 458 P. 2d 194 (Cal. 1969), cert. denied, 397 U.S. 915 (1970); *State v. Barquet*, 262 So. 2d 431 (Fla. 1972).

A right to privacy would be anemic if it did not span widely enough to encompass a woman's decision to terminate a pregnancy. This is such a simple truth that it is almost difficult to imagine how one could seriously argue otherwise. Pregnancy is a unique human condition. There are few, if any, other instances in which one human being sustains existence by drawing consistently on the bodily resources of another human being. Perhaps the only close analogy is that of conjoined twins who share a vital organ. But even that analogy must fail because the twins are on equal footing in important respects. That is not so with a pregnant woman and her fetus. Instead, the pregnant woman gives sustenance to the fetus, but the fetus does not give such sustenance to her. Instead, it takes from her. It is her blood, her heart, and her body that experience the wear and tear that comes from pregnancy. Even the best of pregnancies bring physical consequences and potential indignities. Swollen feet, expanded girth, heartburn, thinning hair, nausea, and vomiting are common pregnancy experiences. And of course the impacts of pregnancy can go beyond the inconvenient to the dangerous. Women can experience temporary or permanent disability and even death as a consequence of pregnancy. These are just the physical realities of pregnancy, but its social consequences are also remarkable as discussed in greater depth in the next section.

The recourse available to women who experience unwanted pregnancies varies across different categories of women, especially on the basis of economic status. Appellant Roe well represents this class divide. When women who are financially secure find themselves pregnant and wish to terminate those pregnancies, they can leave their home states or even leave the country in order to secure safe and legal abortions elsewhere. Travel is not an option for women who are poor or who have other responsibilities that make it impossible for them to cross state lines or leave our borders to access a right that should be theirs under the Constitution. For these women, the only choice they can exercise is between seeking out a potentially unsafe illegal abortion, thus putting their lives and health at significant risk, or remaining pregnant against their will and giving birth to unwanted children. One can imagine how desperate women in this situation must feel – so desperate that each year many thousands of them are treated in emergency rooms for grievous wounds or dangerous infections as a result of illegal or self-induced abortions. Br. for Org. and Named Women as Amici Curiae in Support of Appellants in Each Case, at 28.

That so many women willingly become pregnant is a testament to their desire to bear the risk of pregnancy and, for many, eventual parenting because of the value that they or perhaps others around them ascribe to a woman's role as child bearer and mother. To make that sacrifice by choice is seen by many as ennobling and by others as the natural and expected course of a woman's life. But the large number of women who pursue pregnancy by their own design should not blind us to the fact that pregnancy, for many other women, is a burden and not a blessing. It is this latter category of women for whom access to abortion is most salient. If our abortion jurisprudence focuses, as it rightly should, on those women for whom remaining pregnant is an unwanted burden, not a freely pursued choice, the importance of a fundamental right to terminate an unwanted pregnancy becomes stunningly clear.

Where, as here, we find that a fundamental right exists, the state may not deny that right unless it has a compelling interest in doing so and chooses a narrowly tailored means of asserting that interest. *Kramer v. Union Free School District*, 395 U.S. 621, 637 (1969); *Shapiro v. Thompson*, 394 U.S. 618, 634 (1969); *Sherbert v. Verner*, 374 U.S. 398, 406 (1963); *Griswold v. Connecticut*, 381 U.S. at 485; *Aptheker v. Secretary of State*, 378 U.S. 500, 508 (1964). Justice Blackmun's opinion employs a trimester framework premised on the stages of pregnancy to sort the strength of the fundamental right and the various points during a pregnancy when that right must bend to an asserted state interest. The majority would allow the state to override a woman's fundamental right to terminate her pregnancy based on the following taxonomy:

(a) For the stage prior to approximately the end of the first trimester, the abortion decision, and its effectuation must be left to the medical judgment of the pregnant woman's attending physician.

(b) For the stage subsequent to approximately the end of the first trimester, the State, in promoting its interest in the health of the mother, may, if it chooses, regulate the abortion procedure in ways that are reasonably related to maternal health.

(c) For the stage subsequent to viability, the State in promoting its interest in the potentiality of human life may, if it chooses, regulate, and even proscribe, abortion except where it is necessary, in appropriate medical judgment, for the preservation of the life or health of the mother.

Roe, 410 U.S. at 164–65.

Seeking refuge in the objectivity of medicine and science is tempting in a case such as this, which touches upon an intimate part of the human experience. But mapping a pregnant woman's rights based on the trimester framework is an exercise in futility. First, the idea that medicine is wholly objective is complicated by the reality that appeals to science and medicine can mask completely non-medical motives such as political ideology or religious convictions. The history of obstetrics and gynecology in particular is one in which research shows that beliefs about women's roles, the sway of religious dogma, and a desire to wrest control of pregnancy and childbirth away from the woman-dominated field of midwifery all played roles in how "objective" physicians, mostly male, described and sought to control the experience of pregnancy.

Second, the lines we draw today will become largely irrelevant long before controversy about abortion goes away. For instance, current abortion techniques have become sufficiently safe such that at a point in pregnancy the risks to a woman's health are greater if she continues the pregnancy to term than if she terminates that pregnancy. *Roe*, 410 U.S. at 149. As science and medicine continue to progress, as they inevitably will, the medical procedures by which a woman can procure an abortion will become increasingly safer deeper into a pregnancy and increasingly less intrusive early in a pregnancy. One can imagine a time when a woman can safely terminate an early pregnancy at home with little need for any interaction with a physician, thus making regulation even more suspect and invasive.

Similarly, the line of fetal viability will shift. We can only hope that the ability to sustain the lives of children delivered very prematurely will slip closer to the middle of the second trimester rather than its end. As that line moves, Justice Blackmun's window within which a woman could choose to cease being pregnant risks becoming vanishingly small, thus leaving women to shoulder the weight of undesired pregnancies with no legal means of relief.

Third, the trimester framework operates from the premise that at some point during a pregnancy, despite the fact that the Court does not determine a fetus to be a constitutional person,[26] the state interest in potentiality warrants depriving women of the opportunity to end a pregnancy. This conclusion does not comport with a robust conception of the fundamental right to terminate a pregnancy that the Court otherwise espouses. Thus, I reject the trimester framework as deeply flawed and unworkable. Instead the proper test is the same test for evaluating fundamental rights that this Court uses in all such cases – does the state have a compelling state interest and are the means chosen to effectuate that interest narrowly tailored? The Texas laws fail both prongs of the test.

The majority offers several state interests related to abortion regulation including the legitimate and important interest in the safety of the abortion procedure so as to protect the health of the pregnant woman. *Roe*, 410 U.S. at

---

[26] Justice Blackmun's opinion implies that were this Court to grant constitutional personhood to a fetus, the conclusion in this case would be foregone. Given its most obvious definition, a fetus is, at best a potential person and a potential recipient of the rights guaranteed in our Constitution. A fetus has no power to compel another to sacrifice on its behalf and the state cannot do that which the fetus could not compel on its own. To declare a fetus to be worthy of constitutional rights on par with – let alone exceeding those of – a pregnant woman is to tell that woman that she, too, is simply a thing with potential. Our Constitution compels us to treat pregnant women with the respect due to all those who command its protection by virtue of their status as constitutional persons. And, however it may be defined in other realms, a fetus is not a constitutional person.

162. The state also claims an interest in "protecting prenatal life" premised on the potential of the fetus. *Id.* The slope atop which this reasoning rests is precarious indeed. But even assuming arguendo that the interest in potential life is legitimate, even compelling, along with the interest in women's health, the means chosen to effectuate those interests fails to meet the threshold of being narrowly tailored.

The broad legislative stroke that Texas has used in order to make it nearly impossible for most women in the state to procure a safe and legal abortion cannot be justified by either an interest in women's health or an interest in potential fetal life. As for the interest in women's health, the state's claim is belied by its callous decision to stand in the way of safe abortion procedures. Instead it dooms thousands of women each year to seek abortion services from untrained, unlicensed and, in many cases, unscrupulous abortion providers. Br. for Planned Parenthood Fed'n of Am., Inc. and Am. Ass'n of Planned Parenthood Physicians as Amici Curiae, at 46–47. This care far too frequently ends both pregnancies and the lives of the women who sought to terminate those pregnancies. *Id.* True concern for the health of women requires a system of laws that allows women to access a deeply desired medical service within our existing system of medical care with its attendant safeguards. Were the state to regulate abortion care commensurate with how it regulates other forms of healthcare, specifically by focusing on medicine and science, it could immediately begin saving the lives and health of thousands of women who would otherwise die or suffer great harm as they sought to terminate unwanted pregnancies without access to safe care. Laws that allow physicians to provide quality abortion care best serve women's health. The state's denial of access to a wanted medical procedure performed in a safe setting is not protective of women's health.

As for the interest in potential life, the Court writes of the state's interest in the life of the fetus as though the fetus is a separate being to be considered apart from the rights of the pregnant woman. But, until the point of delivery, the fetus is not separate from the woman who gestates it and treating it as a separate entity gives rise to the false impression that women, especially women who are pregnant, are subject to uniquely significant and burdensome deprivations of rights. In stark contrast to this view, I would hold that whatever compelling interest a state has in a fetus must yield in the face of a woman's right to control her body and her future.

I decline the state's invitation to use this case to declare a fetus to be a constitutional person. As Justice Blackmun explains, there is nothing in our nation's history to lead one to believe that the Constitution was written with fetuses in mind. *Roe*, 410 U.S. at 159. Even if a fetus were a constitutional person, it is impossible to decide when one constitutional person, a pregnant woman, must save the life of another by allowing it to gestate inside of her until such time as it can be safely delivered. The life of a fetus cannot take precedence over a woman's right to determine what will happen in her body.

Though our cases have long allowed states to act as *parens patriae* on behalf of living children, *see, e.g., Prince v. Massachusetts*, 321 U.S. 158 (1944), to extend the power of the state so far as to allow it to exercise control over the body of a pregnant woman for the sake of her fetus is repugnant in a constitutional order that protects the sanctity of individual decision making about our own bodies. *See, e.g., Rochin v. California*, 342 U.S. 165 (1952) (rejecting forced stomach pumping). It is axiomatic that a state could not, for instance, force a stranger to submit to a bodily intrusion in order to spare the life of an ailing child, no matter how slight the intrusion and how desperate the child's need for assistance. It might be argued that parents are different and the law should be able to compel them in ways that are inappropriate for a stranger. Here, too, the state's power to act in the interest of children must yield to greater interests. Even in the context of live children, the state cannot force a parent to use her own body to save or sustain a child's life. The state could not demand that a parent give blood for a child desperately in need of a blood transfusion or that a parent donate a kidney to a dying child. And the sacrifice that women are being asked to make when the state tells them that they must carry a pregnancy to term is far greater than asking a parent to donate blood or even a kidney. We might find a parent's refusal to do these things morally repugnant, as some would say of a woman's decision to abort a pregnancy, but moral repugnance is not the foundation upon which constitutional rights rise or fall.

That a woman has a right to terminate a pregnancy and to do so without anyone's permission other than her own does not mean that others cannot seek to persuade her to make a different choice or, perhaps even better, to help avoid unplanned or unintended pregnancies in the first instance. The decision this Court makes today says nothing of what conversations a woman might have with her religious advisor, a trusted friend, her husband, her romantic partner, her parents, or others whose counsel she trusts and might seek before ending a pregnancy. But the state holds no such position of trust in a woman's life, and she is not bound to seek the state's permission or counsel before making a medical decision of such consequence.

That states cannot demand that women carry pregnancies to term against their will does not mean that the state has no power to show respect for fetal life, but the state must act based on a balance in which the life, health, and bodily integrity of the pregnant woman are always paramount throughout a pregnancy. Perhaps the best way for a state to show respect for fetal life is to consider the needs of the pregnant woman who carries that fetus. Thus, where a state so chooses, it is welcome to use its resources as a carrot to encourage women to choose childbirth over abortion by, for instance, offering free or low-cost prenatal care, free or low-cost high-quality childcare, incentives and social support programs to help women begin or return to careers after having children, or creating educational programs for young women who want to combine parenting with completing an education. States can encourage childbirth by creating systems that support the voluntary and uncoerced choice to place a child for adoption. Further, the state could flex its regulatory muscle and make it illegal to take adverse employment actions against a woman because of her reproductive capacity or because she is pregnant, thus making workplaces more stable for women who become pregnant and choose to carry those pregnancies to term. To reduce the risk of unwanted pregnancy in the first instance, the state could provide high-quality sex education to young men and women, including information about contraception, so that they are well equipped to make decisions about their own sexual activity. None of these basic public health and anti-discrimination efforts would seem to create potential constitutional conflicts. Thus, barring a state from legislating so as to force women to bear children when they would prefer not to do so still leaves states with a wide range of opportunities to influence procreative behavior so long as they do not inappropriately infringe on constitutional rights.

As for the regulation of abortion as medical care, the state may, commensurate with its other powers related to healthcare, create medically supportable standards for who may provide abortions and in what setting. Therefore, state regulation of abortion as a medical procedure should be in line with how the state regulates other medical procedures. Regulation that is subterfuge for making it difficult or even impossible for women to choose to terminate a pregnancy must yield to the superiority of the woman's right to end her pregnancy. Abortion, like all surgical procedures, already has become much safer, and this trend will continue. Thus state regulation premised upon an interest in women's health must conform to competent medical evidence about the risks and benefits of any given procedure. Where the state lacks such evidence, its claim of medical need must be rejected.

A statutory scheme like the one before us bars women from exercising pregnancy-related choice, without a legitimate medical purpose, and thus offends basic notions of fair play. It does not appear that Texas requires such onerous procedures for any other type of medical care a woman receives, including for care with potentially dangerous or life-ending consequences, including childbirth. And, of course, there are no medical procedures that require men to first secure the consent of strangers before they can have the care they seek.

It may well become the case in some wild future that fetuses can be removed from a woman's body and brought to term inside an artificial womb or perhaps even transferred into the uterus of another woman who desires to carry that fetus to term. At such time, a future Court might need to decide what that turn of events means for a woman's right to terminate her pregnancy, which does not necessarily or always mean a right to fetal demise. In the early part of a pregnancy, there is no doubt that, at our present stage of scientific knowledge, terminating a pregnancy is synonymous with terminating fetal life, and the right that we find today must also include a right to terminate fetal life in order to vindicate a woman's interest in her own body and in steering the course of her own life. As medicine progresses, fetuses will become viable earlier during a pregnancy. How the state deals with this will become ever more complicated, but it cannot address future scientific progress by conscripting women into compulsory pregnancies.

Thus, fetal viability, rather than being the linchpin of the abortion right as Justice Blackmun's opinion might be read to suggest, is irrelevant to the question of whether a woman can terminate a pregnancy. It becomes relevant only to the extent that once a fetus is removed from a pregnant woman's body, the state has a *parens patriae* interest in the life and health of that child. This interest, critically, is compelling only as to a child and not as to a fetus which, by definition, is the unborn young from the end of the eighth week after conception to the moment of birth. As such, the state cannot require procedures that trade off the health, life, or decision-making control of the pregnant woman in favor of increasing the chance that a fetus will become a live child. Again, at all stages, it is the woman's right to make decisions about terminating a pregnancy.

Though I have assumed that the state interest in women's health and in the potential represented by fetal life are compelling for the purpose of the due process analysis, I think it prudent to consider the difficulty this Court would face if it ever embraced the idea that the state has a compelling interest in fetal life. Presumably, any asserted state interest in fetuses would extend from the existing state *parens patriae* interest in children. But a fetus is no more a child than a packet of flower seeds is a garden. A fetus requires time, nurturing, and a confluence of factors coming together in order for it to eventually become a child. Thus, a state interest in potential life grants unwieldy power as that interest could also extend to eggs and sperm which, with the right combination of time, nurturing, and a confluence of factors can eventually produce a child. The state could not, under a rational set of secular arguments, assert a compelling interest in the uses to which men put their sperm by, for instance, demanding that men get permission from a healthcare provider before having a vasectomy. Beyond the invasiveness of regulation of this sort, the rights to control the bodies of pregnant women that flow from this claimed interest in potential life are staggering. States could arrest pregnant women for behavior during pregnancy that impacts a fetus or require a pregnant woman to submit to a specific childbirth choice in order to benefit a fetus. Government employers could refuse to hire any woman with childbearing potential lest she come in contact with potentially pregnancy-ending or fetus-affecting chemicals. At the end of the potentiality spectrum lies state regulation that would manifestly offend the Constitution.

The state's interest in fetal life is at best important, but never compelling. The state's interest in that fetus only becomes compelling when the fetus becomes a living child and the fetus becomes a living child only after it ceases to be sustained inside the womb of a pregnant woman post-birth. At that point, and only at that point, the state can bring all of its power to bear, with the understanding that this power must be weighed against a parent's fundamental right to care, custody and control of her child. *Prince v. Massachusetts*, 321 U.S. 158 (1944); *Meyer v. Nebraska*, 262 U.S. 390 (1923).

IV

While the determination that the right to terminate a pregnancy is fundamental is a sufficient finding to allow us to decide this case, it is prudent to note that the Texas scheme also implicates the Fourteenth Amendment's equal protection guarantee. Thus the abortion restrictions in this case should fall as a matter of sex equality. I am mindful that past courts have not seen fit to strike down abortion restrictions on this basis, but this Court is not bound to reinforce static notions of equality. As Justice Douglas wrote:

> [T]he Equal Protection Clause is not shackled to the political theory of a particular era. In determining what lines are unconstitutionally discriminatory, we have never been confined to historic notions of equality, any more than we have restricted Due Process to a fixed catalogue of what was at a given time deemed to be the limits of fundamental rights. Notions of what constitutes equal treatment for purposes of the Equal Protection Clause do change.
> *Harper v. Virginia State Bd. of Elections*, 383 U.S. 663, 669 (1966)
> (internal citations omitted).

The right to equal protection articulated here works in tandem with the right to due process. Statutes that restrict access to abortion tread on the sanctity of a woman's body and her private right to make decisions regarding that body, but they also position women as second-class citizens by requiring women, and only women, to maintain pregnancies in contravention of their desire to cease being pregnant. We forget the history and present of women's inequality under the law at our peril and at the peril of the women who look to this Court to ensure that they are treated as equal citizens under the law.

Notions of the proper role of women in the public and private realm have shifted and continue to do so in favor of recognizing and protecting a woman's right to pursue a life outside of the roles of wife and mother. To seek the fullness and richness of her life, a woman may find that motherhood now or ever does violence to the life plans she has constructed. In such a case, to demand that she use her body to pursue the plans of another, whether a fetus, the state, a husband, a boyfriend, or a physician, is to treat her as unequal to other competent adult decision makers. As Judge Lumbard of the Connecticut District Court wrote in striking down that state's restrictive abortion law, "The changed role of women in society and the changed attitudes toward them reflect the societal judgment that women can competently order their own lives and that they are the appropriate decision makers about matters affecting their fundamental concerns." *Abele v. Markle*, 342 F. Supp. 800, 802 (D. Conn. 1972).

Our nation's history is replete with examples of state policies that were premised upon a belief that women were either inferior to men or only fit for certain functions, including mothering. In *Bradwell v. Illinois*, 83 U.S. 130 (1873), this court upheld an Illinois decision that barred women from the practice of law. In his concurring opinion, Justice Bradley wrote,

> It is the prerogative of the legislator to prescribe regulations founded on nature, reason, and experience for the due admission of qualified persons to professions and callings demanding special skill and confidence. This fairly belongs to the police power of the State; and in my opinion, in view of the peculiar characteristics, destiny, and mission of woman, it is within the province of the legislature to ordain what offices, positions, and callings shall be filled and discharged by men.
>
> *Id.* at 142; *see also Goesaert v. Cleary*, 335 U.S. 464 (1948) (barring women from work as bartenders to protect against moral and social problems).

Laws that compel pregnancy similarly rest upon antiquated notions of the proper role and place for women in society.

The fundamental concerns referenced in the *Abele* case include that the ability to control procreation plays an indispensable role in allowing women to become and remain active members of their personal and professional communities. *Abele*, 342 F. Supp. 800. The advent of oral contraceptives has already proven a boon in terms of the ability of some women to pursue a range of life projects before, or indeed in the stead of, building a life with children. That the state has long cherished and valued the status of motherhood for some women does not mean that it is a status that always serves women well.

We do a grand disservice to all women when we let a romantic view of pregnancy and motherhood blind us to the reality that pregnancy is experienced by many women as benefit and burden. On one hand, the fact of being pregnant or capable of becoming pregnant marks some women as special and worthy of praise and the law's protection.[27] On the other hand, the fact of being pregnant or being capable of pregnancy leaves all women at risk for poor outcomes physically, psychologically, professionally, and socially. As described earlier, pregnancy can lead to disability or death in addition to its more common inconveniences. Being pregnant with a child that a woman does not wish to carry to term can bring enormous emotional burdens, especially but not exclusively when the pregnancy results from rape or incest. Weighing options about whether to keep a child or put a child up for adoption; perhaps contending with stigma and shame associated with being pregnant out of wedlock and single motherhood; risking the opprobrium of friends, family, and even strangers; taking on the life-changing experience of motherhood when one is ill-equipped to do so; and accepting the bodily shifts associated with pregnancy even when one's deepest desire is to not be pregnant can exact a significant psychological toll on women. No doubt some women forced to carry a pregnancy to term will willingly embrace motherhood, but there is also no doubt that many women will not.

Within the professional realm, pregnancy's consequences can also be stark. For women who are in the paid workforce, pregnancy can end a promising career, as there is no federal law that explicitly protects women from adverse work decisions because of their pregnancies. There is no federal policy that allows women to take protected leave from their jobs while pregnant and return to those jobs at the same status and with the same pay at a later point. There are no federal statutes creating paid maternity leave policies for women who wish to spend time with their children after giving birth. Young women seeking higher education as a prelude to professional careers can be expelled from their colleges or universities because of an unintended or out-of-wedlock

---

[27] Reverence for pregnancy as a special state has been denied to large groups of women throughout our history. For instance, for Black women who were enslaved in this country, pregnancy was not a badge of honor because of any respect for the wonders of the human condition. Rather, pregnancy was an economic tool that allowed slave owners to reap more monetary benefit from the bodies to which they laid claim, and motherhood as a special status did not extend to enslaved women. *See generally*, E. Franklin Frazier, The Negro Family in the United States 33–36 (1966).

pregnancy. They may even be ostracized from their faith communities or their own families because of such a pregnancy. Br. for Org. and Named Women as Amici Curiae in Supp. of Appellants in Each Case at 28–34.

Further, the burdens of pregnancy will not be experienced evenly across populations of women. Women with sufficient financial wherewithal will leave paid employment behind to contend with an unwanted pregnancy, but other women will find that the loss of work status attendant to pregnancy puts their entire family at risk for an economic catastrophe. There are many workplaces that will not accept women workers who are pregnant, especially pregnant and unmarried, thus denying women access to a range of potentially high paying sectors of employment. For poor Black women, out-of-wedlock pregnancies have been blamed for the crisis in their communities. Office of Policy Planning and Research, United States Department of Labor, *The Negro Family: The Case For National Action* (March 1965). Pregnancy, in this case, is unfairly used as a proxy for irresponsibility and selfishness. It is narrow-minded and naive to assume that pregnancy is a benefit to all women who experience it.

That a woman is pregnant, no matter the circumstances of becoming pregnant, does not signal her assent to remaining pregnant or becoming a mother. Women are not simply vessels through which babies emerge into the world. Treating pregnancy as a period when women cease to be able to lay claim to their own bodies fails to take seriously this simple proposition. It is substantially through the ability to control childbearing with some reliability, with contraceptives and abortion, that women find success in the public sphere. The decision about where and how to find success is a decision to be made by women, not by others. Even for those women whose lives have the outward appearance of being sufficiently stable to allow for motherhood, the state asks too much when it demands that a woman use her body in the interest of the state in a way that would not, and indeed could not, be asked of a man.

That a woman consents to sexual intercourse does not change the analysis of the fundamental right at stake. Sexual intercourse is an act with consequences, no doubt, but this truth does not justify denying women access to the tools of ending pregnancies once they have begun any more than it countenances denying women access to tools to prevent pregnancy in the first instance.

No doubt the reasoning that supports the fundamental rights claims intertwines with the reasoning that supports the Equal Protection arguments being made here. Classifications that expressly discriminate on the basis of gender are subject to scrutiny under the Equal Protection Clause, *Reed v. Reed*, 404 U.S. 71, 75 (1971). The government must justify why it treats like things in a disparate manner, but it can sometimes more readily justify treating unlike things in an unlike manner. In the context of pregnancy, men and women are differently situated because the ability to become pregnant and carry a pregnancy to term is a uniquely female trait. Standing alone, however, this should not end our inquiry, for it is right to draw some distinction between benefits and burdens in the context of classifications drawn on the basis of sex. Here, the state singles out women not for the purpose of assisting them in conquering hurdles related to discrimination or compensating for past wrongs. Instead, when the state forces women to carry pregnancies to term which they wish to terminate, it demands that women take on a uniquely life-affecting status that can work to their detriment. Women are not served by a state-sanctioned policy that denies their competence to make their own healthcare decisions; that likens them to criminals; that subjects them to the potential for serious physical and psychological strain; and that interferes with the relationship between a woman and her healthcare provider in making some of the most intimate decisions that a woman can ever be called upon to make. Even if the state did have legitimate interests in controlling a woman's decision to terminate a pregnancy, it strains credulity to seek to protect those interests by forcing continued pregnancy upon unwilling women. Thus in regard to the fundamental right arguments and Equal Protection arguments, the means chosen to effectuate the state interest cannot withstand any level of constitutional scrutiny.

V

The state's forays into the world of procreative regulation often coincide with shameful parts of this nation's history. Forced sterilizations and state-sponsored eugenics, *Buck v. Bell*, 274 U.S. 200 (1927), *Skinner v. Oklahoma ex rel. Williamson*, 316 U.S. 535 (1942), and racist laws of family formation, *Loving v. Virginia*, 388 U.S. 1 (1967), are legacies of state attempts to control who procreates and with whom. Childbearing or not, all women suffer when the state wields its limited power to regulate procreation as a tool of denigration. And a law that tells women that they cannot make medical decisions in consultation with trusted healthcare providers, family members, friends, religious advisors, or others is a law that denigrates women by discounting their decision-making capacities and denying them the level of agency that the law accords as a fundamental right to other competent constitutional persons.

In holding that a right to privacy emanating from a number of constitutional amendments is broad enough to protect a married couple's right to possess contraception, Justice Douglas wrote that the marital relationship is protected by "a right of privacy older than the Bill of Rights – older than our political parties, older than our school system." *Griswold v. Connecticut*, 381 U.S. 479, 486 (1965). Similarly, the right that we recognize today is a constitutional right with roots that emanate from the most basic truth of our human bodies that have the capacity for creating new life. To embrace that capacity and use one's body in the service of bringing forth a new human form is a momentous task and one which should never be undertaken under duress. The Texas abortion law is a form of governmental duress that we cannot endorse as a constitutional means of enforcing state interests in fetuses, women's health, or the medical profession. Simultaneously, placing the burden of unwanted pregnancy upon women unconstitutionally infringes their rights to equal protection by forcing them to use their bodies in service of the state's interest in ways that are not and cannot be asked of men.

It is likely that this will not be the last time that the issue of abortion regulation comes before this Court. I take this opportunity, then, to be clear about what I hold today. First, a woman, throughout her pregnancy, has a fundamental right to choose whether she wishes to remain pregnant. At no point in pregnancy may the state weaken a woman's right to privacy, her health, or her life by insisting that she remain pregnant when she does not consent to do so. That a woman has a right to cease to be pregnant does not mean that she has a right to demand the termination of the life of a *born child*. Thus, a state may assert an interest in sustaining the life of a born child who has been removed from the womb of a woman who no longer wishes to remain pregnant. In this case, the relevant state interest is the longstanding *parens patriae* interest which comes to fruition only for a child, not for a fetus. Thus the state cannot make demands on the pregnant woman, such as insisting on any specific procedure that will benefit a fetus but that offers no benefit to the pregnant woman, or worse, that actually compromises her life or health in the interest of increasing the life chances of the fetus.

The person with the greatest interest in what happens to a fetus is the woman who carries that fetus in her body. It is women, those constitutional persons, to whom the state owes respect. That respect begins and ends with treating women and their bodies with the same dignity accorded to all others. At no point in a pregnancy can the state substitute its own judgment about the value of pregnancy or the value of fetal life for a woman's judgment about whether she wishes to carry a fetus to term in her body.

I concur in Justice Blackmun's opinion as to result, but not as to its reasoning.

9

Commentary on *Frontiero v. Richardson*

Iselin M. Gambert

INTRODUCTION

"Hot damn!"

These were the words self-described "flaming feminist" Sharron Frontiero joyously uttered when she learned that the U.S. Supreme Court's decision in her landmark 1973 case, *Frontiero v. Richardson*,[1] would allow female military personnel to receive the same dependency benefits for their husbands as their male counterparts were already getting for their wives.[2]

Frontiero was a significant victory for the feminist movement, though not an uncomplicated one.[3] The number of laws on the books in the early 1970s reflecting and reinforcing traditional gender roles was dizzying,[4] and courts – including the U.S. Supreme Court – routinely upheld them. *Frontiero* was only the second case in which the Court invoked equal protection principles to hold unconstitutional a law that discriminated against women.[5] It was also the first case Ruth Bader Ginsburg argued before the Court, helping solidify her role as "the leading Supreme Court litigator for gender equality" in the 1970s.[6] The original decision in *Frontiero* marks the closest the Court has

---

[1] *Frontiero v. Richardson*, 411 U.S. 677 (1973).

[2] A *"Flaming Feminist" Lauds Court*, N.Y. Times, May 22, 1973, at 36.

[3] Serena Mayeri, *"When the Trouble Started": The Story of* Frontiero v. Richardson, *in* Women and the Law Stories 57, 84–85 (Elizabeth M. Schneider and Stephanie M. Wildman eds., 2011).

[4] Gender equality litigators used Appendix E, "a treasure trove" from *Moritz v. Comm'r*, 469 F.2d 466 (10th Cir. 1972), that listed U.S. Code provisions "containing differentiations based upon sex-related criteria," to identify sex discrimination cases. Ruth Bader Ginsburg, Assoc. Justice, U.S. Supreme Court, Remarks at the Woodrow Wilson International Center for Scholars: Presentation for Litigating for Gender Equality in the 1970s (May 21, 2002), www.wilsoncenter.org/event/presentation-litigating-for-gender-equality-the-1970s (hereinafter Ginsburg Remarks).

[5] *See* Mayeri, *supra* note 3, at 59–61.

[6] Wendy W. Williams, *Ruth Bader Ginsburg's Equal Protection Clause: 1970–80*, 25 Colum. J. Gender & L. 41, 41 (2013).

come to recognizing sex as a suspect class[7] – Ginsburg's ultimate goal in a creative and sometimes controversial litigation strategy. But because Justice Brennan's opinion establishing strict scrutiny review for sex-based classifications garnered only a plurality of the Court, *Frontiero* left behind a messy legacy.[8]

In her feminist revision, Professor Dara Purvis, writing as Justice Purvis, gives Ginsburg the strict scrutiny majority for which she strategized so long and hard. Purvis's opinion is grounded in a social constructionist vision of feminism that views all gender stereotypes – including those found in "policies that seemingly honor women's contributions" – as harmful.[9] What is unclear is whether Purvis's feminist judgment, had it been the actual majority opinion, could have done more to mitigate the potential dangers of strict scrutiny seen in recent years.[10]

GINSBURG'S TEMPERATURE-RISING STRUGGLE
FOR STRICT SCRUTINY

In reflecting on her time as a gender equality litigator in the 1970s, Justice Ginsburg noted that "[o]ur starting place was not the same as that of advocates" fighting race discrimination because policies treating the sexes differently were often regarded "as operating benignly in women's favor."[11] Lawmakers and judges were "overwhelmingly white, well-heeled, and male," and "generally considered themselves good husband[s] and fathers. Women, they thought, had the best of all possible worlds" – they could choose to work, serve on juries, and enlist in the military – or they could choose to stay home.[12]

It was against this cultural, political, and legal backdrop that Ginsburg crafted her litigation strategy, designed to unravel all laws that discriminated against women, even those ostensibly implemented to "protect" them. Her strategy was bold – so bold that at times she lacked allies among even her closest colleagues.[13]

---

7   Mayeri, *supra* note 3, at 79.
8   *Frontiero v. Richardson*, 411 U.S. 677 (1973) (4–3–1–1 decision).
9   Dara E. Purvis, *The Origin of Parental Rights: Labor, Intent, and Fathers*, 41 Fla. St. U. L. Rev. 645, 691 (2014).
10 *See* Mayeri, *supra* note 3, at 85–87.
11 Ginsburg Remarks, *supra* note 4.
12 *Id.*
13 *See* Letters between ACLU and S. Poverty Law Ctr. (October 17, 1972–December 20, 1972) (on file with the Library of Congress, Ginsburg Collection, ACLU File, Container 3) (hereinafter Correspondence).

Ginsburg joined the "turning point" case of *Reed v. Reed* after asking the lead lawyer whether "having a woman co-counsel would be appropriate,"[14] and penned what is now known as the "grandmother brief."[15] Ginsburg argued that sex-based classifications should be deemed suspect and subject to the same strict scrutiny review as race-based classifications.[16] The Court ultimately declined to explicitly adopt Ginsburg's vision of sex as a suspect class. However, in unanimously striking down the law at issue in the case, *Reed* marked the first time the Court "acted favorably on a woman's complaint that she had been denied equal protection by any state or federal law."[17] Importantly, *Reed* noted that the classification at issue was "subject to scrutiny" – "impl[ying] that sex classifications warrant something more than the traditionally restrained rational basis test" and thus implicitly recognizing Ginsburg's argument for heightened scrutiny.[18]

Reed "delighted" Ginsburg, who said she "never expected the Court to buy our [strict scrutiny] argument. That would have been a giant step for even a more liberal tribunal."[19] Ginsburg co-founded the ACLU Women's Rights Project and turned her attention to *Frontiero*.[20] With *Frontiero*, Ginsburg sought to exploit the ambiguity in *Reed*, using it to "pressure the Court" to adopt strict scrutiny "by appealing to their obligation to create a clear rule for lower courts to follow," and to "advocate adoption of her alternative position of an intermediate level scrutiny, or 'rational basis with a bite'" should the Court reject strict scrutiny.[21]

Ginsburg's co-counsel, Joe Levin at the Southern Poverty Law Center, did not share her strategic vision. Specifically, while he agreed that statutes in the employment arena, like that in *Frontiero*, "must surely carry a much heavier burden of justification" for sex-based classifications, Levin believed that other "[t]rue protective, remedial, or even neutral ... statutes could be judged by

---

[14] Deborah L. Markowitz, *In Pursuit of Equality: One Woman's Work to Change the Law*, 11 *Women's Rts. L. Rep.* 73, 78, 80 (1989) (citing letters from Ginsburg to then-ACLU director Mel Wulf and Mr. Sonnenfeld).

[15] Mayeri, *supra* note 3, at 59.

[16] Br. for Appellant at 14–24, *Reed v. Reed*, 404 U.S. 71 (1971) (No. 70–74). *See also* Markowitz, *supra* note 14, at 78–79.

[17] Ginsburg Remarks, *supra* note 4. *See also Reed*, 404 U.S. at 75–77.

[18] Markowitz, *supra* note 14, at 79.

[19] *Id.* at 80 (quoting Interview with Ruth Bader Ginsburg, in Washington, D.C. (February 24, 1986) (available at the Schlessinger Library for Women's History at Radcliffe College)).

[20] Mayeri, *supra* note 3, at 66; *Tribute: The Legacy of Ruth Bader Ginsburg and WRP Staff*, ACLU, www.aclu.org/tribute-legacy-ruth-bader-ginsburg-and-wrp-staff (last visited August 11, 2015).

[21] Markowitz, *supra* note 14, at 83.

the rational basis test[.]"[22] Ginsburg rejected this distinction, noting that "[t]he pedestal upon which women have been placed has all too often, upon closer inspection, been revealed as a cage."[23]

There were other disagreements, most notably over oral argument. Levin wanted to argue the case, while Ginsburg emphasized "the importance of argument by a woman attorney in a case of this significance[.]"[24] Levin commented that "[t]here is nothing chauvinistic in our desire ... I do not believe it makes one iota of difference whether a male or female makes this argument."[25] Ginsburg responded by calling off a joint meeting, commenting that elements of Levin's remarks had "made my temperature rise."[26] The two parted ways, each advancing their own distinct arguments in separate briefs to the Court.[27] Given the fractured series of opinions emerging from the case, one wonders whether a more unified litigation strategy between Levin and Ginsburg might have produced a clearer and more cohesive precedent.

A MORE EXPANSIVE AND INCLUSIVE FEMINIST OPINION

While Justice Brennan's *Frontiero* opinion can itself be seen as feminist, Purvis's feminist revision departs from and expands on Justice Brennan's reasoning in several meaningful ways. First, Purvis discusses the harm of gender stereotypes writ large, instead of solely focusing as Justice Brennan did on discrimination against women. Noting the "burden" experienced by men and women who "wish to order their lives differently than the stereotype of their gender," Purvis emphasizes that "men will [also] benefit from subjecting sex-based classifications to strict scrutiny."

Second, Purvis argues that the potential ratification of the Equal Rights Amendment would be "irrelevant" to the case, saying its ratification would make her holding "doubly clear." Justice Brennan did not address the issue.[28] Given that three justices cited the ERA as a "compelling [] reason" to hold

---

[22] Br. for Appellants at 32, *Frontiero v. Richardson*, 411 U.S. 677 (1973) (No. 71–1694).

[23] Br. for ACLU as Amicus Curiae at 29, *Frontiero v. Richardson*, 411 U.S. 677 (1973) (No. 71–1694).

[24] Correspondence, *supra* note 13, at Folder 9.

[25] *Id.*

[26] *Id.*

[27] Levin authored the Appellant Brief and Ginsburg the Amicus Brief. They submitted a joint Reply Brief and divided the oral argument time. Mayeri, *supra* note 3, at 68.

[28] Justice Brennan mentioned the ERA only once, using it to bolster his argument rather than to explain why his opinion was necessary despite the pending amendment. *Frontiero*, 411 U.S. at 687–88.

off on recognizing sex as suspect,[29] Purvis's approach might have swayed one
or more of them to join her, thereby changing a messy plurality into a clear
majority opinion.

Finally, Purvis leaves room for future recognition of a broader range of
classes as suspect. While Justice Brennan used the language of "immutability" and "visibility" of sex and race to show how both classifications must be
deemed suspect,[30] Purvis's analogy between women and racial minorities
intentionally ignored those characterizations. She instead focused on sex and
race as being "biological trait[s] bearing little (if any) relevance to abilities
[that have] been used throughout history as a reason to deny people the ability
to participate in society[.]" The distinction is significant: not only are race and
sex often impossible to determine visually, but some scholars have argued that
Justice Brennan's use of "visibility" as a distinguishing trait has thwarted efforts
to recognize sexual orientation, gender identity, and other invisible statuses as
suspect.[31]

CONCLUSION

When *Frontiero* was decided, co-plaintiff Joseph Frontiero "burst out with a
loud whoop," happy that the couple's efforts "gave a real lift to the feminist
movement."[32] More measuredly, Ginsburg found Justice Brennan's opinion "a
joy to read,"[33] though she thought he "moved too soon" given the lack of clear
precedent.[34] Purvis's majority would have clarified the legal landscape in a way
that Justice Brennan's plurality failed to do,[35] but other, less desirable consequences might have followed. While Ginsburg seemed confident in her quest
for strict scrutiny, Dara Purvis noted in a conversation about this project that
she wrestled with whether to adopt the standard, recognizing that some contemporary scholars view it as "no longer the prize it once had seemed" given
its use to invalidate laws designed to benefit historically discriminated-against
groups.[36] It is unclear whether Ginsburg or Justice Brennan foresaw these

[29] *Id.* at 692 (Powell, J., concurring). In the end, the ERA never became law, and courts grappled
      for years with *Frontiero*'s fractured ruling. Mayeri, *supra* note 3, at 81.
[30] *Frontiero*, 411 U.S. at 686.
[31] *See* Kenji Yoshino, *Assimilationist Bias in Equal Protection: The Visibility Presumption and the
      Case of Don't Ask, Don't Tell,* 108 *Yale L. J.* 485, 496 (1998).
[32] A *"Flaming Feminist" Lauds Court, supra* note 2, at 36.
[33] Mayeri, *supra* note 3, at 79 (quoting Letter from Ruth Bader Ginsburg, ACLU, to Jane
      Lifset (May 15, 1973) (on file Ruth Bader Ginsburg Papers, Container 10, Folder: *Weinberger
      v. Wiesenfeld,* Correspondence, 1972–1973)).
[34] Markowitz, *supra* note 14, at 84.
[35] Mayeri, *supra* note 3, at 85.
[36] *Id.* at 86.

long-term consequences, or whether Purvis, who ultimately adopted strict scrutiny, could have done more in her opinion to mitigate them. What is more certain is that had the Frontieros read Purvis's opinion in 1973, they likely would have whooped even louder, celebrating a decision that breaks open the cage of societal expectations and stereotypes that has long trapped women and men alike.

Frontiero v. Richardson, 411 U.S. 677 (1973)

Justice Dara E. Purvis delivered the judgment of the Court.

We are presented with a military benefits program that allocates funds differentially based upon sex. Male service members who claim their wives as dependents categorically receive certain supplemental housing allowances and medical coverage, whereas each female member claiming her husband as a dependent must prove that her husband earns less than half the money necessary to support himself. Appellants argue that this classification violates the Due Process Clause of the Fifth Amendment. They are correct.

I

Sharron Perry joined the Air Force in October of 1968. In December of 1968, she married Joseph Frontiero, himself a veteran. Joseph Frontiero is a full-time student at Huntingdon College, and holds a part-time job from which he earns approximately $30 per month. He also receives $205 per month in veteran's benefits for his education. Otherwise his expenses, which total about $345 per month, are paid by Sharron Frontiero, now an Air Force lieutenant.

Various provisions of federal law provide benefits to members of the uniformed services for the support of dependents. Under 37 U.S.C. §§ 401 and 403, members of the armed forces who live off-base may apply for a supplemental housing allowance, which increases with the number of dependents claimed. 37 U.S.C. §§ 401, 403 (1962). A spouse may be claimed as a dependent, but under existing law, eligibility is different according to whether the spouse is female or male. Male military personnel may claim their wives as dependents regardless of the wives' expenses and income – wives are categorically viewed as dependents. By contrast, a female soldier who wishes to claim her husband as a dependent faces further hurdles. First, she must submit evidence of her husband's expenses and income. Second, a husband is categorized as a dependent only if over half of his expenses are paid by his wife's earnings. Furthermore, even if the husband relies upon his wife for the majority of his support, his status as dependent will still be denied unless he is physically or mentally incapable of supporting himself. Dep't of Defense, *Military Pay & Allowance Entitlements Manual* § 30242 (1967).

In the fall of 1970, Lieutenant Frontiero requested a housing allowance that included a supplement for her husband. Largely because of the educational benefits Mr. Frontiero receives under the G.I. Bill, Lieutenant Frontiero could not demonstrate that her husband was dependent upon her for over half of his expenses. Her application for the supplemental housing allowance was thus denied. In November 1970, she submitted a formal complaint, which was again denied one week later.

One month later, Sharron and Joseph Frontiero filed a complaint in the U.S. District Court for the Middle District of Alabama, Northern Division, arguing that the difference in treatment according to the sex of the purportedly dependent spouse discriminates against female military personnel and thus violates the Due Process Clause of the Fifth Amendment. A three-judge district court panel was convened under 28 U.S.C. §§ 2282 and 2284, and in April 1972 entered a judgment against the Frontieros. A two-member majority of the panel found that administrative efficiency was a rational basis for the regulations. This appeal followed.

II

The Due Process Clause of the Fifth Amendment provides that no person "shall be deprived of life, liberty, or property, without due process of law." U.S. Const. amend. V. The Fifth Amendment prohibits discrimination that is "so unjustifiable" that it lacks due process, and thus in some circumstances overlaps with the Fourteenth Amendment's guarantee of equal protection of the laws. *See Bolling v. Sharpe*, 347 U.S. 497, 499–500 (1954); *Schneider v. Rusk*, 377 U.S. 163 (1964); *Shapiro v. Thompson*, 394 U.S. 618, 641–42 (1969). We have held, moreover, that equal treatment under the law includes equal treatment regardless of sex, in at least some circumstances. *See Reed v. Reed*, 404 U.S. 71 (1971).

It is not yet clear, however, to what level of scrutiny classifications turning upon the sex of affected persons are subject. Last term this Court found that a state statute specifying that males must be preferred to females in appointing administrators of estates violated the Fourteenth Amendment's Equal Protection Clause, holding that the statute's distinction between male and female administrators was "wholly unrelated to the objective" of the statute providing for appointment of administrators. *Reed*, 404 U.S. at 75–76. While the Court was undoubtedly correct that the classification did not "bear[] a rational relationship to a state objective that is sought to be advanced by" the statute providing for appointment of administrators, it left open the question of whether other classifications on the basis of sex should be subject to a level of scrutiny higher than the deferential rational basis test. *Id.* at 76.

We resolve that question today, holding that classifications on the basis of sex must be assessed under the strictest judicial scrutiny. The government has not convinced us that distinguishing between male and female members of the uniformed services is a narrowly tailored means of achieving a compelling government interest. The challenged classification must therefore be struck down.

In considering whether classifications based on sex should be considered suspect, as this Court has previously used the term, it is useful to compare sex to another characteristic, that of race. Sex can be analogized to race in many useful ways: both are biological traits bearing little (if any) relevance to abilities. Both have been used throughout history to limit or eliminate the right to vote; to hold property; sign contracts; hold employment; and other restrictions too numerous to count. There are, however, important differences between sex and race. One justification for why racial minorities are treated as a suspect class is that they are a discrete and insular minority, a description that plainly does not apply to women in that they constitute approximately half of the population. *See U.S. v. Carolene Prods.*, 304 U.S. 144, 152–53, n.4 (1938). Appellees also argue that classifications based upon race are presumed suspect because race almost never has any relevance to a legitimate purpose, whereas sociological and physiological differences between the sexes are frequently relevant to legislative and regulatory goals. Br. for Appellees at 17. Finally, while few would quibble with the observation that legislative discrimination against racial minorities has arisen from outright prejudice and bigotry, many of the statutes mandating different treatment according to sex are allegedly benign and protective, and may not have been founded upon animosity towards women.

Each of these arguments against recognizing sex as a suspect class fails upon examination. Although women are not easily characterized as a discrete and insular minority, discrimination against women operates to prevent them from vindicating their own rights and interests through the political process, notwithstanding their numbers. Assertions that sociological differences between men and women constitutionally justify sex-based laws and regulations not only beg the question, but demonstrate the insidious power and unquestioning acceptance of gender stereotypes. Finally, restrictions in the name of protecting women and their special roles and vulnerabilities may not be motivated by animus, but such a patronizing view of women is just as constitutionally infirm as outright prejudice is.

Justice Stone suggested in *United States v. Carolene Products* that "prejudice against discrete and insular minorities" may justify heightened constitutional scrutiny due to the curtailing of the "political processes ordinarily to be relied upon to protect minorities." 304 U.S. at 152–53, n.4. Appellees would have us employ this logic to find that women need only use the political process to ensure equal protection of the law, given that women constitute approximately one-half the population and "surely are not disabled from exerting their substantial and growing political influence." Br. for Appellees at 16. This is a startling assertion, given the history of both overt and subtle government obstacles to female political participation.

The most literal instrument of political influence is obviously the vote, a right to which women were not constitutionally entitled until 1920. It seems scarcely necessary to catalog the legal disabilities imposed upon women historically, so universal was the dominant view of women as less able than men. The doctrine of *coverture* suspended "the very being or legal existence" of married women, denying them every cognizable legal right in favor of their husbands. 1 William Blackstone, *Commentaries on the Law of England* 442 (3d ed. 1768). The Women's Rights Convention of 1848 in Seneca Falls listed the incapacities then imposed on women because of their sex: women could not vote, could not own property, could not choose honorable or profitable employment, could not seek higher education. 1 *History of Woman Suffrage* 70–73 (Elizabeth Cady Stanton, Susan B. Anthony and Matilda Joslyn Gage eds., Fowler and Wells 1881). It is true that some of the most egregious legal infirmities visited upon women have been removed, but having the right to vote for fifty years has not erased the systemic gendered hierarchy in American law. Only last term, we found that a categorical preference for male administrators of estates over female candidates was an arbitrary preference that bore no rational relationship to the state goal of efficiently selecting administrators. *Reed v. Reed*, 404 U.S. 71, 76–77 (1971). Yet Idaho's arbitrary and irrational sex-based statute is common: Appellant's briefs in that case provided several pages listing similarly gendered statutes from states across the country. Br. for Appellant, App. at 69–88. It is beyond dispute that the rolls of our nation's laws are full of lines drawn between men and women to specify very different legal rights for each, and mere numerical significance has not manifested in equality under the law.

It is true that one way to subvert the political power of a disfavored group is to literally segregate them, as has been done with members of racial minority groups. The paradigmatic example of a discrete and insular group, racial minorities have been told where they may and may not live, work, and even sit. It is self-evident why isolation and segregation prevent the affected people from using the political process to protect themselves.

This does not mean, however, that segregation is the only means by which a group may be silenced. Women have been systematically told to stay home – not only by social or cultural norms, but also by the operation of the law. This is not to say that there is a prohibition of labor by women – a century ago, enslaved women were given no choice as to whether to work. Today, millions of women work to support themselves and their families, generally in lower-paid and lower-status occupations. Employment outside the home is treated for many women, however, as a questionable choice that should not be encouraged or supported. Many paths to higher-status jobs are barred outright to women. For example, although Lieutenant Frontiero joined the Air Force in part to finance her college education at the University of Connecticut, the more prestigious route into the officer corps via the Air Force Academy was unavailable to her, as her gender makes her ineligible for admission to any of the military academies. Until 1967, the proportion of women in military service was capped at two percent, and female soldiers were ineligible for the ranks of general and admiral. Pub. L. No. 90–130, 81 Stat. 374 (1967).

The myriad restrictions placed upon women keep them from economic self-sufficiency, keep them from educational achievements, and keep them from political mobilization. A distinguished member of this Court said a century ago, "The natural and proper timidity and delicacy which belongs to the female sex evidently unfits it for many of the occupations of civil life. The constitution of the family organization, which is founded in the divine ordinance, as well as in the nature of things, indicates the domestic sphere as that which properly belongs to the domain and functions of womanhood." *Bradwell v. Illinois*, 83 U.S. 130, 141 (1873) (Bradley, J., concurring). Even though woman's place in the domestic sphere has always been a myth, the law has restrained female performance outside the home – and if one is kept busy at the hearth, one cannot be active at the polls.

Women of this country may not be a discrete group, but they are individually isolated by social pressure to avoid employment if possible. Even if women hold employment outside the home, they are burdened in the domestic sphere with the home responsibilities and caregiving labor from which men are deemed free. Many women might choose this division of labor freely, but given the current legal disabilities placed upon women's full participation in the marketplace, it is impossible to tell what a truly equal female population would achieve as free members of society. Equal protection of the laws is guaranteed by the Constitution in precisely this context: a history of legal discrimination that prevents members of a group from vindicating their rights in the political process.

Appellees would have us distinguish between racial classifications, which are inherently suspect, and classifications based on sex, which are presumptively valid in their eyes, for another reason: that race is almost never germane to a legitimate goal, whereas the realities of gender in modern life demonstrate that it is frequently and understandably material to all manner of regulatory distinctions. Again, this argument fails. American society is rife with judgments that turn upon sex. As Alexis de Tocqueville wrote over a century ago, "In no country has such constant care been taken as in America to trace two clearly distinct lines of action for the two sexes ... in two pathways which are always different." 2 Alexis de Tocqueville, *Democracy in America* 259 (Henry Reeve tr. 1898). Only a few decades later Justice Bradley famously wrote, "The paramount destiny and mission of women are to fulfill the noble and benign offices of wife and mother... [T]he rules of civil society must be adapted to the general constitution of things, and cannot be based upon exceptional cases." *Bradwell v. Illinois*, 83 U.S. 130, 141–42 (1873) (Bradley, J., concurring).

It is not clear, however, that such judgments as to women's mission have any basis in reality. The logic that race bears no relationship to permissible legislative goals whereas sex does is consistent only if one builds an edifice of social expectation and stereotype upon the relatively minor biological differences between men and women. Society binds women to hearth and home, then decades later presents a gendered society as a fait accompli. Even where there might be arguably relevant differences between men and women statistically, such generalizations cannot justify different and adverse treatment of individual women. Men may be on average stronger than women, but not every man is stronger than every woman. Longstanding categorical exclusions of women from occupations such as fire fighters and soldiers were based on little more than such blunt generalizations, yet in times of need such as World War II, women ably stepped into those positions. Exclusions of women from legal, medical, and other professions lack even the purported justification of average abilities, yet are just as powerful and persistent.

It is irrelevant for our purposes that some would justify classifications based on sex as benign or even protective of women rather than oppression. It is true that this Court has repeatedly upheld statutes classifying on the basis of sex where such classifications are supposedly justified by the need to protect women. As the Senate Judiciary Committee recently explained, however, "it is under the guise of protection that much of the sex discrimination in this country [has been] perpetrated." U.S. Senate Committee on the Judiciary, Equal Rights for Men and Women, S. Rep. No. 92–689, at 20 (2d. Sess. 1972). Sex discrimination has not been enforced because of bare hatred of women, but has been more commonly defended with women's perceived vulnerabilities and the need to preserve them for their responsibilities in the domestic sphere.

The language of our own precedents demonstrates the point. At the beginning of this century, this Court upheld against constitutional challenge an Oregon statute prohibiting women from working more than ten hours in one day. *Muller v. Oregon*, 208 U.S. 412 (1908). The Court compared women to children in that both need "especial care" for protection, particularly because

> woman's physical structure and the performance of maternal functions place her at a disadvantage ... [C]ontinuance for a long time on her feet at work, repeating this from day to day, tends to injurious effects upon the body, and, as healthy mothers are essential to vigorous offspring, the physical well-being of woman becomes an object of public interest and care in order to preserve the strength and vigor of the race.
>
> *Id.* at 421.

Similarly, Justice Frankfurter wrote forty years later that Michigan could legitimately prohibit women from working as bartenders due to the "moral and social problems" that may arise in that profession – unless female bartenders were the spouse or daughter of the man who owned the bar, in which case he could provide protection from those dangers. *Goesaert v. Cleary*, 335 U.S. 464, 466 (1948). This Court's own decisions, still binding as precedent on lower courts throughout the nation, cast women as comparable to children: susceptible both physically and morally to harm from being out in working society. Such paternalistic sentiments are problematic not only because of their patronizing attitude towards women, but also because they beg the question. Women have been deemed in need of protection by men only because women have been precluded from demonstrating their strength and ability to protect themselves.

Another thread of justifications for discrimination operates by keeping women focused on domestic responsibilities. In *Muller*, this Court rationalized that "a proper discharge of [woman's] maternal functions – having in view not merely her own health, but the well-being of the race – justif[ies] legislation to protect her from the greed as well as the passion of man." *Muller*, 208 U.S. at 422. More recently this Court found unobjectionable a statute placing women on juries only if they voluntarily opted into such service, as

> woman is still regarded as the center of home and family life. We cannot say that it is constitutionally impermissible for a State ... to conclude that a woman should be relieved from the civic duty of jury service unless she herself determines that such service is consistent with her own special responsibilities.
>
> *Hoyt v. Florida*, 368 U.S. 57, 62 (1961).

Both explanations – woman's vulnerability and her domestic responsibilities – are founded upon stereotypes, and have the effect of restricting women to the home. The brunt of such supposedly protective and benign discrimination has been felt by women, whose choices and lives have been constrained for centuries.

It is important, however, to note that recognizing women as a suspect class benefits men as well. All sex-based classifications are subject to strict scrutiny, and sex-based classifications affect both sexes. Just as women have been told to remain at home, men have been told to leave it – using gender as a proxy for responsibilities and roles tells both men and women that if they wish to order their lives differently than the stereotype of their gender, the law will act as a burden upon their lives. Both Sharron and Joseph Frontiero are affected by the regulations and statutes at issue here, as are all other families in which the wife chooses to serve her country in the military, by higher administrative burdens to receive benefits or by denial of benefits that a family with the gender roles reversed would receive automatically. As we saw last term in *Stanley v. Illinois*, an unmarried father can be harmed by sex-based classifications as well. 405 U.S. 645 (1972). In that case, Illinois created an inflexible statutory presumption that unmarried fathers were unfit parents, even though unmarried mothers were not similarly judged, and even though many unmarried fathers such as Peter Stanley provided care for their children. *Id.* In this case, assumptions regarding employment outside the home apply financial pressure against families in which wives provide economic support through military service. Men have been so busy building a wall to keep women from the market and inside the home that they have barely noticed that they have walled themselves out as well.

Statutes that draw a distinction based on sex must therefore be subjected to the highest constitutional scrutiny. Such distinctions presumptively violate the equal protection of the laws, and will survive scrutiny only if the state proves that the classification is narrowly tailored to achieve a compelling government purpose. In assessing such laws, courts will ask whether the state's explanation rests upon gender stereotypes and if the purpose or effect of the classification is to strengthen such stereotypes. If the result of a classification is to make it more difficult for women to hold employment outside the home, to subordinate women's earning capacities to their domestic or reproductive capacities, to cast men as the breadwinners for their families, or to otherwise underscore gender stereotypes, then the classification is inherently discriminatory and unconstitutional.

It is possible that in the next few years, this decision could receive additional textual support in the form of the Equal Rights Amendment (ERA), currently being considered by the states for ratification. We see no need to hold our decision or analysis because of this. The prospect of future legislative, even constitutional, reform and revision does not change the meaning of the Constitution's present form. At the same time, the Constitution is a living document, in that the values it enshrines must be vindicated as the passage of time often grants us a clearer understanding of those values. It is unsurprising that members of the judicial and legislative branches would come to a fuller understanding of equality at roughly the same time as state legislatures and society as a whole. It is worth noting that the sponsors of the ERA themselves view the proposed amendment as redundant, in that they too understand the Equal Protection Clause to already mandate equal treatment regardless of sex. Br. of ACLU as Amicus Curiae at 19.

This Court need not be, and indeed has never universally been, paces ahead of every evolution in America's understanding of the Constitution and its guarantees. If after this decision the ERA is ratified and becomes part of the Constitution that this Court is charged with interpreting, then our holding today is doubly clear. That possibility does not, however, change the meaning of the Equal Protection Clause today.

III

With this framework in mind, we turn our analysis to the statutes and regulations at issue. At present, all wives of military personnel are considered dependents for the purpose of allocating supplemental housing and medical benefits. By contrast, husbands of military personnel are treated as dependents only if the soldier proves that her husband relies upon her for over half of his expenses. This is plainly a classification based upon sex, and thus will be permitted only if it is necessary to achieve a compelling government purpose and neither rests upon nor promotes gender stereotypes.

The goal of offering such benefits to military personnel is to support members of the United States military and presumably to make military service affordable and appealing to Americans. This is a goal of the highest order. The means used to pursue this goal, however, apply different and incompatible evaluation systems to male and female members of the armed forces. Female soldiers are burdened in two ways as compared to male soldiers: first, some number of soldiers will be unable to receive the benefits at issue, because the spouse provides over half of his expenses, as is the case with Sharron and Joseph Frontiero. Second, even soldiers who are eligible for the benefits must overcome the administrative requirements of submitting evidence of all income and other received support for both themselves and their husbands, as well as documenting their husbands' expenses.

The government would justify these comparative hardships with administrative convenience. Faced with the administrative cost of individually examining applications from each married soldier for dependency, it has lit upon sex as a proxy, citing the historical state of affairs that men are employed more frequently and at higher wages than women are. Administrative convenience in the abstract is not a compelling government interest, and Appellees fail to demonstrate the classification at issue furthers that non-compelling goal.

Even a cursory examination reveals numerous faults with Appellees' argument. To begin with, even if we take as true the government's assumption that on average, men earn higher wages than women, that does not demonstrate dependency as the military defines it.[37] If simply being the lesser-earning spouse makes one dependent, then Joseph Frontiero would be clearly dependent upon Lieutenant Frontiero, as his monthly income from all sources is approximately half of his wife's. Instead, the military takes yet another factor into account – the expenses of the purportedly dependent spouse – and compares the non-military spouse's income to his expenses. The government has provided no reason as to why gender should serve as a proxy not only for lower income, but also higher expenses relative to that lower income, as well as how the soldier spouse's income compares to both of these figures. A far simpler inference – that men on average have achieved higher education and have more employment experience, and thus would make more competent administrators of estates – was held to be irrational last term. *See Reed v. Reed*, 404 U.S. 71 (1971). If *Reed*'s use of gender as proxy did not withstand scrutiny, use of gender as proxy for expenses and income cannot either.

Furthermore, the government has given no evidence supporting the stereotype that wives of soldiers are dependent while husbands of soldiers are not. Appellants marshal plenty of statistics in their favor, however. For example, to test the assumption that wives of male soldiers are dependent upon them, one could compare the median salary of men in the military with the median salary of women generally – yet if these figures are juxtaposed, women make

---

[37] It is worth noting, however, that this assumption elides significant employment and earning by women, which is according to some statistics comparable to the median salary of male servicemembers. *See* U.S. Women's Bureau, Dep't of Labor, Fact Sheet on the Earnings Gap 1 (1971) (finding the 1970 median income for women employed full-time to be $5,323); The President's commission on an All-Volunteer Armed Force, The Report of the President's Commission on an All-Volunteer Armed Force 51, 181 (1970) (finding the 1970 median salary of male servicemembers to be $3,686).

significantly *more* than male soldiers. Br. for Appellants at 51. Given that almost 60 percent of married women living with their husbands are employed, it is quite possible that the *majority* of the time, the wife of an individual soldier is both employed and earns enough to pay for half of her expenses. Br. of ACLU as Amicus Curiae at 45. It may be that these median and statistical figures combine to a different result in individual couples, but the fact remains that the only tangible facts upon which we can judge the accuracy or appropriateness of administrative convenience uniformly indicate that the government's explanation is not only unsupported, but likely inaccurate. If the goal of the supplemental benefits program is to provide for dependent spouses, the classification is both under- and over-inclusive: some female spouses are not dependent, and some male spouses are.

It is also relevant that in multiple other contexts, the federal government has rejected gender as proxy for administrative convenience. The Equal Employment Opportunity Commission specifies that it is "an unlawful employment practice for an employer to make available benefits for the wives and families of male employees where the same benefits are not made available for the husbands and families of female employees." 29 C.F.R. § 1604.9 (1972). In December 1971, Congress amended statutes regulating benefits for federal employees to equalize a number of supplemental benefits granted to male and female employees, including elimination of a comparable test for dependency in awarding widow and widower benefits. Pub. L. No. 92–187, 85 Stat. 644 (1971). Even more tellingly, Congress has recently discarded use of the same gendered definition of dependency as it applies to educational benefits awarded to veterans. Pub. L. No. 92–540, 86 Stat. 1074 (1972). It seems questionable at best for the government to assert administrative convenience when in multiple other arenas the government is not only eliminating this very regime but labeling it as discriminatory.

In any case, the justification of administrative convenience rests firmly upon impermissible gender stereotypes. Sex-based classifications that rest upon or strengthen gender stereotypes – in this case an assumption that men earn more than women, making it easier for men to receive employer-granted benefits – must be eliminated if we are ever to achieve gender equality. Even if the government performed an individualized assessment of every military member, and every married male soldier had a dependent wife while not a single married female soldier had a dependent husband, administrative convenience would not justify using gender as an ongoing proxy. Equality is not always the cheapest option, but it remains the only constitutional option nonetheless.

IV

Having found that the statutes and regulations at issue violate the Constitution, the question of remedy still lies before us. Given that use of gender as a categorical proxy for dependency is inappropriate, we could either declare the regime equally operative as to all, or equally inoperative as to all. *See Skinner v. Oklahoma ex rel. Williamson*, 316 U.S. 535, 541–43 (1942). In other words, we could either declare that the military must assume all spouses are dependent, or that no spouses are dependent, and thus individual applications must be made and assessed for all personnel.

In settling upon the appropriate remedy, we must consider the legislative purpose of the benefits program as a whole. *See Moritz v. Comm'r*, 469 F.2d 466, 469 (10th Cir. 1972). It is clear that the supplemental benefits in the instant case were extended in order to support our nation's military and to make continued military service more appealing. Furthermore, as discussed above, the government has eliminated similar use of gendered proxies by extending the benefits to all soldiers, rather than making all soldiers individually apply.

We hold that the gendered nature of the supplemental benefits programs at issue violates the Due Process Clause of the Fifth Amendment. Benefits should be granted to female service members according to the same process, presumptions and judgments by which they are granted to male service members.

Reversed.

10

Commentary on *Geduldig v. Aiello*

Maya Manian

INTRODUCTION

In *Geduldig v. Aiello*,[1] the U.S. Supreme Court infamously held that pregnancy discrimination is not sex discrimination under the Equal Protection Clause of the Fourteenth Amendment. The *Geduldig* decision upheld a California state disability insurance program that denied benefits for pregnancy-related disability, while granting benefits for virtually every other disabling event ranging from prostatectomies to cosmetic surgery.[2]

The legal community and the public reacted with ridicule and rejection.[3] Although the Court later attempted to apply *Geduldig*'s logic to the federal statutory prohibition on sex discrimination in employment[4] – including *Geduldig*'s notoriously obtuse declaration that pregnancy exclusions differentiate not between women and men but between "pregnant women and nonpregnant persons"[5] – Congress quickly overturned that decision with the Pregnancy Discrimination Act of 1978.[6] Despite sustained criticism, the *Geduldig* decision has never been explicitly overruled and continues to constrain women's access to substantive equality and reproductive liberty.

---

[1] *Geduldig v. Aiello*, 417 U.S. 484 (1974).
[2] *See id.* at 499–500 (Brennan, J., dissenting).
[3] *See* Sylvia A. Law, *Rethinking Sex and the Constitution*, 132 U. Pa. L. Rev. 955, 983, 1037 (1984) (describing widespread criticism of *Geduldig*).
[4] *See General Electric Co. v. Gilbert*, 429 U.S. 125 (1976).
[5] *Geduldig*, 417 U.S. at 496 n.20.
[6] Pub. L. No. 95–555, § 1, 92 Stat. 2076 (1978) (codified at 42 U.S.C. § 2000e).

THE *GEDULDIG* OPINION

In *Geduldig*, the Court was asked to decide whether California invidiously discriminated against women in violation of equal protection doctrine by excluding disabilities related to "normal" pregnancy and childbirth from its otherwise comprehensive employment disability insurance program. At the time, the U.S. Supreme Court had not yet clearly articulated that heightened scrutiny must apply for sex-based classifications, although it had strongly suggested as much in two recent cases, *Reed v. Reed* and *Frontiero v. Richardson*.[7] The Court had also recently emphasized the importance of reproductive liberty in *Cleveland Board of Education v. LaFleur*,[8] which struck down employers' forced maternity leave policies. Furthermore, the lower court opinion in *Geduldig* had held that California's pregnancy exclusion denied equal protection to women. The three-judge district court opinion had emphasized in particular that under the standard articulated in *Reed*, states cannot impose statutory classifications based upon gender stereotypes.[9]

Yet six justices, led by Justice Stewart, rejected the plaintiffs' claims. Most striking to many critics, the Court refused to recognize pregnancy discrimination as sex discrimination. The Court rejected the plaintiffs' argument that the heightened level of "rational basis" scrutiny applied in *Reed* and *Frontiero* should apply to the California statute, because the statute was "a far cry from cases like [*Reed* and *Frontiero*] involving discrimination based upon gender as such."[10] Instead, the Court declared: "There is no risk from which men are protected and women are not. Likewise, there is no risk from which women are protected and men are not."[11] The Court elaborated on this assertion in a crucial footnote, explaining:

> Absent a showing that distinctions involving pregnancy are mere pretexts designed to effect an invidious discrimination against the members of one sex or the other, lawmakers are constitutionally free to include or exclude pregnancy from the coverage of legislation such as this on any reasonable basis, just as with respect to any other physical condition. The lack of identity between the excluded disability and gender as such under this insurance program becomes clear upon the most cursory analysis. The program

---

[7] *Reed v. Reed*, 404 U.S. 71 (1971); *Frontiero v. Richardson*, 411 U.S. 677 (1973).
[8] *Cleveland Bd. of Educ. v. LaFleur*, 414 U.S. 632 (1974).
[9] *See Aiello v. Hansen*, 359 F. Supp. 792, 797–801 (N.D. Cal. 1973).
[10] *Geduldig*, 417 U.S. at 496 n.20.
[11] *Id.* at 496–97.

divides potential recipients into two groups – pregnant women and non-pregnant persons.[12]

This exceedingly narrow definition of sex discrimination both ignores the obvious and elides the profound social and economic effects of pregnancy on women. The *Geduldig* majority proclaimed that gender was not even at issue, ignoring the long history of women's subordination based on their capacity for pregnancy and making no mention of the lower court's finding that the program's pregnancy exclusions both rely on and reinforce sex role stereotypes about women.[13]

Having decided that pregnancy discrimination is not sex discrimination, the Court applied minimal rational basis review and accepted the state's cost-based rationales. The Court declared that California's policy interests in a 1 percent employee contribution rate, the existing rate of benefits, and the solvency of the program at those rates provided "an objective and wholly noninvidious basis" for the program.[14] In justifying its conclusion, the Court emphasized that California intended the program to "function essentially in accordance with insurance concepts" and noted that women already received more from the fund than they contributed.[15] The Court failed to address the lower court's counterpoint that California's disability insurance program was in fact designed "so that its likely effect will be that those earning small incomes will receive more in benefits than they contribute" and that California had made no "consistent attempt to limit benefits of various groups based upon actuarial considerations."[16]

Geduldig's abstract illogic and ahistorical analysis severed women's reproductive liberty from sex equality analysis, impoverishing both strands of interdependent doctrines.

THE FEMINIST JUDGMENT

Professor Lucinda Finley, writing as Justice Finley, responds to the faulty formalist logic of the original opinion in distinctively feminist ways. First, the revised opinion foregrounds women's experience of pregnancy-related discrimination and places the statute within that historical context. Incorporating understandings of the long history of sex discrimination and women's lived

---

[12] *Id.* at 496 n.20.
[13] *See Aiello v. Hansen*, 359 F. Supp. at 797–801.
[14] *Geduldig*, 417 U.S. at 496.
[15] *Id.* at 492, 497 n.21.
[16] *Aiello v. Hansen*, 359 F. Supp. at 800.

experiences of that discrimination into legal discourse has been a central goal of legal feminists.[17] Unlike the original opinion, Finley's feminist judgment takes as its starting point the historical context and contemporary reality of widespread disadvantages imposed upon women based on their reproductive capacities. Finley embeds women's experiences throughout, from explaining the "intuitively obvious" reasons why pregnancy-based classifications constitute sex-based discrimination to highlighting why the state's alleged cost concerns actually reflect gender stereotypes.

Second, Finley's judgment accomplishes the key feminist move of unmasking the invisible male norm undergirding the Court's supposed formal equality approach. Finley's judgment makes clear that the government's argument fails even a formal equality analysis. Turning to the proper framework of comparison – focusing on the effect of pregnancy exclusions rather than the risks covered – Finley's judgment reveals how the law, by enshrining male biology as the norm, treats men more favorably. California's scheme provided disability coverage for all men's health care needs but not for all women's health care needs. Yet, Finley's judgment reaches further than formal equality, embracing a richer vision of equality that also aims for anti-stereotyping and anti-subordination. Moving beyond the "treat likes alike" formula, Finley's judgment exposes the sex role stereotypes animating the exclusion of pregnant women from workplace benefits. The judgment calls for rejection of stereotypes about women's natural roles as mothers and the subordination that results from those stereotypes.

Third, Finley's judgment takes on the crucial task of linking women's reproductive liberty to sex equality. She emphasizes how women's reproductive capacity has long been used as a rationale to promote "separate spheres" ideology and to exclude women from employment, education, and civic participation.[18] Finley's feminist revision of *Geduldig* recognizes that the right to reproductive liberty and the right to sex equality are inextricably intertwined rights of full citizenship, a vision legal feminists had been fighting for at the time of the decision.[19]

In sum, Finley's feminist judgment reaches beyond the formal appearance of justice and seeks substantive fairness for women in the public sphere.

---

[17] *See* Martha Chamallas, Introduction to Feminist Legal Theory 1–15 (3d ed. 2013).

[18] *See* Lucinda M. Finley, *Transcending Equality Theory: A Way Out of the Maternity and the Workplace Debate*, 86 Colum. L. Rev. 1118, 1119–122 (1986) (describing and critiquing separate spheres ideology and traditional equality analysis).

[19] *See* Deborah Dinner, *Recovering the LaFleur Doctrine*, 22 Yale J.L. & Fem. 343, 347–48, 387–94 (2010).

IMPLICATIONS

Geduldig's impact on the law has been widespread and lasting, diminishing the law's understandings of sex equality, reproductive liberty, and the relationship between the two. *Geduldig's* parsimonious logic reverberates through judicial decisions governing women's access to abortion care, contraception, and protection from discrimination.

For example, the U.S. Supreme Court implicitly relied on *Geduldig's* reasoning in holding that the federal government did not violate constitutional equality or reproductive liberty principles by denying Medicaid funding for poor women's abortion care – even for medically necessary abortions.[20] *Geduldig's* echoes can be heard in the U.S. Supreme Court's recent decision in *Burwell v. Hobby Lobby*, which held that for-profit corporations could claim religious liberty exemptions from the Affordable Care Act's contraceptive coverage mandate.[21] As in *Geduldig*, the *Hobby Lobby* decision erased concern for women's right to equal treatment from its analysis of women's right to receive employee benefits related to their reproductive health.[22]

Geduldig also continues to affect the interpretation of statutes protecting against pregnancy-related discrimination in employment. Although the Pregnancy Discrimination Act (PDA) reversed the U.S. Supreme Court's decision in *General Electric Co. v. Gilbert*,[23] which applied *Geduldig's* reasoning to Title VII, *Geduldig's* imprint reveals itself in some courts' cramped interpretations of the PDA. Lower courts have parroted *Geduldig's* logic in upholding the exclusion of contraceptive coverage from employer health insurance plans.[24]

The landscape of sex equality law would look dramatically different if the Court had adopted Finley's feminist judgment – a tantalizing possibility since the intellectual foundations for this feminist judgment existed at the time. Many scholars have noted that integrating sex equality arguments with reproductive liberty arguments would have provided a stronger constitutional

[20] *See Maher v. Roe*, 432 U.S. 464 (1977); *Harris v. McRae*, 448 U.S. 297 (1980). In contrast to the U.S. Supreme Court, some state courts have concluded that denying coverage to women for medically necessary abortions while providing coverage for all of men's medical needs constitutes sex discrimination. *See, e.g., New Mexico Right to Choose/NARAL v. Johnson*, 975 P.2d 841, 850–57 (N.M. 1998).

[21] *Burwell v. Hobby Lobby Stores, Inc.*, 134 S. Ct. 2751 (2014).

[22] *See* Elizabeth Sepper, *Gendering Corporate Conscience*, 38 Harv. J.L. & Gender 193, 194–95, 202–12 (2015).

[23] *General Electric v. Gilbert*, 429 U.S. 125 (1976).

[24] *See, e.g., In re Union Pacific Railroad Employment Practices Litigation*, 479 F.3d 936 (8th Cir. 2007).

foundation for abortion rights, and ensured equal access to abortion care for women without economic means.[25] By severing the link between reproductive liberty and sex equality, *Geduldig* impeded both conceptual and doctrinal development of the law in ways that could have provided firmer ground for abortion rights.

Similarly, the feminist *Geduldig* opinion would likely have expanded protection for women's access to contraception. Perhaps *Hobby Lobby* would have come out differently if a more robust foundation had been laid for recognizing that women's claims to reproductive justice fundamentally intersect with sex equality. Certainly, Finley's feminist judgment would have led to reversal of lower court decisions concluding that it is not sex discrimination to exclude contraceptive coverage from employer health insurance plans.

Furthermore, *Gilbert* would surely have come out differently in its interpretation of Title VII. Even with the enactment of the PDA, Finley's feminist version of *Geduldig* could have guided courts to less stingy interpretations of legislation barring pregnancy-related discrimination.

Geduldig continues to cast a long shadow over women's interdependent claims to reproductive liberty and gender equality. It remains to be seen whether, despite *Geduldig*, the law will yet develop a richer vision of sex equality based on a less formalist and more substantive understanding of the links between women's capacity to reproduce and women's subordination.[26]

Geduldig v. Aiello, 417 U.S. 484 (1974)

Justice Lucinda M. Finley delivered the opinion of the Court.

I

Women's ability to become pregnant and bear children has long been used as a rationale to deprive them of the economic security and independence, intellectual development, societal opportunity and respect that can come from full participation in the workplace. Through the operation of employer policies and federal and state laws, women have been barred from certain professions or

---

[25] *See, e.g.*, Elizabeth M. Schneider, *The Synergy of Equality and Privacy in Women's Rights*, 2002 U. Chi. Legal F. 137, 147–54 (2002).

[26] In *Nevada Dept. of Human Resources v. Hibbs*, 538 U.S. 721 (2003), the Court for the first time held that legal regulation of pregnant women based on sex-role stereotypes may violate the Equal Protection Clause, but did not explicitly overrule *Geduldig*. *See also* Reva B. Siegel, *You've Come A Long Way, Baby: Rehnquist's New Approach to Pregnancy Discrimination in Hibbs*, 58 Stan. L. Rev. 1871, 1882–97 (2006) (discussing implications of *Hibbs* for future interpretations of *Geduldig*).

subjected to limited work hours due to assumptions about the implications of their maternal role. *Bradwell v. Illinois*, 83 U.S. 130 (1873) (prohibiting a woman from the practice of law); *Muller v. Oregon*, 208 U.S. 412 (1908) (limiting the number of hours women can work in laundries). They have been subjected to mandatory leave or discharge due to pregnancy. *Cleveland Bd. of Educ. v. La Fleur*, 414 U.S. 632 (1974); *Struck v. Secretary of Defense*, 460 F.2d 1372 (9th Cir. 1971), *vacated and remanded to consider mootness*, 409 U.S. 1071 (1972). They have been barred from returning to work for several months after childbirth. *LaFleur*, 414 U.S. at 634–35. They have been denied seniority accumulation while on forced periods of leave; they have been excluded from utilizing sick leave benefits or from receiving unemployment compensation when absent from work due to the effects of pregnancy; they have often been denied coverage under employer-provided health insurance for health care costs related to pregnancy. *See* Citizens' Advisory Council On The Status of Women, *Job Related Maternity Benefits* (1970); Colquitt Walker, *Sex Discrimination in Government Benefits Programs*, 23 Hastings L.J. 277, 282–85 (1971); Br. for Am. Fed'n of Labor and Council of Indus. Org. as Amicus Curiae; Br. for ACLU as Amicus Curiae; Trudy Hayden, *Punishing Pregnancy: Discrimination in Education, Employment and Credit* (ACLU 1973).

Indeed, it is fair to say that most of the disadvantages imposed on women in the workforce derive from the capacity of women to become pregnant and from the societal and legal responses to the real or supposed implications of this reality. Assumptions and stereotypes about the physical and emotional effects of pregnancy and motherhood, about the appropriate role of women in society and the workplace stemming from the physical fact of childbearing, and about the perceived response of women to childbearing, have contributed more than any other factor to the disadvantageous treatment of women in the workplace and to their economically subordinated position in society.

It is in light of this historical context and contemporary reality that this case comes before us, and requires us squarely to decide whether exclusionary workplace policies constitute discrimination on the basis of sex when they are based on pregnancy and operate to disadvantage women. If so, does the Equal Protection Clause of the Fourteenth Amendment to the Constitution prohibit disadvantageous treatment of pregnancy and related conditions that may render women temporarily unable to work?

Plaintiff-Appellees are four women who became pregnant, were temporarily unable to work due to physical conditions related to their pregnancies, and were ineligible for payments under California's temporary disability insurance system solely because their temporary disabilities were due to pregnancy. California Unemployment Insurance Code § 2626 excludes from its otherwise

comprehensive disability insurance coverage "any injury or illness caused by
or arising in connection with pregnancy up to the termination of pregnancy
and for a period of 28 days thereafter." Plaintiffs challenged this exclusion as a
violation of their right to the equal protection of the law.

II

Concerned about the economic hardship that workers can experience when
they are temporarily unable to work due to physical or mental conditions,
California enacted a comprehensive disability insurance program in 1946.
The program's stated purpose is "to compensate in part for the wage loss sustained by individuals unemployed because of sickness or injury and to reduce
to a minimum the suffering caused by unemployment resulting therefrom."
Cal. Unemp. Ins. Code § 2601. The statute further commands that "it shall
be construed liberally in aid of its declared purpose to mitigate the evils and
burdens which fall on the unemployed" and their families. Id.

The disability program is funded by mandatory employee contributions. At
present, employees must contribute 1 percent of their salary up to a maximum
of $85 per year. Id. §§ 984, 985, 2901. In order to be eligible to receive benefits,
an employee must have contributed 1 percent of a minimum income of $300
during a one-year base period previous to the time of disability. Id. § 2652. For
up to twenty-six weeks, an eligible employee may receive a basic benefit level
currently varying between $25 and $119 per week depending on the amount
earned during the base period. Id. §§ 2653, 2655. Benefits can begin after the
eighth day of disability, or can begin on the first day of hospitalization if the
employee is hospitalized. Id. §§ 2627(b), 2802. Claims must be substantiated
by the affidavit of a licensed medical practitioner attesting to the disability, and
employees may also be required to submit to reasonable examinations. Id. §§
2627(c), (d), 2708, 2710.

Reflecting its broad prophylactic purpose of buffering the adverse economic impact of being temporarily unable to work regardless of the reason,
the program provides benefits for incapacities stemming from virtually all
conditions or activities. The sole exception is that during pregnancy and for
twenty-eight days after childbirth or pregnancy termination, women may
not receive benefits for any temporary work incapacity stemming from the
pregnancy itself or from any illness or injury caused by or arising in connection with the pregnancy. Id. § 2626.[27] Plaintiff-Appellees, all of whom

---

[27] The legislation establishing the disability insurance program restricts the eligibility of those
who have been judicially ordered to be confined to an institution due to drug addiction

were denied disability benefits when they experienced temporary disabilities in connection with their pregnancies, challenge the disadvantageous treatment they suffered as a result of § 2626 as a denial of their right to the equal protection of the law.

Plaintiff Carolyn Aiello, who is self-supporting, had to stop work as a hairdresser in late June 1972, when she had to be hospitalized because she was suffering from an ectopic pregnancy. After surgery to terminate this life-threatening condition, her physician advised her to remain off work for over a month to recuperate. She promptly applied for temporary disability benefits, which were denied solely because her disability arose in connection with pregnancy.

Plaintiff Augustina Armendariz works as a secretary, and she is the sole economic support for herself, her husband, and their young son. In early May 1972, she began to bleed while pregnant, and had to be rushed to the hospital, where she suffered a miscarriage. Her physician ordered her not to return to work until the end of May. She applied for temporary disability benefits, and her claim was also denied on the sole basis that her disability arose in connection with pregnancy.

Plaintiff Elizabeth Johnson works as an operator for the telephone company, and her job provides the primary economic support for her household, which includes herself and her five-year-old son. Ms. Johnson entered the hospital on May 22, 1972, after experiencing intense abdominal pain, swelling in the legs, back pain, and general illness. She was diagnosed as having a tubal pregnancy and, in order to save her life, an operation was performed to terminate the pregnancy. She was discharged from the hospital on May 30, and her physician advised her not to return to work until July 10. Her disability insurance claim was denied for the sole reason that her disability was disqualified by § 2626's pregnancy exclusion.

The final individual plaintiff, Jacqueline Jaramillo, works to provide the sole economic support for herself, her husband who is a student, and their infant. While she did not experience any of the life-threatening pregnancy complications endured by the other plaintiffs, she did require a period of rest and recuperation after her normal vaginal delivery, during which she could not work. She seeks disability benefits for the period she was incapacitated from working due to the delivery of her child.

---

or sexual psychopathology. *Id.* § 2678. At oral argument, however, counsel for Appellant California conceded that such judicial orders are artifacts no longer used, so that this exclusion does not in fact exclude anyone. Tr. of Oral Arg.

Plaintiffs sued, seeking a declaratory judgment that § 2626 violated the Equal Protection Clause of the Fourteenth Amendment by excluding pregnancy, a condition that only women experience. They also sought to enjoin enforcement of the statute as well as to recover the disability insurance payments they would be entitled to if § 2626 is invalid. Because their suit sought to enjoin a state statute, it was heard by a three-judge court pursuant to 28 U.S.C. § 2281.

The lower court, in a divided 2–1 opinion, concluded that the exclusion of pregnancy-related conditions constituted discrimination on the basis of a sex-linked condition. The district court also ruled that the appropriate standard of review to determine whether the pregnancy exclusion was a denial of equal protection of the law was the "heightened scrutiny" we applied in *Reed v. Reed*, 404 U.S. 71 (1971), for sex-based classifications, where we did not simply accept, without critical examination, any proffered rational basis put forth by the state. The lower court determined that the exclusion was based on the same sort of stereotypes about women's maternal role versus their public and workplace role that led us to invalidate the automatic preference for male estate administrators in *Reed*. Under this more rigorous standard of review, the exclusion of pregnancy was not at all related to the statutory purpose, since women who are experiencing temporary disability related to pregnancy are just as much in need of economic support as are workers who are experiencing temporary work disruption because of the physical effects of any other condition. The lower court thus rejected California's proffered rationale that fiscal concerns for the solvency of the program under the current contribution and benefit structure warranted the exclusion of pregnancy, noting that the state had numerous sex-neutral options for maintaining fiscal solvency while covering disabilities relating to pregnancy. *Aiello v. Hansen*, 359 F. Supp. 792 (N.D. Cal. 1973).

California appealed.

III

Before turning to the merits, we must determine whether recent revisions to the interpretation of California's pregnancy exclusion render the claims of three of the four plaintiffs moot, and if so, how to reframe the issue we must decide. Just prior to the lower court ruling, the California Court of Appeal determined that § 2626 did not bar disability benefits for work absences necessitated by conditions related to complications associated with an abnormal pregnancy, such as ectopic pregnancy. *Rentzer v. California Unemp. Ins. Bd.*, 32 Cal. App. 3d 604 (1973). This decision was issued just days before the district court ruling here, and the lower court rejected California's motion to reconsider its decision in light of *Rentzer*. The state accepted the statutory construction adopted by the court in *Rentzer*, and subsequently issued administrative guidelines that the exclusion of pregnancy-related conditions in § 2626 applied only to exclude payment for "maternity benefits," i.e., hospitalization and disability benefits for normal pregnancy, delivery, and recuperation. Based on *Rentzer* and the new administrative guidelines, Appellees Aiello, Armendariz, and Johnson, who suffered from the disabling effects of ectopic pregnancies and miscarriage, became eligible for benefits, and their claims have now been paid. Their claims are thus moot, and only the challenge of Ms. Jaramillo continues to present a live controversy. Consequently, the issue we must decide in this appeal is whether the exclusion from California's otherwise comprehensive disability insurance program of temporary disabilities associated with normal pregnancy and childbirth constitutes a sex-based exclusion that disadvantages women and perpetuates their economic and social subordination, and thus violates the Equal Protection Clause.

IV

To determine whether California's exclusion of conditions associated with normal pregnancy violates the Equal Protection Clause, we must first determine whether it is based on or related to sex, and if so, operates to disadvantage women. The lower court assumed that exclusion based on pregnancy, which only women experience, and which thus adversely impacts only women, is sex related and discriminatory. While this conclusion seems obvious, Appellant and Justice Stewart and the other dissenting justices strenuously contend that pregnancy-based classifications are not sex-based discrimination. Thus, before embracing the intuitively obvious, we must examine the issue in greater depth, being ever mindful of the historical context we outlined at the outset.

The capacity to become pregnant and bear children quintessentially distinguishes women from men. Thus, pregnancy is inextricably a sex-based distinction – only women can become pregnant. Appellant contends that this biological fact makes pregnancy unique and that as a result, pregnant women simply are not similarly situated to men, and so classifications based on pregnancy thus do not inevitably constitute sex discrimination. As Justice Stewart puts it in his dissent, by excluding only pregnancy from the covered risks, "there is no risk from which men are protected and women are not. Likewise, there is no risk from which women are protected and men are not." 417 U.S. at 496–97.

There are several flaws in this reasoning. First, Appellant's and the dissenters' focus on the "uniqueness" of pregnancy, and their comparison of the physical risks women are protected from with those that men are protected from,
are irrelevant to the purpose and structure of California's disability insurance
program. As explicitly stated in California Unemployment Insurance Code §
2601, the program's broad purpose was to protect workers from the economic
hardship of periods of being physically or mentally unable to work, regardless
of the reason for the disability or the nature of the underlying physical condition that caused the disability. California's program simply was not structured
to protect workers only from some physical risks, and not others. The uniqueness of a physical condition to one sex or the other is of no import. Indeed,
with the notable exception of pregnancy, the program covers disabilities stemming from several sex-specific risks, including prostatectomies, hysterecto-
mies, and treatment for endometriosis.

The question whether the exclusion of pregnancy-related disabilities leaves
women similarly situated to men cannot be answered by facile resort to the
uniqueness of pregnancy. It must be answered solely with reference to the
purpose of the program, not to the nature of the underlying risk or cause of
the temporary disability. *See Reed*, 404 U.S. at 76. Thus, the relevant comparison to determine whether women are treated equally is whether women have
as comprehensive coverage as men do for all the normal and likely conditions
and risks that may render them temporarily unable to work. Using the purpose
of the insurance program as the frame for analysis, the relevant comparative
group is not, as the dissent proposes, the women-only group of pregnant persons versus the mixed gender group of non-pregnant persons. Rather, it is the
male-only group of workers who receive disability payments when temporarily unable to work due to any condition or risk that they might conceivably
face, and the group, including only women, who receive a much less comprehensive level of protection, since women cannot receive insurance payments
when temporarily disabled due to a condition they commonly experience.
Normal pregnancy, like all the other conditions whose effects men are protected from, requires medical care, can lead to periods of sickness, hormonal
imbalance, hospitalization, and surgery such as episiotomies, and can require
periods of rest and absence from work in order to recover from its physical
and mental effects. Absences from work due to the effects of pregnancy and
childbirth can lead to economic hardship for women and their families. The
effects of pregnancy, physical and economic, are no different from the effects
of all the conditions for which men receive disability insurance payments. By
excluding pregnancy-related conditions, California creates a vast difference
in the comprehensiveness of coverage for men and women, and fails to treat

the uniquely female condition of pregnancy the same as any and all conditions that render male workers temporarily unable to work. This constitutes sex-based discrimination.

This framework of comparison for determining whether women workers are treated equally to male workers is consistent with the interpretation of the Equal Employment Opportunity Commission (EEOC), the federal agency charged with interpreting and enforcing Title VII of the 1964 Civil Rights Act, 42 U.S.C. § 2000e *et seq.* (1970 ed. Supp. II), the federal statute prohibiting employment discrimination, including discrimination on the basis of sex. The EEOC has declared:

> Disabilities caused or contributed to by pregnancy, miscarriage, abortion, childbirth, and recovery therefrom are, for all job-related purposes, temporary disabilities and should be treated as such under any health or temporary disability insurance or sick leave plan available in connection with employment. Written and unwritten employment policies and practices involving matters such as the commencement and duration of leave, the availability of extensions, the accrual of seniority and other benefits and privileges, reinstatement, and payment under any health or temporary disability insurance or sick leave plan, formal or informal, shall be applied to disability due to pregnancy or childbirth on the same terms and conditions as they are applied to other temporary disabilities.
>
> 29 CFR § 1604.10 (b).

The EEOC adopted this interpretive guideline for Title VII's ban on sex discrimination in employment after carefully scrutinizing both employer practices and their crucial impact on women. Based on this examination, "it became increasingly apparent that systematic and pervasive discrimination against women was frequently found in employers' denial of employment opportunity and benefits to women on the basis of the childbearing role, performed solely by women." Br. for EEOC as Amicus Curiae at 10.

While this case requires us to interpret the Constitution, rather than Title VII, the EEOC's expertise in what constitutes sex discrimination in employment is highly instructive. The agency's conclusion that the failure to treat pregnancy-related disabilities the same as all other conditions that render workers temporarily unable to work constitutes sex-based discrimination bolsters our similar determination that California's exclusion of pregnancy-related conditions deprives its women workers of equal treatment under the law.

In addition to using an irrelevant comparative framework focused on the nature of the risk rather than the effect of the condition, Appellant's and the dissent's focus on the "uniqueness" of pregnancy raises the question of why women should be deprived of workplace benefits for engaging in procreative activity when men are not. Surely a better justification than the uniqueness of women's way of procreating compared with men's should be required before women are disadvantaged. Moreover, the assertion that pregnancy is unique and that pregnancy's "uniqueness" removes it from the reach of the Equal Protection Clause simply enshrines male biology, needs, benefits, and privileges as the supposedly objective norm against which all equal protection claims for sex discrimination should be assessed. Pregnancy is "unique" only because it is not something that males experience. The physical risks that men are protected from – even those that are biologically unique to men – should not become the sole yardstick for assessing whether women are adequately covered for all the risks they might experience. While failing to accord women who are similarly situated to men the same treatment as men can certainly violate the Equal Protection Clause, see Reed, 404 U.S. at 76, it is not the only type of gender-based distinction that can deprive women of the equal protection of the law. An equality doctrine that implicitly says that women can claim equality only insofar as they are just like men is an impoverished concept of equality, unable to protect women from the disadvantages they have long suffered because of sex role stereotypes often based on their biological, reproductive "uniqueness." Being biologically different from men does not have to mean that women should be disadvantaged or subordinated due to their difference. Women are entitled not only to equal treatment with men, but also to equal opportunities for education, employment, and civic participation without barriers emanating from laws and policies that are based on stereotypes about women's "natural" roles. See Pauli Murray and Mary Eastwood, Jane Crow and the Law: Sex Discrimination and Title VII, 34 Geo. Wash. L. Rev. 232 (1965).

The way in which women contribute to procreation, by becoming pregnant and giving birth to a child, has accompanying physical risks that can lead to a period of physical inability to work. The way in which men contribute to procreation, by impregnating, does not have similar physical risks. Thus, a disability insurance plan that excludes physical conditions related to pregnancy imposes an economic penalty on women who engage in procreative activity, but imposes no such economic deprivation on men. As we intimated earlier this term in LaFleur, when we found it unconstitutional to make unpaid maternity leave mandatory at a predetermined point during pregnancy regardless of an individual's ability to work, laws and policies that deny equal employment opportunities to women because of their procreative role can infringe on their right to reproductive liberty. The present case makes it evident that denial of equal employment opportunity to women because they are pregnant not only infringes reproductive liberty, but it also undermines equality between the sexes. Men are not at risk of loss of employment, disability protection, seniority, or economic security when they decide to procreate. Women too often are, not because of the uniqueness of their procreative role, but because of the way laws and workplace policies choose to treat that role. Laws such as California's exclusion of pregnancy-related conditions from the disability insurance plan place economic burdens on women for procreating that no man ever has to face for his procreative activity.

For all these reasons, we reject as fatally flawed the arguments against regarding differential treatment on the basis of pregnancy as a form of sex discrimination. The focus on the unique biological differences between men and women distracts from the salient question of whether the state may enact laws that make women's biological difference a justifiable reason for economic and social inequality. The "uniqueness" of pregnancy does not exempt from the scrutiny of the Equal Protection Clause the kind of policies and laws that single out pregnant workers for adverse treatment. Indeed, pregnancy's unique association with women, and the long history of stereotypes about women's capacities and proper roles that have led to so many forms of excluding women from the workplace due to the capacity to bear children, make it all the more essential to determine whether the sex discrimination effectuated by such policies and practices violates women's right to equal protection of the laws.

V

Having concluded that California's exclusion of pregnancy-related disabilities from its disability insurance program constitutes discrimination on the basis of sex, we must determine the appropriate standard of review for analyzing whether this discrimination violates the Equal Protection Clause.

California argues that as a social welfare program, exclusions from coverage should be reviewed under the deferential rational basis standard of review. *Dandridge v. Williams*, 397 U.S. 471, 483 (1970). Under this standard of review, absent a showing that the distinction involving pregnancy is a mere pretext intended invidiously to discriminate against women, the state's lawmakers are constitutionally free to include or exclude pregnancy from the coverage of this social welfare legislation on any reasonable basis, just as with respect to any other physical condition.

The state's argument for the rational basis standard of review, however, is inextricably linked to its rejected contention that the exclusion of pregnancy is not a form of sex-based discrimination. As our recent decisions in *Reed*, 404 U.S. 71, and *Frontiero*, 411 U.S. 677, make clear, when a legislative

classification is based on sex, as the exclusion of pregnancy in § 2626 undoubtedly is, we must apply a standard of scrutiny more strict than the mere rational
basis review accorded to general social welfare legislation.

In *Reed*, we unanimously applied what an eminent constitutional scholar
has labeled a heightened rational basis test "with bite" to invalidate a statutory
preference for males as estate administrators over females. Gerald Gunther,
*The Supreme Court, 1971 Term – Foreword: In Search of Evolving Doctrine on
a Changing Court: A Model for a New Equal Protection*, 86 Harv. L. Rev. 1,
12, 20 (1972). We ruled that the Equal Protection Clause denies "to States the
power to legislate that different treatment be accorded to persons placed by
a statute into different classes on the basis of criteria wholly unrelated to the
objective of the statute." 404 U.S. at 75–76. "A classification 'must be reasonable, not arbitrary, and must rest upon some ground of difference having a
fair and substantial relation to the object of the legislation, so that all persons
similarly circumstanced shall be treated alike.'" *Id.* at 76. We then concluded
that the preference for men over women was rooted in irrational stereotypes
about the relative capabilities and experience of men and women, and bore
no relation to the purpose of achieving efficient administration of estates.

In *Frontiero*, a plurality of this Court went further, and declared that "classifications based upon sex, like classifications based upon race, alienage, or
national origin, are inherently suspect and must therefore be subjected to
close judicial scrutiny." 411 U.S. at 682. We reached this conclusion based
on our nation's long history of discrimination against women, noting that the
discrimination was often based in romantic paternalism and stereotypes about
women's capacity due to their maternal roles and household responsibilities.
We further noted that sex-based classifications, like racial classifications, often
bear no relationship to the ability to perform or to contribute to society, or to
the actual capabilities or needs of individual women and men. *Id.* at 686–87.

It is now time to take the next step in the natural evolution from *Reed*
to *Frontiero*, and definitively hold that sex-based legislative distinctions that
rest on stereotypes that constrain equal opportunity, or that cause or perpetuate economic or social disadvantage or subordination, should be subjected to
strict scrutiny. The need for heightened scrutiny is especially warranted when
a sex-based distinction affects the fundamental right to reproductive liberty,
as in the area of pregnancy, and the decision whether or not to bear a child
without government-imposed restrictions or burdens. *See, e.g., Eisenstadt
v. Baird*, 405 U.S. 438 (1972); *Roe v. Wade*, 410 U.S. 113 (1973); *LaFleur*, 414
U.S. 632. The government must advance a compelling interest when it makes
a sex-based classification, and the classification must be necessarily related to
achieving that compelling interest.

This does not imply that any sex-based classification or benefit or program should automatically be invalid, or that the sexes must always be treated exactly the same for all purposes. After all, while inequality can result from not treating men and women as alike when they are, it can also result from treating men and women as the same when they are in fact differently situated for a relevant purpose. Heightened scrutiny does not mean blindness to the fact that differences between the sexes may warrant policies or practices supporting truly different needs, such as job-protected pregnancy leave, or opportunities to breast feed at work, or to take breaks in order to pump milk. Nor would strict scrutiny automatically invalidate laws or programs intended to facilitate participation in the public sphere in order to alleviate historical discrimination. *See, e.g., Kahn v. Shevin*, 416 U.S. 351 (1974). Laws aimed at overcoming structural impediments that have caused or exacerbated traditionally subordinated status or denial of opportunity stemming from real differences or from stereotypes about the import of differences may also be justified under a heightened standard of review. Nor does strict scrutiny mean that widely accepted social practices resting on notions of privacy and safety, such as sex-segregated public restrooms, which, unlike racially segregated public facilities, do not seem to subordinate or stigmatize any group, would be invalid.

As we recounted at the outset of this opinion, the long history of women's exclusion from equal opportunities in employment, education, and civic participation – most often due to their reproductive capacity – demonstrates the need to subject the purported justifications for sex-based distinctions to searching examination, ever sensitive to the potential that stereotypes about women's capacity and supposed natural role lurk beneath the law. There is a persistent, deeply entrenched ideology in our society and legal system that men and women are naturally suited to different roles and prefer to, or should, primarily occupy different, separate spheres. The male sphere has been the public world of the workplace, of politics, and culture, while the female sphere is the private world of family and home. Ingrained stereotypes, cultural attitudes, institutional structures, and legal classifications that seem natural actually operate to entrench the separate spheres, thus constraining and limiting the lives of women and men. The presumably well-meaning celebration of women's unique role in bearing children has, in effect, denied women equal opportunity to develop their individual talents and capacities, and has constrained them to accept a dependent, subordinate status in society. See Br. for the ACLU as Amicus Curiae. Women are often pushed out of the public sphere of the workplace when they exercise their reproductive capacity, relegated to the home, dependency, and economic insecurity. The "male breadwinner" ideology also limits men from more active engagement in the realm of the home and the joys and challenges of child-rearing, often to the detriment of their emotional and physical well-being.

California offers two principal justifications for excluding pregnancy from its disability insurance program. First, the state asserts that normal pregnancy is a voluntary condition, and thus pregnancy does not conceptually fit within a program to compensate for illness and injury. This argument is a variant of the focus on the difference or "uniqueness" of pregnancy. Second, and most prominently, California contends that the exclusion is based on cost concerns, and the need to maintain the fiscal solvency of the disability insurance program and its current structure of employee contributions and benefits. California asserts that it would cost upwards of $120 million per year to cover pregnancy-related illnesses, and this cost would soon overwhelm the program, necessitating either sharp increases in premiums or drastic reductions in benefits.[28]

The voluntariness of many normal pregnancies does not withstand scrutiny as a real, rather than a litigation-inspired, rationale for excluding pregnancy-related conditions. Not all pregnancies are voluntary or desired. And no doubt the temporary physical disabilities that can accompany normal pregnancy are neither voluntary nor desired. Moreover, the comprehensive disability program covers other temporary disabilities, illnesses, and injuries that result from numerous voluntary activities or medical procedures. Workers temporarily unable to work because they choose to have voluntary, non-medically-necessary cosmetic surgery or sterilization procedures are fully covered. Workers temporarily disabled due to injuries incurred as a result of voluntary and normal activities, such as playing sports and driving cars, are fully covered. To single out pregnancy from all the other voluntary activities covered by the program is arbitrary, and thus an illegitimate reason under any standard of review.

Turning to the rationale that it would be too costly to cover temporary disabilities related to normal pregnancy, California asserts that based on experience in other states, well over half of the payments from the fund would have to go to cover these disabilities. While the precise amount of increased cost cannot be verified, and Appellees contend that the cost would be far less than California estimates,[29] it is undisputed that benefit

---

[28] This is substantially the same argument that the State advanced and the court accepted in *Clark v. California Employment Stabilization Comm'n*, 332 P. 2d 716 (Cal. App. 4th Dist. 1958), that is, that the exclusion of pregnancy-related disabilities is necessary to protect the solvency of the disability insurance program.

[29] Appellant estimates the increased cost of including normal pregnancy at $120.2 million to $131 million annually, a 33 percent and 36 percent increase. Appellees estimate the increased

costs will increase with an expansion of coverage. It is also undisputed that California would likely have to increase the required level of employee contributions above the current 1 percent, or would have to slightly raise the current $85 cap on annual contributions, thus making the program somewhat more costly for workers.

California also contends that because women workers generate a greater rate of claims, women already receive a greater share of benefits from the fund than men. Appellant submitted to the district court data indicating that both the annual claim rate and the annual claim cost are greater for women than for men. As the district court acknowledged, "women contribute about 28 percent of the total disability insurance fund and receive back about 38 percent of the fund in benefits." 359 F. Supp. at 800.

This latter contention about women generating more claims and receiving a greater share of benefits cannot be California's actual reason, or a legitimate reason, for excluding pregnancy-related disabilities.[30] It is an argument based on actuarial principles, and California deliberately and carefully structured its fund so as not to rest on actuarial calculations. For example, workers' contributions are not set according to their level of individual risk of incurring conditions that will generate claims, or the likely cost and duration of those claims. Contributions do not rise for any group of workers when their group generates a large percentage of claims. All workers pay 1 percent of their income up to $85 per year, regardless of individual or group actuarial risk. Indeed, the program has a scale of benefits designed so that its likely effect will be that those earning small incomes (a group disproportionately composed of women workers, see Tr. of Oral Arg.) will receive more in benefits than they contribute. See Cal. Unemp. Ins. Code § 2655. California conceded in the lower court that under its system, "the right to benefits should not have any relationship to the amount contributed to the fund." 359 F. Supp. at 800. Because the purpose and structure of the California disability compensation program do not limit benefits to various groups based upon actuarial considerations, the state certainly cannot justify limiting benefits for pregnant women on this basis.

cost at $48.9 million annually, a 12 percent increase. California assumes that most women will remain out of work for twelve weeks or longer after childbirth, while Appellees contend that most leaves will be six to eight weeks, the time that the American College of Obstetrics and Gynecologists estimates the average woman is physically disabled from working after childbirth. Br. for Appellees at 59–60.

[30] Similarly, under the EEOC's Guidelines on Discrimination Because of Sex, "[i]t shall not be a defense under title VIII to a charge of sex discrimination in benefits that the cost of such benefits is greater with respect to one sex than the other." 29 CFR § 1604.9 (e).

The state's contention that including pregnancy will undermine the solvency of the program similarly does not withstand even a modest level of scrutiny. As the lower court noted:

> Even using defendant's estimate of the cost of expanding the program to include pregnancy-related disabilities, however, it is clear that including these disabilities would not destroy the program. The increased costs could be accommodated quite easily by making reasonable changes in the contribution rate, the maximum benefits allowable, and the other variables affecting the solvency of the program. For example, the entire cost increase estimated by defendant could be met by requiring workers to contribute an additional amount of approximately [0.364] percent of their salary and increasing the maximum annual contribution to about $119.
>
> 359 F. Supp. at 798.

Appellant contends, however, that California should be able to abide by its reasonable policy choice to limit contributions to their current threshold, and to pay the current level of maximum benefits. While this may well be the case under the *Dandridge v. Williams* rational basis standard of review, 397 U.S. at 483, it is not a sufficient justification for sex-based discrimination, especially one that also burdens women's exercise of their reproductive liberty. California's interest in preserving the fiscal integrity of its disability insurance program as currently constituted simply cannot render its use of a suspect classification constitutional. For while "a State has a valid interest in preserving the fiscal integrity of its programs[,] ... a State may not accomplish such a purpose by invidious distinctions between classes of its citizens ... The saving of welfare costs cannot justify an otherwise invidious classification." *Shapiro v. Thompson*, 394 U.S. 618, 633 (1969). Thus, when a statutory classification is subject to strict judicial scrutiny, the state "must do more than show that denying [benefits to the excluded class] saves money." *Memorial Hospital v. Maricopa County*, 415 U.S. 250, 263 (1974); *see also Graham v. Richardson*, 403 U.S. 365, 374–375 (1971).

When California's particular explanations for why it would be too costly to cover disabilities related to normal pregnancy are more closely examined, it becomes evident that the program's disadvantageous treatment of women due to their reproductive capacity rests on the same illegitimate stereotypes about women's presumed physical limitations and their proper and natural role within the home that underlie other forms of employment discrimination against pregnant women.

Sex-role stereotypes can easily lead to an exaggeration of the feared costs of pregnancy disability benefits. California's anticipation that most women will require lengthy periods of post-childbirth leave longer than six to eight weeks rests on the same stereotypes about the physical frailty and incapacity of all pregnant women that we recently rejected in *LaFleur*, 414 U.S. at 644. Like the forced maternity leave at issue in *LaFleur*, the denial of benefits for pregnancy-related disabilities seems to have its roots in the belief that all pregnant women are incapable of work for long periods of time, and therefore, they will generate large disability claims.[31] The truth of this belief is certainly suspect. As we noted in *LaFleur*, while striking down mandatory maternity leave for pregnant schoolteachers commencing well before and extending for three months after delivery, not all women are physically affected by pregnancy in the same way and for the same duration. Many women will be fully physically capable of returning to work within a few weeks after childbirth; others will require longer leaves.

As the district court pointed out:

> the treatment of pregnancy in other cultures shows that much of our society's views concerning the debilitating effects of pregnancy are more a response to cultural sex-role conditioning than a response to medical fact and necessity ... Indeed, a realistic look at what women actually do even in our society belies the belief that they cannot generally work throughout pregnancy ... Nevertheless, the belief that pregnant women are disabled for substantial periods results in their being denied the opportunity to work, unemployment compensation benefits designed to aid those able to work, and – because of the belief that they will submit large claims – disability insurance benefits.
>
> 359 F. Supp. at 799 (citations omitted).

The sex-role stereotypes in operation are even more starkly revealed by an additional argument advanced to substantiate California's fear that it will cost too much to remove the pregnancy exclusion. The state argues that the pregnancy exclusion is necessary to prevent abuse of the program by women who have no desire to return to work because they prefer to remain home with their children. 359 F. Supp. at 800. The state's argument depends on several unsubstantiated assumptions: These women – presumably many or most – will be able to find sympathetic physicians who support women staying home with their babies, and who will certify them as disabled for as many weeks as possible, so that the women can reap maximum benefits. Many of these women will then never return to work. In other words, California argues that

---

[31] Indeed, as noted above, the starkly differing cost estimates of Appellants and Appellees stem from differing assumptions about the length of leaves that women will take. California assumes leaves will average longer than eight weeks, while Appellees take individual's varying physical and economic situations into account and estimate that most women will require shorter leaves.

the pregnancy exclusion is necessary to prevent women from using the disability program as a maternity leave program. Indeed, the state explicitly defended the pregnancy exclusion on this basis when it was initially challenged on equal protection grounds in state court. *Clark v. California Employment Stabilization Com.*, 332 P.2d 716 (Cal. App. 4th Dist. 1958). The state court uncritically accepted this rationale: "[T]o award disability compensation to women employees on account of illness caused by pregnancy, [would] in effect, constitute[] a maternity benefit plan for a limited group, i.e., women employees. The purpose of the unemployment disability program is to afford relief to employees sustaining loss of wages on account of illness, and not to confer maternity benefits." *Id.* at 719.

This rationale for the pregnancy exclusion is inextricably rooted in the archaic sex-role stereotypes that underlie the separate spheres ideology. The exclusion reflects the idea that women are mothers first, and workers second. This ideological belief assumes that most women will, and should, leave the workforce when they have children. *See* Br. for ACLU as Amicus Curiae. These are precisely the type of sex-role stereotypes that led us recently to reject sex-based laws in *Reed* and *Frontiero*. Moreover, this archaic stereotype ignores the greatly increased workforce participation of women (currently almost 39 percent of women with children under six are in the workforce), and the fact that nearly two-thirds of all women who work do so of necessity: either they are unmarried or their husbands earn less than $7,000 per year. *See* United States Department of Labor, Women's Bureau, *Why Women Work* (rev. ed. 1972); United States Department of Labor, Employment Standards Administration, *The Myth and the Reality* (May 1974 rev.). Appellee Jaramillo, for example, is the sole economic support for her family, and she juggles work outside the home and family responsibilities while her husband pursues his education. The other Appellees are also the sole economic support for their households. They are far more typical of working women than Appellant's stereotyped assumptions acknowledge.

To the extent that some women do in fact leave the workforce when they bear children, California's exclusion of pregnancy has all the earmarks of a self-fulfilling prophecy. If women are treated by the state and their employers as detached from the workforce when pregnancy disables them, it is not surprising that some respond to the disincentives barring their way to return and thus fulfill Appellant's stereotyped vision of women's place post-childbirth. Br. for ACLU as Amicus Curiae.

Concerns about the cost of providing equal disability coverage to women are not a sufficient rationale for the sex-based exclusion of pregnancy-related disability, especially where, as here, these cost concerns evince stereotypes about women's role in reproduction as incompatible with workforce participation. This case highlights that barriers to women's full workforce participation are caused not by women's biological differences from men, but by the way our laws, governments, and employers choose to treat those differences.

The stay previously issued by this Court is vacated, and the judgment of the District Court striking down the pregnancy exclusion in California Unemployment Insurance Code § 2626 is *affirmed*.

11

Commentary on *Dothard v. Rawlinson*

Brenda V. Smith

INTRODUCTION

Dothard v. Rawlinson[1] is among the most important early cases applying Title VII of the Civil Rights Act of 1964 to gender. It was the first case that considered whether a seemingly neutral job requirement like height and weight could violate Title VII if it had a disparate impact on women in the workplace. It was also the first case to address Title VII's bona fide occupational qualification ("BFOQ"), which allows employers to use sex in employment decisions if it is "reasonabl[y] necessary ... to the normal operation of that business or enterprise."[2]

Dothard involved employment in Alabama's state correctional facilities. The female plaintiffs in *Dothard* argued that the prison's height and weight requirements created a disparate impact by excluding 41 percent of women and only 1 percent of men.[3] They also challenged the prison's categorical exclusion of women from contact positions, arguing that maleness was not a BFOQ for employment in Alabama's male prisons.

The U.S. Supreme Court found that Alabama's height and weight requirements violated Title VII because the state offered no evidence that the requirements were necessary to the job. The Court found, however, that sex was a BFOQ permitting Alabama to exclude women from contact positions in its maximum-security prisons. Acknowledging that its reasoning echoed the "romantic paternalism" that it explicitly forbade in *Frontiero v. Richardson*,[4]

---

[1] *Dothard v. Rawlinson*, 433 U.S. 321 (1977).

[2] 42 U.S.C § 2000e-2 A (e) (2012).

[3] The Alabama Department of Corrections (DOC) required that all correctional officers be at least 5 feet 2 inches and weigh at least 120 pounds.

[4] *See generally Frontiero v. Richardson*, 411 U.S. 677 (1973).

the Court nonetheless balked at permitting women to act as prison guards. Describing the men's maximum security prison as a "jungle atmosphere," the Court reasoned that female staff's "very womanhood" would undermine security in the prison and might incite sexual assault by prisoners "deprived of a normal heterosexual environment."[5]

The feminist judgment by Professor Maria Ontiveros, writing as Justice Ontiveros, challenges the legal and logical underpinnings of the Court's opinion. She criticizes the Court's disparate impact analysis for not providing adequate guidance when a challenged job requirement, like height and weight, is a proxy for sex.[6] She is even more critical of the Court's BFOQ analysis, finding that it enshrines sexist stereotypes of women as the cause of sexual assault, permits de facto sex segregation in the workplace, and limits the self-determination of female workers.[7] Ontiveros's opinion illuminates the sexism that is codified in Title VII's BFOQ and reified in U.S. Supreme Court jurisprudence, and provides an alternative to the Court's cramped view of gender equality.

THE FEMINIST JUDGMENT

Adopting the majority's recitation of facts, Ontiveros concurs in part and dissents in part from the majority decision. Ontiveros concurs with the disparate impact ruling, but writes separately, emphasizing important points missing from the majority's analysis. First, she emphasizes that after a plaintiff has successfully presented the prima facie case of discriminatory effect, the employer's burden of proving the necessity of the discriminatory requirement is heavy. The court must scrutinize the alleged necessity of the job requirement, and, where the requirement serves as a proxy for another job qualification, the court must also evaluate the nexus between them. So, if an employer asserts that a particular height and weight is necessary because employees must be strong, the court must evaluate whether strength, as opposed to skill or special training, is truly required for the job. The court, however, must also evaluate whether height and weight are legitimate proxies for strength and not simply impermissible sex stereotypes.

Additionally, Ontiveros addresses underlying structural discrimination that can lead to sex-segregated workplaces, emphasizing that most workplace structures are created by employers and that courts must closely scrutinize workplace structures used to justify job qualifications with discriminatory effects. For

[5] See Dothard v. Rawlinson, 433 U.S. 321, 336 (1977).
[6] Id. at 324.
[7] Id. at 335.

example, in *Dothard*, prison design created undue risks of violence and security breaches for all staff, not just women. As that design was not a legitimate business necessity, it could not justify a strength requirement for prison guards.

Then, Ontiveros dissents from the Court's application of the BFOQ. Drawing on Susan Estrich's critique of rape law,[8] and echoing Catharine MacKinnon's indictment of the *Dothard* Court as speaking for "the reasonable rapist,"[9] Ontiveros argues that the Court's reasoning reduces women to rape objects. Ontiveros reasons that the Court essentialized men and women by equating femaleness with rapability and manhood with rapaciousness.

Additionally, Ontiveros criticizes the Court for the inherent racism embedded in the decision, *e.g.*, the "jungle atmosphere."[10] Noting the likely racial composition of the prison, Ontiveros argues that the court's decision evokes white fear of black male sexual aggression, particularly against white women. Rejecting these racist-sexist tropes, Ontiveros implicitly relies on the work of Catharine MacKinnon and Reva Siegel,[11] as well as the seminal work of Angela Harris warning of the dangers of gender and race essentialism in law.[12]

Finally, Ontiveros rejects the majority's finding that workplace tolerance of the risk of rape can be the basis for a BFOQ defense. Accepting the prison's rationale, the majority normalizes rape of women as tolerable and permits employers to maintain sex-segregated workplaces by creating workplaces hostile to women's work participation. In Ontiveros's view, *Dothard* should have been the Court's first hostile work environment sexual harassment case. She writes that the prison's own description of itself as a workplace where the rape of women was a substantial and foreseeable risk would likely support a Title VII claim under hostile work environment sexual harassment theory.

THE LEGACY OF *DOTHARD* AND THE LIMITATIONS OF THE FEMINIST JUDGMENT

While the feminist judgment tackles many of the pronounced gender and racial stereotypes at work in *Dothard*, it does not address more nuanced issues of gender and sexual norms that undergird the decision and its progeny.

---

[8] Susan Estrich, Real Rape 29 (1988).
[9] Catharine MacKinnon, *On Difference and Dominance*, in Feminism Unmodified: Discourses on Life and Law 38 (1987).
[10] *Dothard*, 433 U.S. at 335; *Pugh v. Locke*, 406 F. Supp. 318, 325 (M.D. Ala. 1976).
[11] Adrienne D. Davis, *Slavery and the Roots of Sexual Harassment*, *in* Directions in Sexual Harassment 467 (Catharine A. MacKinnon and Reva B. Siegel eds., 2003).
[12] Angela P. Harris, *Race and Essentialism in Feminist Legal Theory* 42 Stan. L. Rev. 581, 585 (1989).

First, the feminist judgment does not address the double bind feminists face if they reject uncritically the notion of women as rape objects. The truth is, women are vulnerable to rape, and the rape of women is normalized by American law and society.[13] In particular, the female maximum security prison counterpart to the male prison in *Dothard* was plagued by physical and sexual violence against female prisoners by male staff.[14] The difference is that the female prisoners were largely black. As such, while the *Dothard* Court was protecting white women from potential sexual assault, they ignored and made the physical and sexual vulnerability of primarily black female inmates legally invisible.[15]

A positive legacy of *Dothard's* gender stereotyping was to allow female inmates greater protection from physical contact with male prison staff. *Dothard's* reasoning about women's sexual vulnerability and male sexual predation was the foundation for litigation by female prisoners challenging male supervision, sexual abuse,[16] and their greater need for physical privacy because of past histories of trauma.[17] The legacy of this litigation is that, by and large, male staff can work in women's facilities, but are not permitted to be alone with female inmates, search female inmates, or view them while they disrobe, shower, or toilet.[18]

As much as *Dothard's* reasoning helped female prisoners, its simplistic and stereotyped approach to gender norms and sexual assault turned out to be a double-edged sword. Although helpful to female inmates, the stereotypes of male inmates as predatory and violent embodied in *Dothard's* reasoning caused great damage for male inmates in employment lawsuits by women seeking jobs in men's prisons. *Dothard's* reasoning led courts to conclude that male inmates had minimal modesty concerns and little need for protection from predation.[19] In the context of male prisons, *Dothard's* legacy is that female staff members are permitted to conduct intrusive body searches of men

---

[13] Catharine A. MacKinnon, Toward a Feminist Theory of the State 176–81 (1989) (rape is not prohibited, it is "regulated.").

[14] *See Cooper v. Rogers*, 2012 WL 2050577 (M.D. Ala. 2012). *See also* Department of Justice, Justice Department Releases Findings Showing That the Alabama Department of Corrections Fails to Protect Prisoners from Sexual Abuse and Sexual Harassment at the Julia Tutwiler Prison for Women (January 22, 2014).

[15] Justice Dep't Findings, supra n. 14.

[16] *See, e.g., Women Prisoners of District of Columbia Dep't of Corr. v. District of Columbia*, 93 F.3d 910 (D.C. Cir. 1996).

[17] *See Jordan v. Gardner*, 986 F.2d 1521, 1523–24 (9th Cir. 1993).

[18] *See generally Colman v. Vasquez*, 142 F. Supp. 2d 226 (D. Conn. 2001).

[19] *See* Teresa A. Miller, *Keeping the Government's Hands Off Our Bodies: Mapping a Feminist Legal Theory Approach to Privacy in Cross-Gender Prison Searches*, 4 Buff. Crim. L. Rev. 861, 865 (2001).

including the genital area,[20] and view men while they are naked.[21] Neither *Dothard* nor the feminist judgment contemplates female aggression or predation – sexual or otherwise – which is a significant and alarming problem.[22] The feminist judgment does not address this damaging stereotype of masculinity – particularly black masculinity – in *Dothard* or the disturbing consequences of that stereotype.

Finally, an unexplored narrative in both opinions is the sexual milieu in correctional facilities. In the original *Dothard*, the majority referred to sexual assault as the predictable result of inmates being "deprived of a normal heterosexual environment." The Court's incorrect assumption that heterosexuality is the norm and that male inmates will attempt to alleviate sex deprivation by assaulting women ignored the shocking prevalence of male-on-male rape in prisons,[23] and a host of issues related to LGBTQIA[24] violence in prisons. It took decades before these issues even began to be resolved,[25] and that delay is due in part to *Dothard*'s naïve reasoning; it is notable that the feminist judgment does not mention this aspect of *Dothard*'s problematic reasoning.

In sum, *Dothard* casts a long shadow. Its embrace of gender stereotypes related to sexual assault has led to a rough justice in correctional systems that on the one hand discounts the sexual abuse of men and boys in custody by female staff,[26] and on the other hand fails to address the complicated issues of misogyny that have made women's advancement in male-dominated professions difficult and dangerous.[27] Ontiveros's feminist judgment makes significant headway on many of these issues, but perhaps demonstrates the limits of what one opinion can achieve. This is particularly so when there are

---

[20] *See Johnson v. City of Kalamazoo*, 124 F. Supp. 2d 1099 (W.D. Mich. 2000); *Wilson v. City of Kalamazoo*, 127 F. Supp. 2d 855 (W.D. Mich. 2000). Read together, these cases note a modest privacy interest in that female staff cannot view men nude for an extended period of time under the Fourth Amendment right to bodily privacy.

[21] *See Wilson*, 127 F. Supp. 2d 855.

[22] For example, female staff members are the most likely perpetrators of staff sexual abuse in adult and juvenile male facilities. *See* Allen J. Beck, Bureau of Just. Stat., Sexual Victimization in Prisons and Jails Reported by Inmates, 2008–09 (2010) *available at* http://bjs.ojp.usdoj.gov/content/pub/pdf/svpjri0809.pdf.

[23] 42 U.S.C. § 15601(2) (2012) (the Prison Rape Elimination Act).

[24] This acronym means "lesbian, gay, bisexual, trans*, queer/questioning, intersex and asexual." It is meant to be inclusive of all sexualities and genders. The asterisk after "trans*" signifies all persons who identify as gender non-conforming.

[25] The Department of Justice made some strides in addressing these problems in the National Standards to Prevent, Detect, and Respond to Prison Rape. National Prison Rape Elimination Commission, Standards for the Prevention, Detection, Response, and Monitoring of Sexual Abuse in Adult Prisons at 11, 39–40 (2009).

[26] *See Wood v. Beauclair*, 692 F.3d 1041 (9th Cir. 2012).

[27] *Freitag v. Ayers*, 468 F.3d 528 (9th Cir. 2006).

overlapping narratives and currents of race, gender and sexuality which call for different theories and judgments depending on multiple prisms of race, gender and sexuality.

Dothard v. Rawlinson, 433 U.S. 321 (1977)

Justice Maria L. Ontiveros, concurring in part and dissenting in part.

Title VII of the Civil Rights Act of 1964, 78 Stat. 253, as amended, 42 U.S.C. § 2000e et seq. (1970 ed. and Supp. V), was passed to promote economic opportunity for all, regardless of race, color, sex, religion, or national origin. As we stated in *Griggs v. Duke Power*, 401 U.S. 424 (1971), "[t]he objective of Congress in the enactment of Title VII is plain from the language of the statute. It was to achieve the equality of employment opportunities and remove barriers that have operated in the past to favor an identifiable group of white employees over other employees." *Id.* at 429–30. Although *Griggs* discussed discrimination based on race, we have only briefly addressed Title VII as it applies to discrimination based on sex. In *Phillips v. Martin Marietta Corp.*, 400 U.S. 542 (1971), we held in a one-paragraph opinion that the defendant could not have a different hiring policy for men than women, unless it could prove that the policy (in its case refusing to hire women with pre-school-age children, but allowing employment of men with pre-school-age children) was a "bona fide occupational qualification reasonably necessary to the normal operation of that particular business or enterprise," as permitted under section 703(e) of the Act.[28] *Id.* at 544.

Thus, we come to this case with an almost clean slate, and it is incumbent upon us to apply Title VII in a manner that gives full respect to the importance of guaranteeing equal employment opportunity to women in the United States. Some suggest that the inclusion of "sex" was a mere afterthought, joke, or attempt to defeat the Act because "sex" was added late in the legislative development of the Act, as an amendment during debate on the floor of the House of Representatives. That argument, however, ignores efforts by the National Women's Party to include sex in nondiscrimination legislation, as well as the passage of the Equal Pay Act of 1963, 29 U.S.C. § 206(d), guaranteeing equal pay for women, and the long history of the fight for women's equality. More importantly, it runs counter to congressional intent evidenced in the

[28] In our other case, *Gilbert v. General Electric Co.*, 429 U.S. 125 (1976), we found that an employer's failure to cover pregnancy-related disabilities was not discrimination based on sex. Congress is currently considering legislation to overturn that decision. Senate Bill 995 was introduced on March 3, 1977; House Bill 6075 was introduced on April 5, 1977. So, I will not rely on *Gilbert* in my opinion.

House Judiciary Committee Report when it passed the 1972 amendment to the Act, the Equal Employment Opportunity Act of 1972, Pub. L. No. 92–261, Mar. 24, 1972, 86 Stat. 103. The Report stated:

> The situation of the working women is no less serious [than that of minorities] ... Women are subject to economic deprivation as a class. Their self-fulfillment and development is frustrated because of their sex. Numerous studies have shown that women are placed in the less challenging, the less responsible and the less remunerative positions on the basis of their sex alone ... The Committee believes that women's rights are not just judicial divertissements. Discrimination against women is no less serious than other forms of prohibited employment practices and is to be accorded the same degree of social concern given to any type of unlawful discrimination.
>
> H.R. Rep. No. 92–238, 92nd Cong., 2d Sess. at 4–5 (1971). *See also* S. Rep. No. 92–415, 92nd Cong., 1st Sess. 7–8 (1971).

This case provides the ideal vehicle to draw the parameters of the Act's equal employment guarantee because it involves two different types of discrimination against women: a neutral practice with a discriminatory effect and a facial policy barring all women from employment. Therefore, we are able to outline the application of disparate impact analysis and analysis of the bona fide occupational qualification (BFOQ) as applied to sex discrimination. This case also allows us to address the issue of how to treat arguments about women's sexuality in the workplace. A BFOQ which is based on stereotypes of women's sexuality, including the inevitability of her being sexually assaulted, is no more valid than a BFOQ based on stereotypes about women's strength or ability to impose discipline. If, on the other hand, a workplace truly creates or tolerates a sexually abusive atmosphere that negatively affects women, the employment conditions constitute a form of sex discrimination, which lower courts have labeled sexual harassment.

The facts recited by the majority fairly sum up the case. To reiterate briefly, Appellee Dianne Rawlinson sought employment with the Alabama Board of Corrections as a prison guard and was refused employment because she failed to meet the statutory minimum 120-pound weight requirement. The statute also establishes a height minimum of 5 feet 2 inches.

While Rawlinson's class action suit regarding the height and weight requirements was pending, the Alabama Board of Corrections adopted Administrative Regulation 204, which establishes explicit gender criteria for correctional counselors in "contact positions" in maximum-security institutions. Contact positions are those requiring continual close physical proximity to inmates. Because most of Alabama's prisoners are held at four maximum-security male penitentiaries, 336 of the 435 correctional counselor jobs were in those institutions. A majority of them were concededly in the "contact" classification. Under Regulation 204's gender criteria, therefore, women applicants could compete equally with men for only about 25 percent of the correctional counselor jobs available in the Alabama prison system. Thus, as the majority notes, Regulation 204 "explicitly discriminates against women on the basis of their sex." *See Dothard v. Rawlinson*, 433 U.S. 321, 323–28, 333 (1977).

I

Disparate impact analysis

On the whole, I concur with the majority in its analysis of disparate impact discrimination found in Part II of its opinion to the extent it reaffirms our earlier decisions and applies them to this case. That is, I agree that to make out a prima facie case of disparate impact, all the plaintiffs need to show is that facially neutral requirements, like the height and weight requirements here, result in a significant discriminatory pattern of exclusion. *See Griggs v. Duke Power Co.*, 401 U.S. 424 (1971); *Albemarle Paper Co. v. Moody*, 422 U.S. 405 (1975). The plaintiff need not show a purposeful discriminatory motive. Once the plaintiff establishes a prima facie case, the employer must show that the requirement has a "manifest relationship" to the job. *Griggs*, 401 U.S. at 432. If the employer shows that the requirement is job related, the plaintiff can counter by showing that other requirements without a similar discriminatory effect would serve the needs of the employer.

Here, there is no question that the plaintiffs made out a prima facie case of disparate impact. As the District Court found, the height and weight requirements, combined, would exclude 41.13 percent of the female population while excluding less than 1 percent of the male population. Rather, the case focused on whether these requirements were "job related." The majority found that they were not, in part because the employer offered no evidence to support a correlation between the requirement and "strength."

I write separately for several reasons. First, I write to emphasize the majority's holding that disparate impact analysis applies to discrimination based on sex, no less so than to discrimination based on race. Second, our application of disparate impact in this case survives our recent decision in *Washington v. Davis*, 426 U.S. 229 (1976), which took a different approach to disparate impact analysis under the U.S. Constitution. In *Washington*, we emphasized

the purpose of the Equal Protection Clause of the Fourteenth Amendment
as a prohibition against intentionally discriminatory treatment by official conduct. *Washington*, 426 U.S. at 239. In *Washington*, we also reaffirmed that
under Title VII, "when hiring and promotion practices disqualifying substantially disproportionate numbers of blacks are challenged, discriminatory
purpose need not be proved." *Id.* at 246–47. This is because Title VII goes
beyond a prohibition on negative conduct taken by an employer. It focuses
on providing full economic opportunity for all employees, despite their membership in a protected classification. The affirmative guarantee of equal opportunity found in Title VII goes beyond the intent based, non-discrimination
approach of the Fourteenth Amendment and encompasses the broader goal
of full economic participation of women and other members of protected
classes. As we implied in *Griggs*, the statute must be read broadly to give
meaning to this congressional intent.

Finally, I write to provide guidance on how courts should evaluate an
employer's response to a prima face case of discrimination based on disparate
impact. In this case, the employer offered no evidence that strength was necessary for the job or of a relationship between its height and weight requirements
and the specified job requirement of "strength." This utter lack of evidence
makes it an easy case to decide. In the future, though, employers may come
forward with evidence, and it is incumbent upon us to provide guidance for
how to evaluate that evidence. These guidelines are grounded in the stated
nature of Title VII as an affirmative statute with a purpose of providing full
economic participation for protected classes.

Because the prima facie disparate impact case establishes that a discriminatory effect in fact exists, the burden of persuasion shifts to the employer to
justify the discriminatory requirement. The employer's burden is a heavy one.
It must be. Otherwise, economic opportunities will be foreclosed to members
of a protected class.

The court must first evaluate carefully an employer's assertion that a job
qualification is necessary. Here, for example, the court would begin the analysis by assessing whether "strength" – as opposed to special skills or abilities –
is actually necessary to the job of correctional officer. Then, if an employer
uses a specific employment practice or requirement, such as the height and
weight requirement here, by alleging that the requirement serves as a proxy
for a specific job qualification (here, strength), courts must also closely scrutinize whether the nexus between the qualification and the requirement is
sufficiently close to justify the use of the proxy.

These two steps are especially important when the asserted job qualification
may include stereotypes based on sex or another protected characteristic. For

example, in this case, because the employer suggests that prison guards must be "strong," the employer must prove why guards need to be strong and how much strength they need to perform the job. Otherwise, the qualification of "strength" could be used to illegally exclude women from jobs. This is particularly important because society often views strength as a masculine trait, so it carries with it a significant danger of sexual stereotyping. Moreover, the employer would also need to show that height and weight are so related to strength that they are accurate proxies for strength. This second step is critical to preventing employers who would otherwise be prohibited from saying "no women in this job" from using superficially neutral criteria, such as height and weight, to accomplish the same result.

I also disagree with the assertion in the concurring opinion by Justice Rehnquist that a simple statement by the employer that "the appearance of strength" is a necessary qualification for the job of correctional officer would be sufficient to rebut the prima facie case here. The employer must do more than simply assert, without supporting evidence, a reason that could easily be a pretext used to exclude women from these jobs. Instead, the employer would have to adduce convincing evidence that the "appearance of strength" is an actual business necessity.

More importantly, disparate impact analysis must also be used to examine the structure that the employer has chosen for its workplace, especially if this structure is used to justify discriminatory qualifications. In most situations, the design of a workplace is not a given. The employer makes conscious choices about how to structure the workplace. Those choices must also be justified under the doctrine of business necessity when they have a discriminatory impact. In this case, for instance, the employer has chosen to operate its prison with inadequate staffing and facilities. It has chosen not to classify or segregate its population by type of offense or level of dangerousness, despite testimony that such procedures are essential to effective prison administration. *Dothard*, 433 U.S. at 334–35. It has also designed prisons in a dormitory style and incorporated extensive farming operations that it argues require a large number of strip searches. Each of these choices might lead to a certain "qualification" that has a disparate impact. If it does, then the employer must justify the choice as a business necessity. If it cannot, then the workplace design or structure violates Title VII because it is restricting the economic opportunities available to members of a protected class. An employer outside the prison context also makes certain choices about workplace design, including the schedules, hours and shifts that it requires of employees and ways in which it sets compensation. When these choices have a disparate impact, the employer must justify them as a business necessity.

II

Bona Fide Occupational Qualification Analysis ("BFOQ")

I dissent from almost the entirety of Part III of the majority opinion and its ana-lysis of the BFOQ. The BFOQ deals with the most egregious form of discrimin-ation – an outright, facial prohibition against the employment of all members of a protected class. I agree with the majority to the extent that it describes the BFOQ as "an extremely narrow exception to the general prohibition of discrimination on the basis of sex." *Dothard*, 433 U.S. at 334. The majority quotes with approval the findings from lower courts that facial "discrimination based on sex is valid only when the *essence* of the business operation would be undermined by not hiring members of one sex exclusively." *Diaz v. Pan Am. World Airways, Inc.*, 442 F.2d 385, 388 (5th Cir. 1971) (emphasis in original). And, an employer may only utilize the BFOQ defense when it has "reasonable cause to believe, that is, a factual basis for believing, that all or substantially all women would be unable to perform safely and efficiently the duties of the job involved." *Weeks v. S. Bell Tel. & Tel. Co.*, 408 F.2d 228, 235 (5th Cir. 1969). This language flows logically from the restrictive language of the Act, which states that facial discrimination is allowable only "in those certain instances where ... sex ... is a bona fide occupational qualification reasonably necessary to the nor-mal operation of that particular business or enterprise." 42 U.S.C. § 2000e-2(e).

When addressing the requirements of a BFOQ, the majority agrees with all lower federal courts and the guidelines published by the Equal Employment Opportunity Commission that "it is impermissible under Title VII to refuse to hire an individual woman or man on the basis of stereotyped characterizations of the sexes." It would seem obvious that it is equally impermissible to use the BFOQ defense to refuse to hire an individual woman or man based on a dis-criminatory work environment, inhospitable to a particular gender, that has been created by the employer.

The majority errs in its finding that the defendant's situation meets the strict BFOQ standard. The majority reasons:[29]

> The environment in Alabama's penitentiaries is a peculiarly inhospitable one for human beings of whatever sex. Indeed, a Federal District Court has held that the conditions of confinement in the prisons of the State, character-ized by "rampant violence" and a "jungle atmosphere," are constitutionally intolerable. *Pugh v. Locke*, 406 F. Supp. 318, 325 (MD Ala. 1976). The record

---

[29] The majority's reasoning is reproduced here at length because, as described below, it illustrates the sexist assumptions and attitudes at the heart of this case.

in the present case shows that because of inadequate staff and facilities, no attempt is made in the four maximum-security male penitentiaries to classify or segregate inmates according to their offense or level of dangerousness – a procedure that, according to expert testimony, is essential to effective penological administration. Consequently, the estimated 20% of the male prisoners who are sex offenders are scattered throughout the penitentiaries' dormitory facilities.

The essence of a correctional counselor's job is to maintain prison security. A woman's relative ability to maintain order in a male, maximum-security, unclassified penitentiary of the type Alabama now runs could be directly reduced by her womanhood. There is a basis in fact for expecting that sex offenders who have criminally assaulted women in the past would be moved to do so again if access to women were established within the prison. There would also be a real risk that other inmates, deprived of a normal heterosexual environment, would assault women guards because they were women. In a prison system where violence is the order of the day, where inmate access to guards is facilitated by dormitory living arrangements, where every institution is understaffed, and where a substantial portion of the inmate population is composed of sex offenders mixed at random with other prisoners, there are few visible deterrents to inmate assaults on women custodians.

The likelihood that inmates would assault a woman because she was a woman would pose a real threat not only to the victim of the assault but also to the basic control of the penitentiary and protection of its inmates and the other security personnel. The employee's very womanhood would thus directly undermine her capacity to provide the security that is the essence of a correctional counselor's responsibility.

Dothard, 433 U.S. at 334–36.

The majority's analysis is flawed for several reasons.

A

The BFOQ and women's ability to perform the job

First, the employer cannot support the argument that being male is a BFOQ for the job of correctional officer because evidence from across the nation shows that women can – and do – effectively perform the job of correctional officer in other prison systems. This reveals the employer's asserted BFOQ as an unsupported assumption based on a sex stereotype that women cannot perform the job. The State of Washington uses female guards within the state's male adult correctional institutions. Harold Bradley, Director of the Washington Division of Adult Corrections, testified that women guards perform the same duties as male guards and have not experienced any security-related concerns. Br. for Washington State Human Rights Comm'n as Amicus Curiae at 16–17. Female prison guards have also been used effectively in the Metropolitan Correctional Center in Chicago, a federal maximum security institution. The warden of that institution found their performance to be "very satisfactory" and their presence to have exerted a positive, normalizing effect on the Center. Mem. for the United States as Amicus Curiae at 30.

The State of California has integrated women into the staff of all male correctional facilities for over ten years. In its Amicus Brief, California states that women can perform adequately and safely within the all-male penitentiary and properly categorize the contrary evidence produced by Alabama as "subjective feelings" of prison administrators. Br. for State of California as Amicus Curiae at 9–12. California argues that "[f]or this court to elevate the subjective feelings of prison administrators to the status of law would be to destroy thirteen years of progress toward equal employment opportunities for women." *Id.* at 11. One year into the integration of female guards into contact positions with male prisoners, the Deputy Director of the California Department of Corrections reported "[g]enerally, female officers are functioning successfully in male institutions ... A captain who ten months ago felt that women had a limited place in corrections, now, after supervising women custodial personnel who perform all officer post assignments, states 'They have been accepted by male personnel and inmates ...'" Motion of ACLU for Leave to File and Br. Amicus Curiae at 21. With regard to Alabama, in particular, as the concurring opinion noted, "the record shows that the presence of women guards has not led to a single incident amounting to a serious breach of security in any Alabama institution." 433 U.S. at 344 (Marshall, J., concurring). Substantial evidence adduced at trial and found in the lower court's opinion in this case shows that the presence of women in all-male penal institutions contributes to the normalization of the prison environment and has a positive psychological effect upon the prisoners. *Mieth v. Dothard*, 418 F. Supp. 1169, 1184 (M.D. Ala. 1976). The evidence fails to meet the majority's BFOQ standard that all or substantially all women would be unable to perform safely and efficiently the duties of the job involved.

Second, I agree with Justice Marshall's concurrence that the unique and hostile nature of the Alabama prisons cannot be the basis of a BFOQ. 433 U.S. at 341–42 (Marshall, J., concurring) ("[a] prison system operating in blatant violation of the Eighth Amendment is an exception that should be remedied with all possible speed" and should not justify "conduct that would otherwise violate a statute intended to remedy age-old discrimination.").

Third, the arguments that are used by the employer to justify the restriction run afoul of Title VII because they are based on stereotypes about women as being physically inferior and not as tough as men. As my brethren stated in their concurrence: "[m]uch of the testimony of appellants' witnesses ignores individual differences among members of each sex and reads like 'ancient canards about the proper role of women.' The witnesses claimed that women guards are not strict disciplinarians; that they are physically less capable of protecting themselves and subduing unruly inmates; that inmates take advantage of them as they did their mothers, while male guards are strong father figures who easily maintain discipline, and so on." *Id.* at 343 (Marshall, J., concurring) (citations omitted).

As the majority agreed and we found in *Martin Marietta*, gender stereotypes cannot form the basis for a BFOQ. Facial prohibitions must be based on fact, not conjecture, especially not conjecture that serves to reinforce the very discriminatory attitudes that have kept women out of certain jobs. Title VII's prohibition on sex discrimination invalidates the notion that there are "men's jobs" and "women's jobs." Indeed, Title VII was meant to ameliorate the far too prevalent sex segregation of jobs in the United States. When women are crowded into certain jobs, pay for those jobs falls due to an artificial over-supply of applicants. The working conditions and status of these jobs also lag behind those of jobs primarily occupied by men. The lack of availability of certain jobs will often foreclose a woman's ability to get the training and experience she needs in order to advance in her career. Sex segregation, then, works to prevent the equal participation of women in the United States economy, and gender stereotypes have been the primary justification for keeping women out of certain jobs. *See generally* Theodore Caplow, The Sociology of Work (1954). Title VII is meant to reverse this trend. If properly applied, in twenty years, Title VII should mean the end of the notion that certain jobs are "non-traditional" for women.

Finally, if a job is dangerous to both sexes, a woman must have just as much right to decide whether to accept that risk as a man. An employer cannot make that decision for women. Such paternalism is not permitted by Title VII. A striking example of this type of paternalism is found in the portion of the lower court opinion in this case that dealt with the companion case of *Mieth v. Dothard*. In that case, Brenda Mieth was denied a position as an Alabama State Trooper. When she met with Colonel E.C. Dothard, the Director of the Department of Public Safety of the State of Alabama, to request a waiver of the height and weight restrictions, "Colonel Dothard refused this request, informing Ms. Mieth that he would never put a woman on the road because of the dangers involved. Before departing, the director, in a courtly gesture, presented Ms. Mieth with a certificate making her an 'Honorary State Trooper.'" *Mieth v. Dothard*, 418 F. Supp. 1169, 1174 (M.D. Ala. 1976). While

Colonel Dothard may have meant this as a "courtly gesture," it is patronizing and demeaning. Women must have the agency to make their own decisions about accepting dangerous work, to the same extent that men do. Otherwise, they will be delegated to "honorary" rather than real jobs. When dealing with this issue, the majority approvingly cites *Weeks v. S. Bell Tel. & Tel. Co.*, 408 F.2d 228, 236 (5th Cir. 1969). In that case, the Fifth Circuit wrote, "Title VII rejects just this type of romantic paternalism as unduly Victorian and instead vests individual women with the power to decide whether or not to take on unromantic tasks. Men have always had the right to determine whether the incremental increase in remuneration for strenuous, dangerous, obnoxious, boring or unromantic tasks is worth the candle. The promise of Title VII is that women are now to be on equal footing." *Id.*

The majority argues that this case is different because, in the unique case of prison guards, where the essential function of the job is to maintain order and security, an attack upon a woman could put more people in danger than just the individual female employee. The argument fails because it ignores the fact that attacks on male prison guards also occur and have the same exact effect on overall order and security. Further, the argument ignores the experience of other prisons utilizing female prison guards without incident. Some female prison guards will be bigger and stronger than male prison guards. Female prison guards will also be equipped with specialized skills and training to draw upon in the event of an attack. The only examples of attacks in the record involve an attack on a female clerical worker in Alabama and a hostage incident involving a female student who was visiting the prison. By offering these as justification for its position, the majority ignores the special qualifications of female prison guards and assumes that they are in the same position as the clerical worker and student simply by virtue of their sex.

As a final matter, I note that some of the evidence suggests a racist, as well as sexist, motive for the employer's paternalism here. The federal district court, which concluded that the conditions within the all-male penitentiary system were unconstitutionally cruel and unusual, described the "rampant violence and *jungle atmosphere*" inside the prisons. *Pugh v. Locke*, 406 F. Supp. 318, 325 (M.D. Ala. 1976) (emphasis added). The majority repeated this description as justification for its holding. *Dothard*, 433 U.S. at 334–35. According to the U.S. Department of Justice, the population of the Alabama penitentiary system is over 50 percent black. Bureau of Prisons, U.S. Department of Justice, *Prisoners In State and Federal Institutions for Adult Felons 1968, 1969, 1970*, 47 Nat'l Prisoner Statistics Bulletin, at 3, table 2 (1972). The phrase "jungle atmosphere" plays on racial stereotypes of blacks as inhuman savages. Ms. Rawlinson is a young, twenty-two-year-old, petite white woman, standing just

5'2" and weighing only 115 pounds. The history of the American South is filled with lynching and other practices designed to protect white women from black male sexuality. Kenneth M. Stampp, *The Peculiar Institution: Slavery in the Ante-Bellum South* 190–91 (1956); Arnold Rose, *The Negro in America* 185–86 (1964). Black men have historically been viewed as sexual predators who need to be controlled. Susan Brownmiller, *Against Our Will: Men, Women and Rape* 194, 211–13 (1975). When one court utilizes and this Court emphasizes the term "jungle," one can easily reach the conclusion that the race of the prisoners coupled with the race of the female job applicant played a part in the perceived need to protect Ms. Rawlinson.

B

The BFOQ and women's sexuality

The biggest disagreement I have with the majority opinion is with its treatment of sex and sexuality. Women, the majority argues, cannot serve as guards because of their very "womanhood." Or as the Commissioner of the Board of Corrections, Judson Locke, crassly put it, "She is a sex object." Mem. for the United States as Amicus Curiae at 27. The majority accepts the argument of the State of Alabama that women cannot be prison guards because sexual assaults of female guards are inevitable, and, as a result, Alabama cannot maintain order and security in the prison if women are present. The majority's acceptance of this argument reinforces the subordination of women, in general, and of female workers in particular. As such, and because it is based on a particularly insidious stereotype about women, it cannot be the basis for a BFOQ.

In addition, an employer discriminates against women on the basis of sex and violates Title VII if it creates a work environment that allows and justifies the sexual assault of women. Some lower courts have described an employer's failure to end and prevent sexual assault as sexual harassment in violation of the law. *E.g. Williams v. Saxbe*, 413 F. Supp. 654 (D.C. 1976). The facts in this case demand that we continue the development of this aspect of Title VII.

1

The employer's arguments are based on stereotypes about women as sexual objects who inevitably cause sexual assault

The majority's line of reasoning reinforces the stereotypes that women are, first and foremost, sexual objects whose very presence cause sexual assault. It also relies on the unstated premise that the stereotype is fixed, normal and natural, and nothing can be done to change it. So long as a woman is a woman, she will be viewed primarily as "a sex object." The stereotype of women as sexual objects negatively impacts workers when, as in this case, it precludes them from holding jobs. My brethren, in their concurrence, stated the argument this way:

> With all respect, this rationale regrettably perpetuates one of the most insidious of the old myths about women that women, wittingly or not, are seductive sexual objects. The effect of the decision, made I am sure with the best of intentions, is to punish women because their very presence might provoke sexual assaults. It is women who are made to pay the price in lost job opportunities for the threat of depraved conduct by prison inmates. Once again, "(t)he pedestal upon which women have been placed has ... upon closer inspection, been revealed as a cage." *Sail'er Inn, Inc. v. Kirby,* 5 Cal.3d 1, 20, 95 Cal.Rptr. 329, 341, 485 P.2d 529, 541 (1971).
>
> *Dothard,* 433 U.S. at 345 (Marshall, J., concurring).

The negative effects of the stereotype are even more insidious than the concurrence suggests, though, because they impact even those female workers who are not completely excluded from jobs because of their sexuality. When female workers are viewed first and foremost as sex objects, they are not viewed primarily as workers. Because of the division between the world of sex and the world of work, a person who is viewed primarily through the lens of sex will never be evaluated first and foremost through the lens of job performance. That is why male workers, especially in nontraditional jobs, who do not want women competing for their jobs, will emphasize their female coworkers' sexuality. Whether it is a seemingly innocent compliment on how she looks; a reference to her sex life; a proposition; or offensive name-calling based on a female body part, such comments recast the woman as sex object, instead of woman as worker. The majority's wholesale adoption of this stereotype as an adequate basis for a BFOQ makes it almost impossible for female workers to be judged fairly on the basis of their work performance and not their sex.

This line of reasoning also reinforces disturbing stereotypes about sexual assault. It assumes that sexual assaults are inevitable because of women's sexual allure. In this world view, it is the woman's sexuality – her very womanhood – which causes the assaults. In fact, rape has nothing to do with sexual allure; it is a crime of violence. Brownmiller, *Against Our Will, supra,* at 15. Linking rape with women's sexual allure creates and validates a culture where rape and sexual assault become quasi-acceptable because of the notion that they are an extension of men's natural sexual response and cannot be prevented. In this version of the world, rape is a biological imperative rather than a deviant criminal act of the assailant. Because it locates the cause of sexual assault in women's sexuality, this line of reasoning also leads rather quickly to blaming violent assaults on the victim, rather than focusing on the acts of the assailant.

This approach to sexual assault is problematic because it makes the act of rape less troubling to society and less likely to be prosecuted. As a result of attitudes like the ones embodied in the majority's reasoning, real, violent harms to women are ignored and downplayed. Male dominance of women, physically and sexually, is seen as a normal part of maleness and masculinity. Taken to its logical end, this perspective, which is embedded in the majority reasoning, means women have no independent agency and no right to control their bodily integrity. As a result of this victim blaming, a woman who "cries rape" is put on trial herself. She must prove that she did not provoke the assault and that she fought back against her assailant. No other crime requires the victim to do such things. Stereotypical assumptions about sexual assault are particularly prevalent in the prison environment where there is a disturbing prevalence of prisoner-on-prisoner rape. Within the prison system, even more than outside, rape is viewed as commonplace and quasi-acceptable. Rape can be viewed as anything from a welcome diversion to an additional form of punishment meted out against a deserving offender. It sometimes serves as a punch line for jokes. But, for the prisoner victims of rape, it is not a joke. The majority's acceptance of the "rape is inevitable" trope will only make things worse for those incarcerated in our nation's prisons.

For all these reasons, the majority's reasoning that primarily defines women as objects of sexual desire and therefore inevitable victims of sexual assault cannot form the basis of the BFOQ.

2

It is irrational to allow an employer to argue that by establishing a sexually abusive workplace it has created a BFOQ allowing it to exclude women

The majority's reasoning misses on two critical points. First, the majority should have recognized that an employer who creates or tolerates a sexually abusive workplace that negatively affects women discriminates against women in violation of Title VII. Second, a violation of Title VII such as this cannot form the basis for a BFOQ; rather, it is an illegal employment practice that

needs to be corrected. The second point seems obvious. To justify a discriminatory action as necessary because of existing, underlying discrimination is cir-
cular reasoning at its worst. If a stereotype cannot be used as the basis for a
BFOQ, then certainly outright discrimination cannot be used as justification
either. Essentially, the prison argues that because it has created a workplace
that is unsafe for women, Title VII should allow it to exclude women from the
workplace. The prison bears responsibility for the fact that the workplace is
unsafe for women because it has, apparently, taken no action to stop rape and
sexual violence against women, nor does it plan to take any action. It cannot
use its failure to end and prevent sexual assault to justify not hiring women.
Such a conclusion would make a mockery of the BFOQ and Title VII's goal
of ending discrimination.

A job that is dangerous to a woman because of her sexuality is discriminatory. An employer cannot create or tolerate a sexually hostile environment
without violating Title VII. Lower courts have recently begun to confront
these issues. Some courts, adopting the same "sexual assault is inevitable
when women are in the workplace" trope found in the majority's opinion,
have ruled that "sexual harassment and sexually motivated assault do not constitute sex discrimination under Title VII." *E.g. Tomkins v. Pub. Serv. Elec. &
Gas Co.*, 422 F. Supp. 553, 556 (D.N.J. 1976). For the reasons described above,
that outcome cannot be accepted and those cases should be overturned.

Other courts have found that sexual harassment would be prohibited only
if it were part of "an employer's active or tacit approval, of a personnel policy."
E.g., Miller v. Bank of America, 418 F. Supp. 233 (N.D. Cal. 1976). The actions
of the employer in this case would violate Title VII even under this restrictive
view, because the employer has admitted that acceptance of sexual violence
against female employees is the policy of the system. The reasoning of this
line of cases is, however, too restrictive to be consistent with the goals of Title
VII. An employer must be held accountable not just for harassing conduct
which is part of an employer's policy. To truly realize the goal of Title VII to
achieve equality of employment opportunities and remove barriers, employers
must be held accountable if they tolerate discriminatory conduct, even if that
conduct is not part of an acknowledged policy.

The lower courts that we should follow today are those that have begun to
recognize a type of discrimination violating Title VII called "sexual harassment," *see, e.g., Williams v. Saxbe*, 413 F. Supp. 654 (D.C. 1976) or "racial
harassment," *see, e.g., Rogers v. EEOC*, 454 F.2d 234 (5th Cir. 1971). In these
cases, employees are targeted for poor treatment because of their membership
in a protected class. In the sexual harassment cases, female employees are
subjected to sexual advances, sexual assault or comments of a sexual nature.

Women are the target of these actions because they are women. Thus the actions are discrimination on the basis of sex. The harm caused by the harassment does not need to result in a discharge to be actionable. Since the purpose of Title VII is to provide for full economic opportunity and participation, any employer activity that interferes with full economic opportunity and participation of a protected group can be reached by the statute. As Judge Goldberg wrote in discussing ethnic harassment in *Rogers*:

> We must be acutely conscious of the fact that Title VII of the Civil Rights Act of 1964 should be accorded a liberal interpretation in order to effectuate the purpose of Congress to eliminate the inconvenience, unfairness, and humiliation of ethnic discrimination ... the employees' psychological as well as economic fringes are statutorily entitled to protection from employer abuse, and that the phrase "terms, conditions, or privileges of employment" in Section 703 is an expansive concept which sweeps within its protective ambit the practice of creating a working environment heavily charged with ethnic or racial discrimination.
>
> 454 F.2d at 238.

In the instant case, the employer admits that it has created a work environment that is abusive and hostile to women, as women. An atmosphere hostile to women as women violates Title VII because it is harder for women to succeed in such a workplace. It denies them equal opportunity for full economic participation. The employer has an obligation to eliminate and prevent this type of behavior. If it fails to do so, as the employer has in this case, it violates Title VII.

For these reasons, I dissent from the majority's ruling as it applies to the BFOQ.

12

Commentary on *City of Los Angeles Department of Water and Power v. Manhart*

Cassandra Jones Havard

INTRODUCTION

Marie Manhart, a former employee of the City of Los Angeles Department of Water and Power, brought a class action lawsuit on behalf of herself and current and former employees, challenging the Department's requirement that female employees contribute approximately 15 percent more than male employees to the Department's retirement plan.[1] The Department used sex-based actuarial tables to classify employees and determine the amount of an employee's contribution. The plaintiffs alleged that because identically situated male employees paid less, the policy constituted discrimination based on sex under Title VII of the Civil Rights Act of 1964.[2] The plaintiffs argued that the Department impermissibly classified employees by sex and not as individuals to determine the amount of the contributions.

The Department defended the differential treatment, asserting that women on average had longer life expectancies than men.[3] It argued that Title VII did not apply because actuarial longevity factor was a "factor other than the [employee's] sex."[4] In the original majority opinion written by Justice Stevens, the U.S. Supreme Court agreed with the lower courts that the employer discriminated by reducing the take-home pay of women.[5] The Court found retroactive relief inappropriate, however, because of the potential impact on the employer and economy.[6]

---

[1] *City of L.A. Dept. of Water & Power v. Manhart*, 435 U.S. 702, 705 (1978). The annual disparity was approximately $6,000, with women making payments of approximately $18,171.40 compared to $12,834.53 paid by men.

[2] 42 U.S.C. § 2000e-2(a)(1) (Supp. V 1970).

[3] *Manhart*, 435 U.S. at 712.

[4] *Id.*

[5] *Manhart*, 435 U.S. at 717.

[6] *Id.* at 718–733.

In an opinion concurring in part and dissenting in part, Justice Marshall reasoned that the *Manhart* plaintiffs were wrongly denied restitution, a refund of the wages improperly deducted from their take-home pay.[7] Relying on the foundational case *Albemarle Paper Co. v. Moody*,[8] Justice Marshall posited that Title VII authorized the district court to fashion appropriate relief, with a presumption favoring retroactive relief. Examining the record for clearly erroneous factual findings and abuse of discretion, Justice Marshall concluded that this presumption in favor of retroactive relief was not overcome.[9]

THE FEMINIST JUDGMENT

In the *Manhart* feminist judgment, a re-imagined majority opinion, Professor Tracy Thomas, writing as Justice Thomas, explores how legal systems may operate to economically oppress women. The judgment implies that sex- or gender-based discrimination is systematic, patriarchal, and hierarchical, effectively suppressing and subordinating women. This is especially true when assumptions and stereotypes go unquestioned. From Thomas's opinion, one infers her belief that failure to award damages, as the original *Manhart* opinion did, operates to validate the legal and economic marginalization of female workers. Advancing gender equality, therefore, required invalidating the Department's classification and awarding damages. Thomas's opinion rejects the traditional notions about women that are embedded in law and policy and that often surface as *post hoc* rationales.[10] Decision making must be scrutinized for stereotypes and generalizations, implicit biases and inconsistencies in order to completely eradicate the unequal treatment of the sexes.

Thomas's feminist judgment is in substantial agreement with Justice Marshall's partial concurrence and dissent. The rewritten majority opinion demonstrates that sex-based classifications are impermissible under Title VII. Thomas's opinion expresses the underlying concern that gendered assumptions may result in the economic oppression of women. The judgment takes a feminist approach by drawing attention to three aspects of gendered economic subordination: the pension plan's stereotype of female employees is overly broad and does not evaluate them based on individual characteristics; second, prior precedents are structurally flawed because of their gender-based

---

[7] *Id.* at 732–733 (Marshall, J., concurring in part and dissenting in part).

[8] *Albemarle Paper Co. v. Moody*, 422 U.S. 405 (1975).

[9] *Manhart*, 435 U.S. at 733 (Marshall, J., concurring in part and dissenting in part).

[10] *See, e.g.*, Ruth Milkman, Gender at Work: The Dynamics of Job Segregation by Sex During World War II 26 (1987) (discussing how employers' explicit designation of "women's jobs" in the auto and electrical industries during the 1920s became an industry norm).

classifications; and third, it would be inequitable for the Court to award Title
VII back pay for male workers in a preceding retirement benefits case, but not
in this one.[11]

GENDERED ECONOMIC ASSUMPTIONS

Traditionally, American culture associated men with work and wages and
women with home and family.[12] That norm changed as women entered the
paid workforce out of both necessity and choice.[13] Slower to change were workplace rules and policies.[14] At the heart of the *Manhart* controversy is the conflict between actuarial logic and formal equality. While actuarial techniques are
often labeled as impartial, they are also based on social norms.[15] Thomas's feminist judgment clarifies the female employees' discrimination claim by showing
how the longevity factor treats them differently based on sex. She isolates the
substantive flaws in what appears to be neutral decision making, the application
of precedent, and the appropriate relief for victims of discrimination.

GENDERED STEREOTYPES

Insurance companies have long taken the view that economic discrimination
is fair if there is an actuarial basis for differential treatment. Supporters of classifications based on sex or race posit that such classifications are both neutral
and beneficial.[16] An issue arises, however, if the criteria used to define the differences are based on generalizations or stereotypes.[17] There is a long, sordid
history of improper racial classifications in the insurance industry.[18] Using race
as a proxy for longevity, insurance companies, until prohibited by law, routinely sold more expensive (but less valuable) policies to African-Americans.[19]

---

[11] See *Fitzpatrick v. Bitzer*, 427 U.S. 445 (1976).
[12] Herbert A. Applebaum, The American Work Ethic and the Changing Work Force: An
     Historical Perspective 119–120 (1998).
[13] World War II contributed to the changing role of the paid woman worker. *See generally*
     Douglas R. Hurt, The Great Plains During World War II 84–85 (2008).
[14] *See, e.g.*, Raymond Gregory, Women and Workplace Discrimination: Overcoming Barriers to
     Gender Equality 23 (2002).
[15] Spencer L. Kimball, *The Purpose of Insurance Regulation: A Preliminary Inquiry in the Theory
     of Insurance Law*, 45 Minn. L. Rev. 471, 495 (1961).
[16] Jonathan Simon, *Ideological Effects of Actuarial Practices*, 22 Law & Soc'y Rev. 771, 781 (1988).
[17] *See generally* Regina Austin, *The Insurance Classification Controversy*, 131 U. Pa L. Rev. 517,
     534–548 (1983).
[18] *See generally* Mary L. Heen, *Ending Jim Crow Life Insurance Rates*, 4 Nw. J. L. & Soc. Pol'y.
     360 (2009).
[19] Insurance companies used racially explicit mortality tables to provide separate pricing. *See
     Lange v. Rancher*, 56 N.W.2d 542, 543 (Wis. 1953).

This actuarial practice was mirrored in *Manhart* in the selected gender classification.

A critical feature of the feminist judgment is Thomas's reliance on *Califano v. Goldfarb*, which also struck down gender-specific requirements regarding male widowers' receipt of Social Security benefits.[20] Thomas implies that *Manhart's* failure to follow *Califano* would be yet another glaring injustice of the Court's intentionally restricting women's employment opportunities. That historical perspective is crucial in invalidating this unintentional yet discriminatory structure. Thomas acknowledges that longevity could have been one of several appropriate factors used to determine any employee's contribution, but that sex is not an appropriate proxy for longevity. Not only will some men live longer than the projected life expectancy, but some women will not live as long as projected. Thus, reducing every female employee's take-home pay was based on an over-simplified belief that is factually untrue.

INCONSISTENT PRECEDENTS

Title VII prohibits an employer from discriminating on the basis of sex. In this and previous cases, the Court had difficulty delineating gendered circumstances and even recognizing sex-based discrimination. In *General Electric v. Gilbert*,[21] relying on the equal protection case of *Geduldig v. Aiello*,[22] pregnancy was excluded as a disability and an insurance benefit, respectively. This exclusion applied to both men and women. Although pregnancy is unique to women, the Court found no Title VII violation in either case, reasoning that the employer's classification of affected employees was "pregnant women" and "nonpregnant persons," not a classification based on sex. The original decision in *Manhart* distinguished *Gilbert*, finding that the Department's classification was one based solely upon sex, and because women were disadvantaged.[23] Thomas implies that *Gilbert* and *Geduldig* were wrongly decided. She hints, "It may very well be that these pregnancy cases require re-examination." Had Thomas's feminist judgment been the actual majority decision in *Manhart*, her decision would have paved the way for the Court to revisit those cases. Such action proved unnecessary, however, as six months later Congress overruled *Gilbert* by amending Title VII to expressly provide that discrimination "because of sex" included pregnancy discrimination.[24] Broadly construed,

---

[20] *Califano v. Goldfarb*, 430 U.S. 199 (1977).
[21] *General Electric v. Gilbert*, 429 U.S. 125 (1976).
[22] *Geduldig v. Aiello*, 417 U.S. 484 (1974).
[23] *Manhart*, 435 U.S. at 715.
[24] 42 U.S.C. § 2000e(k) (2000), as an amendment to Title VII of the Civil Rights Act of 1964.

the feminist judgment in *Manhart* stands for the proposition that exclusively female classifications discriminate against individual women and therefore are impermissible. Thus classifications based on pregnancy would fail.

INEQUITABLE REMEDIES

Justice Stevens' original opinion reevaluated the appropriateness of relief, focusing on the employer's good faith and potential economic harm to deny restitution for the past harm. Thomas departs from the original *Manhart* decision in applying the *Albemarle* presumption. Echoing Justice Marshall's language, Thomas said that any allegation of economic harm to innocent parties was "chimerical."[25] The feminist judgment notes that the Court is bound by the precedent in *Fitzpatrick v. Bitzer*.[26] In that case, male employees who had been subject to a discriminatory retirement plan were awarded retroactive relief. It is axiomatic, then, in Thomas's opinion that the discriminated female employees in *Manhart* should receive back pay or restitution, having actually made the very payments now declared illegal. Thomas is not swayed by arguments about potentially cataclysmic impacts on the nation's pension system. This is, in part, because of her capacious understanding of remedies. Thomas recognizes that EEOC rules permit reimbursement for only a two-year period, and that structured payment systems or reductions on women's contributions for a limited time could accomplish the correct result without disastrous financial consequences to anyone.

CONCLUSION

Feminist law reform requires revealing how traditional, accepted notions perpetuate female inequality including economic subordination. The *Manhart* feminist judgment exposes the stereotypes, assumptions, and implicit biases that result in economic subordination of women. Thomas's feminist revision points out how the original majority's multiple missteps, incorrect standard of review, and failure to invalidate gendered economic assumptions in the prior precedents and to award restitution in *Manhart* are contrary to Title VII's purpose and frustrate the statutory scheme of eradicating discrimination. The Court's denial of retroactive liability devalued the female employees in substantially the same way as the employer did. It also made the victims' victory hollow. The feminist judgment, by awarding back pay and attorney's fees,

[25] *Manhart*, 435 U.S. at 732 (Marshall, J., concurring in part and dissenting in part).
[26] *Fitzpatrick v. Bitzer*, 427 U.S. 455 (1976).

which even Justice Marshall had not considered,[27] forces the employer to bear full responsibility for its past wrong acts and to restore women to a formally equal position.

City of Los Angeles Department of Water & Power v. Manhart, 435 U.S. 702 (1978)

Justice Tracy A. Thomas delivered the opinion of the Court.

Women working for the City of Los Angeles Department of Water and Power take home less pay than men for the same work because they are required to make greater contributions to their employer's pension fund. The Department assesses all women approximately 15 percent more than men for the same pension plan which pays employees a monthly annuity at retirement. This is a significant disparity as illustrated by the record of one woman whose annual contribution to the fund was $18,171.40 while a similarly situated man contributed only $12,843.53 for the same monthly benefit in retirement. The Department claims that the surcharge is justifiable because women as a class live longer on average than men do, and thus women will receive retirement benefits longer than men will. We reject this use of a sex-based classification for employment benefits. We thus affirm the holdings of the courts below finding that the Department's retirement contribution plan violates Title VII of the Civil Rights Act of 1964, as amended by the Equal Employment Opportunity Act of 1972, 42 U.S.C. § 2000e-2(a)(1), and affirm the award of retroactive monetary relief.

I

The long and winding road

The Department's practice of discriminating against women in employment benefits is part of a "long and unfortunate history of sex discrimination." *Frontiero v. Richardson*, 411 U.S. 677, 684 (1973) (plurality). Its use of gender-based actuarial tables follows a pattern since the mid-nineteenth century of using such statistics to justify higher costs or reduction of benefits to women. *See* Henry Moir, *Sources and Characteristics of the Principal Mortality Tables* 10, 14 (1919). The assumptions behind this gender-differentiated practice were grounded in traditional notions of women's dependency in the home and men's primary breadwinner role. The reduced economic benefit

---

[27] *Manhart*, 435 U.S. at 728–733 (Marshall, J., concurring in part and dissenting in part).

for women reflected the belief that women did not need the same financial security as men because they were not supporting themselves or their families. Similarly here, the Department seems to assume that women have less need for their monthly income and can accept earning 15 percent less for the same work as men.

This Court has, in the past, perpetuated such stereotypes about women's subordinate role in the workplace. In *Bradwell v. Illinois*, 83 U.S. 130 (1873), the Court denied Myra Bradwell's right to practice law. The concurrence explained that "[t]he paramount destiny and mission of woman is to fulfill the noble and benign offices of wife and mother." *Id.* at 141 (Bradley, J., concurring). Citing divine and natural law, it concluded that "the female sex evidently unfits it for many of the occupations of civil life." *Id.* Instead, it explained, women properly belong to the domestic sphere, which was "repugnant to the idea of a woman adopting a distinct and independent career from that of her husband." *Id.* Decades later, in *Muller v. Oregon*, 208 U.S. 412 (1908), this Court again found women's nature made them less capable and less dependent on the workplace, thereby justifying maximum-hour laws for women that limited their work and pay.

In recent years, however, the Court has challenged such acceptance of sex-based economic assumptions. In *Califano v. Goldfarb*, 430 U.S. 199 (1977), we struck down gender-based distinctions in the federal Social Security Act that allowed all widows, but only dependent widowers, to obtain survivor's benefits. The law was based on the gendered assumption that all women were dependent on their spouses, while most men were not. The Court rejected such a gender-based rule "when supported by no more substantial justification than archaic and overbroad generalizations, or old notions, such as assumptions as to dependency, that are more consistent with the role-typing society has long imposed, than with contemporary reality." *Id.* at 207 (citations omitted). The decision in *Califano* thus clearly signaled that the Court will closely scrutinize sex-based classifications for economic benefits like the one presented here.

The Department requires its female employees to make larger contributions to its pension fund than male employees. Upon retirement, each employee is eligible under the pension plan for a monthly retirement benefit computed as a fraction of salary multiplied by years of service. The plan is funded by employee contributions matched by 110 percent compulsory employer contributions plus interest earned. The monthly benefits for men and women of the same age, seniority, and salary are equal. Based on a study of mortality tables and its own experience, the Department determined that its 2,000 female employees, on average, will live a few years longer than its

10,000 male employees. The cost of a pension for the average retired female is greater than for the average male retiree because more monthly payments must be made to the average woman who lives longer. The Department therefore required all women to make extra monthly contributions to the fund that were 14.84 percent higher than the contributions required of similarly situated male employees. Employee retirement contributions were withheld from paychecks, and thus women received less take-home pay for equal work because of their sex.

On April 5, 1972, the Equal Employment Opportunity Commission (EEOC) amended its regulations to clarify that this type of sex-based contribution differential is illegal. The EEOC regulations provided that it shall not be a defense to a charge of sex discrimination in benefits that "the cost of such benefits is greater with respect to one sex than the other." 29 CFR § 1604.9(e); *see also id.* §§ 1604.9(b&f). The Department thus should have been on notice of the illegality of its retirement contribution plan, but took no action to change it. In 1973, five women and their union brought this suit in the United States District Court for the Central District of California on behalf of a class of women employed or formerly employed by the Department. They requested an injunction prohibiting the future operation of the sex-based pension contribution plan, restitution of the excess contributions, and attorney's fees. While this action was pending, the California Legislature enacted a law prohibiting certain municipal agencies from requiring female employees to make higher pension fund contributions than males. Cal. Gov't. Code Ann. § 7500 (1975). The Department thus amended its plan on January 1, 1975. The current plan draws no distinction on the basis of sex.

The District Court granted a preliminary injunction and subsequently granted summary judgment for the plaintiffs, ruling that the extra assessment against women violated Title VII. *Manhart v. City of Los Angeles, Dep't. of Water & Power*, 387 F. Supp. 980 (1975). It ordered a refund of the excess contributions paid since April 5, 1972, the date of the EEOC regulations, measured by the difference between the amount the women paid versus the amount men paid, and adding 7 percent interest. It also awarded reasonable attorney's fees. The United States Court of Appeals for the Ninth Circuit affirmed and denied rehearing en banc. *Manhart v. City of Los Angeles, Dep't. of Water & Power*, 553 F.2d 581 (1976).

On appeal, the Department and *amici curiae* argue that the contribution surcharge does not constitute sex discrimination because it is based on longevity, a factor "other than sex," which differently situates women and justifies their different treatment. *See* 42 U.S.C. § 2000e-2(h); *Gen. Elec. Co. v. Gilbert*, 429 U.S. 125 (1976). We reject these contentions as the evidence shows that the

Department explicitly and singularly relies only on sex in treating employees differently in clear contravention of the law. Accordingly, we affirm the decisions of the courts below.

II

The same yet different

There are both real and fictional differences between women and men. The question is whether these differences bear any legal significance. Our past cases have struck down discriminatory decisions predicated on economic stereotypes about women. *Califano*, 430 U.S. 199; *Frontiero*, 411 U.S. at 690; *Weinberger v. Wiesenfeld*, 420 U.S. 636, 642 (1975). The Civil Rights Act of 1964 forbids employers from discriminating against individuals because of their sex, and by this law "Congress intended to strike at the entire spectrum of disparate treatment of men and women resulting from sex stereotypes." *Sprogis v. United Air Lines, Inc.*, 444 F.2d 1194, 1198 (7th Cir. 1971).

The Department claims this case is distinguishable because its practice is not based on stereotypes of women, but on the statistical fact that women live longer than men. We have noted, however, that stereotypes may contain an element of truth. *Weinberger*, 420 U.S. at 642. In a context similar to the case here, we found that the assumption of the Social Security law that men were more likely than women to be the primary supporters of their children was "not entirely without empirical support." Nevertheless, we struck down the law because "such a gender-based generalization cannot suffice to justify the denigration of the efforts of women who do work and whose earnings contribute significantly to their families' support." *Id.* at 642. The statistically valid fact that more men than women were breadwinners did not save the sex-based classification. The infirmity was in applying that factual observation about a group to an individual for whom it might not have been true.

Thus, in the analogous context of race, the use of statistical facts is no longer a valid reason for providing unequal economic benefits. Actuarial statistics show a higher mortality rate for blacks as a group, but using that race-based distinction to charge individuals more for insurance has been struck down as illegal and has otherwise been discontinued. *See Lange v. Rancher*, 56 N.W.2d 542 (Wis. 1953). A distinction based on sex like that based on race is judicially suspect. *See Frontiero*, 411 U.S. at 688. "Since sex, like race and national origin, is an immutable characteristic determined solely by the accident of birth, the imposition of special disabilities upon the members of a particular sex because of their sex would seem to violate 'the basic concept of our system

that legal burdens should bear some relationship to individual responsibility.'"
Id. at 686.

Despite the Department's claims, the evidence does not show that it is relying on longevity as the determinative factor in assessing retirement contributions. A retirement plan using longevity would connect the surcharge to
projected lifespan, for example assessing a surcharge after twenty years to those
employees who draw longer on the retirement benefits. Or a retirement plan
relying on longevity might predict an individual's projected lifespan based on
the relevant factors of health, genetics, obesity, and behaviors like smoking
and alcohol consumption. Sex is not an accurate proxy for longevity because
it is not the biological fact of sex that makes women on average live longer, but
rather the fact of other behaviors or circumstances. For example, more men
are heavy smokers, but it is the fact of smoking, not sex, that is determinative
of lifespan. Robert D. Retherford, *The Changing Sex Differential In Mortality*
71–82 (1975). The Department claims that a more individualized assessment
would be cost prohibitive, and thus for administrative ease it must instead
rely on the proxy of sex. This Court, however, has repeatedly rejected administrative convenience as an excuse for sex discrimination. *Califano*, 430 U.S.
199; *Reed v. Reed*, 404 U.S. 71, 76 (1971); *Frontiero*, 411 U.S. at 690. Indeed,
in *Cleveland Board of Education v. LaFleur*, 414 U.S. 632, 644, 647 (1974),
we criticized an employer's use of administratively convenient presumptions
about women and its failure to make individualized determinations about the
relevant health factors for women. The excuse of administrative convenience
is no more defensible here.

The Department's employee classification also shows that it is regulating
by sex, not longevity. Unlike our recent decision in *Gen. Elec. Co. v. Gilbert*,
429 U.S. 125 (1976), where the employer classified by an identifiable physical condition, the Department here expressly classifies on the basis of sex.
In *Gilbert*, the employer excluded pregnancy from its disability plan, and the
question was whether that pregnancy distinction was a factor "other than sex"
or merely a pretext for sex-based classification. *Id.* at 134. It was persuasive to a
majority of the divided Court that pregnancy distinctions were not sex-based
because women were included in both the disadvantaged pregnant group and
the advantaged non-pregnant group. *Id.* at 135; *see also Geduldig v. Aiello*,
417 U.S. 484, 496–497 (1974). It may very well be that these pregnancy cases
require re-examination. But we need not do that here.

The Department retirement plan expressly differentiates based on sex.
Employees are not grouped according to longevity, but solely by sex. As the
Court of Appeals noted, "it is not reasonable to say," as the Department does,
"that an actuarial distinction based entirely on sex is 'based on any other factor

other than sex.' Sex is exactly what it is based on." *Manhart*, 553 F.2d at 588. The Department's classification creates two groups of employees composed entirely and exclusively of members of the same sex, and then assigns all disadvantage to the women. All women pay the surcharge and receive reduced pay; all men pay no surcharge and receive full pay. This classification is overly broad, because it includes women who will not in fact live longer than average. The rule is also under-inclusive because it excludes men who will have longer lifespans and increased retirement costs. Perhaps more telling, 84 percent of women and men live to the same age. Gerald D. Martin, *Gender Discrimination in Pension Plans*, XLIII J. of Risk & Ins. 203 (1976). Thus, in the vast majority of cases, there is no statistical difference in longevity based upon sex.

Insurance works by grouping people together in order to share the costs and risks across a wide spectrum. However, Title VII prohibits the grouping of those risks solely on the basis of sex. Today we hold that an employer may not discriminate against women by requiring them to make unequal, higher contributions to an employer-operated pension fund. Nor may the employer circumvent this holding by moving the sex-based classification to the end payout stage by paying women retirees less in their monthly benefit. Whether by higher costs or reduced benefit, the discrimination is the same. Title VII may not have envisioned a revolution in the insurance industry, but it has produced one. Congress clearly intended to eradicate all sex-based decisions in employment, including in the provision of insurance and retirement benefits like the plan challenged here.

III

Ubi jus, ibi remedium

The question remains as to the appropriate relief in this case. It is a standard proposition of law that *ubi jus, ibi remedium*: "where there's a right, there must be a remedy." As we held in the early days of this Court, the very foundations of justice and jurisprudence require that violations of rights are vindicated with meaningful remedies. *Marbury v. Madison*, 5 U.S. 137 (1803). "It is a settled and invariable principle, that every right, when withheld, must have a remedy, and every injury its proper redress." *Id.* For in the absence of such tangible, meaningful relief, legal rights become empty, unenforceable aspirations that are not supported with concrete action forcing defendants to internalize the consequences of their wrongful behavior. Without specific consequences, defendants have no incentives to avoid such discriminatory misconduct.

That is the case here. The Department seeks to avoid all consequences for its history of sex discrimination. While injunctive relief and an intervening California law have ended the use of this discriminatory plan, they do not redress the years of overcharges and lost monies to the plaintiff class. The Civil Rights Act provides that a court in a Title VII case may "order such affirmative action as may be appropriate, which may include, but is not limited to, reinstatement ... with or without back pay ... or any other equitable relief as the court deems appropriate." 42 U.S.C. § 2000e-5. Back pay is limited to two years prior to the filing of the case with the EEOC. *Id.* at 5(g). Courts also have discretion to award prevailing plaintiffs attorney's fees. *Id.* at 5(k). In accordance with the statute, the District Court ordered the refund of all overcharges going back to April 5, 1972, the date of the EEOC regulations. 13 Fair Empl. Prac. Cas. at 1625. This was a shorter period of time than permitted by the statute, which would have allowed retroactive relief to June 5, 1971. The court also awarded reasonable attorney's fees.

While the Department challenges this retroactive refund as inappropriate, the Court has previously established a "presumption in favor of retroactive liability" in Title VII cases which "can seldom be overcome." *Albemarle Paper Co. v. Moody*, 422 U.S. 405 (1975). The strong presumption is that "the injured party is to be placed, as near as may be, in the situation he would have occupied if the wrong had not been committed." *Id.* at 418. Retroactive relief "should be denied only for reasons which, if applied generally, would not frustrate the central statutory purposes of eradicating discrimination throughout the economy and making persons whole for injuries suffered through past discrimination." *Id.* at 421. Retroactive monetary relief makes plaintiffs whole and provides the consequences for discriminatory conduct and the incentives for required egalitarian treatment. Such retroactive relief is the usual default remedy in both Title VII and the law more generally. The only required showing is loss to the plaintiff. No heightened standard of bad faith or evil intent is required because the statutory purpose is compensatory, not punitive.

> If backpay were awardable only upon a showing of bad faith, the remedy would become a punishment for moral turpitude, rather than a compensation for workers' injuries. This would read the "make whole" purpose right out of Title VII for a worker's injury is no less real simply because the employer did not inflict it in "bad faith."
>
> *Id.* at 422.

Thus, it is immaterial whether the plan administrators were conscientious or recalcitrant in the face of intervening EEOC guidelines. What is relevant is the economic loss to the plaintiffs from the charges illegally withheld from their paychecks. We measure the amount of this loss by awarding the difference between contributions made by female employees and those made by male employees. While the inability to assess the discriminatory surcharge might have required the Department to adopt a different, undifferentiated actuarial table that would have reassessed contributions for both women and men, we cannot use this hypothetical past to calculate monetary relief nor can we rectify a precise accounting by deducting pay from the checks of the male employees who are not parties to this action. Instead, our goal is to ensure the "employee is placed in no worse a position than if" the conduct had not occurred, and the return of the improper contributions as actually paid is necessarily required to provide that meaningful relief as envisioned by Title VII. *Mt. Healthy City Sch. Dist. Bd. of Educ. v. Doyle*, 429 U.S. 274, 286 (1977).

We recently approved such retroactive relief for a class of men in a Title VII case similarly challenging a retirement plan. *Fitzpatrick v. Bitzer*, 427 U.S. 445 (1976). In *Fitzpatrick*, the Court held that a state retirement plan that allowed women to retire five years earlier than men discriminated on the basis of sex and that the Eleventh Amendment did not bar retroactive payment of retirement benefits as an appropriate remedy. Denying this same retroactive relief in the case here when confronted with a similar discriminatory retirement plan would establish the perverse rule that allows damages for men, but not women. Such a result would clearly "frustrate the central statutory purposes of eradicating discrimination" under Title VII by re-inscribing sex inequality via the remedial mechanism. *Albemarle Paper Co.*, 422 U.S. at 421.

The Court has, however, been sensitive to special circumstances in exercising our equitable powers under Title VII to fashion an appropriate remedy. 42 U.S.C. § 2000e-5(g); *Albemarle Paper Co.*, 422 U.S. at 418–419; *see Chevron Oil Co. v. Huson*, 404 U.S. 97, 105–09 (1971). Special circumstances that might be relevant in a case like this involving a government pension fund include the potential economic impact of the remedy on the public employer, the solvency of the pension fund, or the benefit or harm to third-party employees or retirees. No devastating or detrimental impacts such as these are raised by the facts of this case. The Department itself admitted it could cover this lump sum payment out of city revenues. Pet. for Cert. 30–31. Thus, the Department would pay for this Title VII award in the same way that it would have to pay any ordinary back pay award arising from its discriminatory practices. The payment would not risk insolvency to the pension fund nor any disruption in benefit to the retirees or employees. Hence the possibility of harm falling on innocent retirees or employees is chimerical.

Moreover, the alleged risk of crippling impact on other pension plan defendants following this precedent is minimized by our approach. Our remedial evaluation includes equitable sensitivity, as stated above, to account for unique circumstances of different employers and plans. Second, the EEOC rules permit reimbursement for only a two-year time period prior to the filing of the case, 42 U.S.C. § 2000e-5(g), thus limiting the financial impact of the award. Finally, there other remedial accounting options available to address the practical problems of implementation. A structured payment system that incrementally pays the amount owed over a period of months or years is a common remedial structure. Alternatively, an employer could reduce the amount of women employees' future retirement contributions until the deficit is closed, for example, by having women pay 85 percent of the contribution amount for a period of time.

In this case, however, there are no special factors to overcome the usual presumption of awarding retroactive relief in order to accomplish the primary make-whole purpose of Title VII. The District Court was not clearly erroneous in its factual findings, nor did it abuse its discretion. *See Albemarle Paper Co.*, 422 U.S. at 424. Accordingly, we affirm the judgment below including the award of monetary relief and attorney's fees.

It is so ordered.

13

Commentary on *Harris v. McRae*

Mary Ziegler

INTRODUCTION

The Hyde Amendment, the law at the heart of *Harris v. McRae*,[1] arguably represents the anti-abortion movement's most important victory since the U.S. Supreme Court held in *Roe v. Wade* that the Constitution protects a woman's right to choose abortion. Since September 1976, Congress has banned the use of federal dollars for the reimbursement of most abortion services under the Medicaid program. *McRae* matters most simply because the U.S. Supreme Court rejected a constitutional challenge to the Hyde Amendment, enabling the federal and state governments to ban funding for abortion. As Professor Leslie Griffin's opinion shows, *McRae* might have done even more damage to the cause of women's rights when the Court closed the door on Establishment Clause claims against abortion restrictions.[2]

BACKGROUND

The story of *Harris v. McRae* began in the immediate aftermath of *Roe v. Wade*, when abortion opponents across the country gathered to respond to the U.S. Supreme Court's decision. From the beginning, the movement fixed its sights on a constitutional amendment banning abortion. The Hyde Amendment emerged from an equally important tactical response to *Roe* – one intended to limit access to the procedure as much as possible under the current law.[3]

---

[1] *Harris v. McRae*, 448 U.S. 297 (1980).
[2] For the text of the 1980 version of Hyde Amendment considered by the Court in *McRae*, see Pub. L. No. 96-23 § 109, Stat. 926.
[3] For discussion of the history of the early anti-abortion movement, see Mary Ziegler, After *Roe*: The Lost History of the Abortion Debate 27–95 (2015); Keith Cassidy, *The Right to Life Movement: Sources, Development, and Strategies, in* The Politics of Abortion and Birth Control in Historical Perspective 128–51 (Donald T. Critchlow ed., 1996).

As Representative Henry Hyde of Illinois recognized, Medicaid played a vital part in the realization of the right to choose abortion. Created in 1965, Medicaid provided financial support to participating states to reimburse certain costs incurred in the treatment of needy patients. Because Medicaid operated as a cooperative federal-state program, some states had already banned the use of most abortion funding at the time Hyde pushed his proposal in Congress.[4]

Just the same, Hyde understood the significance of a federal ban. Before 1976, Medicaid funded roughly 33 percent of all abortions. A study conducted in the late 1970s by *Family Planning Perspectives* found that, but for the Hyde Amendment, roughly 23 percent of women who carried a pregnancy to term would have made a different choice. On the day Congress enacted the initial version of the Hyde Amendment, Rhonda Copelon, Sylvia Law, and others – the attorneys for Cora McRae and those challenging the Hyde Amendment – filed suit. Americans United for Life, a group that increasingly embraced incremental restrictions on abortion, quickly sought to intervene and represent Representative Hyde and several congressional allies. A year later, in *Maher v. Roe*, the U.S. Supreme Court upheld a state Medicaid funding ban, reasoning that the law "place[d] no obstacles ... in the pregnant woman's path to an abortion."[5]

At trial, the feminist attorneys focused primarily on distinguishing the Hyde Amendment from the law upheld in *Maher*. While the Connecticut law at issue in that case required the funding of "medically necessary abortions," the Hyde Amendment allowed for funding only when a woman's life would be endangered if she carried a pregnancy to term. The plaintiffs put on extensive expert testimony about the new health risks women would face if the Hyde Amendment stayed in place. Feminist attorneys also amended the complaint to include arguments based on the Religion Clauses of the First Amendment. As Copelon and Law explained, arguments based on the Religion Clauses "provided an additional answer to the holding of *Maher*." In Copelon and Law's view, religion-clause reasoning also strengthened the political case against the Hyde Amendment, exposing "the heavy hand of religious belief and institutions in the battle over Medicaid and abortion."[6]

---

[4] *See* Laurence Tribe, Abortion: The Clash of Absolutes 151 (1992).

[5] *Maher v. Roe*, 432 U.S. 464, 474 (1977). For the *Family Planning Perspectives* article, see James Trussell, Jane Menken, Barbara L. Lindheim, and Barbara Vaughan, *The Impact of Restricting Medicaid Financing for Abortion*, 12 *Family Planning Perspectives* 120, 120 (1980).

[6] Rhonda Copelon and Sylvia Law, *"Nearly Allied to Her Right to Be"* – Medicaid Funding for Abortion: The Story of Harris v. McRae, *in* Women and the Law Stories 222 (Elizabeth M. Schneider and Stephanie Wildman eds., 2011).

The district court's decision shaped the strategy both sides pursued before the U.S. Supreme Court. Trial evidence highlighted the extent to which religious beliefs about the fetus motivated passage of Hyde's rider. Just the same, the district court rejected feminists' Establishment Clause argument. The court insisted that tradition rather than religious belief explained the Hyde Amendment – a secular, "general and long held social view." By contrast, the court held that the Hyde Amendment violated the Free Exercise Clause, framing the abortion decision as a matter of conscience for all women, including those with "religiously formed conscience."[7]

On appeal before the U.S. Supreme Court, feminists continued to press Establishment Clause claims. However, Copelon and her colleagues did not dig below the surface of the "traditionalist" explanation for the Hyde Amendment adopted by the district court. Copelon and Law later wondered whether they should have "take[n] the Establishment Clause argument further and [...] demonstrate[d] more precisely the discriminatory nature of the view of women that underlay the Church's absolutist position on contraception." For tactical reasons, however, feminists mostly stayed away from such a claim, worrying about the "slipperiness of motivational analysis" and the barriers created by the U.S. Supreme Court's past decisions denying that pregnancy discrimination and sex discrimination were one and the same. By contrast, Free Exercise Clause claims seemed easy to reconcile with the ideas of choice and freedom of conscience that the U.S. Supreme Court had already deployed.[8]

The Court's opinion in *McRae* rejected all of the feminists' arguments. The Court first took up the question of whether Title XIX of the Social Security Act required states participating in the Medicaid program to continue funding abortions. The *McRae* majority rejected this claim, emphasizing that Medicaid involved cooperative federalism and therefore did not require the states to unilaterally pay the cost of any procedure, let alone one for which Congress had withdrawn funding. The Court also rejected the distinction plaintiffs had drawn between *Maher* and *McRae*, reiterating that the Due Process Clause in no way "confer[red] an entitlement to such funds as may be necessary to realize all the advantages of that freedom."[9]

The Court's treatment of the Religion Clauses was even more dismissive. Because none of the individual plaintiffs sought an abortion for religious reasons, the *McRae* majority easily set aside arguments about the free exercise

7 *McRae v. Califano*, 491 F. Supp. 630, 738–39, 741–42 (E.D.N.Y. 1980).
8 Copelon and Law, *supra* note 6, at 223.
9 *McRae*, 448 U.S. at 309–10, 316–18.

of religion on standing grounds. The Court further found that the Women's Division of the United Methodist Church did not meet the requirements for standing for a group bringing a claim on behalf of its members because the claim required the participation of individual members to illustrate the burden that the Hyde Amendment imposed on their religious beliefs. Nor did the Court find merit in the Appellees' Establishment Clause argument. Rejecting evidence that the Hyde Amendment reflected one set of religious views, *McRae* suggested that the moral beliefs reflected in the law simply coincided with the values animating certain religions. As the Court stated, the Hyde Amendment was "as much a reflection of 'traditionalist' values towards abortion as it is an embodiment of the views of any particular religion."[10]

REWRITING *MCRAE*

Professor Leslie Griffin, writing as Justice Griffin, illuminates the promise of a path not taken by either the Court's opinion in *McRae* or feminist attorneys at the time: one focused on the Establishment Clause. Griffin cuts through the secular explanations for the Hyde Amendment, taking its legislative history seriously. Her opinion spotlights the lack of concern for medical evidence in the legislative record and shows that the cost-saving concerns some advocates later articulated merely concealed the personal, religious arguments that had originally motivated the framers of the Hyde Amendment. Griffin also offers a new angle on the equal protection argument against the Hyde Amendment. Rather than focusing on the differing treatment of childbirth and abortion, Griffin highlights the overlap between the religious purpose of the Hyde Amendment and animus against poor pregnant women.

Griffin offers a more feminist vision for *McRae* first by creating an opportunity for attorneys to challenge restrictions on reproductive rights under the Religion Clauses. The Court's original opinion in *McRae* ignored compelling evidence in the record. By contrast, Griffin illustrates a possible path for future Establishment Clause challenges – one based both on close examination of legislative history and a mismatch between the stated secular ends of a law and its actual statutory text and effect.

Beyond reviving Establishment arguments, Griffin explicitly makes the connection that the feminist attorneys litigating *McRae* left unspoken, exploring how the religious principles underlying the Hyde Amendment stand in tension with women's rights. As Griffin notes, the framers of the Hyde Amendment showed almost no concern for women's reproductive liberty or

[10] *Id.* at 319.

health and wellbeing. In Griffin's rendering, *McRae* would pave the way for more feminist claims relying not only on Establishment Clause reasoning but also exposing how and when organized religion rejects the principles of equality and autonomy for women.

Perhaps most provocatively, Griffin hints at a feminist Religion Clause jurisprudence that explicitly rejects Free Exercise as a foundational argument. Honoring conscientious objection for women choosing abortion, as Griffin explains, would lead logically to the recognition of similar rights of conscience for those opposed to rights for women. Rather than deescalating conflict, a conscience-based approach would only ignite further battles.

A more feminist *McRae* might have dramatically reshaped the landscape defining both reproductive justice and religion and the law. Griffin's *McRae* would first ensure that poor women could still access a full range of reproductive services under Medicaid, finally undermining the two-tiered system that has long characterized abortion care.

Written in Establishment Clause terms, *McRae* would also set the stage for more Establishment Clause challenges to restrictions on access or funding for reproductive health services. Rather than dismissing questions about the connections among hostility to abortion, religion, and anti-feminism, attorneys might have better odds in bringing the intersection of the three to the surface. A feminist *McRae* would have set the stage for a different outcome in *Bray v. Alexandria Women's Health Clinic*,[11] a case asking whether anti-abortion blockades were motivated by sex discrimination in contravention of the Civil Rights Act of 1871. Recognizing the connections among religious belief, anti-feminism, and a moral objection to abortion would also radically change the Court's understanding of the purpose of many abortion restrictions, including the federal Partial Birth Abortion Act upheld by the Court in *Gonzales v. Carhart*.[12] With an Establishment Clause framework in place, the purposes vindicated by the Court in *Carhart* – the integrity of the medical profession, the prevention of post-abortion regret, and the morals of the larger society – might well have seemed less than secular.

Finally, Griffin's *McRae* might have set the conscience wars on a very different course. As the *McRae* litigation reminds us, Free Exercise Clause arguments once appealed to Americans across the ideological spectrum, including the feminist attorneys who challenged the Hyde Amendment. To many, respect for conscience seemed likely to lower the stakes of conflict, bolster pluralism, and demonstrate that feminists, as well as conservatives, valued religion.

---

[11] *Bray v. Alexandria Women's Health Clinic*, 506 U.S. 263 (1993).
[12] *Gonzales v. Carhart*, 550 U.S. 124 (2007).

Griffin's opinion reveals the dark side of a Free Exercise Clause strategy. Without an Establishment Clause foundation, feminists have likely had a harder time questioning the spread of conscience-based objection in areas from same-sex marriage to the contraceptive mandate. Under Griffin's version of *McRae*, Establishment Clause arguments might well have provided a better foothold not only for fighting religious exemptions but also for protecting women's own freedom of conscience. Rather than closing the door on Establishment Clause reasoning, as Griffin reminds us, *McRae* could have made the Religion Clauses a key component of sex equality jurisprudence.

Harris v. McRae, 448 U.S. 297 (1980)

Justice Leslie C. Griffin delivered the opinion of the Court.

This case concerns the constitutionality of the Hyde Amendment, which denies public funding for medically necessary abortions. In invalidating the amendment, the district court ruled that the Hyde Amendment violated the equal protection component and Due Process Clause of the Fifth Amendment. It also found a violation of the Free Exercise Clause but not the Establishment Clause of the First Amendment. *McRae v. Califano*, 491 F. Supp. 630 (E.D.N.Y. 1980). We affirm the ruling of the district court, but use different reasoning. We conclude that the Hyde Amendment violates both the Establishment Clause and equal protection. As we explain below, when Congress enacted a personal moral principle unrelated to the Medicaid Act into law, it passed legislation lacking a secular purpose in violation of the Establishment Clause. That moral principle bore no rational relationship to Medicaid's provision of medically necessary services in violation of the equal protection considerations of the Fifth Amendment.

I

The Medicaid Act, which makes federal money available to the states for health care, has as its goal "to furnish (1) medical assistance on behalf of families with dependent children and of aged, blind or disabled individuals, whose income and resources are insufficient to meet the costs of necessary medical services, and (2) rehabilitation and other services to help such families and individuals attain or retain capability for independence or self-care." 42 U.S.C. §§ 1396(1)–(k). Pursuant to the Medicaid Act, and prior to the passage of the first Hyde Amendment in September 1976, the federal government funded approximately 250,000 to 300,000 abortions annually. *McRae*, 491 F. Supp. at 639–40.

In 1976, Representative Henry Hyde of Illinois began a single-minded legislative campaign to prohibit all abortions in the United States. On the floor of the
House, Hyde remarked, "I certainly would like to prevent, if I could legally, any-
body having an abortion, a rich woman, a middle-class woman, or a poor woman.
Unfortunately, the only vehicle available is the HEW [M]edicaid bill." *Id.* at 773.

The HEW Medicaid bill was the only vehicle available in 1976 because,
immediately before the Hyde Amendment was introduced, a proposed constitutional amendment banning all abortions failed to reach the floor for debate in
the House of Representatives. Unable to overturn this Court's ruling protecting
the constitutional right to choose abortion in *Roe v. Wade*, 410 U.S. 113 (1973),
by constitutional amendment, the House instead considered a statutory amendment restricting abortion. Although the Hyde Amendment ostensibly banned
only *funding* for abortions, the district court found that "the amendment was
intended to prevent abortions, not shift their cost to others, and rested on the
premise that the human fetus was a human life that should not be ended."
McRae, 491 F. Supp. at 641, 644 ("The debates demonstrate that the purpose of
the funding restriction was to its proponents a means of preventing abortions.").

The district court's conclusion is supported by the amendment's legislative
history. When Representative Hyde first introduced his amendment in June
1976, his suggested language proposed a *complete* ban on abortion funding:

> None of the funds appropriated under this Act shall be used to pay for abor-
> tions or to promote or encourage abortions.
>
> *Id.* at 743.

No medical testimony was considered during the debate over the amendment, and the amendment originally introduced by Hyde, as worded above,
mentioned nothing about the woman patient's life or health. Instead, Hyde
identified his *sole* goal as protecting the "unborn child":

> The unborn child facing an abortion can best be classified as a member of the
> innocently inconvenient and since the pernicious doctrine that some lives
> are more important than others seems to be persuasive with the pro-abortion
> forces, we who seek to protect that most defenseless and innocent of human
> lives, the unborn, seek to inhibit the use of Federal funds to pay for and thus
> encourage abortion as an answer to the human and compelling problem of
> an unwanted child.
>
> *Id.* at 744.

The woman's life, health, medical necessity, and constitutional right to choose
abortion were unmentioned at the initial stage of the bill's consideration as
fetal life took absolute priority.

The Hyde Amendment passed the House of Representatives in this initial, absolute, and exception-free wording. After the initial Hyde Amendment passed the House of Representatives, the Senate rejected it completely. Some Senators expressed their concern that the Hyde Amendment used "language more restrictive than that of the proposed constitutional amendments, that under it even the health and life of the mother could not be protected if an abortion were the only way of protecting that life." *Id.* at 747.

Only after the Senate rejected the amendment did Senators during the Senate–House conference meetings add language denying funding for abortion "except where the life of the mother would be endangered if the fetus were carried to term." *Id.* at 763. President Gerald Ford then vetoed the appropriations bill containing the abortion funding restriction because of its expense. Congress overrode the President's veto, and the amendment entered into law. Representative Hyde commented that although he agreed with the President's *financial* reasons for vetoing the legislation, Hyde's own *moral* opposition to abortion motivated him to approve the legislation:

> I am, nevertheless, voting to override the President's veto because within this legislation is a provision forbidding the use of Federal funds to pay for abortions. In starkest terms, the potential exists of saving some 300,000 lives which otherwise might be destroyed with the use of taxpayers' funds. The saving of these lives far outweighs the economic considerations involved in this legislation. It is unfortunate that the choice is between a sensible veto and the saving of so many human lives, but human life cannot be measured in terms of dollars, and so my choice is as clear as it is unpleasant. I reluctantly vote to override the President's veto.
>
> *Id.* at 770.

Thus the first Hyde Amendment, enacted over the President's veto, included one endangerment exception: "None of the funds contained in this Act shall be used to perform abortions except where the life of the mother would be endangered if the fetus were carried to term." *Id.* at 763.

Over the next several years, annual House–Senate Conferences adopted different versions of the Hyde Amendment. At first the Conference Committee Report concluded that it was not "the intent of the Conferees to prohibit medical procedures necessary for the termination of an ectopic pregnancy or for the treatment of rape or incest victims; nor is it intended to prohibit the use of drugs or devices to prevent implantation of the fertilized ovum." *Id.* at 772. Federal funds would be available for rape and incest victims, however, only "where the physician has certified that the life of the mother would be endangered if the fetus were carried to term." *Id.* In 1977 and 1978, Congress added an exception for "those instances where severe and long-lasting physical health damage to the mother would result if the pregnancy were carried to term when so determined by two physicians." *Id.* at 835. The 1977 and 1978 amendments also excepted rape and incest victims as long as they reported the rape or incest within sixty days after it occurred. *Id.* at 836–37.

The amendment thus had its origins in one Representative's absolute personal moral opposition to abortion and from then on was the subject of sustained moral disagreement and debate among members of the House and Senate. The Hyde Amendment is an appropriations amendment to the Medicaid Act. The Medicaid Act promotes individual health and an efficient health care system by funding medically necessary services. The Hyde Amendment, however, is not health-related or economically efficient. Thus, as we explain below, when Congress enacted a personal moral principle unrelated to the Medicaid Act into law, it passed legislation lacking a secular purpose in violation of the Establishment Clause. Moreover, because Congress's moral principle bore no rational relationship to human health care and Medicaid's provision of medically necessary services, the Hyde Amendment violates the equal protection considerations of the Fifth Amendment.

II

"Government in our democracy, state and national, must be neutral in matters of religious theory, doctrine, and practice." *Epperson v. Arkansas*, 393 U.S. 97, 103–04 (1968). In the legislative context, this Court ensures religiously neutral government by requiring that all legislation have a valid secular purpose. See *Committee for Public Education v. Nyquist*, 413 U.S. 756, 773 (1973) ("to pass muster under the Establishment Clause, the law in question, first, must reflect a clearly secular legislative purpose"); *Lemon v. Kurtzman*, 403 U.S. 602, 612 (1971) ("[T]he statute must have a secular legislative purpose"). Just like the Arkansas anti-evolution statute that we invalidated in *Epperson*, "[n]o suggestion has been made that [the Hyde Amendment] may be justified by considerations of state policy other than the religious views of some of its citizens. It is clear that fundamentalist sectarian conviction was and is the law's reason for existence." 393 U.S. at 107–08.

The district court found that the debate over the amendment was not motivated by financial or medical concerns, but was instead guided by irreconcilable differences over personal moral principles. As noted above, Representative Hyde's initial, exception-free amendment was rooted in his complete moral opposition to the constitutional right to abortion. The first version of the amendment to pass both houses, allowing funding only "where the life of the mother would be endangered if the fetus were carried to term," was also based on moral, not financial or medical, justifications. *McRae,* 491 F. Supp. at 641.

At the economic level, the district court found that the amendment would cost the government more money than it saved. Cutting funding for abortion raises Medicaid costs because childbirth is more expensive than abortion, bringing with it additional costs of public assistance for the first year after childbirth. *Id.* at 746. Although the President vetoed the legislation because of its high cost, supporters like Representative Hyde admitted that the moral aspects of the bill were more important to them than any financial or cost-saving aspect of Medicaid funding. *Id.* at 770. Thus, Congress had no secular purpose to control or manage health care costs when it passed the Hyde Amendment.

The district court also found that the life endangerment standard was "not a term used in the medical profession as a standard for determining medical procedures, and that it is not susceptible of any agreed definition among medical practitioners." *Id.* at 665. In contrast to Congress in the Hyde Amendment, "the medical profession does not treat pregnancy, the threat of complications in pregnancy, and the factor of the pregnant woman's attitude toward her pregnancy and child bearing in terms related to determining whether 'the life of the mother would be endangered if the fetus were carried to term.'" *Id.* at 667. Instead, doctors regularly understand and employ the "medical necessity" standard of Medicaid, which allows them to exercise their medical expertise to protect women's health.

Testimony in the district court established that doctors must evaluate each pregnancy contextually, taking into account the duration of the pregnancy and the health and life of the mother. Focusing only on "life endangerment" does not help a doctor to identify a medically necessary abortion. Thus, as the district court found, the "life endangerment test is simply alien to the medical approach when put forward as a sole test, for it extends only over an indeterminate range of instances that appears to exclude significant instances in which before *Roe v. Wade,* and the first changes in the state statutes, the therapeutic abortion committees of hospitals were approving abortion." *Id.* at 667.

The district court also found that the Hyde Amendment made pregnancy more dangerous for women because lack of funding delays abortions until they become riskier. *Id.* at 673. Most important, testimony in the district court also established that many "medically necessary" abortions would not qualify for coverage under the endangerment standard. *Id.* at 667.

The medical evidence in this case shows there was no health-related reason for the legislation and so it confirms that Congress had no secular purpose when it passed the Hyde Amendment. Instead, the entire debate about

the amendment was moral and religious, not medical or financial. *See id.* at
641 ("Both houses viewed the issue as a moral and not a financial issue ...
[T]hroughout there were references to religion and morality and the moral
implications of the positions taken in the debate."). The Senators' and
Representatives' personal moral beliefs opposing the constitutional right to
abortion did not provide a secular purpose for the legislation.

This conclusion that the amendment is not related to any secular purposes
is confirmed by the direct correspondence between Representative Hyde's
original amendment and his Roman Catholic faith. Roman Catholic theology
identifies the fetus as a full human person from the time of fertilization. *Id.* at
693. From fertilization onwards, it gives the fetal life absolute preference over
the mother's life and health. Abortion is not permitted even to save the life of
the mother. Representative Hyde identified this same goal to protect fetal life
absolutely as his purpose in proposing the amendment.

This absolute preference for fetal life over maternal life is inconsistent
with the constitutional framework established in *Roe v. Wade*, 410 U.S. 113,
164 (1973), which allows even late-term abortions if they are necessary to preserve the health or life of the mother; it is inconsistent with the purposes of
the Medicaid Act; it can be explained only by its faith-based origins. Absent
any consideration of the statutory goals of health and well-being or the constitutional protection of a woman's right to choose abortion, we conclude
that the Hyde Amendment originated in a desire to impose a comprehensive moral principle unrelated to the legislation's purposes. This sectarian moral purpose does not meet the secular purpose standard of *Lemon
v. Kurtzman*, and leads us to invalidate the Hyde Amendment as a violation
of the Establishment Clause.

The district court ruled that because the final version of the first Hyde
Amendment, which allowed abortion if the woman's life was endangered,
did not correspond exactly to Roman Catholic theology, no establishment
violation occurred. *McRae*, 491 F. Supp. at 692–93. This analysis misses
the point. The Establishment Clause requires that every law has a secular
purpose. *Lemon*, 403 U.S. at 612. We recognize that, as described above,
after Representative Hyde first proposed his amendment in June 1976, it
evolved through the legislative process to permit some exceptions to the
absolute ban on funding. To violate the Establishment Clause, however,
those modifications did not have to exactly correspond to one church's theology, as the district court concluded. Instead, the legislation fails in all
its modifications because it lacks a secular purpose. The legislative history
of the Hyde Amendment, which was summarized by the district court in
exquisite detail, confirms "[i]t was more than once agreed that the issue

under debate was a moral one and that religious conviction entered into the positions taken." *McRae*, 491 F. Supp. at 645.

As the comprehensive Annex compiled by the district court demonstrates, after Representative Hyde first introduced *his* personal moral principle governing abortion into the House debate, the Representatives and Senators engaged in a prolonged moral, philosophical, and religious discussion about abortion, with each individual proposing his or her own moral code as the proper rule to regulate abortion. *Id.* at 743–844. The debate was consistently about religion and morality, not health or medical necessity. Throughout Congress's deliberations, "secular and religious teachings" were "so intertwined" that an Establishment Clause violation occurred. *Lemon*, 403 U.S. at 613. This moral, rather than legal, financial, or medical focus, explains why the House and Senate debates were so "extended and bitter" and "contentious," *McRae*, 491 F. Supp. at 640, and confirms the wisdom of the Establishment Clause's prohibition of the "active involvement of the sovereign in religious activity." *Walz v. Tax Comm'n of City of New York*, 397 U.S. 664, 668 (1970).

Just as in *Epperson*, where Arkansas banned the teaching of evolution "for the sole reason that it is deemed to conflict with a particular religious doctrine," 393 U.S. at 103, in this case "sectarian conviction was and is the law's reason for existence." *Id.* at 108. Sectarian laws are never religiously neutral and require invalidation under the Establishment Clause. Thus we disagree with the district court's rejection of the Establishment Clause challenge and invalidate the law under the First Amendment.

III

In contrast to the district court, we decide this case on establishment grounds, not those of free exercise.

In the last two paragraphs of its opinion, the district court confusingly mingled due process and religious liberty arguments when it concluded that the Hyde Amendment "raise[s] grave First and Fifth Amendment problems affecting individual liberty." *McRae*, 491 F. Supp. at 741. The court ruled that the constitutional right to abortion, which is rooted in the Due Process Clause, is "*doubly protected* when the liberty is exercised in conformity with religious belief and teaching protected by the First Amendment." *Id.* at 742 (emphasis added). The Hyde Amendment violates free exercise, the court concluded, because individuals enjoy a constitutional right of "conscientious decision and conscientious nonparticipation." *Id.*

That analysis misinterprets the constitutional law of abortion and free exercise. Appellees enjoy neither a constitutional right to abortion *funding, Maher v. Roe*, 432 U.S. 464 (1977), nor a constitutional right to government funding of the exercise of religion. Indeed, government funding of religious exercise violates the Establishment Clause. *Nyquist*, 413 U.S. 756; *Everson v. Bd. of Educ. of Ewing Twp.*, 330 U.S. 1 (1947).

Moreover, the plaintiffs' constitutional right to abortion is protected by the Due Process Clause, not the Free Exercise Clause. The district court's "doubly protected" analysis would provide religious women extra rights to abortion that non-religious women do not enjoy. The Free Exercise Clause does not require such privileging of religious conscience, and the Establishment Clause prohibits it. *Everson*, 330 U.S. at 15 ("The 'establishment of religion' clause of the First Amendment means at least this: neither a state nor the Federal Government ... can pass laws which aid one religion, aid all religion, or prefer one religion over another."). If we were to rule in this case that women's conscientious decision to choose abortion is protected as a matter of free exercise, we see no reason why Representative Hyde and the members of Congress who passed his amendment would not enjoy a similar right of conscientious objection to refuse abortion funding to the very same women. Such back-and-forth battles of conscience would be "extended and bitter," as were the Congress's religious and moral debates about the Hyde Amendment. *McRae*, 491 F. Supp. at 640.

As we clarified in our opinions addressing conscientious objections to war, "Our cases do not at their farthest reach support the proposition that a stance of conscientious opposition relieves an objector from any colliding duty fixed by a democratic government." *Gillette v. United States*, 401 U.S. 437, 461 (1971). Instead, as we explained in Part II, the Establishment Clause protects freedom of conscience by requiring laws that serve a secular purpose and invalidating laws that impose personal morality.

Women enjoy no free exercise right of conscience to abortion; they enjoy the fundamental right of privacy recognized in *Roe v. Wade*, 410 U.S. 113 (1973). Because we invalidate the Hyde Amendment on establishment grounds, we need not revisit here the scope of the fundamental constitutional right to abortion, *Roe*, 410 U.S. 113, or the law of abortion funding, *Maher*, 432 U.S. 464.

IV

Like the district court, we conclude that the Hyde Amendment violates the equal protection component of the Fifth Amendment by irrationally depriving poor pregnant women of medically necessary care. "Under traditional equal protection analysis, a legislative classification must be sustained, if the classification itself is rationally related to a legitimate governmental interest." *U.S. Dep't of Agric. v. Moreno*, 413 U.S. 528, 533 (1973).

The Hyde Amendment creates a classification distinguishing medically necessary services available to all persons from medically necessary services related to abortion. As demonstrated in Part II, however, no medical considerations were taken into account in creating this classification. Instead, Congress's moral agenda bore no relationship to the goals of the Medicaid Act: "to furnish (1) medical assistance on behalf of families with dependent children and of aged, blind or disabled individuals, whose income and resources are insufficient to meet the costs of necessary medical services, and (2) rehabilitation and other services to help such families and individuals attain or retain capability for independence or self-care." 42 U.S.C. §§ 1396(1)–(k).

The Hyde Amendment is similar to the Food Stamp Act amendment that we invalidated in *Moreno*, 413 U.S. at 533. In *Moreno*, Congress passed an amendment distinguishing households of related persons from households containing one or more unrelated persons, allowing food stamps to the former but not the latter. *Id.* at 534. We recognized that this classification was irrelevant to the Food Stamp Act's purpose to enhance personal nutrition. *Id.* at 533–34. Similarly, the Hyde Amendment is irrelevant to the Medicaid Act's purpose of providing medically necessary services to the poor and needy.

In *Moreno*, we also concluded that the legislative history indicated that Congress had acted out of unconstitutional animus because it "intended to prevent so-called 'hippies' and 'hippie communes' from participating in the food stamp program." *Id.* at 534. We summarized the holdings of our equal protection cases by stating "if the constitutional conception of 'equal protection of the laws' means anything, it must at the very least mean that a bare congressional desire to harm a politically unpopular group cannot constitute a legitimate governmental interest." *Id.* Here, as in *Moreno*, Congress expressed its desire to harm a politically unpopular group, namely poor pregnant women. The constitutional conception of equal protection of the laws does not recognize the targeting of poor pregnant women as a legitimate governmental interest. Congress's obligation is to protect the health of all, not to express its moral disapproval of pregnant women or to mandate its own moral code upon them.

Because we conclude that Congress's moral disapproval of poor pregnant women and its imposition of morality upon these targeted victims cannot survive rational basis review, we do not address whether the targeting of some pregnant women in the Hyde Amendment was a sex-based classification subject to intermediate scrutiny. See *Frontiero v. Richardson*, 411 U.S. 677 (1973). The denial of medically necessary services to some Americans but not others is not a legitimate governmental interest and cannot survive rational basis scrutiny.

The decision of the district court invalidating the Hyde Amendment is *affirmed*.

14

Commentary on *Michael M. v. Superior Court*

Margo Kaplan

BACKGROUND

At around midnight on June 3, 1978, a seventeen-and-a-half-year-old boy named Michael and his two friends approached a sixteen-and-a-half-year-old girl named Sharon and her sister at a California bus stop. According to Sharon's testimony, Michael and Sharon walked to some railroad tracks, and then over to a bush.[1] Michael began to kiss Sharon, who at first responded by kissing him back. Sharon then asked Michael to stop and slow down.[2] Although he agreed to stop, he did not do so until Sharon's sister and Michael's friends rejoined them.[3]

After the others left, Sharon and Michael walked to a park, sat down on a bench, and began kissing again.[4] As they were lying on the bench, Michael told Sharon to take her pants off.[5] When Sharon verbally refused and tried to stand up, Michael struck her in the face with his fist two or three times.[6] Sharon testified, "I just said to myself 'Forget it,' and I let him do what he wanted to do … ."[7] Michael took Sharon's pants off and had sexual intercourse with her.

Rather than charge Michael with rape,[8] the State of California prosecuted him under its statutory rape statute.[9] At the time, this offense punished only unlawful sexual intercourse with a woman under 18. Men or boys who

---

[1] *See Michael M. v. Superior Court*, 450 U.S. 464, 466 (1981).
[2] *Id.* at 483–86 (Blackmun J., concurring).
[3] *Id.*
[4] *Id.*
[5] *Michael M.*, 450 U.S. at 483–86.
[6] *Id.*
[7] *Id.*
[8] Cal. Penal Code § 261 (1970).
[9] *Id.* § 261.5 (1970).

had sex with female minors were therefore subject to criminal charges that women and girls who had sex with male minors escaped. Michael challenged the statute as a violation of the Equal Protection Clause of the Fourteenth Amendment based on its disparate treatment of men and women. The trial court, the California Court of Appeal, and the California Supreme Court all upheld the statute. The U.S. Supreme Court granted certiorari and affirmed as well.

ORIGINAL OPINION

The Petitioner's argument reflected a growing backlash against the paternalism of statutory rape laws intended to protect the chastity of young women. Under this view, gender-specific statutory rape laws reinforce outmoded norms about both male and female sexuality, framing women as passive recipients or resisters of male sexual urges. According to the Petitioner, upholding such stereotypes would conflict with Court precedent that the legislature may not justify sex-based distinctions with "overbroad generalizations based on sex which are entirely unrelated to any differences between men and women or which demean the ability or social status of the affected class."[10]

Justice Rehnquist's brief plurality opinion upholding the statute tried to distance itself from gender stereotypes by arguing that, in the context of statutory rape, a young woman's ability to become pregnant makes her not similarly situated to men. It argued that the state has a legitimate interest in preventing teen pregnancy, which poses unique social, medical, and economic harms to young women.[11] The plurality reasoned that it made sense to punish only men and boys, as the "natural sanction" of pregnancy would deter teen girls from having sex.[12]

Justice Blackmun and Justice Stewart filed concurring opinions that hinted at the more insidious gender stereotypes at play in the case. Justice Blackmun expressed concern that Sharon's case was "an unattractive one to prosecute" because Sharon "appears not to have been an unwilling participant in at least the initial stages of the intimacies."[13] According to Justice Blackmun, Sharon's decision to drink and kiss a "nonacquaintance" and "encourage" his attentions undermined her ability to claim she didn't consent to intercourse.[14]

[10] See Michael. M., 450 U.S. at 469 (citing Parnham v. Hughes, 441 U.S. 347, 354 (1979) (plurality opinion of Stewart, J.)).

[11] See id. at 469.

[12] See id. at 473.

[13] See id. at 483, 485 (Blackmun, J., concurring).

[14] See Frances Olsen, Statutory Rape: A Feminist Critique of Rights Analysis, 63 Tex. L. Rev. 387, 416–17 (1984).

The dissenting opinions focused on the California law's weak relationship to its purported goals. Justice Brennan's dissent, for example, argued that the deterrent effect of the laws was questionable. He countered the state's argument that gender-neutral laws would be harder to enforce by noting that the thirty-seven other states with gender-neutral statutory rape laws had suffered no unusual enforcement problems.

THE FEMINIST JUDGMENT

Cynthia Godsoe's dissent provides a much deeper analysis of the myriad feminist issues that the plurality, concurring opinions, and dissents either misinterpret or ignore. Professor Godsoe, writing as Justice Godsoe, acknowledges the very real and disparate negative impact that pregnancy and childbirth can have on women and on young women in particular. But she rejects the plurality's simplistic argument that pregnancy creates a "real difference"[15] that justifies the California law. Instead, she cites the social, cultural, and legal causes of both teen pregnancy and its negative consequences, such as sex role stereotypes, lack of access to contraception and abortion, and lack of support for mothers. She argues that the California law does not address these causes and, in some cases, exacerbates them by reinforcing troubling sex-role stereotypes. Godsoe notes how the law "endorses and perpetuates the notion that boys are aggressive and lustful, girls passive, non-sexual, and incapable of informed choices." By encouraging boys and men to be sexually aggressive at the expense of girls' and women's sexual autonomy, such stereotypes create a culture conducive to rape. Moreover, as Godsoe writes, "stereotypes of girls as passive are self-fulfilling, leaving them more susceptible to coercion, both physical and emotional" and less likely to have their reports of sexual assault believed if they "do not conform to traditional notions of feminine behavior." The law's bolstering of sex stereotypes is therefore likely to increase incidence of rape and decrease reporting. This undermines California's argument that the law encourages women to report rapes; as Godsoe notes, the reluctance, if not refusal, of police and prosecutors to pursue cases "where the victim does not fulfill the chaste, feminine ideal" deters women from reporting sexual assaults.

Godsoe also analyzes the insidious effect that such sex stereotyping has on young men. She notes that the stereotypes it perpetuates – that sexual aggression is natural in men and boys, passivity in women and girls – are over- and

---

[15] *See* Ann E. Freedman, *Sex Equality, Sex Differences, and the Supreme Court,* 92 Yale L. J. 913, 921 (1983).

underinclusive. They also reinforce the very behaviors that contribute to the sexual assault of both sexes, in particular the beliefs that sexual aggression against and coercion of women is a natural part of courtship, and that men cannot be raped because they always desire sex. She further notes how the law undermines the sexual autonomy of young men by refusing to acknowledge that many young men and boys are the victims of sexual assault.

Godsoe's dissent provides a richer feminist analysis of the equal protection issues at stake in the *Michael M.* case than the existing dissenting opinions. While Justice Brennan's dissent discusses the law's reliance on sex stereotypes in passing, its primary focus is on the statute's poor fit with its legislative goal. Similarly, Justice Stewart finds California's justification for sex-specific laws unconvincing, arguing that a law that seeks to prevent teenage pregnancy should apply to teenage girls as well as men and boys.[16] Godsoe agrees with the dissents that the statute is not sufficiently related to the legislative goal of preventing pregnancy. Unlike either the plurality or dissents, Godsoe acknowledges that the unique vulnerabilities of women and girls should not be ignored at the risk of achieving formal equality over substantive equality. She notes that young women may face unique coercion to engage in sexual activity. But Godsoe argues that California's statute does not strengthen respect for a young woman's sexual autonomy as much as perpetuate the idea that women are the chaste gatekeepers to sex.

Godsoe also provides a far more nuanced and feminist analysis of the issues of sexual violence that the case raises, as well as their relationship with sex equality. The opinion begins with a pointed discussion of the justices' failure to acknowledge the forcible nature of the victim's rape. It rightly criticizes Justice Blackmun for inferring that the victim's initial consent to kissing the defendant constituted consent to sex. Godsoe uses Justice Blackmun's opinion to make a broader point about how sex stereotypes strengthen and sustain a norm of violence against women. She argues that sex equality requires a more fundamental change in the way the criminal justice system – and society as a whole – views sexual violence and violence against women.

It would be impossible in a limited commentary to discuss in its entirety the rich history of feminist scholarship that Godsoe's opinion reflects, but it is useful to discuss some of the most salient work. Ann Freedman's *Sex Equality, Sex Differences, and the Supreme Court* is particularly relevant.[17] Freedman places the *Michael M.* case in the larger context of U.S. Supreme Court jurisprudence on sex equality. The plurality reflects the Rehnquist-Stewart "real

---

[16] *See Michael M. v. Superior Court*, 450 U.S. 464, 499–502 (1981) (Stevens, J., dissenting).

[17] *See* Freedman, *supra* note 15.

differences" approach to equal protection, in which sex discrimination is permissible if the state can point to a difference that makes men and women not similarly situated for the purposes of the law – in the case of *Michael M.*, pregnancy. Freedman contrasts the "Brennan-Marshall" approach of focusing on the poor fit between the law and the purported state goal. Like Freedman, Godsoe rejects each of these approaches and adopts a more normative approach to sex-based classifications and a deeper analysis of the true causes and costs of sex inequality. Specifically, Godsoe's opinion discusses the underlying causes of violence against women and the lack of reported sexual assaults, as well as the more fundamental reasons that girls bear the costs of teen pregnancy.

Similarly, Godsoe's dissent reflects Frances Olsen's analysis of *Michael M.* in her work *Statutory Rape: A Feminist Critique of Rights Analysis*.[18] Olsen shares Godsoe's skepticism of Justice Blackmun's narrow view of female sexual autonomy and the Court's general unwillingness to condemn the damaging gender stereotypes underscoring California's law. Godsoe's opinion echoes Olsen's analysis of how the law implicated both male and female sexual autonomy in ways the Court failed to grasp.[19] Olsen is careful, however, to argue that real sex differences exist in the way that boys and girls experience sexual exploitation,[20] a point that Godsoe endorses.

Godsoe also puts the discussion of violence against women at the forefront of her opinion, drawing on Catharine MacKinnon's work, *Reflections on Sex Equality under Law*, demonstrating the inextricably intertwined nature of sexual violence and sex discrimination.[21] Godsoe's recognition of the unique vulnerability of young women and girls reflects Michelle Oberman's important work on statutory rape laws.[22] Like Oberman's work, Godsoe's opinion struggles with how to achieve substantive equality in the law of statutory rape, and in particular how to further a feminist vision of statutory rape laws without perpetuating the patriarchal attitudes that underlie the history of these laws and the criminal justice system in which they are enforced.

Godsoe's feminist vision of a *Michael M.* dissent uses these and other feminist ideas to present a more progressive and thoughtful approach to U.S.

---

[18] *See* Olsen, *supra* note 14.

[19] *See id.* at 418–19.

[20] *See id.* at 426–27.

[21] *See* Catharine A. MacKinnon, *Reflections on Sex Equality under Law*, 100 Yale L. J. 1281 (1991).

[22] *See, e.g.*, Michelle Oberman, *Girls in the Master's House: Of Protection, Patriarchy and the Potential for Using the Master's Tools to Reconfigure Statutory Rape Law*, 50 DePaul L. Rev. 799 (2001); Michelle Oberman, *Turning Girls Into Women: Re-Evaluating Modern Statutory Rape Law*, 85 J. Crim. L. & Criminology 15 (1994).

Supreme Court jurisprudence on sex equality and sexual violence. Her opinion calls for the Court, and lower courts, to take a more robust and progressive stance on sexual violence, sexual autonomy, and sex discrimination.

Michael M. v. Superior Court, 450 U.S. 464 (1981)

Justice Cynthia Godsoe, dissenting.

The gender-based classification at issue here is a California statute that defines statutory rape as "an act of sexual intercourse accomplished with a female ... under the age of 18 years." Cal. Penal Code § 261.5 (West 1980). The statute presumes non-consent for girls and young women under the age of majority. This classification is based, in large part, on socially constructed rather than biological differences. Enshrining these in law perpetuates stereotypes harmful to both sexes. We must, however, be careful not to mistake formal equality for substantive equality. Girls are more susceptible than boys to both forced and non-consensual sexual activity. Indeed, the victim in this case said "no" and was struck in the face repeatedly. Nonetheless, I conclude that the most narrowly tailored proxy for vulnerability and exploitation is age rather than sex. Accordingly, I dissent on the grounds that the statute violates the Equal Protection Clause.

I

I am compelled for several reasons to begin my opinion with forcible rape. First, the facts of this case show that the defendant Michael used force to compel Sharon to have sex with him. Indeed, the State of California acknowledges this in describing Michael M. as "utiliz[ing] his apparent physical superiority to force the victim to submit to intercourse." Br. for Resp't at 3. Second, California also admits that it frequently uses the statutory rape statute to prosecute forcible rapes. None of my colleagues noted this pattern; indeed one suggests that Sharon's abuse was, in part, her fault. *Michael M.*, 450 U.S. at 464 (Blackmun, J., concurring). This attitude speaks volumes about our failure to recognize the ongoing gender hierarchy in sexual relations and helps to explain why rape remains the most underreported and underconvicted crime.

The scant facts we have reveal that this case is not about sexual activity that would be consensual simply if Sharon were older. In contrast, she was forcibly raped. At the preliminary hearing, Sharon testified that "at first" she kissed Michael back. Soon after, she "was telling him to slow down and stop." Although he said "okay, okay ... he just kept doing it." Her sister and the other boy present left, and Michael convinced her to lie down on a park bench.

They continued kissing and "he told [her] to take her pants off." She said "No," and tried to get up but "he hit [her] back on the bench ... slugg[ing her] in the face ... two or three times" and causing bruises. Only then did she "let him do what he wanted to do and he took [her pants] off" and had forced sexual intercourse. *Michael M.*, 450 U.S. at 484–85.

This type of encounter is sadly too common. A girl or woman's initial consent to kissing or petting is deemed to be consent to any further actions, including intercourse. Her verbal protestations are ignored and the blows she is subjected to overlooked. All too typical is the reaction of my colleague Justice Blackmun. He feels "it is only fair" that he note that Sharon "appears not to have been an unwilling participant in at least the initial stages of the intimacies." *Id.* at 483. He then opines that Sharon's behavior, behavior he views as unfitting of a "true" victim, makes this case "an unattractive one to prosecute *at all*" and particularly as a felony of forcible rape. *Id.* at 483–85 (emphasis added). The conduct my colleague finds problematic is that Sharon did not know Michael before this encounter, that she drank alcohol, separated from the other young people, and consensually kissed Michael. Justice Blackmun characterizes this behavior as "foreplay" to the rape. He says that Sharon "willingly participated [in]" and even "encouraged" Michael's actions. This latter finding does not seem to be supported by the transcript. Although it is uncontested that Sharon was below the age of consent, and that the defendant knew that, *id.* at 485, Justice Blackmun only "reluctantly conclude[s]" that these facts meet even that crime. *Id.* at 487.

Scrutinizing a victim's conduct and blaming her for the sexual assault is the frequent response of police, prosecutors, judges and juries, rendering even forcible rape a very difficult crime to prosecute.[23] Both in California and nationally, rape has the highest acquittal rate of any felony. Note, *Rape and Rape Law: Sexism in Society and Law*, 61 Cal. L. Rev. 919, 927 (1973) (citing California data from the 1960s); Federal Bureau of Investigation, Uniform Crime Report: 1979 (same). At every stage of the process, rape is treated differently than other crimes, particularly other violent crimes. Fewer cases are reported, charged, prosecuted, and convicted, and fewer defendants are incarcerated. See *Rape and Rape Law* at 927 (reporting on one study of 1,219 men charged with rape, half of whom were acquitted or had their cases dismissed, and only 10 percent of whom were incarcerated). Much of this differentiation occurs at the front end by government gatekeepers; police "unfound" about

---

[23] A recent Department of Justice report notes this problem. *See* National Inst. of Law Enforcement and Crim. Justice, U.S. Dep't of Justice, Forcible Rape: Final Project Report (1978).

one-fifth of rape complaints and prosecutors are reluctant, if not unwilling, to bring cases where the victim does not fulfill the chaste, feminine ideal. *See* Uniform Crime Report, *supra*, at Ch. 6. *See also* Vivian Berger, *Man's Trial, Woman's Tribulation: Rape Cases in the Courtroom*, 77 Colum. L. Rev. 1 (1977) (describing the harms the legal system inflicted on rape victims during prosecutions of their alleged attackers). This law-enforcement gatekeeping, coupled with the exposure of a victim's prior sexual history and mental health at trial, deters victims from reporting rapes; the Federal Bureau of Investigation estimates that rape is the most unreported crime by a large margin. *See* Uniform Crime Report, *supra*, at 15. Accordingly, one of the most harmful and traumatic personal crimes goes largely unpunished.

    I am mindful that these flaws in our criminal justice system render statutory rape, which requires only a showing of the victim's age, a valuable tool for prosecutors to secure convictions against more violent and dangerous defendants. Br. for the U.S. as Amicus Curiae at 16, nn.17–18 (arguing that statutory rape laws "serve to facilitate the prosecution of forcible rapes involving young victims"). The State of California acknowledges that the instant case is one of forcible rape and is undoubtedly sincere in claiming that the statutory rape law is "commonly employed in situations involving force, prostitution, pornography or coercion due to status relationships." Br. for Resp't at 3. Indeed, it repeatedly articulates its interest in "prohibiting forcible intercourse," and notes the harm to girls of forcible rape, rather than of sexual intercourse itself. *Id.* Amicus the United States reports that the majority of reported statutory rape decisions outline facts indicating forcible rape. Br. for the U.S. as Amicus Curiae, at n.18; *see also* Forcible Rape: Final Project Report Nat'l Institute of Law Enforcement and Criminal Justice, at 17 (reporting that almost one-third of forcible rape victims are under 18 years old, and 20 percent are under 12 years old). Tellingly, one of the only courts to find a gender-specific statutory rape law unconstitutional specifically noted the facts in that case, a consensual encounter between two young people, and distinguished them from most other statutory rape cases. *See Meloon v. Helgemoe*, 564 F.2d 602, 605 n.4 (1st Cir. 1977) ("It is not unlikely that a court's reasoning on this issue would be colored by the fact that an actual rape occurred as opposed to the statutory consensual offense.").

    Although I am sympathetic to the difficulties of prosecuting these cases, reliance on statutory rape laws to punish forcible rape perpetuates the current failure to take forcible rape seriously. The defendant here could have been charged with felony forcible rape, as the state appears to acknowledge, but instead was only charged with the instant offense which carries significantly lighter penalties. *See* Br. for the U.S. as Amicus Curiae at n.10 (noting that forcible intercourse with a girl could be charged under three statutory provisions, including forcible rape).

Truly eliminating gender discrimination in the criminal justice system and achieving the state's goal of protecting its citizens from forcible and unwanted sexual intercourse requires not a gender-distinctive statute, but rather ensuring that the existing statutes are fully and fairly enforced.[24] There are heartening steps being taken to this end including law enforcement training; the elimination of resistance requirements, corroboration requirements, and chastity exceptions; and the prohibition against introducing a victim's prior sexual activity at court. See Nat'l Institute of Law Enforcement and Criminal Justice, *supra*, n.1 (outlining reforms). Nonetheless, the prosecution of this case as statutory rather than forcible rape, and my Brothers' ignorance or implicit condonation of Michael's assault of Sharon, indicate that we still have far to go to address this gendered violence.

II

I now turn to California Penal Code § 261.5. Gender-based classifications survive constitutional scrutiny only if they are "substantially related" to the achievement of "important governmental objectives." *Craig v. Boren*, 429 U.S. 190, 197 (1976). California offers two rationales for its male-only statute, arguing first that it prevents teenage pregnancy, and also contending more broadly that the statute helps protect children from exploitation. Br. for Resp't at 3, 22–24. Although these are both important legislative goals, the gender classification here is not substantially related to either. Accordingly, the statute fails intermediate scrutiny.

I first consider the prevention of teenage pregnancy. I agree with my dissenting colleagues Justices Brennan, White, and Marshall that California Penal Code § 261.5 is not substantially related to that purpose. *Michael M. v. Superior Court of Sonoma County*, 450 U.S. 464 (1981) (Brennan, J., dissenting). The statute covers sexual intercourse with girls too young to become pregnant, defendants who use birth control, and the slightest penetration, all situations very unlikely to result in pregnancy. The causes of increased teen pregnancy are complex, including a "radical change in teenage sexual mores," and many minors' lack of access to contraception and abortion. Br. for ACLU

---

[24] The number of reported rapes has risen dramatically over the last two decades, far outpacing the increase in other crimes. *See* Federal Bureau of Investigation, Uniform Crime Reports 1960–1980 (17,190 reported rapes in 1960 versus 82,990 in 1980). While some view this as cause for alarm, I view this as a positive development, believing that increased dialogue about rape and sensitivity to its victims has led to increased reporting of a crime that was always occurring.

as Amicus Curiae at 15; Br. for Pet. at 23 (citing statistics that nationally 45 percent of adolescent females are sexually active). These causes are not substantially addressed by criminally sanctioning only one party to the encounter.

Moreover, the unequal consequences of teenage pregnancy for mothers
that California points to are largely based on gender stereotypes rather than
biological differences. Although girls are much more physically affected than
boys by pregnancy and childbirth, the financial and social burdens of young
parenthood that California articulates are cultural constructs rather than biological realities. Our decision less than a decade ago in *Geduldig v. Aiello*
clarifies that the "most cursory analysis" reveals "the lack of identity between
[pregnancy] and gender as such." 417 U.S. 484, n.20 (1974) (holding that a
statute declining to pay disability benefits for pregnancy did not discriminate
on the basis of sex). The law should not endorse inequitable stereotypes, but
rather should work to eradicate them.

III

I turn now to the secondary rationale California offers: that the male-only
statutory rape law serves to protect girls and young women from exploitation. Although this is also an important governmental objective, I find that
this rationale and its nexus likewise fail intermediate scrutiny. I do so for
several reasons. First, protection, even if well-intentioned, is largely based
on impermissible gender stereotypes. Second and relatedly, the statute protects only some girls, those who conform to feminine norms of chastity.
Third, the statute does not protect boys from exploitation. A truly protective statute would attempt to shield all young people from adult sexual
predation.

The statute is not saved because the California legislature seeks to protect girls. Discriminatory legislation has long been justified by the need to
protect women. *See, e.g., Muller v. Oregon*, 208 U.S. 412 (1908) (limiting
women's work hours in factories and laundries); *Bradwell v. Illinois*, 83
U.S. 130, 131 (1873) (prohibiting women from the practice of law). Much
purportedly protective legislation includes women with children, thus
equating the two in terms of capacity and autonomy. *See West Coast Hotel
Co. v. Parrish* 300 U.S. 379, 394 (1937) (affirming a minimum wage law
applicable to women and children). Here, the omission of certain young
women from protection, those deemed unchaste, belies a truly protective
purpose.[25] See *Goesaert v. Cleary*, 335 U.S. 464, 468 (1948) (Rutledge, J.,

---

[25] All states had chastity exceptions to rape at one point, and a number of states still do.

dissenting), *disapproved of by Craig v. Boren*, 429 U.S. 190 (1976) (Court in *Craig* noting that the exclusion of some women from protection, there the wives and daughters of bartenders, contradicts "the assumption that the statute was motivated by a legislative solicitude for the moral and physical well-being of [all] women"). Even if the legislature were driven by truly benign motives, protection cannot justify impermissible gender classifications. As we noted in *Frontiero v. Richardson*, "romantic paternalism" usually "put women, not on a pedestal, but in a cage." 411 US 677, 684 (1973).

As in the cases discussed above, California Penal Code § 261.5 relies not on biological differences between males and females, but rather on sex-role stereotypes. Specifically, it endorses and perpetuates the notion that boys are aggressive and lustful, girls passive, non-sexual, and incapable of informed choices.[26] Yet there is no showing of a biological basis for this dichotomy.[27] To the contrary, it perpetuates a long history of treating female sexuality, particularly virginity, as a "treasure" to be guarded. Tellingly, statutory rape was originally framed as a property crime, with a girl's father as the victim. *See* Note, *Forcible and Statutory Rape: An Exploration of the Operation and Objectives of the Consent Standard*, 62 Yale L.J. 55, 76 (1952). The exemption of wives from statutory rape and other rape laws further demonstrates the persistence of this property view of women's sexuality. *See* Cal. Penal Code § 261.5 (punishing sexual intercourse with girls under eighteen only where "they are not the wife of the perpetrator.") More broadly, notions of female virtue as a tangible thing of value, and young women as needing protection from their own incompetent choices, continue to underlie the law today. *Michael M.*, 450 U.S. at 495–96 (Brennan, J. dissenting).

We have previously decided "a State is not free to make overbroad generalizations based on sex which are entirely unrelated to any differences between men and women or which demean the ability or social status of the affected class." *Parham v. Hughes*, 441 U.S. 347, 354 (1979). The statute here relies on socially created differences, even mere stereotypes, to demean both males and females. By imposing gendered scripts on sexual encounters, it limits the autonomy of all adolescents. Boys are always assigned the role of

---

[26] On the contrary, empirical findings specifically indicate that minor females are capable of and do make intelligent decisions about sexual activity. *See* Melvin Zelnik and John F. Kantner, *Sexual and Contraceptive Experience of Young Unmarried Women in the United States, 1976 and 1971*, 9 *Family Planning J.* 55 (1971).

[27] A wealth of recent research indicates that many attributes long considered "female" or "male" are, in fact, the product of culture and psychology, not biology. *See, e.g.,* Todd Tieger, *On the Biological Basis of Sex Differences in Aggression*, 51 *Child. Dev.* 943 (1980).

initiator or decision-maker, thus culpable for sex with other adolescents or even with adults. Girls are deemed incapable of consent and those who are appropriately feminine are designated the victims of all sexual encounters, even those with other teens or adolescents younger than them. These scripts may describe the context of some, even many, adolescent sexual encounters. They also, however, oppress the numerous young men and women who do not conform to these historic gender roles.

These stereotypes are both overinclusive *and* underinclusive. Boys are punished even when not more culpable than their sexual partners, and girls are protected even when they are not being exploited. At the same time, California's statutory rape framework ignores the trauma of all young male victims. Male victims of sexual exploitation have long been ignored, even by my colleagues finding the instant statute discriminatory in punishing only boys. 450 U.S. at 489 (Brennan J., dissenting). It may also exclude girls who are being exploited but who have previously been sexually active. Although California no longer maintains a statutory chastity exception, many informal barriers impede the equal treatment of victims, including gatekeeping by police and prosecutors of which cases will even be prosecuted. See discussion *supra*. Indeed, Justice Stevens suggests that the law might be more effective if it punished only "promiscuous" young women rather than the young men they use and "discard[]." *Id.* at 502. Race also plays a significant role in the determination of victims and offenders; the rape of White girls and women by Black boys and men has long been punished far more harshly than other rape cases. *See* Marvin E. Wolfgang and Marc Riedel, *Rape, Racial Discrimination, and the Death Penalty, in Capital Punishment in the United States* 118–119 (Hugo Adam Bedau and Chester M. Pierce, eds. 1976) (reporting study showing that, nationally, Blacks have been disproportionately punished for rape). Accordingly, I find that the statute impermissibly uses sex as an "inaccurate proxy" for vulnerability and harm. *Craig*, 429 U.S. at 198.

The fact that men comprise the overwhelming majority of sexual abuse and rape offenders does not affect the equal protection analysis here. *See* Susan Brownmiller, *Against Our Will: Men, Women and Rape* 278 (1975) (citing a study finding that 97 percent of offenders are male). First, this discrepancy could, in part, be due to the sex-role stereotypes discussed above, which deter minors victimized by women, particularly boys, from reporting any assaults. Second, men rape boys and adult men as well, even if at lower rates than they rape girls and women. *Id.* (reporting that 10 percent of child sex abuse victims are male). *See also* A. Kaufman, *Male Rape Victims: Noninstitutionalized Assault*, 137 Am. J. of Psychiatry 221 (1980).

IV

Although I conclude that immutable, biological differences between males and females do not justify this gender-specific law, I am compelled to point out that there are significant differences in victimization between young men and young women – differences my colleagues have ignored. Girls are more likely to be victims of statutory rape and child sexual abuse than are boys, 450 U.S. at 464 n. 8 (Brennan, J., dissenting); see also Br. for Resp't at 22–23 (both outlining data). Long-entrenched norms of feminine passivity render girls more susceptible to coercion, both physical and emotional. This is stated not to blame the victim, but rather to contextualize adolescent sexual interactions. As the state argues, girls are also more vulnerable to physical and other harms from early sex. The prevalence of forcible or non-consensual sexual intercourse, and the concomitant fear of most girls and women that they will be victimized, powerfully operates to limit women's options. *See generally* Brownmiller, *supra*. Sometimes the state itself limits women's options based on this fear. For instance, in *Dothard v. Rawlinson*, a majority of this Court permitted women to be restricted in employment as prison guards, out of a completely undocumented fear that they would be disproportionately likely to be raped, 433 U.S. 321 (1977). Justice Marshall correctly pointed out in his dissent that all of the evidence demonstrated that guards, male and female, were at risk of rape because they were guards, and were best able to protect themselves through training and appropriate staffing procedures in prisons. *Id.* at 343, 345–46.

One of the great difficulties in addressing discrimination is appropriately recognizing the differences between the sexes. Treating males and females the same poses the risk of allowing formal equality to obscure substantive inequality. Sex-based differences are particularly pronounced in sexual interactions and ignoring this context is problematic. Yet, because they are primarily socially constructed, rather than biological, enshrining these differences in law would be counterproductive and would further inequality. Instead, the legislature should be mindful of these differences in enforcing neutral laws so as best to protect victims and punish offenders, regardless of their sex.

V

Age rather than sex constitutes the real axis of victimhood; the harm to be addressed by statutory rape laws is the exploitation or coercion of younger by older.[28] Many states acknowledge this by punishing more severely sex with

---

[28] This is not to say that adult women are not more vulnerable to sexual exploitation and rape than men. They are; a powerful gender hierarchy persists in sexual relations. Nonetheless,

children significantly below the age of consent, whether male or female.[29] California itself accords greater punishment to those who have sex with a boy or girl under fourteen years of age. Cal. Penal Code § 288 (West 1980) ("lewd and lascivious acts"). Most of these statutes are gender-neutral, reflecting the reality that sexual activity is harmful both to young boys and young girls. This trend makes the differential treatment of adolescent and adult males and females puzzling – why does California deem all boys to become autonomous, even predatory to girls, at age fourteen? Further undercutting this dramatic change in the treatment of young men are the harsh punishments for sodomy of minors of either sex. Cal. Penal Code § 286 (defining sodomy as "sexual contact between the penis of one person and the anus of another person.")[30]

The age of the offender is relevant as well. Adults, particularly those out of their teenage years, are more able to coerce and exploit adolescents, again of either gender. Recognizing this dynamic, at least thirty states take into account the age differential between the parties in assessing criminal sanctions and the level of punishment.[31] Relatedly, a majority of states set a minimum age for offenders. Rita Eidson, Comment, *The Constitutionality of Statutory Rape Laws*, 27 UCLA L. Rev. 757, n.294 (1980). This age differential is a much more appropriate proxy for offending and victimhood than gender. Age represents what my colleague terms "a legislative judgment that one [party to sexual activity] is more guilty than the other." *Michael M*, 450 U.S. at 500 (Stevens, J., dissenting). Accordingly, statutory rape statutes should focus on the respective ages of the victims and offenders, rather than gender. They should also be expanded to include all forms of sexual intercourse, including sodomy. Criminal sanctions and the severity of punishment should not vary dependent upon whether the offender is homosexual or heterosexual.

---

because a statutory rape law is at issue here, I focus on sexual intercourse with those under the age of consent.

[29] We recently remarked upon several states that maintained the death penalty for cases of rape "where the victim was a child and the rapist an adult." *Coker v. Georgia*, 433 U.S. 584, 595 (1977) (listing three state statutes, and declining to rule on the constitutionality of the death penalty for child rape, while finding it an unconstitutional punishment for adult rape). As to states punishing sexual intercourse with young children more severely than with older minors, *see, e.g.*, Ala. Code § 13A-6-66 (1978); Alaska Stat. §11.41.440 (1978); Ark. Code. Ann. § 41–1810 (1977).

[30] The state recently exempted sodomy between consenting adults. *Statutes and Amendments to the Codes of California 1975*, page 1957, ch. 877, enacted September 18, 1975, effective January 1, 1976. California's sodomy law carries more severe punishment than its statutory rape law, reflecting the view of same-sex relations as "deviant."

[31] For instance, Maryland, New Jersey and Wyoming all require that the offender be four years older than the victim. Md. Code Ann. art. 27, §§ 463(a)(3), 464C(a)(3), (1979); N.J. Stat. Ann. §§ 2C:14-2, -3 (West 1979); Wyo. Stat. Ann. §§ 6-4-303(a)(v), (c), -305 (1977). Other states vary punishment based on the respective ages. See, e.g., Alaska Stat. §§ 11.41.410(a)(3), 440(a)(1) (1978); Ariz. Rev. Stat. Ann. § 13–1405(1978); Ark. Code. Ann. §§ 41–1804 to -1810 (1977).

Statutory rape prosecutions, like the one at hand, often involve two adolescents who are close in age. Eidson, *supra*, at 769, 775–76. I agree with Justice Stevens that the law here is unjust in punishing only the male, yet I do not endorse his argument that a gender-neutral statutory rape law should be applicable to both boys and girls under the age of consent.[32] As we noted recently in invalidating a different age of majority for men and women, "[a] child, male or female, is still a child." *Stanton v. Stanton*, 421 U.S. 7, 14 (1975). Because such a scheme would create two significant problems, I believe that neither boys nor girls should be punished for sex with another minor. First, such a scheme would leave up to prosecutors whom to designate the offender and whom the victim, where both were below the age of consent. This overly broad discretion risks perpetuating gender and other stereotypes even with a facially neutral law.[33] Second, it would punish young people in the name of protecting them. This type of punitive paternalism is overly harsh, particularly because statutory rape is a strict liability crime in most jurisdictions. It is also ineffective, as it would deter reporting of sexual abuse and rape, which are already at very low levels. Finally, such a scheme is at peril of being overly vague because it does not clearly identify when a young person is a victim and when she is an offender. We recently held a criminal vagrancy statute to be void for vagueness because it "fail[ed] to give a person of ordinary intelligence fair notice that his contemplated conduct is forbidden" and "encourag[ed] arbitrary and erratic arrests and convictions." *Papachristou v. City of Jacksonville*, 405 U.S. 156, 162 (1979).

Where a state's purposes "are as well served by a gender-neutral classification as one that gender classifies, and therefore carries with it the baggage of sexual stereotypes, the state cannot be permitted to classify on the basis of sex." *Orr v. Orr*, 440 U.S. 268, 283 (1979). I believe a gender-neutral statute considering the age difference between two parties, and increased attention to prosecution of forcible rape, would best meet the state's goals without relying on overly broad sex stereotyping.

I would hold that California Penal Code § 261.5 violates the Equal Protection Clause of the Fourteenth Amendment, and would reverse the judgment of the California Supreme Court.

---

[32] Justice Stewart also appears to endorse the punishment of at least some females below the age of consent. *Michael M.*, 450 U.S. at 477 (Stewart, J., concurring) (noting that girls could be charged with aiding and abetting under the statutory rape statute).

[33] Selective enforcement is already a significant problem with underenforced crimes such as statutory rape. Sanford H. Kadish, *The Crisis of Overcriminalization*, 374 Annals Am. Acad. Pol. & Soc. Sci. 157 (1967).

15

Commentary on *Rostker v. Goldberg*

Jamie R. Abrams

Without the dissent by Justice Thurgood Marshall and the historic context, the reader of *Rostker v. Goldberg*[1] might wonder why this opinion was selected for a feminist re-envisioning. The U.S. Supreme Court in *Rostker* upheld Congress's Military Selective Service Act (MSSA) determination that only men must register for military service. Based on its strong deference to Congress's war powers, the majority opinion defined the constitutional standard for review of gender equality almost entirely out of the case. The reader must read ten pages into the *Rostker* majority before finding the acknowledgement that the Constitution prohibits the state from denying men or women equal protection of the laws. Yet everything about the case's political, legal, and social context positioned gender equality at the center of the issue presented, rather than as merely an incidental byproduct of a question about military readiness.

THE ORIGINAL OPINION

Perhaps the centrality of gender equality was lost in *Rostker* because it began as a class action filed by men fighting against the Vietnam War itself, not by litigants fighting for gender equality.[2] The male plaintiffs alleged that the male-only registration requirement violated the Equal Protection Clause, leveraging *Reed v. Reed*'s iconic shift in constitutional review of gender classifications. A year earlier, in *Reed*, the Court had struck down a mandatory male preference in an estate administration hierarchy.[3] Although the *Reed* opinion

---

[1] *Rostker v. Goldberg*, 453 U.S. 57 (1981).
[2] *Rowland v. Tarr*, 378 F. Supp. 766 (E.D. Pa. 1974) (raising due process, equal protection, and involuntary servitude claims).
[3] *Reed v. Reed*, 404 U.S. 71 (1971).

did not explicitly define a heightened standard of review, the Court's striking down the statute despite its administrative convenience appeared to signal a new era of heightened scrutiny.[4]

While *Rostker* was pending for many years,[5] the Court's equal protection review of sex classifications became increasingly clear and vigorous throughout the 1970s. The *Rostker* class action was dormant after President Ford revoked the draft in 1975, returning to an All-Volunteer Force and pushing for a rigorous review of the selective service program.[6] In 1980, President Carter reinstated the draft and asked Congress to include women in registration.[7]

The registration requirement reinvigorated the *Rostker* class action and positioned it squarely within the context of recent equal protection cases establishing heightened standards of review for sex-based classifications. In *Frontiero v. Richardson*, a Court plurality struck down a statute treating male and female dependent allowances differently based on a presumption that women were economically dependent on their spouses, but men were not.[8] In *Craig v. Boren*, the U.S. Supreme Court articulated the governing intermediate scrutiny test under which "a gender-based classification cannot withstand constitutional challenge unless the classification is substantially related to the achievement of an important governmental objective."[9]

Interrupting this strong decade-long line of precedent, the 6–3 opinion in *Rostker* upheld male-only registration.[10] The Court's first paragraph focused squarely on Congress's power to "raise and support Armies." The Court concluded that Congress is entitled to more deference in its actions relating to military readiness than in its governance legislation. Framing the MSSA's purpose as to "facilitate any eventual conscription,"[11] the majority reasoned that Congress has the power to raise an army, this power receives great deference, the MSSA registration requirement is designed to raise troops for combat, and the lawsuit did not challenge the underlying ban of women from combat.

---

[4] From Fourteenth Amendment ratification until 1971, Courts applied the deferential rational basis review to gender classifications.

[5] *Rostker* was first held to present a non-justiciable political question in 1972 (with its original litigants). *Rowland*, 378 F. Supp. at 766.

[6] *See* Proclamation No. 4360, 40 Fed. Reg. 14567 (Mar. 29, 1975) (ceasing the existing selective service registration procedures and stating that a new approach would be followed going forward).

[7] *See* Jimmy Carter, U.S. President, State of the Union Address (Jan. 23, 1980), *in* Public Papers of the Presidents of the United States: Jimmy Carter 1980–81, 194, 198 (1981).

[8] *Frontiero v. Richardson*, 411 U.S. 677 (1973).

[9] *Craig v. Boren*, 429 U.S. 190 (1976).

[10] *Rostker*, 453 U.S. 57.

[11] *Id.* at 59.

As a result, the Court was required to defer to Congress's decision to require male-only registration since only men can serve in combat.

The *Rostker* majority explicitly declined the Government's invitation to apply rational basis review based on military deference, expressing concern that this "refinement" to the levels of "scrutiny" might "all too readily become [a] facile abstraction[] used to justify a result."[12] Citing *Craig*, the majority suggested that it would require the government to prove an important government interest and that the means selected were substantially related to achieving that interest. But the majority repeatedly emphasized that it was "giving great deference to the judgment of Congress."[13] Though the majority purported to apply intermediate scrutiny, it merely concluded that exempting women was "not only sufficiently, but also closely, related to Congress'[s] purpose in authorizing registration."[14] Had the Court applied intermediate scrutiny, the government would have been required to show "that registering women would substantially impede its efforts to prepare for such a draft."[15] The government never claimed that it could not prepare for a draft of combat troops by registering both men and women. And any arguments based solely on administrative convenience or outdated stereotypes would fail the intermediate scrutiny test.[16] Thus, in reality, the Court applied a test so profoundly deferential to Congress – even reverential – that it was no more than rational basis scrutiny. The *Rostker* decision thus shifted the momentum away from more rigorous intermediate scrutiny toward more deferential review, a ratcheting down that might be explained by the Court's deference to Congress in military matters or by a larger shift that would be reflected in subsequent gender equality cases.

The *Rostker* dissents focused on women's role in military service and the practical realities of induction. Justices White and Brennan conceded that there would no reason to register women if war mobilization meant that all positions must be filled with combat-qualified persons, but argued that combat qualifications were often not required.[17] Nor was it clear from the record that all the positions for which women were eligible would be filled by volunteers, so as to render women's registration unnecessary.[18]

---

[12] *Id.* at 69–70.
[13] *Id.* at n.6.
[14] *Id.* at 79.
[15] *Rostker*, 453 U.S. at 94.
[16] *Id.* at 95.
[17] *Id.* at 83–85. ("On the contrary, the record … supports … that the services would have to conscript at least 80,000 persons to fill positions for which combat-ready men would not be required.")
[18] *Id.* at 85.

Justices Marshall and Brennan framed the issue as an equal protection violation that excluded women from "a fundamental civic obligation."[19] They critiqued the majority's reasoning that "women may be excluded from registration because they will not be needed in the event of a draft."[20] Invoking congressional "war power," argued their dissent, "does not remove constitutional limitations safeguarding essential liberties." Rather, intermediate scrutiny required the government to defend women's exclusion as substantially related to military effectiveness, a burden the government could not meet given the 150,000 women who were presently volunteering in the military and the historic and future contributions that women would make to the armed forces.[21]

THE FEMINIST JUDGMENT

Writing as Justice Cohen, Professor David S. Cohen positions military women, men, and the President at the center of his rigorous application of the intermediate scrutiny test. Cohen summarizes the self-defeating circularity of the *Rostker* majority opinion – that it is acceptable to exclude women from registration because they are excluded from combat – when he concludes that "reliance on the combat exclusion is an attempt to justify one policy's ostensible constitutionality by pointing to another policy that is likely unconstitutional." Cohen finds that Congress's role in military oversight does not justify shirking equal protection scrutiny, but instead the role of the military underscores the necessity for judicial oversight.[22] As he puts it: "War is not a blank check for the government when it comes to the rights of the nation's citizens."[23]

Cohen's opinion applies the intermediate scrutiny test authentically and rigorously, consistent with existing precedent. As applied, the test requires the government to meet its burden to prove that the exclusion of women was substantially related to its registration goals. Notably, Cohen does not endorse intermediate scrutiny over the strict scrutiny of the *Frontiero* plurality.

In the *Rostker* majority opinion, Congress was the central actor; concerns about women's role in society and gender equality fell outside the analysis.

---

[19]   *Id.* at 86.

[20]   *Rostker*, 453 U.S. at 94.

[21]   *Id.* at 90–91.

[22]   Cohen's reasoning here cites the underlying primary sources later used influentially by Peter Irons to reveal the government's suppression and alteration of evidence in lawsuits challenging the internment of Japanese Americans. *See generally* Peter Irons, Justice at War: The Story of the Japanese-American Internment Cases (1993).

[23]   This language is the same powerful language that Justice O'Connor later used regarding the detention of enemy combatants in *Hamdi v. Rumsfeld*, 542 U.S. 507, 536 (2004).

The *Rostker* majority and dissent read like a series of volleys back and forth regarding the statistics supporting registration as it relates to induction. While the dissents reached the same outcome as Cohen, they largely argued on the majority's turf, limiting their later impact. Cohen injects a feminist perspective by staying out of this debate over deference and approaching *Rostker* consistent with the underlying anti-stereotyping principles that aligned and synthesized *Reed, Frontiero, Craig,* and other cases before *Rostker.*

Cohen's opinion begins where *Rostker* did not – highlighting both the historical centrality of women's contributions to the military and the burden that men have shouldered. In doing so, Cohen reveals that a critical examination of the underlying gender stereotypes was notably absent from the Court's majority opinion. Women's exclusion from registration deprives them of access to full political citizenship,[24] undermines men's role as nurturers and family caregivers, and burdens only men with the civic duty of military service. Cohen powerfully outlines the harms that women's exclusion from the registration requirement perpetuates on women, on men, and even on the military.[25]

The *Rostker* majority had distinguished prior cases striking down sex-based classifications under the intermediate scrutiny test on the basis that in *Rostker,* Congress did not act "unthinkingly" or "reflexively," but rather it considered women's registration only to ultimately reject it. In the majority's opinion, this congressional discussion meant that women were not excluded merely because of traditional thinking or stereotypes.[26] Cohen, however, refuses to look so superficially at Congress's deliberations. Rather, he analyzes the question of intention in depth and concludes that the role of legislators in categorizing men and women monolithically "cannot escape the effect of deeply ingrained beliefs about traditional sex roles."[27] Cohen demands that before the Court upholds the requirement, it must find that Congress acted upon

---

[24] Cohen connects military registration directly to citizenship itself. He argues that women's military exclusion also violates "principles of equal protection as clarified by the Nineteenth Amendment." This analytic approach applies the transformative work of Reva Siegel, *She the People: The Nineteenth Amendment, Sex Equality, Federalism, and the Family,* 115 *Harv. L. Rev.* 947 (2002).

[25] In articulating the harms to men and to the limited construction of masculine identities, Cohen layers into his analysis the teachings of masculinities theory, a strand of gender scholarship and sociology that later emerged to interrogate hegemonic masculinity and the hegemony of men.

[26] *See Rostker,* 453 U.S. at 74.

[27] To support this point, Cohen powerfully and effectively draws upon the work of Charles Lawrence in *The Id, the Ego, and Equal Protection: Reckoning with Unconscious Racism,* 38 *Stan. L. Rev.* 317 (1987) as well as modern framings of implicit bias.

accurate descriptions of men and women, stating that any outdated or inaccurate generalizations supporting the classification "doom[] the classification."[28]

The feminist judgment demonstrates that the original decision obscured the longstanding contributions of women in our armed forces, positioned women as vulnerable marginal outsiders in the military, and pretended that male military service is innate and natural. These stereotypes sit at the heart of modern military challenges. Had Cohen's rigorous anti-stereotyping analysis instead been applied in *Rostker*, it might have catalyzed far broader changes in military service and gender equality. Even today as women are formally integrated in the military, they are not required to register for the draft. The modern military faces a growing sexual assault crisis, disproportionately impacting women, and a mental health crisis leaving 22 veterans a day committing suicide, disproportionately impacting men.[29] Cohen's opinion reveals how a re-envisioned *Rostker* opinion might have provided essential early support for legal, political, and social shifts toward achieving gender equality.

Rostker v. Goldberg, 453 U.S. 57 (1981)

Justice David S. Cohen delivered the opinion of the Court.

There is no denying that women have become an essential part of our military. Their participation rates have been steadily increasing, with the expectation that they will rise even more quickly in the future.

While large numbers of men have also served and sacrificed for our country, some men have objected to being a part of the machinery of war. They object for many reasons, including their religion, their politics, or their pacifism. For other men, serving in the military is inconsistent with how they see themselves as men.

Nonetheless, despite many women serving our military with honor and many men objecting to military service on matters of deep principle, Congress requires that all men and no women register for the draft. Because this requirement perpetuates archaic and malignant stereotypes about both men and women, we hold that the current male-only registration system violates the principle of equal protection embedded in the Fifth Amendment's Due Process Clause.

---

[28] This analytic approach applies the scholarly work developed by Mary Ann Case, *The Very Stereotype the Law Condemns*, 85 *Cornell L. Rev.* 1447 (2000).

[29] James Dao and Andrew W. Lehren, *Baffling Rise in Suicides Plagues the U.S. Military*, N.Y. Times (May 15, 2013). *See* www.nytimes.com/2013/05/16/us/baffling-rise-in-suicides-plagues-us-military.html.

I

For the first ninety years that women served in the United States military, they did so almost exclusively as nurses. Florence Nightingale organized the first female military nurses in the Crimea in 1854. Women served as civilians until the Spanish–American War in 1902 when women became uniformed personnel as part of the Army Nurse Corps. In World War I, the first women were granted military rank, and in World War II, women held nursing, administrative, and clerical jobs, but they also worked in intelligence and communication.

Since World War II, women's roles have continued to expand, as they have entered many other areas of the military, including logistics and maintenance. In fact, over the past decade, the Department of Defense has opened all occupational specialties to women except those related to combat. As a result, women's participation in the military has increased from the post-World War II level of about 2 percent of the Armed Forces to more than 8 percent in 1980. *See generally* Anne Hoiberg, *Military Occupations: The Cutting Edge for Women?*, Naval Health Research Center (1980); Nancy Goldman, *The Changing Role of Women in the Armed Forces*, 78 Am. J. Soc. 892 (1973).

Women's participation in the military has been a success. Then-General Dwight D. Eisenhower noted as much in 1948:

> Like most old soldiers I was violently against women soldiers. I thought a tremendous number of difficulties would occur, not only of an administrative nature … but others of a more personal type that would get us into trouble. None of that occurred … In the disciplinary field they were a model for the Army. More than this their influence throughout the entire command was good. I am convinced that in another war they have got to be drafted just like men.
>
> *Hearings on S.1614 before the Subcomm. on Organization and Mobilization of the House Comm. on Armed Services,* 80th Cong., 2d Sess., at 5563–64 (1948) (statement of Dwight D. Eisenhower, General, U.S. Army).

Based on this record, when President Carter recommended reinstating the requirement that young people register for the draft last year, he recommended that both women and men be subject to the requirement. *Presidential Recommendations for Selective Service Reform – A Report to Congress Prepared Pursuant to Pub. L. 96–107,* House Comm. on Armed Services, 96th Cong., 2d Sess., at 20–23 (Comm. Print No. 19, 1980) (hereinafter *Presidential Recommendations*). The President has the authority to require registration pursuant to the Military Selective Service Act, 50 U.S.C.S. App. § 451 *et seq.*

The purpose of that law is to provide a pool of people who could be drafted into military service if the need arises. During the Vietnam War, men were required to register for the draft, but President Ford discontinued that requirement in 1975. Early last year, President Carter determined that, because of the Soviet invasion of Afghanistan, mandatory registration should begin again. Jimmy Carter, U.S. President, State of the Union Address, 16 Weekly Comp. of Pres. Doc. 198 (1980).

In his recommendations to Congress, the President explained that "women are capable of high quality performance in many military skills." As a result, the President recommended removing statutory restrictions on women's assignments so as to provide the military "greater flexibility" in assigning women. The report offered three reasons for this change: women are already successfully performing a "large number of military jobs," drafting women would "free more men for close combat jobs," and requiring women to register would promote equity. The recommendation concluded: "In order to expand the potential personnel pool available during a national emergency, women as well as men should be subject by law to registration, induction and training for service in the Armed Forces." *Presidential Recommendations, supra*, at 20–23.

Nonetheless, despite this recommendation from the Commander in Chief, Congress decided to omit women from the registration requirement. Congress allocated funds for registration but limited those funds to only those necessary to register men. S. Rep. No. 96–789, at 1 nn.1, and 2 (1980). On July 2, 1980, acting pursuant to this authority, President Carter ordered registration of men only to begin July 21. Proclamation No. 4771, 45 Fed. Reg. 45247 (July 2, 1980).

President Carter's actions in reinstating the registration requirement were directly relevant to a case that had lain dormant in the Eastern District of Pennsylvania for years. In 1971, several men subject to the then-applicable registration requirement filed suit against the Selective Service System alleging, among other things, that the system discriminated against them based on sex[30] and thus violated the Fifth Amendment's Due Process Clause.[31]

After an initial decision that the case was not moot, *Rowland v. Tarr*, 378 F. Supp. 766 (E.D. Pa. 1974), nothing happened until 1979 when the clerk

[30] Our cases have previously referred to "gender," not "sex," but that is an error. Sex refers to a person's biology; gender refers to traits or characteristics that a person presents to the world. Ann Oakley, Sex, Gender and Society 16 (1972). To make this perfectly clear, masculine women are not covered by the registration requirement, while effeminate men are.
[31] The Fifth Amendment's Due Process Clause contains an implied equal protection component that we interpret the same as the Fourteenth Amendment's Equal Protection Clause. *See, e.g., Califano v. Webster*, 430 U.S. 313, 316–17 (1977).

of the court, acting pursuant to a local rule about inactive cases, proposed dismissing the case. The court denied the motion to dismiss early last year, *Goldberg v. Tarr*, 510 F. Supp. 292 (E.D. Pa. 1980), and then certified the case as a class action, with the class defined as "all male persons who are registered or subject to registration under 50 U.S.C. App. § 453 or are liable for training and service in the armed forces of the United States under 50 U.S.C. App. 454, 456(h) and 467(c)." *Goldberg v. Rostker*, 509 F. Supp. 586, 589 (E.D. Pa. 1980).

On July 18, 1980, three days before the new registration requirement was scheduled to take effect, the three-judge panel found that the Military Selective Service Act was unconstitutional because it discriminates between men and women. *Id.* at 605. Justice Brennan, acting as the Circuit Justice for the Third Circuit, immediately stayed the decision, allowing the registration requirement to take effect on July 21 pending the outcome of the case in this Court. 448 U.S. 1306 (1980).

II

Over the past decade we have been engaging in the long-needed process of revisiting our understanding of how the Constitution addresses sex discrimination. Although our work is incomplete, we need not complete our mission today. The constitutional standard that we apply here – the intermediate scrutiny standard – is not as responsive to the harms of sex discrimination in modern society as the strict scrutiny standard; nonetheless, it is sufficient for the task at hand.

A

Standard of review

Until 1971, this Court had never struck down a law as unconstitutional because it discriminated based on sex. In fact, in an unbroken string of cases dating back to the early days of the Fourteenth Amendment, we had given our blessing to government entities treating women like second-class citizens. We approved Illinois' refusal to allow women to be lawyers, *Bradwell v. Illinois*, 83 U.S. (16 Wall.) 130 (1873); Oregon's restricting women from working the same hours as men, *Muller v. Oregon*, 208 U.S. 412 (1908); Michigan's prohibition on most women being bartenders, *Goesaert v. Cleary*, 335 U.S. 464 (1948); and Florida's requirement that women opt in to jury service while men are automatically included, *Hoyt v. Florida*, 368 U.S. 57 (1961). Our decisions were based on the stereotyped notion that women inhabited a separate sphere from men. As we stated most recently in *Hoyt*, "[d]espite the enlightened emancipation of women from the restrictions and protections of bygone years, and their entry into many parts of community life formerly considered to be reserved to men, woman is still regarded as the center of home and family life." *Id.* at 61–62.

In 1971, we signaled a change when we declared unconstitutional an Idaho law that enabled the state to preferentially appoint men over women to administer estates. *Reed v. Reed*, 404 U.S. 71 (1971). We ruled that the law violated the Equal Protection Clause because there was no rational basis for this sex-based preference. *Id.* at 76–77. Although we stated that we were applying rational basis review, in hindsight, the only real explanation of the case's reasoning was that we had, in fact, applied a more stringent form of review. Gerald Gunther, *Foreword: In Search of Evolving Doctrine on a Changing Court: A Model for a Newer Equal Protection*, 86 Harv. L. Rev. 1, 34 (1972).

Reed was the first case decided amidst increasing calls to apply strict scrutiny to classifications based on sex. As articulated by Professor Ruth Bader Ginsburg before this Court in a subsequent case, sex is "a visible, immutable characteristic bearing no necessary relationship to ability" and "has been made the basis for unjustified or at least unproved assumptions concerning an individual's potential to perform or to contribute to society." Women have been excluded from the political process and stigmatized as inferior in efforts to protect them. Tr. of Oral Arg., *Frontiero v. Richardson*, 411 U.S. 677 (1973).

Despite these compelling arguments for applying strict scrutiny, to this date, this Court has applied an intermediate scrutiny test in judging classifications based on sex. We came one vote short of strict scrutiny in *Frontiero* because otherwise sympathetic justices believed we should wait for the outcome of the then-pending Equal Rights Amendment on the political stage rather than deciding the issue ourselves. *See id.* at 691–692 (Powell, J., concurring in judgment). So far, the Equal Rights Amendment has not been ratified, leaving our concerned colleagues looking inappropriately timid. Nonetheless, we do not need to revisit the very strong case for strict scrutiny today, as the intermediate scrutiny test is sufficient to decide this case.

In 1976, we first announced the standard that we apply today. In *Craig v. Boren*, 429 U.S. 190 (1976), we addressed an Oklahoma law that allowed women between the ages of 18 and 21 to drink beer with 3.2 percent alcohol but did not allow men to do so. Very clearly departing from our previous application of the rational basis test, we stated that all classifications based on sex "must serve important governmental objectives and must be substantially related to achievement of those objectives." *Id.* at 197.

This standard requires that the government have an exceedingly persuasive, though not necessarily compelling, reason for the sex classification and that the means used are very closely related to, though not necessarily narrowly tailored to, its goals. Although this test will allow a small number of government classifications based on sex, it will find most unconstitutional. The reason for this test is, as Professor Ginsburg so clearly explained, that sex is rarely a relevant basis for the government to differentiate between two people.

B

The anti-stereotyping principle

Though the mechanics of the intermediate scrutiny test are clear – substantial relationship to an important government interest – what has formed the real basis for our analysis in our past cases has been whether the government classification promotes or relies upon stereotypes about men and women. In fact, if you dig deep enough into our cases about sex discrimination, what emerges is the principle that, in order for a sex classification to survive, the classification must be an accurate description of all men or all women (or both). Any deviation, no matter how slight, from this requirement dooms the classification as unconstitutional. Our cases make this abundantly clear. Beginning with *Frontiero*, our case law has consistently decried "gross, stereotyped distinctions between the sexes." 411 U.S. at 685 (Brennan, J., plurality opinion). This stereotyping, as Justice Brennan's plurality opinion explained, has oppressed women in ways that black people have also been historically oppressed – limited access to civil, political, and social institutions. *Id.* at 685–686. Women as a group, like black people, were viewed as not having the characteristics needed to be full participants in society.

An excellent example of this anti-stereotyping principle comes from *Wengler v. Druggists Mutual Insurance Company*, 446 U.S. 142 (1980). In *Wengler*, we evaluated the constitutionality of a Missouri law that treated widowers different from widows for purposes of receiving workers' compensation death benefits. The law allowed a widow to receive benefits without proving dependence on her husband's earnings, but required a widower to prove dependence on his wife's earnings. Missouri attempted to justify the distinction on the generalization that "most women are dependent on male wage earners" and that in comparison there are only "few cases in which men might be dependent." *Id.* at 151.

We rejected Missouri's argument, even though we were willing to admit that there "may be [] empirical support for the proposition that men are more likely to be the principal supporters of their spouses and families." *Id.* Missouri's attempt to rely on this possibly true empirical argument was nothing other than reliance on an overbroad stereotype about men and women. Stereotypes, as *Wengler* and other cases have explained, are a matter of administrative convenience at the expense of individualized determinations about merits. *Id.* at 151–152. Administrative convenience, of course, is not always prohibited; rather, if it is to be a valid basis for law, it must be applied equally for men and women, or not at all. That is, the state can opt for the administrative ease of assuming all men *and* all women provide for their spouse, requiring no individualized determinations; or it can assume that no men *and* no women provide for their spouse, requiring individualized determinations for everyone. But these are the state's only options; principles of equal protection place stereotyping one group or the other off the table.

The reason this anti-stereotyping principle is at the heart of our sex classification cases is that stereotyping men and women based on a belief that is not true of all men or all women harms both men and women in serious ways that offend basic constitutional principles. Stereotyping offends notions of equality by removing opportunities from people who should otherwise have access to them, instead placing them in a subordinate position relative to the favored group. Stereotyping also offends notions of liberty by conveying the message that men and women should act in accordance with prescribed notions of gender rather than being free to act in ways that their own individuality compels. For these reasons, our case law has taken a strong stand against sex stereotyping.

C

Military context

That the sex classification arises in the context of the military does not change our analysis;[32] in fact, if anything, history teaches us that we should be even more skeptical of identity-based classifications in the military context.

Korematsu v. United States, 323 U.S. 214 (1944), is instructive. There, we approved the removal and imprisonment of Japanese-Americans during World War II. We purported to apply what we now call "strict scrutiny." *Id.*

---

[32] Appellant argues that because Congress is responsible under Article I, Section 8 of the Constitution for raising the military, the Court must defer to Congress's actions. If that argument were true, it would prove too much, as it would mean that this Court would never be able to scrutinize any of Congress's actions taken pursuant to an enumerated power.

at 216. However, we were overly deferential to military claims that linked Japanese-Americans to espionage and sabotage on the West Coast and analyzed the case under a standard that is a far cry from the highly critical eye we cast upon racial classifications today. The only explanation of our deviation from what we *said* in *Korematsu* – that we were applying "the most rigid scrutiny" – and what we *did* in *Korematsu* – defer to the military – is that we believed the military context necessitated a different approach to an equal protection claim.

We were wrong to be deferential in that context, and we now repudiate the reasoning and outcome of *Korematsu*, one of the darkest decisions in this Court's history. Our deference led us to approve the imprisonment of over 110,000 American citizens based on nothing more than their ancestry. Not only is this antithetical to the basic principles of our Constitution as amended by the Reconstruction Amendments, but it was also based upon the federal government's intentional deception of this Court. The Solicitor General at the time, Charles Fahy, intentionally omitted key government documents from the Court record that showed that the government knew there was no general threat of espionage from Japanese Americans. Eleventh Naval Dist. Branch Intelligence Office, Lt. Comm. Kenneth D. Ringle, Serial LA/1055/re, Report on Japanese Question (1942). Solicitor General Fahy also withheld from this Court information from the Federal Bureau of Investigation and the Federal Communications Commission that indicated there was no proof supporting allegations of unauthorized radio communications between Japanese Americans and the Japanese military. Memorandum from FBI Director Edgar J. Hoover to Attorney General Francis Biddle (Feb. 7, 1944); Memoranda from FCC Chairman James L. Fly to Attorney General Francis Biddle (April 1 and 4, 1944). Perhaps most appalling, in his argument before this Court, Solicitor General Fahy explicitly vouched for a report that said the exact opposite, even though he knew at the time that this was false. Memorandum from Assistant Attorney General Ennis & Deputy Attorney General John Burling to Deputy Attorney General Herbert Wechsler (September 2, 1944).

Our deference to the government in *Korematsu* allowed us to accept everything the government asserted about espionage and sabotage at face value. We refuse to repeat that same mistake here. War is not a blank check for the government when it comes to the rights of this nation's citizens. The Equal Protection Clause, as applied to the federal government through the Fifth Amendment's Due Process Clause, admits no exceptions in the military context. *See also Frontiero v. Richardson*, 411 U.S. 677 (scrutinizing sex-based military policies no differently than non-military policies).

III

We apply the intermediate scrutiny test as developed here – that the law must have an important government purpose and be substantially related to that purpose. No one before the Court contends that having the best possible military is not an important government purpose. The issue before us, then, is whether requiring only men to register for the draft is substantially related to that purpose. Because this method of reaching the goal of military excellence is based on gross stereotypes and generalizations about women and men, we hold that it fails intermediate scrutiny and is thus unconstitutional.

A

Stereotyping women

As Justice Brennan has written, military service is "one of the highest duties of American citizenship." *Trop v. Dulles*, 356 U.S. 86, 112 (1958) (Brennan, J., concurring). By excluding women from being part of the pool of people from whom military service could be demanded, the registration exclusion stereotypes women in a way that unconstitutionally treats them as inferior second-class citizens.

As history shows and President Eisenhower learned when he was this nation's highest-ranking general, women are more than capable of being excellent members of the military. Yet, by excluding women from registration, the United States stereotypes women as incapable of performing this service in a time of need and thus incapable of being full citizens. Professor Norman Dorsen eloquently explained this point to the Senate Judiciary Committee in 1970: "[W]hen women are excluded from the draft – the most serious and onerous duty of citizenship – their status is generally reduced. The social stereotype is that women should be less concerned with the affairs of the world than men." *Equal Rights 1970: Hearings on S.J. Res. 61 and S.J. Res. 231 Before the Senate Judiciary Comm.*, 91st Cong., 2d Sess., at 326 (1970).

The negative stereotype about women goes beyond the invidious notion that they are less concerned with the world and politics than men. It also treats women, as a group, as weak, passive, and incapable of participating in public life. Simply put, this is a gross overgeneralization about women that is reminiscent of our discarded case law treating women differently because they are "regarded as the center of home and family life." *Hoyt*, 368 U.S. at 61–62.

To be sure, there are undoubtedly some women who fit these descriptions. But there are many men who fit these descriptions. However, those men are

required to register for the draft, no matter how much their individual characteristics may deviate from what is most beneficial for the military. No women,
regardless of how capable they are at performing military duties if drafted, are
required to register for the draft – though, as President Eisenhower noted, we
know from history that many women excel at military service.

By treating all men, even those who are not fit to be drafted, one way, and
all women, even those who are fit to be drafted, in a different way, the Military
Selective Service Act has the same constitutional infirmity as laws that we
have previously struck down as unconstitutional based on sex stereotyping. For
instance, in *Orr v. Orr*, 440 U.S. 268 (1979), we recognized that more women
might need financial assistance after the death of a spouse than men; nonetheless, we still found that the law stereotyped women in an unconstitutional
manner. By labeling all women "needy spouses," the law "carried with it the
baggage of sexual stereotypes" about the inferior position of women in society.
Id. at 282–283. We stated, as a general matter, that "[l]egislative classifications
which distribute benefits and burdens on the basis of gender carry the inherent risk of reinforcing the stereotypes about the 'proper place' of women." *Id.*
at 283.

Similarly, in *Weinberger v. Wiesenfeld*, 420 U.S. 636 (1975), we recognized
that there is empirical support for the "notion that men are more likely than
women to be the primary supporters of their spouses and children." *Id.* at
644–645. Nonetheless, we found a Social Security Act provision granting
benefits to women whose spouse dies with a surviving child, but not to men, a
"gender-based generalization [that] cannot suffice to justify the denigration of
the efforts of women who do work and whose earnings contribute significantly
to their families' support." *Id.* at 645.

Here, it is true that men are, by virtue of the federal law prohibiting women
from serving in combat roles,[33] capable of serving in a greater number of roles
in the military than women. However, we have never allowed this type of
sex-based classification that stereotypes women and denigrates their contributions to society. Allowing Congress to omit women from registration requirements is the same type of "gender-based generalization" that denigrates
women that we have struck down in the past.

Moreover, when Congress omits women from such a basic element of citizenship as mandatory registration for the military, Congress is also violating
the principles of equal protection as clarified by the Nineteenth Amendment.
For those who claim that principles of equal protection were not originally
understood to include a protection against sex discrimination, the Nineteenth

---

[33] For further discussion of the combat exclusion, see *infra* Section IV.B.

Amendment makes clear that women are required to be treated as equal citizens.

Although it specifically covers only voting, the Nineteenth Amendment has a broader purpose: granting the most basic citizenship rights to women. The Amendment's specific language about voting is just one way that women can be made equal citizens in our democracy, but the language does not limit other ways. Read in the context of the debates of the time that led to its passage, the Amendment speaks broadly to women's equal participation in society. Voting is merely the foundation upon which equal citizenship status is built.

Among those citizenship rights that we can read as a part of the Nineteenth Amendment and its implications for equal protection is the broad right not to be a second-class citizen. When women are excluded from registration, they are being treated as second-class citizens not worthy of serving their country in a time of need. The Nineteenth Amendment, read in conjunction with the Fifth and Fourteenth Amendments, prohibits such subordination of women.

B

Stereotyping men

Almost by necessary implication, every law that stereotypes women also stereotypes men. Just as we have struck down laws that apply overbroad generalizations about women as unconstitutional, we have done the same with overbroad generalizations about men. By stereotyping men as violent, aggressive, strong, and powerful, the registration requirement is unconstitutional.

That the constitutional concern about sex stereotyping extends to classifications that stereotype men as well as women is abundantly clear from our case law. Starting with *Stanley v. Illinois*, 405 U.S. 645 (1972), we decried the overbroad generalizations that limit men to a particular type of masculine behavior. In that case, the State of Illinois declared that children of unmarried fathers were automatically wards of the state upon the death of their mother. *Id.* at 649, 658. We held that this presumption was unconstitutional. Illinois had argued that the presumption was based on the stereotype that "unmarried fathers are so seldom fit that [a state] need not undergo the administrative inconvenience of inquiry in any case." *Id.* at 656. We dismissed this argument as an unconstitutional stereotype, noting that "all unmarried fathers are not in this category; some are wholly suited to have custody of their children." *Id.* at 654.

We followed a similar course in *Califano v. Westcott*, 443 U.S. 76 (1979), and *Stanton v. Stanton*, 421 U.S. 7 (1975). In both cases, we addressed policies that presumed that men had the "primary responsibility to provide a home and its essentials" whereas women were the "center of home and family life." *Califano*, 443 U.S. at 89. These overbroad assumptions about men (and women) were rejected because, as we wrote in *Stanton*, "[n]o longer is the female destined solely for the home and the rearing of family, and only the male for the marketplace and the world of ideas." 421 U.S. at 14–15. The problem with these laws was not just that they stereotyped women; they were also unconstitutional because they assumed that all men acted in a particular way and that the state could treat them according to that overbroad generalization.

The registration requirement fails for the same reasons. By requiring all men to register for the draft, the law assumes that all men, solely by virtue of their sex, are the type of people who would be valuable to the military effort. Indisputably, many men fall within this category. Just as indisputably, many men do not. Some men are pacifists who want nothing to do with the war effort. Others are unsuited to be a part of an organization that relies on aggressive interactions between superiors and subordinates. Still others have personal characteristics that do not fit the mold of a regimented organization such as the military.

Just as capable women are lumped into a group that will never be drafted, these men who do not fit the mold of stereotypical masculinity are lumped into a group that will be eligible to be drafted into the military based on no criteria other than their sex. Because believing that all men are the same is an overbroad generalization, principles of equal protection prevent the government from requiring all men, by virtue of their sex alone, to act in the same way. These assumptions about men are "loose-fitting characterizations incapable of supporting [the government] scheme[] that [was] premised upon their accuracy." *Craig*, 429 U.S. at 198–199. As such, they are unconstitutional.

C

Stereotyping's harm

Stereotypes cause serious harm. Rather than amounting to a trivial mismatch between a classification and its goal, stereotypes treat all men as separate from all women and attribute essential traits to each group based solely on sex. These generalizations harm women, men, and the country at large in ways that raise constitutional issues related to both equality and liberty.

For women, the harms are legion. They begin with the loss of the numerous benefits that flow from military service. *See generally* Barbara A. Brown et al., *The Equal Rights Amendment: A Constitutional Basis for Equal Rights for Women*, 80 Yale L.J. 871, 968 and n.252 (1973). By being excluded from registration, they lose out on these benefits in two ways. First, the message is communicated that they are less fit for the military than men, so they would logically volunteer for the military in smaller numbers than men. Second, if there were ever a draft based on the mandatory registrants, women would not be a part of the drafted contingent. Both of these mechanisms deflate the number of women in the military, which leads to far fewer women receiving service benefits than men. In this way, women are subordinated to men with respect to government benefits.

Women lose out in other ways as well. By excluding women from registration, the government is sending a message about how women are supposed to express their identity. Even if society has progressed to allow women more entry into public life and no longer limit women to the family sphere, that progress is not complete. Women are essentially told that they can break free from traditional notions of gender, but only so much.

Women are also harmed in another insidious way that relates to the stereotypes about men that are furthered by the registration requirement. Men are told by the government that they are the more violent and aggressive sex. Moreover, the men who are drafted as a result of registration are then trained in violence by the government. By sending this message and then training some men in the ways of war, the government reinforces the cultural acceptance of male violence, including male violence against women. *See* Murray Straus, U.S. Comm'n on Civil Rights, *Wife Beating: Causes, Treatment, and Research Needs, in Battered Women: Issues of Public Policy* 471, 482 (1978) (finding that "examples of governmental violence provide powerful models for the behavior of individual citizens" and that "the frequency of interpersonal violence" rises dramatically following major wars). Compounding the problem, the message conveyed to both men and women is that women are incapable of addressing violence. This is a very real harm that women suffer daily. *See* Dane Archer and Rosemary Gartner, *Violent Acts and Violent Times: A Comparative Approach to Postwar Homicide Rates*, 41 Am. Soc. Rev. 937 (1976).

Men are also harmed. For the men who register, their chances of being drafted are doubled because women are excluded. Though being drafted may have very positive results for some people, for others it may lead to life-long emotional trauma, physical injury, or death. Only men are subject to these risks when a draft occurs.

Beyond those men who may be drafted as a result of registration, the requirement that men, and men alone, register for the draft harms men by contributing to society's dominant view of how men are expected to act. As history consistently teaches, those men who do not fit within the expected mold of masculinity are subject to oppression from those who exhibit stereotypically dominant masculine traits. They are verbally and physically abused, bullied, and harassed as a result. As one factor that constructs this culturally dominant male identity, the male-only registration requirement helps to subordinate those who do not conform.

Moreover, the male-only registration requirement affects all men in a way that restricts their liberty to act as they see fit, not just those who already do not conform. When a particular notion of male behavior is presented as the model or assumed as universal, that notion contributes to limited expressions of identity for all men. Men then struggle to live up to conceptions of the ideal male. They adopt personas that are not true to themselves and find it difficult to deviate from society's expectations. In other words, when society tells men that they are supposed to be aggressive wage-earners who value strength over caring, men will try to adopt that persona while fighting any inclination they may have to do otherwise. This constraint on men's liberty is not just the result of the male-only registration requirement, but such stereotyping plays an important role.

Finally, society at large is negatively affected by this requirement. First, the American people are deprived of the best military they can possibly have. When military requirements are based on sex rather than competence, two classifications that are not equivalent, the resulting military will not be as strong as one based solely on competence.

Second, outside of the military context, the registration requirement reinforces the notion that men and women are inherently different and accordingly must be treated differently. For the past decade our cases have begun the work of breaking down these distinctions based on sex because we have realized the insidious nature of this assumption. To uphold this distinction would make our work of the past decade almost meaningless. We refuse to do that today.

D

Failing intermediate scrutiny

We have so far focused our attention on the ways that the Military Selective Service Act relies on harmful stereotypes of men and women. Based on our now well-established precedent, that alone is enough for a statute to be declared unconstitutional.

In conducting the above analysis, we are not ignoring the particulars of the intermediate scrutiny test. As established in *Craig v. Boren*, a sex-based classification "must serve important governmental objectives and must be substantially related to achievement of those objectives." 429 U.S. at 197. Though we do not question the importance of the military's need to have the best force possible, our analysis of the stereotypes behind the law indicates that excluding women from the registration requirement is not "substantially related to the achievement" of that objective. Overbroad generalizations about women and men can never satisfy that test, which is why we conclude that the registration requirement violates the principles of equal protection implicit in the Fifth Amendment Due Process Clause and is thus unconstitutional.

IV

The chief arguments put forth in Justice Rehnquist's dissenting opinion require our attention but do nothing to change our reasoning or conclusion about the registration requirement's unconstitutionality. At heart, the dissent puts forth a vision of the Constitution that allows the government to rely on stereotypes that harm equality and liberty, a vision that we have consistently rejected for the past decade.

A

Congress's intentional act

One of the dissent's primary arguments is that Congress acted intentionally and after much thought and debate when it excluded women from registration. In making this argument, the dissent completely misunderstands that sex discrimination is unconstitutional whether based on careful consideration or not.

The dissent attempts to establish a clear dichotomy. On the one hand, there are sex classifications that legislatures enact "unthinkingly" or "reflexively and not for any considered reason." 453 U.S. at 72 (Rehnquist, J.). These types of sex classifications are unconstitutional because they reflect an "accidental by-product of a traditional way of thinking about females." *Id.* at 74 (quoting *Califano*, 430 U.S. at 320). On the other hand, there are sex classifications, like the registration requirement at issue here, that are the "subject of wide-ranging public debate," "extensively considered," and based on Congress's "clearly expressed []purpose and intent." *Id.* at 72–74. These types of sex classifications, according to the dissent, are constitutional when based on sound understandings of the differences between men and women.

The very existence of this dichotomy is questionable. Even legislators who carefully consider distinguishing between men and women cannot escape the effect of deeply ingrained beliefs about traditional sex roles. For instance, here, as the dissent explains in detail, the presidential recommendation to register women was debated and then rejected by both houses of Congress. The Senate Armed Services Committee adopted findings supporting the exclusion of women, and both Houses of Congress later adopted those findings. The dissent then concludes that these findings are "considerably more significant than a typical report of a single House." *Id.* at 74.

However, nothing about this process, no matter how lengthy and well-considered, means that the members of Congress who voted against registering women were able to act without being influenced by sex-based overgeneralization. The power of sex stereotypes stems from their persistence, even in the face of evidence to the contrary and despite reasoned debate on the matter. People who have reflexive beliefs that women are not fit for certain parts of public life may never acknowledge those beliefs, but may act on them nonetheless, even when they do not know they are doing so. Thus, the distinction the dissent draws is one that has no basis in the way that discrimination based on sex (or race, or any other characteristic) works.

Moreover, even if this distinction between intentional, well-thought-out sex classifications and unthinking, reflexive sex classifications did exist, it would not help the dissent's case. Merely because a legislature carefully considered a classification based on a particular characteristic does not change the analysis. For instance, in our most iconic equality case, *Brown v. Board of Education*, 347 U.S. 483 (1954), if the legislatures of the segregated states had carefully considered, debated, and then rejected integrating their schools, our analysis would have been no different. The children would still have suffered the grave indignity of being separated based on nothing other than their race, something that is no less of a constitutional violation based on how much the legislators discussed the issue.

The same is true in the context of our sex discrimination cases. For instance, if the legislature of Alabama had considered in depth the issue of providing alimony for divorced men who would qualify but then decided that men as a class do not need alimony, our decision in *Orr v. Orr* would still be the same. The legislature acted based on overly broad generalizations about women and men, generalizations that are unconstitutional regardless of how extensively they are considered. 440 U.S. at 281–283. In fact, in all of the foregoing hypotheticals, the legislature's intentional resort to discriminatory classifications is possibly of even greater constitutional concern. *See Personnel Administrator of Mass. v. Feeney*, 442 U.S. 256 (1979).

We will not belabor the point by going through all of the other sex discrimination cases we have decided in the past decade because the point is clear. A sex classification that is based on stereotypes fails intermediate scrutiny regardless of whether those stereotypes are reflexively adopted or carefully debated. The dissent's attempt to absolve the exclusion of women from the registration requirement for being extensively considered misses the mark.

B

Combat exclusion

The dissent emphasizes the prohibition on women serving in combat roles in the military. This exclusion is statutory for the Navy and Air Force, *see* 10 U.S.C. § 6015 (Navy), § 8549 (Air Force), and a matter of policy for the Army and Marine Corps. *Rostker*, 453 U.S. at 76 (Rehnquist, J.). The Senate Report rejecting the registration of women endorsed the combat restriction. "Current law and policy exclude women from being assigned to combat in our military forces, and the Committee reaffirms this policy ... Women should not be intentionally or routinely placed in combat positions in our military services." S. Rep. No. 96–826, at 157–160. The President's report recommending including women in mandatory registration did not question this policy of excluding women from combat. *Presidential Recommendations*, *supra*, at 3.

According to the dissent, this exclusion from combat roles dooms the constitutional challenge here. Because women cannot serve in combat roles, they are not "similarly situated for purposes of a draft or registration for a draft" and their exclusion from the registration requirement is "closely related" to the requirement's purpose, thus satisfying intermediate scrutiny. *Rostker*, 453 U.S. at 78–79 (Rehnquist, J.). This argument has two chief flaws: first, it overstates the connection between registration and combat; and second, it relies on a policy that is itself of questionable constitutionality.

First, the military draft is not exclusively for the purpose of filling combat positions. As the District Court found, if there were a draft, the military would need to conscript at least 80,000 people to fill positions that do not require combat readiness. *Goldberg v. Rostker*, 509 F. Supp. at 600. Because these positions could be filled by women, there is no rational basis, let alone one that satisfies intermediate scrutiny, for excluding women from the pool of people eligible to be drafted into these positions.

To say women can be excluded is to denigrate the contributions and service of the 150,000 women who are currently in active service. By statute and policy, these women are not eligible to serve in combat roles; nonetheless, they are making positive contributions to the military every day. As the District Court concluded after reviewing the evidence, "[t]here can be no doubt that the experience of women in the all[-]volunteer army has been a success story." *Id.* at 603. Moreover, the Appellant in this case, Bernard Rostker, the Director of the Selective Service System, stated earlier this year that "[t]here is no distinction possible, on the basis of ability or performance, that would allow the President to exclude women from an obligation to register." *Department of Defense Authorization for Appropriations for Fiscal Year 1981: Hearings on S. 2294 Before the Senate Comm. on Armed Services*, 96th Cong., 2d Sess., at 1804 (1980).

Requiring women to register to be drafted if the need arises to fill more positions for which women are eligible recognizes women's current military service. Excluding them is a grave insult to those who currently serve, as it is a not-so-veiled statement that women are unnecessary, or worse, to the military. Neither we, nor the Constitution, can countenance such a position.

Moreover, the dissent's reliance on the combat exclusion is an attempt to justify one policy's ostensible constitutionality by pointing to another policy that is likely unconstitutional. The combat exclusion is not before us today, so we cannot make a final determination about its constitutionality. Nonetheless, we stress here that the combat exclusion suffers from many of the same infirmities as the registration exclusion. There is no question that there are some women who are stronger, quicker, fiercer, and would make better combat soldiers than some men. Nonetheless, those men are eligible to serve in combat roles; those more qualified women are not. The reason for this difference is nothing other than overbroad sex-based stereotypes with the same constitutional problems we have already described.

Perhaps even more fundamentally, we cannot allow one sex-based policy before the Court to be justified by another sex-based policy not before the Court. The absurdity of this proposition is apparent if we once again think about *Brown v. Board of Education.* Before the Court in that case was the issue of segregation based on race in elementary and secondary schools. We would never have allowed the states to justify segregation's constitutionality by pointing to separate universities that were segregated by law, under a theory that many elementary and secondary school students go on to attend college.

We decline to commit that same error here today. The likely unconstitutional combat exclusion is no defense to the unconstitutionality of the registration exclusion.

C

Administrative convenience

Finally, the dissent reveals its true concern at the end of its opinion when it writes that "assuming that a small number of women could be drafted for non-combat roles, Congress simply did not consider it worth the added burdens of including women in draft and registration plans." *Rostker*, 453 U.S. at 81 (Rehnquist, J.). In other words, the dissent is basing the registration exclusion's constitutionality on the administrative convenience of not including women in registration.

If there is one thing that has been unquestioned for the past decade of our developing jurisprudence about sex classifications, it is that administrative convenience cannot serve as the basis for a sex classification's constitutionality. We stated as much in our first case in this area of constitutional law, *Reed v. Reed.* "To give a mandatory preference to members of either sex over members of the other, merely to accomplish the elimination of hearings on the merits, is to make the very kind of arbitrary legislative choice forbidden by the Equal Protection Clause of the Fourteenth Amendment." 404 U.S. at 76. Our anti-stereotyping jurisprudence that has developed since *Reed* teaches the same lesson. Legislatures cannot generalize men and women merely to eliminate the administrative burden involved with investigating individual characteristics. *See also Wengler*, 446 U.S. at 152.

That principle applies with equal strength today. Sex equality can never take a back seat to administrative convenience.

V

We note in conclusion that although the short-term remedy for the registration requirement being found unconstitutional is obvious, the long-term remedy is not. In the short term, the current registration scheme is struck down as unconstitutional. Accordingly, because we have no authority to create a system other than that Congress has created, there is no registration requirement. Our only authority is to pass judgment on the system before us, a system that we have determined violates the Constitution.

However, Congress is free to respond to this decision with a new system that it thinks is best for this country *and* passes constitutional muster. Thus, for those who challenged the registration requirement because they were pacifists, like the plaintiffs in this case, or who are opposed to registration and the draft because of feminist concerns about the militarization of society, no matter how valid those concerns, today's decision might be a short-lived victory. Congress may very well react to today's decision by instituting the system the President recommended – a system that requires both men and women to register for the draft. This is the nature of an equal protection challenge. As Justice Jackson wrote decades ago:

> Invalidation of a statute or an ordinance on due process grounds leaves ungoverned and ungovernable conduct which many people find objectionable. Invocation of the equal protection clause, on the other hand, does not disable any governmental body from dealing with the subject at hand. It merely means that the prohibition or regulation must have a broader impact.
> *Railway Express Agency, Inc. v. New York*, 335 U.S. 106, 112 (1949) (Jackson, J., concurring).

Because we find the registration requirement a violation of equal protection principles, Congress is not, by virtue of this opinion, disabled from requiring registration. Rather, if Congress continues to want a registration requirement, it must do so with "a broader impact."

The decision of the District Court is accordingly *affirmed*.

16

Commentary on *Meritor Savings Bank v. Vinson*

Kristen Konrad Tiscione

INTRODUCTION

Meritor v. Vinson[1] marks the first time the U.S. Supreme Court recognized hostile work environment sexual harassment as a violation of Title VII. It held that sexual harassment is not limited to *quid pro quo* harassment, where a woman is fired or financially punished for refusing a supervisor's sexual demands.[2] Sexual harassment that is severe or pervasive enough to alter the conditions of employment and create an abusive working environment also violates Title VII. Although feminists welcomed *Meritor's* recognition of *quid pro quo* and hostile environment sexual harassment, the decision written by Justice Rehnquist has proved problematic for plaintiffs. Professor Angela Onwuachi-Willig, writing as Justice Onwuachi-Willig, rectifies many of these problems in her feminist judgment.

First, she brings race and its historical intersection with gender and rape to the fore. Rehnquist does not acknowledge that the complainant and her alleged harasser were African-American nor how that might have shaped Mechelle Vinson's working environment or the responses of the various courts that addressed her case. Second, Onwuachi-Willig holds that sexual harassment is actionable if it unreasonably interferes with the work environment, creates a hostile or intimidating environment, or preserves sex segregation in the workplace. This is a significant departure from the majority rule,

---

[1] *Meritor Sav. Bank v. Vinson*, 477 U.S. 57 (1986). Title VII of the 1964 Civil Rights Act prohibits employers from discriminating against any individual "with respect to his compensation, terms, conditions, or privileges of employment, because of such individual's race, color, religion, sex, or national origin." 42 U.S.C. 2000e-2(a) (1) (2012).

[2] When Vinson filed suit, only two courts had held that sexual harassment violates Title VII, and they were in *quid pro quo* cases. *See Barnes v. Costle*, 561 F.2d 983 (D.D.C. 1977) and *Williams v. Saxbe*, 413 F. Supp. 654 (D.D.C. 1976), *rev'd sub nom.*, *Williams v. Bell*, 587 F.2d 1240 (D.C. Cir. 1978).

which required the harassment to be "severe or pervasive" and "unwelcome," thus creating an "abusive working environment." Although some lower courts later adopted a reasonable person standard for evaluating harassment claims, Onwuachi-Willig holds they are to be evaluated from the perspective of a reasonable victim in the complainant's shoes (here, an African-American woman) because the traditional standard can perpetuate dominant or white male norms about appropriate behavior in the workplace. Third, Justice Onwuachi-Willig holds that a complainant's manner of dress is not relevant, shifting the focus from the complainant's "voluntary" participation in the alleged harassment to the defendant's conduct and the impact of that conduct on the working environment. Finally, in a bold move, Onwuachi-Willig holds employers strictly liable for hostile environment harassment of subordinate employees even without any form of notice.

THE U.S. SUPREME COURT DECISION

In the original majority decision, the Court addressed three main issues.[3] First, it held that *quid pro quo* and hostile environment sexual harassment violate Title VII.[4] To be actionable, the sexual advances must be "unwelcome" and "sufficiently severe or pervasive 'to alter the conditions of [the victim's] employment and create an abusive working environment.'"[5]

Second, it summarily concluded that Vinson's clothing and speech were "obviously relevant" to the merits of her claim. Since EEOC guidelines instruct triers of fact to look at "the totality of the circumstances, such as the nature of the sexual advances and the context in which the alleged incidents occurred," Rehnquist reasoned that Vinson's dress and sexually explicit speech were part of the totality.[6] Although a trial court could presumably exclude this kind of evidence as unduly prejudicial, he stated there was no *per se* rule excluding it.[7]

Third, the majority concluded that while Vinson's failure to report the harassment and the lack of notice to the Bank did not insulate it from liability, employers are not automatically liable for hostile environment sexual

---

3 The majority consisted of Rehnquist, Burger, White, Powell, Stevens, and O'Connor. Marshall filed an opinion concurring in the judgment, which Brennan, Blackmun, and Stevens joined. Stevens also filed a concurring opinion, stating his belief that the majority and concurring opinions were consistent.

4 477 U.S. at 64–65.

5 *Id.* at 67–68 (quoting *Henson v. Dundee,* 682 F.2d 897, 902 (11th Cir. 1982) and *Rogers v. EEOC,* 454 F.2d 234 (5th Cir. 1971)).

6 *Id.* at 69 (quoting 29 C.F.R. § 1604.11(b) (1985)).

7 The majority was silent on the admissibility of evidence that Taylor had harassed Vinson's co-workers, some of which the trial court excluded.

harassment by supervisors.[8] Somewhat inexplicably, Rehnquist reasoned that Congress's decision to define "employer" to include "any agent" indicated its intent to restrict, as opposed to expand, employer liability. Declining to articulate a definitive employer rule, he referred lower courts to agency principles, specifically those in the Restatement (Second) of Agency §§ 219–237 (1958).

THE AFTERMATH

In the wake of *Meritor*, lower courts had to construe the meaning of "severe or pervasive" conduct and "unwelcome" advances, decide whether "severe or pervasive" should be judged by a "reasonable person" or "reasonable woman" standard, and determine the scope of employer liability in hostile environment cases.[9] The Eleventh Circuit's pre-*Meritor* definition of unwelcome is still used,[10] but federal circuits are split on the appropriate standard for determining whether conduct is "severe or pervasive."[11] Courts struggled for years with agency principles to determine the proper scope of employer liability;[12] then in 1998, the Supreme Court decided that if no tangible employment action was taken against the employee, as is the case with most hostile environment cases, employers are not liable if they can show that they took reasonable steps to prevent and correct the behavior, and the complainant unreasonably failed to take advantage of available opportunities to avoid the harm.[13] These defenses are not available to the employer in cases where a tangible employment action was taken against the employee, such as with most *quid pro quo* cases.[14] Moreover, the Court has also recently adopted a narrow definition of "supervisor" to mean only those empowered to take tangible employment action against the complainant.[15]

---

[8] *Id.* at 72. In his concurring opinion, Marshall stated that sexual harassment by a supervisor should be imputed to the employer regardless of notice. *Id.* at 78.

[9] In 1993, the Court held in *Harris v. Forklift Systems, Inc.* that "severe or pervasive conduct" has a subjective and objective element: both the victim and a reasonable person must find the work environment abusive. 510 U.S. 17, 21–22 (1993).

[10] "Unwelcome" conduct is that which an employee did not solicit or incite and which is regarded as undesirable or offensive. *Henson v. Dundee*, 682 F.2d 897, 903 (11th Cir. 1982).

[11] *See, e.g.*, V. Blair Druhan, *Severe or Pervasive: An Analysis of Who, What, and Where Matters When Determining Sexual Harassment*, 66 *Vand. L. Rev.* 355, 361–65 (2013).

[12] *See, e.g.*, Michael J. Phillips, *Employer Sexual Harassment Liability Under Agency Principles: A Second Look* at Meritor Savings Bank v. Vinson, 44 *Vand. L. Rev.* 1229, 1237–238 (1991).

[13] *Burlington Indus., Inc. v. Ellerth*, 524 U.S. 742 (1998) and *Faragher v. Boca Raton*, 524 U.S. 775, 807–808 (1998).

[14] *Faragher*, 524 U.S. at 807–808.

[15] *Vance v. Ball State Univ.*, 133 S. Ct. 2434, 2439 (2013). Tangible employment actions include "hiring, firing, failing to promote, reassignment with significantly different responsibilities, or a decision causing a significant change in benefits." *Ellerth*, 524 U.S. at 761.

THE FEMINIST JUDGMENT

Onwuachi-Willig reaches the same result as the Court but departs from the majority in significant ways. First, she instructs courts to consider the social and historical context in which sexual harassment occurs, including the race, class, age, and status of the parties, and its influence on the parties' behavior and the work environment. Because Vinson and Taylor were African-American, the pervasive stereotype of "the African-American male rapist" must be considered. As a result, "challenged behaviors, which may be viewed as benign when performed by white men, may be read as overly sexual or aggressive when performed by African-American men."

Similarly, the stereotype of black women as "so loose, sexually promiscuous, and lacking in sexual morality that they were deemed legally unrapable" has been used for centuries to justify or deny their claims of sexual assault and rape. As Onwuachi-Willig explains, acknowledging these racial stereotypes may help explain why no one stopped Taylor despite witness testimony that he openly harassed Vinson or why others might have assumed Vinson was "a strong African American woman who needed no help," "immoral and loose," or even "incapable of being sexually harassed and harmed." Additionally, Onwuachi-Willig hypothesizes Vinson might have been hesitant to report Taylor, a successful African-American man in a largely white business, for fear of contributing to this stereotype.

Second, Onwuachi-Willig criticizes the trial court for failing to develop an adequate and clear record, including its failure to find whether the parties even had sexual relations and the nature of Taylor's conduct in the workplace. In her judgment, finding these facts was crucial in ruling on the merits of Vinson's potential *quid pro quo* and hostile environment claims. Despite these insufficiencies, Onwuachi-Willig proceeds to address several of the legal issues to guide the lower court.

She turns first to the elements of a hostile environment sexual harassment claim. Rejecting the majority's rule that advances be "unwelcome" and sufficiently "severe or pervasive"[16] to "create an abusive working environment," she holds the question is whether they "unreasonably interfere with the victim's work environment and performance, create a hostile or intimidating environment, or preserve patterns of sex segregation in employment." Onwuachi-Willig greatly expands the basis for liability, providing three

---

[16] The majority's "severe or pervasive" requirement has been criticized for implying that significant yet sporadic harassment does not cause actionable harm. *See* Susan Estrich, *Sex at Work*, 43 *Stan. L. Rev.* 813, 843 (1991).

alternative bases for recovery. Since defendants in existing cases often use a complainant's acquiescence to alleged advances to justify their behavior, Onwuachi-Willig focuses on the defendant's behavior and its effect both on the complainant and the work environment. Where the harassment tends to reinforce "the notion of the dominant and powerful man over the subordinate woman," she would find a hostile environment.

The next major change is Onwuachi-Willig's requirement that the nature of the work environment be evaluated from the perspective of a "reasonable victim in the complainant's shoes."[17] On remand, the court must examine Taylor's conduct from the perspective of an African-American woman in Vinson's circumstances – a single woman with limited education who is dependent on her job to support her family. While the more generic "reasonable person" standard may look objective, it can conceal a masculine, white perspective. Onwuachi-Willig's particularized standard thus avoids perpetuating racial, cultural, and gender bias.[18] Moreover, it acknowledges that women are more likely than men to view certain behavior as harassment[19] and some women are less likely to resist or complain given their economic circumstances and the racial and gender hierarchy in their work environments.[20]

Onwuachi-Willig also rejects the controversial "welcomeness" requirement of the majority. Whether or not the harassment was "welcome" distracts the decision maker from what should be the central inquiry: the behavior of the harasser and the effect of that behavior on both the workplace and the victim.[21] Moreover, it is difficult for a court to gauge either "voluntariness" or "welcomeness" because of the significant power differentials between supervisor and subordinate, especially a subordinate as vulnerable as Vinson. In these situations, it is common for a subordinate woman to say (or otherwise appear to say) "yes" to a supervisor's advances in order to be accepted, get promoted, or save her job.

One of the most controversial aspects of the original *Meritor* opinion was Rehnquist's assumption that a complainant's manner of dress is "obviously

---

[17] Since *Meritor*, the circuit courts have been split on whether to evaluate claims of harassment on a reasonable person or a reasonable woman standard. *Compare Hirschfeld v. New Mexico Corrections Dep't*, 916 F.2d 572 (10th Cir. 1990), *with Ellison v. Brady*, 924 F.2d 872 (9th Cir. 1991).

[18] *See, e.g.,* Leslie M. Kerns, *A Feminist Perspective: Why Feminists Should Give the Reasonable Woman Standard Another Chance*, 10 Colum. J. Gender & L. 195, 211–15 (2001).

[19] *See, e.g.,* Kathryn Abrams, *Gender Discrimination and the Transformation of Workplace Norms*, 42 Vand. L. Rev. 1183, 1202–203 (1989); Druhan, *supra* note 11, at 365–66.

[20] *See, e.g.,* Kerns, *supra* note 18, at 217–21.

[21] *See, e.g.,* Estrich, *supra* note 16, at 826–834; Margaret Moore Jackson, *A Different Voicing of Unwelcomeness: Relational Reasoning and Sexual Harassment*, 81 N.D. L. Rev. 739 (2005).

relevant" in determining the welcomeness of an alleged harasser's conduct.[22] Not surprisingly, since she dispenses with the welcomeness requirement, Onwuachi-Willig holds that "dress is never relevant to a determination of hostile environment sexual harassment." Evidence of a complainant's manner of dress not only improperly focuses attention on the complainant but also reinforces gender and racial stereotypes. For example, men may find a particular kind of outfit on a white woman professional or fashionable but inappropriate or sexually provocative on an African-American woman. Onwuachi-Willig thus rejects the notion that clothing choices reflect how a complainant wishes to or should be treated by work colleagues. She also challenges the notion that women invite sexual attack by causing men to lose control.[23]

As to the admissibility of a complainant's sexually provocative speech, Onwuachi-Willig finds it may sometimes be relevant but only if it tends to show the alleged harasser's actions did not create a hostile environment or unreasonably interfere with the complainant's work. If the complainant used explicit sexual speech in the workplace, the court must then "engage in a complex analysis" to determine whether the complainant's speech indicated she did not find the work environment hostile or the complainant used it as "a means of surviving in a workplace culture permeated by masculine norms or gender inequality."[24]

Finally, Onwuachi-Willig tackles the employer liability standard that has arguably caused the most problems for sexual harassment plaintiffs. Rejecting a distinction between *quid pro quo* and hostile environment cases, she holds employers strictly liable for their supervisors' harassment in both kinds of cases. Acknowledging the centrality of work in people's lives and their need to earn a living, Onwuachi-Willig finds that employers are in the best position to control how their employees treat each other in the workplace. In her view, the alleged harasser's actual authority is irrelevant; what matters is whether complainants perceive their supervisor to have "the right and power to supervise and evaluate their work." In that situation, even the perception of power can be used "to abuse or otherwise terrorize employees" and create an environment "so hostile or polluted with discrimination as to affect the

---

[22] *See, e.g.,* Christina A. Bull, Comment, *The Implications of Admitting Evidence of a Sexual Harassment Plaintiff's Speech and Dress in the Aftermath of* Meritor Savings Bank v. Vinson, 41 *UCLA L. Rev.* 117 (1993).

[23] *See, e.g.,* Lynne Henderson, *Rape and Responsibility,* 11 *Law & Phil.* 127 (1992).

[24] On the related evidentiary issues, Onwuachi-Willig holds the trial court erred in excluding witness testimony on Taylor's harassment of Vinson because it was directly relevant to Vinson's harassment claims. She also holds the evidence of Taylor's harassing other bank employees relevant for establishing a pattern of harassment or to show the reason why Vinson did not report the alleged harassment to superiors.

terms and conditions of [their] employment, including [their] emotional and psychological state and performance in the workplace." In turn, a hostile and polluted atmosphere can work to "preserve[] patterns of sex segregation in the workplace." Because an employer grants this power to its supervisors by virtue of their title and position, employer and supervisor are one and the same.

Onwuachi-Willig's strict liability approach is of great importance. After *Meritor*, courts and scholars struggled with common law agency principles to articulate clear and predictable rules, often confusing actual, implied, apparent, and imputed authority concepts.[25] Strict liability for employers in both kinds of supervisor harassment cases would have prevented this confusion. And it would have sent a strong message to employers that sexual harassment is unacceptable; in the workplace, it is the employers' job to prevent it. As the law stands today, a complainant's perception of her supervisor's power is not enough to hold an employer strictly liable in a hostile environment case. The supervisor must have had the ability to take tangible employment action against her.[26] Strict liability in all harassment cases would also have encouraged businesses to take reasonable steps to create and ensure workplaces that are fair, equal, and welcoming to employees of all genders, races, and ethnicities.

Meritor Savings Bank v. Vinson, 477 U.S. 57 (1986)

Justice Angela Onwuachi-Willig delivered the opinion of the court.

This case presents important questions concerning claims of workplace "sexual harassment" brought under Title VII of the Civil Rights Act of 1964, 78 Stat. 253, as amended, 42 U.S.C. § 2000e *et seq.* These questions include (1) whether the factual record was sufficiently developed to render decisions on either a *quid pro quo* claim or a hostile environment claim, (2) whether sexual harassment leading only to psychological harm violates Title VII, (3) whether the "voluntariness" of the complainant's participation in sexual activity is pertinent in a hostile environment case, (4) whether the complainant's manner of dress or sexually provocative speech is relevant to determining whether sexual harassment occurred, (5) whether the trial court erred in excluding testimonial evidence from other women who claimed to have been harassed by the alleged wrongdoer and to have seen him harass the complainant, and (6) whether employers are automatically liable for sexual harassment by their supervisory personnel regardless of notice to the employer.

---

[25] *See, e.g.*, Phillips, *supra* note 12, at 1239–252.
[26] *See, e.g.*, Vance, 133 S. Ct. at 2439.

I

Facts

In September 1974, a nineteen-year-old African-American woman named Mechelle Vinson met Sidney Taylor, an African-American man who served as Assistant Vice President and Branch Manager for what is now Petitioner Meritor Savings Bank. Taylor ran into Vinson on the street and struck up a conversation with her. To Vinson, an impressionable teenager who had grown up in an impoverished environment, Taylor led an impressive life. For Vinson (and for many others), Taylor represented the American dream. Taylor had worked his way up from janitor to Assistant Vice President. He also possessed high status within his social community, serving as a church deacon. At trial, Taylor's lawyer described him as "something of an Eagle Scout."

During their initial meeting, Vinson asked Taylor about the possibility of employment at the Bank. Taylor responded by encouraging Vinson to apply for a job at his branch of the Bank. Vinson immediately followed Taylor's advice, completing and turning in her application the very next day. That same afternoon, Taylor offered Vinson a position as a teller-trainee, from which she could be promoted to teller if she performed satisfactorily. Vinson accepted the offer, becoming one of the more than 80 percent of women who worked as bank tellers nationwide. Prior to that, Vinson, a high school drop-out with a GED, had worked in lower-level, female-dominated jobs in the service industry, having performed the duties of a temporary employee in an exercise club, a food store, and a shoe store.

On September 9, 1974, Vinson began working at the Bank. She quickly proved to be a highly competent employee, earning promotions from teller to head teller and then to assistant branch manager. The District Court indicated that "[Vinson's] promotions were based on merit alone." *Vinson v. Taylor*, No. 78–1793, 1980 WL 100, at *1, 7 (D.D.C. Feb. 26, 1980).

During the first few months of her employment, Vinson enjoyed a pleasant, father-daughter-like relationship with Taylor, a man who was old enough to be her father. Taylor even once helped Vinson by giving her money to assist her in obtaining an apartment. Furthermore, Vinson confided in Taylor about a number of personal matters, including that she was raised in violence; had a troubled relationship with her own father; and was going through the process of separation from her then-husband, an older man who impregnated her when she was just fourteen.[27]

---

[27] She later miscarried.

Ultimately, the relationship between Vinson and Taylor proved to be problematic. According to Vinson's trial testimony, by May of 1975, Taylor began to make unwelcome sexual advances towards her. Speaking about the first advance, Vinson testified that Taylor took her to dinner at a local Chinese restaurant and then suggested during dinner that they go to a motel to engage in sexual relations. Vinson contended that she initially declined Taylor's invitation, but that Taylor refused to take "no" for an answer, insisting that she owed him because he had given her a job. Vinson explained at trial, "He said just like he could hire me, he could fire me … He told me that he was my supervisor. He gave me my pay check, and I had to do what he wanted me to do." Trial Tr. vol. II, 51, 59. Vinson further declared that, despite her resistance, Taylor drove her to a motel and left her waiting in the car while he registered for a room. According to Vinson, Taylor then took her to the motel room and asked her to wait while he showered. Thereafter, Vinson indicated, she engaged in sexual relations with Taylor because she was afraid that she would lose her job if she did not perform sexual favors for him.

Vinson further testified that, after this incident, Taylor continued to demand sexual favors from her, usually at the Bank itself. According to Vinson, Taylor frequently forced her to engage in sexual intercourse with him inside the bank vault as well as in other rooms such as the storage area in the bank basement, both during and after work hours. Vinson estimated that, between May 1975 and 1977, she and Taylor had sexual contact somewhere between 40 to 50 times. Vinson also asserted that Taylor sexually harassed her in other ways. For example, she testified that Taylor exposed himself to her many times and groped her breasts and buttocks on the job, both in the presence of co-workers and in the women's restroom when she was there alone. Vinson also claimed that Taylor fondled other female workers and made suggestive remarks in their presence. At trial, Vinson attempted to call upon witnesses, such as Christine Malone and Mary Levarity, who could support her claims about Taylor's harassment of her and other women at the Bank. The District Court, however, excluded much of this evidence, proclaiming that Vinson could not present "wholesale evidence of a pattern and practice relating to sexual advances to other female employees in her case in chief." *Vinson*, 1980 WL 100, at *1, n. 1. Instead, the District Court advised that "she might well be able to present such evidence in rebuttal to the defendants' cases." *Vinson*, 753 F.2d at 144.

Most important, Vinson indicated that all of these actions by Taylor were against her will. She proclaims that Taylor often assaulted or raped her, once so brutally that she suffered serious vaginal bleeding for weeks and had to seek a doctor's care.

In 1977, Vinson began to have a steady boyfriend. At this point, she contends, Taylor stopped making sexual demands upon her, but continued to fondle, grope, and otherwise harass her at work. Vinson also testified that Taylor advised her in 1977 that she would be given her own branch managership and advised her in June 1978 that she would be promoted to a branch manager position at the company's Tacoma Park branch in December 1978. Vinson ultimately turned down this opportunity.

Taylor denies ever engaging in sexual relations with Vinson. He asserts that he never fondled Vinson, never made suggestive remarks to her, and never even asked her to have sex with him. He admits to taking Vinson to lunch, but he claims that he took her to lunch only when Christine Malone was also present and that he never took Vinson to lunch or dinner alone. He also testified that Vinson was a scorned woman who had made advances towards him, which he declined.

According to Taylor, in late summer or early September 1978, he and Vinson had a disagreement over which employee Vinson should train to become the next head teller. Taylor indicates that he instructed Vinson to begin to train Dorethea McCallum as head teller, but Vinson instead began to train Karen Kirkland. Taylor argues that Vinson has brought these charges against him because of this disagreement and his rejection of her advances towards him.

At trial, McCallum, whom Vinson refused to train, asserted that Vinson wore revealing clothing and spoke frequently about sexual fantasies in the workplace. McCallum proclaimed that Vinson "had a lot of sexual fantasies." McCallum testified, "[Vinson] talked quite a bit about sex. I guess more than half of her conversation was related to sex." She further alleged that Vinson's "dress wear was very explosive." McCallum explained that "most of the days [Vinson] would come in with, if not a third of her breasts showing, about half of her breasts showing; and some days, short dresses; or if she did wear a skirt, something that had a slit in it." Ironically, Taylor asserted during his deposition that, as a general matter, Vinson wore appropriate clothing to work and that she never did anything to suggest that she wanted to have sex with him.

Beginning on September 21, 1978, Vinson stopped reporting to work. She contends that she was forced to stop coming to work because Taylor began to tamper with her personnel records, made false complaints against her with management, denigrated her in front of other employees, entrapped her into work errors, threatened her life when she asserted she would report him, and engaged in a campaign of fault-finding against her. When Taylor contacted Vinson about her absence from the workplace, she told him that she was ill and that her absence from work would be indefinite. On November 1, 1978, the Bank informed Vinson that she was terminated due to excessive use of sick leave. On the exact same date, Vinson sent the Bank a letter indicating that she was forced to offer her "constructive resignation." J.A. 17.

Despite the fact that the Bank had a blanket policy against discrimination and a complaint procedure for reporting discrimination (though the Bank did not have any policies relating specifically to sexual harassment), Vinson never reported Taylor's actions to any of his supervisors. She never otherwise followed the Bank's complaint procedure, which mandated that an employee had to "state his grievance in writing and present it to his supervisor ... only after oral representation has been made and it is felt that the grievance has not been fully resolved." Pl.'s Ex. 13 at 11.

Following her termination, Vinson brought this lawsuit against Taylor and the Bank, alleging that she was constantly subjected to sexual harassment by Taylor in violation of Title VII. Vinson asserts that she never reported this harassment during her employment because she was afraid of Taylor. She asserts that he had threatened to kill her and have her raped like Christine Malone, another employee of the Bank. While there is no evidence that connects Taylor to Malone's rape by an unknown assailant in 1974, Malone confided in Vinson after the rape, and Vinson recalls that a disturbed Malone was never the same after the crime. Explaining the effect of Taylor's alleged threats on her, Vinson testified, "My life was put on the line. I didn't know what might happen to me. Christine was raped. She almost lost her mind. I saw things that went on in the bank and I didn't want anything to happen to me. My life was very valuable to me." Trial Tr. vol. IV, 28. Vinson further claims that Malone and another woman, Mary Levarity, previously complained to Vice President David G. Burton about Taylor's sexually harassing behavior toward them, but that Burton took no action. Vinson further claims that, when she raised Taylor's mistreatment of women in the office to him, he said "that's my way of relaxing them, and if they didn't like it, they can get the hell out and I can get the hell out." Trial Tr. vol. III, 48.

The Bank argues that, even if the alleged sexual advances were made by Taylor, it should not be held liable because it did not know about such behavior and, as a result, could not have consented to and/or approved such activities.

II

After a bench trial, the District Court decided the question regarding whether the Bank "received notice of the alleged sexual harassment directed against [Vinson] and allegedly other female employees" and whether the Bank should be liable for Vinson's acts. *Vinson*, 1980 WL 100, at *4–6. The court held that the Bank could not be held liable for the actions of Taylor, even assuming they were true, because neither Vinson nor any other employee had notified the Bank of the alleged actions by Taylor, "the bank had a policy asserting its dedication to equal treatment and employee rights," and there was no evidence to suggest that Taylor's status as an officer in the Bank was anything more than "honorary." *Id.* at *6. The District Court noted that Taylor had no authority to hire, fire, or promote employees. Finally, after acknowledging "that sexual harassment of female employees in which they are asked or required to submit to sexual demands as a condition to obtain employment or to maintain employment or to obtain promotions falls within protection of Title VII," the District Court determined that Vinson was not a victim of sexual harassment or sexual discrimination. *Id.* at *8. Although the District Court issued twenty-one factual findings, it never offered a finding as to whether sexual activity occurred between Taylor and Vinson. Instead, it indicated the following: "If [Vinson] and Taylor engaged in an intimate or sexual relationship during the time of Vinson's employment ... that relationship was a voluntary one by [Vinson] having nothing to do with her continued employment at [the bank] or her advancement or promotions at that institution." *Vinson v. Taylor*, 753 F.2d 141, 145 (D.C. Cir. 1985).

On appeal, the D.C. Circuit began its review of the case by identifying two different forms of sexual harassment that reflected the definitions originated by Professor Catharine MacKinnon: (1) *quid pro quo* sexual harassment, which occurs when a complainant is asked to perform sexual favors in order to maintain her job or receive a promotion, and (2) hostile environment sexual harassment, defined as "[u]nwelcome sexual advances, requests for sexual favors, or other verbal or physical conduct of a sexual nature ... hav[ing] the purpose or effect of unreasonably interfering with an individual's work performance or creating an intimidating, hostile, or offensive work environment." *Id.* at 145. *See also* Catharine A. MacKinnon, *Sexual Harassment of Working Women* 32–47 (Yale Univ. 1979). Ultimately, the D.C. Circuit reversed the District Court's decision, concluding that the trial court's holding was inconsistent with the intent of Title VII.

Deferring to the District Court's factual finding that Vinson "was not required to grant Taylor ... sexual favors as a condition of either her employment or in order to obtain promotion," the D.C. Circuit left standing the District Court's conclusion that Vinson was not a victim of *quid pro quo* harassment. *Vinson*, 753 F.2d at 145. The D.C. Circuit concluded, however, that the District Court failed to properly consider and evaluate whether Vinson had been the victim of hostile environment sexual harassment and noted the ambiguity of the District Court's finding about the existence and nature of the sexual relationship between Vinson and Taylor. The D.C. Circuit explained:

> This finding leaves us uncertain as to precisely what the court meant. It could reflect the view that there was no Title VII violation because Vinson's employment status was not affected, an error to which we already have spoken. Alternatively, the finding could indicate that because the relationship was voluntary there was no sexual harassment – no "[u]nwelcome sexual advances, requests for sexual favors, or other verbal or physical conduct of a sexual nature ... ha[ving] the purpose or effect of unreasonably interfering with an individual's work performance or creating an intimidating, hostile, or offensive working environment."
>
> *Id.* at 146.

Given this ambiguity and the District Court's failure to consider a possible hostile environment violation, the D.C. Circuit remanded the case for an examination of Vinson's hostile environment sexual harassment claim. Petitioner, Meritor Savings Bank, appeals this decision.

III

Before this Court begins its review of the legal questions in this case, it first acknowledges that evaluating any particular sexual harassment claim requires an understanding of the historical and social context in which the alleged harassment occurred. The presence and persistence of sexual harassment may be influenced not only by gender dynamics but also by racial, class, age, status hierarchy, and other relevant dynamics within the workplace. For example, this case involves an allegation of sexual harassment, including claims of rape, against an African-American man by an African-American woman. Although both parties in this case are African-American, awareness of race, and in particular, awareness of racial stereotypes and the history of racism against both African-American men and women in sexual misconduct cases are pertinent to our understanding of the claims in this lawsuit. Such stereotypes and history not only may have influenced how and why each party acted as he or she did during their workplace relationship; they also may have shaped the lens through which management and employees viewed the two parties' interactions with each other and through which the factfinder and the Court of Appeals evaluated the legal claims.

In examining the claims in this lawsuit, this Court must be cognizant of widespread and long-standing racialized tropes and stereotypes that have placed race at the center of common definitions and understandings about what rape or sexual misconduct is. Despite the fact that most sexual misconduct and rape occurs between individuals within the same racial group, the most dominant and pervasive trope regarding rape and other forms of sexual misconduct centers on an African-American male perpetrator and a white female victim. *See* Jennifer Wriggins, *Rape, Racism, and the Law*, 6 Harv. Women's L.J. 103, 105, 114 (1983); *see also* Angela Y. Davis, *Women, Race, & Class* 173–190 (1983). Since slavery, African-American men have been cast as sexually immoral, overly aggressive predators who lack self-control when it comes to sexual urges, particularly when it comes to white women. *See, e.g.,* Susan Brownmiller, *Against Our Will: Men, Women, and Rape* 194, 211–213 (1975). In part due to these racialized stereotypes and the lack of credibility that comes along with them, African-American men, even when the evidence against them is weak and, in fact, doubtful, have found themselves to be vulnerable and easy targets of wrongful convictions in sexual misconduct cases. One particularly disturbing example comes from the conviction of the nine young Scottsboro boys who spent many years in prison as a result of two white women who lied about being raped by them during the 1930s. *See* Davis, *supra,* at 198. Indeed, in some states, juries could consider race, or rather blackness itself, as evidence of a defendant's intent to engage in sexual crimes. *See* Wriggins, *supra,* at 111, 120. Due to the pervasiveness of the stereotype of the African-American male rapist, courts must be careful to examine sexual harassment claims with an understanding that challenged behaviors, which may be viewed as benign when performed by white men, may be read as overly sexual or aggressive when performed by African-American men. In sum, courts must evaluate claims of harassment against the backdrop of African-American men's historical and current vulnerability to false claims of rape and harassment.

Similarly, as this particular case involves an African-American female complainant, this Court must analyze this claim against the backdrop of a long history of sexual assault, rape, and harassment of African-American women as well as the history of African-American women's extreme vulnerability to sexual misconduct in the workplace and otherwise, both by white and non-white men. Historically, African-American women were viewed as so loose, sexually promiscuous, and lacking in sexual morality that they were deemed legally unrapable. In other words, for decades upon decades, the rape of African-American women was legal. *See* Davis, *supra,* at 6–12, 182–184; Beverly Smith, *Black Women's Health: Notes for a Course, in All the Women Are White, All the Blacks Are Me, But Some of Us Are Brave* 110–111 (Gloria T. Hull *et al.* eds., 1982). *See, e.g.,* Harriet Jacobs, *Incidents in the Life of a Slave Girl* (1861). In a vicious cycle of racist sexual violence, the pervasive raping of African-American women was used as evidence of their purported sexual immorality, which in turn was used to legally justify the rape and sexual assault against them. Indeed, indictments against alleged rapists were frequently dismissed for failure to allege that the victim was white. *See* Wriggins, *supra*, at 106–107. Here, Taylor's claim that Vinson is a sexually aggressive scorned woman seeking revenge for his rebuffing her invokes race and gender stereotypes that have pervaded much of rape history. In fact, such stereotypes may help to explain why no one stopped Taylor's alleged harassment of Vinson, which Vinson and others testified was open and obvious. For example, other supervisors in the workplace may have felt no need to interfere on Vinson's behalf if they had internalized stereotypes of Vinson as either a strong African-American woman who needed no help or an immoral and loose African-American woman who invited Taylor's attention or was simply incapable of being sexually harassed and harmed.

In places where African-American women have toiled, they have been particularly vulnerable to rape. In addition to being frequent victims of sexual assault and rape by their white masters during slavery, African-American women often worked in domestic spaces where they were continually exposed to their employers' sexual aggression. *See id.* at 118–119. Furthermore, perpetrators of crimes against African-American women have received and continue to receive less harsh punishment than perpetrators of crimes against white women. *See generally* Howard Myers, *The Effect of Sexual Stratification by Race on Arrest in Sexual Battery Cases,* 9 Amer. J. Crim. Just. 172 (1985). When African-American women report sexual misconduct, they are also less likely to be believed than white women. *See* Wriggins, *supra*, at 122. Not surprisingly, the result of this long history has been that African-American women are less likely to report sexual misconduct than white women are, even though they are more likely to be victims of sexual harassment and misconduct. *See id.* at 122–23, n.122 (citing a 1976 study that found that "[w]hite rape victims were much more likely to report the crime to the police (59%) than were Black rape victims (26%)").

The history of African-American women and rape may shed light on why Vinson did not report Taylor's alleged raping and harassment of her to anyone in the workplace. This history of racism and sexism is further complicated by the difference in status between Taylor and Vinson. Vinson knew that Taylor was a bank vice president, a church deacon, and the father of seven, while she was a high-school dropout and divorcée. Moreover, bank policy required Vinson to report the harassment to her supervisor, who, in this case, was the man who was harassing her. When the context of this case is closely examined through a historical lens, it is not hard to see why Vinson failed to report Taylor's alleged assaults.

Questions about racial and gender dynamics, including that the parties were working in a predominantly white work environment, may have also shaped how they behaved. For example, African-American women can feel strong pressure not to reveal, particularly to the white community, so-called "dirty laundry" about African-American men given the subordinate status of African-American men in society. *See* bell hooks, *Feminist Theory: From Margin to Center* 18, 68–69, 73–75 (1984). Thus, Vinson may have feared reporting Taylor because she did not want to be viewed as a traitor to her race for turning in a successful African-American man, especially given his success in a white-dominated work environment. That fear may have been further intensified by her knowledge of the historical and current injustices in the legal system against African-Americans.

Age, class, and status differences between Vinson and Taylor are also relevant to the analysis. In fact, the power dynamics connected to the status hierarchy at the Bank appear to be rooted in both gender and age differences, with young women overwhelmingly working in the subordinate and entry-level position of teller, while older men dictated and governed their work as management. For example, Vinson testified that one of the reasons why she did not complain to management about Taylor's harassment was because she, a woman of limited education, feared losing the job of her dreams and because she lacked similar economic alternatives. Indeed, Vinson took legal action in this case only when her lawyer, whom she went to see about her divorce, learned of the harassment and suggested she should sue.

The basic point is that, in considering the legal questions in this lawsuit, the Court must be careful to examine all claims against historical and societal circumstances and through the various lenses that may be consciously or unconsciously affecting the behavior of the key parties.

IV

In this case, not only did the fact finder – here, the District Court – fail to evaluate Vinson's claims within their historical and social context, it also failed to develop a sufficient factual record. Most important, the District Court failed to provide a finding of fact as to whether sexual relations occurred between Vinson and Taylor.

The first problem with this hypothetical "factual finding" by the District Court is that it is not a factual finding at all and fails to resolve one of the most critical questions in the case. As this Court has previously held, lack of clarity or unsoundness in a material fact "sufficiently clouds the record to render the case an inappropriate vehicle" for a final determination. *Jones v. State Bd. of Educ. of Tennessee*, 397 U.S. 31, 32 (1970) (per curiam). Here, a determination as to whether Vinson and Taylor had sexual intercourse and whether Vinson did so to maintain her employment must occur before any court can determine the merits of a potential *quid pro quo* claim.

Indeed, factual determinations as to whether Vinson and Taylor had sexual intercourse from May 1975 to 1977, whether Taylor accosted and fondled Vinson within the workplace, why Vinson engaged in intercourse with Taylor (if she did), and whether Taylor's actions are what pushed Vinson to take an indefinite leave from the workplace are also crucial determinations to Vinson's other potential *quid pro quo* claim based upon the link between the sexual favors and Vinson's claimed constructive discharge. Similarly, the District Court must make a factual determination regarding the existence of a sexual relationship before a decision can be made about whether the Bank violated reasonable expectations for establishing and maintaining a productive and welcoming work environment for Vinson and its other employees.

Additionally, a finding concerning sexual relations between Vinson and Taylor is an important step in determining whether Vinson was constructively discharged from the Bank. If Taylor's repeated requests for sexual favors and his retaliatory attacks on Vinson's work eventually caused Vinson's indefinite sick leave, which was the very basis for the Bank's decision to fire her, then Vinson's refusal to give in to Taylor's requests for sexual intercourse easily go to the heart of any *quid pro quo* claims. Indeed, the quintessential *quid pro quo* case involves the loss of a job because of a refusal to perform sexual acts with one's supervisor. At trial, Vinson addressed the toll that Taylor's alleged actions had on her decision to stop coming to work. She asserted, "[H]e would touch me practically every day … Whenever he felt like it … Each day was a touching day. Each day was a mental day … I felt humiliated. I felt powerless. I was afraid of him." Trial Tr. vol. II, 66, 71, 80. Her resignation letter specifically cited the harassment as the reason for her leaving. J.A 17.

The second problem with the District Court's hypothetical "factual finding" is that it is ambiguous. As the Court of Appeals explained, the finding could mean that there was no violation under Title VII because Vinson's job position, particularly her job status, in the workplace did not change in the negative. If the District Court intended this meaning, it is incorrect as a matter of law. One, it mistakenly presumes that a negative change in job status is required to assert a *quid pro quo* claim. Any demand that an employee engage in sexual relations to maintain her employment provides a sufficient basis for asserting a *quid pro quo* claim regardless of any change in status. Here, Vinson asserts that she engaged in sexual intercourse with

Taylor because she feared losing her job. She explained at trial that she felt that she "had no other choice" because of her lack of power and lack of viable economic alternatives. Trial Tr. vol. IV, 50. This is enough for a *quid pro quo* claim. That Vinson was a highly competent employee who earned her promotions due to her superior work performance should not defeat her claim. To hold otherwise would be to punish Vinson for being an excellent employee and reward Taylor for selecting a highly competent employee to be his victim. Taylor still may have been willing to punish Vinson, whether highly competent or not, by firing her if she refused his advances. The *quid pro quo* claim protects against the threat of retaliation and does not require that the retaliation actually occur. Here, of course, however, Vinson may have actually suffered a forced change in position as she asserts that she ultimately resigned due to Taylor's alleged harassment. Moreover, the District Court's "factual finding" about Vinson and Taylor's sexual relationship ignores Vinson's potential hostile environment claim, which this Court discusses in more detail below.

V

Next, we address several legal questions raised by this factual record to guide the District Court on remand.

A

The first question concerns whether a Title VII violation occurs only when sexual harassment victims suffer tangible or economic injury. The Bank argues that statutory language that prohibits discrimination with respect to "compensation, terms, conditions, or privileges" of employment indicates that Congress was concerned with injuries of an economic or tangible character only, not psychological or otherwise intangible injuries. We reject this argument.

As numerous courts have held, hostile environment sexual harassment, which tends to result in non-tangible or non-economic injury, "erects barriers to participation in the work force of the sort Congress intended to sweep away by the enactment of Title VII." *See, e.g., Katz v. Dole,* 709 F.2d 251, 254 (4th Cir. 1983). Indeed, a number of federal courts have recognized that "[s]exual harassment which creates a hostile or offensive environment for members of one sex is every bit the arbitrary barrier to sexual equality at the workplace that racial harassment is to racial equality." *Henson v. City of Dundee,* 682 F.2d 897 (11th Cir. 1982). *See also Bundy v. Jackson,* 641 F.2d 934, 934–944 (D.C. Cir. 1981).

In racial harassment cases, courts have recognized that some "working environments [may be] so heavily polluted with discrimination as to destroy completely the emotional and psychological stability of minority group workers." *Rogers v. EEOC*, 454 F.2d 234, 238 (5th Cir. 1971). Similarly, this Court recognizes that certain workplaces may be so hostile to men or women based on sex and gender that workers cannot remain emotionally and psychologically stable in their jobs. For this type of hostile environment sexual harassment to be actionable, however, the challenged conduct must unreasonably interfere with the complainant's work performance, create a hostile or intimidating environment, and/or help to preserve patterns of sex segregation in employment.

In determining whether hostile environment harassment has occurred, courts must examine the allegations of harassment from the standpoint of a reasonable victim in the complainant's shoes, here a reasonable African-American woman. Examining the allegations from the perspective of a reasonable person with the complainant's identity characteristics is key because courts must be careful not to reify existing inequalities by adopting a purportedly objective perspective that simply offers the outlook of a reasonable man or a reasonable white man. For example, a male bank vice president might believe it is acceptable to tell a female subordinate that "her dress fits her body well" while a female subordinate may find such comments discomforting or offensive because they focus on her looks as opposed to her work. In fact, because of differing experiences with and distinct vulnerabilities to sexual assault and rape, women frequently hold different viewpoints from men about the same factual circumstances. Furthermore, not examining the allegations from a reasonable complainant's perspective disregards how harassers frequently target victims they know are vulnerable. For example, a male harasser may target a female subordinate of limited education or a single mother dependent on her income precisely because he knows she has fewer viable economic alternatives than a woman with more education or a married woman with other resources. In this case, Taylor knew of Vinson's vulnerabilities as a result of her impoverished upbringing, limited education, crumbling marriage, past work history in low-level service jobs, and financial burdens.[28] Viewed from the perspective of a victim with Vinson's background and characteristics, the evidence offered supports Vinson's claim of a hostile and intimidating work environment.

Furthermore, Taylor's actions, if true, also may have unreasonably interfered with Vinson's work performance and helped to preserve patterns of sex

---

[28] Indeed, the record here intimates that Taylor may have harassed other women like Vinson – young, African-American, poor, and "hungry for work" – by hiring them or loaning them money and then asserting that they owed him.

segregation and inequality in the workplace. First, testimony from this case describes the most severe forms of sexual misconduct. Criminal conduct involving sexual assault and rape easily satisfies the standard for proving a hostile or intimidating environment. It is difficult to imagine any actions that could more readily create an intimidating and hostile environment than the rape and other physical intrusions of the body, such as the fondling of private parts, that Vinson testified that she suffered at the hands of Taylor.

Vinson has also presented evidence, which if believed, could support a finding that Taylor's alleged actions unreasonably interfered with her work performance. At trial, Vinson testified that she suffered serious psychological and physical consequences, such as extreme nervousness and stress, an inability to eat or sleep, and loss of hair due to Taylor's harassment. She further indicated that, despite years of excellent job performance, she ultimately was unable to come to work to perform her job. Trial Tr. vol. II, 71, 77–80; Trial Tr. vol. III, 51, 64; Trial Tr. vol. IV, 65.

Finally, Vinson's allegations, if believed, detail behavior that would work to preserve patterns of sex segregation and inequality in the workplace. Here, Taylor's harassment and the Bank's failure to respond to it likely made harassed female subordinates feel powerless and voiceless. This dynamic can help sustain sex segregation between female tellers and male management by reinforcing the notion of the dominant and powerful man over the subordinate woman.

Therefore, Vinson's allegations, if proven, would suffice to establish hostile environment sexual harassment.

B

The second remaining question concerns whether the complainant's "voluntary" participation in sexual episodes is pertinent in a hostile environment sexual harassment case. Related to that question are two more legal issues before this Court, which are (1) whether the District Court erred in excluding Vinson's evidence from alleged female victims of Taylor and witnesses of Taylor's harassment of Vinson, and (2) whether a complainant's dress or sexually provocative speech is relevant in evaluating hostile environment sexual harassment claims.

1

Regarding the relationship between "voluntariness" and sexual harassment, the Court concludes that voluntariness is not the central inquiry in a hostile environment sexual harassment claim. The gravamen of any such claim is whether the challenged conduct unreasonably interfered with the plaintiff's work environment or performance, created a hostile or intimidating environment, or worked to preserve patterns of sex segregation in employment. Even if one could call Vinson's capitulation to Taylor's alleged sexual demands voluntary, that determination would not resolve the question of whether Taylor's actions constituted hostile environment sexual harassment. While the welcomeness of the advances might shed light on whether the conduct helped to create a hostile or intimidating environment or affected the complainant's work performance, as suggested by the EEOC in 29 C.F.R. § 1604.11(a) (1985), welcomeness is a digression from the heart of Title VII's purpose in addressing sex discrimination: eradicating sex segregation in jobs and arbitrary barriers to employment and advancement for people of all sexes. More so, focusing on welcomeness inappropriately reinforces the notion that sexual harassment is all about sex or sexual attraction when it is truly about power and subordination. Indeed, Vinson's testimony that Taylor's advances stopped once she had a steady boyfriend reveals how masculine power and norms about "ownership" of women were at play in this situation. Finally, parsing "unwelcomeness" or "voluntariness" in interactions between a male manager and female subordinate is problematic. For instance, sexual activity by a subordinate is hardly voluntary if the subordinate acquiesced only because she feared losing her job; in far too many instances, a subordinate may want to say "no" to a supervisor but may instead reply "yes" as a means of pleasing him to maintain her job. In the end, what is most relevant to claims of hostile environment sexual harassment is the behavior of the alleged harasser and its effects on the complainant and her workplace environment.

2

Relatedly, this Court holds that the District Court erred in not allowing Vinson to present all of her evidence about other employees' accounts of Taylor's harassment of Vinson during her case in chief. Witnesses Christine Malone and Mary Levarity were prepared to testify in support of Vinson's claims about Taylor's harassment of Vinson. For example, both Malone and Levarity were ready to testify about seeing Taylor sexually accost and handle Vinson, and seeing Vinson visibly become upset and repeatedly ask him to stop harassing her. Trial Tr. vol. I, 34–38, 40 (Testimony of Malone); Trial Tr. vol. VI, 25 (Testimony of Levarity). This evidence is directly relevant to whether Vinson found the environment at the Bank hostile and intimidating and whether Taylor's actions affected her work performance, and/or promoted and maintained gender inequality and segregation in the workplace.

Additionally, this Court holds that the District Court erred in not allowing Vinson to present evidence about Taylor's alleged harassment of other female employees during her case-in-chief. Both Malone and Levarity claimed Taylor sexually accosted and harassed them, too. For example, Malone stated that Taylor "put his hands on [her] breasts and he would put his hands on [her] backside." Trial Tr. vol. I, 21. While such evidence is inadmissible to show Taylor's character or propensity for sexual harassment under Fed. R. Evid. 404, it could have been admitted as habit evidence or evidence of routine practice under Fed. R. Evid. 406. It may have been helpful in assessing Vinson's testimony about why she did not report Taylor's alleged harassment to any supervisors at the Bank, as seeing a supervisor harass other women with impunity could discourage a reasonable woman from thinking any action would be taken on her complaints.

In the end, the exclusion of Malone and Levarity's testimony about Taylor's behavior deprived Vinson of the opportunity to build a factual record in support of her case. For this reason, too, we remand this case to the District Court to correct its error.

3

On the remaining issue concerning the relevancy of dress and sexually provocative speech, this Court concludes that dress is never relevant to determinations on hostile environment sexual harassment claims. It further holds that sexually provocative speech is relevant only to the extent that it can be used to discredit claims that the alleged harasser's actions either unreasonably interfered with the complainant's work environment and performance, created a hostile or intimidating environment, or worked to preserve patterns of sex segregation in the workplace.

At the outset, this Court notes that the EEOC Guidelines stress that the factfinder must evaluate the question of workplace sexual harassment in light of "the record as a whole" and the "totality of the circumstances, such as the nature of the sexual advances and the context in which the alleged incidents occurred." 29 C.F.R. § 1604.11(b) (1985). The totality of circumstances, however, does not include everything within the context, only those factors that might shed light on the central issues.

Holding that a complainant's mode of dress is relevant to a sexual harassment determination improperly takes the focus away from the alleged harasser and places it on the complainant. It allows the assumptions and interpretations that others make about the meaning of an individual's choice of clothing, even when erroneous, to dictate how that individual can be treated. Employees should feel free to select the clothing they will wear to work each day (assuming it complies with the employer's dress code) without worrying about what others may presume from it. For this reason, a complainant's clothing or dress has no probative value in workplace sexual harassment cases. Moreover, allowing such evidence may work to reinforce racial and gender stereotypes if the same type of clothing is viewed as having a different, provocative meaning when worn by women of a particular race or ethnicity or women with particular body types.

Unlike with dress, however, sexually provocative speech may sometimes have limited relevance to a determination about sexual harassment. For example, if an alleged harasser's actions are in direct response to an explicit invitation by the complainant, it would be more difficult to show that the challenged conduct created a hostile environment or affected the complainant's work performance.

We emphasize, though, that the probative value of sexually provocative speech is limited and must be evaluated with care. An alleged harasser may even respond in offensive and intimidating ways to an explicit invitation by a complainant. Moreover, a complainant may engage in sexually explicit speech as a defensive mechanism or a means to minimize gender differences, especially in sex-segregated workplaces or workplaces where masculine norms and sexual banter are part of workplace culture. For example, if a complainant offered a sexually related retort in response to sexually crude language directed at her or other women in the workplace, courts would have to engage in a complex analysis evaluating whether the complainant's response revealed that she did not find the workplace hostile, or was merely a means of surviving in a workplace culture permeated by masculine norms or gender inequality.

C

Finally, this Court decides whether an employer is automatically liable for sexual harassment by its supervisory personnel, even if it was never notified of the complained-of conduct. The Court answers this question with an understanding of the central meaning that work holds in many individuals' lives and with an understanding of most individuals' need for paid work to survive and support themselves and their families. The Court also acknowledges that one party, the employer, best controls or directs the environment within any

particular workplace. Indeed, this Court finds the following rationale by the
Court of Appeals convincing:

> Instead of providing a reason for employers to remain oblivious to conditions
> in the workplace, we think the enlightened purpose of Title VII calls for an
> interpretation cultivating an incentive for employers to take a more active
> role in warranting to each employee that he or she will enjoy a working envir-
> onment free from illegal sex discrimination … Employer responsiveness to
> on-the-job discrimination at the supervisory level is an essential aspect of
> the remedial scheme embodied in Title VII. It is the employer alone who is
> able promptly and effectively to halt discriminatory practices by supervisory
> personnel … .
>
> Vinson, 753 F.2d at 151.

Given the primacy and urgency of work in many people's lives as well as
the reality that employers are the ones best positioned to communicate to all
employees how they must treat others in the workplace, this Court holds that
an employer is strictly liable for a hostile environment created by a supervisor's conduct. The employer need not have notice of the supervisor's actions
because the supervisor is an agent of the employer and, as such, his or her acts
are imputed to the employer.[29]

The supervisor's actual authority to hire, fire, or promote employees is
irrelevant. The ultimate question is whether the workplace environment
for an employee has become so hostile or polluted with discrimination as to
affect the terms and conditions of his or her employment, including his or her
emotional and psychological state and performance in the workplace, and
whether it preserves patterns of sex segregation in the workplace. A supervisor
who controls the day-to-day aspects of an employee's work, or has the ability to
evaluate or offer input about the employee's work, can alter the conditions of
employment regardless of the supervisor's actual ability to hire, fire or demote.

The key point is that supervisors, by virtue of the title and position conferred on them by the employer, exercise control and authority over employees. Whether they truly have the ability to hire and fire is less important than
whether their title creates the perception that they do. As long as employees
believe that a supervisor has the right and power to supervise and evaluate
their work, that power can allow the supervisor to abuse or otherwise terrorize
employees. Because the employer has granted that authority (or perceived
authority) to the supervisor by virtue of his title and position, the employer and
supervisor are one and should be treated as such.

---

[29] We note that here, if the harassment was as open as Vinson and her witnesses indicate, the
Bank certainly had constructive notice of the harassment.

Should Vinson be able to prove the facts of her case on remand, this lawsuit is an excellent example of a supervisor and employer who are one. Here, regardless of the Bank's claim that Taylor had no authority to hire, fire, or promote employees, Vinson believed otherwise. As Vinson explained at trial, "He told me that he was my supervisor. He gave me my pay check, and I had to do what he wanted me to do." Trial Tr. vol. II, 59. In fact, everything that Vinson knew about Taylor seemed to suggest that he had the power to hire, promote, or fire her. Taylor had hired Vinson or caused her to be hired. He was her direct supervisor and evaluated her, at least he evaluated her enough to know about her work performance and that her promotions were based on merit. He directed her to train certain people for other positions, and he informed her of future promotions. To deprive Vinson and other potential complainants of the possibility of redress under Title VII merely because the employer claimed to have no notice of the actions of its own supervisors would cut against the purpose of Title VII, which is to eliminate discrimination and harassment in the workplace.

CONCLUSION

In sum, this Court holds that (1) the District Court failed to establish a sufficient factual record to determine the viability of either a *quid pro quo* claim or a hostile environment claim because it failed to determine whether sexual relations actually occurred between Vinson and Taylor and under what circumstances they occurred; (2) sexual harassment that results in non-economic injury or injury that is not otherwise tangible can violate Title VII; (3) the focus of the inquiry in a hostile environment claim is on the conduct of the alleged harasser and its effects on the complainant and the work environment; (4) the trial court erred in excluding testimonial evidence from other women who claimed to have been harassed by the alleged wrongdoer and to have seen him harass the complainant; (5) a complainant's manner of dress is not relevant to the inquiry of welcomeness, and a complainant's sexually provocative speech is relevant only to the extent that it helps to determine whether the challenged conduct unreasonably interfered with the complainant's work environment and performance, created a hostile or intimidating environment, or worked to preserve patterns of sex segregation in the workplace; and (6) employers are automatically liable for sexual harassment by their supervisory personnel regardless of whether they were aware of such conduct.

17

Commentary on *Johnson v. Transportation Agency*

Deborah Gordon

INTRODUCTION

In *Johnson*, the U.S. Supreme Court upheld a voluntary affirmative action plan that the defendant agency (the "Agency") implemented in response to a significant lack of female workers in its "skilled," and therefore supervisory and higher-paying, positions.[1] Justice Brennan, for the majority, found that the plan did not violate Title VII even though it allowed the Agency to take into account a job applicant's sex; the Court reasoned that this preference was used to remedy a "manifest" imbalance in job classifications for which women had been traditionally underrepresented and, in doing so, did not "unnecessarily trammel" the rights of male workers or create an absolute bar to their advancement.

Extending approval of race-based affirmative action programs to gender-based programs, the *Johnson* Court also recognized that treating women "equally" with men did not necessarily mean treating women identically to men. And yet, by accepting that the male applicant in question was "more qualified" than the female, *Johnson* embraces the notion that merit can be objectively and fairly determined. Professor Deborah Rhode, writing as Justice Rhode, rewrites the decision to highlight and debunk this fundamental misunderstanding and to confront directly how limits on women's traditional employment opportunities are not simply matters of choice.

JOHNSON: FACTS AND DOCTRINE

Diane Joyce was the first woman at the Agency to hold a road maintenance position, a prerequisite to the dispatcher job at the center of the dispute in

---

[1] *Johnson v. Transportation Agency*, 480 U.S. 616 (1987).

this case. At the time Joyce applied to be dispatcher, the Agency had never employed a woman in that position or in any of its 238 "skilled craft" positions.

One of Joyce's review panels included two Agency employees who had sexually harassed Joyce in the past. Although this panel recommended promoting Petitioner Paul Johnson over Joyce, the Agency Director decided to promote Joyce instead. In response, Johnson filed a complaint alleging that he had been denied a promotion on the basis of sex in violation of Title VII.

The district court found that Johnson was "more qualified" for the dispatcher position than Joyce and that Joyce's gender was the "determining factor in her selection"; it further held that the Agency's plan violated *Steelworkers v. Weber*, 443 U.S. 193 (1979). The Ninth Circuit Court of Appeals reversed, and the U.S. Supreme Court affirmed, finding that the Agency's hiring preference was put in place to remedy the historic, systematic underrepresentation of women in the occupational categories at issue. The Court reasoned that the decision to promote Joyce over Johnson was consistent with the purposes of Title VII because it was made pursuant to a plan that addressed a "manifest imbalance" of women in skilled craft jobs. An affirmative action plan need not be adopted to remedy the employer's own discriminatory practices, the Court held, but rather could rely on an imbalance in traditionally segregated job categories, so long as it did not authorize blind hiring by numbers or statistics. Here, the plan satisfied *Weber* because it did not "unnecessarily trammel" the rights of male employees or create an absolute bar to their advancement.

The *Johnson* opinion did not address, however, how the harassment prevalent in the Agency's regular hiring process contributed to the male-dominated nature of the workplace. The opinion noted the potential unfairness of the Agency's promotion process in footnotes, but left intact the underlying premise that the process was fair and objective and that Johnson was "more qualified" for the job.

JOHNSON'S LEGACY

Johnson is regarded as important to feminist scholars primarily because it is the first example of the U.S. Supreme Court's applying the concept of "substantive" equality to gender. Formal equality advocates who oppose affirmative action preferences assume that employers' policies are purely merit based and, therefore, neutral. In holding that the Agency's affirmative action plan was consistent with Title VII's purpose of eliminating the effects of employment discrimination, the *Johnson* Court recognized that men and women are situated differently, so applying identical rules to them may produce inequitable outcomes. But by accepting the premise that Johnson was inherently "more qualified" for the promotion, *Johnson* reinforces the idea that determining merit involves a fair, objective process and does not depend on the biases of the evaluators or even the very system that fostered or impeded the female employee's desire to seek a particular job in the first place.

Rhode's feminist judgment deliberately does not question or reject the Court's adoption of the *Weber* standards, including that an affirmative action program must address a "manifest imbalance" and must not "unnecessarily trammel" the rights of other employees. While this language "takes a political toll,"[2] Rhode, having clerked for Justice Marshall, had some experience with what it takes to build a majority on the Court. Although she recognized that the Court missed some opportunities in *Johnson* that would have made greater strides for women and other groups for whom affirmative action is important, Rhode did not want to disrupt the slender majority of five who were willing to put forth their collective belief that this gender-based affirmative action program was needed, legitimate, and "embodies the contribution that voluntary employer action can make in eliminating the vestiges of discrimination in the workplace."[3]

THE FEMINIST JUDGMENT

Rhode's feminist judgment centers on the Court's important failure to consider, confront, and re-characterize what "merit" and "equality" mean. To that end, Rhode highlights the implicit biases embedded in the Agency's evaluation process of Joyce and takes issue with deeply ingrained notions of why women are often perceived as less deserving than their male counterparts. Rhode was one of the first, and most prolific, feminist scholars to discuss what she has described as a "misleading myth of meritocracy," which is the misguided but prevalent idea that benefits, advancement, and opportunity result purely from hard work and merit, untainted by bias or discrimination.[4] This false premise of gender neutrality influences our thinking about employment opportunities but also extends to many other legal rules

---

[2] Ann C. McGinley, *The Emerging Cronyism Defense and Affirmative Action: A Critical Perspective on the Distinction Between Colorblind and Race-Conscious Decision Making Under Title VII*, 39 *Ariz. L. Rev.* 1003, 1035 (1997).

[3] Justice Brennan's majority was joined by Justices Marshall, Blackmun, Powell, and Stevens. Justices Stevens and O'Connor filed separate concurrences, and Justices White and Scalia filed dissents, in which Chief Justice Rehnquist joined.

[4] Deborah L. Rhode, Speaking of Sex 147 (1998); Anne Lawton, *The Meritocracy Myth and the Illusion of Equal Employment Opportunity*, 85 *Minn. L. Rev.* 587, 594–599 (2000); Deborah L. Rhode, *Myths of Meritocracy*, 65 *Fordham L. Rev.* 585, 588 (1996).

and institutions that purport to treat women "equally" while simultaneously ignoring the reality of women's lives that makes their experiences substantively different from men's.[5]

The feminist judgment underscores how deciding who is "best qualified" for a job is complicated, inherently subjective, and often tainted by bias. It does so by highlighting, in a separately numbered Part II of the opinion, facts about Joyce's prior harassment at the hands of two men who played a key role in deciding whether to promote her. The original opinion had relegated these critical details to footnotes, literally marginalizing Joyce's experiences of harassment and marking them as irrelevant to the question of the fairness of the review process and to the legal issue of affirmative action. Rhode strengthens the point by adding more details from the lower court decisions and amicus briefs to show how the record "casts serious doubt" on the premise that Johnson was better qualified than Joyce. Ultimately, however, the feminist judgment refrains from a finding that the district court's determination that Johnson was "more qualified" than Joyce was clearly erroneous. Rhode deliberately took a more nuanced approach because the U.S. Supreme Court rarely would take such a step, and, more importantly, because this approach allowed her to reach the key issue of the affirmative action plan's legitimacy, which would have been unnecessary had she ruled Joyce was the more qualified applicant.

The added details highlight the subjectivity of the Agency's allegedly "merit-based" evaluation process. Rhode's feminist judgment thus shows the evaluators' open gender bias – evident in the one evaluator's prior refusal to give Joyce the same coveralls received by her male counterparts and another's characterizing her as a "rebel-rousing, skirt-wearing person" and as "not a lady," based on her use of "vulgar profanity." Marginalizing women's individual experiences – and deeming them legally irrelevant – has made women and their experiences invisible in law.[6] In choosing to bury important facts about Joyce's work history, the U.S. Supreme Court (and each of the lower courts) accepted the promotion process as purely "merit" based, despite ample evidence that it was not.

---

[5] *See* Catharine A. MacKinnon, *Feminism, Marxism, Method, and the State: Toward Feminist Jurisprudence*, 7 *Signs* 515, 518 (1982); *see also* Katharine T. Bartlett, *Feminist Legal Methods*, 103 *Harv. L. Rev.* 829 (1990).

[6] *See, e.g.*, Kim Lane Scheppele, *Just the Facts, Ma'am: Sexualized Violence, Evidentiary Habits, and the Revision of Truth*, 37 *N.Y.L. Sch. L. Rev.* 123 (1992); Margaret E. Montoya, *Mascaras, Trenzas, y Grenas: Un/Masking the Self While Un/braiding Latina Stories and Legal Discourse*, 17 *Harv. Women's L.J.* 185 (1994); *see also* Mari Matsuda, *Affirmative Action and Legal Knowledge: Planting Seeds in Plowed-Up Ground*, 11 *Harv. Women's L.J.* 1 (1988).

The narrative of Joyce's prior dealings with her supervisors, fleshed out with testimony about other similar experiences during her Agency tenure, show that Joyce was arguably *more* rather than less qualified to be dispatcher; she achieved her excellent performance record under far more challenging conditions than did her male counterparts. Seemingly small acts of prejudice, such as failing to give women the required tools (like coveralls), telling them constantly that they cannot do the job, and wearing them down psychologically, contribute to making it harder for women to succeed. By highlighting the kind of discrimination that Joyce suffered, and that is typical of male-dominated workplaces, the feminist judgment reinforces the need for affirmative action programs of the type the Agency adopted. Rather than an issue of "preferences," affirmative action programs help level otherwise unfair playing fields.

Rhode's decision also makes clear that taking affirmative account of an applicant's sex is "special" only if one assumes that the status quo is gender-neutral. Rhode takes on the law's putative neutrality by challenging the notion that women "choose" not to advance in certain male-dominated jobs. Feminist scholars have long questioned whether women's career and employment "choices" are truly voluntary given a society that is replete with sexual harassment and other forms of oppression.[7] Rhode directly confronts the dissent's assertion that women's underrepresentation in "skilled craft" jobs is a result of women's free choice – their deliberate refusal, in Justice Scalia's words, to "shoulder pick and shovel." The feminist judgment debunks the dissent's unsupported claim that it is "absurd" to attribute the absence of women on road maintenance crews to the systematic exclusion of women. It does so by presenting a mass of statistical evidence to the contrary, including Agency testimony, Department of Labor statistics, and construction industry data, to show that pervasive discrimination rather than lack of desire accounts for women's traditional underrepresentation in the type of positions at issue in *Johnson*. Rhode's majority thus topples the deep-seated and incorrect assumptions about women's choice and neutrality embodied by the dissent – assumptions that contribute, to this day, to women's underrepresentation in certain fields and to a significant gender-based wage gap.

There are many ways to approach a feminist judgment. The author could choose to radically revise the opinion and not speculate about whether she would have the votes to command a majority. The author could concur or dissent. Here, Rhode takes a path that, at first glance, appears to make only minor changes to the original, but on reflection is far more profound. Rhode

[7]   See, e.g., Nicole Buonocore Porter, *The Blame Game: How the Rhetoric of Choice Blames the Achievement Gap on Women*, 8 F.I.U. L. Rev. 447, 450–451 (2013).

placed herself in the position of a feminist justice at the time *Johnson* was decided. She surmised that the majority's decision to include the facts about the Agency's biased review process, albeit in footnotes, meant that underscoring those facts would likely not cause loss of any votes; acknowledging the subjectivity of performance evaluations and the potential for bias to affect them would, however, enhance the decision's educational value. In sum, she thought deeply about what it would take to incorporate certain important feminist ideas into the opinion while still preserving the delicate majority of votes that allowed the Court to reach its important recognitions about gender equality.

Johnson v. Transportation Agency, 480 U.S. 616 (1987)

Justice Deborah L. Rhode delivered the opinion of the Court.[8]

Respondent, Transportation Agency of Santa Clara County, California, promulgated an Affirmative Action Plan. In selecting applicants for the position of road dispatcher, the Agency passed over Petitioner Paul Johnson and promoted Diane Joyce. The question for decision is whether in making the promotion the Agency impermissibly took into account the sex of the applicants in violation of Title VII of the Civil Rights Act of 1964, 42 U.S.C. §§ 2000e *et seq*. After receiving a right-to-sue letter from the Equal Employment Opportunity Commission (EEOC), Johnson filed suit in the District Court for the Northern District of California. It held that Respondent had violated Title VII. The Court of Appeals for the Ninth Circuit reversed. *Johnson v. Transportation. Agency*, 770 F. 2d 752 (9th Cir. 1984). We granted certiorari, *Johnson v. Transportation Agency*, 478 U.S. 1019 (1986). We affirm.

I

In December 1978, the Santa Clara County Transit District Board of Supervisors adopted an Affirmative Action Plan (Plan) for the County Transportation Agency. The Plan implemented a County Affirmative Action Plan, which had been adopted, declared the County, because "mere prohibition of discriminatory practices is not enough to remedy the effects of past practices and to permit attainment of an equitable representation of minorities, women and handicapped persons." J.A. 31. The Agency Plan provides

---

[8]   This opinion draws heavily on the language of the original opinion, authored by Justice Brennan, concerning the factual backdrop of the case in Part I and the analysis of the permissibility of the affirmative action plan under *Steel Workers v. Weber* in Part IV.

that, in making promotions to positions within a traditionally segregated job classification in which women have been significantly underrepresented, the Agency is authorized to consider as one factor the sex of a qualified applicant.

In reviewing the composition of its work force, the Agency noted in its Plan that women were represented in numbers far less than their proportion of the County labor force in both the Agency as a whole and in five of seven job categories. Specifically, while women constituted 36.4 percent of the area labor market, they composed only 22.4 percent of Agency employees. Furthermore, women working at the Agency were concentrated largely in EEOC job categories traditionally held by women: women made up 76 percent of Office and Clerical Workers, but only 7.1 percent of Agency Officials and Administrators, 8.6 percent of Professionals, 9.7 percent of Technicians, and 22 percent of Service and Maintenance Workers. As for the job classification relevant to this case, none of the 238 Skilled Craft Worker positions was held by a woman. J.A. 49. The Plan noted that this underrepresentation of women in part reflected the fact that women had not traditionally been employed in these positions, and that they had not been strongly motivated to seek training or employment in them "because of the limited opportunities that have existed in the past for them to work in such classifications." J.A. 57. The Plan also observed that, while the proportion of ethnic minorities in the Agency as a whole exceeded the proportion of such minorities in the County work force, a smaller percentage of minority employees held management, professional, and technical positions.

The Agency stated that its Plan was intended to achieve "a statistically measurable yearly improvement in hiring, training and promotion of minorities and women throughout the Agency in all major job classifications where they are underrepresented." J.A. 43. As a benchmark by which to evaluate progress, the Agency stated that its long-term goal was to attain a work force whose composition reflected the proportion of minorities and women in the area labor force. J.A. 54. Thus, for the Skilled Craft category in which the road dispatcher position at issue here was classified, the Agency's aspiration was that eventually about 36 percent of the jobs would be occupied by women.

The Plan acknowledged that a number of factors might make it unrealistic to rely on the Agency's long-term goals in evaluating the Agency's progress in expanding job opportunities for minorities and women. Among the factors identified were low turnover rates in some classifications, the fact that some jobs involved heavy labor, the small number of positions within some job categories, the limited number of entry positions leading to the Technical and Skilled Craft classifications, and the limited number of minorities and women qualified for positions requiring specialized training and experience.

J.A.56–57. As a result, the Plan counseled that short-range goals be established and annually adjusted to serve as the most realistic guide for actual employment decisions. Among the tasks identified as important in establishing such short-term goals was the acquisition of data "reflecting the ratio of minorities, women and handicapped persons who are working in the local area in major job classifications relating to those utilized by the County Administration," so as to determine the availability of members of such groups who "possess the desired qualifications or potential for placement." J.A. 64. These data on qualified group members, along with predictions of position vacancies, were to serve as the basis for "realistic yearly employment goals for women, minorities and handicapped persons in each EEOC job category and major job classification." J.A. 64.

The Agency's Plan thus set aside no specific number of positions for minorities or women, but authorized the consideration of ethnicity or sex as a factor when evaluating qualified candidates for jobs in which members of such groups were poorly represented. One such job was the road dispatcher position that is the subject of the dispute in this case.

On December 12, 1979, the Agency announced a vacancy for the promotional position of road dispatcher in the Agency's Roads Division. Dispatchers assign road crews, equipment, and materials, and maintain records pertaining to road maintenance jobs. J.A. 23–24. The position requires at minimum four years of dispatch or road maintenance work experience for Santa Clara County. The EEOC job classification scheme designates a road dispatcher as a Skilled Craft Worker.

Twelve County employees applied for the promotion, including Joyce and Johnson. Joyce had worked for the County since 1970, serving as an account clerk until 1975. She had applied for a road dispatcher position in 1974, but was deemed ineligible because she had not served as a road maintenance worker. In 1975, Joyce transferred from a senior account clerk position to a road maintenance worker position, becoming the first woman to fill such a job. Trial Tr., 83–84, August 10, 1982. During her four years in that position, she occasionally worked out of class as a road dispatcher.

Petitioner Johnson began with the County in 1967 as a road yard clerk, after private employment that included working as a supervisor and dispatcher. He had also unsuccessfully applied for the road dispatcher opening in 1974. In 1977, his clerical position was downgraded, and he sought and received a transfer to the position of road maintenance worker. Trial Tr. 127. He also occasionally worked out of class as a dispatcher while performing that job.

Nine of the applicants, including Joyce and Johnson, were deemed qualified for the job, and were interviewed by a two-person board. Seven of the

applicants scored above 70 on this interview, which meant that they were certified as eligible for selection by the appointing authority. The scores awarded
ranged from 70 to 80. Johnson was tied for second with a score of 75, while
Joyce ranked next with a score of 73. A second interview was conducted by
three Agency supervisors, who ultimately recommended that Johnson be
promoted.

Prior to the second interview, Joyce had contacted the County's Affirmative
Action Office because she feared that her application might not receive dis-
interested review. Joyce testified that she had had disagreements with two of
the three members of the second interview panel. One had been her first
supervisor when she began work as a road maintenance worker. In performing
arduous work in this job, she had not been issued coveralls, although her male
coworkers had received them. After ruining her pants, she complained to her
supervisor, to no avail. After three other similar incidents, ruining clothes on
each occasion, she filed a grievance, and was issued four pairs of coveralls the
next day. Trial Tr. 89–90.

Joyce had dealt with a second member of the panel for a year and a half in
her capacity as chair of the Roads Operations Safety Committee, where she
and he "had several differences of opinion on how safety should be implemented." Trial Tr. 90–91. This same panel member had earlier described
Joyce as a "rebel-rousing, skirt-wearing person." Trial Tr. 153. He also referred
to her as "not a lady," based on her use of "vulgar-type profanity." Trial Tr.
161–162. However, he acknowledged that such language was used on the roads
with some frequency among the men, a fact that he did not seem to hold
against them. Trial Tr. 162.

The Affirmative Action Office contacted the Agency's Affirmative Action
Coordinator, whom the Agency's Plan makes responsible for, *inter alia*, keeping the Director informed of opportunities for the Agency to accomplish its
objectives under the Plan. At the time, the Agency employed no women in
any Skilled Craft position, and had never employed a woman as a road dispatcher. The Coordinator recommended to the Director of the Agency, James
Graebner, that Joyce be promoted.

Graebner, authorized to choose any of the seven persons deemed eligible,
thus had the benefit of suggestions by the second interview panel and by the
Agency Coordinator in arriving at his decision. After deliberation, Graebner
concluded that Joyce should receive the promotion. As he testified: "I tried
to look at the whole picture, the combination of her qualifications and Mr.
Johnson's qualifications, their test scores, their expertise, their background,
affirmative action matters, things like that … I believe it was a combination of
all those." Trial Tr. 68.

The certification form naming Joyce as the person promoted to the dispatcher position stated that both she and Johnson were rated as well qualified for the job. The evaluation of Joyce read: "Well qualified by virtue of 18 years of past clerical experience including 3½ years at West Yard plus almost 5 years as a [road maintenance worker]." J.A. 27. The evaluation of Johnson was as follows: "Well qualified applicant; two years of [road maintenance worker] experience plus 11 years of Road Yard Clerk. Has had previous outside Dispatch experience but was 13 years ago." J.A. 27. Graebner testified that he did not regard as significant the fact that Johnson scored 75 and Joyce 73 when interviewed by the two-person board. Trial Tr. 57–58. He did consider it relevant that Joyce was seeking a position that had never been held by a woman. In his view, while the promotion of Joyce "made a small dent, for sure, in the numbers," nonetheless "philosophically it made a larger impact in that it probably has encouraged other females and minorities to look at the possibility of so-called 'non-traditional' jobs as areas where they and the agency both have samples of a success story." Trial Tr. 64.

Petitioner Johnson filed a complaint with the EEOC alleging that he had been denied promotion on the basis of sex in violation of Title VII. He received a right-to-sue letter from the EEOC on March 10, 1981, and on March 20, 1981, filed suit in the United States District Court for the Northern District of California. The District Court found that Johnson was more qualified for the dispatcher position than Joyce, and that the sex of Joyce was the "*determining factor* in her selection." App. to Pet. for Cert. 4a (emphasis in original). The court acknowledged that, since the Agency justified its decision on the basis of its Affirmative Action Plan, the criteria announced in *Steelworkers v. Weber*, 443 U.S. 193 (1979), should be applied in evaluating the validity of the Plan. App. to Pet. for Cert. 5a. It then found the Agency's Plan invalid on the ground that the evidence did not satisfy *Weber's* criterion that the Plan be temporary. App. to Pet. for Cert. 6a. The Court of Appeals for the Ninth Circuit reversed, holding that the absence of an express termination date in the Plan was not dispositive, because the Plan repeatedly expressed its objective as the attainment, rather than the maintenance, of a work force mirroring the labor force in the County. *Johnson v. Transp. Agency*, 770 F.2d 752, 756 (9th Cir. 1984). The Court of Appeals added that the fact that the Plan established no fixed percentage of positions for minorities or women made it less essential that the Plan contains a relatively explicit deadline. *Id.* at 757. The Court held further that the Agency's consideration of Joyce's sex in filling the road dispatcher position was lawful. The Agency Plan had been adopted, the court said, to address a conspicuous imbalance in the Agency's work force, and neither unnecessarily trammeled the rights of other employees, nor created an absolute bar to their advancement. *Id.* at 757–759.

II

Although the district court determined that Johnson was better qualified than Joyce, (Finding of Fact No. 18), the record casts serious doubt on that conclusion. No evidence before the court suggested that the test procedures, the questions asked, or the scoring system employed by either panel were validated as job-related in conformity with professionally accepted validation procedures or federal guidelines. Nor was there any evidence that the difference of 2.5 in scores was significant and beyond the range of error inherent in the scoring system.

Moreover, substantial evidence indicated that Joyce compiled her excellent performance record despite significant discrimination and harassment on the job. When Joyce first interviewed for position of account clerk, she was told that "you know we wanted a man." Trial Tr. 110–111. In addition to the incidents of bias by her interviewers noted earlier, Joyce recollected six other incidents. Trial Tr. 119. She testified that "[m]any times I felt I was discriminated against because of my sex, but I don't think I ever filed … any formal grievances because of it, simply because it would be very difficult to prove." Trial Tr. 118. In effect, Joyce had compiled an outstanding performance record, almost equivalent to that of her male rival, under far more difficult conditions and biased evaluation processes. Given all the facts, Joyce is arguably more qualified than Johnson, not slightly less.

We raise these concerns about the district court's conclusion because they underscore a broader point about "merit-based" evaluation criteria. Often ostensibly objective criteria mask subjective processes that open the door to bias. So too, as the brief for the American Society for Personnel Administration notes, "[i]t is a standard tenet of personnel administration that there is rarely a single 'best qualified' person for a job. An effective personnel system will bring before the selecting official several fully qualified candidates who each may possess different attributes which recommend them for selection … [F]inal determinations as to which candidate is 'best qualified' are at best subjective." Br. for the Am. Soc'y for Pers. Admin. as Amicus Curiae Supporting Resp'ts at 13. Here, the Agency's personnel system did what is recommended in providing several candidates, and the supervisor in charge made a well-founded decision that Joyce was the best for the job. There was no convincing basis for the district court to reverse that decision.

However, we do not need to find the court's finding clearly erroneous in order to sustain the personnel decision made by the Agency because we find that the decision was in accordance with a fully justified affirmative action plan.

III

As a preliminary matter, we note that Petitioner bears the burden of establishing the invalidity of the Agency's Plan. Only last term, in *Wygant v. Jackson Board of Education*, 476 U.S. 267, 277–278 (1986), we held that "[t]he ultimate burden remains with the employees to demonstrate the unconstitutionality of an affirmative-action program," and we see no basis for a different rule regarding a plan's alleged violation of Title VII. This case also fits readily within the analytical framework set forth in *McDonnell Douglas Corp. v. Green*, 411 U.S. 792 (1973). Once a plaintiff establishes a prima facie case that race or sex has been taken into account in an employer's employment decision, the burden shifts to the employer to articulate a nondiscriminatory rationale for its decision. The existence of an affirmative action plan provides such a rationale. If such a plan is articulated as the basis for the employer's decision, the burden shifts to the plaintiff to prove that the employer's justification is a pretext and the plan is invalid. As a practical matter, of course, an employer will generally seek to avoid a charge of pretext by presenting evidence in support of its plan. That does not mean, however, as Petitioner suggests, that reliance on an affirmative action plan is to be treated as an affirmative defense requiring the employer to carry the burden of proving the validity of the plan. The burden of proving its invalidity remains on the plaintiff.

The assessment of the legality of the Agency Plan must be guided by our decision in *Weber*, 443 U.S. 193. In that case, the Court addressed the question whether the employer violated Title VII by adopting a voluntary affirmative action plan designed to "eliminate manifest racial imbalances in traditionally segregated job categories." *Id.* at 197. The respondent employee in that case challenged the employer's denial of his application for a position in a newly established craft training program, contending that the employer's selection process impermissibly took into account the race of the applicants. The selection process was guided by an affirmative action plan, which provided that 50 percent of the new trainees were to be black until the percentage of black skilled craftworkers in the employer's plant approximated the percentage of blacks in the local labor force. Adoption of the plan had been prompted by the fact that only 1.83 percent of skilled craftworkers at the plant were black, even though the work force in the area was approximately 39 percent black.

Because of the historical exclusion of blacks from craft positions, the employer regarded its former policy of hiring trained outsiders as inadequate to redress the imbalance in its work force.

We upheld the employer's decision to select less senior black applicants over the white respondent, for we found that taking race into account was consistent with Title VII's objective of "break[ing] down old patterns of racial segregation and hierarchy." *Id.* at 208. As we stated:

> It would be ironic indeed if a law triggered by a Nation's concern over centuries of racial injustice and intended to improve the lot of those who had 'been excluded from the American dream for so long,' 110 Cong.Rec. 6552 (1964) (remarks of Sen. Humphrey), constituted the first legislative prohibition of all voluntary, private, race-conscious efforts to abolish traditional patterns of racial segregation and hierarchy.
>
> *Id.* at 204.

We noted that the plan did not "unnecessarily trammel the interests of the white employees," because it did not require "the discharge of white workers and their replacement with new black hires." *Id.* at 208. Nor did the plan create "an absolute bar to the advancement of white employees," since half of those trained in the new program were to be white. *Id.* Finally, we observed that the plan was a temporary measure, not designed to maintain racial balance, but to "eliminate a manifest racial imbalance." *Id.* As Justice Blackmun's concurrence made clear, *Weber* held that an employer seeking to justify the adoption of a plan need not point to its own prior discriminatory practices or even to evidence of an "arguable violation" on its part. *Id.* at 212. Rather, it need point only to a "conspicuous ... imbalance in traditionally segregated job categories." *Id.* at 209. In so holding, we recognized that voluntary employer action can play a crucial role in furthering Title VII's purpose of eliminating the effects of discrimination in the workplace, and that Title VII should not be read to thwart such efforts. *Id.* at 204.

In reviewing the employment decision at issue in this case, we must first examine whether that decision was made pursuant to a plan prompted by concerns similar to those of the employer in *Weber*. Next, we must determine whether the effect of the Plan on males and nonminorities is comparable to the effect of the Plan in that case.

The first issue is therefore whether consideration of the sex of applicants for skilled craft jobs was justified by the existence of a "manifest imbalance" that reflected underrepresentation of women in "traditionally segregated job categories." *Id.* at 197. In determining whether an imbalance exists that would justify taking sex or race into account, a comparison of the percentage of minorities or women in the employer's work force with the percentage in the area labor market or general population is appropriate in analyzing jobs that require no special expertise, *see Teamsters v. United States*, 431 U.S. 324 (1977), or training programs designed to provide expertise, *see Steelworkers v. Weber*, 443 U.S. 193 (1979). Where a job requires special training, however, the comparison should be with those in the labor force who possess the relevant qualifications. *See Hazelwood School District v. United States*, 433 U.S. 299 (1977). The requirement that the "manifest imbalance" relate to a "traditionally segregated job category" provides assurance both that sex or race will be taken into account in a manner consistent with Title VII's purpose of eliminating the effects of employment discrimination, and that the interests of those employees not benefiting from the plan will not be unduly infringed.

A manifest imbalance need not be such that it would support a prima facie case against the employer. Application of the "prima facie" standard in Title VII cases would be inconsistent with *Weber's* focus on statistical imbalance, and could inappropriately create a significant disincentive for employers to adopt an affirmative action plan. *See Weber*, 443 U.S. at 204 (Title VII intended as a "catalyst" for employer efforts to eliminate vestiges of discrimination). An organization is hardly likely to adopt a plan if in order to do so it must compile evidence that could be used to subject it to a colorable Title VII suit.

It is particularly important that employers not be discouraged from implementing affirmative action initiatives that can address women's gross underrepresentation in nontraditional occupations. Nationally, women comprise only 2.4 percent of skilled crafts workers, and a smaller percentage of construction workers.[9] Justice Scalia attributes this underrepresentation to women's reluctance to "shoulder pick and shovel." But a vast array of evidence suggests that discrimination, not simply women's preferences, plays a dominant role in gender- segregated workforces. In this case, Myra Beals, the former Assistant Personnel Officer for the Agency, testified about a number of Agency practices that excluded women. Supervisory employees had expressed the view that it "wasn't appropriate to hire women, but particularly not pregnant women." Trial Tr. 256. Women also "were prevented from getting the training that was given to men in the identical position," and supervisors in the Road Division had acknowledged that they would assign work based on feelings about "what was appropriate for women to do and what was not appropriate." Trial Tr. 231, 253.

---

9   U.S. Dep't of Labor, Bureau of Labor Statistics, Employment and Earnings 46–7, Tables A-23 and A-24 (May 1986).

National data make clear that such bias is pervasive. The experience of
the Department of Labor is that "there are women available and interested
in entering the skilled trades. However, the longstanding reputation of the
trades for excluding women discourages many women from applying for these
jobs."[10] For example, witnesses at hearings conducted by the Office of Federal
Contract Compliance Programs on the construction industry testified that it
was discrimination, not the lack of interested female applicants that was keeping the percentage of women at such low levels. The data collected were full
of illustrations of women applying for jobs once they become available.[11] The
Office concluded that "unless specific affirmative action steps are prescribed,
construction employment opportunities will not reach the female workforce
of this country."[12]

To avoid a similar result in road work, the Santa Clara Transportation
Agency took reasonable remedial measures. The Agency Plan acknowledged the "limited opportunities that have existed in the past," J.A. 57, for
women to find employment in certain job classifications "where women
have not been traditionally employed in significant numbers." J.A. 51. As a
result, women were concentrated in traditionally female jobs in the Agency,
and represented a lower percentage in other job classifications than would
be expected if such traditional segregation had not occurred. Specifically,
nine of the ten Para-Professionals and 110 of the 145 Office and Clerical
Workers were women. By contrast, women were only two of the 28 Officials
and Administrators, five of the fifty-eight Professionals, twelve of the 124
Technicians, none of the Skilled Craft Workers, and one – who was Joyce –
of the 110 Road Maintenance Workers. J.A. 51–52. The Plan sought to remedy these imbalances through "hiring, training and promotion of … women
throughout the Agency in all major job classifications where they are underrepresented." J.A. 43.

Initially, the Agency adopted, as a benchmark for measuring progress in
eliminating underrepresentation, the long-term goal of a work force that
mirrored in its major job classifications the percentage of women in the area
labor market. Even as it did so, however, it acknowledged that such a figure

---

[10] Equal Employment Opportunity in Apprenticeship and Training, 43 Fed. Reg. 20760, 20763
(May 12, 1978).

[11] Construction Contractors – Affirmative Action Requirements, 42 Fed. Reg. 41379 (August
16, 1977).

[12] Construction Contractors – Affirmative Action Requirements, 43 Fed Reg. 14888, 14892 (April
7, 1978). For other evidence on discrimination rather than women's preferences as the driver
of sex-segregated jobs, *see* Women's Work, Men's Work – Sex Segregation on the Job 77, 80
(Barbara Reskin and Heidi Hartmann eds., 1986); Women's Bureau, U.S. Dep't of Labor,
A Woman's Guide to Apprenticeship 4 (1980).

could not, by itself, necessarily justify taking into account the sex of applicants for positions in all job categories. For positions requiring specialized training and experience, the Plan observed that the number of minorities and women "who possess the qualifications required for entry into such job classifications is limited." J.A. 56. The Plan therefore directed that annual short-term goals be formulated that would provide a more realistic indication of the degree to which sex should be taken into account in filling particular positions. J.A. 61–64. The Plan stressed that such goals "should not be construed as 'quotas' that must be met," but as reasonable aspirations in correcting the imbalance in the Agency's work force. J.A. 64. These goals were to take into account factors such as "turnover, layoffs, lateral transfers, new job openings, retirements and availability of minorities, women and handicapped persons in the area work force who possess the desired qualifications or potential for placement." J.A. 64. The Plan specifically directed that, in establishing such goals, the Agency work with the County Planning Department and other sources in attempting to compile data on the percentage of minorities and women in the local labor force that were actually working in the job classifications constituting the Agency work force. J.A. 63–64. From the outset, therefore, the Plan sought annually to develop even more refined measures of the underrepresentation in each job category that required attention.

By contrast, had the Plan simply calculated imbalances in all categories according to the proportion of women in the labor pool, and then directed that hiring be governed solely by those figures, it would raise significant questions. If a plan failed to take distinctions in qualifications into account in providing guidance for actual employment decisions, it would dictate mere blind hiring by the numbers, for it would hold supervisors to "achievement of a particular percentage of minority employment or membership ... regardless of circumstances such as economic conditions or the number of available qualified minority applicants ... " *Sheet Metal Workers v. EEOC*, 478 U.S. 421, 495 (1986) (O'Connor, J., concurring in part and dissenting in part).

The Agency's Plan emphatically did *not* authorize such blind hiring. It expressly required taking into account numerous factors in making employment decisions, including the qualifications of female applicants for particular jobs. Thus, despite the fact that no precise short-term goal was yet in place for the Skilled Craft category in mid-1980, the Agency's management nevertheless had been clearly instructed that they were not to hire solely by reference to statistics. The fact that only the long-term goal had been established for this category posed no danger that personnel decisions would be made by reflexive adherence to a numerical standard.

Given the obvious imbalance in the Skilled Craft category, and given the Agency's commitment to eliminating such imbalances, it was plainly not unreasonable for Graebner to consider as one factor the sex of Ms. Joyce in making his decision. The promotion of Joyce thus satisfies the first requirement enunciated in *Weber*, since it was undertaken to further an affirmative action plan designed to eliminate Agency work force imbalances in traditionally segregated job categories.

IV

We next consider whether the Agency Plan unnecessarily trammeled the rights of male employees or created an absolute bar to their advancement. In contrast to the plan in *Weber*, which provided that 50 percent of the positions in the craft training program were exclusively for blacks, and to the consent decree upheld last term in *Firefighters v. Cleveland*, 478 U.S. 501 (1986), which required the promotion of specific numbers of minorities, the Santa Clara Plan sets aside no positions for women. The Plan expressly states that "[t]he 'goals' established for each Division should not be construed as 'quotas' that must be met." J.A. 64. Rather, the Plan merely authorizes that consideration be given to affirmative action concerns when evaluating qualified applicants. As the Agency Director testified, the sex of Joyce was but one of numerous factors he took into account in arriving at his decision. Trial Tr. 68. The Plan thus resembles the "Harvard Plan" approvingly noted by Justice Powell in *Regents of University of California v. Bakke*, 438 U.S. 265, 316–319 (1978), which considers race along with other criteria in determining admission to the college. As Justice Powell observed: "In such an admissions program, race or ethnic background may be deemed a 'plus' in a particular applicant's file, yet it does not insulate the individual from comparison with all other candidates for the available seats." *Id.* at 317. Similarly, the Agency Plan requires women to compete with all other qualified applicants. No persons are automatically excluded from consideration; *all* are able to have their qualifications weighed against those of other applicants.

In addition, Petitioner had no absolute entitlement to the road dispatcher position. Seven of the applicants were classified as qualified and eligible, and the Agency Director was authorized to promote any of the seven. Thus, denial of the promotion unsettled no legitimate, firmly rooted expectation on the part of Petitioner. Furthermore, while Petitioner in this case was denied a promotion, he retained his employment with the Agency, at the same salary and with the same seniority, and remained eligible for other promotions.

Finally, the Agency's Plan was intended to *attain* a balanced work force, not to *maintain* one. The Plan includes ten references to the Agency's desire to "attain" such a balance, but no reference whatsoever to a goal of maintaining it. The Director testified that, while the "broader goal" of affirmative action, defined as "the desire to hire, to promote, to give opportunity and training on an equitable, non-discriminatory basis," is something that is "a permanent part" of "the Agency's operating philosophy," that broader goal "is divorced, if you will, from specific numbers or percentages." Trial Tr. 48–49.

The Agency acknowledged the difficulties that it would confront in remedying the imbalance in its work force, and it anticipated only gradual increases in the representation of minorities and women. It is thus unsurprising that the Plan includes no explicit end date, for the Agency's flexible, case-by-case approach was not expected to yield success in a brief period of time. Substantial evidence shows that the Agency has sought to take a moderate, gradual approach to eliminating the imbalance in its work force, one which establishes realistic guidance for employment decisions, and which visits minimal intrusion on the legitimate expectations of other employees. Given this fact, as well as the Agency's express commitment to "attain" a balanced work force, there is ample assurance that the Agency does not seek to use its Plan to maintain a permanent racial and sexual balance.

In evaluating the compliance of an affirmative action plan with Title VII's prohibition on discrimination, we must be mindful of "this Court's and Congress's consistent emphasis on 'the value of voluntary efforts to further the objectives of the law.'" *Wygant*, 476 U.S. at 290 (O'Connor, J., concurring in part and concurring in judgment) (quoting *Bakke*, 438 U.S. at 364). The Agency in the case before us has undertaken such a voluntary effort, and has done so in full recognition of both the difficulties and the potential for adverse effects on men and nonminorities. The Agency has identified a conspicuous imbalance in job categories traditionally segregated by race and sex. It has made clear from the outset, however, that employment decisions may not be justified solely by reference to this imbalance, but must rest on a multitude of practical, realistic factors. It has, therefore, committed itself to annual adjustment of goals so as to provide a reasonable guide for actual hiring and promotion decisions. The Agency earmarks no positions for anyone; sex is but one of several factors that may be taken into account in evaluating qualified applicants for a position. As both the Plan's language and its manner of operation attest, the Agency has no intention of establishing a work force whose permanent composition is dictated by rigid numerical standards.

We therefore hold that the Agency appropriately took into account as one factor the sex of Diane Joyce in determining that she should be promoted to the road dispatcher position. The decision to do so was made pursuant to an affirmative action plan that represents a moderate, flexible, case-by-case approach to effecting a gradual improvement in the representation of minorities and women in the Agency's work force. Such a plan is fully consistent with Title VII, for it embodies the contribution that voluntary employer action can make in eliminating the vestiges of discrimination in the workplace. Accordingly, the judgment of the Court of Appeals is

Affirmed.

18

Commentary on *Price Waterhouse v. Hopkins*

Dale Margolin Cecka

INTRODUCTION

As the first U.S. Supreme Court decision to explore sex stereotyping in depth, *Price Waterhouse v. Hopkins*[1] was a landmark decision, with unforeseen and often progressive results in cases involving LGBQT rights and sexual harassment. However, on balance, its effect on women plaintiffs in glass ceiling cases has been disappointing to feminists because the opinion failed to define "stereotyping" in a way that gave legal meaning to the concept of implicit bias. The Court did not connect the dots between stereotyping, subconscious behavior, and disparate gender impact in corporate culture. It is no surprise, therefore, that even in 2015, a new generation of women faces a corporate culture startlingly similar to the one Ann Hopkins faced over twenty-five years ago.[2]

Professor Martha Chamallas, writing as Justice Chamallas, strengthens the original opinion by clarifying that decision makers often stereotype unconsciously. She also makes clear that, especially in cases involving "token" women in male-dominated workplaces, courts should pay close attention to expert testimony. The feminist judgment provides a framework for lower courts to identify implicit gender stereotyping and define actionable violations of Title VII.

---

[1] 490 U.S. 228, 256 (1989).

[2] *See, e.g.,* David Streitfeld, *In Ellen Pao's Suit vs. Kleiner Perkins, World of Venture Capital is Under Microscope* (March 5, 2015), www.nytimes.com/2015/03/06/Technology/In-Ellen-Paos-Suit-Vs-Kleiner-Perkins-World-Of-Venture-Capital-Is-Under-Microscope.html (female venture capitalist in Silicon Valley told to "[s]peak up – but don't talk too much. Light up the room – but don't overshadow others. Be confident and critical – but not cocky or negative.").

DOCTRINAL SUMMARY

In *Price Waterhouse*, the Court established the "mixed motive" framework of discrimination cases. The "mixed motive" framework supplemented the *McDonnell-Douglas* test in which a plaintiff can succeed by showing that an employer's proffered "legitimate" reason for the employment decision was a "pretext" for discrimination.[3] By contrast, "mixed motive" cases recognize that employment decisions can be the result of a combination of legitimate and illegitimate reasons. The burden then shifts to the employer to prove it would have made the same decision without the illegitimate factors. Plaintiff Ann Hopkins succeeded because her case involved several "smoking gun" comments by the male partners that showed their decision had relied on explicitly gender-based stereotyping. But the limitations of *Price Waterhouse* stem in part from these "smoking gun" comments, because the Court failed to clarify how, in future cases without such comments, plaintiffs could prove an illegitimate "motive."[4]

The other weakness of *Price Waterhouse* is that the Court seemed to reaffirm the assumption that bias is always deliberate and conscious. Therefore, subsequent plaintiffs were circumscribed from proffering evidence about subconscious bias or about inherently biased male-dominated work environments with broad-based disparate impacts on women. *Price Waterhouse* was a perfect case for the Court to address the subtlety and complexity of sex-based discrimination, but instead it extended existing doctrinal frameworks that simplistically ignore the reality that an employer's reasons are not necessarily known or knowable.

Price Waterhouse is primarily known for its addressing of sex stereotyping. The word "stereotype" appears ten times in the various opinions of *Price Waterhouse*, but the Court did not clarify what kind of stereotype-influenced behavior and workplace environment is illegal. The Court had in the record extensive expert testimony from Dr. Susan Fiske about stereotyping, but it dismissed that testimony as mere "icing on the cake"[5] and it was not integral to the holding. The Court concluded summarily that partners reacted "negatively to [Hopkins's] personality because she is a woman."[6] It alluded to the "possible ways of proving that stereotyping played a motivating role in an

---

[3] 411 U.S. 792 (1973).

[4] The 1991 Amendments to Title VII established that discriminatory motives could not be a "motivating factor" in employment decisions but otherwise were silent about how plaintiffs could prove those motives. 42 U.S.C. 2000e-5(2)(B).

[5] *Price Waterhouse v. Hopkins*, 490 U.S. 228, 256 (1989).

[6] *Id.* at 235.

employment decision."[7] But, it expressly declined to decide "which specific facts, 'standing alone,' would or would not establish a plaintiff's case."[8]

The Court's failure to provide a framework for evaluating stereotyping led lower courts to become entangled over whether, for example, a statement by an employer is just an innocuous "stray remark" or evidence of illegal bias.[9] Other courts also have become preoccupied with the status of the speaker of the comment and who, if anyone, heard or paid attention to it.[10] As Chamallas points out, this confusion undercuts the progressive holding of *Price Waterhouse* and makes what could have been a ground-breaking decision on women's rights a paper tiger. Twenty-six years after *Price Waterhouse*, women still earn less and have a lower status in the workplace, even controlling for factors such as qualifications, personal preferences, job responsibilities, occupation type, and industry.[11]

GENDER DISPARITIES AND BIAS IN THE AFTERMATH OF *PRICE WATERHOUSE*

Many feminist scholars agree that discrimination against women has changed: it has become less intentional and overt and more entrenched, repressed, and subconscious.[12] The prevalence of implicit bias has also been the subject of an increasing number of scientific studies and experiments.[13]

The U.S. Supreme Court has never recognized implicit bias against women. Indeed, in 2011, it found that Wal-Mart had not discriminated against

---

[7] *Id.* at 251–52.

[8] *Id.* at 252.

[9] *See, e.g., Ortiz-Rivera v. Astra Zeneca LP*, 363 F. App'x 45, 47 (1st Cir. 2010); *Montgomery v. J.R. Simplot Co.*, 916 F. Supp. 1033, 1039–40 (D. Or. 1994); *Millan-Feliciano v. Champs Sports*, No. 11–1823, 2012 U.S. Dist. LEXIS 148264, at *16–20 (D.P.R. October 15, 2012).

[10] *See* Kerri Lynn Stone, *Clarifying Stereotyping*, 59 U. Kan. L. Rev. 591, 610 nn. 110–11 (2011).

[11] Christi Corbett, *The Simple Truth About the Gender Pay Gap*, aauw 1, 8 (2015), www.aauw.org/files/2015/02/The-Simple-Truth_Spring-2015.pdf.

[12] Stone, *supra* note 10, at 626; *See generally* Ann McGinley, *¡Viva La Evolucion!: Recognizing Unconscious Motive in Title VII*, 9 Cornell J.L. & Pub. Pol'y 415 (2000); Linda Hamilton Krieger and Susan T. Fiske, *Behavioral Realism in Employment Discrimination Law: Implicit Bias and Disparate Treatment*, 94 Cal. L. Rev. 997 (2006).

[13] *See, e.g.,* Nicholas D. Kristof, *Our Racist, Sexist Selves*, N.Y. Times, April 6, 2008, www.nytimes.com/2008/04/06/opinion/06kristof.html?_r=3&. According to one study, female politicians with more feminine features ("large eyes and rounded features") tend to win elections, while those with more masculine features ("prominent eyebrows") tend to lose. These judgments took place "380 milliseconds after the presentation of a female politician's face" to study participants. Eric Hehman, Colleen M. Carpinella, Kerri L. Johnson, Jordan B. Leitner and Jonathon B Freeman, *Early Processing of Gendered Facial Cues Predicts the Electoral Success of Female Politicians*, 5 Soc. Psych. and Personality Sci. 815, 821 (May 14, 2014).

1.5 million female employees even though better-performing women were paid less and promoted less often than their male peers and despite comments in the record that women should not make as much money as men. In so doing, the Court rejected expert testimony about stereotyping at Wal-Mart, and instead relied on its own armchair psychology.[14]

THE FEMINIST JUDGMENT

Chamallas's opinion rectifies the confounding legacy of *Price Waterhouse*. The actual *Price Waterhouse* decision was progressive in admitting psychological theory into evidence, but it did not go far enough. Chamallas's opinion explores and defines what stereotyping is; acknowledges the prevalence, complexity, and danger of implicit bias; and explicitly supports the use of interdisciplinary experts to help courts grapple with these thorny issues.

One crucial difference between the feminist judgment and the original *Price Waterhouse* is that Chamallas rejects the focus on conscious intent as the touchstone of "real" discrimination. Relying on theories developed by Linda Krieger, Susan Fiske, and Chamallas herself,[15] Chamallas exposes the pretext/mixed motive differentiation as a false dichotomy, because it assumes people are self-aware. In Chamallas's view, it is much more likely that seemingly "legitimate" reasons will often be tainted by unconscious, if non-malicious, stereotyping. In contrast to the original opinion, the feminist judgment unequivocally rejects that actionable cases of gender stereotyping are limited "to instances in which the decision maker is aware that he or she is relying on a gender stereotype." Chamallas affirmatively recognizes that subconscious stereotyping is a violation of Title VII.

Chamallas also attempts to prevent the array of restrictive and conflicting "tests" created by the lower courts in the wake of the original decision. The treatment of stereotyping by many of the lower courts did not account for the nuances of bias, and is not in line with the spirit of the decision, which was to prohibit employers from allowing stereotypes to infiltrate their decision making. Chamallas's opinion, in contrast to the original, requires courts to look at the totality of a corporate culture. Chamallas's recognition of implicit bias opens a window on the subtle ways that corporate cultures still limit opportunities for women. According to Chamallas, courts should consider the context of

[14] *Wal-Mart*, 131 S. Ct. at 2545, 2553–554.
[15] *See generally* Krieger and Fiske, *supra* note 12; Martha Chamallas, Introduction to Feminist Legal Theory (3d ed. 2012); Martha Chamallas, *Deepening the Legal Understanding of Bias: On Devaluation and Biased Prototypes*, 74 *S. Cal. L. Rev.* 747–53 (2001).

the workplace, statistical evidence of implicit bias, and whether the employer has done anything to prevent stereotyping behavior, rather than fixating on sexist comments. For example, in male-dominated "token" environments like Price Waterhouse and Silicon Valley, the Chamallas decision would require courts to examine how stereotypes influence the clubby and competitive culture at the partner level. In cases like Wal-Mart, where women's representation has reached beyond token levels, Chamallas urges courts to heed expert testimony that explains how stereotypes may still be at play when managers are given complete discretion to make pay and promotion decisions. By granting probative value to scientific findings, the feminist judgment strikes a blow against allowing masculine bias in law to pass as "objectivity."

Twenty- six years after *Price Waterhouse*, the glass ceiling still exists, from big box stores to Silicon Valley.[16] We know that human beings are inherently biased and our culture has ingrained stereotypes.[17] If the law continues to ignore the pervasiveness of implicit bias, discrimination in wages, promotions, and other employment benefits are unlikely to change. Chamallas's opinion is groundbreaking because it recognizes implicit bias and encourages courts to place expert testimony about bias at the center of Title VII discrimination cases.

The research on bias is shocking, but there is a bright side. It can be used to ferret out bad behavior if, as Chamallas would, we allow it a place in discrimination cases. Spreading this knowledge among the judiciary and in the corporate world can also foster good behavior. But in order to right past wrongs, courts would have to follow Chamallas, and recognize the nexus between stereotyping about women, implicit bias, and the glass ceiling.

Price Waterhouse v. Hopkins, 490 U.S. 228 (1989)

Justice Martha Chamallas, concurring.

Ann Hopkins's bid for a partnership at Price Waterhouse, one of the nation's largest accounting firms, requires us to consider the scope of Title VII's ban on sex discrimination, 42 U.S.C. § 2000e, at a time when women are increasingly seeking to advance and attain leadership roles in male-dominated institutions and organizations. Just five years ago, we confronted a similar challenge to a denial of a partnership in a law firm and held for the first time that Title VII

[16] Jillian D'Onfro, *Ellen Pao's Best Piece of Advice for Professional Women Who Feel Like They're Hitting a Glass Ceiling*, Bus. Insider (April 6, 2015), www.businessinsider.com/ellen-pao-after-kleiner-perkins-trial-2015-4/.

[17] Stone, *supra* note 10, at 613–19, 626 (citing McGinley, *supra* note 12, at 425).

applies to the partnership selection process. *Hishon v. King & Spaulding*, 467 U.S. 69, 77–78 (1984). Today, the Court strengthens its commitment to sex equality in employment by ruling that firms must assure that such partnership decisions are not tainted by stereotypes about gender or women, even when some members of the firm couch their objections in neutral terms.

Although we deal here with a case of individual disparate treatment, we must bear in mind that any fair evaluation of a claim of sex, race, or other form of status-based employment discrimination invariably requires us to take account of the larger context in which the alleged discrimination takes place. In litigating her claim, Hopkins has highlighted her status as a "token" woman in a male-dominated workplace and has produced evidence that she was subjected to the kind of gender bias characteristic of the treatment of token women when they are evaluated by supervisors and peers in such settings.[18] Hopkins employs the term "token" in a straightforward, numerical sense to express the fact that women senior managers and women partners are rare at Price Waterhouse, as indeed they are in the other Big-8 accounting firms.[19] Although Title VII's mandate of equality has been in effect for nearly twenty-five years, it is still the case that most women are employed in predominantly female occupations and in predominantly female jobs within occupations. Ann Hopkins's case thus is embedded in the dynamics of tokenism in the workplace and in the conflict that occurs when individuals from groups that were formerly segregated into lower-status positions seek to break into the highest levels of the organization. Her case is what has become known as a "glass ceiling" case, a metaphor used to describe the invisible (glass) barriers facing women employees who can see elite positions but cannot reach them (ceiling).[20] When pioneers such as Ann Hopkins seek to surmount such barriers and pursue paths that traditionally were not open to women, this Court must guarantee that they are afforded equal treatment and an equal opportunity to succeed.

---

[18] The first published use of the term "tokenism" was by Dr. Martin Luther King in an article criticizing the slow pace of racial integration in schools and factories in the South. Martin Luther King, Jr., *The Case Against Tokenism*, N.Y. Times Mag., August 5, 1962, at 11. The term was later used by sociologists to describe the situation of groups that were dramatically underrepresented in organizational settings. *See* Rosabeth Moss Kanter, Men and Women of the Corporation 206–24 (1977).

[19] In 1988, the highest percentage of women partners in a Big-8 accounting firm was 5.6 percent. Price Waterhouse had the lowest percentage with 2 percent women. Eric N. Berg, *The Big Eight: Still a Male Bastion*, N.Y. Times, July 12, 1988, www.nytimes.com/1988/07/12/business/the-big-eight-still-a-male-bastion.html.

[20] Carol Hymowitz and Timothy D. Schellhardt, *The Glass Ceiling: Why Women Can't Seem to Break the Invisible Barrier that Blocks Them from the Top Jobs*, Wall St. J., March 24, 1986, at 1.

Ann Hopkins was a senior manager at Price Waterhouse when the firm turned down her bid for partnership. As a woman seeking partnership, Hopkins was a rarity in the firm. When Hopkins became a candidate for partner in 1982, only seven of the 662 partners at Price Waterhouse were women. All of the partners in her home office were men. *Hopkins v. Price Waterhouse*, 618 F. Supp. 1109, 1112 (D.D.C. 1985). Most significantly, Hopkins was the only woman in the group of eighty-eight persons being considered for partnership that year. *Id.* The firm demographics clearly indicate that Hopkins was a token woman in a large, intensively male-dominated organization.

Although Hopkins never complained of sex discrimination before being rejected for partner, she did encounter other sex-linked obstacles on her way towards achieving her goal of becoming a partner, both during her tenure at Price Waterhouse and before joining the firm. Like many professional women, Hopkins found it difficult to navigate the special "dual career" problems that arise when both spouses work in a professional capacity. Thus, Hopkins had previously worked for Touche Ross, another major accounting firm, where her husband was also employed. *Hopkins v. Price Waterhouse*, 825 F.2d 458, 461 (D.C. Cir. 1987). Because Touche Ross had a policy against both spouses being considered for partnership, Hopkins left that firm, making it possible for her husband to become a partner shortly thereafter. *Id.* To secure the job at Price Waterhouse, Hopkins had to obtain a waiver of a rule that barred employment of anyone whose spouse was a partner in a competing firm. *Id.* The year before she went up for partner at Price Waterhouse, however, the firm informed Hopkins that she would be ineligible to become a partner because of her husband's position. *Id.* at 461–62. At that point, Hopkins threatened to resign as senior manager and the controversy was settled only when her husband left Touche Ross to set up his own consulting firm.[21] *Id.* at 462. Once these barriers were removed, plaintiff was finally nominated for partnership by the partners in her home office. *Id.*

The partners voted on Hopkins's candidacy through a collegial, collective process, with no pre-set standards for determining how much opposition would be fatal to a given candidacy. Of the thirty-two partners who submitted

---

[21] Although Hopkins did not allege that Price Waterhouse's ban on hiring the spouse of a partner in a competing firm amounted to sex discrimination, such bans on the employment of spouses (including no-spouse rules within the same organization) likely have a disparate impact on women because of the societal pressure on women to place their husbands' careers ahead of their own. *See* Anna Giattina, Note, *Challenging No-Spouse Employment Policies as Marital Status Discrimination: A Balancing Approach*, 33 *Wayne L. Rev.* 1111, 1115 (1987) (citing Irving Kovarsky and Vern Hauck, *The No-Spouse Rule, Title VII, and Arbitration*, 32 *Lab. L.J.* 367 (1981)).

evaluations on her candidacy, thirteen supported her, eight partners opposed her, three recommended that her candidacy be placed on hold, and eight indicated that they lacked sufficient information to make a judgment. 490 U.S. at 233. That degree of opposition was enough to put Hopkins's partnership on hold. *Id.* Some months later, after she lost the support of two partners in her home office, she was advised that it was very unlikely that she would ever be admitted to the partnership. 825 F.2d at 463. Hopkins then decided to quit the firm, following the "up and out" practice at Price Waterhouse in which candidates rejected for partnership routinely resigned. *Id.* She set up her own firm and filed this suit for sex discrimination. *Id.* Ultimately, sixty-two men in the group of eighty-eight candidates received partnership offers. *Id.* at 462.

The record demonstrates that, in many respects, Hopkins was a star performer. She compiled an impressive record on tangible measures that usually matter most in the professional world. In the years before she was considered for partner, she brought in more business and billed more hours than any other person nominated for partner in that year. *Id.* Most notably, she won a $25 million contract with the Department of State that Price Waterhouse admitted was a "leading credential" for the firm when it competed for other lucrative contracts. 490 U.S. at 233. The partners in her office initially strongly supported her candidacy, and she was highly regarded by her clients. *Id.* at 234.

According to Price Waterhouse, however, Hopkins was deficient with respect to her social or interpersonal skills, particularly what some partners regarded as her overbearing personal style and harsh treatment of staff. *Id.* at 234–35. Several partners faulted her for not acting more like a lady. *Id.* at 235. During the partnership selection process, for example, a number of partners submitted written evaluation comments framed in terms of Hopkins's sex. *Id.* One partner said she needed to take a course in "charm school." 825 F.2d at 463. Others criticized her for being too "macho" and speculated that she "overcompensated for being a woman." *Id.* Some partners objected to her use of "profanity," and one of her supporters stated that he believed that the negative reaction to Hopkins stemmed from the fact that Hopkins "was a lady using foul language." *Id.* In describing Hopkins's career at the firm, one supporter noted that plaintiff "had matured from a tough-talking, somewhat masculine hard-nosed mgr. [manager] to an authoritative, formidable, but more appealing lady ptr. [partner] candidate." *Id.* The tenor of the firm's objection to her candidacy was summed up by the partner in charge of Hopkins's office who was tasked with explaining to Hopkins why she had been put on hold. *Id.* To increase her chances of making partner, he counseled Hopkins to "walk more femininely, talk more femininely, dress more femininely, wear make-up, have her hair styled, and wear jewelry." *Id.*

The record also reveals that sex stereotyping at Price Waterhouse was not confined to Hopkins's case. In prior years, one woman candidate had been criticized for trying to be too much like "one of the boys," another, because she reminded a male partner of the legendary bank robber, Ma Barker, and another, because she was typecast as a "woman's libber." *Id.* at 467. The starkest example of sexism was a comment made by a partner the year before Hopkins's evaluation who said that he "could not consider any woman seriously as a partnership candidate and believed that women were not even capable of functioning as senior managers." 490 U.S. at 236. The firm never reprimanded the partner, and his vote was recorded in Hopkins's case. *Id.*

Overall, the portrait of Ann Hopkins that emerges from the trial record is that of a non-traditional woman who disrupted gender expectations by excelling in objective (one could say, masculine) measures, such as rainmaking and billable hours, but who was regarded as lacking when it came to soft (feminine) social skills. In a very concrete way, this case tests whether the promise of equal access and equal opportunity will be realized for those exceptional and pioneering women who defy gender conventions.

As this Court is well aware, this case is not just about whether to compel one of the leading accounting firms to grant Ann Hopkins a partnership. Instead, our decision is important because the Court endorses a special mixed-motive (or "motivating factor") framework of proof designed to cover a potentially large percentage of employment discrimination cases in which it can be said that both legitimate and biased reasons caused a negative employment outcome, such as a lost job, promotion, or raise. This special framework of proof is tailored to today's workplace realities and is far preferable to the abstract, "but-for" causation test imported from tort law that the dissent would have us apply to Title VII cases. Although some judges and commentators have enlisted tort law as a guide to interpreting Title VII, we should take care not to borrow indiscriminately from that body of private law. It is worth reminding ourselves that one reason Congress felt it necessary to enact Title VII outlawing discrimination by private employers was that tort law had proven so inadequate to protect employees against manifestly unfair and discriminatory decisions. *See* Catharine A. MacKinnon, *Sexual Harassment of Working Women: A Case of Sex Discrimination* 164–74 (1979). Thus, it should come as no surprise that importing tort principles into the realm of Title VII, as the dissent would have us do, is not likely to further Title VII's twin goals of deterring discrimination and making victims of workplace discrimination whole. Title VII is more than simply a federal tort; it is a distinctive body of public law that aims to eliminate longstanding patterns of segregation, stratification, and lack of equal opportunity.

The "motivating factor" framework of proof the Court adopts today will undoubtedly be used in a myriad of future cases in which it can be said that the cause of an adverse employment action is overdetermined, in the sense that several causes (legitimate and illegitimate) contributed to the outcome and it is difficult to ascertain whether a single cause alone would have produced the same result. Given employees' limited access to proof and lack of intimate knowledge of the employers' practices and procedures, it is enough to require the employee to prove that sex was a motivating factor or played a role in the adverse decision. The employer is in a better position to prove the counterfactual in such cases, namely, to convince the court that the same decision would have been made even absent consideration of plaintiff's sex.

Equally important, today's decision makes it clear that sex stereotyping is a form of sex discrimination. For two decades, this Court has condemned sex stereotyping in constitutional cases when states have sought to justify sex-based classifications on the basis of outmoded stereotypes about women and men. See Orr v. Orr, 440 U.S. 268, 282–83 (1979); Califano v. Goldfarb, 430 U.S. 199, 215–17 (1977); Weinberger v. Wiesenfeld, 420 U.S. 636, 650–53 (1975); Frontiero v. Richardson, 411 U.S. 677, 688–91 (1973). In those cases, the Court ruled that government benefit schemes may not be premised on traditional assumptions about the roles of men and women, namely, that the man is (or should be) the "breadwinner" in a household, while the woman is (or should be) the "homemaker" responsible for performing domestic duties. The constitutional cases indicate that such "separate spheres" ideology is incompatible with the mandate of equal protection because it denies individuals the right to participate in society free of pre-conceived and often denigrating beliefs about their gender group. See Nadine Taub and Elizabeth M. Schneider, Perspectives on Women's Subordination and the Role of Law, in The Politics of Law: A Progressive Critique 124–30 (David Kairys ed., 1982).

Today we expand anti-stereotyping theory to condemn decisions by private employers motivated by stereotypical assumptions about the differing traits, talents and behaviors of the sexes or normative views about the proper (and different) roles of men and women. I wholeheartedly concur in Justice Brennan's observation that "we are beyond the day when an employer could evaluate employees by assuming or insisting that they matched the stereotype associated with their group." 490 U.S. at 251. Like the plurality, I agree "that an employer who acts on the basis of a belief that a woman cannot be aggressive, or that she must not be, has acted on the basis of gender." Id. at 250. By so explicitly tying gender stereotyping to prohibited sex discrimination under Title VII, we implement Congress's commitment "to strike at the entire spectrum of disparate treatment of men and women resulting from sex stereotypes." *City of L.A. Dep't of Water & Power v. Manhart*, 435 U.S. 702, 707 n.13 (1978).

The key role stereotyping plays in producing and perpetuating gender inequality in the workplace was addressed by plaintiff's expert in this case, Dr. Susan Fiske. Although the use of experts has become commonplace in Title VII litigation, this is the first case we have considered in which a social psychologist versed in stereotyping theory has offered her expertise regarding an employer's decision-making process. Unlike the plurality, I do not regard Dr. Fiske's testimony as mere "icing on the cake." 490 U.S. at 256. Nor am I inclined to dismiss her knowledge and insights as illegitimate or self-serving, as does the dissent. Instead, I regard Dr. Fiske's testimony as providing the district court with a psychologically informed concept of sexual stereotyping and bias that may prove valuable as we struggle to define cognate legal concepts. I value Fiske's interdisciplinary insights not for their own sake but because her body of knowledge may deepen our understanding of how actual decisions are made in the contemporary workplace. Such a deep understanding of the specific mechanisms and expressions of bias in the workplace is necessary if this Court is to remain true to its word that Title VII reaches not only blatant but subtle forms of discrimination. *See McDonnell Douglas Corp. v. Green*, 411 U.S. 792, 801 (1973).

Dr. Fiske's analysis starts by recognizing that certain workplace cultures tend either to foster or to inhibit stereotyping. For social psychologists such as Fiske, the key inquiry is whether it is likely that stereotyping has infected decision making in an organization. Fiske's focus is on the organizational level; notably, she and her colleagues do not purport to make judgments about the biased mindset of any particular individual. For Fiske, it was highly significant that Price Waterhouse was a male-dominated organization, with few women at the upper levels. The paucity of women at the firm meant that decisions were most often made by an all-male group who only rarely were called upon to judge the qualifications of a woman. Fiske explained how such skewed demographics in a firm increased the likelihood that stereotyping would occur, particularly if the firm took no overt steps to counteract it. Under such conditions of tokenism, there is a higher risk that a woman will be judged not as an individual but rather as a member of her gender group.

Dr. Fiske's expertise also enabled her to detect signs of stereotyping at Price Waterhouse. Drawing on the psychological literature, as amplified by the amicus brief filed by the American Psychological Association, Br. for American Psychological Association as Amicus Curiae in Support of Resp't (hereinafter Br. for APA), Fiske's method was to examine the comments of the partners who cast votes on Hopkins's partnership looking for evidence of two types of stereotypes: (1) descriptive stereotypes, which tell a stock or culturally familiar story about how people with certain characteristics behave and where their talents and abilities lie, and (2) prescriptive stereotypes, which tell a story about how people from a certain group should behave. *See* Br. for APA at 13–16. Beyond identifying the two types of stereotypes, the social science research that Fiske drew upon has also documented what scholars call the "double bind," i.e., the dilemma facing professional women based on an inherent conflict between socially approved views of femininity and professional competence. Br. for APA at 33–37. Thus, well-entrenched gender stereotypes cognitively associate women (and femininity) with "personal warmth, empathy, sensitivity, emotionalism, grace, charm, compliance, dependence, and deference." Nadine Taub, *Keeping Women in their Place: Stereotyping Per Se As a Form of Employment Discrimination*, 21 B.C. L. Rev. 345, 356 (1980). The contrasting gender stereotypes cognitively associate men (and masculinity) with "aggressiveness, egotism, emotional detachment, persistence, ambition and drive." *Id.* The double bind comes into play when professional women are required to display masculine attributes to be successful in their jobs, yet are penalized for being the wrong "type of woman" because they fail to conform to the feminine script. *See id.* at 356–58.

In Fiske's view, a variety of prescriptive stereotyping was likely operating at Price Waterhouse. Under her theory, the explicitly sex-based comments, detailed above, were a predictable response to Hopkins's status as a token woman who did not conform to the conventional feminine mold. Fiske's testimony thus provided Hopkins with a theory to explain why some partners might have reacted so negatively to her seemingly unfeminine behavior – why deviation from expected sex-linked behavior would be viewed as a personal shortcoming and result in a penalty.

Beyond the explicitly gender-based comments, Fiske discerned evidence of stereotyping and tokenism in the intensely hostile reaction of some partners who knew Hopkins only slightly. Opponents tended to exaggerate the negative and discount the positive. Claims were made, for example, that Hopkins was universally disliked, potentially dangerous, and likely to abuse authority. Tr. Test. of Dr. Susan Fiske, R. at 39, 55 (hereinafter "Tr. Test."). Fiske noted that the risk of stereotyping and negative reactions to an unconventional token woman was greatly facilitated by the standardless, subjective process by which partners were selected at Price Waterhouse. 618 F. Supp. at 1117–18. Although discretionary decision making is common in professional firms such as Price Waterhouse, we must recognize that exercise of such discretion makes it easier to mask or hide bias. In this case, for example, if only objective measures were used in the partnership selection process, Price Waterhouse would have had a much more difficult time explaining its decision to reject Hopkins's candidacy.

In many respects, I fully concur with Justice Brennan's thoughtful plurality opinion. I would note, however, that despite his "icing on the cake" character-ization of Dr. Fiske's testimony, the plurality opinion goes a long way toward translating and incorporating many of Fiske's insights into Title VII law.

First, I wholeheartedly agree that the *McDonnell Douglas* "pretext" model is not the sole framework of proof permissible in individual disparate treat-ment cases under Title VII. *McDonnell Douglas Corp.*, 411 U.S. at 802–05. The mixed-motives framework of proof that the Court endorses today is neces-sary to supplement the pretext model. In the most common type of "pretext" (or single-motive) case, plaintiffs will seek to prove that there is no legitimate basis for their adverse treatment and will urge the factfinder to infer, often through a process of elimination, that the real or true reason for the employer's action was race, color, sex, national origin or religion. The evidence adduced in pretext cases is most often circumstantial evidence. Rarely these days will plaintiffs be able to offer direct evidence of discrimination, i.e., "smoking gun" comments or admissions that reveal the decision maker's biased state of mind. Instead, whenever possible, plaintiffs will generally offer comparative evi-dence of discrimination, *i.e.*, evidence of similarly situated employees, outside plaintiff's racial or gender group, who were treated better than the plaintiff. In some cases, comparative evidence can serve as living proof of disparate treatment.

However, in many other discrimination cases, plaintiff will be unable to point to a sufficiently similar comparator. This is particularly true in cases involving professional employees where no two employees may perform identical tasks or work at the same level in the same department or division. Additionally, with respect to high-level positions involving a range of skills, tal-ents, and competencies, an employer can nearly always point to a dimension in which a comparator differs from the individual plaintiff.

In this case, for example, the District Court concluded that Hopkins failed to make out a pretext case under the *McDonnell Douglas* framework of proof. The court ruled that Hopkins's comparative evidence was insufficient to prove pretext because the successful male candidates Hopkins offered as comparators were not similar enough to Hopkins. Given that Hopkins's abrasive personality and asserted lack of social graces were at issue, she attempted to demonstrate that Price Waterhouse had selected male partners who were equally deficient in interpersonal skills. She produced comparative evidence of two men who had been selected as partners, even though the first man had been criticized for acting like a "Marine drill sergeant" and the second man for being "cocky," "abrasive and overbearing," and having a "wise guy attitude." Br. for Resp't at 13. However, the District Court found the cases distinguishable based on Price Waterhouse's claim that each of the male comparators possessed special skills needed by the firm. The Court did not mention why Hopkins's skill in landing a multi-million contract and her reputation for billing the most hours were not "special" enough to warrant a similarly favorable result, despite her abrasiveness. Particularly when it comes to intangible qualities, it is often difficult to persuade a court that another employee is sufficiently similar to the plaintiff. Moreover, there is a risk that gender bias may creep into the very assessment of similarity or comparability. Thus, the candidate likened to a Marine drill sergeant was also praised by a partner for being a "man's man," suggesting a willingness to excuse or discount his lack of social graces because he fit the expected masculine stereotype. Br. for Resp't at 13.

Given the difficulties associated with the availability and interpretation of comparative evidence, it is critically important that today's ruling clarifies that a plaintiff may prove discrimination through evidence of sexual stereotyping, even in the absence of comparative evidence. Thus, candidates such as Ann Hopkins who are able to show that sexual stereotyping infected the decision-making process need not always adduce living proof of a similarly situated man who was treated better. Allowing proof of discrimination via sexual stereotyping means that women employees in sex-segregated positions (where there are no male comparators), women employees in unique positions (where there are no comparable employees), and women employees in organizational settings such as Price Waterhouse where candidates are evaluated on a number of tangible and intangible factors – making comparison exceedingly difficult – will not be denied the protection of Title VII simply because no one is quite like them.

I write separately, however, to elaborate upon the meaning of the core concept of "stereotyping" and to provide guidance to the lower courts as they evaluate the legal sufficiency of evidence relating to stereotyping. The record in this case demonstrates that sexual stereotypes may operate to infect an employer's decision-making process, in violation of Title VII, even when the decision makers themselves are unaware of their own biases. Perhaps influenced by the testimony of Dr. Fiske, the trial court acknowledged that "the stereotyping by individual partners may have been unconscious on their part," but nonetheless held Price Waterhouse liable because "the maintenance of a system that gave weight to such biased criticisms was a conscious act of the partnership as a whole." 618 F. Supp. at 1119. Thus, in fashioning a claim of discrimination centered on sexual stereotyping, the district court contemplated that plaintiffs would pursue such claims – and might well prevail on their claims – even if those responsible for making the adverse decision sincerely believed that they were free of bias and did not realize that bias had distorted the decision-making process.

Unfortunately, the plurality's use of the term "stereotyping," is ambiguous, creating uncertainty that could cause confusion and potentially undercut the force of today's ruling. Thus, at one point in the plurality opinion, Justice Brennan states that gender may be said to have played "a motivating part in an employment decision" in those cases where "if we asked the employer at the moment of the decision what its reasons were, and if we received a truthful response, one of those reasons would be that the applicant or employee was a woman." 490 U.S. at 250. The import of this statement is that gender bias, motivated by gender stereotyping, cannot exist if the employer sincerely believes that gender did not play a role in the adverse action. The plurality's statement could thus be read to limit actionable cases of gender stereotyping to instances in which the decision maker is aware that he or she is relying on a gender stereotype, excluding cases in which a person harbors sex stereotypical attitudes or even utters sex-based generalizations about men and women, but (erroneously) believes that gender did not drive his or her decision in any way.

Although one can argue that Hopkins has proven the kind of conscious gender bias that the Court's statement envisions, many cases of sex-based disparate treatment will involve unconscious (or semi-conscious) gender bias and stereotyping. As Dr. Fiske explained in her testimony, unconscious stereotypes may "motivate" or "cause" a person to reach a negative judgment – in the sense that stereotypes provide a stimulus to action – even when the evaluator sincerely believes he is basing his judgment on neutral grounds. Thus, for example, a decision maker may reject an Asian American candidate with an impressive record of achievement because he cognitively associates Asians with hard work, but lack of creativity, and does not realize that his subjective assessment of the candidate is a product of a widely held descriptive stereotype about Asians rather than the individual candidate's record. In such a case, a white candidate for the position may seem to be more creative to the decision maker simply because he enters the competition without any preconceived notions about his creative abilities. The important point here is that disparate treatment fueled by unconscious stereotypes is no less injurious than disparate treatment prompted by consciously articulated stereotypes. Thus, in the gender discrimination context, it matters little whether the plaintiff is a victim of conscious or implicit bias because, in both situations, the plaintiff has been treated less favorably because of her sex and has been denied a valuable job benefit that she would have received if she were a man.

Because prescriptive and descriptive stereotypes can operate beneath the surface and may not manifest themselves in explicitly gender-based comments, I object to Justice O'Connor's insistence that discrimination plaintiffs provide "direct" evidence of bias, in the form of gender-based comments by decision makers, before they are entitled to invoke the mixed-motives framework established by the Court today. 490 U.S. at 276. It goes without saying that now that the Court has called attention to and condemned the gender-based stereotypical comments that surfaced in Price Waterhouse's partnership selection process, we can expect employers to take steps to clean up or sanitize their process, making sure they put fewer comments on the record and instructing decision makers not to refer to a plaintiff's gender in direct or indirect ways. Lest our decision today merely provide a recipe for evading Title VII liability, we should make it clear that gender-based unequal treatment – from whatever source, and however proven – violates Title VII.

At a more fundamental level, I write separately to express my view that, while I endorse the development of a new mixed-motive framework of proof under Title VII, I am of the firm belief that we should not attempt to tightly constrain the methods of proof or arguments plaintiffs offer in future cases. In real life, cases cannot be neatly separated into single-motive (or pretext) cases – where the only question is whether the employer was motivated by the employee's sex or by a legitimate, nondiscriminatory reason – and mixed-motive (or motivating factor) cases where the debate centers on the degree of causal influence exerted by the legitimate versus the illegitimate reason. Instead, in many sex discrimination cases, it simply may be impossible to tell whether the asserted nondiscriminatory reason for the employer's action is itself a product of gender bias or gender stereotyping.

Indeed, the case before us provides a good illustration of the false dichotomy between single and mixed-motive cases. For the most part, this case has been approached by the courts and the litigants as a mixed-motive case. On a strategic level, this is understandable because the District Court expressly found that Ann Hopkins's lack of social graces constituted a legitimate, non-fabricated reason for the firm's refusal to offer her a partnership. 618 F. Supp. at 1114. Thus, if Hopkins was to succeed in her Title VII action, she had to persuade the court that sex also played a role in the partnership denial and to convince the court to place the burden on the employer to prove that it would have made the same decision even if she were a man, an evidentiary burden Price Waterhouse was unable to shoulder. Viewed as a mixed-motive case, Hopkins has won, primarily because she was able to offer explicitly gender-based comments made by decision makers proximate to the time the decision was made.

However, in my view there is another, more instructive way of approaching Hopkins's case. On this record, it is far from clear that the partners' perceptions of Hopkins as lacking in social graces and as having an abrasive personality qualify as legitimate, nondiscriminatory reasons for the partnership denial. Instead, Hopkins has made a convincing case that these perceptions themselves were tainted by sexual stereotyping, thereby undercutting the categorization of this case as a mixed-motive case. Thus, if the purportedly legitimate reasons cannot be said to be free of sex bias, we are then left with only sex-based reasons for the adverse decision.

Central to understanding why these apparently legitimate reasons may be tainted by gender bias is the testimony and approach of Dr. Fiske. Rather than focusing on abstract concepts of motive or causation to determine what happened at Price Waterhouse, Fiske placed paramount importance on the structural features of the workplace at Price Waterhouse, particularly the fact that Hopkins was a token woman in a large organization. Tr. Test. at 26–7. Fiske explained how this condition of rarity can have a significant impact on how a person is viewed within a given organization, describing what psychologists call selective perception. In line with gender stereotypes, many people expect token individuals to fit preconceived views regarding traits of the group (e.g., that women are more caring and nurturing than men) and are apt to scrutinize women more closely on feminine dimensions such as interpersonal skills and personality. Id. at 31. It does not take an expert to appreciate that women, in the professions and in other settings, are often noticed and rated on a scale applied to women only, focusing selectively on their style of dress, their appearance, their social graces, and other traits not directly linked to their ability to perform the job. The phenomenon of selective perception described by Fiske can easily translate into disparate treatment, given that men are not as likely to be judged negatively because of their lack of social graces, allowing even a "man's man" to be blunt and assertive and yet still make partner.

This kind of biased attention can be particularly harmful to a woman such as Ann Hopkins who acts counter to the stereotype. When highly visible individuals defy expectations, they often elicit intensely negative reactions from some people in the organization. In this case, for example, several partners had an intensely negative view of Hopkins even though they had had little personal contact with her, suggesting a predisposition against a woman being aggressive or forceful. Most tellingly, the very same traits that elicited a negative reaction by some were viewed by others as acceptable, even laudable. Thus, supporters viewed Hopkins as "outspoken, sells her own ability, independent, [has] the courage of her convictions," Tr. Test. at 37, while detractors found her "over-bearing, arrogant, abrasive, runs over people, implies she knows more than anyone in the world about anything and is not afraid to let anyone know it." *Id.* at 64. At the very least, this split image of Hopkins made it very difficult to ascertain the accuracy of differing partners' evaluation of her personality.

In her testimony, Fiske also explained how token women in male-dominated organizations are liable to be slotted into role traps that mimic patterns associated with women outside the workplace, such as mother, little sister, seductress, or militant. Tr. Test. at 31. Once an individual is so typecast, her behavior is more likely to be perceived as fitting the preconceived role, creating a tendency to view that person through such a distorted lens. Thus, there is a tendency to characterize "mixed" behavior (tough and assertive, yet warm and funny) as being all of one type (tough and assertive), suppressing the interpretation that does not fit the preconceived role. In this respect, the personality of the token individual is very much a social construct, the majority's distorted image of the individual, with little room for individuality or diversity within the token group. Given her token status, it is possible that Hopkins was typecast as a militant and that the softer side of her personality was obscured by a preconceived view of Hopkins as hard-nosed, abrasive and aggressive. Certainly the advice given to Hopkins – to soften her style by dressing and talking more femininely – suggests that some partners believed that perceptions of Hopkins might change if her appearance changed and that there was nothing inalterable or deep seated about her personality that made her unfit for a partnership at Price Waterhouse.

Given the dynamics of tokenism, the split view of Hopkins by the partners at Price Waterhouse was likely not simply a function of the slice of Hopkins's behavior that each individual evaluator had witnessed. Nor can we be confident that the collective assessment of Hopkins as competent, but also rude and abrasive, was fair and accurate. Instead, even with all the evidence in, the "real" Ann Hopkins does not clearly emerge simply from putting the pieces together. One lesson we can learn from this case is that when gender stereotyping and unconscious bias color perceptions, it is exceedingly difficult to discover the objective truth about an individual. In the final analysis, it may be impossible to separate Hopkins's "real" personality from the environment in which she worked.

In this case, however, what we do know is that Price Waterhouse did nothing to decrease the chances that gender bias and gender stereotyping would infect its decision-making process. It did not reprimand the partner who openly voiced his opposition to women joining the ranks of partner. It did not instruct the partners that each candidate should be judged on his or her performance or merit, rather than on sex-linked traits, such as social graces or personal appearance. It did nothing to limit possible abuse of discretion by partners, for example, by specifying with some precision the criteria to be used in the partnership decision and seeking the partners' assessment of the candidates only on those measures. Perhaps most importantly, it did not take any steps to ensure that the few women who served as senior managers, such as Ann Hopkins, had a clear path for advancement and an opportunity to remedy any perceived shortcomings before they went up for partner.

In my view, this is an easy Title VII case. Simply put, Ann Hopkins deserved to win her suit because she handily met and exceeded the objective, performance-based measures of success – she proved her ability to attract clients, to generate billable hours, and to handle major projects for the firm. As a token woman in the firm, she also presented compelling evidence that she was vulnerable to sex bias and sexual stereotyping, bias that surfaced in the written comments of several partners during the selection process. Because Price Waterhouse did nothing to inhibit or counteract stereotyping in its organization, it cannot now rely on subjective assessments of the personality of a female candidate to justify its adverse decision, particularly given the high risk that such assessments are themselves tainted by sexual bias.

I concur separately today to underscore my view that Title VII plaintiffs should be able to make out a viable claim for sex stereotyping not only in mixed-motive cases where proof of sex stereotyping is used to discharge the plaintiff's initial burden of proving that sex was a "motivating factor" in a decision based on legitimate and discriminatory reasons, but also in other types of discrimination cases in which the employer's asserted "legitimate" reason may itself be tainted by impermissible sex stereotypes. Additionally, I would adopt a psychologically informed definition of stereotyping for use in Title VII cases that encompasses commonly held descriptive and normative generalizations about a group, whether those beliefs are explicitly stated by decision makers, through direct evidence of gender-based or sexist comments, or simply can be inferred from the fact that an exceptional candidate from an underrepresented group has been rejected by an organization which lacks diversity and has done little to minimize the risk of stereotyping in its organization. Our decision today should alert employers that they are responsible for taking steps to assure that neither conscious nor unconscious stereotyping distorts the processes by which they select and make key decisions about their employees, including monitoring and structuring discretionary decisions to focus on job-related criteria, skills and performance.

Undoubtedly, we will be called upon in the future to decide more difficult cases, in which women are denied advancement in gender-integrated settings or are judged deficient on performance-based, objective measures that tend to favor male candidates. In such cases, plaintiffs will likely be required to point to a different set of organizational features or individual facts to convince the factfinder that they have been subjected to disparate treatment because of their sex. Today, we have the relatively easy task of declaring that Title VII prohibits an employer from denying an exceptional candidate the opportunity to ascend to the highest ranks of her profession simply because some members of her firm judged her not feminine enough for their tastes.

19

Commentary on *Planned Parenthood of Southeastern Pennsylvania v. Casey*

Macarena Sáez

After *Roe v. Wade*,[1] the polarization of supporters and detractors of the right to abortion resulted in both legislative restrictions on abortion and legal battles to protect *Roe*. The U.S. Supreme Court had several opportunities to revisit *Roe*, and each time the Court upheld it, albeit weakening its foundations.[2] Between 1988 and 1989 Pennsylvania's legislature passed five amendments to the Pennsylvania Abortion Control Act of 1982. The provisions required that women must give express consent and receive specific information at least 24 hours prior to the procedure; underage girls must obtain parental consent or judicial authorization; married women must sign a statement indicating that they had notified their husbands; and abortion clinics must comply with a series of reporting requirements. In *Planned Parenthood of Southeastern Pennsylvania v. Casey*, the U.S. Supreme Court upheld all but the spousal notification requirement.[3] It even reversed sections of prior decisions to uphold the information and waiting-period requirements.[4]

Casey came as a surprise to conservatives and liberals.[5] It reaffirmed *Roe*, clarifying what the majority viewed as its "essential holding": (1) recognition of the right to choose an abortion before viability without undue interference from the State; (2) "confirmation of the State's power to restrict abortions after fetal viability," with limited exceptions; and (3) recognition of a state interest from the outset of the pregnancy in "protecting the health of the woman and

---

[1] *Roe v. Wade*, 410 U.S. 113 (1973).

[2] E.g., *Akron v. Akron Ctr. for Reprod. Health, Inc.*, 462 U.S. 416 (1983); *Thornburgh v. American Coll. of Obstetricians & Gynecologists*, 476 U.S. 747 (1986); *Webster v. Reprod. Health Servs.*, 492 U.S. 490 (1989). *Roe*, 41 U.S. 113, was decided 7–2; *Akron*, 462 U.S. 416, was a 6–3 decision; *Thornburgh*, 476 U.S. 747, and *Webster*, 492 U.S. 490, were decided 5–4.

[3] *Planned Parenthood of Se. Pa. v. Casey*, 505 U.S. 833 (1992).

[4] See id. at 870, 882–87 (referring to *Akron*, 462 U.S. 416, and *Thornburgh*, 476 U.S. 747).

[5] As Lawrence H. Tribe stated, both sides felt defeated by the decision. Lawrence H. Tribe, Abortion: The Clash of Absolutes 244 (1992).

the life of the fetus that may become a child."[6] *Casey* relaxed *Roe's* standard
of review by moving from strict scrutiny to "undue burden." Under the new
standard, the means chosen by states to further their interest in potential life
pre-viability "must be calculated to inform the woman's free choice, not hinder it."[7] Given that *Casey* upheld all but the spousal notification, the bar for
what constitutes a "substantial obstacle" was left very high. *Casey* also ended
the trimester system, and viability became the dividing line between women's
liberty to choose and the right of a state to ban abortions. As a result, the time-
frame during which women have access to abortion is more uncertain than
Roe envisioned.[8]

Although in practice *Casey* reduced women's opportunities to access safe
abortions by giving more deference to states' interest in potential life, parts of
its reasoning supported women's citizenship and equality, something *Roe* did
not do. Most post-*Casey* decisions, however, have not advanced arguments
on citizenship and equality and have reduced the opportunities for women to
obtain safe abortions.

One important feminist legal method is what Katharine Bartlett has called
"asking the woman question," or examining how women have been disadvantaged by or absent from the law.[9] Although *Casey* formally upheld *Roe*,
it did not center on the experience of women affected by Pennsylvania's
abortion restrictions. The "woman question," if present, was answered by
contemplating a mythical woman with unlimited human and economic
resources, with no disabilities, no connections to anyone, and no responsibilities. For *that* woman, very few burdens would be so substantial as to
prevent her from accessing abortion. The only instance in which the *Casey*
court referred to specific women was in discussing the spousal consent provision, which it struck down because of the risk imposed on women who could
suffer domestic violence.

Writing a re-imagined majority opinion as Justice Pruitt, Professor Lisa
Pruitt places actual women at the center of her reasoning. Her feminist opinion reaffirms *Roe*, striking down all amendments to the Pennsylvania Abortion
Control Act. Pruitt uses strict scrutiny instead of the undue burden standard,
and she maintains *Roe's* trimester system. Her opinion overall rejects *Casey's*
premise that women's liberty and states' interest in potential life should be

[6] *Casey*, 505 U.S. at 846.
[7] *Id.* at 877.
[8] Restrictions based on viability may target pregnancies even at 19 weeks. Bonnie Hope Arzuaga and Ben Hokew Lee, *Limits of Human Viability in the United States: A Medicolegal Review*, 128 *Pediatrics* 1047, 1051 (2011).
[9] *See generally* Katharine T. Bartlett, *Feminist Legal Methods*, 103 *Harv. L. Rev.* 829 (1990).

afforded equal weight. Using Justice Blackmun's reasoning, Pruitt maintains that a state's interest in protecting fetal life is not grounded in the Constitution and can only be justified on pragmatic or humanitarian grounds. Given its weak source, this interest merely allows a minimal intervention on the rights of women to choose an abortion.

Pruitt intentionally incorporates verbatim parts of Justices Stevens' and Blackmun's separate opinions, some parts of the majority's opinion and some parts of the District Court's opinion. For example, she adopts Justice Stevens' discussion of the 24-hour waiting period; and she incorporates Justice Blackmun's explanation of the balance between the state's interest and women's interest, his support of strict scrutiny, his argument that the state interest is not grounded in the Constitution, and the unconstitutionality of mandatory reporting. Pruitt also adopts the majority reasoning on the risk of domestic violence in cases of spousal notification and the District Court's arguments on the 24-hour waiting period. Her opinion, however, is unique because it looks at the lives of actual women. She writes that the issue is "the fundamental rights of millions of women in Pennsylvania." Pruitt does not refer to "women" as if all women in every place were subject to the same constraints when faced with the same restrictions. She analyzes how abortion restrictions impact differently rural, poor, and Native American women.

Pruitt strikes down the waiting period and informed consent requirement after considering who would be harmed by these restrictions. Her focus on concrete women leaves no doubt that a 24-hour waiting period makes access to abortion almost impossible for women who live far from abortion clinics, do not have the economic means, rely on public transportation, or have no job flexibility. In the case of spousal notification, as *Casey* acknowledged, the relevant group is married women who may suffer domestic violence. Pruitt recognizes the risks of analyzing a restriction based on whether it affects the "majority" or a "large percentage" of women. The original *Casey* decision referred to this problem but it missed the opportunity to establish a better standard. The feminist judgment does not establish a percentage of women needed for a statute to become facially unconstitutional but it strongly rejects the use of large percentages to determine constitutionality. The most vulnerable groups are unlikely to be significant enough to become a "large percentage" of women.

The most original part of Pruitt's opinion comes from her analysis of rural women in Pennsylvania. This section of her opinion explains the concrete reality of women with whom most people living in urban centers, including judges, are unfamiliar. Through her opinion, readers can understand the burdens of rural women trying to access abortion procedures.

One similarity between this judgment and the original *Casey* opinion is the use of viability as the moment when the state interest becomes compelling enough to restrict and even ban most abortions. A less pragmatic feminist decision might have avoided the use of a medical term to determine the moment women lose control over their bodily integrity. *Casey*, however, was decided at a delicate moment when pressures to overturn *Roe* were dangerously strong. Pruitt's judgment reflects her sense that it was important to maintain as much of *Roe*'s reasoning as possible. Viability, therefore, acts as a compromise that keeps *Roe*'s trimester system in place, giving women a few more weeks of unrestricted access to abortion.

The original opinion in *Casey* referred in several passages to bodily integrity as tied to *Roe*, but it used *Roe* only to strike down the spousal notification requirement.[10] Pruitt, instead, borrows Justice Blackmun's words to stress the harm of abortion restrictions to women's bodily integrity. She refers to "compelled continuation of a pregnancy" and the right to control one's person without interference.[11] Taking this statement seriously inevitably reduces the freedom of states to hinder women's access to abortion. Pruitt replicates Justice Stevens' feminist assertion that the "authority to make such traumatic and yet empowering decisions is an element of basic human dignity."[12] Pruitt also includes Justice Blackmun's equal protection reference, missing in *Casey*'s majority opinion. Her argument about rural and poor women might have been the springboard for an equal protection analysis. Although not pursued, the opinion leaves the door open for future decisions to expand on the issue of equal protection. Such analysis in *Casey*'s original majority opinion might have allowed the success of equal protection arguments dismissed by other courts in later cases.[13]

Pruitt's judgment keeps *Roe* formally and substantially in place. While *Casey* balanced the constitutional right to bodily integrity and the state interest in fetal life, this feminist judgment reinforces the preeminence of constitutional rights over state interests not grounded in the Constitution. Pruitt's conclusions are not based on the impact of the restrictions on women as if there were one model that fits all. They provide a method of legal reasoning that judges should use more often, thinking of laws' burdens from the perspective of those who suffer on account of a particular restriction. That requires a complex analysis, on

---

[10]   See *Planned Parenthood of Se. Pa. v. Casey*, 505 U.S. 833, 835, 838, 857 (1992).

[11]   *Id.* at 927 (Blackmun, J., concurring in part, concurring in the judgment in part, and dissenting in part).

[12]   *Id.* at 916 (Stevens, J., concurring in part and dissenting in part).

[13]   E.g., *Planned Parenthood of Mid-Missouri & E. Kan., Inc. v. Dempsey*, 167 F.3d 458, 464–65 (8th Cir. 1999); *Tucson Women's Clinic v. Eden*, 379 F.3d 531, 543–44 (9th Cir. 2004).

a case-by-case basis, where the target group is not just women, but individuals situated in a particular context. Pruitt's argument is compelling: "Pennsylvania regulations do not fall with equal measure upon rich and poor" and she refuses "to adopt middle class and affluent women as a norm."

It is unclear how the political scenario would have changed if this opinion had been *Casey's* majority. The feeling after *Casey* of being "one Justice away" from overturning *Roe* fueled the 1992 presidential election.[14] A feminist judgment may have energized more conservative masses, perhaps changing the course of the presidential election, creating an even more complex scenario for women in later cases. Elections, however, are decided on several factors and a feminist decision may have not been enough to change the course of political history. In any case, it would have resulted in a stronger protection of women. Pruitt's decision would have left no doubt that states' interest in potential life could not supersede women's liberty. *Casey* declared that any regulation creating a structural mechanism to "express profound respect for the life of the unborn" was permissible as long as it did not impose a substantial burden.[15] The lack of concrete analysis, however, made almost any obstacle unsubstantial.

Pruitt's opinion would have changed the course of many post-*Casey* decisions. It would have been impossible for a court to affirm *Casey* and uphold regulations imposing medically unnecessary requirements for drug-induced abortions, and Targeted Regulation of Abortion Providers laws (TRAP).[16] While new cases keep testing the undue burden criteria based on a mythical "ideal woman," more than forty-four states have passed some form of TRAP laws seriously reducing access to abortion to women with real budgets, real dependents, and real limitations. A feminist opinion in 1992 would have given true meaning to women's constitutional right to bodily integrity.

Planned Parenthood of Southeastern Pennsylvania v. Casey, 505 U.S. 833 (1992)

Justice Lisa R. Pruitt delivered the opinion of the Court.

At issue in this case are the fundamental rights of millions of Pennsylvania women. Several provisions of the Pennsylvania Abortion Control Act of 1982,

---

[14] William Schneider, *The Battle for Saliency: The Abortion Issue in This Campaign*, The Atlantic Online (Oct. 1992) www.theatlantic.com/politics/abortion/batt.htm.

[15] *Planned Parenthood of Se. Pa. v. Casey*, 505 U.S. 833, 877 (1992).

[16] E.g., *Planned Parenthood Sw. Ohio Region v. DeWine*, 696 F.3d 490 (6th Cir. 2012); *Greenville Women's Clinic v. Comm'r, S.C. Dep't of Health & Envtl. Control*, 317 F.3d 357 (4th Cir. 2002); *Women's Health Ctr. of W. Cty., Inc. v. Webster*, 871 F.2d 1377 (8th Cir. 1989); *Planned Parenthood of Greater Tex. Surgical Health Servs. v. Abbott*, 748 F.3d 583 (5th Cir. 2014).

as amended in 1988 and 1989 ("the Act"), threaten the rights and health of Pennsylvania's reproductive-age female population. We strike these provisions as unconstitutional and contrary to the fundamental right to privacy and our holding in *Roe v. Wade*.

We consider the following provisions of the Act: (1) Unless certain exceptions apply, a married woman seeking an abortion must sign a statement indicating that she has notified her husband of her intended abortion. 18 Pa. Cons. Stat. § 3209 (1989). (2) A woman seeking an abortion must give informed consent prior to the abortion procedure, and she must be provided with certain information at least 24 hours before the abortion is performed, which results in a minimum delay of 24 hours before the abortion can be performed. *Id.* § 3205. (3) For a minor to obtain an abortion, the informed consent of one of her parents is required, although a judicial bypass option is available for a minor who does not wish to or cannot obtain a parent's consent. *Id.* § 3206. The Act exempts compliance with these three requirements in the event of a "medical emergency." *Id.* §§ 3203, 3205(a), 3206(a), 3209(c). (4) Finally, the Act imposes certain reporting requirements on facilities that provide abortion services. *Id.* §§ 3207(b), 3214(a), 3214(f).

Petitioners are five abortion clinics and one physician representing himself and a class of physicians who provide abortion services. Before any of the Pennsylvania provisions took effect, these Petitioners brought this suit seeking declaratory and injunctive relief. The Petitioners challenge each provision of the Act as unconstitutional on its face. The District Court entered a preliminary injunction against the enforcement of the regulations and, after a three-day bench trial, held all provisions unconstitutional and entered a permanent injunction against Pennsylvania's enforcement of them. *Planned Parenthood of Se. Pa. v. Casey*, 744 F. Supp. 1323, 1325, 1396–97 (E.D. Pa. 1990). The Court of Appeals for the Third Circuit affirmed in part and reversed in part, upholding all of the regulations except the spousal notification requirement. *Planned Parenthood of Se. Pa. v. Casey*, 947 F.2d 682, 687 (3d. Cir. 1991). We granted certiorari.

We affirm in part and reverse in part.

I

This Court today reaffirms that the Constitution protects a woman's right to terminate her pregnancy in its early stages. Today, no less than yesterday, the Constitution and decisions of this Court require that a state's abortion restrictions be subjected to the strictest of judicial scrutiny. Under this standard, all challenged provisions of the Pennsylvania Act must be invalidated.

We today reaffirm the long recognized rights of privacy and bodily integrity. "No right is held more sacred, or is more carefully guarded by the common law, than the right of every individual to the possession and control of his own person, free from all restraint or interference of others ... " *Union Pac. Ry. Co. v. Botsford*, 141 U.S. 250, 251 (1891). Throughout this century, this Court also has held that the fundamental right of privacy protects citizens against governmental intrusion in such intimate family matters as procreation, childrearing, marriage, and contraceptive choice. Personal decisions that profoundly affect bodily integrity, identity, and destiny should be largely beyond the reach of government. *See Eisenstadt v. Baird*, 405 U.S. 438, 453 (1972). In *Roe v. Wade*, this Court correctly applied these principles to a woman's right to choose abortion. 410 U.S. 113, 169–70 (1973).

State restrictions on abortion violate a woman's right of privacy in two ways. First, compelled continuation of a pregnancy infringes upon a woman's right to bodily integrity by imposing substantial physical intrusions and significant risks of physical harm. During pregnancy, women experience dramatic physical changes and a wide range of health consequences. Labor and delivery pose additional health risks and physical demands. Restrictive abortion laws thus force women to endure physical invasions far more substantial than those this Court has held to violate the constitutional principle of bodily integrity. *See, e.g., Winston v. Lee*, 470 U.S. 753, 766 (1985) (finding that state may not compel a murder suspect to undergo surgical removal of bullet in search for evidence); *Rochin v. California*, 342 U.S. 165, 172–74 (1952) (finding that police violated plaintiff's due process rights when they required his stomach to be pumped in order to obtain suspected drugs).

Further, when the state restricts a woman's right to terminate her pregnancy, it deprives a woman of the right to make her own decisions about reproduction and family planning – critical life choices that this Court long has deemed central to the right to privacy. The decision to terminate or continue a pregnancy has no less an impact on a woman's life than decisions about contraception or marriage. *See Roe*, 410 U.S. at 152–53. Because motherhood has a dramatic impact on a woman's educational prospects, employment opportunities, and self-determination, restrictive abortion laws deprive her of basic control over her life. For these reasons, "[t]he decision whether or not to beget or bear a child" lies at "the very heart of this cluster of constitutionally protected choices." *Carey v. Population Servs. Int'l*, 431 U.S. 678, 685 (1977).

A state's restrictions on a woman's right to terminate her pregnancy also implicate constitutional guarantees of gender equality. State restrictions on abortion compel women to continue pregnancies they otherwise might terminate. By restricting the right to terminate pregnancies, the state forces women to continue pregnancies, suffer the pain of childbirth, and in most instances, provide years of maternal care. The state assumes that women owe this duty as a matter of course. This assumption – that women can simply be forced to accept the "natural" status and incidents of motherhood – appears to rest upon a conception of women's role that has triggered the Equal Protection Clause. *See, e.g., Miss. Univ. for Women v. Hogan*, 458 U.S. 718, 724–26 (1982); *Craig v. Boren*, 429 U.S. 190, 198–99 (1976).[17] These assumptions about women's place in society are no longer consistent with our understanding of the family, the individual, or the Constitution.

The Court has held that limitations on the right of privacy are permissible only if they survive "strict" constitutional scrutiny – that is, only if the governmental entity imposing the restriction can demonstrate that the limitation is both necessary and narrowly tailored to serve a compelling governmental interest. *Griswold v. Connecticut*, 381 U.S. 479, 485–86 (1965). We have applied this principle specifically in the context of abortion regulations. *Roe*, 410 U.S. at 155. To say that restrictions on a right are subject to strict scrutiny is not to say that the right is absolute. Regulations will be upheld if they have no significant impact on the woman's exercise of her right and are justified by important state health objectives. *See, e.g., Planned Parenthood of Cent. Mo. v. Danforth*, 428 U.S. 52, 65–7, 79–81 (1976) (upholding requirements of a woman's written consent and record-keeping). But we today reaffirm the essential principle of *Roe* that a woman has the right to choose to have an abortion before viability and to obtain it without undue interference from the state. Under *Roe*, any interference that is more than *de minimis* is an undue burden and therefore unconstitutional.

Roe implemented these principles through a framework that was designed to ensure that the woman's right to choose *must* not become so subordinate to the state's interest in promoting fetal life that her choice exists in theory but not in fact. *Roe* identified two relevant state interests: an "interest in preserving and protecting the health of the pregnant woman" and an "interest in protecting the potentiality of human life." 410 U.S. at 162. With respect to the state's interest in the health of the mother, "the 'compelling' point ... is at approximately the end of the first trimester," because this is the point when the mortality rate

---

[17] A growing number of commentators are recognizing this point. *See, e.g.*, Reva Siegel, *Reasoning from the Body: A Historical Perspective on Abortion Regulation and Questions of Equal Protection*, 44 Stan. L. Rev. 261, 350–80 (1992); Cass R. Sunstein, *Neutrality in Constitutional Law (With Special Reference to Pornography, Abortion, and Surrogacy)*, 92 Colum. L. Rev. 1, 31–44 (1992); Catharine A. MacKinnon, *Reflections on Sex Equality Under Law*, 100 Yale L.J. 1281, 1308–24 (1991); *cf.* Jed Rubenfeld, *The Right of Privacy*, 102 Harv. L. Rev. 737, 788–91 (1989) (similar analysis under the rubric of privacy).

in abortion approaches that in childbirth. *Id.* at 163. "With respect to the State's ... interest in potential life, the 'compelling' point is at viability" because it is at this point that the fetus "presumably has the capability of meaningful life outside the mother's womb." *Id.* In order to fulfill the requirement of narrow tailoring, "the State is obligated to make a reasonable effort to limit the effect of its regulations to the period [when] ... its health interest will be furthered." *Akron v. Akron Ctr. for Reprod. Health, Inc.*, 462 U.S. 416, 434 (1983).

This analytical framework is as warranted now as when seven members of this Court adopted it in *Roe*. Strict scrutiny of state limitations on reproductive choice still offers the most secure protection of the woman's right to make her own reproductive decisions. No majority of this Court has ever agreed upon an alternative approach. The factual premises of the trimester framework have not been undermined, *see Webster v. Reprod. Servs.*, 492 U.S. 490, 553–54 (1989) (Blackmun, J., concurring in part and dissenting in part), and the *Roe* framework is far easier to administer and far more difficult to manipulate than alternative standards proposed by Pennsylvania and by others.

Roe held that an abortion is not "the termination of life entitled to Fourteenth Amendment protection," *Roe*, 410 U.S. at 159, and no member of this Court – nor for that matter, the Solicitor General – has ever questioned that holding. Accordingly, a state's interest in protecting fetal life is not grounded in the Constitution. It also cannot be grounded in a theological or sectarian interest, lest it run afoul of the Establishment Clause. *See Thornburgh v. Am. Coll. of Obstetricians & Gynecologists*, 476 U.S. 747, 778 (1986) (Stevens, J., concurring). The interest in fetal life is instead grounded in humanitarian or pragmatic concerns.

The question then is how best to accommodate the state's minimal interest given the constitutional liberties of pregnant women. *Roe*'s trimester framework does not ignore the state's interest in prenatal life. The state may take steps to ensure that a woman's choice is thoughtful and informed, but serious questions arise when a state attempts to persuade the woman to choose childbirth over abortion. The state may not impose its own views upon a woman's most personal deliberations.

In sum, *Roe*'s requirement of strict scrutiny, as implemented through a trimester framework, must not be disturbed. No other approach is more protective of the woman's fundamental constitutional right in relation to the state's very limited interest in potential life. Application of the strict scrutiny standard results in the invalidation of all the challenged provisions. Indeed, this Court has invalidated virtually identical provisions in prior cases, and *stare decisis* requires that we again strike them down.

We turn now to the Act's specific provisions.

II

SPOUSAL NOTIFICATION REQUIREMENT

Section 3209 of Pennsylvania's abortion law provides that, except in cases of medical emergency, "no physician shall perform an abortion on a married woman" without receiving a signed statement from the woman that "she has notified her spouse that she is about to undergo an abortion." 18 Pa. Cons. Stat. § 3209 (1989). The woman has the option of providing an alternative signed statement certifying that her husband is not the man who impregnated her; that her husband could not be located; that the pregnancy is the result of spousal sexual assault which she has reported; or that the woman believes that notifying her husband will cause him or someone else to inflict bodily injury upon her. A physician who performs an abortion on a married woman without receiving the appropriate signed statement will have his or her license revoked and is liable to the husband for damages.

The District Court heard the testimony of numerous expert witnesses and made detailed findings of fact regarding the effect of this statute. These findings included:

> 279. The 'bodily injury' exception could not be invoked by a married woman whose husband, if notified, would, in her reasonable belief, threaten to (a) publicize her intent to have an abortion to family, friends or acquaintances; (b) retaliate against her in future child custody or divorce proceedings; (c) inflict psychological intimidation or emotional harm upon her, her children or other persons; (d) inflict bodily harm on other persons such as children, family members or other loved ones; or (e) use his control over finances to deprive of necessary monies for herself or her children ...
>
> 283. The required filing of the spousal consent form would require plaintiff-clinics to change their counseling procedures and force women to reveal their most intimate decision-making on pain of criminal sanctions. The confidentiality of these revelations could not be guaranteed, since the woman's records are not immune from subpoena.
>
> 284. Women of all class levels, educational backgrounds, and racial, ethnic and religious groups are battered ...
>
> 287. Battering can often involve a substantial amount of sexual abuse, including marital rape and sexual mutilation ...
>
> 289. Mere notification of pregnancy is frequently a flashpoint for battering and violence within the family ...
>
> 290. Secrecy typically shrouds abusive families. Family members are instructed not to tell anyone, especially police or doctors, about the abuse

and violence. Battering husbands often threaten their wives or her children with further abuse if she tells an outsider of the violence[.]

> 744 F. Supp. 1323, 1360–62 (E.D. Pa. 1990) (citations omitted).

The District Court found that women qualifying for an exception to the spousal notification requirement would not likely invoke the exception because they would not understand its relevance or because practical reasons would deter them from doing so.

> 294. A woman in a shelter or a safe house unknown to her husband is not 'reasonably likely' to have bodily harm inflicted upon her by her batterer[;] however her attempt to notify her husband pursuant to section 3209 could accidentally disclose her whereabouts to her husband. Her fear of future ramifications would be realistic under the circumstances.
>
> 295. Marital rape is rarely discussed with others or reported to law enforcement authorities, and of those reported only few are prosecuted.
>
> 296. It is common for battered women to have sexual intercourse with their husbands to avoid being battered. While this type of coercive sexual activity would be spousal sexual assault as defined by the Act, many women may not consider it to be so and others would fear disbelief.
>
> 297. The marital rape exception to section 3209 cannot be claimed by women who are victims of coercive sexual behavior other than penetration[;] ... further ... many ... women may be psychologically unable to discuss or report the rape for several years after the incident.
>
> 744 F. Supp. at 1362 (citations omitted).

These findings are supported by studies of domestic violence. A summary of the recent research published by the American Medical Association (AMA) indicates that approximately two million women are the victims of severe assaults by their male partners each year. A 1985 survey of women revealed that nearly one in every eight husbands had assaulted their wives during the past year. The AMA views these figures as "marked underestimates" because the nature of these incidents discourages women from reporting them, and because surveys typically exclude the very poor, those who do not speak English well, and women who are homeless or in institutions or hospitals when the survey is conducted. According to the AMA, "[r]esearchers [on family violence] agree that the true incidence of partner violence is probably *double* the above estimates; or four million severely assaulted women per year. Studies on prevalence suggest that from one-fifth to one-third of all women will be physically assaulted by a partner or ex-partner during their lifetime." AMA Council on Scientific Affairs, *Violence Against Women* 7 (1991) (emphasis in original). Nearly 11,000 U.S. women are severely assaulted by their male partners on an average day, and many such incidents involve sexual assault. *Id.* at 3–4.

Other studies complete this troubling picture. Physical violence is only the most visible form of abuse. Psychological abuse, particularly forced social and economic isolation of women, is also common. *See* Lenore E. Walker, *The Battered Woman Syndrome* 27–8 (1984). Many victims of domestic violence remain with their abusers, perhaps because they perceive or have no better alternative. *See* Benigno E. Aguirre, *Why Do They Return? Abused Wives in Shelters*, 30 J. Nat'l Ass'n Soc. Workers 350, 352 (1985). Many abused women who find temporary refuge in shelters return to their husbands, in large part because they have no other source of income. *Id.*

The limited research that has been conducted about notifying one's husband of an abortion also supports the District Court's findings of fact. The vast majority of women notify their male partners of their decision to obtain an abortion. Where the husband is the father, the primary reason women do not notify their husbands is that the husband and wife are experiencing marital difficulties, often accompanied by violence. *See* Barbara Ryan and Eric Plutzer, *When Married Women Have Abortions: Spousal Notification and Marital Interaction*, 51 J. Marriage & Fam. 41, 45–46 (1989).

This information and the District Court's findings reinforce what common sense suggests. In well-functioning marriages, spouses discuss important intimate decisions such as whether to bear a child, but millions of women in this country are not in well-functioning marriages. Many women are the victims of regular physical and psychological abuse at the hands of their husbands. Should these women become pregnant, they may have very good reasons for not wishing to inform their husbands of their decision to obtain an abortion. Many have a reasonable fear that notifying their husbands will provoke further instances of abuse of themselves or their children, yet these women will not enjoy an exemption from section 3209's notification requirement. Many will fear devastating forms of psychological abuse from their husbands, including verbal harassment, threats of future violence, the destruction of possessions, physical confinement to the home, the withdrawal of financial support, or the disclosure of the abortion to family and friends. This psychological abuse may act as even more of a deterrent to notification than the possibility of physical violence, but women who are the victims of this kind of abuse are not exempt from section 3209's notification requirement. And many women who are pregnant as a result of sexual assault by their husbands will be unable to avail themselves of the exception for spousal sexual assault because of the requirement that the woman has notified law enforcement, which in turn triggers notice of that report to her husband.

The spousal notification requirement would thus impose more than a *de minimis* burden – and therefore an undue one – on the privacy rights of a significant number of women. We must not ignore the plight – or the rights – of these women.

These cases are distinguishable from those involving a living child raised by both parents. In those cases, the parents' interests in a child's welfare are presumptively equal. *See Stanley v. Illinois*, 405 U.S. 645, 651–52 (1972); *see also Quilloin v. Walcott*, 434 U.S. 246 (1978); *Caban v. Mohammed*, 441 U.S. 380 (1979); *Lehr v. Robertson*, 463 U.S. 248 (1983). Before birth, however, the issue takes on a very different cast. It is an inescapable biological fact that state regulation with respect to the fetus a woman is carrying will have a far greater impact on the mother's liberty than on the father's. The effect of state regulation on a woman's protected liberty is doubly deserving of scrutiny in such a case because the state is intervening not only upon the traditionally private sphere of the family but also upon the very bodily integrity of the pregnant woman. The Court has held that "when the wife and the husband disagree on this decision, the view of only one of the two ... can prevail." *Danforth*, 428 U.S. at 71. Because the woman is "more directly and immediately affected by the pregnancy, as between the two, the balance weighs in her favor." *Id.*

Danforth remains our guide. For the great many women who are victims of abuse inflicted by their husbands, or whose children are the victims of such abuse, a spousal notice requirement enables the husband to wield an effective veto over his wife's decision. Whether the prospect of notification itself deters such women from seeking abortions, or whether the husband, through physical force, or psychological pressure or economic coercion, prevents his wife from obtaining an abortion until it is too late, the notice requirement will often be tantamount to the veto found unconstitutional in *Danforth*. The women most affected by this law – those who most reasonably fear the consequences of notifying their husbands that they are pregnant – are in the gravest danger.

If a husband's interest in the potential life of a child outweighs a wife's liberty, the state could require a married woman to notify her husband before she uses a post-fertilization contraceptive. Next might come a statute requiring pregnant married women to notify their husbands before engaging in conduct with risks to the fetus, e.g., drinking alcohol or smoking. Perhaps married women should notify their husbands before using contraceptives or before undergoing any type of surgery that may have complications affecting their own reproductive organs. If a husband's interest justifies notice in any of these cases, one might reasonably argue that it justifies what the *Danforth* Court held it did not justify: a requirement of the husband's consent. A state may not give to a man dominion over his wife.

Respondents attempt to avoid the conclusion that section 3209 is invalid by pointing out that it imposes almost no burden at all for the vast majority of women seeking abortions. They begin by noting that only about 20 percent of the women who obtain abortions are married, and 95 percent of these women notify their husbands of their own volition. Br. for Resp'ts at 85. Thus, Respondents argue, section 3209 has consequences for perhaps 1 percent of women who obtain abortions: married women who are subject to spousal abuse and who do not wish to notify their husbands. Br. for Resp'ts at 86. Respondents assert the statute cannot be invalid on its face because it has an impact on too few women. Br. for Resp'ts at 91–92.

Respondents' analysis is deeply flawed. Our analysis does not end with the women upon whom the statute operates; it begins there. Legislation is measured for consistency with the Constitution by its impact on those whose conduct it affects. The proper focus of constitutional inquiry is the group for whom the law is a restriction, not the group for whom the law is irrelevant.

By selecting as the controlling class women who wish to obtain abortions, rather than all women or all pregnant women, Respondents, in effect, concede that section 3209 must be judged by reference to those for whom it is an actual, rather than an irrelevant, restriction. Of course, section 3209's real target is narrower even than the class of women seeking abortions: it is married women seeking abortions who do not wish to notify their husbands and who do not qualify for one of the statutory exceptions to the notice requirement. The unfortunate yet persisting conditions we document above will mean that in a significant number of the cases in which section 3209 is relevant, it will operate as an undue burden on a woman's choice to terminate a pregnancy.

Section 3209 is repugnant to our understanding of marriage and of the nature of the rights the Constitution secures. Women do not lose their constitutionally protected liberty when they marry. Section 3209 creates an undue burden on a significant number of women and is, therefore, unconstitutional.

III

INFORMED CONSENT AND WAITING PERIOD REQUIREMENTS

We next consider the "informed consent" and waiting period requirements of the Act, section 3205. Except in a medical emergency, the statute requires that at least 24 hours before performing an abortion, a physician must inform the woman of the nature of the procedure, the health risks of the abortion and of childbirth, and the "probable gestational age of the unborn child." 18 Pa. Cons. Stat. § 3205 (1989). The physician or a qualified non-physician must inform the woman of the availability of printed materials published by the state describing the fetus and providing information about medical assistance for childbirth, information about child support from the father, and a list of agencies providing adoption and services that are alternatives to abortion. *Id.* Under this law, an abortion may not be performed unless the woman certifies in writing that she has been informed of the availability of these printed materials and has been provided them if she chooses to view them. *Id.* We find this provision unconstitutional because it imposes an undue burden on the constitutional right to an abortion while serving no medical purpose. In short, the law is a thinly disguised effort to delay abortion, and ultimately to deter it, by making abortion more difficult and expensive to obtain. The law thus fails strict scrutiny.

As with any medical procedure, the state may enact regulations to further the health or safety of a woman seeking an abortion. Pennsylvania may thus require that the patient be informed of the nature of the procedure, the health risks of the abortion and of childbirth, and the probable gestational age of the fetus, *Akron,* 462 U.S. at 445 n. 37. But no vital state need dictates that the information be provided by a physician rather than a counselor. *Id.* at 448. The District Court found that the physician-only requirement would necessarily increase the cost of an abortion. 744 F. Supp. at 1380. Because trained counselors are more numerous than physicians and often have more time to spend with patients, the physician-only disclosure requirement is not narrowly tailored to serve Pennsylvania's purported interest in protecting maternal health.

The mandatory delay imposed by section 3205 rests upon assumptions that are either outmoded or unacceptable about the decision-making capacity of women or, alternatively, upon the belief that the decision to terminate the pregnancy is presumptively wrong. This is contrary to the District Court's finding that "[a] very small percentage of women are ambivalent concerning whether to have an abortion when they come to a clinic. Arrangements for special counseling sessions are made for women demonstrating any ambivalence about her decision." 744 F. Supp. at 1351 (citations omitted). The requirement that women consider this obvious and slanted information for an additional 24 hours will influence the woman's decision, if at all, in improper, coercive ways. The vast majority of women will already know this information. For the few who do not, this information is less likely to change their minds than either the realization that the state opposes their choice; the need once again to endure abuse and harassment on return to the clinic; or the added cost and effort associated with two trips to the abortion provider.

Unnecessary health regulations that have the purpose or effect of imposing an undue burden on a woman seeking an abortion are unconstitutional. Even regulations that serve the laudable purpose of health enhancement will be invalid if they constitute an undue burden. A woman considering abortion faces a choice with serious and personal consequences. The authority to make such significant and empowering decisions is an element of basic human dignity. A woman's decision to terminate her pregnancy is nothing less than a matter of conscience. "Our whole constitutional heritage rebels at the thought of giving government the power to control men's minds." *Stanley v. Georgia*, 394 U.S. 557, 565 (1969). That heritage similarly rebels at the thought of giving government the power to control women's bodies.

As we stated in *Thornburgh*, "[t]his type of compelled information is the antithesis of informed consent," 476 U.S. at 764, and it goes far beyond merely describing the general subject matter relevant to the woman's decision. "That the Commonwealth does not, and surely would not, compel similar disclosure of every possible peril of necessary surgery or of simple vaccination, reveals the anti-abortion character of the statute and its real purpose." *Id.*

The 24-hour waiting period following the provision of the foregoing information is also patently unconstitutional because it creates an undue burden. The District Court found that the 24-hour delay would, in practice, frequently result in delays in excess of twenty-four hours because most plaintiff-clinics and plaintiff-physicians do not perform abortions on a daily basis. 744 F. Supp. at 1351. Indeed, the District Court found that the provision would effectively impose delays of forty-eight hours to two weeks on the majority of Pennsylvania women. *Id.* at 1351. Such delays increase health risks. *Id.* at 1379. Because the provision would require two visits to the abortion provider, it would increase travel time and financial cost. *Id.* at 1351, 1379. We invalidated a similarly arbitrary and inflexible waiting period in *Akron* because, as here, it furthered no legitimate state interest. *Akron*, 462 U.S. at 450–51.

The meaning of any legal standard can only be understood by considering the actual situations in which it applies. Just as the spousal notification provision does not fall with equal measure on all women, neither does the waiting-period requirement. The latter provision has a much greater impact on the poor and on those living far from an abortion provider. This makes it inappropriate to adopt middle class, affluent, and/or urban women as norms in our analysis. In applying the undue burden standard, courts must seriously consider the impact of statutory restrictions on the wide range of real world contexts in which women live. The female experience, like the human experience, is hardly monolithic. In this regard, we endorse the thinking of feminist and other critical scholars who caution against abstract reasoning. *See generally* Patricia J. Williams, *The Alchemy of Race and Rights* 44–51 (1991); Mari J. Matsuda, *Looking to the Bottom: Critical Legal Studies and Reparations*, 22 Harv. C.R.-C.L. L. Rev. 323 (1987); Carrie Menkel-Meadow, *Portia in a Different Voice: Speculations on a Women's Lawyering Process*, 1 Berkeley

Women's L. J. 39 (1985). Any analysis of whether a law that regulates or restricts the provision of abortion burdens the right to privacy necessarily examines that burden on a wide range of women, including groups rarely given specific mention in constitutional jurisprudence. In the context of the waiting period requirement, those facing particular obstacles to abortion include poor women, rural women and Native American women. For these women, too, are guaranteed the constitutional right to privacy.

We turn first to poor women. Poverty and its consequences can be difficult for the Court to grasp. As Justice Marshall admonished nearly two decades ago, "no one who has had close contact with poor people can fail to understand how close to the margin of survival many of them are." *United States v. Kras*, 409 U.S. 434, 460 (1973) (Marshall, J., dissenting). Indeed, though we hear much talk about diversity on the bench, socioeconomic diversity is sadly and sorely lacking. Truly poor people are not appointed as federal judges. Regardless of race, ethnicity, or sex, judges are not selected from the class of people who live in trailers or urban ghettos. Further, those who grow up poor but nevertheless become lawyers rarely acquire the sort of elite credentials that get them appointed to the bench. The everyday problems of people who live in poverty are thus not close to our hearts and minds. Yet handicapped as we are in truly comprehending the day-to-day deprivation associated with poverty, we refuse to ignore poor women.

One reason to attend to poor women in particular is that they constitute a high proportion of the women who utilize abortion services. Women with family incomes less than $11,000 are nearly four times more likely to have an abortion than women with family incomes greater than $25,000. Rachel B. Gold, *Abortion and Women's Health: A Turning Point for America?* 16 (1990). At least one study indicates that, for women below the poverty level, 60 percent of births are unintended, *i.e.*, unwanted or mis-timed, while only 30 percent of births to women above 200 percent of the poverty level are unintended. Stephen E. Radecki, *A Racial and Ethnic Comparison of Family Formation and Contraceptive Practices Among Low-Income Women*, 106 Pub. Health Rep. 494, 500 (1991). This greater incidence of unintended pregnancies is no doubt a consequence of the lesser availability of affordable and effective contraceptive options for poor women. The Alan Guttmacher Institute, *Abortions and the Poor: Private Morality, Public Responsibility* 20 (1979). Poor women are less able to afford children, which may prompt their decision to terminate a pregnancy because they cannot afford a child. Finally, restrictions on the right to abortion fall most heavily on poor women because they are in a worse position to overcome barriers of cost (including child care and time away from work), availability or delay imposed or generated by abortion regulations. *See* James P. O'Hair, A *Brief History of Abortion in the United States*, 262 JAMA 1875, 1878–79 (1989). Only thirteen states permit the use of state funds for medically necessary abortions. National Abortion Rights Action League Foundation, *Who Decides? A Reproductive Rights Manual* 10 (1990).

The District Court concluded that for those women who have the fewest financial resources, those who must travel long distances, and those who have difficulty explaining their whereabouts to husbands, employers, or others, the 24-hour waiting period will be "particularly burdensome." 744 F. Supp. at 1352. We agree. We find that the waiting period provision would so severely restrict the ability of poor women to obtain abortions that it would render illusory the right to make a private, procreative choice. For many poor women, the obstacles would not be merely burdensome; they would be insurmountable.[18] The delay and added costs imposed by the waiting period – exacerbated by the likelihood of scheduling difficulties at overcrowded facilities where poor women receive care – will actively interfere with the ability of poor women to obtain abortions.

This brings us to the situation of rural women, those outside the major metropolitan areas where most abortion providers are located. Not only are many rural women also poor, these women face the added challenges of distance and mobility. Among the District Court's detailed findings of fact related to these women was that "[i]n 1988, 58% of the women obtaining abortions in Pennsylvania resided in only five of the Commonwealth's counties. Women who live in any of the other 62 counties must travel for at least one hour, and sometimes longer than three hours, to obtain an abortion from the *nearest* provider." 744 F. Supp. at 1352 (citations omitted) (emphasis in original).

The need to travel long distances already presents a substantial barrier to care for many women. For example, one of the plaintiff clinics in this case, the Women's Health Services (WHS) in Pittsburgh, serves an area of thirty-four counties within Pennsylvania, portions of Ohio, West Virginia, Maryland and New York. Patients travel great distances, and "it is not unusual for women to travel three, four hours to get to the clinic. Sometimes it's much longer

---

[18] *See* Richard Lincoln, Bridgitte Doring-Bradley, Barbara L. Lindheim and Maureen A. Cotterill, *The Court, the Congress and the President: Turning Back the Clock on the Pregnant Poor*, 9 *Fam. Plan. Persp.* 207, 210–11 (1977); *see generally* Lisa M. Koonin, Kenneth D. Kochanek, Jack C. Smith and Merrell Ramick, *Abortion Surveillance, United States, 1988*, 40 *Morbidity and Morality Wkly. Rep.* 15 (1991). Even the informal networks built by women to ensure pregnant women's access to abortion are often inaccessible to women of color and the solutions offered unaffordable. Byllye Avery, *A Question of Survival/A Conspiracy of Silence: Abortion and Black Women's Health, in* From Abortion to Reproductive Freedom: Transforming a Movement 75 (Marlene Gerber Fried ed., 1990).

because they have to take buses to get in." Tr. Test. of WHS Executive Dir. Roselle, Vol. II, 80.

Consider, for example, the situation of a woman living in nonmetropolitan Greene County, in the state's southwest corner, where the poverty rate is 21.4 percent. A woman living in the rural Springhill township of Greene County, where the poverty rate is higher, even, than elsewhere in the county, will travel twenty-three miles just to reach the county seat, Waynesburg. Because she must travel on mountainous, secondary roads, that trip will take thirty-nine minutes – if she has access to a private vehicle; public transportation is not available. From Waynesburg, the woman will travel fifty-two miles – about one hour by private vehicle – to Pittsburgh, the location of the nearest abortion provider. Again, however, no public transportation is available between Waynesburg and Pittsburgh. For one of the county's many poor residents, then, getting to an abortion provider in Pittsburgh will be extremely difficult. Getting there twice, or staying there up to two weeks between her two appointments, may well prove impossible. Her situation will be aggravated if she is young, must arrange time off from work, or already has children. By any measure, the obstacle that Pennsylvania has put in the woman's path – requiring her to make the journey twice – is much more than a *de minimis* burden on her constitutional right. It is, therefore, an unconstitutional, undue burden.

That woman's situation is not atypical within our nation. Indeed, it is the proverbial tip of the iceberg – the iceberg being laws that impose waiting periods that prevent many women from procuring abortion services. In 1985, 82 percent of all counties in the United States – counties in which one-third of all reproductive-age women lived – had no identified abortion provider. Stanley K. Henshaw, Jaqueline Darroch Forrest, and Jennifer Van Vort, *Abortion Services in the United States, 1984 and 1985*, 19 Fam. Plan. Persp. 63, 65–6 (1987). This shortage is especially acute in rural areas. Nine out of ten non-metropolitan counties (91 percent) in the United States have no abortion provider. *Id.* at 65. For example, just one clinic provides abortions for 24 counties in northern Minnesota. Lisa Belkin, *Women in Rural Areas Face Many Barriers to Abortion*, N.Y. Times, July 11, 1989, at A1. Imagine how much greater the burden would be if a woman in one of those remote Minnesota counties – already situated much farther than our hypothetical woman in Greene County, Pennsylvania from the Pittsburgh clinic – had to make two trips to her nearest abortion provider. Such waiting-period requirements are far too disruptive of the exercise of constitutional rights to survive constitutional muster, especially when they offer no proven benefit to women's health.

Among those most burdened by waiting-period requirements are Native American women living in Indian Country, often remote from metropolitan areas where abortion services are available. The burden on these women is aggravated because Indian Health Services, which may be the only familiar provider of health care and the one in closest proximity, are prohibited from performing abortions, even if the woman has money to pay for the procedure. Laurie Nsiah-Jefferson, Reproductive Laws, Women of Color, and Low-Income Women, in Reproductive Laws for the 1990s 26–7 (Sherrill Cohen and Nadine Taub eds., 1989).

Indeed, the District Court recognized the burden of distance in combination with other factors associated with low-income women in concluding:

> 197. The mandatory 24–hour waiting period would force women to double their travel time or stay overnight at a location near the abortion facility. This will necessarily add either the costs of transportation or overnight lodging or both to the overall cost of her abortion. Additionally, many women may lose ... wages or other compensation as a result of the mandatory 24-hour delay, if forced to miss work on two separate occasions. Two trips to the abortion provider may cause the women to incur additional expenses for food and child care ...
>
> 199. The mandatory 24–hour waiting period will be particularly burdensome to those women who have the least financial resources, such as the poor and the young, those women [who] travel long distances, such as women living in rural areas, and those women [who] have difficulty explaining their whereabouts, such as battered women, school age women, and working women without sick leave.
>
> 744 F. Supp. at 1352 (citations omitted).

This analysis speaks to the effects of the state-imposed burden. But a burden may be undue not only because its effects are severe but also because it lacks a legitimate justification. Pennsylvania's 24-hour delay requirement also fails this second test. The findings of the District Court establish the severity of the burden that the 24-hour delay imposes on many pregnant women. 744 F. Supp. at 1351–52. Yet, even for those women for whom the delay is not as onerous (e.g., the wealthy, the urban), it is "undue" because Pennsylvania has presented no evidence that it serves a useful or legitimate purpose. No legitimate reason exists for requiring a woman, who has already made her decision, to leave the clinic or hospital and return another day. While a general requirement that a physician notify her patients about the risks of a proposed medical procedure is appropriate, a rigid requirement that all patients wait twenty-four hours or much longer – as evidence suggests will occur in practice – to evaluate the significance of information that is either common knowledge or irrelevant fails the strict scrutiny test.

Finally, the waiting period does not advance the state's "interest in maternal health," and it "infringes the physician's discretion to exercise sound medical judgment," 744 F. Supp. at 1378. Indeed, delaying abortion – as the waiting period will do – has adverse health consequences for women. Empirical evidence establishes that significant delays in obtaining abortions increase dramatically the health risks associated with abortions. "[A]ny delay increases the risk of complications to a pregnant woman who wishes an abortion." William Cates, Jr., Kenneth F. Schulz, David A. Grimes, and Carl W. Tyler, Jr., *The Effect of Delay and Method Choice on the Risk of Abortion Morbidity*, 9 Fam. Plan. Persp. 266, 268 (1977) (emphasis in original). *See also* Tr. Test. of Allen, Vol. I, 45. The total morbidity rate rises 20 percent when abortion is delayed from the eighth to the twelfth week, and the complication rate increases 91 percent for that same delay. Cates, Jr. *et al.*, *supra*, at 268. Poor women of color, who disproportionately suffer from illnesses exacerbated by pregnancy, will likely be most affected by significant delays in obtaining abortion services. Again, we turn to the District Court's findings:

> 200. In some cases, the delays caused by the 24–hour waiting period will push patients into the second trimester of their pregnancy[,] substantially increasing the cost of the procedure itself and making the procedure more dangerous medically.
>
> 201. A delay of 24 hours will have a negative impact on both the physical and psychological health of some patients, as well as increase the risk of complications.
>
> 202. While an abortion is still substantially safer than carrying a pregnancy to term, after the eighth week of the pregnancy, delay in the performance of the abortion increases the risk of death to the woman. A substantial increase in the risk of death from an abortion procedure occurs when the pregnancy moves from the earlier stages of the second trimester to the middle portion of the second trimester (16 to 20 weeks of gestation).
>
> 203. A mandatory 24–hour waiting period between the receipt of informed consent information and the performance of the abortion serves no legitimate medical interest.
>
> 744 F. Supp. at 1352 (citations omitted).

Accordingly, we re-instate the District Court's invalidation of section 3205.

IV

REQUIREMENT OF INFORMED CONSENT FOR MINORS

We next consider the parental consent provision. Relevant parts of the Pennsylvania law provide that, except in a medical emergency, an unemancipated woman under eighteen may not obtain an abortion unless she and a parent or guardian provide informed consent. If no parent or guardian provides consent, a court may authorize an abortion upon a determination that the young woman is mature and capable of giving informed consent and has, in fact, given her informed consent, or that an abortion would be in her best interests.

We have been over most of this ground before. Binding precedents establish, and we reaffirm today, that a state may require a minor seeking an abortion to obtain the consent of a parent or guardian, so long as an adequate judicial bypass procedure exists. *See, e.g., Ohio v. Akron Ctr. for Reprod. Health*, 497 U.S. 502, 510–20 (1990); 497 U.S. at 497–501 (Kennedy, J., concurring in the judgment in part and dissenting in part); *Hodgson v. Minnesota*, 497 U.S. 417, 461 (1990) (O'Connor, J., concurring in part and concurring in the judgment in part); *Bellotti v. Baird*, 443 U.S. 622, 643–44 (1979) (plurality opinion).

Based on evidence in the record, the District Court concluded that, in order to fulfill the informed-consent requirement, generally accepted medical principles would require an in-person visit by the parent to the facility. 744 F. Supp. at 1382. We disagree. Although the Court "has recognized that the State has somewhat broader authority to regulate the activities of children than of adults," the State nevertheless must demonstrate that there is a "[s]*ignificant state interest* in conditioning an abortion … that is not present in the case of an adult." *Danforth*, 428 U.S. at 74–5 (emphasis added). The requirement of an in-person visit would carry with it the risk of delay of several days or possibly weeks, even where the parent is willing to consent. While the state has an interest in encouraging parental involvement in the minor's abortion decision, section 3206 is not narrowly drawn to serve that interest. The statute imposes more than a *de minimis* burden on the right.

The judicial-bypass provision of the Pennsylvania statute does not cure this violation. The law requires more than parental involvement or approval; it requires that the parent receive information designed to discourage abortion in a face-to-face meeting with the physician. Conversely, the Minnesota law approved in *Hodgson* did not impose that in-person requirement. Minn. Stat. § 144.343 (1986). The Pennsylvania bypass procedure cannot ensure that the parent would obtain the information because, in many instances, the parent would not even attend the hearing, which is essentially the purpose of the bypass option. A state may not place such a restriction on a young woman's right to an abortion simply because it has provided an opportunity for judicial bypass.

V

RECORD-KEEPING AND REPORTING REQUIREMENTS

Finally, the Act requires every facility performing abortions to report its activities to the Commonwealth. Pennsylvania contends that this requirement is valid under *Danforth*, in which this Court held that record-keeping and reporting requirements "reasonably directed to the preservation of maternal health and that properly respect a patient's confidentiality are permissible." 428 U.S. at 80. Pennsylvania attempts to justify its required reports on the ground that the public has a right to know how its tax dollars are spent. A regulation designed to inform the public about public expenditures does not further Pennsylvania's interest in protecting maternal health. Accordingly, such a regulation cannot justify a legally significant burden on a woman's right to an abortion.

The confidential reports concerning the identities and medical judgment of physicians involved in abortions, at first glance, may seem valid, given Pennsylvania's interest in maternal health and enforcement of the Act. The District Court found, however, that, notwithstanding the confidentiality protections, "many physicians, particularly those who have previously discontinued performing abortions because of harassment, [would] refuse to refer patients to abortion clinics if their names were to appear on these reports." 744 F. Supp. at 1392. Pennsylvania has failed to show that the name of the referring physician either adds to the pool of scientific knowledge concerning abortion or is reasonably related to Pennsylvania's interest in maternal health. We therefore agree with the District Court's conclusion that the confidential reporting requirements are unconstitutional insofar as they require the name of the referring physician and the basis for his or her medical judgment.

VI

CONCLUSION

In sum, we affirm the judgment of the District Court with respect to all except the provisions relating to minors seeking abortions, and we thus affirm in part and reverse in part the Court of Appeals. We remand the matters for further proceedings.

It is so ordered.

20

Commentary on *United States v. Virginia*

Christine M. Venter

INTRODUCTION

In 1996, in *United States v. Virginia*,[1] Justice Ruth Bader Ginsburg wrote one of her first important women's rights opinions. The case was initiated by the Justice Department after an unidentified woman complained that she was denied the opportunity to attend Virginia Military Institute ("VMI"), a public military college, because of her gender. In writing for the majority that VMI's male-only admissions policy was unconstitutional under the Equal Protection Clause of the Fourteenth Amendment, Justice Ginsburg noted that "[h]owever 'liberally' this plan serves the Commonwealth's sons, it makes no provision whatever for her daughters. That is not *equal* protection."[2]

Reading her majority opinion from the bench, Justice Ginsburg made clear that the Constitution does not permit women to be excluded from public educational opportunities. VMI vehemently opposed the decision, and debated taking the institution private, a proposal narrowly defeated by its Board of Visitors. Although women's groups responded optimistically to the decision, the actual legacy has not proven quite as rosy. At VMI today, women comprise only about 10 percent of the VMI student body, and many leadership roles are still held by men. Moreover, equal protection remains elusive for the women of VMI, as the Department of Education Office of Civil Rights recently found violations of Title IX at VMI, including that VMI created an "environment hostile to [women] both in the barracks and in the classroom" and maintained discriminatory tenure and promotion standards for women faculty.[3]

[1] *United States v. Virginia*, 518 U.S. 515 (1996).
[2] *Id.* at 540.
[3] Letter from Alice B. Wender, Reg'l Office Dir., U.S. Dep't of Educ., Office for Civ. Rts. to Gen. J.H. Binford Peay III, Superintendent, Va. Military Inst. (May 9, 2014), www.inside highered.com/sites/default/server_files/files/VMI%20letter.pdf (last visited August 27, 2015).

THE FACTUAL AND LEGAL ISSUES

At the time of the litigation, VMI was a publicly funded, elite, single-sex military institute, founded in 1839, when Virginia offered public education only to men. VMI prided itself on creating "citizen soldiers" who were prepared for military and civilian life through the "adversative" method as well as strict physical and mental discipline and a strong moral code. This type of training and formation, combining rigorous academics with demanding military training based on a moral code, was unavailable elsewhere in Virginia.

The Justice Department sued, alleging that VMI's male-only admission policy violated equal protection. The District Court ruled in VMI's favor, and Justice appealed. The Court of Appeals for the Fourth Circuit reversed and suggested that VMI had three options: it could admit women, establish a parallel program, or reject state funding and go private. In response, VMI established a parallel program, creating the Virginia Women's Institute of Leadership ("VWIL"). Although VWIL was much smaller and did not offer engineering degrees or VMI's type of military training, the District Court found that VWIL had created a similar, parallel educational opportunity for women, noting that it did not have to be a "mirror image" of VMI.[4] On appeal, the Fourth Circuit affirmed.[5]

THE U.S. SUPREME COURT DECISION

The U.S. Supreme Court acknowledged that "our Nation has had a long and unfortunate history of sex discrimination."[6] While the Court conceded that single-sex education could be beneficial, it noted Virginia's long history of denying women access to higher education, and rejected the notion that VMI's male-only admission policy was in furtherance of diversity, finding rather that it offered a "unique educational benefit only to males."[7]

The Court similarly rejected VMI's contention that admitting women would destroy the adversative method. Justice Ginsburg found it likely that some women who were capable of succeeding in the adversative system would want to attend the institution, although no actual plaintiff had alleged this, as the Justice Department had brought the complaint and the factual record was limited.[8]

[4] *United States v. Virginia*, 852 F. Supp. 471, 481 (W.D. Va. 1994).
[5] *United States v. Virginia*, 44 F. 3d 1229 (4th Cir. 1995).
[6] 518 U.S. 515, 531 (1996) (citing *Frontiero v. Richardson*, 411 U.S. 677, 684 (1973)).
[7] *Id.* at 540.
[8] *Id.* at 542–43.

The Court then examined whether VWIL would pass constitutional muster by placing women in "the position they would have occupied in the
absence of [discrimination]."[9] The Court noted that the academic requirements for students and faculty were less rigorous for VWIL, and that the college incorporating VWIL offered fewer degrees and had a substantially lower
endowment than VMI.[10] Instead of VMI's adversative method, VWIL offered
a cooperative form of ROTC.[11] The Court, therefore, found no "substantial
equality" between the two schools because of the vast disparity in resources,
opportunities and reputation.[12]

The Court used new language to describe the standard of scrutiny, requiring an "exceedingly persuasive" justification for Virginia's males-only policy.[13]
Chief Justice Rehnquist wrote separately to criticize this phrasing, which he
argued would introduce uncertainty.[14] In his dissent, Justice Scalia also criticized the new language, calling it an abandonment of intermediate scrutiny
that would render single-sex public education "functionally dead."[15]

THE FEMINIST JUDGMENT

Professor Valorie Vojdik, the lead attorney for Shannon Faulkner in the *Citadel*
case, is an ideal person to revisit the VMI decision from a feminist perspective.
It is worth asking, however, why VMI was chosen for inclusion in the volume,
given that the majority opinion was authored by feminist Justice Ruth Bader
Ginsburg, and the Justice Department prevailed in its quest to integrate VMI.

As a matter of feminist history, the VMI case exemplifies the disagreement
in feminist legal theory between equality feminists, who find that "differences"
between men and women are largely socially constructed stereotypes, and difference feminists, who argue that the differences between men and women
are real and important and should be equally valued.[16] In the 1990s, difference feminists who looked beyond biological sex differences found support in

---

[9] *Id.* at 547 (citing *Milliken v. Bradley*, 433 U.S. 267, 280 (1977)).
[10] *Id.* at 552.
[11] 518 U.S. 515, 548 (1996).
[12] *Id.* at 554.
[13] *Id.* at 556. Intermediate scrutiny usually requires gender classifications to be "substantially
     related" to an "important" government interest. *Craig v. Boren*, 429 U.S. 190 (1976).
[14] *United States v. Virginia*, 518 U.S. 515, 572 (1996) (Rehnquist, J., concurring).
[15] *Id.* at 596 (Scalia, J., dissenting).
[16] *See, e.g.*, Wendy W. Williams, *The Equality Crisis: Some Reflections on Culture, Courts,
     and Feminism*, 14 Women's Rts L. Rep. 151 (1992); Catharine A. MacKinnon, *Difference and
     Dominance: On Sex Discrimination, in* The Moral Foundations of Civil Rights 144 (R.K.
     Fullinwider and C. Mills eds., 1986) (describing equality and difference theories).

the work of Carol Gilligan, who famously chronicled variations in male and female moral reasoning.[17]

The equality/difference debate was evident from the amici briefs. Feminist law professor Susan Estrich participated in writing an amicus brief supporting VWIL, finding value in its more diverse approach to education and leadership.[18] By contrast, an amicus brief listing Gilligan as co-author argued that VWIL embodies "the very stereotype that the law condemns" and denounces the physiological and psychological sex differences VMI uses to support VWIL's program as a distortion of the scientific data, including Gilligan's.[19]

Vojdik's opinion reaches the same result as the majority, initially aligning with equality feminism. Like the majority, she rejects the diversity rationale offered by VMI. She also agrees that VWIL is an insufficient remedy. Vojdik's concurrence, however, is rooted in the anti-stereotyping tradition of feminist jurisprudence as well as the anti-subordination theories articulated by Ruth Colker and others.[20] With respect to her analysis of stereotyping, Vojdik's reasoning both exposes and critiques the hegemonic masculinity that runs rampant at hyper-masculinized single-sex institutions like VMI. She asserts that the activities, language, symbols and culture of VMI all reinforce the notion that men are the antithesis of feminine, are heterosexual, and are physically aggressive. In this way, Vojdik aligns herself with theorists like Ann McGinley, Pierre Bourdeau, and Raewyn Connell,[21] who argue that single-sex environments foster discursive practices and structures that encourage men to perform in a stereotypical masculine way, and relegate women to a stereotypical feminine role that is disparaged and reviled.

---

[17] Carol Gilligan, In a Different Voice: Psychological Theory and Women's Development (1982). Gilligan has distanced herself somewhat from the notion that her data proves true gender "difference." See Carol Gilligan, Revisiting "In a Different Voice," Keynote Address at the Carr Center for Reproductive Justice Conference, Reproductive Rights Law: Where is the Woman? (April 1, 2014), http://socialchangeharbinger.com/2015/03/11/revisiting-in-a-different-voice-2/.

[18] Br. for Dr. Kenneth E. Clark, et al. as Amici Curiae in Support of Resp'ts, U.S. v. Virginia, 518 U.S. 515 (1996) (No. 94–1941). See also Br. of Women's Sch. Together, Inc., et al. as Amici Curiae in Support of Resp'ts, U.S. v. Virginia, 518 U.S. 515 (1996) (No. 94–1941) (supporting VWIL).

[19] Br. for the Am. Ass'n of Univ. Professors, et al. as Amici Curiae in Support of Pet'r, United States v. Virginia, 518 U.S. 515 (1996) (No. 94–1941). See also Br. for Nat'l Women's Law Ctr., et al. as Amici Curiae in Support of Pet'r, United States v. Virginia, 518 U.S. 515 (1996) (No. 94–1941) (arguing against VWIL remedy and in favor of strict scrutiny for gender classifications).

[20] See Ruth Colker, The Anti-Subordination Principle: Applications, 3 Wisc. Women's L.J. 59 (1987).

[21] See Ann C. McGinley, Creating Masculine Identities: Bullying and Harassment "Because of Sex", 79 U. Colo. L. Rev. 1151 (2008); Pierre Bourdieu, Masculine Domination (2001); Raewyn Connell, Gender: In World Perspective (2d ed. 2009).

Beyond stereotyping, Vojdik emphasizes that the wrong committed by VMI was not merely in categorizing women as a group incapable of fulfilling VMI's demanding program, but also in devising an educational policy that reinforced the systematic subordination of women by excluding them from access to all of the rights, resources, privileges and accouterments of full citizenship. She rejects that the state may attempt to preserve its resources, like public education, solely for men in an attempt to perpetuate the subordination of women.

Vojdik performs an historical analysis of the role of the state with regard to the exclusion of women from full citizenship rights through the lens of anti-subordination feminist jurisprudence. She notes that during our country's history, women were initially denied the right to vote, denied the right to serve on juries, not permitted to practice law, restricted from certain jobs or overtime pay, and denied access to public education. Vojdik's concurrence identifies VMI's refusal to admit women as part of a deliberate and continual effort to support this system of women's subordination. In her view, Virginia's insistence on excluding women from VMI sends the message that by their very sex, women threaten and damage an important state institution.

Explicitly rejecting that women are different and inferior, Vojdik dismisses the arguments that admitting women to VMI will "destroy" the institution, noting that women have successfully been integrated into the armed forces. Vojdik finds the arguments advanced in favor of the exclusion of women from VMI to be "deeply misogynistic." She interprets the exclusion of women as "the denigration of women as a class" because VMI believes it will be "contaminated" by the admission of women, whom the institution considers "other." Vojdik finds these arguments strikingly similar to, and equally as unpersuasive as, the arguments raised against interracial marriage in *Loving v. Virginia*.[22]

Vojdik also tackles the standard for gender classifications, finding such classifications inherently suspect and noting that courts have had difficulty applying intermediate scrutiny in a way that distinguishes "real physical differences from paternalistic classifications that stereotype or exclude women." Rejecting the majority's somewhat ambiguous standard, Vojdik explicitly requires strict scrutiny for gender classifications, though she carves out an exception for gender classifications that serve remedial purposes such as rectifying past discrimination.

In terms of remedy, Vojdik concludes that merely opening the doors of VMI to women will be insufficient to dismantle the gendered practices of VMI, because the denigration of women is integral to the culture and pedagogy of VMI. Vojdik points out that VMI must change the structures, language, traditions and highly gendered norms of its educational policies to achieve fully the goal of integration.

[22] 388 U.S. 1 (1967).

Vojdik's challenge to VMI to develop a plan to integrate women and eliminate discrimination "root and branch" by eradicating practices based on the superiority of men echoes Article 5(a) of the 1981 Convention on the Elimination of All Forms of Discrimination Against Women, which calls on all states that are parties to "modify the social and cultural patterns of conduct of men and women, with a view to achieving the elimination of prejudices and customary and all other practices which are based on the idea of the inferiority or the superiority of either of the sexes or on stereotyped roles for men and women."[23]

CONCLUSION

Since *United States v. Virginia* was decided, intermediate scrutiny continues to be the standard for gender-based classifications. Courts also rarely acknowledge that gendered assumptions and stereotyped roles for men and women serve to exclude women from the public and political sphere. Had Vojdik's opinion been the opinion of the Court, perhaps the integration of women into institutions of male privilege (like VMI) would have occurred more rapidly and smoothly. As Vojdik noted, "we are long past the time when a state can treat its daughters so differently from its sons."

United States v. Virginia, 518 U.S. 515 (1996)

Justice Valorie K. Vojdik, concurring.

The wholesale exclusion of qualified women from the Virginia Military Institute (VMI) categorically denies an entire class of persons the benefits of a unique and prestigious public college, solely because of their sex. At a time when women are serving alongside men in the Persian Gulf, putting themselves in harm's way to defend our nation, VMI and the Commonwealth of Virginia have waged a six-year battle to preserve VMI free from women. VMI concedes that some women are qualified for VMI's military-style program, and that its military-style methodology is not inherently unsuitable for women. It continues to argue, however, that men and women are fundamentally different and that the "very presence" of women will "destroy" VMI. Rather than admit women, Virginia has created a separate, and admittedly unequal, program for women at a private women's college.

Since *Reed v. Reed*, 404 U.S. 71 (1971), this Court has never upheld a state classification that perpetuates the exclusion of women from an important

[23] Convention on the Elimination of All Forms of Discrimination Against Women, G.A. Res. 34/180, U.N. GOAR Supp. No. 46, U.N. Doc. A/34/46, at 193 (December 18, 1979).

state benefit, let alone public education. I agree with the majority that Virginia has failed to justify its discriminatory admission policy or offer an adequate remedy for those women who seek the advantages of VMI's unique program. I write separately, however, to emphasize four points. First, the exclusion of women from VMI is not merely based upon stereotypical views about men and women or the alleged value of single-gender education. Rather, it is an essential part of a legal and political system that subordinated women, denying them full citizenship and dignity. The exclusion of women is one of the defining features of the institution, premised upon traditional notions of masculinity that demean and stigmatize women as different and unequal.

Second, the time has come for this Court to hold that gender classifications denying women equal access to opportunities or benefits because of their sex or gender are presumptively invalid and should be subject to strict scrutiny. The long history of discrimination against women, and the persistent confusion in the lower courts in distinguishing real physical differences from paternalistic classifications that stereotype or exclude women, warrants application of the same skeptical review of gender classifications as afforded all other protected classes.

Third, Virginia's decision to relegate women to a separate program, the Virginia Women's Institute for Leadership ("VWIL"), does not remedy the violation, but compounds it. I agree with the majority that VWIL is but a pale shadow of VMI, unequal in resources, reputation, and the other tangible and intangible qualities offered to men at VMI. But I write separately to emphasize that even if VWIL were somehow identical, the creation of a separate-but-equal program for women does not satisfy the requirements of equal protection. "Separate educational programs are inherently unequal." *Brown v. Bd. of Educ.*, 347 U.S. 483, 495 (1954).

Finally, I write to highlight that admitting women to VMI is not enough to satisfy equal protection. VMI must make changes to its program. Just as we held that states must dismantle racially segregated colleges "root and branch," so we must require VMI to identify and eliminate all vestiges of its discriminatory, males-only policy to fully include women.

I

Founded in 1839, VMI restricted admission to only men, not because of any "pedagogical" belief in the benefits of "single-gender" education, but because of the "unquestioned general understanding of the time about the distinctively different roles in society of men and women." *United States v. Virginia*, 44 F.3d 1229, 1243 (4th Cir. 1995) (Phillips, J., dissenting). Throughout most of the nineteenth century, Virginia offered public education to males only; state officials recognized in 1879 that Virginia "has never, in any period of her history," provided for the higher education of her daughters, though she "has liberally provided for the higher education of her sons." 2 Thomas Woody, *A History of Women's Education in the United States* 254 (1929). The University of Virginia did not abandon its males-only admission policy until 1972, following a bitter lawsuit that resulted in a court order.

VMI's mission underscores its goal and commitment to produce not military leaders, but "educated and honorable men … prepared for the varied work of civil life, imbued with love of learning, confident in the functions and attitudes of leadership, possessing a high sense of public service, advocates of the American democracy and free enterprise system, and ready as citizen-soldiers to defend their country in time of national peril." *United States v. Virginia*, 766 F. Supp. 1407, 1425 (W.D. Va. 1991) (quoting Mission Study Committee of the VMI Board of Visitors, Report, May 16, 1986). VMI is not a federal service academy, but a state college that educates its students in a military-style environment similar to West Point. As the courts below describe, VMI organizes cadets into companies within battalions; cadets wear uniforms and live in barracks, subject to a student chain of command that is similar to the military. *Id.* at 1422–24. Entering freshmen, called "rats," are subjected to the "ratline," a system of rules and discipline which is designed to "break down" individual freshmen and rebuild them as "VMI Men." *Id.* at 1422–23.

Following our decision in *Miss. Univ. for Women v. Hogan*, 458 U.S. 718 (1982), holding that Mississippi could not justify the exclusion of men from its all-female nursing school, VMI formed a commission to review its males-only admission policy. Officials at West Point advised the commission that gender integration had been successful there, that the introduction of women did not significantly change West Point, and that VMI graduates will "probably be considered disadvantaged in the coed Army" because they do not come from a coed environment. 766 F. Supp. at 1428. The commission reaffirmed VMI's males-only policy in a brief one-and-a-half page report that provided no real rationale for the decision. *Id.* at 1429.

After the United States filed suit in federal court challenging its males-only admission policy, VMI sought to justify its wholesale exclusion of women by advancing two justifications: (1) offering men the opportunity for a "single-gender education" advances the diversity of Virginia's higher education system and (2) the admission of women would destroy the unique methodology used to train its male students, depriving both men and women of what they seek at VMI.

The District Court concluded that VMI's policy was justified, despite finding that some women could succeed at VMI; that the presence of women would improve the ability of male cadets to learn to work with women; and that the policy denied women "a unique educational opportunity that is available only at VMI." *Id.* at 1407, 1432. In support of its decision, the District Court offered numerous "findings" that men and women fundamentally differ in their cognitive, psychological, and physical needs and abilities, as well as in their educational needs. *Id.* at 1432–34. These "differences," the court held, were "real" and "not stereotypes." *Id.* at 1432.

The District Court also agreed with VMI that the admission of women would materially change certain aspects of its program. *Id.* at 1414. Specifically, the court noted that "allowance for personal privacy would have to be made," "[p]hysical education requirements would have to be altered, at least for the women," and the adversative environment could not survive unmodified. *Id.* at 1412–13.

Reversing, the Court of Appeals held that VMI's males-only admission policy was not substantially related to an important government interest because it failed to justify offering "the unique benefit of VMI's type of education and training to men and not women." *United States v. Virginia*, 976 F.2d 890, 898 (4th Cir. 1992). But while the Court of Appeals found that "some women" would qualify for and benefit from VMI, it refused to require their admission "in light of ... the generally recognized benefit" that VMI offers men and the changes that would occur if women were admitted. *Id.* at 896–97, 900. Instead, the Court of Appeals allowed VMI to propose an alternative remedy that might include "parallel" programs or institutions, or "other more creative options." *Id.* at 900.

Rather than admit women, Virginia created and funded a separate and deliberately unequal program for women, the VWIL, at Mary Baldwin College, a private women's college near VMI. 44 F.3d at 1233–34. Turning back the constitutional clock for women, the District Court and the Court of Appeals held that VWIL satisfied equal protection, even though it differed substantially from VMI and lacked "those intangible qualities of history, reputation tradition, and prestige that VMI has amassed over the years." *United States v. Virginia*, 852 F. Supp. at 475; 44 F.3d at 1241. In approving VWIL, the Court of Appeals declined to apply the heightened standard of review required by our precedent and instead crafted its own, lesser standard of review: the remedial plan need not be equal to VMI, as long as the benefits provided were "substantively comparable" and the program did not tend "by comparison to the benefits provided to the other, to lessen the dignity, respect, or societal regard of the other gender." 44 F.3d at 1237.

II

The exclusion of women from VMI, as the majority holds, is based upon generalizations and stereotypes repeatedly rejected by this Court since *Reed v. Reed*, 404 U.S. 71 (1971). Virginia's decision to continue to preserve VMI for men only by creating a new, separate and different program for women does not remedy the violation, but compounds it. Rather than admit women, Virginia chose to perpetuate its discriminatory policy, ratifying its belief that men and women are fundamentally different and stigmatizing women as less deserving of the educational opportunities bestowed upon its male citizens.

Under our modern equal protection doctrine, this Court has never upheld a state classification that perpetuates the historical exclusion of women from an important state benefit, let alone public education. Instead, we have repeatedly recognized that women have suffered "a long and unfortunate history of sex discrimination," including in public education, where they still face "pervasive" discrimination. *See Frontiero v. Richardson*, 411 U.S. 677, 685–86 (1973); *see also Mathews v. Lucas*, 427 U.S. 495, 506 (1976). Like mistaken beliefs about racial difference, claims about "differences" between men and women have been used throughout our nation's history to privilege men and relegate women to a separate and inferior position in our society, denying women participation in our nation's political, social, and economic life. States may no longer rely on claims of so-called gender "differences" to constrain or deny benefits or opportunities to women or to denigrate or demean members of either sex.

As the majority holds, Virginia's proffered justification violates these fundamental principles. Virginia's argument that offering men, but not women, a single-gender education advances diversity in higher education is unsupported by the record and contradicted by the history of education in the state. At the time VMI was founded, Virginia denied all women access to public education; since then, all the other universities and colleges that were segregated by sex have become coeducational. Virginia's "diversity" argument "is, at best, a stratagem to achieve the Commonwealth's real objective – preservation of VMI ... from the unwelcome intrusion of women." *United States v. Virginia*, 52 F.3d 90, 92 n.3 (4th Cir. 1995) (Motz, J., dissenting from denial of rehearing). VMI admits that some women would benefit and succeed at VMI and, as the majority holds, VMI cannot exclude qualified women based upon alleged differences between "most" women and men. VMI presented no evidence that any such changes would impair the ability of male cadets to learn to become leaders or citizen-soldiers, nor earn their undergraduate degree.

In dismissing Virginia's proffered justifications, the majority characterizes these arguments as outmoded stereotypes, predictions "hardly proved," no different than other similar predictions of doom made throughout history to rationalize the exclusion of women from other all-male preserves, including higher education, the military, and the law. *United States v. Virginia*, 518 U.S. 515, 542–43 (1996). These arguments have historically been used by gatekeepers of male privilege to preserve the benefits of social institutions for men alone.[24] Given the widespread integration of women into the U.S. military and service academies, the notion that women would "destroy" VMI is based neither on fact nor reasoning, but upon demeaning beliefs about the proper role and interests of women that are "relic[s] of the nineteenth century." *See Faulkner v. Jones*, 51 F.3d 440, 451 (4th Cir. 1995) (Hall, J., concurring).

To focus solely on stereotyping as the constitutional wrong, however, suggests that Virginia's decision to bar all women from VMI is ultimately a mistake or error in judgment or classification. This misperceives the nature and effect of Virginia's discriminatory policy. The exclusion of women from VMI is not merely a mistake in classification, but the defining feature of the institution, which "not only practices inequality, but celebrates it." *See Faulkner v. Jones*, 10 F.3d 226, 234 (4th Cir. 1993) (Hall, J., concurring).

At the time of its founding, VMI was part and parcel of a system of subordination that preserved the public sphere and full citizenship for white men only. The exclusion of women from VMI symbolizes and reinforces a traditional view of masculinity and femininity that has been used by state actors throughout our nation's history to justify the separation of men and women into different and unequal spheres, enforced by law. *See* Kenneth L. Karst, *The Pursuit of Manhood and the Desegregation of the Armed Forces*, 38 UCLA L. Rev. 499, 508 (1991).

VMI's mission is to create "men," not merely leaders, who exhibit qualities traditionally considered to be masculine in our society. Its "adversarial, military-style system is a highly specialized program designed for the distinctive physiological and developmental characteristics of males." Br. for Appellees at 20. VMI claims that it seeks to "draw out the man" in its young male students through rigorous physical and mental testing, discipline, and punishment.

---

[24] It is important to note that not all men were equally privileged. For too much of this nation's history, men of color were also denied equal rights and opportunities.

"The barracks provides a total training environment," VMI argues, "in which the spartan conditions, complete absence of privacy, military demands, and minute regulation of behavior produce stress for the purpose of *drawing out the man*." *Id.* at 24 (italics added).[25]

Like the military, VMI considers itself a proving ground for men to demonstrate their manhood, premised upon a particular masculine identity, in which men are defined as the opposite of women. Its system pits male students against each other, "setting the aggressiveness of one person against another through conflict, egalitarianism, lack of privacy and stress – both physical and mental." 44 F.3d at 1239. First-year male students must conform to the minute regulation of every aspect of their behavior, enforced by discipline and punishment meted out by upperclassmen, including push-ups and sprints.

This rigorous, stressful and aggressive system is based upon, and reinforces, the identity of a cadet as male and masculine, defined in opposition to women and femininity. *See* Christine L. Williams, *Gender Differences at Work: Women and Men in the Nontraditional Occupations* 47 (1989). VMI argues that men are, and should be, masculine – strong, aggressive, in need of rigor and challenge – and that women are, and should be, the opposite – lacking self-esteem and in need of nurturing and support. Its system, VMI asserts, is suitable only for men and one in which most women cannot, or should not, succeed. The exclusion of women from admission into this highly masculinized culture, like the integration of women into the military, threatens the belief that men are fundamentally superior to women. *See* Karst, *supra*, at 523–545.[26] If women can succeed at VMI after all, then its program, by definition, no longer "draws out the man." The admission of women to VMI fundamentally threatens the ideology of masculinity and the construction of gender as difference that serves to privilege men and subordinate women.

VMI's males-only policy is a vestige of this system of gender subordination, not merely a mistake in classification. In seeking to preserve VMI for men only, Virginia sends an unmistakable message to its citizens: women are not only inherently different and inferior to men, but must be segregated into a

---

[25] VMI also prescribes rules of conduct and norms of behavior for its male students in a written pamphlet called the "Code of a Gentleman."

[26] A recurring explanation for the military's opposition to the integration of women has similarly focused on the need to preserve the military as a place where men can "prove" and "celebrate" their manhood. Retired Navy Admiral James Webb, for example, has argued that the military provided a "ritualistic rite of passage into manhood," and the integration of women into the military makes troops "feel stripped symbolically and actually." James Webb, *Women Can't Fight*, The Washingtonian, Nov. 1979, at 280. He queried, "The real question is this: Where in the country can someone go to find out if he is a man? And where can someone who knows he is a man go to celebrate his masculinity?" *Id.*

separate program because their very presence at VMI would destroy a venerable state institution.[27] This claim is strikingly similar to the argument made by Virginia in *Loving v. Virginia*, 388 U.S. 1 (1967) in defense of its anti-miscegenation statute, which banned white persons from marrying persons of other races. The Virginia Supreme Court upheld that the law as a legitimate means "to preserve the racial integrity of its citizens," explaining "nations and races have better advanced in human progress when they cultivated their own distinctive characteristics and culture and developed their own peculiar genius." *Naim v. Naim*, 87 S.E.2d 749, 756 (Va. 1955). This Court struck down the Virginia statute, holding that its enforcement of the legal separation of the races was a means to preserve white supremacy. The exclusion of women from VMI similarly is based upon the belief that each sex has separate needs and characteristics that should be preserved; Virginia's fear that women will change or "destroy" VMI is similarly rooted in the belief system of male supremacy.

Like the exclusion of women from the jury box, Virginia's decision to continue to deny women admission to VMI reinvokes a history of exclusion of women from the public sphere and brands women as a class as different and inferior to men. *See J.E.B. v. Ala. ex rel. T.B.*, 511 U.S. 127, 142 (1994). As David Riesman, one of VMI's experts, observed:

> The pluralistic argument for preserving all-male colleges is uncomfortably similar to the pluralistic argument for preserving all-white colleges ... The all-male college would be relatively easy to defend if it emerged from a world in which women were established as fully equal to men. But it does not. It is therefore likely to be a witting or unwitting device for preserving tacit assumptions of male superiority – assumptions for which women must eventually pay.
>
> *United States v. Virginia*, 518 U.S. at 535 n.8 (citing Christopher Jencks and David Riesman, *The Academic Revolution* 297–98 (1st ed. 1968)).

III

Virginia's continued exclusion of qualified women, based solely on their sex and regardless of their individual accomplishments, is not substantially related to any important state interest and thus cannot survive even so-called

---

[27] In a deposition taken in the parallel litigation in *Faulkner v. Jones*, the superintendent of VMI, Josiah Bunting, testifying as an expert witness regarding the effect of the admission of women on The Citadel, the only other males-only military-style public college, described women as a "toxic virus" whose admission would destroy The Citadel. Deposition of Josiah Bunting at 30, *Johnson v. Jones*, No. 2: 92-1674-2 (D.S.C. 1994).

intermediate scrutiny. On several recent occasions, however, this Court explicitly has reserved the issue of whether strict scrutiny applies to gender classifications. *J.E.B.*, 511 U.S. at 137 n.6 ("once again [the Court] need not decide whether classifications based on gender are inherently suspect"); *Harris v. Forklift Sys. Inc.*, 510 U.S. 17, 26 n.* (1993) (Ginsburg, J., concurring); *Hogan*, 458 U.S. at 724 n.9; *Stanton v. Stanton*, 421 U.S. 7, 13 (1975). The decisions below exemplify serious confusion about intermediate scrutiny among the lower courts and provide an ideal opportunity for this Court to clarify the appropriate standard of review.

Courts repeatedly have complained that the standard for reviewing gender classifications provides little guidance. *See, e.g., Lamprecht v. FCC*, 958 F.2d 382, 398 n.9 (D.C. Cir. 1992); *Coral Constr. Co. v. King County*, 941 F.2d 910, 931 (9th Cir. 1991). Application of the intermediate scrutiny standard by the lower courts often has resulted in confused and erroneous decisions, failing to protect women from state discrimination. Before *J.E.B.*, for example, numerous courts using intermediate scrutiny upheld gender-based peremptory strikes based on traditional and overbroad stereotypes. *See United States v. Nichols*, 937 F.2d 1257, 1262–64 (7th Cir. 1991); *United States v. Broussard*, 987 F.2d 215, 218–20 (5th Cir. 1993); *State v. Culver*, 444 N.W.2d 662, 665–67 (Neb. 1989). This confusion has not abated. The lower courts below held that Virginia could deny qualified women admission to VMI based upon generalizations about "most" men and "most" women – and which would be rejected out of hand if applied to members of racial or ethnic groups.

It is time to declare "what, by now, should be axiomatic: Intentional discrimination on the basis of gender by state actors violates the Equal Protection Clause." *J.E.B.*, 511 U.S. at 130–31. This Court's decisions under the Fourteenth Amendment "reveal a strong presumption that gender classifications are invalid." *Id.* at 152. (Kennedy, J., concurring). In *Frontiero*, a plurality of this Court concluded that "classifications based upon sex, like classifications based upon race, alienage, and national origin, are inherently suspect, and must therefore be subjected to close judicial scrutiny." *Frontiero*, 411 U.S. at 688. That reasoning applies with equal force today. Sex, like race and national origin, is an immutable characteristic that this Court repeatedly has recognized is not usually relevant to any legislative classifications. *See City of Cleburne v. Cleburne Living Ctr.*, 473 U.S. 432, 440 (1985); *Frontiero*, 411 U.S. at 687–88. Gender classifications are unlikely to further a legitimate state interest but instead reflect "invidious, archaic, and overbroad stereotypes about the relative abilities of men and women." *See, e.g., J.E.B.*, 511 U.S. at 131.

As the majority affirms, "there can be no doubt that our Nation has a long and unfortunate history of sex discrimination." *Frontiero*, 411 U.S. at 684.

"While the prejudicial attitudes toward women in this country have not been identical to those held toward racial minorities, the similarities between the experiences of racial minorities and women, in some contexts, overpower those differences." *J.E.B.*, 511 U.S. at 135. "From its beginning, the United States maintained a dual system of law for men and women – separate and unequal." Br. for Nat'l Women's Law Ctr. as Amici Curiae, *et al.*, at 27. Under the Constitution, women were second-class citizens, denied the right to vote until 1920. With respect to jury service, "African Americans and women share a history of total exclusion; ... [s]o well entrenched was this exclusion of women that in 1880 this Court, while finding that the exclusion of African American men from juries violated the Fourteenth Amendment, expressed no doubt that a State 'may confine the selection [of jurors] to males.' *J.E.B.*, 511 U.S. at 131 (citing *Strauder v. West Virginia*, 100 U.S. 303, 310 (1880)).

In the private sphere, state law made the husband the legal "head" of each family and sole guardian of his wife, his children, and their property.[28] A husband also had the sole right to collect wages for his wife's work outside the home, owned his wife's personal property outright, and had the right to manage and control all of her real property, including the right to keep profits from it. *Id.* A wife could not sell her property without her husband's consent. *Id.* at 562. As Justice Black stated, "This rule has worked out in reality to mean that though the husband and the wife are one, the one is the husband." *United States v. Yazell*, 382 U.S. 341, 361 (1966) (Black, J., dissenting).

The position of women throughout much of the nineteenth century "was, in many respects, comparable to that of blacks under the pre-Civil War slave codes." *J.E.B.*, 511 U.S. at 136; *Frontiero*, 411 U.S. at 685. *See also* Gunnar Myrdal, *An American Dilemma: The Negro Problem and American Democracy* 1073 (1944) (recognizing that the legal status of women and children served as a model for the legal status of slaves). Even after the Civil War and the passage of the Fourteenth Amendment, women had neither the right to vote, *Minor v. Happersett*, 88 U.S. 162, 177–78 (1875), nor the right to practice law, *Bradwell v. Illinois*, 83 U.S. 130, 139 (1873), nor serve on juries. Women were long excluded from public education, as the majority explains at length. *United States v. Virginia*, 518 U.S. at 536–38. Virginia exemplifies this history: it resisted the admission of women to its flagship university, the

---

[28] Barbara Allen Babcock, *et al.*, Sex Discrimination and the Law: Causes and Remedies 561 (1975). The husband also was immune from any legal consequences for raping his wife and was effectively immunized for beating her by the law's reluctance to intervene unless she suffered serious and permanent injury. *Id.* at 562–63 and n.8; *see also id.* at 1–2 (describing the dual law system for men and women).

University of Virginia, until forced by a court order. *See Kirstein v. Rector and Visitors of the Univ. of Va.*, 309 F. Supp. 184, 187 (E.D. Va. 1970).

Neither federal nor state legislatures provided a remedy for the exclusion of women from higher education, employment opportunities, or equal pay. During the late nineteenth and early twentieth centuries, states enacted laws explicitly requiring both private and public employers to discriminate against women at work, excluding them from certain occupations and limiting the type of work that could be assigned. Babcock, *supra* note 28, at 261. Until very recently, this Court routinely upheld laws that barred women from employment, the right to vote, and jury service. *See, e.g., Goesaert v. Cleary*, 335 U.S. 464, 466 (1948) (upholding state law prohibiting women from employment as bartenders); *Hoyt v. Florida*, 368 U.S. 57, 62 (1961) (upholding state law exempting women from jury service). In *Hoyt v. Florida*, this Court in 1961 reaffirmed the constitutionality of excluding women wholesale from jury service, noting that "woman is still regarded as the center of home and family life." *Id.* at 62. In addition, *Hoyt* held that states were constitutionally permitted to categorically exclude women, making individual exceptions. *Id.* It was not until 1975 that this Court finally struck down a state law exempting women from jury service. *See Taylor v. Louisiana*, 419 U.S. 522, 537 (1975). Even then, many states continued to exclude women through registration requirements and automatic exemptions to deter them from exercising their right to jury service. *See, e.g., Fay v. New York*, 332 U.S. 261, 289–90 & n.31 (1947).

Congress itself has acknowledged that "classifications based upon sex are inherently invidious," enacting specific laws to ameliorate some, but not all, types of gender-based discrimination. *Frontiero*, 411 U.S. at 687–88; *see, e.g.*, Title IX of the Education Amendments of 1972, 20 U.S.C. § 1681(a) (1994) (generally prohibiting sex discrimination in federally funded education programs); Title VII of the Civil Rights Act of 1964, as amended, 42 U.S.C. § 2000e-2 (1988) (prohibiting sex discrimination by employers with fifteen or more employees).[29] Such remedies are not coextensive, however, with remedies for discrimination based upon race, color, national origin, or disability.

Nearly twenty years after the application of intermediate scrutiny to sex-based classifications in *Reed v. Reed*, "women still face pervasive, though at times more subtle, discrimination," that continues to exclude them from full citizenship and public spheres of power. *See Frontiero*, 411 U.S. at 686.

---

[29] Title VI of the Civil Rights Act, 42 U.S.C. § 2000d (1988), prohibits discrimination in federally funded programs on the basis of race, color, or national origin. The Rehabilitation Act of 1973 (§ 504), 29 U.S.C. § 794 (1988), provides similar protection from discrimination based on disability. There is no parallel federal statutory protection, however, from government-sponsored discrimination based on sex.

Although women now compose nearly half the U.S. workforce, they are still relegated to jobs that generally pay less and provide fewer benefits.[30] In 1994, women earned an average of 72 cents for every dollar earned by men.[31] The Federal Glass Ceiling Commission concluded that gender stereotyping continues to block the full advancement of women in the workplace.[32] In the political process, women also remain underrepresented, a fact hardly surprising given this country's history regarding exclusion of women from the right to vote. See Ruth Bader Ginsburg, *Women as Full Members of the Club: An Evolving American Ideal,* 6 Hum. Rts. 1, 4 (1976).[33]

The persistence of these social, economic, and political disparities confirms that women remain a disadvantaged group adversely affected by pernicious gender stereotypes and norms. These are vestiges of the legal system that subordinated women, relegating them to second-class citizenship. This longstanding and continuing history of discrimination against women continues to infect the processes of governmental and judicial decision making. Because gender stereotypes are deeply rooted in this history of exclusion of women under law, political leaders and courts alike often have difficulty in recognizing discrimination. See, e.g., Wendy Williams, *The Equality Crisis: Some Reflections on Culture, Courts and Feminism,* 7 Women's Rts. L. Rep. 175 (1982). As this case demonstrates, sex discrimination has often been justified by lawmakers and courts alike under the guise of protectionist concerns for women's supposed health and welfare. See, e.g., *Goesaert,* 335 U.S. at 466; *Michael M. v. Superior Court,* 450 U.S. 464, 470–73 (1981); Nancy Gertner, *Bakke on Affirmative Action for Women: Pedestal or Cage?* 14 Harv. C.R.-C.L.

---

[30] Women occupy predominantly administrative support jobs nationwide across all industries. Moreover, women are underrepresented in many professional and technical jobs, comprising only 8.6 percent of all engineers, 3.9 percent of airplane pilots and navigators, 18.6 percent of architects, and little more than 20 percent of doctors and lawyers. See Br. for Nat'l Women's Law Center, ACLU, *et al.* as Amici Curiae in Support of Pet'r at 32; Bureau of the Census, U.S. Dep't of Commerce, Statistical Abstract of the United States 1994 at 407–09 (114th ed. Sept. 1994).

[31] Nat'l Comm. on Pay Equity, The Wage Gap: 1993 (citing U.S. Dep't of Commerce, Bureau of the Census, Current Population Reports, Series P-60).

[32] Federal Glass Ceiling Commission, Good for Business: Making Full Use of the Nation's Human Capital at 26–29 (1995).

[33] In 1995, women constitute only 8 percent of all U.S. Senators and 10.8 percent of all U.S. Representatives, 20.7 percent of state legislators, 25.9 percent of all state elective executive offices, and there is only one woman governor in all 50 states. See Br. for Nat'l Women's Law Ctr., ACLU, *et al.* as Amici Curiae, *supra* note 7, at 36 (citing Center for the American Woman and Politics, Women in Elective Office 1995 (1995) (fact sheet) and Center for the American Women and Politics, Women Candidates and Winners in 1992 (1992) (fact sheet)). No woman has ever served as President or Vice President of the United States, a Secretary of State, Secretary of the Treasury, Secretary of Defense, or Speaker of the House. *Id.* at 36.

L. Rev. 173, 184–89 (1979). The difficulty of distinguishing real physical differences from paternalistic classifications that stereotype or exclude women mandates the same level of strict scrutiny for gender-based classifications as those based upon race, national origin, or religion.

For these reasons, gender classifications, like classifications based upon race, are inherently suspect and should be subject to strict scrutiny. Strict scrutiny requires courts to evaluate carefully governmental classifications based on gender – a characteristic that, like race, seldom provides a relevant basis for disparate treatment. States that seek to justify the use of gender classifications must demonstrate that they are narrowly tailored to meet a compelling government interest.

Strict scrutiny would not prohibit all gender or sex classifications or prevent states from using sex classifications for certain remedial purposes – "to compensate women for particular economic disabilities they have suffered, to promote equal employment opportunity, [and] to advance full development of the talent and capacities of our Nation's people." *United States v. Virginia*, 518 U.S. at 533 (citations and quotations omitted). The use of gender classifications, narrowly tailored to remedy past discrimination against women as a class, could survive scrutiny, for example, where the state can prove there are no less restrictive or discriminatory means of achieving redress. But the heightened level of scrutiny would insure that all persons, regardless of their sex, are treated equally under the law, free from the subtle forms of discrimination and gender bias that thus far have artificially limited the full development of the talents and contribution of our female citizens.

IV

A

Virginia compounds the harm of its wholesale exclusion of women based on discredited gender stereotypes by proposing to establish and maintain a segregated system of leadership education – a military-style program for men at VMI and a non-military program for women at VWIL – that is intentionally different and unequal.

Our remedial principles are clear: a remedial decree must place those persons unconstitutionally denied an opportunity or advantage in "the position they would have occupied in the absence of [discrimination]," *Milliken v. Bradley*, 433 U.S. 267, 280 (1977), and "eliminate [so far as possible] the discriminatory effects of the past" and "bar like discrimination in the future." *Louisiana v. United States*, 380 U.S. 145, 154 (1965). The Court of Appeals erred when it approved Virginia's remedial proposal. In holding that VWIL was "sufficiently comparable" to VMI to justify preserving the unique benefits of VMI for men only, the Court of Appeals replaced the well-established test of intermediate scrutiny with a highly deferential standard that fell below the protections of the now-discredited "separate but equal" test in *Plessy v. Ferguson*, 163 U.S. 537, 540 (1896). In so doing, the Court of Appeals jettisoned modern equal protection jurisprudence, reverting to precedent prior to *Reed v. Reed*, when gender-based classifications were routinely upheld.

In *Sweatt v. Painter*, 339 U.S. 629, 635–36 (1950), this Court rejected a similar effort by Texas to create a new law school for blacks solely to preserve the University of Texas Law School for whites only. Similar to the "remedy" in *Sweatt*, which was grounded in the racist view that the presence of black students would sully the University of Texas, VWIL is grounded in an inherently debased view of women as inferior and "toxic" to VMI. Funded in large part by VMI alumni, VWIL's "primary, overriding purpose is not to create a new type of educational opportunity for women, nor to broaden the Commonwealth's educational base for producing a special kind of citizen-soldier leadership, nor to further diversify the Commonwealth's higher education system ... but ... to allow VMI to continue to exclude women." 44 F.3d 1229, 1247 (4th Cir. 1995) (Phillips, J., dissenting). VWIL thus expresses Virginia's core belief that women are different and unequal to men and that their very presence will destroy what is valuable about VMI. This is not a remedy; it is misogyny.

Even if VWIL somehow provided women with the same level of prestige and opportunities as VMI, it would still fail to provide women with equal protection under the law. Virginia cannot remedy its violation by relegating women who are interested in VMI to a separate program for women. This Court recognized in *Brown v. Board of Education* that "education is perhaps the most important function of state and local governments" and that "the opportunity of an education[] ... where the state has undertaken to provide it, is a right which must be made available to all on equal terms." 347 U.S. 483, 493 (1955); *see also United States v. Fordice*, 505 U.S. 717 (1992). As this Court held in *Brown*, "separate educational facilities are inherently unequal." *Brown*, 347 U.S. at 495.

This is just as true when states segregate students based upon sex as it is when states segregate students based upon race. Like the racial segregation of students in public schools, state policies that segregate men and women into separate educational programs historically have been rooted in the belief that men and women are inherently different and unequal. Sex-segregated public educational programs that are based upon generalizations about "most" men or women are just as pernicious as those based upon race. All persons "have the right not to be excluded summarily because of discriminatory and stereotypical presumptions that reflect and reinforce patterns of historical discrimination." *J.E.B.*, 511 U.S. at 141–42. Wittingly or unwittingly, such state programs reflect and reinforce our history of treating women as second-class citizens under law, stigmatizing women as different and unequal to men.[34]

B

Having been found to have unconstitutionally excluded women from its public educational program, VMI must not only eliminate its discriminatory policy but also eliminate the effects of past discrimination and prevent future discrimination. The ultimate objective is to make whole the victims of discrimination and achieve a school system "wholly free from [...] discrimination." *Milliken*, 433 U.S. at 280, 283. In *Brown v. Board of Education*, and subsequent cases, this Court has recognized that segregated educational facilities are part of a system of subordination that must be eliminated "root and branch." *See, e.g., Green v. County Sch. Bd.*, 391 U.S. 430, 438 (1968).

In the context of higher education, for example, we have held that the establishment of race-neutral policies alone is not sufficient to discharge a state's obligation to dismantle a formerly *de jure* segregated system. *Fordice*, 505 U.S. at 729. "Freedom of choice" is not a talisman, but a means to a constitutionally required end – the abolition of segregation and its effects. *Green*, 391 U.S. at 440. Providing students the choice to attend a previously segregated institution, we have recognized, has tended to perpetuate discrimination, placing the burden of desegregation on the excluded group, sometimes making them targets of violence and reprisal. *Id.* at 440 n.5 (quoting U.S. Comm'n on Civil Rights, *Southern School Desegregation, 1966–1967*, at 88 (1967)). Many policies and factors affect student choice; those that have segregative effects must be eliminated as well. *See Fordice*, 505 U.S. at 729.

To fully eliminate discrimination in higher education, a state institution must closely examine all of its policies, even those that are facially neutral, to determine whether these policies are rooted in the former system and continue to influence student choice or have discriminatory effects. *Id.* It is no

---

[34] This case involves public education and the exclusion of women from a historically males-only public college. It does not present the issue of whether the exclusion of men from private women's colleges could be held to violate the Equal Protection Clause. Resolution of that issue would require a determination that a private college constitutes a state actor and, if so, whether it could justify its exclusionary policy under strict scrutiny as a form of narrowly tailored affirmative action.

defense to argue that a policy does not intentionally discriminate, so long as the policy can be traced back to the prior *de jure* system. *Id.* at 731–32.

Although VMI now objects to changing any aspect of its system to admit women, it voluntarily modified aspects of its system when it admitted African-American male students to better accommodate a racially diverse student body. 766 F. Supp. at 1436. VMI changed its school fight song from the Confederate song "Dixie," and eliminated the requirement that cadets salute the Confederate flag and the tomb of General Robert E. Lee at ceremonies and sports events. *United States v. Virginia*, 518 U.S. at 546 n.16. It also created new programs to facilitate the retention and recruitment of black students, including an academic support program and a social club for black students to provide support to "minority members of a dominantly white and tradition-oriented student body." *Id.*

Just as VMI abandoned some of its traditions in recognition of the need to respect and include a racially diverse student body, so it must modify its system and traditions to respect and fully include women. Incorporating women into its ranks will require VMI to fundamentally change its mission and aspects of its methodology, both of which are designed to create and celebrate a certain narrow view of men and masculinity. To eliminate its discrimination against women root and branch, VMI must identify and eliminate those policies and practices that perpetuate the exclusion of women, disparately impact women, or impede their full participation at VMI. To put women in the same position they would have been absent VMI's males-only policy, VMI must re-examine its policies and practices and eliminate those that assume or reinforce the expectation that cadets are, or should be, male. Because VMI has only admitted male students, its policies and practices have been designed solely with reference to males. Its uniforms are designed for male bodies, for example, as are its grooming and physical fitness standards. Had women been admitted to VMI from the beginning, it is likely that VMI would have made different choices about its standards and practices, taking into account its obligation to maximize the benefits of its program for both men *and* women.

To fully eradicate the vestiges of its discriminatory policy, VMI must also identify and eliminate those policies or practices that assume or reinforce gendered norms of masculinity, particularly those that demean or devalue women. The record in this case does not include detailed testimony from VMI students or alumni as to how the adversative system actually works. Like other traditionally male institutions such as the military, however, VMI reinforces gendered norms of masculinity through practices that challenge men to prove their manhood by distinguishing themselves from women and other men who are not considered adequately masculine. Traditionally male institutions, such as VMI and the U.S. military, are organized around a culture of masculinity that is based upon, and celebrates, certain masculine norms and values while denigrating women and social notions of femininity. *See* Karen O. Dunivin, *Military Culture: Change and Continuity*, 20 Armed Forces & Soc'y 531, 534–37 (1994). Under this view of masculinity, there is "one categorical imperative: don't be a girl." Kenneth L. Karst, *The Pursuit of Manhood*, 38 UCLA L. Rev. 499, 503 (1991). Within these institutions, masculinity is created by and between men, through a range of homosocial interactions that challenge men to prove they are not women. *See* Michael Kimmel, *Manhood in America: A Cultural History* 8 (1st ed. 1996). During basic training, or boot camp, for example, "traditional images of independent, competitive, aggressive, and virile males are promoted and rewarded." Dunivin, *supra*, at 536. This association of the military with masculinity, enforced through a range of institutional practices and rituals, functions to justify the exclusion of women. *See id.* at 534–37.

The District Court found that, prior to the admission of women, West Point cadets were routinely subjected to hazing, "including demeaning or insulting activity." 766 F. Supp. at 1441. Following the admission of women, West Point officially abandoned these hazing rituals. *Id.* VMI was patterned after the U.S. Military Academy at West Point and its "adversative system" may well include similar practices that demean both women and men.[35] Sexually demeaning hazing practices have been reported in the press at both VMI and the Citadel, a similar males-only, military-style state college in South Carolina.[36] Some

[35] There is documentation that suggests that some of VMI's rituals have involved forced nudity, the use of sexualized language, and physical violence that demeans and humiliates both women and men. One of the unofficial cadet activities is a naked shower run. William A. DeVan, Note, *Toward a New Standard in Gender Discrimination: The Case of Virginia Military Institute*, 33 Wm. & Mary L. Rev. 489, 534 n.313 (1992). Freshmen males "are stripped naked and run through the communal shower with some shower heads turned on all hot and others all cold." *Id.* Several cadets were recently suspended for attacking a cadet who had been excused from physical fitness training for medical reasons. Ellen Nakashima, *6 at VMI Suspended in Attack on Cadet Taken Off 'Rat Line'*, Wash. Post, April 17, 1996, at D01. They entered his room at night, "flipped his bunk, held him down," and attempted to shave his head and "spray his testicles with a hot balm." *Id.*

[36] The Citadel is also the subject of a lawsuit challenging its exclusion of women. During a hearing before the District Court in that case, a former cadet testified that "[w]hen you make a mistake, you are either a faggot, a queer, weak, a woman, and then the terms just go right down into the gutter from there." Cadets criticized each other by using sexually explicit and degrading terms for "woman." There have been allegations in the press that the "adversative" system at the Citadel has included sexualized and physical abuse of male cadets. *See* Susan Faludi, *The Naked Citadel*, New Yorker, Sept. 5, 1994, at 62, 67–68, 70 (discussing the adversative method); Rick Reilly, *What Is The Citadel?*, Sports Illustrated, Sept. 14, 1992, at 70 (analysis of the adversative method).

of these rituals include the use of physical or sexualized violence and threats of violence against male cadets, and the use of sexualized and humiliating language that demeans women and men alike. Rituals that demean women or punish men who may not conform to stereotypical notions of masculinity constitute gender discrimination. *See Price Waterhouse v. Hopkins*, 490 U.S. 228, 250 (1989) (holding that an employer who punishes employees who fail to conform to stereotypical expectations of members of his or her sex discriminates on the basis of sex).

As part of its remedial obligations, VMI must identify and eliminate any such practices or traditions to ensure that both men and women are treated with equal respect and dignity. None of these practices is essential to fulfilling its mission of creating leaders. VMI's "adversative" methodology is simply a means to an end – not an end itself. Indeed, Virginia concedes that its goal of producing leaders could be accomplished at VWIL, a radically different and non-military institution.

As VMI opens its doors to women, it must take all necessary steps to create an inclusive environment for all students, regardless of their sex or gender. At a minimum, Virginia and VMI must take affirmative steps to prevent and address the possibility of hostility and harassment of female students. In a similar lawsuit against The Citadel, South Carolina's males-only public college, the prospect of the admission of women has been accompanied by hostility and harassment toward the female plaintiff.[37] The integration of women into the federal service academies beginning in 1976 also was accompanied by widespread harassment and hostility toward women.[38] While we have no evidence in this record of such hostility, VMI officials and alumni have relentlessly opposed the admission of women throughout this lawsuit, devoting millions of dollars to keeping women out. It is now imperative for VMI to take all necessary steps to prevent the harassment of women, including

[37] T-shirts emblazoned with the motto "1,952 Bulldogs and One Bitch" above the image of the Citadel mascot (a bulldog) were sold and worn. Rupert Cornwell, *Knives Sharpen for Haircut of the Century*, The Indep. (London), August 12, 1994, at 9. Bumper stickers proclaiming, "Save the Males" were printed and handed out in the courtroom. Catherine S. Manegold, "'Save the Males' Becomes Battle Cry in Citadel's Defense Against Women," N.Y. Times, May 23, 1994, at A10.
[38] According to a GAO survey of sexual and gender harassment, over half of female cadets in military academies experienced "mocking gestures," whistles and catcalls on a recurring basis and half experienced offensive posters or graffiti and "derogatory comments" on a recurring basis. One in six female cadets reported being repeated targets of "unwanted horseplay or hijinks" while one in seven reported "unwanted sexual advances." U.S. Gen. Accounting Office, GAO/Nsiad-94-6, DOD Service Academies: More Actions Needed To Eliminate Sexual Harassment 21 (1994).

implementing policies prohibiting harassment, training for students and staff, and creating a system for reporting and addressing complaints.

This will take time and commitment. To ensure the adoption of an effective remedial plan, I would order Virginia and VMI to submit a proposed remedial plan within 120 days that provides for the immediate elimination of its males-only policy, eliminates all vestiges of its past discrimination, and prevents future violations. I would remand to the District Court for further proceedings to review the plan to determine whether it satisfies the requirements of equal protection as set forth in this opinion, and retain jurisdiction to oversee the implementation of the plan.

We are long past the time when a state can treat its daughters so differently than its sons. Women who are qualified for the rigors of the military-style program at VMI are entitled not merely to comparable education at a females-only college, but equal access to opportunities for political and economic power that Virginia offers male graduates. 44 F.3d at 1250 (Phillips, J. dissenting). To fully eliminate the vestiges of its males-only policy, and prevent discrimination against women in the future, VMI must develop a plan to guarantee women equal respect and dignity. Rather than destroy VMI, the admission of women is likely to promote policies that cultivate respect and dignity for all cadets, whether male or female, masculine or feminine.

21

Commentary on *Oncale v. Sundowner Offshore Services, Inc.*

Margaret E. Johnson

INTRODUCTION

In *Oncale v. Sundowner Offshore Services, Inc.*,[1] the U.S. Supreme Court decided that same-sex sexual harassment was actionable as a violation of Title VII of the Civil Rights Act of 1964.[2] Under Title VII, an employer cannot take an adverse employment action "because of sex." In *Oncale*, the harassment included physical assaults of a sexual nature, including threatened rape. Importantly, the text of Title VII does not include "sexual orientation" or "gender identity" in its list of protected classes that includes race, color, religion, and national origin, in addition to sex.[3]

As important as the *Oncale* ruling is for plaintiffs subjected to same-sex sexual harassment, it is also problematic. For instance, the U.S. Supreme Court did not include discrimination based on sexual orientation and gender identity as discrimination because of sex. In addition, many courts have interpreted the Court's opinion to limit the theories by which a plaintiff could prove same-sex discrimination to those specifically enumerated by the Court, thereby precluding other theories, such as gender role policing.[4] The feminist judgment, by Professor Ann McGinley writing as Justice McGinley, seeks to correct these and other limitations of the original opinion.

THE U.S. SUPREME COURT DECISION

The facts of *Oncale* are set out in detail in the feminist judgment and need not be reiterated here. Writing for the U.S. Supreme Court, Justice Scalia

---

[1]   *Oncale v. Sundowner Offshore Servs., Inc.*, 523 U.S. 75 (1988).
[2]   42 U.S.C. §2000e-2(a)(1) (2012).
[3]   *Id.*
[4]   *See, e.g., Wasek v. Arrow Energy Servs., Inc.*, 682 F.3d 463, 467–68 (6th Cir. 2012); *La Day v. Catalyst Tech., Inc.*, 302 F.3d 474, 478 (5th Cir. 2002).

provided in the original opinion only limited facts, citing the need for "brevity and dignity." The facts of the majority thus state little more than that during his employment at Sundowner Offshore Inc., Oncale was forcibly subjected to "sex-related, humiliating actions" by male supervisors and coworkers.[5]

On the legal issue, the Court began by holding that "nothing in Title VII necessarily bars a claim of discrimination 'because of ... sex' merely because the plaintiff and the defendant ... are of the same sex."[6] The Court enumerated three ways that a plaintiff could prove that same-sex harassment was because of sex and in violation of Title VII. First, the plaintiff could raise the inference of sex discrimination if the harasser was homosexual, making the harassment motivated by desire. Second, the plaintiff could argue that the harassment used "sex-specific and derogatory terms," evidencing that "the harasser [wa]s motivated by general hostility to the presence of [that specific sex] in the workplace." Third, the plaintiff could "offer direct comparative evidence about how the alleged harasser treated members of both sexes in a mixed-sex workplace." The Court emphasized, however, that "ordinary socializing in the workplace – such as male-on-male horseplay or intersexual flirtation" would not be discrimination because of sex because it would not be sufficiently severe or pervasive enough to create a hostile work environment.[7]

THE CONTEXT OF THE ORIGINAL *ONCALE* OPINION

Two important U.S. Supreme Court cases preceded the *Oncale* decision: *Meritor Savings Bank v. Vinson*[8] and *Price Waterhouse v. Hopkins*.[9] First, in *Meritor*, the Court held that "a plaintiff may establish a violation of Title VII by proving that discrimination based on sex has created a hostile or abusive work environment."[10] Second, in *Price Waterhouse*, the plaintiff claimed she was denied partnership because of her failure to conform to feminine stereotypes. The Court interpreted Title VII's prohibition of discrimination based on sex to require that "gender must be irrelevant to employment decisions."[11] Partners' sex-stereotyping comments during their review of plaintiff for partnership evidenced that gender might have been a "motivating part" of the employment decision in violation of Title VII.[12]

---

[5] *Oncale*, 523 U.S. at 77.
[6] *Id.* at 79.
[7] *Id.* at 81.
[8] *Meritor Savings Bank v. Vinson*, 477 U.S. 57 (1986).
[9] *Price Waterhouse v. Hopkins*, 490 U.S. 228 (1989).
[10] 477 U.S. at 66.
[11] 490 U.S. at 240.
[12] *Id.* at 250–51.

These cases laid important groundwork for *Oncale*, which raised issues of same-sex and sex stereotyping harassment. At the time of *Oncale*, public opinion did not favor legal recognition of rights for lesbians, gays, bisexuals, and transgender people. *Bowers v. Hardwick*, which upheld the constitutionality of sodomy laws on due process grounds, was still the law of the land.[13] *Lawrence v. Texas, U.S. v. Windsor*, and *Obergefell v. Hodges*, finding same-sex relationships and marriage constitutionally protected as a liberty interest, were still years away.[14]

THE IMPACT OF *ONCALE*

The *Oncale* decision both contributes to and hinders the fight for gender justice. It is important for its recognition that harassment is actionable when the harasser and the harassed employee are of the same gender. This holding reaffirms a critical strand of feminist legal theory – equality theory – or the principle that "individuals who are alike should be treated alike, according to their actual characteristics, rather than stereotypical assumptions."[15]

The decision is also important in its recognition that the "desire" of the harasser is one, but not the only, possible motivation for sexual harassment.[16] The recognition of gender hostility as a basis for sexual harassment represents a noteworthy acceptance of the anti-subordination theory that sexual harassment is a manifestation of power used to oppress marginalized persons, and is not necessarily about sexual interest.[17] As such, the decision indicates that gender harassment is part of "the overall institutional oppression" based on gender.[18]

Despite these positive outcomes, however, the legacy of *Oncale* is highly problematic and rich with opportunities for feminist rewriting.

THE FEMINIST JUDGMENT

The feminist judgment retains the outcome of the original decision but substantially alters and adds to its reasoning.

---

[13] *Bowers v. Hardwick*, 478 U.S. 186, 196 (1986).
[14] *Lawrence v. Texas*, 539 U.S. 558, 578 (2003); *United States v. Windsor*, 133 S. Ct. 2675, 2694 (2013); *Obergefell v. Hodges*, 135 S. Ct. 2584 (2015).
[15] Katharine T. Bartlett, *Gender Law*, 1 *Duke J. Gender L. & Pol'y* 1, 1 (1994).
[16] The Court states that such inference should be extended to male–male sexual harassment if the harasser is homosexual. *Oncale*, 523 U.S. at 80.
[17] Catharine A. MacKinnon, *The Sexual Harassment of Working Women*, 1, 9–10 (1979).
[18] Bartlett, *supra* note 15, at 10.

Narrative and dignity

The feminist judgment takes issue with the majority's shying away from the graphic sexual nature of the harassment of Oncale. McGinley emphasizes that dignity requires the Court to provide details of the harassment because "[a] decision not to relate the facts alleged protects those who may have engaged in the behavior and diminishes the perceived severity of the acts." McGinley's account of Oncale's narrative of the harassment is grounded in feminist legal theory, both narrative theory and dignity theory. Narrative theory, drawing from both anti-subordination and anti-essentialism theory,[19] emphasizes the importance of an employee's own personal account of the discrimination because it can provide a "challenge to conventional under-standings of objectivity" and be "a source of empirical truth."[20] By providing Oncale's fuller narrative, McGinley shines a spotlight on Oncale's experience of the brutal harassment and holds his harassers accountable for their extreme behavior. As such, Oncale's experience stands as an alternate narrative to "the dominant stories or universal narratives on which the law is based and give[s] voice to the actual, otherwise submerged, experiences of the dominated."[21]

Providing a full account of the harassment also supports Oncale's dignity because it surfaces his human capacity for surviving, resisting, and responding to the harassment.[22] It offers power to others in similar situations to learn from and organize against similar forms of discrimination. This support for Oncale's dignity is important because dignity makes possible the exercise of agency, such as agency to resist the oppression of sex-based harassment.[23]

---

[19] Id. at 15 (anti-essentialism seeks to attack the assumed "privileged norm – that of the white, middle class, heterosexual woman – and thereby deny or ignore differences based on race, class, sexual identity, and other characteristics that inform a woman's identity.")

[20] Id. at 6.

[21] Id. at 17 and n. 83 (citing Lucie E. White, Subordination, Rhetorical Survival Skills, and Sunday Shoes: Notes on the Hearing of Mrs. G, 38 Buff. L. Rev. 1 (1990)); Martha R. Mahoney, Legal Images of Battered Women: Redefining the Issue of Separation, 90 Mich. L. Rev. 1 (1991); Robin West, The Difference in Women's Hedonic Lives: A Phenomenological Critique of Feminist Legal Theory, 3 Wis. Women's L.J. 81 (1987); Regina Austin, Sapphire Bound!, 1989 Wis. L. Rev. 539; Richard Delgado, Storytelling for Oppositionalists and Others: A Plea for Narrative, 87 Mich. L. Rev. 2073 (1989); Patricia J. Williams, The Alchemy of Race and Rights: Diary of a Law Professor (1991)). But see Kathy Abrams, Hearing the Call of Stories, 79 Cal. L. Rev. 971 (1991) (narratives are problematic when they create an essentialized new truth, seemingly exclude different experiences, or are untrue).

[22] Margaret E. Johnson, A Home with Dignity: Domestic Violence and Property Rights, 2014 B.Y.U. L. Rev. 1, 10 (2014).

[23] Margaret E. Johnson, Redefining Harm, Reimagining Remedies, and Reclaiming Domestic Violence Law, 42 U.C. Davis L. Rev. 1107, 1164 n. 24 (2009) (citing Kathryn Abrams, Subordination and Agency in Sexual Harassment Law, in Directions in Sexual Harassment

Heteronormativity critiqued

The feminist judgment also exposes discrimination law's heteronormativity, which assumes opposite-sex sexual relationships are normal and preferred. Specifically, McGinley notes that decision makers have easily inferred that male-on-female harassment involving sexual activity is discrimination "because of ... sex." McGinley rightly points out that this inference is based on an assumption that a sexual proposition would not be made to a member of the same sex because the majority of people are heterosexual. While the original opinion identified this inference it nonetheless accepted it uncritically. The feminist judgment explicitly addresses and critiques the bias inherent in this view.

Harassment motivated by hostility, not desire

While the original opinion briefly mentions harassment based on hostility, McGinley highlights gender hostility as a bigger problem than sexual attraction in sexual harassment cases. She states that "when the facts of the sexual harassment cases are examined closely, it appears that sexual interest may actually mask hostility rather than sexual attraction." The feminist judgment provides examples that show hostility undergirding harassment "because of ... sex": women who harass other women to ensure their own positions among male employees or to punish women who fail to conform to sex stereotypes. McGinley's opinion clearly understands and establishes that sexual harassment is "better understood as the expression, in sexual terms, of power, privilege, or dominance," not sexual desire.[24] As Katherine Franke has noted, "[w]hat makes it sex discrimination is not ... that the conduct is sexual, but that the sexual conduct is being used to enforce or perpetuate gender norms and stereotypes."[25]

Moreover, as Vicki Schultz has argued, the focus on desire in sexual harassment law often marginalizes the evidence of harassment that involves gender hostility and derogation without any sexual comments or actions. As a result, courts may dismiss claims because they have disaggregated the "sexual" and gendered harassment evidence rather than combining them for a complete

---

Law 112–14 (Catharine A. MacKinnon and Reva B. Siegel eds., 2004) (agency is the "capacity for self-definition and self-direction' despite subordination based on gender").

[24] Katherine M. Franke, *What's Wrong with Sexual Harassment*, *in* Directions in Sexual Harassment Law, 174 (Catharine A. MacKinnon and Reva B. Siegel eds., 2004).

[25] *Id.*

analysis of harassment because of sex.[26] McGinley's reasoning ensures that the law centralizes the importance of gender hostility to the determination of sexual harassment.

Masculinities

The feminist judgment utilizes masculinities theory to identify different ways in which Oncale could prove harassment "because of ... sex" even without a female comparator. As Ann McGinley and Nancy Dowd have argued, masculinities theory deconstructs the "universal man" assumed in some feminist legal theory to examine multiple masculinities and society's gendering of men by constructing what is male.[27] The feminist judgment explains that Oncale could show he was harassed because his male co-workers did not consider him sufficiently masculine. Oncale could also prove male co-workers harassed him because of sex by policing the "masculine boundaries of the job." The feminist judgment rejects the original opinion's minimizing of "hazing" and "roughhousing" as "ordinary socializing in the workplace." Rather, it emphasizes that "hazing" and "rough-housing" are "often gendered behavior occurring because of sex in order to establish the masculinity of the group or to get the newcomer to conform to the masculine behaviors."

Sex stereotyping

Relatedly, the feminist judgment also highlights the importance of sex stereotyping as a theory of discrimination. McGinley relies heavily on *Price Waterhouse*, a precedent conspicuously absent from the original decision. The feminist judgment uses *Price Waterhouse* to demonstrate that "because of ... sex" includes "because of gender" and, more specifically, "not only the biological sex of an individual, but also the societal expectations of a person of a particular biological sex." The feminist judgment thus clarifies that *Price Waterhouse* interprets Title VII to preclude discrimination based on gendered expectations of the employee's sex and sex stereotyping. In this way, the feminist judgment confronts a key issue that has confounded the lower courts since *Oncale* – trying to distinguish between hostility based on sexual orientation and hostility based on sex. The feminist judgment dismantles this artificial

---

[26] Vicki Schultz, *Reconceptualizing Sexual Harassment*, 107 Yale L. J. 1683, 1720–29 (1998). *See also* Franke, *supra* note 24, at 174–75 (the desire paradigm for sexual harassment law leaves out the "gendered" nature of the harassment).

[27] Ann C. McGinley, *Masculinities at Work*, 83 Or. L. Rev. 359, 364–67 (2004); Nancy E. Dowd, *Masculinities and Feminist Legal Theory*, 23 Wis. J.L. Gender & Soc'y 201, 210–11 (2008).

distinction by noting that "separating biological sex from gender is a difficult, likely impossible, proposition."

Integrating research on sex stereotyping and masculinities theory, the feminist judgment further demonstrates that "concepts of masculinity and heterosexuality are so inextricably intertwined that it is virtually impossible to distinguish motivations." Accordingly, an employer should not be able to avoid Title VII liability by arguing that the harasser was motivated by an aversion to homosexuality and not by "sex."

Burden of proof

Finally, McGinley makes gender justice more accessible to Title VII sexual or gender harassment plaintiffs by altering the burden of proof for the "because of sex" element. A plaintiff raises an inference that the harassment occurred because of sex when she proves the harassment included any sexual or gendered words or acts. A plaintiff need not prove the harasser's desire or hostility, nor the dissimilar treatment of a comparable employee. The defendant then bears the burden to prove the behavior did not occur because of sex. McGinley's procedural change makes employers more accountable for words or acts of a sexual or gendered nature while, at the same time, ensuring Title VII prohibits discrimination, not mere incivility, with the additional "unwelcome" and "severe or pervasive" elements.

CONCLUSION

The *Oncale* feminist judgment demonstrates how much influence the reasoning of the U.S. Supreme Court has on the law. By altering the reasoning of the original decision, the feminist judgment furthers gender justice by interpreting Title VII's "because of sex" requirement in a way that honors the goal of the statute to eradicate all forms of discrimination based on sex.

Oncale v. Sundowner Offshore Services, Inc., 523 U.S. 75 (1998)

PER CURIAM (Justice Ann C. McGinley)

I

This case presents the question of whether workplace harassment violates Title VII's prohibition against "discriminat[ion] ... because of ... sex," 42

U.S.C. § 2000e-2(a)(1), when the harasser and the harassed employee are of the same biological sex. We have already concluded, in *Price Waterhouse v. Hopkins*, 490 U.S. 228, 241(1989), that Title VII's prohibition against discrimination because of sex also includes discrimination because of gender, and today we hold that discrimination against a person of the same biological sex or gender violates Title VII if the other requirements of proving illegal sex- or gender-based harassment are met.

The plaintiff, Joseph Oncale, brought suit in the United States District Court for the Eastern District of Louisiana, alleging that his employer, the defendant, Sundowner Offshore Services, Inc. (Sundowner), discriminated against him because of his sex in violation of Title VII. Specifically, the complaint alleged, and the plaintiff's affidavit and deposition avow, that Oncale's male supervisors and coworkers at Sundowner sexually harassed him at work. App. 19–22, 66–70, 76–77. The District Court granted summary judgment to the defendant, relying on the Fifth Circuit's decision in *Garcia v. Elf Atochem North America*, 28 F.3d 446, 451–52 (5th Cir. 1994), which held that Title VII provides no cause of action for same-sex harassment. App. 106. On appeal, a panel of the Fifth Circuit concluded that *Garcia* was binding Circuit precedent, and affirmed. 83 F.3d 118 (5th Cir. 1996). We granted certiorari. 520 U.S. 1263 (1997).

II

Because the District Court granted summary judgment for Respondents, we must assume the facts to be as alleged by Petitioner Joseph Oncale. While the precise details alleged by the plaintiff are disturbing, we believe it is important to relate the facts alleged. Some would argue that the dignity of this Court is sacrificed by the account, but if the allegations are true, the behavior constitutes a much greater insult to Joseph Oncale than to the Court. A decision not to relate the facts alleged protects those who may have engaged in the behavior and diminishes the perceived severity of the acts. Furthermore, the facts alleged here are important to the determination of the case: when taken in the light most favorable to the plaintiff, Joseph Oncale's coworkers and supervisors engaged in serious physical and verbal harassment that emphasized their masculinity and demeaned that of Mr. Oncale.

The facts alleged are as follows: In late October 1991, Oncale was working for Respondent Sundowner Offshore Services, Inc., on a Chevron U. S. A., Inc., oil platform in the Gulf of Mexico. He was employed as a roustabout on an eight-man crew, which included Respondents John Lyons, Danny

Pippen, and Brandon Johnson. Lyons, the crane operator, and Pippen, the driller, had supervisory authority. App. 41, 43, 77. On several occasions, Lyons, Pippen, and Johnson forcibly subjected Oncale to sex-related, humiliating actions against him in the presence of the rest of the crew. Pippen and Lyons also physically assaulted Oncale in a sexual manner, and threatened him with rape. Specifically, the complaint alleges, among other acts, that Pippen and Johnson restrained Oncale while Lyons placed his penis on the back of Oncale's head on one occasion, and on his arm on another occasion, that Lyons and Pippen made repeated threats that they would rape Oncale, and that Lyons forced a bar of soap between Oncale's buttocks while Pippen restrained Oncale in the shower on the employer's premises, App. 66–70, 76.

The complaint further alleges and Oncale avows in his affidavit and deposition that his complaints to supervisory personnel produced no remedial action; in fact, the company's Safety Compliance Clerk, Valent Hohen, told Oncale that Lyons and Pippen "picked [on] him [Hohen] all the time too," calling Hohen "Valene, Valene the Rig Queen," a name suggesting homosexuality. App. 77. Oncale eventually quit his job because he was afraid of his coworkers and supervisors. He repeatedly asked that his pink slip reflect that he "voluntarily left due to sexual harassment and verbal abuse." App. 79. When asked at his deposition why he left Sundowner, Oncale stated: "I felt that if I didn't leave my job, that I would be raped or forced to have sex." App. 71.

III

Title VII of the Civil Rights Act of 1964 provides, in relevant part, that "it shall be an unlawful employment practice for an employer ... to discriminate against any individual with respect to his compensation, terms, conditions, or privileges of employment, because of such individual's race, color, religion, sex, or national origin." 78 Stat. 255, as amended, 42 U. S. C. §2000e-2(a)(1). We have held that this provision not only covers "terms" and "conditions" in the narrow contractual sense, but also "evinces a congressional intent to strike at the entire spectrum of disparate treatment of men and women in employment." *Meritor Savings Bank* v. *Vinson*, 477 U.S. 57, 64 (1986) (citations and internal quotation marks omitted). "When the workplace is permeated with discriminatory intimidation, ridicule, and insult that is sufficiently severe or pervasive to alter the conditions of the victim's employment and [to] create an abusive working environment, Title VII is violated." *Harris v. Forklift Systems, Inc.*, 510 U.S. 17, 21 (1993) (citations and internal quotation marks omitted).

We have held that Title VII's prohibition of discrimination "because of ... sex" protects men as well as women, *Newport News Ship-building & Dry Dock*

Co. v. EEOC, 462 U.S. 669, 682 (1983), and in the related context of racial discrimination in the workplace we have rejected any conclusive presumption that an employer will not discriminate against members of his own race. "Because of the many facets of human motivation, it would be unwise to presume as a matter of law that human beings of one definable group will not discriminate against other members of their group." *Castaneda* v. *Partida*, 430 U.S. 482, 499 (1977). *See also id.* at 515–16, n.6 (Powell, J., joined by Burger, C. J., and Rehnquist, J., dissenting). In *Johnson* v. *Transportation Agency*, 480 U.S. 616 (1987), a male employee claimed that his employer discriminated against him because of his sex when it preferred a female employee for promotion. Although we ultimately rejected the claim on other grounds, we did not consider it significant that the supervisor who made that decision was also a man. *See id.* at 624–25. If our precedents leave any doubt on the question, we hold today that nothing in Title VII necessarily bars a claim of discrimination "because of ... sex" merely because the plaintiff and the defendant (or the person charged with acting on behalf of the defendant) are of the same biological sex. In fact, given the evidence that biological sex is not limited to two and that persons express themselves in a number of genders, "because of ... sex" must have a much broader application.

Courts have had little trouble with the principle that persons can discriminate against others of the same biological sex in cases like *Johnson*, where an employee claims to have been passed over for a job or promotion. But when the issue arises in the context of a "hostile work environment" sexual harassment claim, the state and federal courts have taken a bewildering variety of stances. Some, like the Fifth Circuit in this case, have held that same biological sex sexual harassment claims are never cognizable under Title VII. *See also, e. g., Goluszek* v. *H. R. Smith*, 697 F. Supp. 1452 (N.D. Ill. 1988). Others say that such claims are actionable only if the plaintiff can prove that the harasser is homosexual (and thus presumably motivated by sexual desire). *Compare McWilliams* v. *Fairfax County Board of Supervisors*, 72 F.3d 1191 (4th Cir. 1996), *with Wrightson* v. *Pizza Hut of America*, 99 F.3d 138 (4th Cir. 1996). Still others suggest that workplace harassment that is sexual in content is always actionable, regardless of the harasser's sex, sexual orientation, or motivations. *See Doe v. Belleville*, 119 F.3d 563 (7th Cir. 1997).

We see no justification in the statutory language or our precedents for a categorical rule excluding same biological sex harassment claims from the coverage of Title VII or for a limitation that would permit same biological sex harassment claims only upon proof that the alleged perpetrator is homosexual. But neither do we believe that sexual content in the workplace is always actionable under Title VII whether the behavior harasses members of a different biological sex or of the same biological sex. As some courts have observed, male-on-male sexual harassment in the workplace was assuredly not the principal evil Congress was concerned with when it enacted Title VII. However, statutory prohibitions often go beyond the principal evil to cover reasonably comparable evils; it is ultimately the provisions of our laws rather than the principal concerns of our legislators by which we are governed. Title VII prohibits "discriminat[ion] ... because of ... sex" in the "terms" or "conditions" of employment. Our holding in *Meritor Savings Bank v. Vinson* that this provision bans sexual harassment must extend to sexual harassment of any kind that meets the statutory requirements.

Proof standards

Respondents and their *amici* contend that recognizing liability for same biological sex harassment will transform Title VII into a general civility code for the American workplace. That risk is no greater for same biological sex harassment than for different biological sex harassment, and is adequately met by careful attention to the requirements of the statute. Title VII does not prohibit all verbal or physical harassment in the workplace; it is directed only at "*discriminat[ion] ... because of ... sex.*" In the context of a hostile work environment, the harassment must be sufficiently severe or pervasive to alter the terms or conditions of the plaintiff's employment. We have never held that workplace harassment, even harassment between men and women, is automatically discrimination because of sex because the words used have sexual content or connotations. Nonetheless, we believe that the presence of sexual or gendered content in the harassment is important in helping to determine whether the behavior occurred because of sex.[28] Therefore, we hold here that verbal and/or physical harassment of sexual or gendered content should raise a rebuttable inference that the harassment occurred because of sex. Once the plaintiff establishes the inference, the burden of persuasion on the issue of whether the behavior occurred because of sex shifts to the defendant.[29] Even if the defendant is unable to prove by a preponderance of the evidence that the harassment did not occur because of sex, the plaintiff must still prove by a preponderance of the evidence that the harassment was unwelcome and sufficiently severe or pervasive to alter the terms or conditions of employment.

[28] By gendered content, we mean physical or verbal behavior that is not necessarily sexual in nature but that has the intent or effect of harming a person because of the way the individual performs gender or that generally demeans an identifiable group (i.e., a man is called "effeminate" or "macho;" a woman described as "butch" or "prissy;" or "all men are stupid," "women are terrible drivers," etc.).

[29] If there is harassment but its content lacks sexual or gendered speech or behavior, the plaintiff should retain the burden of persuasion on the "because of sex" element.

These latter requirements impose sufficient limitations on lawsuits brought under Title VII as to avoid converting Title VII into a general civility code.

Defining "because of ... sex"

In harassment cases, courts and juries have found the inference of discrimination automatic in most male–female sexual harassment situations, because they interpret the challenged conduct as involving explicit or implicit proposals of sexual activity. Where the evidence suggests that the motivation of the perpetrator is sexual attraction to the victim, it may seem easy to assume that the proposals would not have been made to someone of the same sex. Of course, this assumption is based in heteronormativity – the belief that most individuals are heterosexual. The inference may be reasonable, but we note that sexuality exists along a spectrum between heterosexual and homosexual, with a number of persons either identifying as bisexual or having orientations that fall somewhere between heterosexual and homosexual. Many individuals who fail to identify as bisexual may adhere to heterosexual or homosexual behaviors exclusively because of societal pressures. By the same token, given that a statistical majority of persons continue to identify as heterosexual, harassing behaviors with sexual content in different sex situations can raise an inference that the behavior occurs because of sex. The same chain of inference would be available to a plaintiff alleging same biological sex harassment, if there were credible evidence that the harasser was homosexual, and that the motivation of the perpetrator is sexual attraction to the victim.

It is important to recognize that harassing conduct need not be motivated by sexual desire to support an inference of discrimination on the basis of sex. Indeed, when the facts of the sexual harassment cases are examined closely, it appears that sexual interest may actually mask hostility rather than sexual attraction. Sex may also be used as a weapon or "technology" of sexism that is motivated by hostility. *See* Katherine M. Franke, *What's Wrong With Sexual Harassment?*, 49 Stan. L. Rev. 691, 693 (1997). In the alternative, motivation that begins as sexual desire may actually convert to hostility if the victim rebuffs the perpetrator's advances. There are many fact patterns that support a finding that the discrimination occurred because of sex, many of which we have no room to mention here, but we will offer a number of examples. These examples do not attempt to provide an exclusive list.

A trier of fact might reasonably find such discrimination, for example, if a female victim is harassed in such sex-specific and derogatory terms by another woman as to make it clear that the harasser is motivated by hostility to the presence of the female victim because she is a woman. Some research suggests that some women engage in discriminatory behavior against other women in order to assure their own position among men. *See generally* Robin J. Ely, *The Effects of Organizational Demographics and Social Identity on Relationships Among Professional Women*, 39 Admin. Sci. Q. 203 (1994). Women can harass other women because of their sex if they fail to adhere to stereotypes of how female employees should dress and behave. *See generally* Karen Lee Ashcraft and Michael E. Pacanowsky, *"A Woman's Worst Enemy:" Reflections on a Narrative of Organizational Life and Female Identity*, 24 J. of App. Comm. Res. 217 (1996). *See also* Laurie A. Rudman, *Self Promotion as a Risk-Factor for Women: The Costs and Benefits of Counterstereotypical Impression Management*, 74 J. Personality & Soc. Psych. 629, 642, 643 (1997). A plaintiff claiming same biological sex harassment may also, of course, offer direct comparative evidence about how the alleged harasser treated members of other sexes in a mixed-sex workplace.

A man like Joseph Oncale in an all-male workplace may produce evidence that suggests that he was harassed because his male colleagues either considered him insufficiently masculine to perform the job and/or because they wanted to prove their own masculinity to the other members of the group and to police the masculine boundaries of the job. Behavior among men at work such as "hazing" and "roughhousing" is often gendered behavior occurring because of sex in order to establish the masculinity of the group, to demonstrate that the newcomer is insufficiently masculine to be a member of the group, or to assure that the male newcomer adopts similar masculine behaviors to bond him to the group. A woman in a traditionally male job may encounter similar harassment by men. Her colleagues may sexually harass her to prove that a woman cannot perform the job as well as a man can and to force her out of the job or generally to demean her and all women doing a man's job. James W. Messerschmidt, *Masculinities and Crime: Critique and Reconceptualization of Theory* 130–33 (1993). Studies of masculinity demonstrate that such behavior enhances the self-worth of the male harassers and establishes gendered requirements for the job in question.

These are some means of demonstrating that the behavior occurred because of sex, but there are others. Persons of indefinable gender and/or sex may suffer from harassment because of sex because they do not conform to social norms in their dress, behavior or performed identities. Clearly, the "because of … sex" language is broad enough to protect persons against discrimination based on their sexual orientation and gender identities, whether they fall into socially approved categories of dress and behavior or not. Of course, a finding that the behavior occurred because of sex does not automatically mean that the plaintiff will win the Title VII cause of action. The plaintiff must also prove that the behavior was unwelcome and sufficiently severe or pervasive to alter the terms or conditions of employment, requirements that will likely eliminate simple flirtation and ordinary socializing depending on the context of the situation. *Harris*, 510 U.S. at 21(citing *Meritor*, 477 U.S. at 67).

IV

Price Waterhouse v. Hopkins and Oncale

Nearly a decade ago this Court decided *Price Waterhouse v. Hopkins*, where we held that sex stereotyping is discrimination "because of … sex." 490 U.S. 228 (1989). In that case, Price Waterhouse refused Ann Hopkins's bid for membership in the partnership in part because of her failure to live up to female stereotypes. *Id.* at 251. The voting partners considered Ms. Hopkins to be insufficiently feminine and too masculine. We concluded that taking an adverse employment action because a person does not adhere to gendered societal stereotypes (i.e., a woman should be feminine; a man should be masculine) is discrimination because of sex. *Id.* In other words, the term "because of … sex" incorporates "because of gender," which we understand to include not only the biological sex of an individual, but also the societal expectations of a person of a particular biological sex, and even the societal expectations that all individuals belong to a particular biological sex or gender. Title VII, then, forbids discrimination based on an individual's failure to live up to, or excessive compliance with, gendered expectations of his or her biological sex. Or, if the person fails to identify as a particular sex or gender, as gender-queer individuals do, Title VII forbids discrimination based on this failure. Thus, had Price Waterhouse refused partnership to Ann Hopkins because she was too feminine or too good-looking or too sexy, or if it was unclear which sex and/or gender to which she belonged, it would have discriminated because of sex. Moreover, given that not all people are born with a defined biological sex and that even some who are do not identify with either male or female gender, the term "because of … sex" must be sufficiently broad to protect persons of all genders and neither biological sex.[30]

---

[30] The only exception to the sex stereotyping rule would be if the employer proves that being of a particular biological sex or adherence or non-adherence to particular gendered expectations is a bona fide occupational qualification of the job ("BFOQ") under 42 U.S.C. Sec. 2000e-2(e) (1). This is an extremely limited exception to the statute's ban on sex discrimination. The "because of … sex" provision of Title VII applies the same whether the discrimination alleged is failure to hire, a firing, or other adverse action because of a person's sex or gender or a sex- or gender-based hostile working environment that alters the person's terms or conditions of employment.

We understand that *Price Waterhouse's* holding on gender combined with our ruling in this case may be interpreted as expanding the term "because of … sex," but separating biological sex from gender is a difficult, likely impossible, proposition that is better left to the realm of biologists and social scientists than the courts. Moreover, biological sex itself is not as easily determined as previously thought. *See generally* John Money, *Gay, Straight and In-Between: The Sexology of Erotic Orientation* (1988). Our decision in *Price Waterhouse* that the definition of "sex" includes the broader categories of sexual stereotypes imposed by gender expectations recognized how intertwined sex and gender are in everyday life.

Even the legislators who originally wrote Title VII in the early 1960s likely understood, either consciously or unconsciously, that the term "sex" includes aspects of gender stereotypes and expectations. Certainly, after the passage of the Act the courts interpreted the term "sex" to indicate more than biology. *See, e.g., Rosenfeld v. Southern Pac. Co.*, 444 F.2d 1219 (9th Cir. 1971) (holding that the defendant's personnel policies that forbade women from certain positions violated Title VII, and discussing approvingly an EEOC Guidance that declared it illegal to make employee assignments based on stereotypes such as men cannot do detail work or women cannot be aggressive salespersons). For example, assume that in 1965 a trucking company refused to hire a woman to do long haul trucking because "women can't be truck drivers." This refusal to hire would violate Title VII even though the reason for the employer's pronouncement did not actually reflect a woman's biological weakness. Instead, the employer's view reflected a socially constructed, stereotypical view of what women can and should do. Even in 1965, this employer could not successfully defend its case by testifying that the refusal to hire the plaintiff was not because of her sex, but rather because of her failure to adhere to societal expectations of her sex. The employer would surely have lost this argument.

In a similar vein, courts have consistently concluded that customer preferences are not a defense to a Title VII lawsuit. *See* 29 C.F.R. Sec. 1604.2 (a)(I)(iii) (1997); *Gerdom v. Cont'l Airlines, Inc.*, 692 F.2d 602, 609 (9th Cir. 1982); *Diaz v. Pan Am. World Airways, Inc.*, 442 F.2d 385, 389 (5th Cir. 1971); *Bollenback v. Bd. of Educ. of Monroe-Woodbury Cent. Sch. Dist.*, 659 F. Supp. 1450, 1472 (S.D.N.Y. 1987). For example, an airline cannot refuse to hire female pilots because customers are more comfortable with male pilots. This rule exists to counteract societal gendered expectations and stereotypes about women. In contrast, by adopting a narrow reading of "because of … sex," courts could have decided that an airline that succumbs to customer expectations and refuses to hire female pilots to soothe customers' nerves does not possess the necessary intent to discriminate against the female applicants because of their sex. But courts chose to interpret the statute in a broader way, because splitting hairs as to the employer's intent would not do justice to the broad purposes of the statute.

Likewise, after this case, plaintiffs will bring suits alleging that sex- or gender-based harassment in all-male workplaces was motivated by the plaintiffs' failure to conform to gendered expectations. Theories of masculinity demonstrate that society pressures men and boys to live up to ideals of masculinity; this pressure leads men to engage in competitive behaviors to prove their masculinity. Because men derive their masculine self-worth in large part from the work they do, especially in all-male workplaces, men compete with one another to prove their masculinity to other men and to affirm their masculinity to themselves. A common behavior among men in traditionally male workplaces is to harass other men, sometimes in a sexual way. In cases where a plaintiff alleges harassment or other discriminatory treatment based on the plaintiff's failure to conform to masculine stereotypes, defendants may attempt to escape liability by arguing that the harassing behavior did not occur because of the plaintiff's failure to comply with gendered expectations, but rather because of the plaintiff's homosexual orientation or perceived homosexual orientation. In other words, defendants would attempt to distinguish between behavior that is motivated by the harassers' aversion to employees who do not meet traditional expectations of masculinity and that which is motivated by the harassers' aversion to homosexuality. Research on masculinity demonstrates, however, that concepts of masculinity and heterosexuality are so inextricably intertwined that it is virtually impossible to distinguish motivations. Michael S. Kimmel, *Masculinity as Homophobia: Fear, Shame, and Silence in the Construction of Gender Identity, in Theorizing Masculinities* 119–41 (Harry Brod and Michael Kaufman eds., 1994).

In typical workplace harassment situations, common terms for homosexuality and lack of masculinity are used in the same breath: men are accused of being limp-wristed, effeminate, "pussies" and "fags." Some of these terms appear to indicate that the harasser is motivated by homosexual orientation, either perceived or real, of the victim, but others appear to indicate the victim's failed masculinity. Especially because the most prevalent expectation about men is that they will be attracted to women, there is no space between discrimination based on sexual orientation and that based on a failure to meet gendered expectations. In fact, perhaps the most notable gendered stereotype is that members of a particular biological sex will be attracted to and have sexual relations with persons who are members of a different biological sex. Even if there were a difference between the sexual orientation and gender, it would be impossible for the courts, juries or even the victims and perpetrators themselves to distinguish between behavior that is motivated by the victim's failure to conform to gender stereotypes and behavior motivated by the victim's sexual orientation. Asking the courts to engage in this hair-splitting would be an affront to the dignity of the courts and of the individuals Title VII was designed to protect. In essence, sexualized comments and behavior are frequently directed at individuals because they do not fit the gender norms of the workplace, which may or may not include a sexual orientation other than heterosexuality. Therefore, we conclude that an employee who suffers unwelcome severe or pervasive harassment of a sexual or gendered nature by employees of the same or different biological sex may satisfy the "because of ... sex" requirement by demonstrating that the perpetrators engaged in the harassment because of the victim's failure to adhere to masculine (or feminine) stereotypes including the real or perceived sexual orientation of the victim.

V

In this case, Mr. Oncale is a slight man (125–135 pounds), App. 68, who complained about the harassing behavior directed at him. He can argue that he was harassed because the defendants thought him to be insufficiently masculine or because they perceived him to be homosexual. In either case, the behavior of Sundowner's employees may be explained by an interest in punishing Mr. Oncale because of his failure to meet their standards of masculinity or as a means of assuring that all members of the oil rig conform to their masculine ideals. Or, he may explain his treatment as the homosexual desires of work colleagues to engage in sexual behavior with him. Whatever his theory of the case, Mr. Oncale has clearly set forth sufficient evidence that the behavior was sexual and/or gendered in content. Therefore, it appears that he has presented sufficient evidence to shift the burden to the defendant to prove that the behavior did not occur because of sex. The defendant should have an opportunity to present this evidence to the trial court and to move once more for summary judgment, if it desires.

 Once the evidence is presented, if there is sufficient evidence for a reasonable jury to conclude that proof establishes that the behavior occurred because of biological sex or gender, and that the behavior was unwelcome to Mr. Oncale, and that the behavior was sufficiently severe or pervasive to alter Mr. Oncale's terms or conditions of employment, the defendant's motion for summary judgment should be denied.

VI

Because we conclude that sex discrimination consisting of same biological sex sexual harassment is actionable under Title VII, the judgment of the Court of Appeals for the Fifth Circuit is reversed, and the case is remanded for further proceedings consistent with this opinion.

It is so ordered.

22

Commentary on *Gebser v. Lago Vista Independent School District*

Michelle S. Simon

INTRODUCTION

In *Gebser v. Lago Vista Independent School District*,[1] the U.S. Supreme Court held that a thirteen-year-old girl who was raped by her teacher did not have a Title IX cause of action against the school district because the district did not have actual notice of the abuse.[2] The consequences of this decision for young victims of sexual abuse by educators have been significant. Unsurprisingly, commentators have criticized the decision as gutting Title IX and creating an unsurmountable hurdle for a victim trying to prove the school liable.[3]

In her feminist judgment, Professor Ann Bartow, writing as Justice Bartow, dissents from the majority opinion. She challenges the decision by focusing on the story of the young student, Alida Gebser, and her abuse by her teacher, Frank Waldrop. This is a story that she believes the various courts euphemized and distorted. Relying on the feminist method of narrative, Justice Bartow attacks the actual notice standard primarily through a retelling of Alida's story, although she also criticizes this standard as unworkable because it allows school districts to disregard inappropriate teacher conduct. Bartow educates the reader about the realities and complexities of child sexual abuse by a trusted authority figure and endorses an agency standard that places the burden of exposing abusive teachers on the school district and its employees.

---

[1] *Gebser v. Lago Vista Indep. Sch. Dist.*, 524 U.S. 274 (1998).
[2] *Id.* at 304 (Stevens, J., dissenting).
[3] *See generally* Martha McCarthy, *Students as Targets and Perpetrators of Sexual Harassment: Title IX and Beyond*, 12 *Hastings Women's L.J.* 177 (2001); Catherine Fisk and Erwin Chemerinsky, *Civil Rights Without Remedies: Vicarious Liability Under Title VII, Section 1983, and Title IX*, 7 *Wm. & Mary Bill Rts. J.* 755 (1999).

TITLE IX, SEXUAL HARASSMENT AND THE COURTS

Title IX's prohibition of sex discrimination in federally funded education programs offers little legislative history guidance. Prior to *Gebser*, the U.S. Supreme Court decided two key Title IX sex discrimination cases: one, *Cannon v. University of Chicago*,[4] found an implied cause of action for Title IX sex discrimination, and the other, *Franklin v. Gwinnett County Public Schools*,[5] held that plaintiffs could recover damages. After *Franklin*, the lower courts struggled with the parameters for Title IX sexual harassment liability.[6]

To address the circuit split,[7] the U.S. Supreme Court granted certiorari in *Gebser*. In a majority opinion written by Justice O'Connor (joined by Justices Rehnquist, Scalia, Kennedy, and Thomas), the Court refused to find the school district liable either when a teacher sexually harasses students by virtue of his position of authority, or where administrators should have known about the unlawful conduct. Ultimately, the Court concluded that there has to be actual notice to a person within the institution who has authority to address the wrongdoing and implement corrective measures, and also that this recipient of actual notice must exhibit deliberate indifference to the discriminatory conduct.[8]

The dissent, written by Justice Stevens and joined by Justices Souter, Ginsburg, and Breyer, determined that agency principles do apply, and that "this case presents a paradigmatic example of a tort that was made possible, that was effected, and that was repeated over a prolonged period because of the powerful influence that Waldrop had over Gebser by reason of the authority that his employer, the school district, had delegated to him."[9] Justice Ginsburg, joined by Justices Souter and Breyer, added that an effective policy to curtail and redress injuries caused by sexual harassment should serve as an affirmative defense for school districts.[10] Since *Gebser*, the lower courts have continued to struggle with the definition of "actual notice" and "deliberate indifference."[11]

---

[4] 441 U.S. 677 (1979).

[5] 503 U.S. 60 (1992).

[6] *See* Sandra J. Perry and Tanya M. Marcum, *Liability for School Sexual Harassment Under Title IX: How the Courts are Failing our Children*, 30 U. La Verne L. Rev. 3, 10 (2008).

[7] *See id.* at 5 n.17 (collecting cases).

[8] *Gebser*, 524 U.S. at 291–93.

[9] *Id.* at 299 (Stevens, J., dissenting).

[10] *Id.* at 306 (Ginsburg, J., dissenting).

[11] *See, e.g., Baynard v. Malone*, 268 F.3d 228 (4th Cir. 2001) (need to have actual knowledge of misconduct); *Bostic v. Smyrna Sch. Dist.*, 418 F.3d 355 (3d Cir. 2005) (actual knowledge of sexual conduct is not necessary); *Williams* ex rel. *Hart v. Paint Valley Local Sch. Dist.*, 400 F.3d 360 (6th Cir. 2005) (knowledge of risk from other students is sufficient); *Kinman v. Omaha Pub. Sch. Dist.*, 171 F.3d 607 (8th Cir. 1999) (as long as a school district did something, it

THE FEMINIST JUDGMENT

Bartow joins Justice Stevens in his dissent, but writes separately. While she agrees that the agency standard is more appropriate than an actual notice standard, her opinion emphasizes that this case is really a story about child abuse. The Court's analysis should not focus on the wording of Title IX and its comparison to Title VI or Title VII; rather the analysis should center on Alida's story, and the responsibility of the justice system to protect children from sexual abuse. Bartow uses narrative to demonstrate that courts have failed to create a standard that guards a child's self-worth and ability to become a functioning member of society.

Narrative has been used by critical scholars, including feminists and race theorists, to offer first-person renditions of experiences with immediacy and passion.[12] Narratives expose actual experiences – like Alida Gebser's rape – that are seldom discussed in public. The voices heard in the narrative are not the voices of judges, but those of women, children, and members of other disadvantaged groups. The narrative itself is the key; it creates the argument without further analysis.[13] By looking at the world through the eyes of a young teenager who has been raped by her trusted teacher, Bartow reveals the injustice of the actual notice standard and the need for a different analysis.

Bartow emphasizes that the recitation of facts by both the U.S. Supreme Court and the Fifth Circuit fails to communicate the turmoil Alida suffered between the ages of thirteen and fifteen at the hands of her trusted and mature teacher. For example, the Court describes them as having a "relationship," when in reality, Alida was repeatedly raped. She was a child and lacked the capacity to consent. Further, the requirement that she attend school and take certain classes meant continuous contact with her abuser over multiple years. Frank Waldrop had both custodial and supervisory control over Alida. Yet, neither the Circuit Court nor the U.S. Supreme Court focused on the facts from Alida's point of view.

Using the technique of feminist practical reasoning,[14] Bartow examines how the law fails to account for the experience and values that are more typical of women than men. She then exposes these features and suggests ways to

---

cannot be deliberately indifferent); *Vance v. Spencer Cty. Pub. Sch. Dist.*, 231 F.3d 253 (6th Cir. 2000) (school must demonstrate deliberate indifference).

[12] *See* Charles R. Lawrence, III, *The Word and the River: Pedagogy as Scholarship as Struggle*, 65 S. Cal. L. Rev. 2231, 2284–85 (1992).

[13] Kathryn Abrams, *Hearing the Call of Stories*, 79 Cal. L. Rev. 971, 975 (1991); Catharine A. MacKinnon, Toward a Feminist Theory of the State 83–105 (1989).

[14] Katharine T. Bartlett, *Feminist Legal Methods*, 103 Harv. L. Rev. 829, 850 (1990).

correct them. She takes particular aim at the Court's choice to adopt the narrow standard of actual notice and deliberate indifference.

The impact of these onerous requirements makes it nearly impossible for young women to recover under Title IX, even if, like Alida, they are raped by a teacher during school hours. Instead of focusing on effectively protecting children against discriminatory practices, the majority focused on Title IX's lack of the word "agency" and the contractual funding Title IX provides. While there are criminal laws to punish teacher-abusers, and student-victims may pursue other civil avenues, these avenues are consistently unsuccessful and fail to consider the lack of power these young girls actually have.[15] Alida's story illustrates this. Despite her strength in standing up for her rights and pursuing all her legal avenues of recovery, the judicial system failed her. Under its analysis, the Court's actual notice standard does not provide any incentive for the school district to develop anti-harassment policies and procedures, or incentive for adults to police each other. The Court failed to protect Alida a second time by denying her monetary damages to compensate for her suffering.

Sexual harassment in the educational setting continues to be a significant issue. While the majority of research on sexual harassment in education has been conducted in the realm of higher education,[16] sexual harassment of younger children is rampant.[17] As Bartow recognizes by looking through the eyes of abused children, elementary and high school students are very uncomfortable talking to administrators.[18] It is unusual for them to tell even their family or friends. Like Alida, a child might be misled into thinking that she is "in a relationship," or be concerned she is being graded by the teacher, or be worried that she has to have the same teacher the following semester.[19] She

---

[15] Diane M. Holben and Perry A. Zirkel, *School Bullying Litigation: An Empirical Analysis of the Case Law*, 47 *Akron L. Rev.* 299, 324 (2014).

[16] Billie Wright Dziech and Michael W. Hawkins, Sexual Harassment in Higher Education: Reflections and New Perspectives (1998); Combating Sexual Harassment in Higher Education (Bernice E. Lott and Mary Ellen Reilly eds., 1995); Catherine Hill and Elena M. Silva, Drawing the Line: Sexual Harassment on Campus (2005); Virginia Lee Stamler and Gerald L. Stone, Faculty-Student Sexual Involvement: Issues and Interventions (1998).

[17] A 1993 study by the American Association of University Women Educational Foundation (AAUW) concluded that 85 percent of girls and 76 percent of boys were sexually harassed in their schools. Hostile Hallways, AAUW 20 (2001). Of those, 25 percent of girls and 10 percent of boys stated that the harasser was a teacher, coach, or other school employee. The AAUW repeated this study in 2001 and again found that eight in ten students reported some kind of harassment in their school lives. *Id.* Less than 12 percent of student-victims report the harassment to a teacher, and less than 25 percent tell a family member. *Id.* at 29.

[18] *Id.* at 35–36.

[19] *See Gebser v. Lago Vista Indep. Sch. Dist.*, 524 U.S. 274, 297 n.10 (1998) (Stevens, J., dissenting).

may be anxious that she needs letters of recommendation, or she might just be ashamed or afraid.[20] Although the agency standard takes some burden of reporting away from the child by making the school responsible for investigating clues that an adult is acting inappropriately, this standard fails to address the reporting issues from a child-victim's perspective. The Court ignores psychological impediments that prevent a child from reporting abuse. By ignoring these facts, the Court has opted to protect and insulate school districts from financial harm instead of protecting young female children.

Bartow critiques *Gebser* through the insights that emerge by viewing the experiences of a young girl who was victimized by her teacher. But is that enough? There must be a clear proposal for change, including a standard for sexual harassment claims brought under Title IX. Child abuse in the educational setting is a serious problem that demands a legal response. Bartow has focused on our youngest victims – female minors in elementary and high school. While these cases are frequently the most egregious and shocking, sexual harassment in any setting toward any victim has serious repercussions. College students may not be minors, but sexual harassment still compromises the educational mission of higher education and reinforces sex discrimination. It does not represent "harmless expressions of interpersonal attraction or adolescent behavior."[21] Sexual harassment in schools negatively affects not only its young women victims, but all students in the educational setting.[22]

Gebser v. Lago Vista Independent School District, 524 U.S. 274 (1998)

Justice Ann Bartow, dissenting.

Today the Court has decided that children who are the victims of sexual harassment in schools warrant weaker legal protections under Title IX than adult victims of sexual harassment in the workplace receive under Title VII. By establishing an actual notice/deliberate indifference standard for teacher-on-student sexual harassment cases in which monetary damages are requested, the majority's holding telegraphs at best complete indifference to child victims of sexual violence, and quite possibly a bias against them.

---

[20] *See, e.g., id.*

[21] Susan Brownmiller, Against Our Will: Men, Women and Rape 394 (1975).

[22] Nancy Chi Cantalupo, *Burying Our Heads in the Sand: Lack of Knowledge, Knowledge Avoidance, and the Persistent Problem of Campus Peer Sexual Violence*, 43 Loy. U. Chi. L.J. 205 (2011); Nancy Chi Cantalupo, *Masculinity & Title IX: Bullying and Sexual Harassment of Boys in the American Liberal State*, 73 Md. L. Rev. 887 (2014).

The Court had the option of construing Title IX's standard of liability in a way that advanced the objectives of the statute by incentivizing school districts to affirmatively train and supervise faculty and staff to reduce the risk of sexual harassment of students. A legal standard that encourages everyone in a school to look out for acts of sexual abuse is the best way to protect children.

Instead, the Court has incentivized school districts to ignore evidence of bad actions by teachers, and to make their reporting procedures as byzantine and opaque as possible to avoid civil liability. This puts minor students at increased risk of sexual assault, the exact opposite of the goals of Title IX.

Justice Stevens' dissenting opinion focuses on the standard of school district liability for teacher-on-student harassment in secondary schools. He notes that the majority's approach is at odds with settled principles of agency law, which would hold the school district responsible for the teacher's misconduct because the existence of the agency relationship is what facilitated commission of the tort. Justice Stevens correctly observes: "This case presents a paradigmatic example of a tort that was made possible, that was effected, and that was repeated over a prolonged period because of the powerful influence that [the teacher] had over [the student] by reason of the authority that his employer, the school district, had delegated to him." *Gebser v. Lago Vista Independent School Dist.*, 524 U.S. 274, 299 (1998) (Stevens, J., dissenting).

I join Justice Stevens' dissenting opinion, but write separately to explain more explicitly what should have been the majority's central understanding of this case: When a teacher sexually assaults a minor student, they are not having a relationship. The sex is non-consensual as a matter of law. *See, e.g.,* Tex. Penal Code Ann. § 21.11 (indecency with a child). The student is being raped. And child rape victims are empirically unlikely to report their sexual assaults to authorities, especially when the rapist is their trusted teacher.[23] That is why student victims of sexual harassment are so desperately in need of legal protection.

The number of children who are negatively affected by the majority's ill-advised ruling is enormous. Department of Justice crime data from 1996 show that teens sixteen to nineteen years of age were approximately three and one-half times more likely than the general population to be victims of rape, attempted rape, or sexual assault. U.S. Dep't of Justice, *Criminal Victimization in United States, 1996 Statistical Tables* at Table 9. An AAUW

---

[23] Anne L. Bryant, *Hostile Hallways, The AAUW Survey on Sexual Harassment in America's Schools*, 63 *Journal of School Health* 355, 357 (1993) (only 7 percent of victims of sexual harassment in school told a teacher, while 23 percent told a parent and another 23 percent told no one at all). *See also* Reuben A. Lang, and Roy R. Frenzel, *How Sex Offenders Lure Children*, 1 *Annals of Sex Res.* 303 (1988).

study conducted in 1993 found that 25 percent of girls and 10 percent of boys are sexually harassed in school by a teacher or other school employee.[24]

I

Title IX provides that: "No person in the United States shall, on the basis of sex, be excluded from participation in, be denied the benefits of, or be subjected to discrimination under any education program or activity receiving Federal financial assistance." 20 U.S.C. § 1681(a) (1986). In *Cannon v. University of Chicago*, 441 U.S. 677 (1979), this Court recognized that Title IX was enforceable through an implied private right of action. In *Franklin v. Gwinnett County Schools*, 503 U.S. 60 (1992), this Court held that sexual harassment can constitute sex discrimination, and that monetary damages are available to private litigants when a teacher sexually abuses a student. *Id.* at 76.

Today, we had the opportunity to clarify how school liability should be determined in a manner consistent with the principal purposes of Title IX: "'[T]o avoid the use of federal resources to support discriminatory practices' and 'to provide individual citizens effective protection against those practices.'" *Gebser*, 524 U.S. at 286 (alteration in original) (quoting *Cannon*, 441 U.S. at 704). Instead the Court abruptly halts the march of progress effectuated by *Cannon* and *Franklin* in protecting what all parties and every member of this Court, *Gebser*, 524 U.S. at 292, agree is a very large number of students who are victimized by teachers.

The Court's ruling means that a student who has been sexually harassed by a teacher may not recover damages under Title IX unless a school district official who has authority to institute corrective measures on the district's behalf has actual notice of, and is deliberately indifferent to, the teacher's misconduct. Without compelling justification, the Court has declined to apply Title VII principles to Title IX cases. In Title VII hostile environment cases, this Court endorsed a "knew or should have known" or "constructive" notice liability standard in *Meritor Savings Bank v. Vinson*, 477 U.S. 57 (1986), and we unanimously concluded that that Congress wanted courts to look to agency principles for guidance with respect to employer liability. *See also Harris v. Forklift Sys., Inc.*, 510 U.S. 17 (1993).

Today, the Court imposes a greater burden on schoolchildren seeking compensation for sexual harassment that is inflicted upon them at school than that which is imposed upon adults who have suffered sexual harassment in the workplace. This is because according to the majority, Title IX is not, like Title

[24]   Bryant, *supra* note 23, at 355–56.

VII, a prohibition on sexual harassment. It is instead a contract under which the federal government agrees to provide money in exchange for an agreement by schools not to discriminate based on sex. The terms of this contract, it turns out, are very favorable indeed for a school district that inadequately supervises its teachers and also fails to distribute an official grievance procedure for lodging sexual harassment complaints or a formal anti-harassment policy, as required by federal regulations. *See* 34 C.F.R. pt. 106.8–9.

As Justice Stevens points out, the majority relies heavily on the notion that because the private cause of action under Title IX is "judicially implied," the Court has "a measure of latitude" to use its own judgment in shaping a remedial scheme. Writing for the majority, Justice O'Connor asserts that enforcing Title IX requires actual notice to relevant school officials and an opportunity for voluntary compliance before administrative enforcement proceedings can commence. The purpose for the actual notice requirement, she asserts, is to avoid diverting educational funds from a school district that is unaware that it is discriminating, and willing to institute prompt corrective measures once it is informed. This standard, she says, is not satisfied by theories based upon agency principles, vicarious liability, or constructive notice. *Gebser*, 524 U.S. at 285. Instead, Title IX places the burden on the plaintiff in a private cause of action against a school board to prove that: (1) the student was subjected to harassment severe enough to compromise the victim's educational opportunities; (2) the recipient of the federal funds had actual knowledge of the harassment; and (3) the recipient exhibited deliberate indifference to the harassment.

In consequence, the best practice for a school district eager to retain federal funding is to remain as unaware as possible about the bad acts its teachers inflict upon its students. Only if actual knowledge of sexual abuse is thrust upon a school official with specific authority to institute corrective measures must corrective measures be instituted, and if they are, the school district can still avoid liability for sexual harassment. This corrosive view of Title IX insulates schools from financial harms they are well positioned to avoid, at the expense of vulnerable children.

II

James Boyd White trenchantly observed that every legal case starts with the client's story, and it ends with a legal decision that offers another version of that story, which is cast into a legal framework. James Boyd White, *Heracles' Bow: Essays on the Rhetoric and the Poetics of the Law* 168 (1985). In 1989 Professor Richard Delgado explained the importance of telling and carefully analyzing legal stories. Richard Delgado, *Storytelling for Oppositionists and Others: A Plea for Narrative*, 87 Mich. L. Rev. 2411 (1989). Narrative storytelling is an important tool for reframing the stories of people, such as Alida Gebser, who have not received justice from the Court. The problems with the majority's holding are best illustrated by the facts of the case, and by a close examination of how the facts are recounted by the courts. Both the Fifth Circuit and the majority here pay inadequate attention to Alida Gebser. When she is discussed, she is often characterized as having made voluntary choices in a situation in which she actually had little power.

Alida Star Gebser's real name is in the caption of this case. The identity of sexual abuse victims is often kept private for their protection. Where it is necessary to protect a person from harassment, injury, ridicule or personal embarrassment, courts have permitted the use of pseudonyms. *See, e.g., United States v. Doe*, 556 F.2d 391, 393 (6th Cir. 1977); *see generally* Charles R. Petrof, *Protecting the Anonymity of Child Sexual Assault Victims*, 40 Wayne L. Rev. 1677 (1994). Though initially appearing in pleadings as Jane Doe when her case was at the District Court level and in the Fifth Circuit, her real name was copiously used after her litigation odyssey brought her victimization to this Court, both in court documents and in media coverage of the matter. I wondered why this Court had decided to expose her in this way. I found the unexpected answer in the Petitioner's Brief, where footnote 1 says "This suit was filed when Alida Gebser was a minor. The pseudonyms 'Jane Doe' and 'Jean Doe' were used to designate her and her mother, Alida Jean McCullough, who sued as her next friend. Alida Gebser having become an adult, the Petitioners have chosen to use their legal names." Pet'r's Br. n.1. Perhaps using her real name before this Court was a way for Alida Gebser to signal that she is not ashamed about what happened, because she knows that while wrongs were inflicted upon her, she herself has done nothing wrong.

This is a message the majority has utterly scrambled. Evidence that she may have been a uniquely mature and motivated teenager is held against her, because she did not somehow call upon these reserves to extricate herself from a bad situation or ascertain how to report her teacher's sexual abuse in the correct way and to the correct school official. If Alida Gebser could not find assistance or relief from the abuse, it is even less likely that a younger or less sagacious student would be able to do so.

The fact that Alida Gebser brought a lawsuit, and then pursued justice all the way to this Court, choosing to use her real name in the caption, suggests she is a strong person. But this strength alone did not protect her from being abused by a teacher. The narrative tone and word choice in the Fifth Circuit's

recitation of the facts of the case reveals embedded and problematic perceptions of Alida Gebser, who is referred to as "Doe":

> Frank Waldrop, a teacher at Lago Vista High School, first met Jane Doe
> while she was a student in his wife's eighth-grade honors class during the
> 1990–91 school year. At that time, she was thirteen. Because Doe needed
> a more challenging academic program, Waldrop's wife referred her to her
> husband's high school discussion group, which Doe participated in for sev-
> eral weeks. When Doe became a ninth-grader, she was assigned to Waldrop's
> class in advanced social studies. Their relationship grew during the academic
> year. Waldrop went out of his way to flatter Doe and spend time alone with
> her, and Doe enjoyed receiving attention from her instructor.
>
> Waldrop initiated sexual contact with her at her home in the spring of
> 1992. Knowing she would be alone, he visited under the pretext of returning
> a book and proceeded to fondle her breasts and unzip her pants. During the
> summer, Waldrop had sex on a regular basis with Doe, who was by then fif-
> teen years old. None of the encounters took place on school property. The
> relationship ended in January of 1993, when a Lago Vista police officer hap-
> pened to discover Waldrop and Doe having sex.
>
> Doe agrees with the school district that "there was no direct evidence
> that any school official was aware of Waldrop's sexual exploitation of Jane
> Doe" until January of 1993. The parents and guardian of two other students
> complained to Michael Riggs, the high school principal, that Waldrop had
> made inappropriate remarks in the presence of female students. Riggs organ-
> ized an investigation into this complaint, Waldrop denied the charges, and
> Riggs did not bring the matter to the attention of Virginia Collier, the district
> superintendent.
>
> Doe v. Lago Vista Indep. Sch. Dist., 106 F.3d 1223, 1224–25 (5th Cir. 1997).

Note that Frank Newton Waldrop and Alida Gebser are described as having a "relationship" that "grew." Alida Gebser is reported to have "enjoyed
receiving attention from her instructor." The court states that the two "had
sex on a regular basis" as if they were an ordinary adult romantic couple.
The word rape is never used. And the court highlights the fact that "[n]one
of the encounters took place on school property," the implication being this
made the nature of the relationship impossible for school officials to discover.
That the sexual abuse took place during school hours, when both student
and teacher should have been on school property, is not mentioned. When
law enforcement officials stop an act of sexual abuse in progress and arrest
Waldrop, the Fifth Circuit characterizes this as the relationship ending when
the two were discovered "having sex." Alida Gebser is painted as a willing
participant in her own sexual abuse, contrary to the undisputed facts in the

pleadings, and then denied the opportunity to pursue her claim against the school district because she did not report her abuser.

When this Court granted certiorari, it must have given Alida Gebser and her mother great hope that justice would finally be theirs. Yet Justice O'Connor's recitation of the facts alone is enough to foreshadow their loss. The sexual abuse appears even more civilized, and less of a reason for concern. Gone from Justice O'Connor's account of the facts are: the intervention by Frank Newton Waldrop's wife, Trudy, that first brought Alida Gebser to Frank Newton Waldrop's attention; Waldrop's instrumental flattery of Alida Gebser; Alida Gebser's alleged enjoyment of same; and specific mentions of Waldrop's initial assault on Alida Gebser's breasts and his unzipping of her pants in her own home. She has edited out these rather salacious aspects of the facts, as if to make the whole story less disturbing.

Added by Justice O'Connor, however, are details that seem meant to be reassuring to readers. These include Waldrop's apology for any unintended offensive remarks he might have made in the presence of students, and a notation that events ended with Waldrop's arrest. Dutifully emphasized is the fact that Waldrop "initiated sexual contact" with Alida Gebser but while "they often had intercourse during class time" it was "never on school property." The physical relationship between the two is described as "sexual intercourse" rather than sexual abuse. The word rape is still nowhere in evidence. This suggests the majority utterly fails to comprehend the magnitude of the wrong at issue.

Alternatively, perhaps the majority understands full well the nature of what occurred and how deeply it appears to have traumatized Alida Gebser, but represses this knowledge in the service of preserving educational funding for a school district that positions itself as innocent and unable to address a problem it was innocently unaware of due to Alida Gebser's inaction. While the prospect of punishing an innocent party is always troubling, as well it should be, the majority fails to recognize that the truly innocent party in this dispute is Alida Gebser. She was an innocent child and the school district put her in harm's way. Being sexually abused by her teacher does not make her less innocent. Failing to report the sexual abuse does not make her less innocent.

The culpability focus should be not on what Alida Gebser did or did not do, but on the acts and omissions of Frank Newton Waldrop, and the school district that employed him. Frank Newton Waldrop was a fifty-something-year-old high school teacher when he formed a book discussion group for high school students in which he often made sexually suggestive comments to and about students during meetings. All of this was possible because he was a school teacher.

When Petitioner Alida Gebser was a vulnerable thirteen-year-old eighth-grade student at a middle school in the Spring of 1991, Frank Newton Waldrop's then-wife Trudy Haas Waldrop, who was also a teacher, identified Alida Gebser as a very bright student she thought could benefit from contact with her high school teacher husband, and persuaded Alida Gebser to join his book discussion group. Pet'r's Br., *supra*, at 2. There is no evidence in the record suggesting Waldrop's wife knew that the interest Frank Newton Waldrop would take in Alida Gebser would be sexual in nature. Nevertheless, by encouraging Alida Gebser to join her husband's book discussion group as its youngest member, fellow Lago Vista Independent School District teacher Trudy Haas Waldrop affirmatively acted to put Alida Gebser into a situation that ultimately contributed to her victimization by a teaching colleague.

Perpetrators of child sexual abuse gain the trust of potential child victims by using a deliberate grooming procedure. This process involves identifying potential victims, gaining their trust, and breaking down their defenses. Grooming facilitates access to the victim, and sets up a relationship grounded in secrecy so that the sexual abuse is less likely to be discovered. See Lang and Frenzel, *supra* note 1, at 314. After Frank Newton Waldrop realized that Alida Gebser was a young girl who might be susceptible to his sexual predations, he began to groom her for physical sexual abuse. In the fall of 1991 and spring of 1992, Alida Gebser was a student in Frank Waldrop's classes. He directed an increasing number of sexually charged comments directly to her during class meetings, in the presence of other students. Petitioners assert: "The remarks seemed in retrospect calculated to flatter her for understanding them while introducing a covert sexuality into their teacher-student relationship. On one occasion during class discussion, for example, he made a reference to 'Tantra' believing that Gebser alone would understand that 'Tantra' was 'sex magic.'" Pet'r's Br., *supra*, at 3. He encouraged her to spend a lot of time alone with him in his classroom. Surprisingly, no one at the school, such as another teacher or an administrator, found this unusual enough to enquire about. Finally, he contrived a visit to her house, ostensibly to give her a book, during which he kissed and touched her inappropriately, groping her breasts and vagina. Alida Gebser testified:

[T]hat incident was, at the time, the first absolutely blatant, no questions, no mistaking, sexual advance that he had made towards me. The other things had all been double entendre and, quote, references, things like that. You know, the sort of thing that if you knew the references that he was making, you would understand, but if you didn't, it would seem innocent.

I was terrified. I had no idea what I was supposed to do. I had trusted him. I had believed him. I–you know, he was basically my mentor. And it was terrifying. He was the main teacher at the school with whom I had discussions, and I didn't know what to do.

Id. at 3–4.

He began raping fourteen-year-old Alida Gebser shortly thereafter.[25] Alida Gebser testified that she was terrified, ashamed and depressed, and "freaked out." Pet'r's Br., *supra*, at 8. Neither the Fifth Circuit nor the majority reference or credit this testimony. Yet these are exactly the sort of negative consequences for a student that a properly functioning Title IX is designed to either prevent or compensate for.

Frank Newton Waldrop continued to rape Alida Gebser through the spring, summer and fall of 1992. Like many young sexual abuse victims, Alida Gebser was confused and conflicted about her situation. She realized that Waldrop's conduct was improper, but she was uncertain how to react. He paid more attention to her than any other teacher did. He seemed to care for her, and had in fact told her he loved her. Resp't's Br. at 3. In certain respects she trusted him. Pet'r's Br., *supra*, at 6 (Waldrop was the teacher Gebser "most trusted"). He treated her as though she was special. *Id.* at 1–3 ("[W]hen she was fourteen ... Waldrop began singling Gebser out for special attention because, she thought, of her intellectual qualities."). He had her convinced that they were in a relationship, so that she was less likely to recognize that she was being exploited and victimized. He also had academic authority over her. Alida Gebser testified that the Gifted and Talented program at Lago Vista High School had been effectively terminated and her "only means of getting the educational programs she needed depended on the good graces of Waldrop; it was Waldrop alone who offered her advanced classes in sociology and psychology, and the record clearly indicates that he used his official position as Gebser's teacher to propose sexual interludes." *Id.* at 4.

Frank Waldrop used his powerful influence over Alida Gebser to persuade her to keep his actions secret. He even encouraged her to have sex with a boy near her age, because he feared it would be suspicious if she didn't maintain a romantic relationship that "the world could know about." *Id.* at 5. Ultimately she sought an avenue of escape that would avoid directly confronting her situation or disclosing the scope of her victimization. Her solution was to try to graduate early from high school as "a way that without being discovered,

---

[25] Because Alida Gebser was 14 years old when Waldrop began sexually abusing her, it was rape under Texas law. Tex. Penal Code Ann. § 21.11 (indecency with a child). Texas also criminalizes sexual conduct between educators and children. *Id.* § 21.12.

without bringing it to light, that I could get out of it without having his disapproval." *Id.* at 9. That Alida Gebser's chosen coping strategy required her to forgo a year of high school reflects the serious and lasting impact that Frank Newton Waldrop's relentless sexual abuse had upon her life. But neither the Fifth Circuit nor the majority opinion even reports these facts, much less acknowledges their significance.

Frank Newton Waldrop also continued to make sexually charged comments in his classes. This, too, is ignored by both the Fifth Circuit and the majority. Those inappropriate sexual remarks were strikingly similar to those employed by Waldrop in the early stages of his approach to Alida Gebser. This is important because it illustrates how the majority opinion fails not just Alida Gebser but every other student Frank Newton Waldrop came into contact with as a teacher. Potentially he was grooming other students for contemporaneous or future victimization of the sort Alida Gebser was suffering:

> Waldrop reportedly made specific references to a girl's figure, and made a suggestive remark in the presence of another concerning a male student's anatomy. In addition, one of the girls told her mother 'that whenever Mr. Waldrop looked at her, she felt like he was looking at her up and down.' Another said that, in a Gifted and Talented class attended only by her and Gebser, most of the time was spent in conversation. And that much of that was strange and uncomfortable to the point of having sexual connotations as well as telling off-colored jokes and stories that Mr. Waldrop found very amusing, but that made [the girl] feel very uncomfortable.
>
> *Id.* at 7–8 (alteration in original) (citations omitted).

Eventually these other students complained about this to their parents. In October of 1992, the parents of two of them took their complaints to the supervising high school principal, Martin Riggs. At a meeting with these parents and the principal, Frank Newton Waldrop denied making offensive remarks, but also sought to defuse the situation by apologizing for any misunderstanding, as if misunderstanding was the problem.

Nothing in the record suggests that Principal Riggs asked any explicit questions about sexual abuse. He accepted Waldrop's denials of any intentional harassment, and failed to make any written notes of the meeting between Waldrop and complaining parents, or any entry in Waldrop's personnel file about the accusations against him. Afterwards, Principal Riggs informed the school guidance counselor about the meeting, but not the district superintendent, even though the superintendent was the district's Title IX coordinator. The district did not have a formal policy against sexual harassment, or an official grievance procedure for lodging sexual harassment complaints.

In January of 1993 a police officer encountered Frank Newton Waldrop raping Alida Gebser in a remote area. See *Texas Educ. Agency v. Waldrop*, No. 169-TTC-293, ¶ 3 (August 1993). Both were naked. *Id.* Alida Gebser informed the police officer that the activity was consensual and lied that she was eighteen years of age. *Id.* ¶ 4. Another police officer demanded to know from Alida Gebser whether "they had used protection," and learned that the answer was no. *Id.* at ¶ 5. Frank Waldrop had represented to Alida Gebser that he was sterile. *Id.*

After the police caught him raping Alida Gebser, Frank Newton Waldrop was arrested. This arrest led to the loss of his teaching position at the Lago Vista Independent School District, and the revocation of his teaching license by the Texas Education Agency. *Id.* at ¶ 5 (conclusions of law). He was convicted of *attempted* sexual assault on a minor, but given only probation as a punishment.[26] Neither the Fifth Circuit nor Justice O'Connor describes what happened to Alida Gebser as rape, even though it clearly met the legal definition. Even the criminal justice system inexplicably seemed to give him a pass: Waldrop was convicted of a far lesser charge, even though statutory rape is putatively a strict liability offense, and served no jail time for his crimes.

III

In early 1992, right before Frank Newton Waldrop began sexually abusing Alida Gebser, this Court expressly and unanimously ruled that Title IX is violated when a teacher sexually abuses a student. *Franklin*, 503 U.S. at 1036–37. The Court had left lower courts the job of hammering out when students who were sexually abused by their teachers would have Title IX-based causes of action against the school districts that employed and ostensibly supervised these predatory teachers. The Fifth Circuit responded by promulgating a liability standard for teacher-student sexual harassment under Title IX that is met "only if a school official who had actual knowledge of the abuse was invested by the school board with the duty to supervise the employee and the power to take action that would end such abuse and failed to do so." *Rosa H. v. San Elizario Indep. Sch. Dist.*, 106 F.3d 648, 660 (5th Cir. 1997); *see also Canutillo Indep. Sch. Dist. v. Leija*, 101 F.3d 393, 401 (5th Cir. 1996) ("Therefore, before the school district can be held liable under Title IX for a teacher's hostile environment sexual abuse, someone in a management-level position must be advised about (put on notice of) that conduct, and that person must fail to take remedial action.").

---

[26] Crim. Disposition, *Texas v. Waldrop*, No. 93–2518 (June 25, 1998).

This made it impossible for at least two children who were sexually abused by school employees in the Fifth Circuit to pursue damage awards against their school districts. In *Leija*, a second grader who was serially molested by a physical education teacher was unable to pursue damages from the teacher's employing school even though Rosemarie Leija told her homeroom teacher about the sexual abuse, Rosemarie Leija's mother also contacted the homeroom teacher about the abuse, and a second student informed the homeroom teacher she was being sexually abused by the same physical education teacher. *Leija*, 101 F.3d at 395, 402. The homeroom teacher simply threatened Rosemarie Leija with "trouble" if she was lying about her accusation and declined to report the allegations to her supervisor or anyone else. *Id.* at 395.

In addition to precluding monetary compensation for the child victim of sexual abuse from the school district that employed both the abuser and the teacher who refused to take action about the abuse reports, this gave the accused abuser the ability to continue to sexually abuse students, and continue he did. Months later, another parent complained to an assistant principal at the elementary school that the physical education teacher had sexually molested her daughter. *Id.* at 402. Finally, a few months after that, four more girls complained of sexual abuse, this time to the principal, who actually reported the incidents to the school district's superintendent, which finally resulted in the sexual abuser's suspension from his teaching duties and a diminution in his access to young students to molest. *Id.*

In *Rosa H.*, the plaintiff was a fifteen-year-old girl who was sexually abused by a karate instructor who had been hired to teach at her school. *Rosa H.*, 106 F.3d at 650. Rosa H. was unable to convince the court that the school district had actual notice of the abuse even though she testified that she informed a high school counselor that she was having sex with the karate instructor, a social worker witnessed inappropriate conduct by the karate instructor toward the student and reported it to the school district's director of special programs, the student's mother made the high school principal aware of the possibility that the student was being sexually pursued by the karate instructor, and the school began more closely supervising the karate instructor based on related sexual abuse concerns. *Id.* at 651. Based on the Fifth Circuit's reasoning, every teacher, staff member and administrator in the school could have known that the karate teacher was serially raping the minor student without incurring liability for the school district, as long as none of them had both supervisory duties and the explicit power and authority to halt the abuse. *Id.* at 660.

In November of 1993, Alida Gebser and her mother filed suit as Jane and Jean Doe against Frank Newton Waldrop and the Lago Vista Independent School District. The Texas Tort Claims Act immunizes school districts from tort liability in cases like this one, so tort law did not offer an option for recovery. The claims against Frank Newton Waldrop were disposed of in state court and are not the focus of the majority opinion, nor of this dissent. It is worth noting, however, that even if Alida Gebser prevailed in a civil action against Frank Newton Waldrop, the recently unemployed teacher might well be judgment proof. Only the school district would be likely to have the financial resources to compensate her in any meaningful way. Ironically, some of these funds would be in the possession of the school district as a result of Title IX educational funding.

Alida Gebser lost her Title IX claim on summary judgment in federal district court. The Fifth Circuit Court of Appeals affirmed the dismissal, relying in part on the *Leija* and *Rosa H.* cases. Rosemarie Leija, Rosa H., and Alida Gebser were all denied opportunities to pursue monetary damages under Title IX because the Fifth Circuit set a very high standard of liability for teachers on student sexual abuse claims, just as the majority does today for the entire nation. It is likely that the extremely high standard of liability has discouraged other child sexual abuse victims in the Fifth Circuit from seeking redress from the legal system at all. This chilling effect on potentially meritorious Title IX suits will now spread through the whole United States.

As Justice O'Connor herself observed, "The number of reported cases involving sexual harassment of students in schools confirms that harassment unfortunately is an all too common aspect of the educational experience." *Gebser*, 524 U.S. at 292. Like Rosemarie Leija, Rosa H., and Alida Gebser, tens of thousands of school children attend schools that now have little motivation to protect them from sexual abuse by teachers or school employees.

IV

Even under the harsh and counterproductive strictures of the liability standard adopted by the majority, there was room for Alida Gebser to prevail based on a closer examination of the undisputed facts. Under a theory of constructive notice, a Title IX plaintiff could prevail by showing that management-level authorities should have known of the misconduct and failed to take steps to end it. Evidence that the Lago Vista Independent School District had constructive notice that Frank Newton Waldrop was acting inappropriately was even judicially noticed. Both the Fifth Circuit and U.S. Supreme Court opinions stress the fact that none of the rapes, which the courts refer to as sexual encounters and sexual intercourse, took place on school premises. Yet it was also indisputably established that many of those rapes took place during class time, when school officials should have noticed that one of the district's teachers was absent from school property, and even more pertinently, should have been aware that a young student was not present on school grounds when she was supposed to be. The school was legally responsible for her during the school day. Wasn't attendance taken? Weren't Alida Gebser's absences noted? Surely the Lago Vista Independent School District knew, or should have known, about Alida Gebser's troubling pattern of going missing during the school day, and should have investigated.

Waldrop even concocted a summer advanced placement course in which Alida Gebser was ultimately the only student enrolled. It was "the only AP class taught in her school that summer, and Gebser's only opportunity to obtain college level credit." Pet'r's Br., *supra*, at 4. Although other students signed up for that class, after the first meeting only Alida Gebser attended, leaving her alone with Waldrop throughout this period. *Id.* Waldrop often raped Gebser during the time allotted for this class. Presumably he got paid for purportedly teaching this course, and if for no other reason than discouraging fraud, one would have expected the school district to make sure the class was actually being appropriately taught. If people within the Lago Vista Independent School District had cared about the wellbeing of Alida Gebser, Frank Newton Waldrop's sexual abuse would have been discovered much sooner. That is why a standard of liability that does not encourage school employees to affirmatively look for signs of child sexual abuse is such an appalling travesty of justice.

V

Under the majority's holding, for a child to recover under Title IX, that child must prove both that the school official responsible for compliance had actual knowledge of the sexual harassment and that the official reacted to that notice with deliberate indifference. In order for Alida Gebser to recover under the majority's standard, she would have had to report that she was being raped by a teacher on whom she depended for advice, grades and recommendations, and who was the only teacher offering college level courses. She would have had to find her way to the superintendent of schools, a complete stranger, to tell that official about the abuse. And, she would have had to do that even though she knew that others had reported inappropriate behavior by the same teacher, but the adults in charge took no action.

An alternative and more humane Title IX jurisprudence understands the vulnerability of students to exploitation by untrustworthy, predatory teachers, and does not blame children for their own abuse, or deny them compensation for failing to report sexual abuse, or for reporting it to the wrong person. Justice Stevens' dissent laments the obvious and appalling consequence of the majority's holding: it provides a powerful motivation for school boards to insulate anyone with "authority to institute corrective measures" from actual knowledge about the sexual abuse of students by teachers. Justice Stevens makes the crucial observation that Frank Newton Waldrop had profound authority and control over Alida Gebser by reason of his position as her teacher, and he grossly misused it. A Title IX that wants to reduce sexual harassment must motivate schools to seek out and punish teachers who sexually abuse their students.

As Justice Stevens observed, an agency theory of Title IX liability that focuses upon teacher authority is the best legal approach to foster the aspirational goals of Title IX. It would put the onus on school districts to actively supervise teachers and other school employees, and to create a culture in which teachers police each other, and report wrongdoing to the appropriate supervisors for investigation.

The standard of liability using the agency law approach is explained by the National Women's Law Center (NWLC) in its amicus brief: a school district is liable under Title IX if a teacher's sexual harassment was "facilitated, either expressly or implicitly, by the teacher's actual or apparent authority as an employee of the school." Br. for Nat'l Women's Law Ctr., Am. Ass'n of Univ. Women, *et al.* as Amici Curiae Supporting Pet'r at 2. This standard of liability properly recognizes "the pervasive role of the school's delegated authority" in facilitating teacher-student sexual abuse. *Id.*

There is an additional, important rationale for an agency law approach for Title IX cases involving teacher-student sexual abuse. Using agency principles for Title IX liability tracks the standards for liability in Title VII cases. As noted by the NWLC, a teacher's sexual abuse of a student is certainly facilitated by the teacher's authority, much like "sexual harassment by a supervisor in the workplace is facilitated by the supervisor's authority over employees." *Id.* (citing *Meritor*, 477 U.S. at 76–77 (Marshall, J., concurring)). Given the similarity in power differentials in the employment and educational contexts, it makes little sense to depart from agency principles for Title IX.

Indeed, an agency standard is arguably even more warranted for cases involving children abused by their teachers than for cases in which adults are sexually harassed while employed. As noted by the NWLC, the power exercised by teachers over students is "more compelling" because of the immaturity of the victims and the often significant differences in age between the victim and the perpetrator. *Id.* at 2. Children are far more vulnerable than adults, who may better understand the process for making a sexual harassment complaint, and who can choose to leave their employment. Compulsory attendance rules require children to attend school every day.

They are less likely than adults to fight back or report abuse, and may experience feelings of shame and stigma which are even more acute than those of adult victims of harassment. See Arthur J. Lurigio *et al.*, *Child Sexual Abuse: Its Causes, Consequences, and Implications for Probation Practice*, 59 Fed. Probation 69, 71 (1995).

The criminal justice system recognizes the vulnerability of children to sexual predation, especially by adults. Indeed the premise of statutory rape laws is that children under a certain age are incapable of consenting to sexual intercourse. *See* Patricia Donovan, *Can Statutory Rape Laws Be Effective in Preventing Adolescent Pregnancy*, 29 Fam. Planning Perspectives 30 (1996). Some statutory rape laws even impose enhanced penalties when the age differential between the victim and the abuser is more than a few years. *See* Michelle Oberman, *Turning Girls into Women: Re-Evaluating Modern Statutory Rape Law*, 85 J. Crim. L. & Criminology 15, 23, 37 (1994). Children, who are far more vulnerable than adults, deserve a standard of liability under Title IX cases that is at least commensurate with what adults are accorded in Title VII sexual harassment cases.

The agency law approach also encourages school districts to have clear and well-publicized procedures for reporting sexual abuse. Alida Gebser testified that she was confused and did not know what to do in response to Frank Newton Waldrop's behavior, stating: "If I had known at the beginning what I was supposed to do when a teacher starts making sexual advances towards me, I probably would have reported it. I was bewildered and terrified and I had no idea where to go from where I was." Pet'r's Br., *supra*, at 9. The majority concedes that during the period in which Alida Gebser was being sexually abused by her teacher, the Lago Vista Independent School District "had not promulgated or distributed an official grievance procedure for lodging sexual harassment complaints; nor had it issued a formal anti-harassment policy." *Gebser*, 524 U.S. at 278. A legal approach to liability that motivates schools to make reporting easy for students and mandatory for teachers and other school employees is far preferable to one that allows a school district to escape liability because its reporting procedures are confusing or inaccessible to child victims.

Ironically, if Frank Waldrop had been employed in the private sector and sexually harassed an adult employee over whom he had supervisory authority, his employer might very well be liable under facts similar to those in this case. The majority acknowledged that students and parents complained to school officials about Waldrop's inappropriate sexual comments. Under a theory of constructive notice, a plaintiff can prevail by showing that management-level authorities should have known of the misconduct and failed to take steps to end it. Pet'r's Br., *supra*, at 10.

Finally, Justice Ginsburg and I have both signed on to the dissent authored by Justice Stevens, and agree on most of the important issues. Yet Justice Ginsburg's dissenting opinion argues in favor of recognizing an effective policy for reporting and redressing such misconduct as an affirmative defense to a Title IX charge of sexual harassment. She would place the burden on a school district to show that "its internal remedies were adequately publicized and likely would have provided redress without exposing the complainant to undue risk, effort, or expense," and then deny Title IX relief to any plaintiff found to have "*unreasonably* failed to avail herself of the school district's preventive and remedial measures." *Gebser*, 524 U.S. at 307 (Ginsburg, J., dissenting) (emphasis added). I believe her general goal of providing school districts with strong incentives to put policies for reporting and redressing sexual harassment into effect is admirable. However, substantial research suggests that most victims will be reluctant to report their sexual abuse no matter how accessible the reporting process appears to adults. Teachers who sexually abuse students desperately do not want to be caught. They go to great lengths to threaten, cajole, or flatter their victims into remaining silent. This is why schools need to supervise teachers closely. It is also why students are unlikely to report their abuse. Removing minor children who are victims of sexual harassment from the protections of Title IX because they are afraid, or are confused about the nature of their physical relationships with their adult teachers and may not understand that it is sexual abuse, is misguided and counterproductive.

An agency theory approach would have created the incentives necessary to achieve Congress's intent that Title IX eliminate sex discrimination in federally funded educational programs by prompting schools to actively prevent sexual harassment. It would have recognized that the power exercised by teachers over students, who are children, and who may not have the option of leaving school, is significant. It would have acknowledged the vulnerability of students, rather than punishing children for their naiveté. Most importantly, it would have motivated school districts to proactively protect their own confused young students, who may understandably fail to recognize their own victimization, blame themselves for the abuse directed at them, or feel reluctant to report teachers in authority whose egregious sexual abuse is mistaken for or conflated with friendship and love.

This Court was willing to recognize that sexual harassment by a supervisor in the workplace is facilitated by a supervisor's authority over employees. *Meritor*, 477 U.S. at 76–77 (Marshall, J., concurring). But today it fails a far more vulnerable group of people, school children.

I respectfully dissent.

23

Commentary on *United States v. Morrison*

Shaakirrah R. Sanders

INTRODUCTION

United States v. Morrison[1] involved the constitutionality of the private cause of action authorized by the Violence Against Women Act (VAWA).[2] The District Court and the Fourth Circuit en banc dismissed Christy Brzonkala's complaint against James Crawford, Antonio Morrison, and Virginia Polytechnic Institution.[3] The U.S. Supreme Court affirmed the dismissal and held that: (1) VAWA's private cause of action exceeded congressional authority under Article I's Commerce Clause because gender-motivated violence was a noneconomic local activity that did not substantially affect interstate commerce; and (2) the Fourteenth Amendment's Enforcement Clause did not allow remedial measures against private actors.[4] Justices Souter and Breyer wrote separate dissents. Both dissenters argued that gender-motivated violence was well within the purview of the commerce power, and neither discussed the validity of VAWA's private right of action under the enforcement power.[5]

Professor Aníbal Rosario Lebrón, writing as a dissenting Justice, details the facts in *Morrison* quite differently than do the original majority and dissenting opinions. For example, Chief Justice Rehnquist's majority opinion briefly and succinctly described Crawford and Morrison's alleged attack on Brzonkala as an "assault[]" and "repeated[] rape[]."[6] Morrison's debasing remarks about what he liked to do with women (delivered some months after the alleged rape) were vaguely described as "vulgar remarks that cannot fail to shock and

---

[1]   *United States v. Morrison*, 529 U.S. 598 (2000).
[2]   42 U.S.C. § 13981(c) (1994), *invalidated by United States v. Morrison*, 529 U.S. 598 (2000).
[3]   *Morrison*, 529 U.S. at 604–05.
[4]   *Id*. at 627.
[5]   *Id*. at 628–55 (Souter J., dissenting); *Id*. at 655–66 (Breyer J., dissenting).
[6]   *Id*. at 602.

offend."[7] The dissenting opinions authored by Justices Souter and Breyer did not mention the terms rape or assault in relation to Brzonkala, nor did the dissenters refer to Morrison's post-attack comments.[8]

Rosario Lebrón's narrative explicitly adopts a situated perspective. Rosario Lebrón challenges neutrality as the proper tone of judicial opinions, as well as the concept that judicial language is somehow disconnected from patriarchy. Rosario Lebrón intentionally excludes a discussion of Brzonkala's race and the race of her alleged attackers, believing that such a discussion detracts from how gender-motivated violence perpetuates both physical and economic dominance over women. Nor does Rosario Lebrón mention that Brzonkala had been drinking prior to the alleged rape, believing that to do so would constitute re-victimization.

Rosario Lebrón's personalization of Brzonkala's story offers more than a strict and legalistic narrative of her "encounter" with Crawford and Morrison. Rosario Lebrón argues that the Court's failure to examine and recognize gender-motivated violence as a form of economic domination allows the Court to ignore the miscarriage of justice that Brzonkala experiences beginning with the filing of the initial complaint against Crawford and Morrison and continuing throughout the federal judicial proceedings against the *Morrison* defendants. Relying on national statistics, Marxist theory, and feminist theory, Rosario Lebrón reveals how Brzonkala is re-victimized by administrative and legal systems that preserve the status quo and permit the subordination of women.

THE COMMERCE CLAUSE IN CONTEXT

The *Morrison* majority excluded non-economic local activities from those that could be regulated under the third and broadest category of Commerce Clause jurisprudence – activities that "substantially affect" interstate commerce. The *Morrison* majority reasoned that the significance of the impact on interstate commerce was a judicial, not a legislative, question.[9] Thus, congressional findings alone were insufficient to sustain legislation under the commerce power.[10]

Rosario Lebrón explains how *Morrison* stands in stark contrast to prior Commerce Clause jurisprudence and how it continues an interpretative shift

[7] *Id.*
[8] *Morrison*, 529 U.S. at 628–55 (Souter J., dissenting); *id.* at 655–66 (Breyer J., dissenting).
[9] *Id.* at 614.
[10] *Id.*

that had begun five years earlier in *United States v. Lopez*.[11] *Lopez* struck down the Guns Free School Zones Act of 1990[12] on the grounds that Congress had attempted to regulate a purely "local" matter, i.e., the possession of a firearm in a school zone.[13] Yet, as explained almost seventy years ago, "[t]he term 'affecting commerce' means in commerce, or burdening or obstructing commerce or the free flow of commerce."[14] Because the term "affecting commerce" is one of inclusion, the focus of the inquiry for Commerce Clause purposes has historically been the *burden* on interstate commerce, "not the *source* of the injury."[15]

Lopez perhaps can be attributed to Congress's failure to establish a legislative record of any "substantial effect" on interstate commerce,[16] but *Morrison* cannot. Rosario Lebrón's argument that gender-motivated violence constitutes a substantial burden on interstate commerce relies on congressional findings, specifically Senate testimony of the aggregate economic and non-economic costs of "violent crime against women."[17] These costs amount to billions annually.[18]

Rosario Lebrón incorporates feminist theory to illustrate gender-motivated violence as an economic operation and cites to Gayle Rubin, who has explored female oppression as a pivotal element of the existing male-dominated economic systems.[19] Rubin unravels the exchange of women, sexual access, genealogical statuses, and rights as the underlying foundations of kinship systems that sustain society.[20] This system relies on gender-based allocations of responsibilities where women do not lead, inherit, or talk to God,[21] and where "the entire domain of sex, sexuality and sex oppression is subsumed."[22] Rosario Lebrón also relies on Catharine MacKinnon to demonstrate how gender-motivated violence is more than just sociopathic or criminal conduct

[11] *United States v. Lopez*, 514 U.S. 549 (1995).
[12] 18 U.S.C. § 922(q)(1)(A) (1988 ed., Supp. V), *invalidated by United States v. Lopez*, 514 U.S. 549 (1995).
[13] *Lopez*, 514 U.S. at 567.
[14] *NLRB v. Jones & Laughlin Steel Corp.*, 301 U.S. 1, 31 (1937).
[15] *Id.* at 32 (emphasis added); *see also United States v. Darby*, 312 U.S. 100 (1941); *Wickard v. Filburn*, 317 U.S. 111 (1942); *Heart of Atlanta Motel, Inc. v. United States*, 379 U.S. 241 (1964); *Katzenbach v. McClung Sr. & McClung Jr.*, 379 U.S. 294 (1964) (same). *But see National Federation of Independent Business v. Sebelius*, 132 S. Ct. 2566 (2012).
[16] *Lopez*, 514 U.S. at 562.
[17] *See* S. Rep. No. 101–545, at 30, 33, 36–37 (1990); S. Rep. No. 103–138, at 41, 54 (1990).
[18] *Id.*
[19] Gayle Rubin, *The Traffic in Women: Notes on the Political Economy of Sex, in* Toward an Anthropology of Women 169–83 (Rayna R. Reyter ed., 1975).
[20] *Id.*
[21] *Id.* at 164.
[22] *Id.*

that is motivated by sexual desire.[23] MacKinnon identifies gender-motivated violence as a mechanism that preserves male domination.[24] Rosario Lebrón's incorporation of Rubin and MacKinnon, among others, places feminist social and legal theory at a level of persuasiveness comparable to other types of scholarship commonly cited by the Court.

Rosario Lebrón exposes how the effects of gender-motivated violence are magnified for young college women, who often truncate their education and curtail their economic prospects after a sexual assault or rape.[25] For some victims, abandoning one's studies is the only way to avoid one's attackers.[26] This certainly proved to be the case for Brzonkala, whose losses were not only physical and emotional, but also economic. After the alleged assault and gang rape, another student allegedly made debasing remarks about Brzonkala to Crawford.[27] Morrison allegedly made public statements about his preference for hard-core sex with women that he would get drunk.[28] Even though he confessed to nonconsensual sex with Brzonkala, Morrison's two-semester suspension was set aside as excessive.[29] These events led Brzonkala to stop attending classes and withdraw from Virginia Tech.[30]

THE ENFORCEMENT CLAUSE IN CONTEXT

The *Morrison* majority's interpretation of the Commerce Clause rejects jurisprudential precedent but its interpretation of the Fourteenth Amendment's Enforcement Clause embraces precedent. *Morrison* relies heavily on the *Civil Rights Cases*,[31] which held that the private right of action created by the Civil Rights Act of 1875[32] could not be enforced against private individuals because the Fourteenth Amendment only applied against state actors.[33] For almost a

---

[23] Catharine A. MacKinnon, *Feminism, Marxism, Method, and the State: Toward Feminist Jurisprudence*, 7 Signs 515, 534 (1983).

[24] *Id. See also* S. Rep. No. 103–108, at 54.

[25] S. Rep. No. 103–108, at 44.

[26] *Id.*

[27] *Id.*

[28] *Brzonkala v. Virginia Polytechnic Inst. and State Univ.*, 169 F.3d 820, 827 (4th Cir. 1999) (en banc) (Motz, J., dissenting).

[29] *United States v. Morrison*, 529 U.S. 598, 603 (2000) (Virginia Tech found insufficient evidence to punish Crawford).

[30] *Brzonkala*, 169 F.3d at 908 (Motz, J., dissenting).

[31] 109 U.S. 3 (1883).

[32] 18 Stat. 335–337 *invalidated by* Civil Rights Cases, 109 U.S. 3 (1883).

[33] *Id.* at 12–14; *see City of Boerne v. Flores*, 521 U.S. 507, 529–536 (1997) (congressional records insufficient to support the use of the enforcement power); *Kimel v. Florida Board of Regents*, 528 U.S. 62, 80–91 (2000) (same).

century after the *Civil Rights Cases*, separate-but-equal laws, which were also upheld under the Fourteenth Amendment, allowed race discrimination to flourish in American society.

The *Morrison* majority, like the *Civil Rights Cases* majority, held that the lack of appropriate state responses to inequality does not always trigger Congress's remedial power under the Enforcement Clause. In contrast, Rosario Lebrón describes the lack of such state action to combat gender-motivated violence as a trigger for congressional remedial power. Commissioned studies from coast to coast have "concluded that crimes disproportionately affecting women are often treated less seriously than comparable crimes against men."[34] Law enforcement officers refuse to take reports, prosecutors encourage defendants to plead to minor offenses, and juries lay blame on the victim.[35] According to one study, approximately 41 percent of judges "believed that juries give sexual assault victims less credibility than other crime victims."[36]

Rosario Lebrón also discusses the United States' international obligation to combat gender-motivated violence under the International Covenant on Civil and Political Rights (ICCPR). The ICCPR was ratified by the United States in 1991[37] and recognized gender-motivated violence as one of the gravest and most pervasive, yet long-ignored, violations of human rights and humanitarian law. The ICCPR recognized non-discrimination based on sex as a non-derogable right, identified gender-based violence as an extreme form of gender discrimination, and required governments to provide remedies for such violence.[38] The U.N. Human Rights Commission also declared the elimination of gender-motivated violence a priority of utmost importance.

According to Rosario Lebrón, the civil remedy created by the VAWA also satisfied the United States' international obligations under the ICCPR. Rosario Lebrón maintains that because a valid treaty existed, Congress had authority to enact legislation that was necessary and proper to meet that treaty's obligations.[39] Moreover, Congress had legislative authority over the subject matter of the ICCPR.[40] Rosario Lebrón concludes that *Morrison* ignores Congress's unquestionable authority to enact legislation to meet international treaty and customary law obligations.

---

[34] S. Rep. No. 102–197, at 43 (1991).
[35] S. Rep. No. 103–138, at 42 (1993).
[36] *Id.*
[37] International Covenant on Civil and Political Rights, S. Treaty Doc. No. 95-20 (1992), 999 U.N.T.S. 171.
[38] *Id.* at arts. 2, 3, 4(1), 14, 26.
[39] *Missouri v. Holland*, 252 U.S. 416, 432 (1920).
[40] *Id.*

CONCLUSION

The legitimacy of addressing gender-motivated violence under the commerce and enforcement powers may be resolved, but the states' inability to adequately remedy such violence remains troubling. Almost fifteen years after *Morrison*, the lack of appropriate responses to gender-motivated violence has again captured the attention of the federal government. The United States Department of Education recently revealed that nearly eighty-five colleges and universities may have failed to properly investigate, report, and prosecute sexual assaults and rapes.[41] Perhaps the civil remedy crafted by the VAWA and struck down in *Morrison* could have prevented the atrocities at the colleges and universities currently under investigation. Regardless, these findings illuminate a larger societal reluctance to address gender-motivated violence.

Congressional findings under the VAWA revealed rape and sexual assault as the leading reason that freshmen women drop out of college.[42] This certainly proved true for Brzonkala who delayed her education to escape her alleged attackers. This ultimately resulted in significant economic costs for Brzonkala, and perhaps countless other college freshmen women nationwide.

United States v. Morrison, 529 U.S. 598 (2000)

Justice Aníbal Rosario Lebrón, dissenting.

With its narrow understanding of our Constitution and gender-motivated violence, the majority lends institutional support to gender violence in our nation. Instead of taking steps that would give women a remedy for the systemic violence that they endure, the majority condones and perpetuates the institutionalized bias against victims of gender-motivated violence that pervades the judicial system. It is precisely this bias that Congress was striving to counteract with the enactment of section 13981 of the Violence Against Women Act of 1994 (hereinafter VAWA), 42 U.S.C. § 13981.

The majority wrongly holds that Congress has no power either under section 8 of Article I of the Constitution or section 5 of the Fourteenth Amendment to create the "federal civil rights cause of action" established in section 13981 of VAWA. The majority reasons that gender violence is beyond the reach of the Commerce Clause because "gender-motivated crimes of violence are not,

---

[41] *Education Department Confirms Sexual Assault Investigations Ongoing at 85 U.S. Schools*, University Herald, Oct. 16, 2014, www.universityherald.com/articles/12215/20141016/education-department-confirms-sexual-assault-investigations-ongoing-at-85-u-s-schools.htm.

[42] *Violence Against Women: Victims of the System: Hearings Before the Senate Comm. on the Judiciary*, 102d Cong. 243 (1991) (statement of National Fed'n of Bus. and Prof'l Women, Inc.).

in any sense of the phrase, [an] economic activity." *Morrison*, 529 U.S. at 613. With this decision, the majority overlooks that gender-motivated violence is an economic operation *per se*. As such, gender violence is an activity susceptible to regulation by Congress under the Commerce Clause.

Furthermore, the majority employs an unreliable distinction between the public and the private spheres in declining to find authority under section 5 of the Fourteenth Amendment for Congress to provide a federal civil remedy for victims of gender-motivated violence. By classifying the remedy established in section 13981 of VAWA as an action between "one citizen against each other," *id.*, when states are effectively discriminating against women, the Court denies victims their constitutional rights. Our previous interpretations of the Constitution do not prohibit such remedies, especially when private actors play a key role in discrimination and in the violation of women's rights.

Last, the majority disregards Congress's international obligation to eradicate gender-motivated violence under the International Covenant on Civil and Political Rights (hereinafter ICCPR), December 16, 1966, S. Treaty Doc. No. 95-20 (1992), 999 U.N.T.S. 171. Overlooking this international commitment reveals the majority's failure to understand gender-motivated violence as a human rights issue as well as its reluctance to acknowledge the role the judicial system has had in perpetuating discrimination. Instead, the majority throws away an important opportunity to become part of the solution.

For the foregoing reasons, I respectfully dissent.

I

Before examining in detail the flaws with the majority's rationale, it is important to retell Christy Brzonkala's story. Even though the majority's recitation of the facts underscores the most legally significant events, its account is completely devoid of the details of the gender-motivated violence that brought about this litigation and the subsequent institutionalized violence experienced by the Petitioner.

Brzonkala was a freshman at Virginia Polytechnic Institute (Virginia Tech), a state institution, in the fall of 1994. In September of that year, Brzonkala's post-secondary education was truncated by the actions of the Respondents, Antonio Morrison and James Crawford, who allegedly took turns raping the then eighteen-year-old student. At the time of the alleged gang rape, which occurred in Brzonkala's own college dormitory, Respondents were student athletes also enrolled at Virginia Tech.

Just thirty minutes after Brzonkala first met the Respondents, Morrison allegedly pushed her down by her shoulders onto a dormitory bed, undressed her, and forced her to submit to vaginal penetration while he pinned her with his hands and pressed his knees against her legs. After Morrison – who admitted to performing the acts even after Brzonkala had told him "no" twice – had finished allegedly raping her, the second Respondent allegedly exchanged places with him. Crawford then allegedly forced Brzonkala to submit to vaginal penetration again while he, like Morrison, allegedly pinned her arms down and placed his knees against her legs. Finally, Morrison and Crawford allegedly changed places for a last time and Morrison allegedly raped Brzonkala for a third time.

However, the violence of the men's attack was not limited to the physical sexual assault. Respondents allegedly abused Brzonkala verbally and endangered her health. Neither Morrison nor Crawford wore condoms while they allegedly took turns raping Brzonkala. Not content with putting Brzonkala's health at risk, after the third unwanted vaginal penetration, Morrison allegedly threatened Brzonkala by stating "you better not have any fucking diseases." *United States v. Morrison*, 529 U.S. 598, 602 (2000) (citing Complaint ¶ 22).

The violence did not stop there. When Respondents finally released Brzonkala, Morrison allegedly stalked her. Continuing his allegedly assaultive and menacing conduct, Morrison allegedly silently followed Brzonkala until she reached her room. Moreover, in the months following the alleged gang rape, Morrison humiliated Brzonkala by allegedly announcing in the dormitory dining hall that he "like[d] to get girls drunk and fuck the shit out of them." *Id.* (citing Complaint at ¶ 31).

Furthermore, the allegedly menacing conduct continued, spreading to other students as well. In early 1995, after Brzonkala filed a complaint with the school against Morrison and Crawford asserting a violation of Virginia Tech's sexual assault policy, she learned that another male student athlete had been overheard allegedly telling Crawford that he should have "killed the bitch [referring to Brzonkala]." *Id.* (citing Complaint at ¶ 42). The effects of the alleged sexual assault were so significant that Brzonkala withdrew from Virginia Tech because she had become depressed to the point that she stopped attending classes. She attempted to commit suicide and had to ask for a retroactive leave from school.

But the gender-motivated violence against Brzonkala did not stop there. After filing her complaint, Brzonkala experienced the institutionalized form of violence that victims of gender-motivated violence commonly undergo. Virginia Tech made any redress for her difficult or ineffective. In fact, the reparation process harmed Brzonkala further and left her in an even more precarious situation than she was in immediately after the alleged gang rape.

During the initial hearing on Brzonkala's complaint, Morrison confessed that he had nonconsensual sexual contact with her. However, while Virginia

Tech found Morrison guilty of sexual assault and sentenced him to immediate suspension for two semesters, it found insufficient evidence to punish Crawford.[43]

Morrison appealed his conviction. In May of 1995, Virginia Tech upheld Morrison's suspension. Nonetheless, two months after that determination, Virginia Tech officials advised Brzonkala that Morrison planned to challenge his conviction in court and that Virginia Tech would not defend its decision to suspend him for two semesters. She was informed that Virginia Tech instead intended to hold a re-hearing to revisit its determination of the Respondent's guilt.

Brzonkala returned to Virginia Tech for the second hearing. She engaged and paid for her own legal representation for this new proceeding. If the ordeal of going through an adversarial hearing for the second time were not enough, Brzonkala was denied equal and fair treatment during the process.

First, in preparation for the hearing, Morrison was permitted full access to the transcript and exhibits from the initial hearing, while Brzonkala allegedly was denied access to these essential documents. In addition, Morrison was given advance notice, sufficient to allow him to procure sworn affidavits from student witnesses who testified at the first hearing, while Brzonkala was allegedly given no such notice. Furthermore, although Brzonkala was informed that the second hearing constituted a *de novo* consideration, she was allegedly instructed to avoid any mention of Crawford in her testimony, which diluted it. Finally, even though there was no proceeding against Crawford, he was notified of the second hearing and was present in an adjacent room during the proceeding.

Notwithstanding the abuses and irregularities in the process, Virginia Tech found Morrison guilty once again and sentenced him to the same two-semester suspension. Yet, inexplicably, Morrison's count of conviction was changed from "sexual assault" to the lesser count of "using abusive language." In addition, after Morrison appealed this revised conviction, Virginia Tech set aside his punishment, allegedly without giving any notice to Brzonkala. Instead, she had to learn from a newspaper that Morrison would return on a full athletic scholarship to Virginia Tech for the fall semester of 1995, the same semester she was planning to return to her college studies.

That event ended Brzonkala's education at Virginia Tech. After learning that Virginia Tech officials had permitted Morrison to enroll again at the school, Brzonkala feared for her personal safety and canceled her plans to return to Virginia Tech. The alleged gang rape by the Respondents and the

[43] There is nothing in the record that explains that decision.

institutionalized violence Brzonkala experienced at this public university limited her career opportunities and earning potential. Moreover, these events created a financial detriment for Brzonkala as she was forced to hire legal counsel to seek redress for the wrongful acts committed against her. In addition, she did not receive a refund of monies that she paid for her room, board, books and fees, nor compensation for the travel expenses associated with the second hearing.

In December of 1995, dissatisfied and frustrated with the way that her case had been handled, Brzonkala decided to bring action against Respondents under the civil rights remedy of VAWA, 42 U.S.C. § 13981. Morrison and Crawford moved to dismiss this complaint on the grounds that it failed to state a claim and that section 13981's civil remedy was unconstitutional. The District Court agreed with the Respondents and dismissed the complaint based on its finding that Congress lacked authority to enact section 13981 under either the Commerce Clause or section 5 of the Fourteenth Amendment. *Brzonkala v. Virginia Pol'c Inst. & State Univ.*, 935 F. Supp. 779 (W.D. Va. 1996). On appeal, a divided panel of the Court of Appeals reversed the District Court, reinstating Brzonkala's § 13981 claim. *Brzonkala v. Virginia Pol'c Inst. & State Univ.*, 132 F.3d 949 (4th Cir. 1997). However, the full Court of Appeals for the Fourth Circuit vacated the panel's opinion when it reheard the case en banc. *Brzonkala v. Virginia Pol'c Inst. & State Univ.*, 169 F.3d 820 (4th Cir. 1999). The en banc court, by a divided vote, affirmed the result and the District Court's rationale that while Brzonkala's complaint sufficiently alleged a gender-motivated crime, Congress lacked the constitutional authority to enact section 13981's civil remedy. *Id.* From this last determination of the Court of Appeals we granted certiorari. *United States v. Morrison*, 527 U.S. 1068 (1999).

II

Brzonkala's case reflects a serious problem that affects our country: gender-motivated violence. Unfortunately, the state governments have not been able to effectively address this problem of national proportions. An estimated four million American women continue to be battered every year by their partners. H.R. Rep. 103–395, at 26 (1993). Studies suggest that three out of four women in the country will become victims of a violent crime at some point during their lifetimes. *Id.* at. 25. This is a problem of significant magnitude in our nation. Today, battering is the single largest cause of injury to females in the United States. S. Rep. No. 101–545, at 37 (1990). Yearly, over a million women in the United States seek medical assistance for injuries resulting from domestic violence. *Id.* at 37. Moreover, it is estimated that "[b]etween 2,000 and 4,000 women die every year from [gender-motivated domestic] abuse." *Id.* at 36.

Figures suggest that gender is the reason behind the violent attacks on women. *Id.* at 30. In fact, when we closely compare the violence men experience *vis-à-vis* that suffered by women, we realize that the great disparity between the two can only be accounted for in terms of gender. For instance, "[s]ince 1974, the assault rate against women has outstripped the rate for men by at least twice for some age groups and far more for others." *Id.*

To make the situation worse, the states have shown a persistent inability to remedy the problem. For instance, arrest rates may be as low as 1% in domestic assault cases in some states. *Id.* at 38. The rate is as staggeringly low for sexual crimes, with an individual who commits rape facing only about a 4% chance of being arrested, prosecuted, and found guilty of any offense. *Id.* at 33. These low rates in the prosecution and conviction of gender-motivated crimes are the product of a systemic discrimination against women that permeates the states from their police enforcement organs up through their judicial apparatus.

"Study after study commissioned by the highest courts of the states – from Florida to New York, California to New Jersey, Nevada to Minnesota – has concluded that crimes disproportionately affecting women are often treated less seriously than comparable crimes against men." S. Rep. No. 102–197, at 43 (1991). For instance, "Police may refuse to take reports; prosecutors may encourage defendants to plead to minor offenses; judges may rule against victims on evidentiary matters; and juries too often focus on the behavior of the survivors – laying blame on the victims instead of on the attackers." S. Rep. No. 103–138, at 42 (1993). Even when the factual evidence is overwhelmingly manifest, police officers rarely take action. Researchers recently found that in Washington, D.C., in 85 percent of cases where a woman was found bleeding, police failed to arrest her attacker. *Id.* at 44.

The implicit bias against women is predicated on patriarchal attitudes and is so prevalent that even state officials can no longer deny its existence. As high as "[forty-one] percent of judges surveyed [in a study] believed that juries give sexual assault victims less credibility than other crime victims." S. Rep. No. 102–197, at 47 (1991). As evidenced by these statistics, gender-motivated violence and the lack of an appropriate government response constitute a national problem that cannot be ignored any longer.

Consequently, in 1994, Congress enacted VAWA. In doing so, Congress acknowledged the urgent need for a general application of the rights of equality and liberty under our Constitution as well as the rights of integrity and dignity under various international treaties. When enacting section 13981, Congress acted pursuant to its affirmative power "under section 5 of the

Fourteenth Amendment to the Constitution, as well as under section 8 of Article I of the Constitution," 42 U.S.C.A § 13981(a) (West 2000), to preserve the right of "[a]ll persons within the United States ... to be free from crimes of violence motivated by gender." *Id.* at § 13981(b). Guaranteeing that the right to be free from crimes of gender-motivated violence would become more than an aspiration, Congress created a civil remedy for victims. Such remedy serves both as a deterrent and as an insurance that aggressors no longer would benefit from the patriarchal impunity they have enjoyed when victims encounter implicit bias while seeking redress.

VAWA's civil remedy provides that a person who commits a gender-motivated crime of violence "shall be liable to the party injured in an action for the recovery of compensatory and punitive damages, injunctive and declaratory relief, and such other relief as a court may deem appropriate." *Id.* at § 13981(c). To be liable under subsection (c), defendants need not be convicted or even prosecuted under criminal laws. The plaintiff, however, must prove by a preponderance of the evidence that the felonious act against her person or her property was "committed because of gender or on the basis of gender, and due, at least in part, to an animus based on the victim's gender." *Id.* at § 13981(d)(1), (e)(1).

III

Today the majority rejects Congress's first steps in combating gender-motivated violence, arguing that Congress lacks the power to do so under section 8 of Article I of the Constitution, the Commerce Clause. Such a conclusion reflects a lack of understanding of both our jurisprudence and gender-motivated violence. Furthermore, the majority's opinion makes manifest how the judicial system has been one of the main players in maintaining the systemic bias women experience in our society.

Although the majority acknowledges that there is no categorical rule against aggregating the economic effects of a non-economic activity to regulate such activity under the Commerce Clause, *Morrison*, 529 U.S. at 613, it refuses to recognize that gender-motivated violence is within the purview of the Commerce Clause. However, the aggregated economic effects of gender-motivated violence on interstate commerce put it squarely within Congress's reach. By not upholding section 13981, the majority has assigned a lesser value to this alleged non-economic activity than to other non-economic activities that we have considered to be appropriate subjects of regulation. *See Wickard v. Filburn*, 317 U.S. 111 (1942) (holding that national quotas for wheat grown for personal consumption on one's own land are permissible under the Commerce Clause because of their aggregated effects on the national economy); *Perez v. United States*, 402 U.S. 146 (1971) (finding that, in aggregate, criminal activity such as loan sharking has a substantial adverse effect on interstate commerce and can be regulated by Congress under the Commerce Clause).

Moreover, the majority adopts today a *de facto* rule against the regulation of non-economic activity by requiring for the first time an express jurisdictional element which might limit the reach of regulation under section 8 of Article I of the Constitution. *Morrison*, 529 U.S. at 613, 614. Surprisingly, the majority ignores the existence of precisely such a limiting jurisdictional element in this case, presumably because it finds unpersuasive the copious evidence gathered by Congress. Yet the majority provides no guidance as to what would be a sufficient limiting element under this new *de facto* requirement.

Yet, even if we accept the majority's proposition that non-economic activity with an aggregated economic effect is not covered by the Commerce Clause without an *effective limiting jurisdictional element*, the Court is ignoring that gender-motivated violence is in and of itself an economic activity. Thus, it falls under Congress's reach.

Under our current understanding of the Commerce Clause, Congress may regulate certain activity if it falls under any of the following three broad premises: (1) channels of interstate commerce; (2) instrumentalities, persons or things in interstate commerce; and (3) activities that substantially affect interstate commerce. *United States v. Lopez*, 514 U.S. 549, 558 (1995). As the majority correctly asserts, the first two categories do not apply here. Regarding the third jurisdictional category, it is this Court's duty to review Congress's assessment of the underlying activity and its connection with interstate commerce under a rational basis standard. *See Wickard*, 317 U.S. at 124–28; *Hodel v. Virginia Surface Mining & Reclamation Assn., Inc.*, 452 U.S. 264, 277 (1981). In other words, we can only look at whether Congress made a rational conclusion that the activity at issue, in the aggregate, has a substantial effect on interstate commerce. We must not review the decision otherwise.

Congress's rationality is uncontested in this case. Congress found that "violent crime against women costs this country *at least 3 billion* … dollars a year." S. Rep. No. 101–545, at 33 (1990) (emphasis added). These costs are the combined effect of significant health care provided to victims, government expenditures in victims' services created to ameliorate the devastating economic effects of gender-motivated violence, and other costs that affect the economy at large. *See id.* at 33, S. Rep. No. 103–138, at 41 (1993).

Apart from the money that women spend for medical attention to treat injuries resulting from domestic violence and other types of gender-motivated crimes, *see* S. Rep. No. 101–545, at 37 (1990), gender-motivated violence forces many victims into poverty. Thus, many victims are then forced to seek government benefits, support and other social services. *Id.* Furthermore, gender-motivated violence has a significant impact on victims' participation and performance in the workforce. Almost 50 percent of rape victims "lose their jobs or are forced to quit in the aftermath of the crime." S. Rep. No. 103–138, at 54 (1993). Even those who remain employed after a rape may experience a prolonged period of decreased productivity. S. Rep. No. 101–545, at 33 (1990). The same holds true for domestic violence victims. The costs of employee absenteeism due to domestic violence may reach $3 billion to $5 billion a year. *Id.*

In this case, the evidence specifically shows the required connection. This case is different from *Lopez*, in which we noted the Government's concession that "[n]either the statute nor its legislative history contain[ed] express congressional findings regarding the effects upon interstate commerce of gun possession in a school zone." *United States v. Lopez*, 513 U.S. at 562. Therefore, the distinction the majority attempts to draw today is superfluous and dangerous, especially when the legislation meets our jurisprudential limits of a rational finding of an aggregated economic effect on interstate commerce.

Moreover, the majority exceeds our reach and goes so far as to suggest that the current Commerce Clause analysis requires Congress to include a jurisdictional element in any law to ensure that the underlying activity being regulated has concrete ties to interstate commerce. *Morrison*, 529 U.S. at 613. This has never been a part of our Commerce Clause jurisprudence. Yet, even if it were, VAWA includes such an element. As mentioned, subsection 13981(e)(1) requires the plaintiff to prove that the criminal activity was gender motivated, which Congress has shown has detrimental effects on interstate commerce. In ignoring that jurisdictional limiting element, the majority shows its lack of understanding of the remedies created by VAWA and the economic dimensions of gender-motivated violence.

The same is true of the majority's suggestion that upholding the constitutionality of this law will open the doors of the federal courts to a whole host of domestic relations disputes, even when the law specifically denies that possibility. *Morrison*, 529 U.S. at 615–616. Congress made clear that nothing in the statute shall be construed "to confer on the courts of the United States jurisdiction over any state law claim seeking the establishment of a divorce, alimony, equitable distribution of marital property, or child custody decree." 42 U.S.C. § 13981(e)(4). Subsection (e)(4) eliminates any possibility of the law's interpretation as a domestic relations regulation. Those two sections place

more than sufficient limits on Congress's actions and restrict its power according to the Tenth Amendment to the Constitution.

The majority's reading of this section reflects a misunderstanding of gender dynamics. The majority deems legal deterrence of gender-motivated
violence as an inappropriate reach into the non-economic domestic sphere.
This limited view is a byproduct of the patriarchal notions that have permeated our legal system for centuries and which place women and the family
in a domestic sphere characterized as diametrically opposite to the market. Gender-motivated violence, however, is in and of itself an economic
activity carefully crafted to maintain women economically, politically, and
socially subordinated. Even if Congress chose to focus instead on the aggregate effects this activity has on interstate commerce, we ought not to do
the same.

As anthropologist Gayle Rubin explains, the operation of the current
social system relies on a clear power distinction between men and women,
and the preservation of that division of power. Gayle Rubin, *The Traffic in
Women: Notes on the Political Economy of Sex, in Toward an Anthropology
of Women* 169–83 (Rayna R. Reyter ed., 1975). Under our capitalist economic
system, that division manifests itself in the historical and moral notions –
which Marxist theorists have already pointed out – of women as a reserve labor
force, lower wages for women that provide a labor surplus, unpaid housework
done by women, and women as administrators of family consumption. *Id.*
at 160. Women have constantly been battling these notions; however, they
have faced resistance at every turn. Domestic violence and other forms of
gender-motivated violence are part of that resistance.

As Engels poignantly summarizes, in order to maintain economic and political control, men exert violence against women predicated solely on their condition as females. Frederick Engels, *Origins of the Family, Private Property, and
the State* 120–22 (International Publishers 1972) (1884). Similarly, Catharine
MacKinnon has explained that rape – one practice of gender-motivated
violence – is a form of men's control over women, not an enactment of sexual desire. Catharine A. MacKinnon, *Feminism, Marxism, Method, and the
State: Toward Feminist Jurisprudence*, 7 Signs 515, 534 (1983). Congress's findings corroborate Engel's and MacKinnon's assertions that gender-motivated
violence is more than patriarchal prejudices and violent behavior, but rather
a fundamental method of ensuring the ongoing subordination of women,
including economic subordination.

For instance, Congress found that gender-motivated violence "deters
women from taking jobs in certain areas or at certain hours that pose a significant risk of such violence." S. Rep. No. 103–108, at 54 (1993). Likewise,

harassment by aggressors reduces women's ability to secure employment. S. Hearing 102–369, at 24–26. Closely related to this case, Congress found that the effects of gender-motivated violence are "often magnified for young women attending college," S. Rep. No. 101–545, at 44 (1990). As in Brzonkala's case, their education is often truncated and their economic prospects curtailed by violence. Female college students who are victims of gender-motivated violence may be forced to leave their studies and careers, as in this case, because they feel it is the only way to avoid their attackers. *Id.* at 44. Finally, it is worth noting that, for similar reasons, many women refrain from using public transportation, being alone in public spaces, shopping, going to public events, or participating in political forums. S. Rep. No. 102–197, at 38 (1991). In sum, gender-motivated violence represents for women lost careers, decreased economic opportunities, and political abstention.

Thus, violence is a tool for maintaining women's economic inferiority. As such, it is an economic operation, even if disguised under the rubric of violence. Therefore, gender-motivated violence not only has aggregated effects on interstate commerce, but it also is an economic activity that affects the national economy. Because gender-motivated violence is an economic activity, it follows that Congress properly exercised its powers when it enacted section 13981.

IV

Further, the majority incorrectly concludes that Congress acted *ultra vires* under section 5 of the Fourteenth Amendment when enacting the civil remedy in section 13981. The majority reasoned that Congress holds no power to enforce civil rights protections between private individuals and that the remedy was "simply not 'corrective in its character, adapted to counteract and redress the operation of ... prohibited [s]tate laws or proceedings of [s]tate officers.'" *Morrison*, 529 U.S. at 624 (citations omitted). The majority relies heavily on the misleading distinction between the public and the private. Yet, the present case is different from *United States v. Harris*, 106 U.S. 629 (1883), and the *Civil Rights Cases*, 109 U.S. 3 (1883), in which we held that section 5 does not authorize Congress to remedy the conduct of private parties under the Fourteenth Amendment.

Those two cases involved exclusively the actions "of private persons, without reference to the laws of the states, or their administration by the officers of the state." *Harris*, 106 U.S. at 640. There was no state action and no link between the private actions and the public actions of state officials. However, as in this case, there is not always a bright line dividing those two spheres that permits us to draw a distinction in which the Fourteenth Amendment is not compromised. Moreover, we should be careful when employing this dichotomy between the private and the public, as it has been used in the past as "a misleading construct, which obscures the cyclical pattern of inequalities between men and women." Susan Moller Okin, *Justice, Gender and the Family* 111 (1989).

The present case is a perfect example of how inequality is obscured by that distinction. Here, the states' failure to provide female victims of gender-based violence comparable treatment to what they offer male victims of other crimes is a state action stemming from state officials' implicit bias. Yet, that bias is linked intrinsically to the actions and identities of the private actors who were the aggressors. Thus, this case is about states' violations of the Equal Protection Clause with links to the actions of private actors.

Since Congress found that states inadequately remedy the implicit biases of state officials who deal with victims of gender-motivated violence, Congress chose to nip the problem in the bud and create a private right of action to deter aggressors while addressing the implicit bias of state officials. Congress's goals in creating such a remedy were threefold: (1) to reduce the rate of gender-motivated violent crimes; (2) to provide reparation to the victims; and (3) to offer a new forum for victims to seek unbiased legal redress. Our Constitution permits Congress to craft such a remedy. The remedy under section 13981 corrects not only for the implicit bias exhibited by government entities against women (by providing them a new and fairer forum), but also for the economic subordination experienced by victims of gender-motivated violence that resulted from the actions of private individuals and the discriminatory state practices.

Our precedents unequivocally hold that the states violate the Equal Protection Clause of the Fourteenth Amendment when they engage in conduct that discriminates against citizens of a particular sex based solely on their gender, inaccurate stereotypes or implicit biases, and when their actions do not further an important government interest in a manner that is substantially related to such interest. *United States v. Virginia*, 518 U.S. 515 (1996) (striking down the Virginia Military Institute's long-standing male-only admission policy); *Kirchberg v. Feenstra*, 450 U.S. 455 (1981) (affirming the unconstitutionality of a Louisiana statute that made husbands head and master of property jointly owned with wives); *Reed v. Reed*, 404 U.S. 71 (1971) (holding unconstitutional a state statute establishing male preference among several persons equally entitled to administer a decedent's estate). In the case of violence against women, Congress found that states have repeatedly been violating the Equal Protection Clause by failing to treat gender-motivated crimes as seriously as other violent crimes.[44] It is difficult for women to obtain justice when "almost a quarter of the judges believe that rape victims 'sometimes' or 'frequently' precipitate their sexual assaults because of what they wear and/ or actions preceding the incidents," S. Rep. No. 102–197, at 47 n.63 (1991), or when judges perceive cases involving domestic violence as trivial. S. Rep. No. 103–108, at 46. (1993). Based on the extensive congressional record of the states' persistent inability to address the implicit biases in the criminal justice system against victims of gender-motivated crimes, the majority erroneously determines that section 13981 was beyond the scope of the Fourteenth Amendment. *See* Section II, *ante*.

While it is true that the Fourteenth Amendment encompasses only state action, *Lugar v. Edmondson Oil Co.*, 457 U.S. 922, 936 (1982), we have never held that Congress's attempts to remedy such violations must be limited to the state actors themselves. Quite the opposite, we have held that the power in the Enforcement Clause of the Fourteenth Amendment is "a positive grant of legislative power." *City of Boerne v. Flores*, 521 U.S. 507, 516 (1997); *Katzenbach v. Morgan*, 384 U.S. 641, 651 (1966). Limiting congressional remedies to the powers proscribed in section 1 would make the Enforcement Clause superfluous.

The Fourteenth Amendment makes a clear distinction between the basis for Congress's taking action under the Amendment and the scope of the remedy crafted under its provision. While we held that Congress cannot act "until some State law has been passed, or some State action through its officers or agents has been taken, adverse to the rights of citizens sought to be protected by the Fourteenth Amendment," *Civil Rights Cases*, 109 U.S. 3, 13 (1883), we have not put such limitations on the *remedies*. Precisely in the *Civil Rights Cases*, we clearly established Congress's ability to enact such corrective legislation as may be necessary and proper for counteracting the actions of the states. *Id.* at 13–14. In fact, the same precedent the majority uses to try to obscure this distinction and hold that a remedy under the Equal Protection Clause could not be directed to non-state actors clearly counters such a proposition. *See id.* at 12–13 (explaining how under the provisions of the Constitution, Congress could provide corrective measures regarding the subject of contracts, even though it is a matter of private parties).

---

[44] Several lower federal courts also have found that states have violated the equal protection rights of victims of gender-motivated crimes. *See, e.g., Hynson v. City of Chester*, 864 F.2d 1026, 1030–31 (3rd Cir. 1988); *Thurman v. City of Torrington*, 595 F. Supp. 1521, 1526 (D. Conn. 1984); *Watson v. City of Kansas City*, 857 F.2d 690, 695 (10th Cir. 1988); *Balistreri v. Pacifica Police Dept.*, 901 F.2d 696, 701 (9th Cir. 1990).

Thus, even though Congress's remedial power under section 5 is not unbounded – as it is restricted by a jurisdictional basis under section 1 – the scope of the remedy does not have such section 1 limitations. The remedy, instead, is bound only by section 5 which requires that the remedy be appropriate. Therefore, congressional acts must bear "congruence and proportionality between the injury to be prevented or remedied and the means adopted to that end." *Boerne v. Flores*, 521 U.S. at 527. There is no distinction between state and non-state actors as the majority purports; such is a patriarchal artifice of the so-called public-private divide.

In the present case, even though the remedy is not addressed toward state actors, it is corrective, congruent, and proportional. The remedy provides victims of gender-motivated crimes with an appropriate forum for their claims while deterring both private and state actors from engaging in discriminatory and subordinating practices. Thus, it follows that the majority wrongly concluded that Congress exceeded its powers under the Fourteenth Amendment when it enacted the civil remedy action under section 13981.

V

Lastly, the majority fails to recognize gender-motivated violence as a human rights issue and ignores this country's obligations under binding international treaties. It is well established in our jurisprudence that Congress has the authority to enact legislation that is necessary and proper to meet our country's obligations under ratified treaties. *Missouri v. Holland*, 252 U.S. 416 (1920). Congress also has the authority to legislate over the subject matter of a valid treaty, whether or not the Constitution provides another source of congressional power to do so. *Id.* at 432 (holding that "[i]f the treaty is valid there can be no dispute about the validity of the statute under Article 1, Section 8, as a necessary and proper means to execute the powers of the Government"). Furthermore, this Court must construe acts of Congress so as not to violate the law of nations, if such an interpretation is possible. *Murray v. Schooner Charming Betsy*, 6 U.S. (2 Cranch) 64, 118 (1804). Thus, if there is a conflict between a treaty and the Constitution, and Congress is acting according to the treaty, it is our duty to reconcile the two in order to allow the United States to fulfill its international obligations that have become part of the law of the land.

The ICCPR – which was ratified by the United States on June 8, 1992 – guarantees individuals the right to be free from gender-based violence and requires party states to provide their citizens with redress and protection from state and privately inflicted forms of gender-motivated violence. S. Treaty

Doc. No. 95-20 (1992). Specifically, the ICCPR guarantees, *inter alia*, the enjoyment of all civil and political rights irrespective of sex; equal treatment in the courts; equal protection of the laws, equal and effective protection against discrimination; the rights to life, liberty and security of person; the freedom from slavery, torture, and other cruel, inhumane, or degrading punishments; the rights to liberty of movement and choice of residence; and the rights to freedom of thought, belief, expression, information and association. *Id.* at arts. 2, 3, 6–9, 12, 18, 25. In addition, article 2 of the ICCPR requires states to "adopt such legislative or other measures as may be necessary to give effect to the rights recognized in the … Covenant." *Id.* at art. 2. That responsibility includes the obligation to ensure that any person whose rights have been violated by state officials or private persons has available "an effective remedy," to be "determined by competent judicial, administrative or legislative authorities or other competent authority." *Id.* at art. 2(3)(a)–(b). The VAWA civil cause of action is such a remedy. Section 13981 gives effect to the ICCPR's right to equal protection of the laws and to equal and effective protection against discrimination.

Because the ICCPR was properly ratified by Congress and it is in complete harmony with our constitutional precedents, section 13981 of VAWA is a valid method of fulfilling our human rights obligations under the treaty. This has been recognized by the United States government itself. The executive branch has stressed internationally how VAWA was a measure undertaken to comply with United States' ICCPR obligations. Summary Record of the 1401st Meeting: United States of America, at ¶ 29, CCPR/C/SR.140 (17/04/95). Taking this into account, the majority should have upheld the obligation to preserve the human rights of our citizens and found section 13981 to be constitutional.

There is no merit to the argument that section 13981 is invalid because Congress did not refer in its legislative history to the ICCPR as a reason for VAWA's enactment. Congress need not state the specific authority for legislation so long as we are able to "discern some legislative purpose or factual predicate that supports the exercise of that power." *EEOC v. Wyoming*, 460 U.S. 226, 244, n.18 (1983). As long as Congress has the authority "as an objective matter, whether it also ha[s] the specific intent to legislate pursuant to that authority is irrelevant." *Coger v. Bd. of Regents*, 154 F.3d 296, 302 (6th Cir. 1998); *Crawford v. Davis*, 109 F.3d 1281, 1283 (8th Cir. 1997); *Ramirez v. Puerto Rico Fire Serv.*, 715 F.2d 694, 698 (1st Cir. 1983). Taking this into account, we should have upheld our tradition of preserving the human rights of our citizens and found Congress's actions under VAWA a proper exercise of its powers.

VI

Section 13981 does not challenge or change the underlying assumptions that give rise to violence against women and cannot provide for an adequate remedy to all victims. Nevertheless, it is a good and constitutional first step to address the problem and improve women's equality. Gender-motivated crimes are within the purview of the Commerce Clause because they are an economic activity leading to the subordination of women. Furthermore, these crimes have aggregated effects on interstate commerce. Likewise, Congress acted within its powers under the Equal Protection Clause when it crafted the civil remedy against the aggressors instead of against state actors. The remedy is congruent and proportional to the corrective measures against political and economic subordination of women. Moreover, upholding the law is consistent with this nation's obligations under international law.

Not following our precedent by attempting to enforce fictitious distinctions between underlying commercial vis-à-vis non-commercial activity and private and public actors, as well as by supplanting rational basis analysis with a new criterion of review for the Commerce Clause, demonstrates how the judicial system can suffer from the same implicit bias against women that Congress was trying to deter with the enactment of VAWA.

Wherefore, I respectfully dissent as I would have reversed the judgment of the Court below d I would have upheld the constitutionality of the law.

24

Commentary on *Nguyen v. INS*

Sandra S. Park

As one of the newest U.S. Supreme Court cases deciding a sex-based equal protection challenge, *Nguyen v. INS*[1] represents a step backwards in constitutional gender jurisprudence. While the Court stated it was applying heightened scrutiny, the decision did not deploy the rigorous analysis of *United States v. Virginia*[2] in determining whether it was constitutional to require fathers to satisfy more onerous criteria to pass on citizenship to their children born abroad. The opinion casts doubt on whether heightened scrutiny meaningfully confines facial sex discrimination. It also illustrates how the Court's equal protection doctrine traditionally has failed to account for intersecting forms of stereotyping and bias.

BACKGROUND

Following feminist advocacy starting in the 1970s, most federal laws that explicitly discriminated based on sex were struck down as unconstitutional or amended to be gender neutral. The Immigration and Nationality Act, however, contains some of the few remaining provisions that expressly treat men and women differently.[3]

One provision governs the acquisition of U.S. citizenship by a child born outside the country to unmarried parents, only one of whom is a U.S. citizen. When the child is born to an unmarried U.S. citizen father, the father must show the following to transmit U.S. citizenship at birth:

---

[1]   *Nguyen v. INS*, 533 U.S. 53 (2001).
[2]   *United States v. Virginia*, 518 U.S. 515 (1996).
[3]   *See, e.g.*, 8 U.S.C. § 1154(f) (granting preferential treatment to children "fathered by United States citizens and born in Korea, Vietnam, Laos, Kampuchea, or Thailand" from 1950 to 1982).

- A blood relationship between the child and the father is established by clear and convincing evidence;[4]
- While the child is under the age of 18 years
  (a) the child is legitimated under the law of the child's residence;
  (b) the father acknowledges paternity of the child in writing under oath;
  (c) the paternity of the child is established by a competent court;[5] or
  (d) the father is physically present in the United States for five years before the child's birth, at least two of which were after the father turned 14 years of age.[6]

In contrast, a U.S. citizen mother need only show that she had U.S. nationality at the time of the child's birth, and that she had been physically present in the United States continuously for one year at any time before the birth.[7]

The U.S. Supreme Court first considered the constitutionality of section 1409(a)(4)'s legitimation requirement in *Miller v. Albright*, ultimately affirming the dismissal of Lorelyn Penero Miller's petition to acquire citizenship through her U.S. citizen father.[8] Because Miller's father had obtained a paternity decree when she was 22 years old, the requirement that this be done before the child turns 18 was not met. None of the opinions garnered a majority on the question of whether the legitimation requirement imposed on U.S. citizen fathers violated the equal protection guarantee when no such requirement was placed on U.S. citizen mothers. However, based on the concurrence and dissents, it appeared that five justices agreed that the provision could not pass constitutional muster.[9]

THE U.S. SUPREME COURT DECISION

In 1969, Tuan Anh Nguyen was born in Vietnam to a Vietnamese woman and a U.S. citizen, Joseph Boulais, who were unmarried. Nguyen came to the United States, lived with Boulais, and became a lawful permanent resident. As an adult, he was convicted of sexual assault and placed into deportation proceedings. Nguyen claimed that he was a U.S. citizen and thus argued that he could not be deported. Nguyen and Boulais brought an equal protection

---

[4] *Id.* § 1409(a)(1).
[5] *Id.* § 1409(a)(4).
[6] *Id.* § 1401(g).
[7] *Id.* § 1409(c).
[8] *Miller v. Albright*, 523 U.S. 420 (1998).
[9] *Id.* at 451 (noting that "[a]lthough I do not share Justice Stevens' assessment that the provision withstands heightened scrutiny…") (O'Connor, J., concurring); *id.* at 460 (Ginsburg, J., dissenting); *id.* at 481 (Breyer, J., dissenting).

challenge to the requirement that the child must be legitimated while under 18 years old.

The U.S. Supreme Court split 5–4, with Justice Kennedy writing for the majority and Justice O'Connor for the dissent.[10] Justice Kennedy purported to apply heightened scrutiny, and thus did not rule on the government's argument that lesser scrutiny was appropriate based on Congress's plenary power over immigration and naturalization. He focused on two governmental interests as justifying the differential treatment of fathers and mothers: (1) "the importance of assuring that a biological parent-child relationship exists"; and (2) "the determination to ensure that the child and the citizen parent have some demonstrated opportunity or potential to develop not just a relationship that is recognized, as a formal matter, by the law, but one that consists of the real, everyday ties that provide a connection between child and citizen parent and, in turn, the United States."

On the first interest, the majority held that section 1409(a)(4) is substantially related to furthering the important governmental interest in obtaining acceptable documentation of paternity. The Court noted that, in most cases, the mother's status is documented at birth. Fathers need not be present at birth, and presence is no guarantee of paternity. Thus, even though section 1409(a)(1) requires establishing a blood relationship, section 1409(a)(4) "represents a reasonable conclusion by the legislature" that the blood link could be established through proof of legitimation.

As for the second interest, the Court found that mothers and fathers are not similarly situated in having an opportunity for a meaningful relationship with a child. For mothers, this opportunity "inheres in the very event of birth," while fathers may not even know that a child was conceived. Citing figures on the millions of young men who served in the military and travel overseas, the Court concluded that section 1409(a)(4) "ensure[s] contact between father and child during the child's minority." The opinion rejected the argument that the statute reflects gender-based stereotyping, asserting: "There is nothing irrational or improper in the recognition that at the moment of birth ... the mother's knowledge of the child and the fact of parenthood have been established in a way not guaranteed in the case of the unwed father."

In dissent, Justice O'Connor forcefully argued that the majority did not properly apply heightened scrutiny.[11] With regard to the first proffered

---

[10] Justice Scalia, with Justice Thomas, filed a concurrence, echoing their *Miller* argument that the Court lacked the power to confer citizenship as a remedy. *Nguyen*, 533 U.S. at 73 (Scalia, J., concurring).

[11] *Id.* at 74 (O'Connor, J., dissenting).

governmental interest, she attacked the inadequate fit between the discriminatory means and the governmental interest. Given section 1409(a)(1) and the ease of DNA testing, a requirement that fathers legitimate their children contributed little to proving paternity.

The dissent condemned the majority's reliance on the second governmental interest as appearing "to rest only on an overbroad sex-based generalization." The majority's assumption that ensuring an opportunity for a relationship would necessarily lead to a "real, practical relationship" was one that "finds support not in biological differences but instead in a stereotype, that is, 'the generalization that mothers are significantly more likely than fathers ... to develop caring relationships with their children.'" Congress could instead have chosen gender-neutral alternatives for a parent to show the nature of his or her relationship with the child.

The dissent examined the gender stereotyping embodied by the statute, pointing out that a stereotype need not be insulting, but instead can reflect an outdated understanding that gender is a useful proxy for other, more germane criteria. Reviewing the legislative history, the dissent illustrated that the statute was rooted in the presumption that mothers of non-marital children took responsibility for them, while their fathers did not. The gendered requirements of section 1409(a)(4) expressed this stereotype by authorizing fathers to transmit citizenship only if they clearly assumed responsibility for their non-marital children.

Nguyen caused great consternation among civil rights advocates and feminist scholars. Only five years earlier, the Court had decided *United States v. Virginia*, a high point in the Court's equal protection jurisprudence that elucidated how exacting heightened scrutiny for gender-based claims should be, requiring the government to provide an "exceedingly persuasive justification."[12] Yet in *Nguyen*, the Court declared that it was applying heightened scrutiny but fell far short of *Virginia*'s requirements and endorsed the age-old stereotype that mothers care for and are responsible for non-marital children.

Nguyen also can be seen as an outlier, a decision driven by the Court's hesitance to interfere in the arena of immigration and citizenship. However, a few courts have cited to *Nguyen* in troubling ways outside the nationality arena, and its full legacy is still unfolding.[13]

---

[12] 518 U.S. at 531.

[13] *See, e.g., Bolden v. Doe* (In re J.S.), No. 20120751, 2014 WL 5573353 (Utah Nov. 4, 2014) (upholding state adoption law requiring the consent only of the biological mother, unless the unmarried biological father met numerous requirements); *Grimes v. Van Hook-Williams*, 839 N.W.2d 237, 241 (Mich. Ct. App. 2013) (upholding state law requiring that in order to later assert paternity, a father must "not know or have reason to know that the mother was married at the time of conception").

THE FEMINIST JUDGMENT

In the feminist judgment, Professor Ilene Durst, writing as Justice Durst, takes an approach similar to Justice O'Connor's dissent, but relies on intersectionality analysis to examine the gender, racial, and illegitimacy biases that infect section 1409(a)(4). Durst convincingly applies heightened scrutiny to the two rationales proffered by the government – the interest in ensuring that a child has a sufficiently recognized relationship to the U.S. citizen parent and the risk of a child becoming stateless (having no recognized citizenship) – and shows that neither is "exceedingly persuasive." Notably, her analysis underlines the government's failure to raise proof of biological parenthood as a governmental interest, despite the majority's reliance on it, and its apparent dismissal of the statelessness justification.

The feminist judgment traces the ways in which discrimination against women, non-marital children, and people of color shaped the nationality law, drawing on the work of scholar Kristin Collins.[14] By limiting the ability of fathers to transmit citizenship to non-marital children born abroad, the government furthered a policy that relieved fathers of responsibility for non-marital children and stigmatized illegitimacy. Because inter-racial marriage was banned in many states, the centrality of marriage for transmission of U.S. citizenship also operated to deny citizenship to bi- or multi-racial children, thereby effectuating racial exclusion.

Durst argues that comprehensive changes to family law that impose parental rights and responsibilities for non-marital children without regard to the sex or race of the parent reveal the lack of governmental justification for the gender distinction in section 1409(a). These legal reforms also reflect the significant shift in the roles of fathers. In 2013, there were an estimated two million single fathers in the United States, and 17 percent of custodial single parents were men.[15] The feminist judgment acknowledges this reality and the injustice of denying a father equal standing to transmit citizenship to a child he has raised.

Under the feminist judgment, a number of sex-based classifications in nationality law would be struck down. For example, in 2011, the Court considered section 1401's longer residency requirement for acquiring citizenship through the father in *Flores-Villar v. United States*.[16] Flores-Villar's father faced

---

[14] Kristin A. Collins, *Illegitimate Borders: Jus Sanguinis Citizenship and the Legal Construction of Family, Race, and Nation*, 123 Yale L.J. 2134, 2204–206 (2014).

[15] National Responsible Fatherhood Clearinghouse, *Dad Stats*, www.fatherhood.gov/library/dad-stats (last visited July 28, 2015).

[16] *United States v. Flores-Villar*, 536 F.3d 990 (9th Cir. 2008), *aff'd*, 131 S. Ct. 2312 (2011) (mem.).

an absolute bar to transmitting citizenship, because he was sixteen when his son was born; thus, he did not have residency in the U.S. for at least five years after the age of fourteen.[17] The sex-based hurdle could not "be satisfied by the father on the day of birth, or the next day, or for the next 18 years."[18] The Court ultimately split 4–4, due to Justice Kagan's recusal, leaving the statute undisturbed. As similar cases wind their way through federal review,[19] the Court may have an opportunity to revisit *Nguyen* and apply heightened scrutiny as the decision in *United States v. Virginia*, and the feminist judgment, demand.

Nguyen v. INS, 533 U.S. 53 (2001)

Justice Ilene Durst delivered the opinion of the Court.

This appeal concerns the right of a United States citizen father, Petitioner Joseph Boulais, to confer citizenship on his biological child, Petitioner Tuan Anh Nguyen, whom Boulais has raised since birth. Petitioners assert that Nguyen derived United States citizenship at birth from his biological father, who is also a United States citizen by birth. The courts below rejected this claim because Nguyen's father was not married to Nguyen's biological mother when Nguyen was born, and no court entered a formal adjudication of paternity prior to Nguyen's 18th birthday, which section 1409(a)(4) of the Immigration and Nationality Act requires when the citizen parent is an unwed father, but not when the citizen parent is an unwed mother.

Petitioners challenge this statute on the basis that it impermissibly awards derivative United States citizenship differently to foreign-born children, based on the citizen parent's sex, imposing a much higher burden on unmarried citizen fathers and their children than on unmarried citizen mothers and their children. We find that the statutory scheme impermissibly discriminates against unmarried citizen fathers and their children because, rather than serving an important governmental purpose, the statute is rooted in, and perpetuates, outmoded stereotypes of sex.[20] Accordingly, section 1409(a) violates the equal protection guarantees of the Constitution.

---

[17] *Id.* Congress later reduced the residency requirement, but it remains longer for fathers than for mothers.

[18] *Nguyen*, 533 U.S. at 71.

[19] *Morales-Santana v. Lynch*, 804 F.3d 520, 528 (2d Cir. 2015) (striking down the longer residency requirement for fathers as violating the equal protection guarantee); *Villegas-Sarabia v. Johnson*, No. 15-CV-122, 2015 WL 4887462, at *1 (W.D. Tex. Aug. 17, 2015) (same).

[20] Had the issue been raised below, we would also discuss the racial discrimination inherent in the statute's historical disparate treatment of offspring of unmarried citizen mothers and of unmarried citizen fathers.

I

Petitioner Joseph Boulais, a United States citizen since birth, was employed in Vietnam when he began a relationship with his son's biological mother. Shortly after his son's birth on September 11, 1969, the couple's relationship ended. Petitioner Nguyen remained with his father, who subsequently married another Vietnamese national. When Saigon fell in 1975, six-year-old Nguyen escaped with his father's wife's family. Within a few months, he entered the United States as a refugee and reunited with his father.

Nguyen has resided here since as a lawful permanent resident, enjoying a bona fide parent-child relationship with his father.[21] Although his father fulfilled all the parental obligations imposed by society and law, paternity was not formally adjudicated until Nguyen was 28 years old. Nguyen presently is in removal proceedings. Boulais and Nguyen assert that Nguyen is a United States citizen since birth and, therefore, not subject to removal.

II

Section 1409(a) of the Immigration and Nationality Act provides that an unmarried citizen father may confer citizenship upon his non-marital foreign-born child as of the date of the child's birth if:

(1) a blood relationship between the person and the father is established by clear and convincing evidence,

(2) the father had the nationality of the United States at the time of the person's birth,

(3) the father (unless deceased) has agreed in writing to provide financial support for the person until the person reaches the age of 18 years, and

(4) while the person is under the age of 18 years,

    (A) the person is legitimated under the law of the person's residence or domicile,

    (B) the father acknowledges paternity of the person in writing under oath, or

    (C) the paternity of the person is established by adjudication of a competent court.

8 U.S.C. § 1409(a).

---

[21] The whereabouts of Nguyen's biological mother are unknown. After the fall of Saigon, Boulais lost contact with her. They never communicated again, and Boulais does not even know if she survived the war.

In contrast, the citizen mother confers citizenship on her foreign-born biological child at the child's birth. Section 1409(c). Unlike the citizen father, the mother need not agree in writing to provide financial support to her child, nor secure a legal adjudication of maternity beyond what an official birth certificate would ordinarily establish. *Id.*

Accordingly, although Boulais and Nguyen enjoy a biological and bona fide parent-child relationship, the courts below have refused to recognize Nguyen's citizenship status because Boulais did not obtain the appropriate adjudication of paternity prior to Nguyen's 18th birthday, as required by section 1409(a)(4).

III

Our jurisprudence over the past 30 years has subjected sex and gender classifications to heightened scrutiny. Accordingly, a sex or gender classification will survive an equal protection challenge if and only if the government establishes an "exceedingly persuasive justification" for its discriminatory classification. *United States v. Virginia*, 518 U.S. 515, 531 (1996). Since 1971, when this Court decided *Reed v. Reed*, 404 U.S. 71 (1971), sex-based classifications have been struck down when they do not meet legitimate government interests. In *Virginia*, this Court found that any "official action that closes a door or denies opportunity to women or to men" minimally must serve "'important governmental objectives' and 'the discriminatory means employed' [must be] 'substantially related to the achievement of those objectives.'" *Virginia*, 518 U.S. at 533 (quoting *Wengler v. Druggist Mut. Ins. Co.*, 446 U.S. 142, 150 (1980)). The state's demanding burden requires that the exceedingly persuasive justification "be genuine, not hypothesized or invented post hoc in response to litigation." *Virginia*, 518 U.S. at 533.

In fact, this Court has recognized that *any* classification based on sex and gender stereotypes likely cannot survive heightened scrutiny. *See, e.g., Miller v. Albright*, 523 U.S. 420, 452 (1998) (O'Connor, J., concurring in judgment); *id.* at 460 (Ginsburg, J., dissenting); *id.* at 472 (Breyer, J., dissenting). This holds true even when the statutory classification appears to favor women over men. *E.g., Miss. Univ. for Women v. Hogan*, 458 U.S. 718, 723–25 (1982). And it remains true regardless of whether the stereotype has some foundation in fact, for "overbroad generalizations about the different talents, capacities or preferences of males and females" will not sustain the burden, even if that generalization has some empirical support. *Virginia*, 518 U.S. at 533. Accordingly, the essential question this Court must answer is whether the sex-based distinction at issue can be replaced by "more accurate and impartial functional" categories. *Miller*, 523 U.S. at 460 (Ginsburg, J., dissenting).

IV

The government contends that imposing more onerous requirements upon the citizen father of a non-marital child than upon the citizen mother is justified. As a prelude to the justifications, the government notes that "Congress's distinction between children born out of wedlock and children born in a marriage – which Petitioners do not challenge – reflects a legislative judgment that children who have no formal relationship with their United States citizen father are less likely to be raised as Americans." Resp't's Br. at 20. The government then proceeds to justify the sex-based distinction on two grounds. For one, the government proposes that "children born abroad out of wedlock to the United States citizen mother and a non-citizen father, unlike children born abroad to a United States citizen father and non-citizen mother, would often be stateless if United States citizenship were not granted liberally." Resp't's Br. at 22–3. Accordingly, the discriminatory classification purports to prevent such children from being stateless. Id. at 25.

Perhaps more importantly, the government also justifies the discriminatory classification as necessary because "an unwed father *typically* will have no legally recognized parental rights or responsibilities toward his child, and will not be similarly situated to an unwed mother or married father, unless he takes steps to formalize the relationship." Id. at 23 (emphasis added). Accordingly, the government has an important interest in "ensuring that children who are born abroad out of wedlock have, during their minority, attained a sufficiently recognized or formal relationship to their United States citizen parent – and thus to the United States – to justify the conferral of citizenship upon them." Id. at 25.

This alleged justification can be broken down into two distinct components: first, ensuring that the relationship between the unmarried citizen father and the non-marital child is a true biological relationship, and second, ensuring that the ties between the United States and the child are established. The requirements of section 1409(a)(4), while potentially concerned with ensuring that a biological parent-child relationship exists, however, must be more concerned with the second issue, ensuring that a relationship exists with the citizen father and with the United States. The first issue is addressed by section 1409(a)(1), not challenged here, which requires that the biological relationship between parent and child be established by clear and convincing evidence. In current times, section 1409(a)(1) can readily be satisfied by DNA testing, providing clear and convincing proof of paternity that is analogously reliable to proof of maternity established through a birth certificate. Therefore, Congress must have intended another or an additional purpose for the 1409(a)(4) requirement of a formal acknowledgement or judicial declaration of paternity, or legitimation.

More likely and consistent with history and concepts of citizenship, Congress wished to ensure that the non-marital child would be able to develop a relationship with the citizen parent, and by extension, the United States, so as not to devalue the dignity of United States citizenship. No one disputes the significance of the conferral of citizenship, nor that such citizenship should bear some relationship to the child's actual familial ties and allegiances to the United States. Nor does anyone dispute the importance to any child, regardless of his or her citizenship, of the opportunity to enjoy a meaningful relationship with both his mother and father, regardless of the quality of the parents' relationship with each other. Therefore, the additional steps required for unwed fathers must reflect the congressional judgment that unwed fathers are situated differently from unwed mothers, specifically in that they will be less likely to develop the necessary ties with their non-marital child in the absence of legitimation, acknowledgment of paternity under oath, or a judicial adjudication of paternity (which presumably does not require the citizen-father's consent or even his knowledge).

V

Unwed mothers may be more devoted than unwed fathers to their biological children. Perhaps one could even discover evidence that mothers are more likely to promote closer ties between their children and the country of citizenship, or that they are more likely to teach their children to appreciate their United States citizenship. Yet, this gender distinction is hardly "an exceedingly persuasive justification" given Congress's professed objective to establish a viable opportunity for such a relationship, or even in connection with the goal of avoiding statelessness. The statute's history, up to and including its current incarnation, clearly privileges unwed citizen mothers over unwed citizen fathers, and once the biological relationship is established, the statute does nothing to ensure that the non-marital child has an actual relationship with either parent or with the United States.

Ironically, the statutory distinction is a relic of the common law and coverture, and the current statute directly descends from those sex- and gender-discriminatory tropes that only recognized the husband's (or father's) citizenship and other legal identities. By virtue of those tenets, an adult woman, once married, lost her right to hold property in her own name, to execute a contract on her own behalf, or to otherwise engage in legal or commercial transactions without the consent of her husband. *See Miller v. Albright*, 523 U.S. at 460–68 (Ginsburg, J., dissenting) (discussing the history of women's and children's citizenship rights from 1790 to the present). By virtue of those same principles, citizenship, like legal and commercial transactions, was conferred based upon this concept of the male as the party with the determinative legal identity. In practice and later by statute, the United States citizen female who married a non-citizen male took the husband's citizenship and relinquished her own.[22] Children born abroad to a married citizen mother and a non-citizen father generally received the father's citizenship. Again, it bears repeating that until the late 1930s, the citizenships of the married wife and the marital children were acquired through the father, the legal identity of the family. As Justice Ginsburg aptly noted, "[P]ages of history place [section 1409] in real-world perspective … During most of our Nation's past, laws on the transmission of citizenship from parent to child discriminated adversely against citizen mothers, not citizen fathers." *Miller*, 523 U.S. at 460–61.

Today's statute continues these tradition-based distinctions, stereotyping the obligations and privileges of men's and women's roles vis-à-vis a child born to an unmarried couple. The corollary to the recognition of the husband as the salient legal identity was the law's refusal to impose any responsibility upon the unwed father for his non-marital offspring. In the absence of marriage (or the modern advanced scientific methods for establishing paternity) the child's legal status depended solely on the man's willingness to recognize the child.[23] Without marriage or the father's recognition, the unwed mother bore sole legal and financial responsibility for their child; society and the law effectively pilloried her for enjoying (or submitting to) sex outside of marriage. Thus, the men were allowed to evade any responsibility for their offspring, presumably because only the woman had the power to avoid or control procreation outside of marriage.

Furthermore, as a practical matter, until the 1960s, unmarried white citizen males were much more likely to travel abroad and/or reside abroad for lengthy periods of time, making it more likely that any children born abroad to an unmarried U.S. citizen would be born to non-citizen mothers.

---

[22] *See, e.g.,* Act of March 2, 1907, § 3, 34 Stat. 1228. The U.S. Supreme Court upheld that statute in *MacKenzie v. Hare*, 239 U.S. 299 (1915). Thus, my grandmother, Lotte Hausner, born in Manhattan in 1891, "lost" her U.S. citizenship when she married my grandfather, a citizen of what was then the Austro-Hungarian Empire, in 1917. She learned that she had lost her citizenship when she chose to appear as a witness at the naturalization interview of her husband's childhood best friend and his wife, both of whom had survived the Holocaust.

[23] *See* Mary L. Shanley, *Unwed Fathers' Rights, Adoption and Sex Equality: Gender-Neutrality and Perpetuation of the Patriarchy,* 95 *Colum. L. Rev.* 60–103 (1995).

Before the current days of easily accessible travel, wealthy elites may have traveled for leisure, but others only traveled or resided abroad as diplomats, businessmen, or members of the military. Given that those groups were largely, if not solely, male, it was much more likely statistically that a male citizen, rather than a female citizen, would become a parent to a child born abroad.

Therefore, throughout United States history, a citizen father who sired a non-marital child abroad had no more obligation to confer citizenship on the child than he did to provide financial support to the child. *See* Nationality Act of 1940. The principles that evolved from the common law further served the nativist interests of United States immigration policy by ensuring that many interracial or non-white children could not claim the benefits of U.S citizenship.[24] When citizen males fathered children abroad, the only means of legitimation generally available was marriage to the non-citizen mother. Yet, well into the 1950s, Asians and other ethnic groups were "ineligible to citizenship" and, accordingly, the citizen male could not confer citizenship upon his child's mother, even if he chose to marry her. *See, e.g.,* Chinese Exclusion Act, ch. 126, § 14, 22 Stat. 58 (1882); *see* Act of May 5, 1892, ch. 60, 27 Stat. 25; Act of Mar. 3, 1875.

Moreover, until the 1960s, interracial marriage was not only socially taboo but illegal in many of the states. Therefore, a marriage between a U.S. citizen and a non-citizen of color, even if lawful abroad, might not have been recognized in the United States.

History shows that initial restrictions on citizens conferring citizenship upon spouses or children were fed by fear of "mass reproduction" of non-whites and certainty of the "moral inferiority" of non-white races. *See, e.g., Guyer v. Smith*, 22 Md. 239 (1864); *Ng Suey Hi v. Weedil*, 21 F.2d 801 (9th Cir. 1927); *Mason ex. rel. Chin Suey v. Tillinghast*, 26 F.2d 588 (1st Cir. 1928); *Louie Wah Yu v. Nagle*, 27 F.2d 573 (9th Cir. 1928). Indeed, the "presumption of legitimacy" that attached to children born of married and common law couples did not apply when the offspring were interracial. Similarly, the dominant white Anglo society perceived women of color as sexually promiscuous, while white women were presumed to be chaste. Therefore, the citizenship restrictions relied on racial stereotypes, as well as sex stereotypes, invoking the concept of

---

[24] Historians have traced maternal descent of citizenship in the U.S. to the slavery system. Children born to female slaves were ipso facto slaves: because the mothers were constitutionally ineligible to citizenship, so, too, were their offspring, regardless of who fathered the children. Similarly, when states enacted laws to determine a resident's race, the maternal line dictated the result.

intersectionality that complicates as well as exacerbates the unequal treatment enshrined in section 1409(a)(4) and its predecessors.[25]

Indeed, the privileging of citizen males abroad, and the discouragement of their marriage to non-Western European women, was further reinforced by military policy. Up through and including recent wars in Vietnam and Indonesia, all military personnel had to request permission to marry a non-citizen spouse. During World War II, male service personnel who sought to marry women of Western European citizenship were freely granted permission, and the U.S. eased the way of the wives' immigration through programs such as the War Brides effort. In contrast, male service personnel who were stationed in ethnically Asian countries, including Japan and the Philippines, were strongly discouraged from marrying women native to those countries. In further perpetuation of the gender distinction, women military personnel stationed abroad were outright prohibited from marrying non-citizens. Accordingly, a child born abroad to an unmarried U.S. citizen father could not derive U.S. citizenship unless the father chose to "claim" the child – action that was discouraged by the U.S. government.

Congress recognized this entrenched racial, ethnic, and gender discrimination and took some steps to rectify it in 1982, when it enacted legislation granting special immigration benefits to children born after 1950 and before October 1982 to unmarried citizen fathers in Korea, Vietnam, Laos, Cambodia, or Thailand. 8 U.S.C. § 1154(f). The immigration benefits required, in part, the citizen father's guarantee of legal custody and financial support, much as is required by the "bona fide" child-parent relationship defined in the current Immigration and Nationality Act. *See* 8 U.S.C. § 1101(b)(1)(D).

                                        VI

The government's argument that the current provisions of section 1409(a) do not discriminate among United States citizens on the basis of sex ignores the sex stereotyping inherent in the historical treatment of unwed parents. The government's argument further fails to acknowledge that United States domestic law has rejected virtually every distinction between the unmarried mother and the unmarried father in terms of their rights and responsibilities to their child. Both parents, regardless of their marital status, bear equal duties to financially support and care for their child. Both have an equal constitutional

---

[25] For a discussion of the role of intersectionality, see Kimberlé Crenshaw, *Demarginalizing the Intersection of Race and Sex: A Black Feminist Critique of Antidiscrimination Doctrine, Feminist Theory and Antiracist Politics*, 1989 *U. Chi. Legal F.* 139 (1989).

right to the care, custody and companionship of their child. Both parents' financial assets are taken into account when the government determines a child's eligibility for needs-based and other government benefits.

In fact, even the U.S. Congress has recognized the unconstitutionality of such a distinction when according preferences for immigration to family members of United States citizens and lawful permanent residents. In 1977, in *Fiallo v Bell*, 430 U.S. 787, this Court rejected a challenge to the then existing statutory definition of "child" for purposes of immigrating to the United States. That definition completely excluded "out of wedlock" children born to unwed fathers who did not legitimate the child under the law of the child's nationality or citizenship.[26] Accordingly, regardless of the strength of the child-father relationship, neither was permitted to confer citizenship or permanent residence on the other in the absence of legitimation, while the biological mother could freely confer such immigration benefits. This Court upheld the sex-based distinction, holding that Congress could treat the parents differently because of the possibility of fraud in claiming a father-child relationship.

In response to *Fiallo*, in 1986, Congress amended the "child" definition to include a child born out of wedlock who enjoys a "bona fide relationship" with the biological father. 8 U.S.C. § 1101(b)(1)(D). Congress recognized that this relationship could have all the attributes of "legal" parenthood, just as it had long recognized the parental relationship between a child and her unwed mother. Moreover, once receiving lawful permanent residence on the basis of this bona fide parent-child relationship, the lawful permanent resident has begun a journey towards U.S. citizenship. If a bona fide relationship, and evidence of biological parentage, is sufficient for lawful permanent residence, such a relationship should support conferral of derivative citizenship, given the explicit connection between lawful permanent residence and naturalization.

In *Miller v. Albright*, a majority of this Court recognized that the sex-based classification of section 1409 is unconstitutional. 523 U.S. at 460–89 (Ginsburg, J., dissenting, joined by Souter, J. and Breyer, J.).[27] Although the Court left the

---

[26] The Immigration and Nationality Act's definition of "child" when the biological parents are unmarried resulted in some tortured reasoning and anomalous decisions. *See, e.g.,* Matter of Mourillon, 18 I. & N. Dec. 122 (BIA 1981) (holding that a naturalized U.S. citizen born abroad out of wedlock was not his biological father's child but was the child of his stepmother, the woman the biological father married when the child was 13).

[27] *Miller's* standing concerns are not at issue here. In *Miller*, the citizen father did not pursue the appeal to the U.S. Supreme Court after he was dismissed at the District Court level; only the non-marital daughter, born in the Philippines, petitioned for and was granted certiorari. 523 U.S. 420. Justice O'Connor's concurring opinion reasoned that the daughter could not raise the equal protection claims of her citizen father. *Id.* at 445–52. Here, both Nguyen and his citizen father are parties to the appeal.

sex-based distinction undisturbed, a majority could not be found for any of
the rationales upholding the statute. Justices O'Connor and Kennedy concurred in the judgment, based upon standing, 523 U.S. at 445–52, but expressly
noted that they disagreed with Justice Stevens' opinion that the provision with-
stood heightened scrutiny. *Id.* at 451. Justices Scalia and Thomas also concurred in the judgment, 523 U.S. at 452–59, paying scant attention to the equal
protection claims because the Court "ha[d] no power to provide the relief
requested: conferral of citizenship on a basis other than that prescribed by
Congress." *Id.* at 453.[28] Only two of nine justices opined that the section 1409
distinction between unwed citizen mothers and unwed citizen fathers did not
violate equal protection guarantees. 523 U.S. at 423–45 (opinion by Stevens,
J. and Rehnquist, J.).

Then and now, the distinction between the requirements that unwed citizen mothers and unwed citizen fathers must meet to establish citizenship
for their children is based upon impermissible stereotypes, rather than the
more accurate and impartial categories demanded by heightened scrutiny.
The statute as written embodies the unconstitutional presumption that the
mother, because of biology, will form ties with the child and ensure that the
child forms ties with the United States. In contrast, the presumption is that the
unwed citizen father, in the absence of a legal adjudication of paternity, will
prefer to abandon or disassociate himself from the child born abroad.

Nguyen's case presents facts even stronger than those in *Miller*, where
the foreign-born non-marital child had no connection or relationship with
her citizen father until she was 22 years old, when she sought to immi-
grate from the Philippines to the United States under her father's sponsor-
ship. 523 U.S. at 423. Here, citizen Boulais has supported and cared for his
son Nguyen since his birth in Vietnam in 1969. Boulais did not obtain an
order of filiation or other legal recognition of their relationship until 1998,
and only when Nguyen was required to establish his citizenship to avoid
removal. Boulais simply had no need for such an order prior to this time: he
knew he had a son, with whom he had a bona fide relationship, and he did
not foresee any threat of disruption to that relationship. In fact, if Boulais
had to establish that Nguyen was his "child" under the current immigration scheme, his conduct would satisfy that definition regardless of a lack of
legitimation or other legal proceeding.

[28] We note that the dissenters' argument that this Court does not have the authority to confer
citizenship outside of the statute is misplaced. By this opinion, this Court confers citizenship
according to a proper constitutional interpretation of the statute, not outside of the statute's
dictates.

VII

Not only does the law discriminate against Boulais on the basis of his sex, but it automatically shrouds him in stigma. For over 40 years now, this Court has rejected distinctions not only based upon gender but also upon marital status. As far back as 1968, this Court has held that legislative distinctions between non-marital and marital children violate equal protection doctrine. *See, e.g., Levy v. Louisiana*, 391 U.S. 68 (1968). Although Petitioners do not challenge the citizenship scheme on this basis, it bears noting that the children of unwed parents and unwed parents themselves still suffer from negative stereotyping. Even the term "out of wedlock" used by the Immigration and Nationality Act situates the child born to unmarried parents outside of the societal mainstream.[29] "The status of illegitimacy has expressed through the ages society's condemnation of irresponsible liaisons beyond the bond of marriage." *Weber v. Aetna Cas. & Sur. Co.*, 406 U.S. 164, 175 (1972). Equal protection law will not permit a state to deny non-marital children the right to inherit from their fathers. *See Trimble v. Gordon*, 430 U.S. 762, 776 (1977).[30]

As late as 1972, members of this Court felt free to impugn the character of unwed fathers and to ascribe to them the stereotypical lack of responsibility discussed above. In *Stanley v. Illinois*, 405 U.S. 645, 649 (1972), even though this Court held that the state could not presume all unwed fathers were unfit parents in the context of dependency proceedings, the majority noted that the state's presumption about unwed fathers was not unusual and that "[i]t may be, as the State insists, that most unmarried fathers are unsuitable and neglectful parents." *Id.* at 654. The dissent went even farther to claim that "[u]nwed fathers as a class are not traditionally quite so easy to identify and locate. Many of them either deny all responsibility or exhibit no interest in the child or its welfare." *Id.* at 665. Clearly displaying its distaste for Stanley, the dissent frequently invoked his failure to marry the mother of his children or to formally adopt his children when he could. Thus, the trope of the irresponsible father pervaded this opinion. Those now-disproven generalizations should not serve to deprive Nguyen of his United States citizenship.

Nor can the sex-based distinctions at issue here survive as a justification for preventing a child's statelessness. If that were truly a concern, the provisions

[29] The state of Alabama, for one, still refers to non-marital children as "bastards" in its statutes. *See, e.g.*, Alabama Code § 26-11-2 ("A father of a bastard child may seek to legitimate it").

[30] Yet, it will allow the Social Security Administration to presume that non-marital children are not dependent on their fathers, again perpetuating the gendered perspective of unwed fathers as irresponsible or not committed to the welfare of their children. *See Mathews v. Lucas*, 427 U.S. 495, 516 (1976).

would liberally grant citizenship regardless of the citizen parent's gender, rather than merely liberalize the residency requirements for citizen mothers. The greater burden placed upon citizen fathers and their non-marital offspring rests upon an outdated historical concern that other countries would not accord citizenship to a child born of an unmarried non-citizen mother, because only fathers could confer citizenship.

In conclusion, the historical legal distinctions between the obligations of biological mothers and biological fathers to their children born outside of marriage surely were bred from the widely held generalizations that women are and were significantly more likely than men to care for and nurture their biological children. Women would not abandon their offspring; men would and did, with the implicit approval of the United States. Although such sex-based generalizations may hold true in some cases today, they are not true in many more cases. In any event, they are a poor proxy for the factors that should determine citizenship: the biological and actual relationship between the U.S. citizen parent and the child, and the child's ties to the United States through the citizen parent. Boulais and his son seek only to enjoy the same constitutional protections provided to their mother-and-child counterparts. Accordingly, section 1409's distinction between unwed mothers and unwed fathers does not survive heightened scrutiny.

We *reverse*.

25

Commentary on *Lawrence v. Texas*

Kris McDaniel-Miccio

In June of 2015, the U.S. Supreme Court decided *Obergefell v. Hodges*.[1] To say that decision represents a seismic shift in law as it pertains to homosexuals and homosexuality is an understatement. In *Obergefell*, Justice Kennedy crafted a majority decision that granted to gay and lesbian couples a fundamental right to marry, and stated unequivocally that laws which prohibit marriage or recognition of out-of-state marriages violate the dignity and humanity of same sex couples and their families.[2] *Obergefell* is closely related to two other decisions authored by Justice Kennedy, *Lawrence v. Texas*[3] and *United States v. Windsor*.[4] In this trifecta of cases, Justice Kennedy authored three decisions that recognized the humanity and legal personage of homosexuals, finally granting a right to privacy (*Lawrence*), equality in allocation of federal rights (*Windsor*), and the fundamental right to marry (*Obergefell*). Without *Lawrence*, neither *Windsor* nor *Obergefell* would have turned out as they did. Justice Scalia was correct when he opined that the confluence of *Lawrence* and *Windsor* would open the door to marriage equality for the lesbian and gay community.[5]

In all three opinions written by Justice Kennedy, he focuses on the idea that constitutional protections in the Fourteenth Amendment are grounded in conceptions of dignity of the individual and of the collective. The thread that ties or links liberty and equality is the dignity and self-worth of the individual. Dignity is not merely a moral canon but a legal principle embedded in conceptions of liberty and equality. Thus, legal personage is a reflection of this canon and principle.

[1] *Obergefell v. Hodges*, 135 S. Ct. 2584 (2015).
[2] *Id.* at 2607–608.
[3] *Lawrence v. Texas*, 539 U.S. 558 (2003).
[4] *United States v. Windsor*, 133 S. Ct. 2675 (2013).
[5] *See Windsor*, 133 S. Ct. at 2709–10 (Scalia, J., dissenting).

IS SEXUAL AUTONOMY A FEMINIST SILVER BULLET?

In the re-write of the *Lawrence* opinion, Professor Ruthann Robson, writing as Justice Robson, rejects the theoretical construct deployed by Justice Kennedy. She raises an important concern; how do we define or unpack "dignity"? Simply put, she asks what is the meaning of dignity and does dignity provide the foundation for liberty and equality embedded in the Fourteenth Amendment. However, rather than interrogate the relationship between liberty and equality and conceptions of human dignity, Robson employs a different theory, that of sexual autonomy.

Sexual autonomy *qua* sexual autonomy as a philosophical concept or legal right has been seriously contested by feminist philosophers. Diane Teitjens Meyers and Marilyn Friedman examine conceptions of autonomy espoused or posited by philosophers such as John Rawls and Immanuel Kant.[6] One feminist critique of autonomy is its reliance on traditional notions of masculinity – a prototype of masculinity captured in literature by such authors as Ernest Hemingway.[7] The autonomous man is separate, distinct, self-reliant; a rational, omnipresent being "above the fray," or, as Lorraine Code remarks, "to view 'from nowhere' the truths the world reveals."[8] As Kant noted, the autonomous man separates the self from norms externally imposed. Kantian notions of autonomy require a disembodied self, freed from the vagaries of the body and the senses – disconnected from himself and from others.[9]

Because classical conceptions of autonomy are gendered, they affect women and sexual outlaws[10] in relation to gender identity and sexual expression. Autonomy, regardless of its modifier, is premised upon rationality. As the feminist relational philosophers point out, women as a class are excluded and homosexuals would be excluded as well because the very act of homosexual sodomy is not only a cultural anathema but irrational and immoral.

---

[6] See Diane Teitjens Meyers, *Personal Autonomy and the Paradox of Feminine Socialization*, 84 J. Phil. 619 (1987); Marilyn Friedman, Autonomy, Gender, Politics (2003); John Rawls, A Theory of Justice (Harvard Univ. Press rev. ed. 1999) (1971); Immanuel Kant, *An Answer to the Question: 'What Is Enlightenment?'*, *in* Kant: Political Writings 54–55 (Hans S. Reiss ed., H.B. Nisbet trans., 1970).

[7] See generally Judith Fetterley, The Resisting Reader: A Feminist Approach to American Fiction (1987).

[8] Lorraine Code, *The Perversion of Autonomy and the Subjection of Women: Discourses of Social Advocacy at Century's End*, *in* Relational Autonomy: Feminist Perspectives on Autonomy, Agency, and the Social Self 181, 185 (Catriona Mackenzie and Natalie Stoljar eds., 2000).

[9] See Kant, *supra* note 6, at 54–55. See also Code, *supra* note 8, at 183.

[10] When I reference sexual outlaws I am referring to all persons who define their sexual identity differently from the traditional male/female dyad. This includes gay men, lesbians, bisexuals, transgendered as well as polyamorous and celibate individuals.

Moreover, the gravamen of classical notions of autonomy rejects subjectivity while privileging objectivity. Friedman observes that ascendant cultural values reflect conceptions of autonomy that are at once privileged and masculine.[11] Moreover, by defining autonomy as the "freedom to make public use of one's reason,"[12] classical theorists deny the "hierarchical divisions that determine whose rational utterances merit public acknowledgement."[13] Whilst sexual autonomy is fundamental to our conceptions of liberty, it is a constitutive element or component rooted in conceptions of dignity. Autonomy, then – whether sexual, personal, political, familial, or religious – is an expression of the dignity and worth of the individual. Moreover, dignity of the individual is fundamental to conceptions of liberty; autonomy is particular *to* both dignity and liberty. Thus, liberty as a right cannot exist in the absence of dignity.

Robson correctly reminds that neither dignity nor autonomy "should … be deployed to … reassert majoritarian or sexist notions of morality," yet the rewritten opinion neither disaggregates nor contests the centrality of masculinity *vis-à-vis* autonomy. Here, it was essential to deconstruct the deeply rooted meaning of autonomy that has operated, regardless of sexual orientation or gender identity, to exclude not only women but gay men.

Many feminist philosophers have abandoned traditional notions of autonomy because objectivism, its core meaning, transforms individuals into mere abstractions, presuming mastery over the external world. Autonomy is attained through rationality and detached objectivity, impervious to the vagaries of relationships.[14]

Indeed, Rawls speaks of the veil of ignorance, coupled with the original position, to determine distribution of social goods, rights and resources. Rawls's thought experiment is an extension of Kant's ideas regarding autonomy – a *nouvelle* take on detached objectivity and the rational man. Gay men and lesbians, as well as all humans, are shaped by social relationships and interaction with race, ethnicity, sexual orientation, gender, and familial status. Because of social relationships as well as cultural iterations of the self, the very notion of detached objectivity is at once false and inauthentic. As sexual beings, gay men and women challenge long-standing notions of the autonomous self because of, not in spite of, gender and sexual conditions that

---

[11] *See* Friedman, *supra* note 6, at 45–47. *See generally* Diana Tietjens Meyers, *Intersectional Identity and the Authentic Self?: Opposites Attract!, in* Relational Autonomy, *supra* note 8, at 151.

[12] Kant, *supra* note 6, at 55.

[13] Code, *supra* note 8, at 183.

[14] *See* Friedman, *supra* note 6, at 38–50.

shape self-awareness. The litigants in *Lawrence*, by being homosexual and engaging in sodomy, contested traditional notions of sexuality in general and sexual autonomy in particular. In *Lawrence*, conduct could not be disconnected from the person because the act was defined by one's sexual identity. Thus, simply importing autonomy from existing cases *sans* analysis could not transform the gendering of autonomy.

LOCATING THE CONTOURS OF JUDICIAL RESPONSIBILITY

Perhaps the most brilliant part of Robson's feminist rewrite is its understanding and then application of conceptions of accountability. Courts make decisions that affect the lives of individuals and discrete groups of people within the community. Neither courts nor the individual justices tend to hold themselves accountable for the human toll exacted by juridical decisions. This is especially true of supreme courts and lower appellate courts whether located in state or the federal court systems. Take the *Shelby* decision handed down in June of 2013.[15] In that decision, Chief Justice Roberts opined that the coverage formula, used to address racial discrimination in voting, conflicted with the constitutional principles of federalism and "equal sovereignty of the states." Additionally, the remedy imposed by the 1965 Voting Rights Act (VRA) was "based on 40-year-old facts having no logical relationship to the present day."[16] Consequently, the Court struck down § 4(b), effectively eviscerating the VRA. The fallout from this one case produced a spate of voter laws in states formerly under the jurisdiction of the VRA that restricted access to the ballot box for minorities, the elderly and young voters. Legal decisions are not sterile or clinical applications of law; they can and do disrupt distribution of social goods and resources as well as dislocate civil and human rights. Thus, law *qua* law is relational.

Lawrence v. Texas, 539 U.S. 558 (2003)

Justice Ruthann Robson delivered the opinion of the Court.

Sexual autonomy and sexual equality are vital in a free and democratic society such as the one guaranteed by our Constitution.

At times the liberty and equality clauses in the Fourteenth Amendment can conflict. In such cases, there might be difficult balancing to do. But this is not one of those cases. Instead, both the Due Process Clause's liberty provision

---

[15] *Shelby Cnty., Ala. v. Holder*, 133 S.Ct. 2613 (2013).
[16] *Id.* at 2629.

and the Equal Protection Clause require we find unconstitutional the Texas statute criminalizing "homosexual conduct," Tex. Penal Code § 21.06(a) (2003).[17] This statute declares that a person commits an offense if he or she engages in "deviate sexual intercourse" as defined in Texas Penal Code section 21.01 (2003),[18] with "another individual of the same sex." This conclusion requires that we overrule *Bowers v. Hardwick*, 478 U.S. 186 (1986), in which we upheld a Georgia statute that criminalized certain sex acts understood to be aimed at same-sex activities.[19]

Relying in part on *Bowers v. Hardwick*, a divided Court of Appeals for the Texas Fourteenth District, sitting en banc, rejected Petitioners' federal and state constitutional claims challenging the Texas statute. *Lawrence v. State*, 41 S.W.3d 349 (Tex. App. 2001). The Petitioners, John Geddes Lawrence and Tyron Garner, two adult males, had been arrested and found guilty of violating the Texas statute. Police officers had entered the home of Lawrence, seemingly properly, and discovered him engaged in a sexual act with Garner. Both men were arrested, held in custody overnight, and were charged and convicted by a Justice of the Peace. They duly raised constitutional challenges to the Texas statute at that time. These contentions were rejected and they were fined $200 each and assessed court costs. After their appeal to the Court of Appeals was unsuccessful, they petitioned this Court for a writ of certiorari.

We granted certiorari, *Lawrence v. Texas*, 537 U.S. 1044 (2002), to consider whether the Texas statute violates the Equal Protection Clause, the Due Process Clause's liberty provision and specifically whether *Bowers v. Hardwick* should be overruled.

We will first discuss due process, then equal protection, and then the overruling of *Bowers v. Hardwick*.

[17] Section 21.06(a) of the Texas Penal Code, entitled "Homosexual Conduct" provides: "(a) A person commits an offense if he engages in deviate sexual intercourse with another individual of the same sex. (b) An offense under this section is a Class C misdemeanor."

[18] Section 21.01 defines "deviate sexual intercourse" as: "(a) any contact between any part of the genitals of one person and the mouth or anus of another person; or (b) the penetration of the genitals or the anus of another person with an object."

[19] The Georgia statute at issue in *Bowers v. Hardwick*, 478 U.S. 186 (1986), Ga. Code Ann. § 16 6 2 (1984), provided:

(a) A person commits the offense of sodomy when he performs or submits to any sexual act involving the sex organs of one person and the mouth or anus of another. A person commits the offense of aggravated sodomy when he commits sodomy with force and against the will of the other person.

(b) A person convicted of the offense of sodomy shall be punished by imprisonment for not less than one nor more than 20 years. A person convicted of the offense of aggravated sodomy shall be punished by imprisonment for life or by imprisonment for not less than one nor more than 20 years.

I

Due process

Sexual autonomy is protected as a fundamental liberty in the Due Process Clause of the Fourteenth Amendment. As such, state statutes, including Texas's statute, that infringe on sexual autonomy are subject to strict scrutiny in which the statute must be narrowly tailored to serve a compelling governmental interest. Morality, without more, is never a compelling governmental interest. This is not to say that at times morality is not co-extensive with other interests, such as preventing harm to a participant in a sexual encounter or promoting equality, but those interests must stand alone and be determined as compelling or not in the particular circumstances of the state prohibition, whether it be prohibition of adult sex activities with minors or prohibition of commercial sexual exchanges.

Moreover, criminalization is not narrowly tailored in this instance as a quick recitation of the facts reveals. While the statute is challenged on its face, we are mindful that the situation came to the attention of the police through a false weapons report and that there was seemingly the exercise of significant police and prosecutorial discretion. Br. for Pet'rs at 2. The men, James Geddes Lawrence and Tyrone Garner, one of whom is white and one of whom is black, were immediately arrested for this misdemeanor, held in custody overnight, and charged and convicted before a Justice of the Peace. The oft-claimed non-enforcement of "homosexual conduct" statutes may be empirically true, but even if rare, this highly discretionary enforcement supports rather than contravenes the lack of narrow tailoring.

A

Our conclusion that sexual autonomy is a fundamental right is uncontrovertible. Our Court long ago stated that "[n]o right is held more sacred ... than the right of every individual to the possession and control of his own person." *Union Pac. R. Co. v. Botsford*, 141 U.S. 250, 251 (1891). In one of our earliest cases construing the liberty protected by the Due Process Clause, we noted that we had "not attempted to define with exactness the liberty thus guaranteed," *Meyer v. Nebraska*, 262 U.S. 390, 399 (1923), but listed rights essentially encompassed by sexual autonomy such as "the right ... to marry, [to] establish a home ... [to] bring up children ... and generally to enjoy those privileges long recognized at common law as essential to [the] orderly pursuit of happiness by free men." *Id.* at 399. As we stated just two years later in *Pierce v. Society of the Sisters of the Holy Names of Jesus & Mary*, the "fundamental theory of liberty upon which all governments in this Union repose excludes any general power of the state to standardize its children." 268 U.S. 510, 535 (1925). While the state's standardization efforts involved in *Pierce* were directed at children, who may enjoy limited autonomy based on their developing capacity, a state's attempt to standardize adults is even more hostile to the liberty protected by the Due Process Clause. Later, we fully recognized adult autonomy in sexual contexts in *Griswold v. Connecticut*, 381 U.S. 479 (1965), and *Roe v. Wade*, 410 U.S. 113 (1973). In *Planned Parenthood of Southeastern Pennsylvania v. Casey*, we continued to recognize that "intimate and personal choices" are "choices central to personal dignity and autonomy, [and] are central to the liberty protected by the Fourteenth Amendment." 505 U.S. 833, 851 (1992).

Obviously, sexual autonomy does not confer an absolute right. We have long held that no right is absolute. *See, e.g., Saenz v. Roe*, 526 U.S. 489, 501–02 (1999) (protections of the "privileges and immunities" Clause of Article IV, section 2, "are not 'absolute,' but the Clause 'does bar discrimination against citizens of other States where there is no substantial reason for the discrimination beyond the mere fact that they are citizens of other States'"); *Emp't Div., Dep't of Human Res. of Or. v. Smith*, 494 U.S. 872, 894 (1990) ("To say that a person's right to free exercise [under the First Amendment] has been burdened, of course, does not mean that he has an absolute right to engage in the conduct."); *Roe v. Wade*, 410 U.S. 113, 154 (1973) ("We, therefore, conclude that the right of personal privacy includes the abortion decision, but that this right is not unqualified and must be considered against important state interests in regulation."); *Chaplinsky v. New Hampshire*, 315 U.S. 568, 571 (1942) ("[I]t is well understood that the right of free speech is not absolute at all times and under all circumstances."); *Near v. Minnesota ex rel. Olson*, 283 U.S. 697, 708 (1931) ("Liberty of speech and of the press is also not an absolute right, and the state may punish its abuse."); *Frisbie v. United States*, 157 U.S. 160, 165 (1895) ("While it may be conceded that, generally speaking, among the inalienable rights of the citizen is that of the liberty of contract, yet such liberty is not absolute and universal. It is within the undoubted power of government to restrain some individuals from all contracts, as well as all individuals from some contracts.").

Moreover, the fundamental right of sexual autonomy is a multi-faceted one encompassing the right to engage in "sex" broadly defined and a concomitant right to refuse to engage in "sex" broadly defined. The right of sexual autonomy has decisional and deliberative aspects as well as physical aspects. Moreover, it is important that definitions of "sex" not be limited to definitions of "sexual intercourse" or "deviant sexual intercourse," but include a range of choices, practices, and decisions.

At times we have used the spatial language of privacy to protect sexual autonomy, but this spatial aspect is synecdoche rather than constitutional principle. In *Griswold*, we mentioned "the sacred precincts of marital bedrooms," but it was clear that the right was the right to maintain a marital relation, which we called "intimate to the degree of being sacred." 381 U.S. at 485–86. Even in *Stanley v. Georgia*, where we protected the possession of obscenity within the confines of the home under the First Amendment, we stressed Justice Brandeis's dissent in *Olmstead v. United States*, 277 U.S. 438, 478 (1928), discussing the Constitution's protection of people in "their beliefs, their thoughts, their emotions and their sensations." 394 U.S. 557, 564 (1969). Thus, while the facts here that gave rise to the challenge to the Texas statute did occur in a home, our conclusion is not reliant on antiquated maxims such as "a man's home is his castle" and is not consistent with attempts to "privatize" patriarchal or domestic violence. *Compare* Catharine A. MacKinnon, *Towards A Feminist Theory of the State* 168, 190–94 (1989) (arguing that privacy theories are not sufficient to protect women from male violence) *with* Elizabeth Schneider, *The Dialectic of Rights and Politics: Perspectives from the Women's Movement*, 61 N.Y.U. L. Rev. 589, 638 (1986) (noting that privacy is often viewed as if it "reinforces and legitimizes the public and private dichotomy which historically has been damaging to women"). Indeed, state sanction of patriarchal or domestic violence, whether within the home or without, is inconsistent with the fundamental right of sexual autonomy.

We have also used the language of "dignity" to encompass a right of sexual autonomy, *Casey*, 505 U.S. at 851 (protecting the right to an abortion as one of the "choices central to personal dignity and autonomy"). Dignity is a vital concept. The Universal Declaration of Human Rights, adopted by the United Nations (UN) General Assembly in 1948, after its drafting by the UN Commission of Human Rights, chaired with great energy by Eleanor Roosevelt, used "dignity" in several of its provisions. United Nations Universal Declaration of Human Rights Preamble, arts. 1, 22, 23 (1948).

Progressive constitutions, such as the South African Constitution (1997), explicitly reference dignity along with equality and freedom. S. Afr. Const. § 10, 1996. The South African Constitutional Court, in *National Coalition for Gay and Lesbian Equality and Another v. Minister of Justice and Others* 1998 (1) SA 6 (CC) (S. Afr.), unanimously concluded that "the common-law crime of sodomy" constitutes "an infringement of the right to dignity which is enshrined in section 10 of our Constitution," noting that "the right to dignity is a cornerstone of our Constitution." *Id.* at para. 28. Likewise, the Supreme Court of Canada has declared the importance of the concept of "dignity" to its Constitution as a source of national pride, and the exclusion of sexual minorities from "dignity" as unconstitutional. *Vriend v. Alberta*, [1998] 1 S.C.R. 493 (Can.).

We therefore do not eschew dignity. However, we recognize that "dignity" does not necessarily solve debates regarding sexual autonomy. Indeed, in *S. v. Jordan* 2002 (6) SA 642 (CC) (S. Afr.), the South Africa Constitutional Court did not find unconstitutional a law criminalizing commercial sex, even as such a law criminalized the sellers and not the buyers in the sexual transaction, reasoning that the "stigma" for sellers was the result of a social attitude and not the result of the law. *Id.* at para. 16. While the concurring justices in *Jordan* would have found the sex discrimination argument more persuasive, they similarly rejected the dignity argument:

> To the extent that the dignity of prostitutes is diminished, the diminution arises from the character of prostitution itself … The dignity of prostitutes is diminished not by the [legislative provision] but by their engaging in commercial sex work. The very character of the work they undertake devalues the respect that the Constitution regards as inherent in the human body.
>
> *Id.* at para. 74 (O'Regan, J., and Sachs, J.).

Indeed, the concurring justices noted that "central to the character of prostitution is that it is indiscriminate and loveless." *Id.* at para. 83. They rejected the notion of autonomy, in part because it was not explicit in the text of their constitution. *Id.*

Thus, while there is certainly power in the term "dignity" – just as there is authority in the term "privacy" – we believe the term "sexual autonomy" or "bodily autonomy" is preferable to stress that the liberty provision of the Due Process Clause guarantees the right to make decisions about and to engage or not engage in "sex" as broadly defined.

We do note that none of these terms is explicit in the text of our centuries-old United States Constitution, as compared to the South African Constitution that is in its first decade. We also note that the Ninth Amendment to our Constitution specifically contemplates the recognition of non-textually specified rights. U.S. Const. amend. IX. Importantly, whatever term is used, it should not be deployed to simply reassert majoritarian or sexist notions of morality. Just as morality can never suffice as a compelling interest in the application of a strict scrutiny test, it cannot function as a constricting camouflage in the assertion of the constitutional guarantee.

Moreover, it would be exceedingly troubling for our courts to assess a right to autonomy based upon the sentiments we ascribed to its exercise.

Whether or not the sexual interaction between Lawrence and Garner was "indiscriminate" or "loveless," *cf. S. v. Jordan* 2002 (6) SA 642 para. 83 (CC) (O'Regan, J. and Sachs, J.) – presuming we could make such a determination as a matter or law or of fact – is irrelevant. In short: our Constitution guarantees a right to sexual autonomy, cognizable even when the choices exercised are considered to be unwise or not self-actualizing. Again, because the right of sexual autonomy includes the decisional aspects and because it encompasses the right to engage in "sex" broadly defined and a concomitant right to refuse to engage in "sex" broadly defined, any moral or sentimental judgments would only be employed to standardize persons into the state's mold of appropriate sexuality.

B

In addition to recognizing that bodily and sexual autonomy are fundamental rights protected by the liberty provision of the Due Process Clause, we reject the narrow formulation for judicial recognition of fundamental rights as articulated in *Washington v. Glucksberg*, 521 U.S. 702 (1997). We do so for three reasons.

First, *Glucksberg's* emphasis on a "careful description" of the right might properly be viewed as a threshold inquiry, but it is highly outcome determinative. 521 U.S. at 703, 721. As *Glucksberg* itself demonstrates, "dying with dignity" as compared to "aiding the commission of suicide" are less "careful" descriptions than persuasive ones. In *Glucksberg*, Justice Rehnquist rejected the en banc Ninth Circuit's and respondents' various descriptions of the interest at stake – "'determining the time and manner of one's death,'... 'a right to die,'... a 'liberty to choose how to die,'... a right to 'control of one's final days,'... 'the right to choose a humane, dignified death,'... and 'the liberty to shape death,'" – in favor of a formulation of the right as a "right to commit suicide which itself includes a right to assistance in doing so." *Glucksberg*, 521 U.S. at 722–23. Any legally crafted "careful description" manifests the very predilections that the *Glucksberg* standard was designed to cabin. Justice Blackmun recognized this when he began the dissenting opinion in *Bowers v. Hardwick* by highlighting the problem with the manner in which the Court had described the right at issue:

> This case is no more about "a fundamental right to engage in homosexual sodomy," as the Court purports to declare ... than *Stanley v. Georgia*, 394 U.S. 557 (1969), was about a fundamental right to watch obscene movies, or *Katz v. United States*, 389 U.S. 347 (1967), was about a fundamental right to place interstate bets from a telephone booth.

Bowers v. Hardwick, 478 U.S. 186, 199 (Blackmun, J., dissenting). Thus, while the *Glucksberg* inquiry is intended to forestall the Court's enactment of its own policy preferences into constitutional mandates, the framing of the issue through a "careful" description of the right does exactly that.

Second, *Glucksberg's* "deeply rooted in this nation's history and traditions" inquiry is deeply flawed. *Glucksberg,* 521 U.S. at 721. Even if Chief Justice Burger, concurring in *Bowers v. Hardwick,* had been correct that "homosexual conduct" had been "subject to state intervention throughout the history of Western civilization" – which we do not believe is accurate – it is immaterial. 478 U.S. at 196. As Justice Frankfurter wrote in 1952, to "believe that this judicial exercise of judgment could be avoided by freezing 'due process of law' at some fixed stage of time or thought is to suggest that the most important aspect of constitutional adjudication is a function for inanimate machines." *Rochin v. California,* 342 U.S. 165, 171 (1952). But whether adjudicated by inanimate machines or all-too-human judges, "freezing" due process rights at some point in our early nationhood will continue to "freeze-out" the people and the interests not cognizable more than two centuries ago. It would allow a state to prohibit married women from owning property or practicing law. It would allow a state to refuse to recognize as criminals married men who physically "chastised" their wives or who raped them. It would be constitutional for a state to prohibit divorce, or limit it to circumstances in which there was adultery by the woman but not the man. And it is not only misogyny and patriarchy that have shaped this nation's history and traditions. Slavery of African-Americans, genocide of Native Americans, Asian exclusion, and indentured servitude are all deeply lamentable features of our early nationhood. Our Constitution and our Fourteenth Amendment were intended to guarantee better futures; we violate their spirit if we shackle them not only to their own time, but to their pasts.

Third and last, the use of *Glucksberg* as a bulwark against *Lochner v. New York,* 198 U.S. 45 (1905), is unnecessary. *Lochner,* which many have criticized and rightly so, is simply inapposite to issues involving sexual or bodily autonomy. In that case, the Court held unconstitutional a state law providing that no employee "shall be required or permitted to work in a biscuit, bread, or cake bakery or confectionery establishment more than sixty hours in any one week." *Lochner,* 198 U.S. at 46 n.†. For the Court, the state law was unreasonable: "the freedom of master and employee to contract with each other in relation to their employment, and in defining the same, cannot be prohibited or interfered with, without violating the Federal Constitution." *Lochner,* 198 U.S. at 64. This "freedom" was in reality a harsh social Darwinism and extreme laissez faire. As Justice Holmes, dissenting, noted, the Court was essentially adopting "Mr. Herbert Spencer's Social Statics." 198 U.S. at 75 (Holmes, J., dissenting). *Lochner* is in disrepute because the liberty it championed was economic and it distorted equality through the guise of liberty for some.

Thus, we reject *Washington v. Glucksberg* as a lodestar for the determination of fundamental rights.

C

We hold that the Texas statute criminalizing "homosexual conduct," Tex. Penal Code Ann. § 21.06(a) (2003), violates the fundamental right of sexual autonomy as grounded in the liberty provision of the Due Process Clause of the Fourteenth Amendment. The Texas statute is clearly unconstitutional. Nevertheless, despite our conclusion that the Texas criminal statute violates the Due Process Clause, the equal protection aspects of the Texas statute deserve our attention.

II

Equal protection

The Texas statute limits its criminalization of the sexual activities in question to those that occur between individuals of the "same sex" and is entitled "Homosexual Conduct." These sexual activities are fundamental rights, as we hold above, and thus cannot be denied on the basis of a classification, unless the classification is narrowly tailored to serve a compelling governmental interest.

A "homosexual conduct" criminal statute cannot satisfy the equal protection concerns we articulated in *Eisenstadt v. Baird,* 405 U.S. 438 (1972), involving a classification between the unmarried and the married, or in *Skinner v. Oklahoma ex rel. Williamson,* 316 U.S. 535 (1942), involving a classification between larceny and embezzlement. This is because the right to sexual autonomy, like the right to contraception involved in *Eisenstadt* and the right to procreation (or at least, not to be sterilized) in *Skinner,* are fundamental rights. They cannot be apportioned through a criminal statute based on classifications that are not narrowly tailored to serve a compelling governmental interest.

There is no compelling interest here, including any attempt to channel people into heterosexuality. Sexual adults, as much if not more so than children, are "not mere creature[s] of the [S]tate" who can constitutionally be "standardize[d]" into some version of humanity that the state prefers. *See*

Pierce v. Soc'y of Sisters, 268 U.S. at 535. Indeed, the true interests here are not only not compelling, they are not even legitimate. Like the interest in *Loving v. Virginia*, 388 U.S. 1, 11 (1967), where we held that Virginia's true interest was to "maintain White Supremacy," the true interest here is to maintain heterosexual hegemony.

Even absent a conclusion that sexual autonomy is a fundamental right, the Texas statute's classifications are not constitutional. The statute makes both a sex classification and a sexual-orientation classification, neither of which can be sustained.

A

The Texas statute defines the conduct as criminal only if an individual "engages in deviate sexual intercourse with another individual of the same sex." Tex. Penal Code Ann. § 21.06(a) (West 2003). While this is not the usual favoring of men over women, *compare United States v. Virginia*, 518 U.S. 515 (1996) (excluding women from the Virginia Military Institute) *with Craig v. Boren*, 429 U.S. 190 (1976) (allowing women aged 18–21, but not men aged 18–21, to purchase 3.2 beer), it nevertheless relies upon sex-based classifications to define the prohibited conduct. The statute is not sex neutral any more than the statute in *Loving v. Virginia* was race neutral. 388 U.S. at 8 ("[W]e reject the notion that the mere 'equal application' of a statute containing racial classifications is enough to remove the classifications from the Fourteenth Amendment's proscription of all invidious racial discriminations."). Additionally, by making the criminality of the sexual conduct dependent upon the sex of one's partner, the statute tells women that only men, and not other women, are appropriate as sexual companions. It enforces by criminal sanction the antiquated view that women who are not married to men are to be considered unfortunate "exceptions to the general rule" that the "paramount destiny and mission of woman" is "to fulfill the noble and benign offices of wife and mother" in accordance with the "law of the Creator." *Bradwell v. Illinois*, 83 U.S. 130, 141–42 (1873) (Bradley, J., concurring).

As the statute makes a sex-based classification, it should be evaluated under the same equal protection standard. As we stated in *United States v. Virginia*, the state has the demanding burden of proffering an "exceedingly persuasive" justification that is genuine, not hypothesized, and not invented post hoc in response to litigation. *See United States v. Virginia*, 518 U.S. at 532–33. The state must show at least that there are "important governmental objectives" and that the "discriminatory means employed" are "substantially related to the achievement of those objectives." *Id.* at 533. The state puts forward two interests: to insulate the statute from a challenge by heterosexual couples and to preserve morality. Br. for Resp'ts at 41–48. These interests do not rise to the level of "at least important" and "exceedingly persuasive," *see United States v. Virginia*, 518 U.S. at 532–33, and we are not convinced that the former interest is genuine and not post hoc. Even if these interests sufficed – which they do not – the "discriminatory means employed" are fatal. In *McLaughlin v. Florida*, 379 U.S. 184, 184 (1964), we held unconstitutional as violative of equal protection a statute criminalizing interracial cohabitation. We did not reject the state's proffered interest in preventing promiscuity, but concluded that there was nothing in the interest that made it "essential to punish promiscuity" of one group and not that of another, and that "legislative discretion to employ the piecemeal approach stops short of permitting a State to narrow statutory coverage to focus on a racial group." *Id.* at 193–94. Similarly, while the standard by which we scrutinize sex classifications is more lenient than the standard by which we scrutinize racial classifications, in the Texas statute there is nothing that makes it essential – or even apparent – that same-sex pairs and not different-sex pairs should be punished for the same "sexual deviant" acts. It is only Texas's "morality" interest in preventing same-sex couplings – as was Florida's interest in preventing different-race couplings – that explains the discriminatory classifications. Texas's interest in insulating the statute from challenge by carving out classifications based on sex is just as fatal here as would have been any argument by Florida that it assumed same-race couples would be more successful in challenging an anti-promiscuity statute. The Texas statute prohibiting same-sex activities fails to satisfy the equal protection standard for sex classifications.

B

The Texas statute is entitled "Homosexual Conduct" and through its criminalization of same-sex but not different-sex "sexual deviant intercourse" between adults, it makes a sexual-orientation classification. We hold that sexual-orientation classifications, like classifications based on sex, must be subject to the standard articulated in *United States v. Virginia*. The state has the demanding burden of proffering an "exceedingly persuasive" justification that is genuine, not hypothesized, and not invented post hoc in response to litigation. *See United States v. Virginia*, 518 U.S. at 532–33. The state must show at least that there are "important governmental objectives" and that the "discriminatory means employed" are "substantially related to the achievement of those objectives." *See id.* at 533. The state cannot satisfy that standard here.

However, we note that even under more lenient standards, the "homosexual conduct" statute violates equal protection. In *Romer v. Evans*, 517 U.S. 620 (1996), we invalidated a state constitutional amendment that forbids anti-discrimination laws, policies, or ordinances based on "homosexual, lesbian, or bisexual orientation." We held that the provision was "inexplicable by anything but animus toward the class it affects; it lacks a rational relationship to legitimate state interests." *Romer*, 517 U.S. at 632. While Colorado did argue it possessed interests other than animus – respect for freedom of association including the "liberties" of landlords or employers who have personal or religious objections to homosexuality and conserving resources to fight discrimination against other groups – we held that the "breadth of the amendment is so far removed from these particular justifications that we find it impossible to credit them." *Romer*, 517 U.S. at 635. Similarly here, Texas raises an interest – or what it names a "reasonable inference" – that the legislature amended the statute to target only same-sex sexual activity "in accordance with what then appeared to be the direction in which constitutional privacy law was heading," *see* Br. for Resp'ts at 39–40, and "to avoid a potentially successful challenge to the State's sodomy law by individuals engaging in consensual heterosexual conduct." *Id.* at 41–42. Yet again, protecting some groups at the expense of another group is a demonstration of animus.

This demonstration of animus need not be born of malice, but might be merely an enactment of majoritarian bias. Considering congressional statements that the law sought to preclude "hippies" from accessing food stamps, in *United States Department of Agriculture v. Moreno*, 413 U.S. 528, 534–35 (1973), we noted that if "the constitutional conception of 'equal protection of the laws' means anything, it must at the very least mean that a bare congressional desire to harm a politically unpopular group cannot constitute a legitimate governmental interest." But that sort of specific malice is not necessary. It was not central in *City of Cleburne v. Cleburne Living Center*, 473 U.S. 432, 450 (1985), in which we found that requiring a special "permit in this case appears to us to rest on an irrational prejudice against the mentally retarded," even if that "prejudice" was in part predicated upon protectionism. Further, "mere negative attitudes[] or fear," even if based on "the wishes or objections of some fraction of the body politic," cannot constitute a legitimate government interest. *Id.* at 448 (quoting *Palmore v. Sidoti*, 466 U.S. 429, 433 (1984) ("Private biases may be outside the reach of the law, but the law cannot, directly or indirectly, give them effect.")).

The role of the courts in a free and democratic society is not only to protect the less empowered from the tyranny of the majority and thus guard our ideals of equality; it also ensures our survival as a free and democratic society.

Creating an "underclass" – whether that underclass be undocumented minors excluded from a basic education as in *Plyler v. Doe*, 457 U.S. 202 (1982), or women excluded from a pre-eminent institution grooming citizen-soldiers as in *United States v. Virginia*, 518 U.S. 515 (1996), or sexual minorities as in the Texas statute criminalizing homosexual conduct before us – is intolerable under the Equal Protection Clause.

C

The Texas statute criminalizing "homosexual conduct" does not satisfy any level of scrutiny as established under our equal protection doctrine. It is, therefore, unconstitutional as a violation of the Equal Protection Clause of the Fourteenth Amendment. We stress, however, that we do not limit our consideration of the constitutionality of the Texas statute to the classification it clearly draws: we should not carve out protection of a right for some because we fear protecting a right for all and the statute is clearly unconstitutional under the Due Process Clause as previously discussed.

III

Stare decisis and apology

Bowers v. Hardwick was incorrect when it was decided and remains incorrect. *Bowers v. Hardwick* is overruled.

The overruling of *Bowers v. Hardwick*, a case less than seventeen years old, implicates stare decisis. Stare decisis has less force in constitutional adjudication, in part because the U.S. Supreme Court is the ultimate arbiter of the Constitution. *See Seminole Tribe of Fla. v. Florida*, 517 U.S. 44, 63 (1996) (noting that stare decisis as a policy rather than "inexorable command" is "particularly true in constitutional cases, because in such cases 'correction through legislative action is practically impossible'"). If we cannot correct the error, it will remain uncorrected. Moreover, when the error results in a denial of constitutional rights, stare decisis has even less validity. The Court should act as quickly as possible to correct its error. *See, e.g., W. Va. State Bd. of Educ. v. Barnette*, 319 U.S. 624 (1943) (recognizing a First Amendment right to refuse to salute the flag) (overruling *Minersville Sch. Dist. v. Gobitis*, 310 U.S. 586 (1940)).

There have been numerous speculations regarding how individual justices reached their conclusions in our closely divided decision reversing the Eleventh Circuit's finding that "the Georgia sodomy statute implicates a fundamental right of Michael Hardwick." *Hardwick v. Bowers*, 760 F.2d 1202, 1212 (11th Cir. 1985). These speculations need not detain us and do not figure in our conclusion that *Bowers v. Hardwick* was wrongly decided. What does – and should –"detain" us, is the consequences of our decision.

It is appropriate that we not only overrule *Bowers v. Hardwick*, but that we apologize.

We regret our decision in *Bowers v. Hardwick* because its consequences, both direct and indirect, have been devastating. Lawrence and Garner should not have been arrested for violating the Texas statute that we today hold unconstitutional.[20] Further, we must count among those people injured by our opinion in *Bowers v. Hardwick*, the original plaintiff, Michael Hardwick, who was a 28-year-old white man working in a gay bar in Atlanta in 1982 when he was subjected to arrest in his home by a police officer who seemingly had a personal vendetta against him. *See* Peter Irons, *The Courage of Their Convictions* 381–82 (1988); *Hardwick v. Bowers*, 760 F.2d 1202, 1204 (11th Cir. 1985). Hardwick was reportedly devastated by our opinion; he became reclusive, and died of complications from HIV/AIDS in 1991. *See* Laura Douglas-Brown, *Bowers v. Hardwick at 15*, Southern Voice, July 12, 2001.

Michael Hardwick's death reminds us that our decision in *Bowers v. Hardwick* was rendered during the HIV/AIDS pandemic. The first cases of what would come to be known as AIDS were reported in the United States in June 1981. Ctrs. for Disease Control & Prevention, Dep't of Health & Human Servs., *Advancing HIV Prevention: New Strategies for a Changing Epidemic – United States, 2003*, 52 Morbidity & Mortality Wkly. Rep. 329–32 (2003). From 1981–2001, approximately 1.3 million to 1.4 million people in the United States were infected with HIV. *Id.* A large proportion of those infected are categorized by the Center for Disease Control and Prevention as men who have sex with men, 5 Ctrs. for Disease Control & Prevention, Dep't of Health & Human Servs., *HIV/AIDS Surveillance Report* 4 (1999), and their acts could therefore be constitutionally criminalized.

The link between criminalization of same-sex encounters and the rates of HIV infection may not be direct, but must be acknowledged. As one scholar

[20] Lawrence and Garner are not unique. At times, the prosecuted crimes were for solicitation of sodomy, a crime that is dependent on the constitutionality of the underlying sodomy crime. *See, e.g., Christensen v. State*, 468 S.E.2d 188 (Ga. 1996); *Williams v. State*, 505 S.E.2d 816 (Ga. Ct. App. 1998); *State v. Moore*, 797 So. 2d 756 (La. Ct. App. 2001); *State v. Bullock*, 767 So. 2d 124, 126 (La. Ct. App. 2000); *State v. Walsh*, 713 S.W.2d 508 (Mo. 1986); *Sawatzky v. City of Oklahoma City*, 906 P.2d 785 (Okla. Crim. App. 1995). At other times, the crime involved heterosexual activity, *see, e.g., United States v. Allison*, 56 M.J. 606 (C.G. Ct. Crim. App. 2001); *State v. Chiaradio*, 660 A.2d 276 (R.I. 1995).

has argued, such criminal laws can prevent people from seeking information and assistance, prevent the dissemination of safe-sex materials, interfere with government data collection, and distort medical research. Christopher R. Leslie, *Creating Criminals: The Injuries Inflicted by "Unenforced" Sodomy Laws*, 35 Harv. C.R.-C.L. L. Rev. 103, 121 n.118 (2000). And as we know, and as the Center for Disease Control documented, the tragedy of HIV/AIDS was not limited to "gay men" or "men who have sex with men," but extended to heterosexual men, women, and children.

Further, the other ill effects of our decision in *Bowers v. Hardwick* were likewise not limited to "gay men." Indeed, our decision had a particularly pernicious effect on lesbians or women perceived to be so. *Bowers v. Hardwick* assumed center stage when Michael Bowers, the Attorney General of Georgia, revoked the offer of employment as an attorney to Robin Shahar when he learned of her planned same-sex marriage. *Shahar v. Bowers*, 114 F.3d 1097, 1099 (11th Cir. 1997). Upholding the denial of employment, the Eleventh Circuit found Bowers's decision reasonable because Shahar's known lesbianism might "interfere with the Department's efforts to enforce Georgia's laws against homosexual sodomy." *Id.* at 1105–06. Our decision was also pivotal in upholding the termination of employment of another woman, one whose job with the police department did not include enforcing anti-sodomy laws, but was administering a community diversion program in Virginia. *Walls v. City of Petersburg*, 895 F.2d 188 (4th Cir. 1990). Teyonda Walls refused to answer Question 40 of a newly instituted background check: the question asked: "Have you ever had sexual relations with a person of the same sex?" *Id.* at 190. The Fourth Circuit declared that the "relevance of this type of question to Walls's employment is uncertain, but because the *Bowers* decision is controlling, we hold that Question 40 does not ask for information that Walls has a right to keep private." *Id.* at 193. Notably, both Shahar and Walls had been acceptable as employees before their employers decided their sexuality was relevant.

Lesbian mothers and their children have also suffered from the consequences of *Bowers v. Hardwick*. Several state supreme courts relied on our mistaken opinion in *Bowers* to determine otherwise appropriate mothers were ill-suited to exercise their parental rights. In the notorious case of Sharon Bottoms, the Virginia courts disregarded the presumption in favor of a "natural parent" to award custody of Ms. Bottoms's toddler to her mother, the child's maternal grandmother, because Ms. Bottoms was sharing her bedroom and her bed with her female lover. *Bottoms v. Bottoms*, 457 S.E.2d 102 (Va. 1995). The trial judge concluded that Sharon Bottoms's conduct was illegal and was a "felony in the Commonwealth of Virginia," therefore rendering Ms. Bottoms an "unfit parent." *Id.* at 109 (Kennan, J., dissenting). The trial court's award of custody to the child's grandmother was upheld by Virginia's highest court. *See id.* at 106–07. Likewise, the Alabama Supreme Court relied on the criminality of same-sex conduct to deny custody to lesbian mothers. In *Ex Parte D.W.W.*, 717 So. 2d 793, 796 (Ala. 1998), the Alabama Supreme Court upheld restricted visitation and a denial of custody to a lesbian mother, citing the Alabama deviate sexual intercourse statute to conclude that "the conduct inherent in lesbianism is illegal in Alabama," and thus the mother "is continually engaging in conduct that violates the criminal law of this state." Similarly, the North Dakota Supreme Court in *Chicoine v. Chicoine*, 479 N.W.2d 891 (S.D. 1992), affirmed a denial of custody and further restricted visitation to a lesbian mother, with one justice writing separately to emphasize the state's sodomy statute and declare that "homosexuals" such as the lesbian mother in question were "committing felonies, by their acts against nature and God." *Id.* at 896 (Henderson, J., concurring in part and dissenting in part).

And while we know the names – or the initials – of some of the people involved in these cases, it is important to acknowledge the countless women and men who feared to litigate because of the reverberations from *Bowers*. The criminalization of same-sex activity has served as a linchpin for the denial of many other constitutional, civil, and common law rights, as well as a justification for private violence. We must apologize for not rendering that linchpin unconstitutional seventeen years ago.

The fact that we have not explicitly apologized for previous incorrect decisions, including *Lochner v. New York*, 198 U.S. 45 (1905), or the travesty of *Plessy v. Ferguson*, 163 U.S. 537 (1896), should not be interpreted as a statement that *Bowers v. Hardwick* is *sui generis*. Instead, our apology is a recognition that the Court must take responsibility for justice, as well as equal protection and due process.

IV

Conclusion

In sum, we find that Texas Penal Code section 21.06(a) is unconstitutional as a violation of the Due Process Clause and as a violation of the Equal Protection Clause. We overrule and deeply regret our decision in *Bowers v. Hardwick*.

The judgment of the Court of Appeals for the Texas Fourteenth District is reversed, and the case is remanded for further proceedings not inconsistent with this opinion.

It is so ordered.

26

Commentary on *Town of Castle Rock v. Gonzales*

Patricia A. Broussard

BACKGROUND

In its 2005 decision in *Town of Castle Rock v. Gonzales*,[1] the U.S. Supreme Court set back state law reforms aimed at protecting the victims of domestic violence. Based on the need to afford broad discretion to police officers, the Court held that Jessica Gonzales and her children had no federal constitutional right to the enforcement of a civil restraining order against her husband and their father. This holding came even when the order was granted pursuant to a Colorado statute and even when both the statute and the restraining order arguably mandated enforcement.[2]

Sometime after midnight on June 23, 1999, Ms. Gonzales's daughters were shot and killed. Their bodies were found in the bed of their father's pick-up truck. The three girls – Rebecca, Katheryn, and Leslie – were aged ten, eight and seven. Although it was not conclusively determined whether the girls were shot and killed by their father before he opened fire on the Castle Rock Police Department or by the hail of return gunfire which ensued in response to his attack, the U.S. Supreme Court assumed that Mr. Gonzales had murdered his daughters.[3]

The Gonzales family lived in Castle Rock, Colorado. Jessica and Simon Gonzales were separated and going through divorce proceedings. During their separation, Ms. Gonzales repeatedly called the police, saying that Mr. Gonzales had threatened and frightened the family. Based on these ongoing

---

[1] *Town of Castle Rock v. Gonzales*, 545 U.S. 748 (2005).
[2] Colo. Rev. Stat. § 18-6-803.5(2)(a), (3), (5) (1999).
[3] *Castle Rock*, 545 U.S. at 754. The facts relied upon in the commentary are drawn from the Supreme Court opinion and from *Lenahan v. United States*, Case 12.626, Inter-Am. Comm'n H.R., Report No. 80/11 (2011), www.oas.org/en/iachr/decisions/2011/USPU12626EN.doc (last visited July 25, 2015).

threats, Ms. Gonzales obtained a permanent restraining order.[4] This mandated that Mr. Gonzales must remain at least 100 yards from Ms. Gonzales and the children and that he could only visit his daughters on alternate weekends. He was allowed to have dinner with the girls one night of each week, provided he arranged to do so in advance.

On the afternoon of June 22, 1999, Ms. Gonzales allowed her daughters to go outside and play near the house, asking that they check in every hour. When they had not checked in with her at the assigned hour and because of the ongoing problems with Mr. Gonzales, Ms. Gonzales immediately believed that her husband had taken the girls. Since Mr. Gonzales was not scheduled to have dinner with the girls that night, nor had he made arrangements to visit with them, Ms. Gonzales concluded that he had violated the permanent restraining order and that she needed police intervention. She contacted police several times that evening, asking them to intervene and enforce the order, but they did not respond.

In her lawsuit against the town and the police officers involved, Ms. Gonzales argued that the police officers' lack of enforcement violated the due process rights of her and her daughters. Moreover, she argued that there was a systematic policy of ignoring restraining orders, and she claimed in a later interview that the police in Castle Rock viewed violations of these orders as merely marital spats.[5]

Ms. Gonzales's lawsuit was dismissed by the District Court, but the U.S. Court of Appeals for the Tenth Circuit reversed. The Tenth Circuit held that although Ms. Gonzales did not have a substantive due process claim, she did have a procedural due process claim.[6]

THE ORIGINAL OPINION

The U.S. Supreme Court reversed the Tenth Circuit in a 7–2 decision. In the majority opinion, Justice Antonin Scalia wrote that the Due Process Clause does not protect all government benefits and, specifically, that due process principles do not create a constitutional right to police protection even if there

---

[4] Historically, civil restraining orders have been used to provide a civil remedy for abused victims. Prior to 1976, only two states had civil restraining order legislation. By 1994, all fifty states had adopted protective order legislation, and in thirty states, violation of a protective order constitutes a criminal offense. Carolyn N. Ko, *Civil Restraining Orders for Domestic Violence: The Unresolved Questions of "Efficacy,"* 11 S. Cal. Interdis. L.J. 361, 362 (2002).

[5] 60 Minutes, *Gonzales v. Castle Rock, Supreme Court to Decide If Mother Can Sue Her Town and Its Police Force*, CBS News (Mar. 17, 2005),www.cbsnews.com/news/gonzales-vs-castle-rock/.

[6] *Gonzales v. Town of Castle Rock*, 366 F.3d 1093 (10th Cir. 2004) (en banc).

is a restraining order. He based the conclusion that there was no due process
right on a tradition of allowing police officers to exercise discretion across a
range of issues. Although Justice Scalia acknowledged that the U.S. Supreme
Court usually defers to the federal circuit courts on the interpretation of state
laws within their jurisdiction, he found such deference to be inappropriate
here. Therefore, it was justifiable for the U.S. Supreme Court to supplant the
Court of Appeals' interpretation of the Colorado law.[7]

Justices Souter and Breyer concurred, also emphasizing the necessity of
preserving the traditional discretion afforded law enforcement officers.[8] They
further found that the Colorado statute did not create a new right, and therefore Ms. Gonzales could not argue that she was denied due process. As they
put it, "To accede to Gonzales's argument would therefore work a sea change
in the scope of federal due process, for she seeks federal process as a substitute
for state process."[9]

In dissent, Justices Stevens and Ginsburg argued that just as a private con-
tractor could grant Ms. Gonzales an entitlement to mandatory individual protection, so could the State of Colorado by creating a statute that is functionally
equivalent.[10] According to the dissent, the Court could have easily found that
the Colorado statute, which arguably envisioned mandatory enforcement by
use of the word "shall," created a protected property interest that was eligible
for constitutional protection. In the words of Justice Stevens:

> The Court's formalistic analysis fails to take seriously the fact that the
> Colorado statute at issue in this case was enacted for the benefit of the narrow
> class of persons who are beneficiaries of domestic restraining orders and that
> the order at issue in this case was specifically intended to provide protection
> to respondent and her children.[11]

The dissent concluded that if the Court viewed the question as one of statutory interpretation, it could have remanded to the Colorado Supreme Court
to decide what its legislature meant by the word "shall," thereby removing
police discretion. Instead, "[t]he failure to observe minimal procedural safeguards creates an unacceptable risk of arbitrary and erroneous deprivation."[12]

The response to the U.S. Supreme Court decision was swift and scathing.
The ACLU urged "[l]egislatures and courts [to] follow the examples of states

[7] *Castle Rock*, 545 U.S. at 757.
[8] *Id.* at 770 (Souter, J., concurring).
[9] *Id.* at 771 (Souter, J., concurring).
[10] *Id.* at 774 (Stevens, J., dissenting).
[11] *Id.* at 779 (Stevens, J., dissenting).
[12] *Id.* at 776–77, 793 (Stevens, J., dissenting).

like Montana and Tennessee and ensure that there are consequences when police arbitrarily fail to follow laws enacted for the protection of victims of domestic violence and their children."[13] Ms. Gonzales filed a petition with the Inter-American Commission on Human Rights (IACHR)[14] alleging that the government violated her human rights when the Castle Rock Police Department failed to protect her and her daughters by enforcing the restraining order and when the U.S. Supreme Court failed to provide them with a remedy. Women's and human rights organizations stated in their amicus briefs to the IACHR that the U.S. Supreme Court decision endangered women and children.[15] And the Commission ruled that "the United States violated its obligations under international human rights laws by failing to use due diligence and reasonable measures to protect Ms. Lenahan (Gonzales) and her daughters from violence by her estranged husband."[16]

THE FEMINIST JUDGMENT

The feminist opinion offered by Professor Maria Isabel Medina, writing as Justice Medina, rejects a formalistic or traditional view and recognizes that property interests come in many different forms. Medina found that the benefit created and granted by the state "is a property interest because a protective order secures to its beneficiaries a bundle of rights that includes a certain level of police protection, an entitlement with ascertainable monetary value, and the holder of that interest was led by the Colorado legislative framework to rely on the security provided by that interest."

The feminist judgment differs from the original in several important ways. First, it provides the historical background of under-recognition and under-enforcement of protective orders that explains why the Colorado legislature decided it was necessary to limit "the discretion that law enforcement may exercise in executing protective orders designed to affirmatively protect women

---

[13] *ACLU Disappointed with Supreme Court Ruling on Domestic Violence Orders of Protection*, ACLU (June 27, 2005), www.aclu.org/news/aclu-disappointed-supreme-court-ruling-domestic-violence-orders-protection.

[14] The IACHR is an organization of the Organization of American States whose mission is to promote and protect human rights in the American hemisphere. Among its functions is to hear cases of alleged human rights violations by its member states. IACHR, *Basic Documents in the Inter-American System*, Org. of Am. States, www.oas.org/en/iachr/mandate/Basics/intro.asp (last visited July 25, 2015).

[15] *See generally* briefs submitted on behalf of organizations dedicated to protecting the rights of women and children and various women's and human rights organizations as *amici curiae* supporting Petitioner Jessica Lenahan (Gonzales) in *Lenahan*, Report No. 80/11, *supra* note 3.

[16] *Lenahan*, Report No. 80/11, *supra* note 3, at 43, 44.

and children from intimate family violence." As Medina writes, "Feminists laid the groundwork for the recognition that the legal system's response to sexual and family violence sheltered and encouraged the violence and reflected the absence of women as active participants in politics and the legal system."

Further, the feminist judgment focuses on the real-life story of Jessica Gonzales and her daughters, illustrating the gravity and human toll represented by violations of the due process rights of domestic violence victims, particularly women and children. This feminist perspective gives voice to and makes visible the woman and children at the center of the opinion, potentially changing the reasoning and the outcome of the case.

Similarly, according to the feminist opinion, Colorado's mandatory arrest policy has the effect of empowering women. Although some have criticized such statutes because they appear to authorize the state to impose its will upon a woman who does not want to pursue legal remedies, Ms. Gonzales willingly invited the state to step in by asking for enforcement of its statute. The power that was given to Ms. Gonzales by the statute was nullified by the police officers.

Finally, the feminist opinion reveals the gender stereotypes that pervaded both the police department's lack of enforcement of the order and the U.S. Supreme Court majority's view of the outcome. Medina points out that these stereotypes are based upon historical "views protecting family and marital privacy as well as the primacy of male spouses as heads of households and stereotypical views of women as naturally submissive, indecisive, and prone to complaint but likely to retract allegations of domestic violence." Although these views have been abandoned in the law, they live on in society. As shown in the record of the *Gonzales* case, police officers often do not believe or trust the women who are the usual victims of domestic violence. Ms. Gonzales contacted police officers numerous times, and each time the police reacted by giving the benefit of the doubt to Simon Gonzales. This bias persisted even though there was documentation of Simon Gonzales's abuse towards the family.

Because of the history of gender stereotypes coupled with a history that artificially deprived women of full representation in decision making, it is even more important, as Medina recognizes, to give full credit "to the Colorado legislature's determination that protective orders today have value."

Town of Castle Rock v. Gonzales, 545 U.S. 748 (2005)

Justice Maria Isabel Medina delivered the opinion of the Court.

This case presents the question whether by limiting the discretion that police may exercise in determining to enforce a protective order, the State of

Colorado created a protected property interest for purposes of the Due Process Clause of the Fourteenth Amendment, thus entitling its beneficiaries, here Jessica Gonzales and her children, to a meaningful opportunity to be heard prior to deprivation of that interest. This Court now holds that the Colorado statute restricting law enforcement's discretion to refuse to enforce mandatory arrest restraining orders created a property interest that entitles its holder to meaningful process under the Due Process Clause. We remand for further proceedings. On remand, the lower court will determine what process would constitute sufficient process under *Mathews v. Eldridge*, 424 U.S. 319 (1976).

I

Before addressing the principles and precedents that govern this case, we review the history of the subject now before the Court.

A

In 1994, the Colorado legislature recognized domestic violence as "the single largest cause of injury to women in the United States, more common than auto accidents, muggings, and rapes combined." H.B. 04-1305, 2004 Colo. Legis. Serv. Ch. 178 § 2 (West) (codified at Colo. Rev. Stat. § 13-14-102(1). *See* Br. of Nat'l Black Police Ass'n *et al.* as Amici Curiae Supporting Resp't (quoting Melody K. Fuller and Janet L. Stansberry, *1994 Legislature Strengthens Domestic Violence Protection Orders*, 23 Colo. Law. 2327 (1994)); Colo. Rev. Stat. §18-6-801.5); Br. for Nat'l Network to End Domestic Violence *et al.* as Amici Curiae Supporting Resp't at 7. In this, Colorado was not alone. *See* Br. for Family Violence Prevention Fund *et al.* as Amici Curiae Supporting Resp't at 10.

Domestic violence was recognized as a national problem in the latter half of the twentieth century. Feminists laid the groundwork for the recognition that the legal system's response to sexual and family violence sheltered and encouraged the violence and reflected the absence of women as active participants in politics and the legal system. *See* Elizabeth M. Schneider, *Battered Women and Feminist Lawmaking* 3–10 (2000). Violence was one of the ways in which men controlled women, particularly in a marriage. Although women engage in intimate partner violence, and domestic violence occurs in same-sex relationships, overwhelmingly domestic violence targets women and children. *See* Patricia Tjaden and Nancy Thoennes, Nat'l Institute of Justice, NCJ 183781, *Full Report of the Prevalence, Incidence, and Consequence of Violence Against Women: Findings from the National Violence Against Women Survey*

(2000). Children are particularly at risk in families that experience abusive relationships. *See* Br. for Family Violence Prevention Fund *et al.* as Amici Curiae Supporting Resp't. According to the National Center for Children Exposed to Violence, "domestic violence has been found to be the single most common precursor to child death in the United States." *See Yale Child Study Center Trauma Section*, Yale School of Medicine, http://childstudycenter.yale.edu/community/nccev.aspx (citing L.G. Mills *et al.*, *Child Protection and Domestic Violence: Training, Practice, and Policy Issues*, 22 Children and Youth Servs. Rev. 315, 332 (2000)).

Traditionally, law treated married women differently than men. Under English and American early common law, men were entitled to use physical force to "correct" wives. Reva Siegel, *"The Rule of Love": Wife Beating as Prerogative and Privacy*, 105 Yale L.J. 2117, 2118 (1996). Women and children were treated as the property of the men in whose control their personal selves (as well as personal property) were placed. Women's primary role was relegated to the "private" domestic sphere focused on the home and the child-care function, whereas men controlled the public sphere, the realm where laws and policy are fashioned and determined. Women, thus, were denied the opportunity to participate in the development of laws and legal institutions. The legal infrastructure on which American law rests today to a large extent was formulated without the meaningful participation of women. Concepts of property were replaced by concepts of marital privacy that prioritized the goal of preserving marital unity above all others. Marriage, in turn, rested on stereotypes about women and men. These stereotypes subjugated women's needs or desires to pursue careers, to have economic independence and a life with both public and private sphere dimensions, that is, a life similar to that enjoyed by men. In a traditional marriage, men could excel in their careers and diminish their roles in the family or marriage to an extent simply unavailable to most women in the United States well into the twentieth century. The doctrine of marital privacy helped shelter from public view or scrutiny the incidence of marital, family, or intimate partner violence. Laws facilitated (and to an extent still facilitate) family violence and made it easy for law enforcement, physicians, hospitals, and courts to ignore assaults that would otherwise be formally prosecuted as a matter of course.

The latter quarter of the twentieth century saw meaningful reform at the federal level through the Violence Against Women Act of 1994 (VAWA), 42 U.S.C. § 13981; the Violent Crime Control and Law Enforcement Act of 1994, 18 U.S.C. § 922(g)(8) (prohibiting a person subject to a state domestic violence protective order from shipping, transporting, possessing, or receiving a firearm that has travelled in interstate commerce); and the Domestic Violence

Offenders Gun Ban of 1996, 18 U.S.C. § 922(g)(9). At the state level, reform ushered in a wave of statutes that included a variety of approaches to stanching intimate violence, including mandatory arrest statutes like Colorado's, and other measures in part fueled by the federal money made available to states under VAWA. VAWA included a full faith and credit provision that requires states to enforce the relief provided by the protective orders of other states as long as the order is "issued for the purpose of preventing violent or threatening acts or harassment against, or contact or communication with or physical proximity to, another person." 18 U.S.C. § 2266(5).

This Court first recognized the problem of domestic violence in *Planned Parenthood of Southeastern Pennsylvania v. Casey*, 505 U.S. 833 (1992), where we found that a state requirement that women notify spouses before terminating a pregnancy imposed an undue burden on their constitutional right to choose to terminate a pregnancy pre-viability. We reasoned that a spousal notification requirement sharply increased the risk that women in abusive relationships faced. In 2000, this Court again dealt with the issue of violence against women. In *United States v. Morrison*, 529 U.S. 598 (2000), we held that Congress lacked power under the Commerce Clause of the United States Constitution or under section 5 of the Fourteenth Amendment to create a private cause of action for damages for victims of crimes of violence motivated by gender animus. *Morrison* restricted the scope of federal power to respond directly to the problem of under-enforcement in domestic violence crimes, but it left intact other VAWA provisions that facilitated and funded state and private initiatives to lessen the impact of domestic violence on American families. M. Isabel Medina, *Justifying Integration of Domestic Violence Throughout the Law School Curriculum: An Introduction to the Symposium*, 47 Loy. L. Rev. 1, 1–20 (2001). *Morrison* recognized that states enjoy primacy in developing effective legal responses to the problem of domestic violence, but *Casey* emphasized that the states were subject to constitutional norms that would prevent them from exacerbating the danger faced by women and children in battering relationships.

In 1994, Colorado, like many other states, enacted statutory reforms expressly designed to better protect individuals and families from domestic violence. One key aspect of this national movement aimed to transform law enforcement response to the victims of intimate violence by communicating clearly a legislative mandate to police to enforce protective orders. *See* Melody K. Fuller and Janet L. Stansberry, *1994 Legislature Strengthens Domestic Violence Protective Orders*, 23 Colo. Law. 2327 (1994); *see also Hearing on H.B. 1253 Before the H. Comm. on the Judiciary*, 1994 Leg. (Colo. 1994) (tr. at 2–5, 40–42); Br. for Nat'l Network to End Domestic Violence *et al.* as Amici Curiae Supporting Resp't at 25–27.

The mandate was important; one of the primary problems identified by advocates for domestic violence victims was the failure by law enforcement to take complaints seriously and to arrest and prosecute perpetrators of intimate violence. Advocates and scholars concluded that "[p]rotection orders ... are only as effective as their enforcement. An order without enforcement can create a false sense of security for victims of domestic violence, and actually increase the chance of danger to the very person or persons the order is intended to protect." Catherine F. Klein and Leslye E. Orloff, *Providing Legal Protection for Battered Women: An Analysis of State Statutes and Case Law*, 21 Hofstra L. Rev. 801, 1095 (1993) (cited in Br. for Family Violence Prevention Fund *et al.* as Amici Curiae Supporting Resp't at 14). *See also* Br. for AARP as Amici Curiae Supporting Resp't at 14 ("Law enforcement officials, who are charged with enforcing protective orders are the gatekeepers of the criminal justice system. However, protective orders are only effective when the restrained party is convinced that the order will be enforced.").

As the amicus brief filed by the National Network to End Domestic Violence notes, every state "has enacted criminal enforcement provisions or criminal sanctions for protective order violations to ensure that these orders are not merely pieces of paper but instead an important barrier between the victim and her abuser." In addition, most states require arrest upon violation, and they and the federal government have developed protective order databases to help law enforcement officers verify those orders. "These states have further determined that judges should determine whether a perpetrator is dangerous to his victim when deciding whether to grant a protective order, and that law enforcement need only decide if he has violated the court's order." Br. for Nat'l Network to End Domestic Violence *et al.* as Amici Curiae Supporting Resp't at 26–27.

The failure to enforce protective orders reflected longstanding views protecting family and marital privacy as well as the unquestioned primacy of male spouses as heads of households and stereotypical views of women as naturally submissive, indecisive, and prone to complaint, but likely to retract allegations of domestic violence. While these views have long been abandoned as a matter of law, they continue to play a role in society. The Colorado statute intentionally limited the discretion that law enforcement may exercise in executing protective orders designed to affirmatively protect women and children from intimate family violence.

Concurrently, the Colorado legislature provided police officers immunity from liability for erroneous arrests made in the course of enforcing protective orders. Colo. Rev. Stat. §18-6-803.5(5). The Colorado legislature thus made clear its commitment to restrict police discretion to ignore protective orders by mandating arrest and protecting police from liability for erroneous arrests.

The problem of under-enforcement of protective orders that Colorado sought to address reflects the structural gender inequalities built into our legal system that make it difficult for that system to respond effectively to a national problem like domestic violence. Protective orders are, in part, a private remedy made necessary because of the failure of the public remedy (law enforcement) to respond effectively. The failure of law enforcement and prosecutors to respond effectively is a result of the historic denial to women of their right to participate as lawmakers, prosecutors, jurors, law enforcers, and judges. It may be, as this case makes clear, a flawed remedy, but from the view of Colorado's and many other state legislatures, it is a necessary remedy that empowers women and children at risk in battering relationships.

B

The facts of this case are uniquely tragic but not uncommon. Jessica and Simon Gonzales became estranged early in 1999. Although the record is not clear, Simon Gonzales apparently had a history of suicidal threats and erratic behavior that led a state court to issue a protective order limiting his contact with the family. The state court issued a temporary restraining order against Simon Gonzales on May 21, 1999, and entered the order into the state's central registry of restraining orders, a computerized database registry accessible to any state or local law enforcement agency, including the Castle Rock Police Department. The order stated that "the court ... finds that physical or emotional harm would result if you are not excluded from the family home," and directed him to stay at least 100 yards away from the home at all times. The order was served on Simon Gonzales on June 4, 1999, and on that same day, the state court made the restraining order permanent, but modified it to allow Simon Gonzales limited visitation with the children. The court allowed him to pick up the three children on alternating weekends commencing after work on Friday evening through 7 P.M. on Sunday evening, for a mid-week dinner visit if it was pre-arranged with Ms. Gonzales with advance notice, and for two non-consecutive weeks during the summer.

The protective order contained the following notice to law enforcement officials:

> You shall use every reasonable means to enforce this restraining order. You shall arrest, or, if an arrest would be impractical under the circumstances, seek a warrant for the arrest of the restrained person when you have information

amounting to probable cause that the restrained person has violated or attempted to violate any provision of this order ... You shall enforce this order even if there is no record of it in the restraining order central registry. You shall take the restrained person to the nearest jail ... You are authorized to use every reasonable effort to protect the alleged victim and alleged victim's children to prevent further violence. You may transport, or arrange transportation for the alleged victim and/or the alleged victim's children to shelter.

In defiance of this restraining order, sometime between 5 and 5:30 P.M., on Tuesday, June 22, 1999, Simon Gonzales abducted his three young daughters from the front of their house. When their mother, Jessica Gonzales, noticed the children were gone, she suspected their father had taken them. Showing considerable restraint, at 7:30 P.M. she telephoned the Castle Rock Police Department for assistance.

The police department dispatched two officers, Brink and Ruisi, to Jessica Gonzales's home. When they arrived, Ms. Gonzales showed them a copy of the restraining order, requested that it be enforced, and asked that the children be returned to her immediately. The two officers told her that there was nothing they could do and suggested that Ms. Gonzales call the police department again if the three children did not return home by 10 P.M.

This initial response set the official tone for subsequent interactions between Jessica Gonzales and the Castle Rock Police Department. At approximately 8:30 P.M., Ms. Gonzales reached Simon on his cellular telephone. He told her that he had the three children at Elitch Gardens amusement park in Denver. Ms. Gonzales again called the police department and was put through to one of the original police officers, Officer Brink. She asked Brink to have someone check for Simon Gonzales or his vehicle at Elitch Gardens and to put out a police alert for Simon Gonzales. Brink refused to do so and again told Ms. Gonzales to wait until 10 P.M. to see if Simon Gonzales returned the three girls home.

Deprived of any police effort to observe or enforce the protective order, Jessica Gonzales waited. At approximately 10:10 P.M. she called the police department again, informing the dispatcher that the three girls were still missing. Again, the police ignored Mr. Gonzales's violation of the protective order, and the mother's concerns over the safety and health of her daughters. The police told her to wait until midnight.

Ms. Gonzales called the police department again at midnight. Nothing appears to have occurred as a result of that call. Ms. Gonzales then went to Mr. Gonzales's apartment but he was not at home. She again called the police on her cellular phone from the apartment. The dispatcher told her to wait there for a police officer to arrive. She waited at Mr. Gonzales's apartment until 12:50

A.M. when she went to the Castle Rock police station. She met with a third police officer, Ahlfinger, who took an incident report from her, but made no effort to locate the children or enforce the restraining order. Instead, he went to dinner.

Simon Gonzales drove to the Castle Rock police station at approximately 3:20 A.M. and opened fire on the station with a semi-automatic handgun he had purchased earlier that evening, shortly after he had abducted the three girls. Police shot Gonzales. The police found the bodies of the three girls in the cab of Simon's truck. The record is uncontested that Mr. Gonzales took the children without advance notice, permission or knowledge of Ms. Gonzales, in defiance of the protective order.

C

Ms. Gonzales, individually and on behalf of her deceased minor children, sued the city of Castle Rock and three individual police officers under 42 U.S.C. § 1983, alleging that the town's police department violated the Due Process Clause and section 1983 because the protective order "created a property right that incurred a duty on the part of the Defendants to protect Plaintiff and the three children"; Defendants "were required by law to protect Plaintiff and the three children by using 'every reasonable means to enforce' the TRO and to 'arrest' or 'seek a warrant for the arrest of' Simon Gonzales"; and Defendants "knowingly failed to perform their duties … willfully, recklessly or with such gross negligence as to indicate wanton disregard and deliberate indifference to the civil rights of Plaintiff and the three children." Compl., Count 1, ¶ 18, 19, 20, 21.

In addition, the Complaint alleged that the city had violated the Due Process Clause in "creating an official policy or custom of failing to respond properly to complaints of restraining order violations" and had "failed to train their officers properly[;] … and [that] this policy is motivated by a deliberate indifference to the rights of persons with whom its police officers come in contact" and "provides for or tolerates the non-enforcement of restraining orders by its police officers." Compl., Count II, ¶ 25, 26, 27.

The defendants moved to dismiss[17] for failure to state a claim on the grounds that a "boilerplate" protective order did not create a property right and thus did not give rise to a viable procedural due process claim. The defendants further contested that Ms. Gonzales could not assert a substantive due process claim because the police department's actions did not "shock the conscience" and

---

[17] The court initially rendered a default judgment, subsequently set aside when the defendants filed an appearance and explained their failure to respond to the complaint.

thus that they were entitled to dismissal of her claims. The individual police officers argued as well that they were entitled to qualified immunity.

The District Court dismissed the claims against the city and police officers, finding that under *DeShaney v. Winnebago Cty. Dep't of Social Servs.*, 489 U.S. 189 (1989), the state could only be held liable under substantive due process "when the State by the affirmative exercise of its power so restrains an individual's liberty that it renders him unable to care for himself, and at the same time fails to provide for his basic human needs." *Id.* at 198, 200. The District Court decided that neither of the two exceptions to the *DeShaney* rule recognized by the Tenth Circuit was applicable (the special-relationship doctrine and the danger-creation theory) because both applied only where the state created the danger and required the plaintiff to establish that defendant's conduct "shock the conscience." Op., Civ. Act. No. 00-D-1285, Pet. for Cert., App. E. That court also held that the plaintiff lacked a legitimate claim of entitlement to a protected property interest. The court reasoned that the protective order was not really mandatory because it required police to exercise discretion in determining probable cause.

On appeal, the Tenth Circuit panel reversed the lower court's dismissal of the procedural due process claim and remanded for further proceedings. The panel affirmed the dismissal of the substantive due process claim. It rejected Ms. Gonzales's argument that the defendants' actions constituted affirmative interference with the protection provided by the restraining order, and instead found that those actions consisted simply of a failure to act. The police officers' failure to enforce the order, the Tenth Circuit reasoned, did not create or enhance the danger to the children and thus the defendants were entitled to a dismissal of that claim. This claim is not now before this Court.

With regards to the procedural due process claim, however, the Tenth Circuit reasoned that under *Board of Regents v. Roth*, 408 U.S. 564 (1972), Ms. Gonzales was entitled to pursue her claim that the state statute at issue gave her an entitlement to receive protective services and that she had been deprived of that protected property interest without due process of law. The panel reasoned that a state statute creates a constitutionally protected property interest when "the regulatory language is so mandatory that it creates a right to rely on that language thereby creating an entitlement that could not be withdrawn without due process." *Gonzales v. Town of Castle Rock*, 307 F.3d 1258 (10th Cir. 2002). The panel concluded that Colorado had, in fact, restrained the discretion of police in enforcing protective orders. The panel further concluded "that defendant police officers used no means, reasonable or otherwise, to enforce the restraining order. Under these circumstances, we conclude that Ms. Gonzales has effectively alleged a procedural due process claim" *Id.* at 1266. That the police exercise some discretion in determining probable cause, the panel reasoned, did not negate the mandatory nature of the order. "The existence of probable cause is an objectively ascertainable matter evaluated on the basis of what a reasonably well-trained officer would know ... It therefore is not a matter committed to the officer's subjective discretion." *Id.*

The defendants petitioned for rehearing en banc, which was granted. The Tenth Circuit en banc agreed with the panel, and reversed the District Court's dismissal of Ms. Gonzales's procedural due process claim. The court also granted the individual officers qualified immunity. 366 F.3d 1093 (10th Cir. 2004). The en banc majority recognized the question to be "whether the state of Colorado created in Ms. Gonzales an entitlement that cannot be taken away from her without procedural due process, and if so, whether the officers' arbitrary denial of that entitlement was procedurally unfair." Applying *Roth*, as the panel below had done, the en banc court found that Colorado had created an entitlement in a restraining order issued by a state court judge, finding irreparable injury if no order were issued, finding that physical or emotional harm would result if Mr. Gonzales was not excluded from the family home, and making it clear that the restrained person could not molest or disturb the peace of the beneficiaries of the protective order. In addition, the order gave notice to the person restrained that he "could be arrested without notice if a law enforcement officer [had] probable cause to believe that [he] knowingly violated the order." *Id.* at 1103.

The en banc opinion explained the limits of police discretion in a probable cause determination to support its conclusion that "a police officer's finding of probable cause is not a wholly discretionary determination which undermines the mandatory edict of the restraining order or statute. While an officer must obviously exercise some judgment in determining the existence of probable cause, the validity and accuracy of that decision is reviewed under objectively ascertainable standards and judged by what a reasonably well-trained officer would know." *Id.* at 1105. That the statutory language commanded officers to use "every reasonable means to enforce this restraining order" did not undermine the mandatory nature of the order. Colo. Rev. Stat. § 18-6-803.5(3)(a). The Tenth Circuit emphasized the legislative history of the statutory scheme at issue and the legislative intent: "to alter the fact that the police were not enforcing domestic abuse restraining orders." 366 F.3d at 1108.

Moreover, the Tenth Circuit reasoned, the conduct of the police department did not constitute an opportunity to be heard at a meaningful time and in a meaningful manner. At a minimum, the court suggested, the Colorado statutes and order required that the police determine whether a valid order exists; whether probable cause exists that the restrained party is violating the order; and whether probable cause exists that the restrained party has notice of the order. Further, the police must provide notification of the results of the officer's decision and the reasons for it to the beneficiary of the protective order. 366 F.3d at 1116. The officers' failure to do so violated Ms. Gonzales's procedural due process rights, and, thus she was entitled to pursue her claim in court.

Castle Rock petitioned for and this Court granted certiorari. This Court now affirms the Tenth Circuit's determination that Colorado law created a protected property interest to which Ms. Gonzales had a legitimate expectation of enforcement.

II

A

To determine whether the kind of benefit Colorado law vested in holders of protective orders is a protected property interest, our starting point is *Board of Regents v. Roth*, 408 U.S. 564 (1972), in which we explained our conceptual framework for modern procedural due process protections. In *Roth* we recognized that procedural due process applies to deprivation of liberty and property interests protected under the Fourteenth Amendment. We rejected rigid or formalistic limitations and "the wooden distinction between 'rights' and 'privileges' that once seemed to govern the applicability of procedural due process rights." *Id.* at 571. We recognized that "liberty" and "property" were terms limited in their meaning. Liberty interests are those that have been recognized by this Court to be protected under the Fourteenth Amendment. With regard to property interests, this Court eschewed a formalistic or traditional view, instead looking to "the security of interests that a person has already acquired in specific benefits." *Id.* at 576. We recognized that property interests could take many forms and could "extend well beyond actual ownership of real estate, chattels, or money." *Id.* at 572. We explained:

> Property interests ... are created and their dimensions are defined by existing rules or understandings that stem from an independent source such as state law – rules or understandings that secure certain benefits and that support claims of entitlement to those benefits. Thus, the welfare recipients in *Goldberg v. Kelly* ... had a claim of entitlement to welfare payments that was grounded in the statute defining eligibility for them. The recipients had not

yet shown that they were, in fact, within the statutory terms of eligibility. But we held that they had a right to a hearing at which they might attempt to do so.

Id. at 578.

To be entitled to the protections of procedural due process, claimants must prove not just the possibility of receiving a benefit, but a legitimate claim of entitlement to it. "It is a purpose of the ancient institution of property to protect those claims upon which people rely in their daily lives, reliance that must not be arbitrarily undermined. It is a purpose of the constitutional right to a hearing to provide an opportunity for a person to vindicate those claims." *Id.* at 577.

This Court has recognized property rights protected by the Due Process Clause to include continued public benefits including a property interest in public employment, *Perry v. Sindermann*, 408 U.S. 593, 601–03 (1972); a public education, *Goss v. Lopez*, 419 U.S. 565, 574 (1975); garnishment of wages by creditors, *Sniadach v. Family Finance Corp.*, 395 U.S. 337, 339 (1969); the right to operate a vehicle on state highways, *Bell v. Burson*, 402 U.S. 535, 539 (1971); professional licenses, *Barry v. Barchi*, 443 U.S. 55, 64 (1979); time limitation on causes of action, *Logan v. Zimmerman Brush Co.*, 455 U.S. 422, 428 (1982); utility services, *Memphis Light, Gas & Water Div. v. Craft*, 436 U.S. 1, 11–12 (1978); disability benefits, *Mathews v. Eldridge*, 424 U.S. 319 (1976); and welfare benefits, *Goldberg v. Kelly*, 397 U.S. 254, 262 (1970). Moreover, whether state law has created a property interest does not depend on how state tort law treats the interest. *See* Br. for Nat'l Ass'n of Women Lawyers and Nat'l Crime Victims Bar Ass'n as Amici Curiae Supporting Resp't.

This Court recognized in *Roth* that property rights may "stem from an independent source such as state law." 408 U.S. at 577. States are free to provide their residents whatever benefits they choose to create, and federalism principles favor deference to a state's decision to create a special benefit for the beneficiaries of a protective order. *See Bishop v. Wood*, 426 U.S. 341, 344 (1976). In *DeShaney*, this Court recognized that a state might afford its residents "an 'entitlement' to receive protective services in accordance with the terms of the statute, an entitlement which would enjoy due process protection against state deprivation under ... *Roth*." 489 U.S. at 195 n.2.

Traditionally, this Court defers to a federal circuit court's determination of the law of a state within its jurisdiction. *Phillips v. Washington Legal Foundation*, 524 U.S. 156, 167 (1998); *see also Bishop*, 426 U.S. at 346, and n.10. This policy reflects "our belief that district courts and courts of appeals are better schooled in and more able to interpret the laws of their respective States." *Brockett v. Spokane Arcades, Inc.*, 472 U.S. 491, 500–501 (1985).

See also Hillsborough v. Cromwell, 326 U.S. 620, 629–630 (1946). We have declined to show deference only in rare cases in which the court of appeals' resolution of state law was "clearly wrong" or otherwise seriously deficient. *See Brockett*, 472 U.S. at 500, n.9; *Leavitt v. Jane L.*, 518 U.S. 137, 145 (1996) (per curiam). This is not such a case and we join with the Tenth Circuit in concluding that state law here created a property interest that entitled its holder to meaningful process before being deprived of her interest.

The benefit that the Colorado statute created, and that the Colorado court which issued the protective order granted to Gonzales, is a property interest because a protective order secures to its beneficiaries a bundle of rights. The bundle includes a certain level of police protection, an entitlement with ascertainable monetary value, and the holder of that interest was led by the Colorado legislative framework to rely on the security provided by that interest.

More specifically, protective orders, like the one here, secure for the beneficiary a bundle of rights that include a limitation on physical access to property by the person restrained; a limitation against the person restrained molesting or disturbing the children's peace; the arrest of the person restrained if police had information amounting to probable cause to believe the person restrained was attempting to or had violated the order; and the mandate to law enforcement to use every reasonable means to enforce the order. The security granted Jessica Gonzales inherent in the bundle of rights plainly has monetary value because at the heart of the protective order is special protection by law enforcement to holders of protective orders.

Were Ms. Gonzales able to afford the cost of private enforcement on the national market, she could have paid for the protection guaranteed to her by the mandatory arrest provision in the protective order she had been issued. Increasingly, communities have turned to private companies for the provision of those services. The benefit at issue in this case is one currently sold on the national and international markets. There is nothing remarkable about treating the interest created by the Colorado statute as a property interest to which Ms. Gonzales had a legitimate entitlement. Our concepts of property now accommodate a vast variety of property interests that include functions that have at some point or another been provided solely by governmental actors, but that now may be provided by governmental and private actors. Thus, many states and municipalities rely on a combination of state and private actors to provide security or police services. While the state and municipal actors may be paid out of city coffers and taxpayer funds, oftentimes communities pay for private security services through special taxpayer assessments or funds. In addition, municipalities or special districts may contract with private security services. Similarly, municipalities may outsource to private actors the provision of services that municipalities themselves previously provided, including the power to arrest or detain in collaboration with the police department. Such an interest has ascertainable monetary value; that it arises out of a function that government actors have always performed – to wit, arresting people who they have probable cause to believe have committed a criminal offense – does not negate that it is a cognizable property interest. This interest is grounded not in a general law enforcement function owed by police to any and all citizens, but in the special protection provided in the particular kind of protective order at issue here.

Colorado was free to create a property interest of the type enacted in its domestic abuse protective order statutory scheme; such a property interest is analogous to that created if Ms. Gonzales had entered into a contract with a private security firm, obligating the firm to provide protection to her family; such a contract has ascertainable monetary value (as does the degree of protection secured by the beneficiaries of a domestic abuse mandatory arrest protective order); and the holder of that property interest is entitled to notice and a meaningful opportunity to be heard before she is deprived of that interest.

B

The plain language of Colorado's mandatory arrest provisions in protective orders makes clear that beneficiaries have a protected interest in enforcement on which they are entitled to rely. Colorado's statute uses unambiguous, mandatory language that sharply restricts the power of police to choose to do nothing in the face of an allegation that a protective order has been violated: "You shall arrest ... You shall enforce this order even if there is no record of it in the restraining order central registry ... You are authorized to use every reasonable effort to protect the alleged victim and alleged victim's children to prevent further violence." Such mandatory language demonstrates that Colorado restricted the power of the police officers to exercise their discretion to refuse or unnecessarily delay enforcement of a protective order, and that Colorado did so by creating a protected interest in the beneficiary that entitled her to a certain degree of process prior to being denied her interest.

Similarly, the legislative history shows that Colorado intended to restrict law enforcement discretion to refuse to enforce protective orders. *See* Br. for Nat'l Coalition Against Domestic Violence and Nat'l Ctr. for Victims of Crime as Amici Curiae Supporting Resp't at 23; Br. of Peggy Kerns, Former Member, House of Rep. of the State of Colorado, and Texas Domestic Violence Direct Serv. Providers as Amici Curiae Supporting Resp't; Br. of Nat'l Black Police Ass'n *et al.* as Amici Curiae Supporting Resp't.

For enforcement orders to protect victims of intimate violence and to discourage perpetrators of such violence, they have to enjoy the weight of the power they carry: they have to be enforced. It is not just the power of the judiciary to order the police to conform, as would be available in the context of any court order; in the case of mandatory arrest orders, it is the power of police to enforce the order and to arrest if the order is violated, which is mandated under the statute. The Colorado statute was designed to achieve the second goal: that police would arrest suspected violators. In doing so, the statute conveyed a property interest to beneficiaries of the order: they were assured of "special" protection beyond that available to other persons who lacked the protections granted by the protective order. Colorado's scheme represented a legislative judgment that this degree of special protection was necessary to overcome long-standing traditional views of gender and marital privacy that insulated domestic violence from law enforcement scrutiny. Colorado determined that this degree of special protection – requiring police to act in cases where long-standing practice had been not to act, not to interfere, and not to arrest – was necessary to overcome stereotypes about women and men and their interactions.

The power to arrest, of course, always carries some degree of discretion on the part of the individual police officer exercising the power. Discretion is necessary to carry out arrests safely, ensuring that neither police nor innocent bystanders are placed at risk. A degree of discretion is also necessary to determine whether in fact the arrest is warranted in any particular case. Thus, police notified that a protective order has been violated are required to engage in some process to determine whether the order has, in fact, been violated, and whether there was probable cause to arrest the violator or whether some other enforcement mechanism was more appropriate. The Colorado statute recognized that arrest in all cases might not be feasible and specified that officers were to "use every reasonable means to enforce the order." The discretion allowed by the statute, however, removed from possible law enforcement responses the ability to ignore alleged violations of protective orders and to refuse, delay, or ignore requests to enforce them. Thus, the limited police discretion the statute allows does not negate Ms. Gonzales's legitimate claim of entitlement to protection.

This is the harm that procedural due process redresses. If police may simply refuse to enforce the order without any process, then they undermine the Colorado legislature's intent.

Here, the Castle Rock police officers had discretion to determine whether the protective order had been violated; whether to arrest; whether to seek a warrant; and whether to use other reasonable means to enforce the order, including sending out an alert to all police to be on the lookout for Simon Gonzales. What the Colorado statute removed from the realm of police discretion was the power to ignore, delay, or simply not respond at all to the alleged violation. This express limit on law enforcement's ability to exercise discretion created a benefit for holders of protective orders. As the Tenth Circuit recognized, precedent demonstrates that this kind of interest constitutes a property interest for purposes of procedural due process.

C

Protective orders were only one part of the 1994 legislative changes, part of a "nationwide movement of States" to eliminate police discretion. Police under-enforcement of protective orders had various causes, "not least of which was the perception by police departments and police officers that domestic violence was a private, 'family' matter and that arrest was to be used as a last resort." Emily J. Sack, *Battered Women and the State: The Struggle for the Future of Domestic Violence Policy*, 2004 Wis. L. Rev. 1657, 1662–63.

Notwithstanding the enactment of federal and state reforms, persons at risk of intimate violence still face substantial resistance by police to enforcement.[18] At the dawn of the twenty-first century, some members of this Court recognized the seriousness of the problem of violence against women, and in particular the failure of local law enforcement to respond appropriately to this violence, in *United States v. Morrison*, 529 U.S. 598, 628–31 (Souter, J., dissenting). This resistance is what drove Colorado to enact its mandatory arrest statutory scheme. *See* Br. for Nat'l Network to End Domestic Violence *et al.* as Amici Curiae Supporting Resp't at 28 (domestic violence researchers concluded after exhaustive review that protective orders' "ultimate efficacy is often greatly compromised when police fail to arrest or prosecutors refuse to prosecute restraining order violations"); Br. for Nat'l Coal. Against Domestic Violence and Nat'l Ctr. for Victims of Crime as Amici Curiae Supporting Resp't at 11, 18 ("Mandatory arrest laws were enacted to combat one of the most serious obstacles to curtailing the epidemic of domestic violence in America – police indifference.") ("the Attorney General called for a 'strong, coordinated

---

[18]   Colorado, like many other states, *see* Br. for Family Violence Prevention Fund *et al.* as Amici Curiae Supporting Resp't at 14, determined that mandatory arrest was necessary to protect women and children when they are most at risk: when they are seeking to break away from the individual who poses a risk. To the extent that claims about personal autonomy and control are valid in the domestic violence context, they do not play a meaningful role when protective orders have been issued and served and when the beneficiary is seeking to enforce the order, as was the case here.

Town of Castle Rock v. Gonzales

effort by the criminal justice system' and issued a report recommending arrest as the standard response to all cases of misdemeanor domestic assault.").

At no time are women and children as much at risk from intimate violence as when they are trying to break away from a relationship, as in the case of Jessica Gonzales. A 2000 report, long available by the time this case came before this Court, found that married women who lived apart from their husbands were nearly four times more likely to report that their husbands had raped, physically assaulted, or stalked them than women who lived with their husbands. Patricia Tjaden and Nancy Thoennes, Nat'l Institute of Justice, NCJ 183781, *Full Report of the Prevalence, Incidence, and Consequence of Violence Against Women: Findings from the National Violence Against Women Survey* (2000). *See* Br. for Family Violence Prevention Fund *et al.* as Amici Curiae Supporting Resp't at 14–15 (citing Laura Crites and Donna Coker, *What Therapists See That Judges May Miss: A Unique Guide to Custody Decisions When Spouse Abuse is Charged*, 27 Judges' J. (1988)).

What few facts we know about this case illustrate the bias that is reflected in the officers' responses to Jessica Gonzales. The officers responded to Jessica Gonzales as if she had overreacted to the actions of the children's father although they were in violation of a protective order. The officers dismissed her concerns, despite the protective order and its express terms, not bothering to investigate, ascertain the exact terms of the order, or follow through on the facts as she communicated them to the officers. The officers assumed or decided that the children's father had a right to take the children, mid-week, without telling the custodial parent when and where he was taking the children, again despite the express terms of the order. Despite clear legal authority directing otherwise, these officers treated Jessica Gonzales's complaint and request for police enforcement as irrational, hysterical, unreasoned, not deserving of any care, consideration, investigation, or minimal follow through, even when the children had been missing well into the early hours of the morning.

These police officers, despite the statistics establishing that beneficiaries of protective orders are particularly at risk when seeking separation or divorce, responded to the protective order as if it were just a "boilerplate order," not deserving of serious, let alone special, enforcement. Def.'s Mot. to Dismiss, August 7, 2000; Def.'s Reply in Support of Mot. to Dismiss, September 15, 2000. The police responded to the escalating series of events as if they were immaterial to the corresponding expectations and duties that the protective order, and the mandatory arrest statute (in addition to the routine duties inherent in their police work), demanded of them. Instead, police officers subordinated Jessica Gonzales's and her children's state-created interests to established and long-standing perspectives informed by systemic gender bias. Colorado's efforts to thwart that subordination warrant respect. Police continue to enjoy some discretion under Colorado's approach, but discretion must be exercised consistently with state legislative priorities.

III

If we were writing on a clean slate, this case might have proceeded along very different lines. Had not systemic gender bias fueled by gender stereotypes produced gross gender inequities throughout the legal system and American society, domestic violence might not be the problem it is today, state legislatures like Colorado's might not have to resort to legislative "reforms" like the one at issue, and Jessica Gonzales might not have had to argue that a mandatory arrest protective order gave her a protected property interest that police arbitrarily deprived her of without giving her a meaningful opportunity to be heard. But we do not write on a clean slate; we write on a slate that reflects almost 150 years of entrenched legal norms that prohibited women's interests from being adequately represented and prohibited the direct participation of women in policy and legislative decision-making. We write on a slate that reflects more than 200 years of gender bias and inequality.

This Court credits the Colorado legislature's determination that protective orders have value. Colorado's legislature has spoken clearly, leaving no doubt as to its intentions. Violators of protective orders engage in public violence, and they and their victims come within the protections of the Due Process Clause. On remand, the lower court, applying *Matthews v. Eldridge*, 424 U.S. 319 (1976), should determine what process constitutes meaningful process. Under *Matthews*, the court must consider (1) the private interest that will be affected by the official action; (2) the risk of an erroneous deprivation of such interest through the procedures used, and the probable value, if any, of additional procedural safeguards; and (3) the government's interest, including the fiscal and administrative burdens that the additional or substitute procedures would entail. 424 U.S. at 332–35.

Plainly, Ms. Gonzales's interest in having the protective order enforced is an interest of the highest order, as it secured her own physical safety and that of her children from a threat the state had determined to be real and serious. Law enforcement's interest is the same as Ms. Gonzales's interest as the primary purpose of providing law enforcement is protection of the community and those individuals residing in it. Law enforcement's interest, however, encompasses providing safety to all residents, not just the Gonzales family, and the lower court must consider this as well. In balancing these interests with the costs of providing persons like Ms. Gonzales the process she was denied by the Castle Rock Police Department, the lower court may determine:

(1) Whether the police officers who responded to Ms. Gonzales's call initially (and in every response to Ms. Gonzales's contacts with the police department) read the protective order;

(2) Whether they determined whether Mr. Gonzales had violated the terms of the order;

(3) Whether they determined that there was probable cause to arrest Mr. Gonzales or made an effort to ascertain the children's wellbeing and whereabouts;

(4) What were the circumstances of Jessica Gonzales's children's death;

(5) Whether the Castle Rock Police Department developed policies responsive to Colorado's enactment of a statutory duty to "use every reasonable means to enforce this restraining order" and "arrest, or, if an arrest would be impractical under the circumstances, seek a warrant for the arrest of the restrained person when you have information amounting to probable cause that the restrained person has violated … any provision of this order";

(6) What policies were in place at the Castle Rock Police Department regarding enforcement of protective orders issued by state courts;

(7) Whether the Castle Rock Police Department provided training to its police officers and dispatch officers in the handling and enforcement of protective orders.

Colorado granted beneficiaries of protective orders a real and cognizable right to mandatory enforcement of a protective order lawfully issued by a state court that foreclosed the discretion of law enforcement to ignore or refuse to enforce the order. The Due Process Clause guarantees to beneficiaries of those protective orders meaningful process at the hands of law enforcement officers prior to deprivation of that interest. The judgment of the Court of Appeals for the Tenth Circuit is affirmed and the case remanded for further proceedings in accordance with this opinion.

It is so ordered.

27

Commentary on *Obergefell v. Hodges*

Erez Aloni

BACKGROUND

In *Obergefell v. Hodges*, decided in June 2015, the U.S. Supreme Court declared unconstitutional state laws in Ohio, Michigan, Kentucky, and Tennessee that defined marriage as a union between one man and one woman only.[1] In effect, this landmark decision legalized same-sex marriage nationwide. The case marks the final stage in a long and contested political and legal struggle to remove such marriage bans.

The first attempts to secure marriage rights through the judicial system date back to the early 1970s, when five same-sex couples filed lawsuits challenging a denial of marriage licenses.[2] Their lawsuits were denied. During the 1980s, the Lesbian Gay Bisexual and Transgender (LGBT) movement itself – mobilized by various legal and societal changes related to sexual relations, gender, and family – led a more organized campaign for legal recognition of same-sex relationships. Two events were particularly strong catalysts: the HIV/AIDS crisis and the "gayby-boom," in which lesbian mothers slammed up against the legal system in trying to secure parental rights.[3] At the time, however, the movement pursued marriage alternatives rather than the right to marry.

The marriage equality movement as we know it gained momentum after the Hawaii Supreme Court's 1993 decision in *Baehr v. Lewin*, the first in the United States that questioned the constitutionality of same-sex marriage bans.[4] (Due to a state constitutional referendum, same-sex marriage did not become

[1] *Obergefell v. Hodges*, 135 S. Ct. 2584 (2015).
[2] Michael Boucai, *Glorious Precedents: When Gay Marriage Was Radical*, 27 Yale J.L. & Human. 101, 102 (2015).
[3] George Chauncey, Why Marriage? The History Shaping Today's Debate over Gay Equality 96–100 (2004).
[4] *Baehr v. Lewin*, 852 P.2d 44 (Haw. 1993).

available in Hawaii.) The *Baehr* decision created a serious political backlash that led to passage of the federal Defense of Marriage Act (DOMA), a law that defined marriage, for federal purposes, as between a man and a woman only.[5]

Despite such hostility, the marriage equality movement made progress, with Massachusetts, in 2003, becoming the first state to legalize same-sex marriage.[6] Following Massachusetts, some states repealed their restrictions on same-sex marriage by either court decision (Iowa, Connecticut) or legislation (Vermont, New York). However, because of DOMA, couples could only enjoy state benefits attendant to marriage, not federal ones.

The tipping point was *United States v. Windsor*, where the U.S. Supreme Court invalidated section 3 of DOMA, ordering the federal government to recognize same-sex marriages performed in states that allow it.[7] Following *Windsor*, marriage equality advocates successfully litigated in four federal circuit courts but lost in the Sixth Circuit.[8] The U.S. Supreme Court took that case – which is *Obergefell*.

ORIGINAL OPINION

In *Obergefell*, the Court's majority decision, written by Justice Kennedy, held that same-sex marriage bans violate the Fourteenth Amendment's Equal Protection and Due Process Clauses, and that states must recognize same-sex marriages entered into in other states.

The majority noted that the right to marry is a fundamental right. While past precedents involving such right had been applied only to opposite-sex couples, the Court found that their underlying premises are also applicable to same-sex couples. The Court noted that four premises make the right to marry fundamental: First, the decision to marry reflects individual autonomy which holds true for all couples. Second, marriage "supports a two-person union unlike any other in its importance to the committed individuals."[9] Same-sex couples, like opposite-sex couples, wish to enjoy this freedom in their intimate relationships. Third, marriage as an institution provides stability and dignity to parents and their children. Same-sex parents are capable parents and deserve the familial safeguards that marriage confers. Fourth, because marriage is a keystone of society, many rights, benefits, and protections are attendant on

---

[5]   Defense of Marriage Act (DOMA), Pub. L. No. 104–199, 110 Stat. 2419 (1996) (codified at 28 U.S.C. § 1738C (2012) and 1U.S.C. § 7).
[6]   *Goodridge v. Dep't. of Pub. Health*, 798 N.E.2d 941 (Mass. 2003).
[7]   *United States v. Windsor*, 133 S. Ct. 2675 (2013).
[8]   *DeBoer v. Snyder*, 772 F.3d 388 (6th Cir. 2014).
[9]   *Obergefell v. Hodges*, 135 S. Ct. at 2599.

marriage. Thus, excluding same-sex couples from all these benefits treats them unequally and violates the Due Process Clause.

The Court then recognized that liberty and equality interests are interconnected and that same-sex marriage bans also "abridge central principles of equality."[10] The majority stated that, especially in light of past discrimination against LGBT individuals, the denial of marriage is grave. However, it did not conduct a traditional analysis of equal protection; it did not indicate whether sexual orientation is a suspect classification, whether same-sex marriage bans constitute sex-based discrimination, and which level of review it used to examine states' interests in marriage bans.

Each dissenting Justice (Roberts, Scalia, Thomas, Alito) filed a separate, angry dissent. They all mourned what they viewed as the majority's acting like super-legislators rather than judges, noting that the decision should have been left to the democratic process.

THE FEMINIST JUDGMENT

For many feminists, *Obergefell* is a double-edged sword. While the decision is a cause for celebration – as same-sex marriage bans are grounded in homophobia, heterosexism, and preservation of traditional gender roles – at the same time, the majority opinion used rhetoric that stigmatizes people in non-marital unions. Moreover, the majority did not adopt a legal theory that will be sufficient for defending women and sexual minorities in future battles. The feminist opinion of Professor Carlos Ball, writing as Justice Ball, blunts some of the sharpest edges of the *Obergefell* sword, showing a way to expand the rights of one group without cost to others. He adopts feminist methodology that uses social science, personal narratives, and emotions to persuade and to challenge stereotypes about biological sex, gender, and sexual orientation. In some parts of his opinion, Ball uses verbatim parts of Justice Kennedy's original opinion to achieve this goal.

Feminism has had a complex relationship with marriage and with the campaign for marriage equality. Marriage's roots in patriarchy and subordination of women have made many feminists skeptical of the wisdom of securing marriage rights for same-sex couples.[11] Even today, unmarried individuals continue to be stigmatized.[12] Thus, some feminists have argued that even if same-sex

---

[10] *Id.* at 2604.

[11] Paula L. Ettelbrick, *Since When Is Marriage a Path to Liberation?*, OUT/LOOK, Fall 1989, at 14.

[12] Erez Aloni, *Registering Relationships*, 87 *Tul. L. Rev.* 573, 619–21 (2013).

marriage bans are unfair, it does not follow that pursuing access to a flawed institution like marriage furthers a just cause.[13] However, other feminists have argued that "elimination of marriage's gender roles is one of marriage equality opponents' worst fears" and that bans derive from the desire to preserve traditional gender specialization.[14] Yet others have criticized the efforts invested in securing marriage equality rather than more imaginative alternatives that will end marriage monopoly.[15]

Unfortunately, the original majority opinion in *Obergefell* adopts a vision of marriage that disparages people who live outside marriage ("No union is more profound than marriage").[16] The opinion includes this attention-getting sentence: "Marriage responds to the universal fear that a lonely person might call out only to find no one there,"[17] implying that married people cannot be lonely or single people cannot flourish.[18] Dismayingly, the Court states that children who live with unmarried parents can "suffer the stigma of knowing their families are somehow lesser."[19]

Ball's opinion strongly rejects this vision. He states that "marriage is [not] the only or, depending on individual circumstances, even the best way of ordering familial and intimate relationships." Moreover, he dismantles some myths about the importance of marriage and traditional gender roles to children's well-being, asserting that no evidence supports the argument that sexual orientation matters in this regard. Ball also responds to the "optimal family" argument that the biological connection between the parents provides the ideal connection to the child. He states that same-sex marriage bans based on such reasoning are discriminatory (the state does not mandate that only "optimal parents" may have children). Further, he presents research finding that mothers and fathers can provide the same love and care to their children, and that categories of "motherhood" and "fatherhood" are largely socially constructed.

Ball's opinion also blunts a crucial sharp edge of the original opinion: its cursory handling of the equal protection argument – especially threatening in light of Chief Justice Roberts's dissent, in which he argued, "[i]n short, our Constitution does not enact any one theory of marriage. The people of a

[13] Claudia Card, *Against Marriage and Motherhood*, 11 Hypatia 1–23 (1996).

[14] Barbara J. Cox, *Marriage Equality is Both Feminist and Progressive*, 17 Rich. J.L. & Pub. Int. 707, 711 (2014); Mary Anne Case, *What Feminists Have to Lose in Same-Sex Marriage Litigation*, 57 UCLA L. Rev. 1199, 1223–24 (2010).

[15] Katherine M. Franke, *Longing for Loving*, 76 Fordham L. Rev. 2685, 2686–87 (2008).

[16] *Obergefell v. Hodges*, 135 S. Ct. at 2594.

[17] *Id.* at 2600.

[18] Bella DePaulo, *Singled Out: How Singles Are Stereotyped, Stigmatized, and Ignored, and Still Live Happily Ever After* (2006).

[19] *Obergefell v. Hodges*, 135 S. Ct. at 2590.

State are free to expand marriage to include same-sex couples, or to retain the historic definition."[20] A reasonable reading of his argument is that states can change marriage laws even in ways that disfavor women – for example, they could reenact fault divorce or even coverture.

Ball's decision remedies the silence of the original opinion's majority. His analysis finds that same-sex marriage bans constitute unjustified sex classifications because they are "predicated on traditional gender role expectations." Following Ball's analysis, it is clear that the Constitution prevents states from adopting a marriage vision grounded in a stereotypical understanding of gender roles. Ball thus echoes the feminist position that same-sex marriage bans leave opposite-sex couples with "an institution reserved for them alone because of and not in spite of its 'traditional' (that is to say, patriarchal) significance."[21] In fact, Ball goes one step further, adopting another feminist position: he expresses hope that inclusion of same-sex couples in marriage will transform marriage by lessening gender norms that are strongly attendant to it.[22]

Further, Ball finds that same-sex marriage bans constitute an impermissible sexual-orientation classification. In so doing, he adjudicates an issue that the Court has failed to rule on in a series of past decisions: whether sexual orientation-based classifications are subject to a heightened level of review. In analyzing whether sexual orientation is a suspect classification, Ball is cautious not to fall into the trap of saying that immutability and lack of political power are essential elements in finding such classification. Indeed, some gay-rights advocates have argued that sexual orientation is immutable – or, that it is at core a trait that one should not be asked to change – and thus deserves recognition as a suspect classification.[23] However, legal scholars have criticized the use of immutability, in part because it transfers the power to decide who deserves the law's protection from the political arena to science and ignores questions of agency and choice.[24]

Ball's opinion clarifies that immutability is not a dispositive factor in deciding what group receives the safeguards of the Equal Protection Clause. In dicta, he notes that, as we learned from the transgender rights movement, it is not clear whether gender is an immutable trait – and yet gender classifications

---

[20] *Id.* at 2611.

[21] Case, *supra* note 14, at 1223.

[22] Nan D. Hunter, *Marriage, Law, and Gender: A Feminist Inquiry*, 1 *Law & Sexuality* 2 (1991); Cox, *supra* note 14 at 710–21.

[23] Jessica A. Clarke, *Against Immutability*, 125 *Yale L. J.* 18–21 (2015).

[24] Janet Halley, *Sexual Orientation and the Politics of Biology: A Critique of the Argument from Immutability*, 46 *Stan L. Rev.* 503, 550–53 (1994).

merit heightened scrutiny. In so doing, he also opens the door to future claims by LGBT individuals.

A few weeks after the Court's decision in *Obergefell*, Justice Ginsburg stated that she did not write a separate opinion because "it was more powerful to have a single opinion."[25] She added that had she written the opinion herself, however, she would have spent more pages explaining an equal protection rationale. In this feminist judgment, Ball pens the opinion that Justice Ginsburg wished to write.

Obergefell v. Hodges, 135 S. Ct. 2584 (2015)

Justice Carlos A. Ball delivered the opinion of the Court.

These consolidated cases raise two questions regarding the constitutionality of same-sex marriage bans: first, whether they violate the Equal Protection Clause of the Fourteenth Amendment; second, whether they violate the liberty protections afforded by the Due Process Clause of that amendment. We answer both questions in the affirmative, as we did in striking down interracial marriage bans almost fifty years ago. *See Loving v. Virginia*, 388 U.S. 1, 12 (1967).

I

As a result of the decades-long political and legal campaigns in favor of marriage equality, the nation has become familiar with the love and commitment that are part of same-sex relationships and families headed by lesbians, gay men, bisexual, and transgender (LGBT) individuals. It might be tempting, therefore, to bypass the Petitioners' individual circumstances in order to address the constitutional questions in these types of disputes, which, as a result of many thoughtful judicial opinions by lower courts, are by now well-framed. But it would be a mistake not to elaborate on at least some of the Petitioners' relationships. There is a tendency in the law to relegate considerations of love and affection to the sphere of emotions, one that is distinct and separate from the law's purported rationality and objectivity. But as several scholars have pointed out, it is important for the law and for considerations of justice generally, to account for the role that emotions play in our lives and aspirations. *See, e.g.*, Kathryn Abrams and Hila Keren, *Who is Afraid of Law and Emotions?*, 99 Minn. L. Rev. 1997 (2010); Martha M. Ertman, *Love's*

---

[25] Mark Joseph Stern, *Ruth Bader Ginsburg Reveals How She Would Have Written the Marriage Equality Decision*, Slate, July 30, 2015.

Promises: How Formal and Informal Contracts Shape All Kinds of Families (2015); Martha C. Nussbaum, *Political Emotions: Why Love Matters for Justice* (2013).

These cases come to us because of the deep love and commitment that the Petitioners, like millions of LGBT people across the country, share with their partners. As a factual matter, the Petitioners' equality and due process claims are grounded in that love and commitment. It was not too long ago that the country's laws and social norms consistently treated sexual and gender-identity minorities as deviant and immoral individuals who were incapable of building healthy, lasting, and committed relationships.

It bears emphasis that, until relatively recently, the state in most Western nations condemned same-sex intimacy as immoral, a belief often embodied in the criminal law. For this reason, among others, many persons did not deem LGBT individuals to have dignity in their own distinct identity. A truthful declaration by same-sex couples of what was in their hearts had to remain unspoken. Even when a greater awareness of the humanity and integrity of LGBT persons came in the period after World War II, the argument that sexual minorities had a just claim to dignity was in conflict with both law and widespread social conventions.

This Court, unfortunately, contributed to the promotion of such biased and prejudiced views when it upheld the constitutionality of laws that targeted the consensual sexual intimacy of lesbians, gay men, and bisexuals by contending that there was no connection between that intimacy, on the one hand, and family, parenting, and marriage, on the other. *See Bowers v. Hardwick*, 478 U.S. 186, 191 (1986) ("No connection between family, marriage, or procreation on the one hand and homosexual activity on the other has been demonstrated ... "). The strong, committed, and loving nature of the Petitioners' relationships is further confirmation of our conclusion in *Lawrence v. Texas*, 539 U.S. 558, 578 (2003), that *Hardwick* "was not correct [from the moment] it was decided."

Petitioner James Obergefell, a plaintiff in the Ohio case, met John Arthur over two decades ago. They fell in love and started a life together, establishing a lasting, committed relationship. In 2011, however, Arthur was diagnosed with amyotrophic lateral sclerosis, or ALS. This debilitating disease is progressive, with no known cure. Two years ago, Obergefell and Arthur decided to commit to one another, resolving to marry before Arthur died. To fulfill their mutual promise, they traveled from Ohio to Maryland, where same-sex marriage was legal. It was difficult for Arthur to move, and so the couple were wed inside a medical transport plane as it remained on the tarmac in Baltimore. Three months later, Arthur died. Ohio law does not permit Obergefell to be listed as the surviving spouse on Arthur's death certificate. By statute, they must remain strangers even in death, a state-imposed separation Obergefell deems "hurtful for the rest of time." He brought suit to be shown as the surviving spouse on Arthur's death certificate.

April DeBoer and Jayne Rowse are co-plaintiffs in the case from Michigan. They celebrated a commitment ceremony to honor their permanent relationship in 2007. They both work as nurses, DeBoer in a neonatal unit and Rowse in an emergency unit. In 2009, DeBoer and Rowse fostered and then adopted a baby boy. Later that same year, they welcomed another son into their family. The new baby, born prematurely and abandoned by his biological mother, required around-the-clock care. The next year, a baby girl with special needs joined their family. Michigan, however, permits only opposite-sex married couples or single individuals to adopt, so each child can have only one woman as his or her legal parent. If an emergency were to arise, schools and hospitals may treat the three children as if they had only one parent. Were tragedy to befall either DeBoer or Rowse, the other would have no legal rights over the children she had not been permitted to adopt. This couple seeks relief from the continuing uncertainty their unmarried status creates in their lives.

Army Reserve Sergeant First Class Ijpe DeKoe and his partner Thomas Kostura, co-plaintiffs in the Tennessee case, fell in love. In 2011, DeKoe received orders to deploy to Afghanistan. Before leaving, he and Kostura married in New York. A week later, DeKoe began his deployment, which lasted for almost a year. When he returned, the two settled in Tennessee, where DeKoe works full-time for the Army Reserve. Their lawful marriage is stripped from them whenever they reside in Tennessee, returning and disappearing as they travel across state lines. DeKoe, who served this nation to preserve the freedom the Constitution protects, must endure a substantial burden.

II

The Petitioners argue that same-sex marriage bans violate the Equal Protection Clause, and we agree. The bans impermissibly classify individuals on the basis of both sex and sexual orientation in violation of that Clause because the state lacks a sufficiently important interest justifying the classifications.

A

There are two different ways in which the marriage bans at issue classify individuals according to sex. First, as a formal matter, whether the bans restrict the ability of individuals to marry depends on their gender. *See Baehr v. Lewin*, 852 P.2d 44 (Ha. 1993). For example, if Petitioner Obergefell had married a woman in Maryland and she had subsequently passed away, Ohio would have listed Obergefell as a spouse on the death certificate. The only reason Ohio refused to recognize Obergefell's marriage to Arthur was because the latter was a man. Clearly, the state took the sex of the deceased into account in refusing to add Obergefell's name to the certificate.

But the marriage bans constitute sex classifications in other crucial, and more historically relevant, ways. For much of the nation's history, marriage, as a matter of law and social expectations, has been a highly gendered institution. Under the common law doctrine of coverture, women's legal and economic identities were subsumed into those of their husbands, leaving the latter with almost complete control over the lives and legal standing of the former. *See generally* Norma Basch, *Invisible Women: The Legal Fiction of Marital Unity in Nineteenth-Century America*, 5 Feminist Stud. 346 (1979); Hendrik Hartog, *Man and Wife in America: A History* (2000); Joan Hoff, *Law, Gender, and Injustice: A Legal History of U.S. Women* (1991). Under the doctrine, wives were expected to serve and obey their husbands, while the latter were expected to support their wives and children. This legally enforceable understanding of spousal roles was based on a socially imposed sexual division of labor, through which men were assumed to be naturally capable of being good providers and women purportedly destined to care for the home and children. This division of labor, and the social expectations that supported it, remained firmly in place decades into the twentieth century.

Notwithstanding the gradual erosion of the doctrine of coverture, invidious sex-based classifications in marriage remained common through the mid-twentieth century. *See* Br. for Appellant at 69–88 (providing an extensive reference to laws extant as of 1971 treating women as unequal to men in marriage). These classifications denied the equal dignity of men and women. One state's law, for example, provided in 1971 that "the husband is the head of the family and the wife is subject to him; her legal civil existence is merged in the husband, except so far as the law recognizes her separately, either for her own protection, or for her benefit." Ga. Code Ann. § 53–501 (1935). Responding to a new awareness, the Court invoked equal protection principles to invalidate laws imposing sex-based inequality on marriage. *See, e.g., Califano v. Westcott*, 443 U.S. 76 (1979); *Orr v. Orr*, 440 U.S. 268 (1979); *Califano v. Goldfarb*, 430 U.S. 199 (1977) (plurality opinion); *Weinberger v. Wiesenfeld*, 420 U.S. 636 (1975); *Frontiero v. Richardson*, 411 U.S. 677 (1973). These precedents show the importance of the Equal Protection Clause in identifying and correcting inequalities in the institution of marriage.

It is against this legal and social backdrop that we must assess the claim that same-sex marriage bans constitute sex classifications. Same-sex relationships question the gender-based expectations, often enforced through law, which have traditionally applied to (and within) the institution of marriage. Our society has traditionally had fixed, rigid, and stereotyped understandings of marital roles as tied to gender. The relationships of same-sex couples challenge those understandings of marriage because they resist the allocation of roles and expectations according to gender.

The notion that marital unions must be between a man and a woman is predicated on traditional gender-role expectations which reject the idea that a marital union can ever be formed by two husbands or two wives. From this perspective, for a union to be marital, there must be a spouse who carries out the male role and another who carries out the female role. Individuals with same-sex sexual orientations, through their relationships and forms of intimacy, question (or, depending on one's point of view, "threaten") this gendered understanding of marriage. Much of the discrimination aimed at sexual minorities is grounded in the notion that, in having sexual relationships with, and in some cases, wanting to marry, someone of the same sex, lesbians fail to act in the way "real women" should and gay men fail to act in the way "real men" should. *See* Andrew Koppelman, *Why Discrimination Against Lesbians and Gay Men is Sex Discrimination*, 69 N.Y.U. L. Rev. 197 (1994); Sylvia Law, *Homosexuality and the Social Meaning of Gender*, 1988 Wis. L. Rev. 187. It is clear to us, therefore, that prohibiting two men or two women from marrying constitutes a gender-based restriction that must be subjected to heightened judicial scrutiny.

B

The marriage bans challenged in these cases also constitute sexual orientation classifications. It has been argued that the marriage bans are sexual-orientation neutral because they do not explicitly take sexuality into account. As the brief on behalf of the Respondent Governor of Kentucky puts it, "[m]en and women, whether heterosexual or homosexual, are free to marry persons of the opposite sex under Kentucky law, and men and women, whether heterosexual or homosexual, cannot marry persons of the same sex under Kentucky law." Br. for Resp't at 26, *Bourke v. Beshear*, 996 F. Supp. 2d 542 (2014) (No. 14–574), 2015 WL 1384105. We reject this highly formalistic, and unrealistic, analysis. The marriage bans at issue in these cases did not aim to prevent heterosexuals from entering into same-sex marriages. Instead, the bans were clearly aimed at "defending" heterosexual marriage from the "threats" presented by the quest by same-sex couples to gain the opportunity to marry. As a result, the bans, as a matter of intent, purpose, and effect, classify on the basis of sexual orientation.

For the last twenty years, this Court has bypassed the opportunity to decide whether sexual orientation classifications merit heightened scrutiny under the Equal Protection Clause. *See United States v. Windsor*, 133 S. Ct. 2675 (2013); *Lawrence*, 539 U.S. 558; *Romer v. Evans*, 517 U.S. 620 (1996). We will bypass no more.

Our case law has consistently relied on two factors to determine whether particular classifications merit heightened scrutiny. These factors are whether the group affected by the classification in question has suffered a long history of invidious discrimination, *see, e.g., United States v. Virginia*, 518 U.S. 515, 531–32 (1996), *Mass. Bd. of Ret. v. Murgia*, 427 U.S. 307, 313 (1976), and whether the trait at issue affects the ability of individuals to perform in or contribute to society. *See, e.g., City of Cleburne v. Cleburne Living Ctr., Inc.*, 473 U.S. 432, 440–41 (1985); *Frontiero*, 411 U.S. at 686. There is little dispute that lesbians and gay men have suffered decades of *de jure* and *de facto* discrimination in our society. *See, e.g., Rowland v. Mad River Local School Dist.*, 470 U.S. 1009, 1014 (1985) (Brennan, J., dissenting from denial of cert.); *Kerrigan v. Comm'r of Pub. Health*, 957 A.2d 407, 433–34 (Conn. 2008); *Varnum v. Brien*, 763 N.W.2d 862, 889–90 (Iowa 2009); *Conaway v. Deane*, 932 A.2d 571, 609–11 (Md. 2007); *Andersen v. King County*, 138 P.3d 963, 974 (Wash. 2006). In addition, the millions of LGBT Americans who, among many other activities, serve as elected officials and jurors, lead corporations, teach at universities, vote and participate in political campaigns, and provide for their families make crystal clear that neither sexual orientation nor gender identity affects the ability of individuals to participate in or contribute to society. *See, e.g., Watkins v. U.S. Army*, 847 F.2d 1329, 1346 (9th Cir. 1988), *opinion withdrawn on reh'g by* 875 F.2d 699 (9th Cir. 1989); *Kerrigan*, 957 A.2d at 434–35; *Varnum*, 763 N.W.2d at 890–92.

Some state courts have concluded that sexual orientation classifications do not merit heightened scrutiny under their state constitutions because sexual orientation may not be immutable and because sexual minorities today have more political power than they did in previous decades. *See, e.g., Conaway*, 932 A.2d at 611–616; *Andersen*, 138 P.3d at 974. Since these courts have sought to follow this Court's analysis for determining when heightened scrutiny is appropriate under the Equal Protection Clause, it is necessary to clarify that neither immutability nor a lack of political power must be established under the Constitution before heightened scrutiny is applied.

It is true that this Court, on some occasions, has addressed considerations of immutability and political power in addressing the question of judicial scrutiny under the Equal Protection Clause. *See, e.g., Bowen v. Gilliard*, 483

U.S. 587, 602 (1987); *Lyng v. Castillo*, 477 U.S. 635, 638 (1986). However, on reflection, it is clear that neither of these factors is dispositive of the heightened scrutiny issue. There are some traits that call for heightened scrutiny despite the fact that they are not immutable. As the nation has learned from the transgender rights movement, one of those traits is gender itself. Before transgender people began coming out of the closet, whether individuals were "male" or "female" was understood to depend entirely on their biological sex. We now know that the concept of gender is less fixed than we once believed, in part because there can be a wide gulf between biological sex (as determined by chromosomes) and the ways in which individuals view and define themselves according to gender. *See M.T. v. J.T.*, 355 A.2d 204 (N.J. Super. Ct. App. Div. 1976). Indeed, the fluidity (or indeterminacy) of sex as a classification is reflected in laws and regulations allowing individuals to change their sex as set forth in legal documents such as birth certificates and drivers' licenses. *See, e.g.*, N.J. Stat. Ann. § 26:8–40.12 (2006); 18 Vt. Stat. Ann. tit. 18 § 5112 (2011). *See also* Dean Spade, *Documenting Gender*, 59 Hastings L.J. 731 (2008). It is not at all clear, therefore, that sex is an immutable characteristic, and yet sex classifications merit heightened scrutiny. *See also Nyquist v. Mauclet*, 432 U.S. 1, 9 n.11 (1977) (holding that alienage classifications are subject to heightened scrutiny despite the ability of some non-citizens to naturalize).

It is also clear that gains in political power do not preclude heightened judicial scrutiny. Racial minorities and women have enjoyed increased political power over the last few decades, and yet both race and sex classifications are still subject to heightened scrutiny. Furthermore, although it cannot be claimed that either men or whites lack political power in our society, the Constitution nonetheless affords them the protections of heightened scrutiny. *See Kerrigan*, 957 A.2d 407 at 441 ("[H]eightened scrutiny is applied to statutes that discriminate against men and against Caucasians.") (citation omitted).

It is therefore inappropriate to focus on either immutability or political power in determining whether sexual orientation classifications merit heightened judicial scrutiny. The fact that sexual minorities have been the victims of decades of discrimination and prejudice and that sexual orientation does not affect the ability of individuals to participate in or contribute to society requires that sexual orientation classifications be subject, at least, to the same degree of judicial scrutiny afforded to sex classifications. As we have explained, under that standard,

> the reviewing court must determine whether the proffered justification is "exceedingly persuasive." The burden of justification is demanding and it rests entirely on the State. The State must show "at least that the

[challenged] classification serves important governmental objectives and that the discriminatory means employed are substantially related to the achievement of those objectives." The justification must be genuine, not hypothesized or invented *post hoc* in response to litigation. And it must not rely on overbroad generalizations about the different talents, capacities, or preferences of males and females.
    United States v. Virginia, 518 U.S. at 533 (internal citations omitted).

Since the Respondents, as explained next, cannot meet their burden under that standard, we leave for another day the question of whether sexual orientation classifications merit the type of strict scrutiny afforded to racial classifications.

C

The Respondents offer only one governmental interest in support of the marital bans challenged in these cases. That interest is helpfully summarized by one of our dissenting colleagues: "States formalize and promote marriage, unlike other fulfilling human relationships, in order to encourage potentially procreative conduct to take place within a lasting unit that has long been thought to provide the best atmosphere for raising children." 133 S. Ct. at 2641 (Alito, J., dissenting).

At its core, this purported state interest is grounded in the notion that the gender and sexual orientation of parents help to create "the best atmosphere for raising children." *Id.* Yet, there is simply no empirical evidence to support the notion that either the gender or the sexual orientation of parents impacts the well-being of children. There is an overwhelming consensus among experts that lesbians and gay men are able to provide their children with the types of caring and nurturing environments that are conducive to children's well-being. *See, e.g.,* Br. for Am. Sociological Ass'n as Amicus Curiae in Support of Pet'rs at 5–14. In short, neither the gender nor sexual orientation of individuals affects their ability to be good parents. To ground marital restrictions on the premise that having parents of certain genders or sexual orientations is crucial for creating "the best atmosphere for raising children" is to base policies on precisely the types of stereotypical assumptions that this Court has found impermissible under the Equal Protection Clause. *See Mississippi Univ. for Women v. Hogan,* 458 U.S. 718 (1982); *Stanton v. Stanton,* 421 U.S. 7 (1975); *Weinberger,* 420 U.S. at 636.

The Respondents' justifications for the marriage bans rely, rather vaguely, on considerations of so-called family optimality. *See, e.g.,* Br. for State of Alabama

in Support of Resp'ts at 3 (defending constitutionality of "man-woman marriage laws" by contending that "States have a legitimate interest in promoting
ties of kinship between children and both of their biological parents because,
in general, those parents together are best suited to provide *optimal* care for
their children.") (emphasis added). From this perspective, households led by
married mothers and fathers who are biologically related to their children constitute the "optimal" family structure for children. *Id.* But it is constitutionally
untenable for the state to raise "optimality" concerns in denying one group
of individuals the opportunity to marry, but not others. The Equal Protection
Clause does not permit the state to promote family "optimality" by targeting
only one class of individuals, in this case lesbians, gay men, and bisexuals.

To illustrate this point, we note that some social science studies suggest, for
example, that children raised by two high-income parents do better in school
than children raised by two low-income parents. *See, e.g.,* Greg J. Duncan,
Pamela A. Morris and Chris Rodrigues, *Does Money Really Matter?
Estimating Impacts of Family Income on Young Children's Achievement with
Data from Random-Assignment Experiments,* 47 Dev. Psychol. 1263 (2011).
Studies also suggest that children raised by parents with more education do
better in school and have fewer behavioral problems than do children of parents with less education. *See, e.g.,* Pamela E. Davis-Kean, *The Influence of
Parent Education and Family Income on Child Achievement: The Indirect Role
of Parental Expectations and the Home Environment,* 19 J. Fam. Psychol. 294
(2005). It could be claimed, therefore, that high-income households in which
parents are highly educated constitute the "optimal" setting for the raising
of children. Yet Respondents do not contend that marriage should be limited to high-income individuals or to those with college degrees. Such social
engineering through marriage eligibility rules would clearly be misguided,
because it would be inconsistent with the intuitive point, supported by the
social science evidence, that there are many factors that account for child outcomes, including not only parental income and education, but also the quality of parent-child relationships, the level of parental care and involvement,
and the child's own abilities and temperament. *See, e.g.,* Michael E. Lamb,
*Mothers, Fathers, Families, and Circumstances: Factors Affecting Children's
Adjustment,* 16 Applied Develop. Sci. 98 (2012). In addition, establishing marriage eligibility rules on the basis of parental income and education considerations would ignore the fact that millions of parents with limited income
and education provide their children with nurturing and caring homes in
which they thrive. It matters constitutionally, therefore, that the Respondents
are seeking to promote so-called family optimality only at the expense of the
interests of same-sex couples and their children.

It bears noting that this Court, in applying the Equal Protection Clause, has rejected the use of family optimality claims to justify the differential treatment of children born out of wedlock. In *Levy v. Louisiana*, 391 U.S. 68 (1968), the Court assessed the constitutionality of a Louisiana law that allowed children to sue in tort for the wrongful deaths of their mothers, but only if those children were born within marriages. The state in *Levy* claimed it was appropriate to deny legal benefits to children born outside of marriage in order to promote its understanding of family optimality. According to the state, "superior rights of legitimate offspring are inducements or incentives to parties to contract marriage, which is preferred by Louisiana as the setting for producing offspring." Br. of Att'y Gen., State of Louisiana, *Levy v. Louisiana*, 391 U.S. 68 (1968), at 4–5.

This Court in *Levy* rejected the state's reasoning, concluding that treating nonmarital children differently was a form of invidious discrimination. *Levy*, 391 U.S. at 71–72. The Court pointed out that those children, when they became adults, had the same legal obligations as everyone else, and yet the state denied them rights and benefits enjoyed by their fellow citizens. Such differential treatment was prohibited by the constitutional mandate requiring equal protection for all. *Id.*

In addition, this Court in *Weber v. Aetna Casualty & Surety Company* addressed the constitutionality of a statute that denied workmen compensation benefits to the nonmarital children of employees. *Weber*, 406 U.S. 164 (1972). We held in *Weber* that whatever interests the government might have in promoting marriage and discouraging the birth of nonmarital children, they were not advanced by denying workmen compensation benefits to those children. This Court found it irrational to believe people would "shun illicit relations" because their children might someday be denied access to particular benefits. *Id.* at 173. Our rulings involving nonmarital children, therefore, make clear that it is constitutionally impermissible to promote so-called family optimality by targeting certain classes of individuals for differential treatment.

In addition to questions of impermissible targeting, the family optimality argument is constructed on troubling notions of gender determinism, that is, on the idea that female parents *because they are women* are able to provide children with certain benefits that male parents *because they are men* are incapable of providing, and vice versa. For example, one of the *amici* briefs supporting the Respondents claims that "[i]n general, mothers have a natural capacity for interacting with their infant children in a way that provides precisely the right amount of stimulation required for the proper development of the infant's brain at any given time." Br. for Org. and Scholars of Gender-Diverse Parenting as Amici Curiae at 5. The brief adds that "[f]athers, in contrast, contribute to cognitive development by virtue of their more hands-off and facilitative parenting style." *Id.*

In assessing the purported connection between gender and parenting capabilities, it is crucial to keep in mind the troubling ways that claims about the "natural" differences between men and women were used in the past to support gender hierarchy, privilege, and subordination. *See, e.g.,* Lucinda M. Finley, *Sex Blind, Separate but Equal, or Anti-Subordination?: The Uneasy Legacy of* Plessy v. Ferguson *for Sex and Gender Discrimination*, 12 Ga. St. U. L. Rev. 1089 (1996). The notion that women are, in effect, hardwired to nurture children and that men are intrinsically more "hands-off" parents is unfortunately consistent with stereotyped notions of what women and men are each capable of accomplishing because of their gender. For the last several decades, our society has progressively moved away from setting policies grounded in gender stereotyping in recognition of the immense harm it has caused both women and men through the generations.

In some ways, parenting abilities and influences may be the last frontier in the necessary effort to discredit notions of biologically determined differences between men and women that purportedly translate into distinct capabilities in performing important social tasks. It therefore bears emphasizing that the differences between how mothers and fathers parent are not as great as is sometimes assumed. A review of studies on the differences between male and female parents found that both groups overlapped considerably in parental attributes and that there was little or no evidence of categorical differences between the two. *See* Bobbi J. Carothers and Harry T. Reis, *Men and Women Are from Earth: Examining the Latent Structure of Gender*, 104 J. Personality & Soc. Psychol. 385 (2013). Although it is possible to find some average differences in discrete activities between fathers and mothers (some studies suggest, for example, that fathers seem to spend a greater proportion of parental time on rough-and-tumble play, *see, e.g.,* Kevin MacDonald and Ross D. Parke, *Bridging the Gap: Parent-Child Play Interaction and Peer Interactive Competence*, 55 Child Dev. 1265 (1984)), examination of a wider set of capabilities and responsibilities finds many more similarities than differences between female and male parents. As child psychologist Michael Lamb, in reviewing the social science literature studying father-child interactions, notes,

> it is now well established that both men and women have the capacity to be good parents. Both parents are physiologically prepared for and changed by parenthood. New mothers and fathers are equivalently competent (or incompetent) at parenting, with most parenting skills learned "on the job." ... It is clear ... that mothers and fathers influence children's development in the

same non-gendered ways – promoting psychological adjustment when they are caring, loving, engaged, and authoritative.

Lamb, supra, at 101.

It is not at all surprising, in a society in which men are still expected to be the primary breadwinners and women the main caretakers of children, that fathers spend less time with their children (and that when they do, they spend a higher percentage of that time playing) and mothers spend more time with them and are therefore usually more involved in caretaking activities. But this does not mean that there is something about male parents that is intrinsically different from female parents (or vice versa). Indeed, the fact that the levels of parental involvement by gender vary across time and cultures significantly undermines the contention that humans are somehow biologically destined to carry out different parental responsibilities depending on their gender. *See* Elizabeth H. Pleck, *Two Dimensions of Fatherhood: A History of the Good Dad – Bad Dad Complex, in The Role of the Father in Child Development* 32 (Michael E. Lamb ed., 4th ed. 2004); Elizabeth H. Pleck and Joseph H. Pleck, *Fatherhood Ideals in the United States: Historical Dimensions, in The Role of the Father in Child Development* 33 (Michael E. Lamb ed., 3d ed. 1997); Catherine S. Tamis-LeMonda, *Conceptualizing Fathers' Roles: Playmates and More,* 47 Human Dev. 220 (2004).

In short, the Respondents have not offered any evidence that lesbians, gay men, and bisexuals are unable to provide their children with caring and nurturing homes that are conducive to their well-being. In addition, the Respondents' selective use of the family optimality claim to justify depriving only one group of individuals (sexual minorities) of the opportunity to marry the individuals of their choice strongly suggests that the purpose behind the claim is to target that group rather than promote children's well-being. Finally, optimality arguments are grounded in troubling and stereotypical notions that link the contributions of mothers and fathers to "natural" differences between the sexes. As a result, we find that the Respondents have failed to meet their burden under the Equal Protection Clause of the Fourteenth Amendment. The marriage bans at issue in these cases are in violation of that Clause.

III

In striking down interracial marriage bans, this Court in *Loving,* as we do today, looked to the Equal Protection Clause. But we also assessed the marriage bans at issue in *Loving* under the Due Process Clause. It is appropriate to do the same here.

It is by now well-established that the Constitution recognizes a fundamental right to marry. In *Loving*, we struck down a ban that prohibited marriage
across racial lines. 388 U.S. at 12. In *Zablocki v. Redhail*, 434 U.S. 374, 384
(1978), we held that a statute prohibiting parents who owed child support from
marrying was unconstitutional. In *Turner v. Safley*, 482 U.S. 78, 95 (1987), we
struck down a regulation barring prisoners from marrying. In all three cases,
we relied on the fundamental right to marry to deem the marriage restrictions at issue unconstitutional. Respondents claim that those rulings are inapposite because they involved instances in which opposite-sex couples sought
to marry.

In assessing the merits of this argument, we note, as an initial matter, the
way in which it is grounded in considerations of sex and sexual orientation.
Whether individuals are eligible for protection under the fundamental right to
marry, the Respondents contend, depends on their sex and sexual orientation.
We believe the Respondents' circumscribed understanding of the fundamental right to marry further supports our conclusion above that the marriage bans
at issue in these cases constitute sex and sexual-orientation classifications.

The Respondents claim that the due process question is not whether the
Petitioners have a right to marry, but is instead whether they have a right to
marry someone of the same sex. The Respondents add that there is no deeply
rooted right in the nation's history to enter into same-sex marriages given that
no state lawfully issued licenses to same-sex couples prior to 2004. However,
this Court in its marriage cases has not framed the constitutional question in
this way. *Loving* did not ask about a "right to interracial marriage"; *Turner* did
not ask about a "right of inmates to marry"; and *Zablocki* did not ask about a
"right of fathers with unpaid child support duties to marry." Rather, each case
inquired about the right to marry in its comprehensive sense, asking if there
was a sufficient justification for excluding the relevant class from the right.
We have already noted that the Respondents have failed to provide a constitutionally permissible justification for denying same-sex couples the opportunity
to marry.

That the Petitioners are covered by the fundamental right to marry is also
clear from our long line of cases that have constitutionally protected the ability of individuals to make important decisions impacting their families and
intimate relationships. In two cases from almost a century ago, we recognized
that parents have a constitutional right to make decisions about the rearing
and educating of their children. *Pierce v. Soc'y of Sisters*, 268 U.S. 510 (1925);
Meyer v. Nebraska, 262 U.S. 390 (1923). We later held that individuals have
a constitutional right to decide whether to procreate and have children, *Roe
v. Wade*, 410 U.S. 113 (1973); *Eisenstadt v. Baird*, 405 U.S. 438 (1972); *Griswold*

v. Connecticut, 381 U.S. 479 (1965), and to engage in consensual sexual intimacy free of government coercion, *Lawrence*, 539 U.S. at 574. These cases protect the liberty interests of individuals in making personal and intimate decisions that impact families and sexual relationships. The fundamental right to marry is entirely consistent with such an understanding of constitutionally protected liberty.

Two of our dissenting colleagues contend that the liberty protected by the Constitution is limited to the negative right of being left alone. Our colleagues reason that the right claimed by the Petitioners to marry their same-sex partners cannot be protected by the Due Process Clause because it requires the government to act affirmatively. *See* 133 S. Ct. at 2620 (Roberts, C.J., dissenting) ("Unlike criminal laws banning contraceptives and sodomy, the marriage laws at issue here involve no government intrusion ... [These] laws in no way interfere with the 'right to be let alone.'"); *id.* at 2634 (Thomas, J., dissenting) ("In the American legal tradition, liberty has long been understood as individual freedom *from* governmental action, not as a right *to* a particular governmental entitlement."). But it cannot be that the Constitution only recognizes negative rights to liberty. After all, everyone involved in the cases before us acknowledges that there is a fundamental right to marry. (The dispute is over *which classes of individuals* are eligible to benefit from the right.) And that right requires the government to act affirmatively to recognize relationships as marital.

It is important in this regard to distinguish *Griswold*, which involved a contraceptive ban that interfered with the liberty interests of *already married* couples, from *Loving*, *Zablocki*, and *Turner*, which involved state refusals to recognize certain relationships as marital. The crux of the constitutional claim in *Griswold* was that the state should leave married couples alone so that they can make important decisions, such as those related to the use of contraceptives, about the intimate components of their relationships. On the other hand, the claimants in *Loving*, *Zablocki*, and *Turner*, like the Petitioners, were not asking that the state leave them alone; instead, they were seeking state recognition (and by implication, state regulation) of their relationships. This Court in those three cases concluded that the denial of that recognition, that is, the *failure* of the state to act, violated the claimants' fundamental right to marry. The harm alleged in *Loving*, *Zablocki*, and *Turner*, therefore, did not arise from state *interference* with intimate relationships; instead, the harm arose from the state's unwillingness to recognize those relationships. If we view the right to marry only in terms of negative liberty, therefore, we are unable to explain fully the kind of affirmative obligation of recognition that the state is under as a result of the Court's rulings in the cases implicating that right.

Our marriage cases show that liberty considerations are not always sufficiently protected by simply asking that the state refrain from acting. In some
settings, such as that involving the legal recognition of relationships as marital,
the government has a constitutional duty to act affirmatively in order to make
the attainment of liberty possible. *Loving, Zablocki,* and *Turner* show that the
meaning of liberty under the Due Process Clause is not limited to considerations of privacy and of being left alone.

IV

We do not intend for our conclusion that the Petitioners are entitled to the protections afforded by the fundamental right to marry to suggest that marriage
is the only or, depending on individual circumstances, even the best way of
ordering familial and intimate relationships. There are millions of Americans
whose personal circumstances or choices lead them to cohabit without raising
children or to raise children alone or with the assistance of their non-marital
partners or family members.

It is one thing to conclude, as this Court has done on many occasions, and
we reaffirm today, that marriage is a fundamental right. It is another matter altogether to conclude that the state is always constitutionally entitled to
privilege marriage by denying certain rights and benefits to individuals who
structure their familial and intimate relationships outside of the institution of
marriage.

But questions regarding the constitutionality of the state's promotion of
marriage, to the possible disadvantage of those who remain outside of that
institution, will have to wait for another day. The Petitioners have sought the
opportunity to marry legally. We hold that the Constitution affords individuals, regardless of sex, sexual orientation, or gender identity, the right to marry
the person of their choice.

The judgment of the Court of Appeals for the Sixth Circuit is reversed.

It is so ordered.

Index

School District; Meritor Savings Bank
v. Vinson; Michael M. v. Superior
Court; Oncale v. Sundowner Offshore
Services, Inc.; rape
sexual autonomy, 101, 486–88, 490–96
sexual freedom, *see* liberty
sexual harassment
actionable, 297–98
employer liability for, 298–99, 302,
307–08, 319–21
exclusion of other women's
testimony, 317–18
hostile work environment, 297–98, 300–01,
308–09, 314–19, 417–18
intersection of race/gender/rape, 297,
300, 309–12
personal appearance, 298, 301, 306, 318–19
provocative speech by complainant,
302, 319
quid pro quo, 298, 302, 308, 312–14
racial stereotypes, 300, 309–12
same-sex sexual harassment, *see also Oncale v.
Sundowner Offshore Services, Inc.*
as actionable, 410
'because of sex' requirement, 408, 409,
412, 413, 414, 415, 416–24
burden of proof, 418–19, 424
Civil Rights Act 1964 Title VII,
416, 417–18
hostile work environment, 417–18
hostility as motivation, 410,
412–13, 419–20
masculinity theory, 413, 421–24
policing gender roles, 420
sex stereotyping, 413–14
Title VII, Civil Rights Act 1964, 408
tangible or economic injury, 314
Title IX Education Amendments of 1972,
298–99, 302, 307–08, 426
Title VII, Civil Rights Act 1964, 226–27,
297, 303, 308, 317
welcomeness and mode of dress, 298, 301,
306, 318–19
welcomeness requirement, 301, 316–17, *see
also Dothard v. Rawlinson; Gebser v.
Lago Vista Independent School District;
Johnson v. Transportation Agency;
Meritor Savings Bank v. Vinson; Oncale
v. Sundowner Offshore Services, Inc.;
same-sex sexual harassment; Virginia
Military Institute (VMI)

sexual liberty, *see* liberty
sexual orientation
classifications, bans on same-sex marriage
as, 536–39, 544–45, *see also* LGBTQI
individuals/families; same-sex
marriage
sexual pluralism, 99, 103
sexual relationships
Fourteenth Amendment, 108
Griswold v. Connecticut, 101–02, 107–09
sexuality
Dothard v. Rawlinson, original opinion
treatment of, 223–27
essentialism, 210, 223–25
legislative changes 1970s, 138–39
radical feminism, 32
spectrum theory, 419, *see also Gebser
v. Lago Vista Independent School
District; Griswold v. Connecticut;
LGBTQI individuals/families; Meritor
Savings Bank v. Vinson; Michael
M. v. Superior Court; Oncale v.
Sundowner Offshore Services, Inc.;
Planned Parenthood of Southeastern
Pennsylvania v. Casey; Price
Waterhouse v. Hopkins; Roe v. Wade;
Virginia Military Institute (VMI)
Shahar v. Bowers, 502
Siegel, Reva, 210, 276n24, 510
Simon, Michelle S., 426
single motive framework, 356–58
situated perspective of decision-makers,
4–5, 9, 448
Slaughter-House cases, 57, 58, 61–62, 63, 64,
65, 66–67, 68–69, 70, 71–73
slavery, 63–64
anti-miscegenation laws, 124–25
marriage in, 123–27
pregnancy during, 164n27
Smith, Brenda, 208
social science, use in judicial opinions, 20, 78,
80, 352
socialist feminism, *see* feminism: Marxist and
socialist
socioeconomic class
abortion, 155
feminism and, 30, 32
intersectionality, 21, 34–35
judiciary, 377
sodomy/sodomy laws, 270, 270n30, 410, 486,
488, 492–93, 494, 499, 500–01